The French Army and the Fil

This is a comprehensive new history of the French Army's critical contribution to the Great War. Ranging across all fronts, Elizabeth Greenhalgh examines the French Army's achievements and failures and sets these in the context of the difficulties of coalition warfare and the relative strengths and weaknesses of the enemy forces it faced. Drawing from new archival sources, she reveals the challenges of dealing with and replenishing a mass conscript army in the face of slaughter on an unprecedented scale, and shows how, through trials and defeats, French generals and their troops learned to adapt and develop techniques which eventually led to victory. In a unique account of the largest Allied army on the Western Front, the book revises our understanding not only of wartime strategy and combat, but also of other crucial aspects of France's war, from mutinies and mail censorship to medical services, railways and weapons development.

ELIZABETH GREENHALGH is QE II Research Fellow in the School of Humanities & Social Sciences at the University of New South Wales, Australia.

Armies of the Great War

This is a major new series of studies of the armies of the major combatants in the First World War for publication during the war's centenary. The books are written by leading military historians and set operations and strategy within the broader context of foreign policy aims and allied strategic relations, national mobilisation and domestic social, political and economic effects.

Titles in the series include:

The American Army and the First World War, by David R. Woodward
The Austro-Hungarian Army and the First World War, by Graydon Tunstall
The British Army and the First World War, by Ian Beckett, Timothy Bowman and Mark Connelly
The French Army and the First World War, by Elizabeth Greenhalgh
The German Army and the First World War, by Robert Foley
The Italian Army and the First World War, by John Gooch

The French Army
and the First World War

Elizabeth Greenhalgh

CAMBRIDGE
UNIVERSITY PRESS

University Printing House, Cambridge CB2 8BS, United Kingdom

Cambridge University Press is part of the University of Cambridge.

It furthers the University's mission by disseminating knowledge in the pursuit of education, learning and research at the highest international levels of excellence.

www.cambridge.org
Information on this title: www.cambridge.org/9781107605688

First published 2014

Printed in the United Kingdom by T. J. International Ltd, Padstow

A catalogue record for this publication is available from the British Library

Library of Congress Cataloguing in Publication data
Greenhalgh, Elizabeth.
The French army and the First World War / Elizabeth Greenhalgh.
    pages   cm. – (Armies of the Great War)
Includes bibliographical references and index.
ISBN 978-1-107-01235-6 (Hardback) – ISBN 978-1-107-60568-8 (Paperback)
1. France. Armée–History–World War, 1914–1918.   2. World War, 1914–1918–Campaigns–Western Front.   3. World War, 1914–1918–France.
I. Title.
D548.G74 2014
940.54′1244–dc23   2014010862

ISBN 978-1-107-01235-6 Hardback
ISBN 978-1-107-60568-8 Paperback

Additional resources for this publication at www.cambridge.org/9781107605688

Contents

Figures

Maps

Tables

Preface

More than eight million French citizens were mobilised during the fifty-two months of the First World War, and the principal battleground in Europe was Northern France, which was devastated as a result. In round figures, of those 8.4 million French soldiers, 1.4 million (including colonials and foreign volunteers) were killed or disappeared during the conflict. A further nine million wounded, gassed or ill men passed through the medical service, some of these, of course, figuring three or four times. Almost two million pensions were being paid to war-wounded veterans in December 1921, of whom 42,000 were blind in one or both eyes and 43,600 had lost either an arm or a leg. These figures exceed comparable statistics for the principal allies on the Western Front, although Russian figures are no doubt higher.

The French Army was fighting to defend home and country, unlike the British and Americans, who occasionally exasperated their 'hosts' by seeming to be prepared to fight to the last Frenchman. It is difficult to imagine the British Army fighting in England with the home counties occupied by the enemy, but enemy occupation is what drove not only those eight million Frenchmen to accept their duty to serve, but also their parents, wives and sisters to work in war factories. Yet, too often, the enormous effort of the French Army of 1914–18 is seen through the prism of 1940, all the more so because its Commander-in-Chief in 1917–18 was Philippe Pétain (who did not sign the 1918 armistice, but is counted responsible for that of 1940). Those volumes of the British official history dealing with 1918 reveal this tendency very clearly, and some American writing on the war reflects a similar tendency to imagine that effete Europeans required an infusion of transatlantic vigour to finish the war.

This book, then, seeks to counteract such features of the anglophone historiography, through an operational history of the First World War as experienced by France's soldiers, politicians and population. More than that, it presents the first institutional account of the French Army during the war and its aftermath. Robert A. Doughty's *Pyrrhic Victory* (2005) has preceded me, offering an excellent account of French strategy and operations, and Anthony Clayton has added to his several studies of the French Army his *Paths of Glory* (2003). In the current work, *The French Army and the First World War*, these are extended to include an analysis of the Army's relationship with the nation-at-war, both as regards industrial mobilisation and civil–military relations. The story is carried into the immediate post-war period, to cover demobilisation and the payment of pensions. In addition, the Army's relationship with the French empire and the three principal allies, Britain, Russia and the USA, is examined. Exterior theatres, Africa, Gallipoli, Greece, Italy, Palestine and Romania are discussed briefly, in the context of alliance relationships.

In the notes, readers will find references not only to recent French research, much of it carried out for doctoral theses by serving French Army officers, but also to the great volume of inter-war professional literature. General histories of the war are absent, in the main, so as not to overload the critical apparatus. Works are cited with full bibliographical details at their first appearance in any chapter, except for the most frequently cited, which appear in the abbreviated form to be found in the list of abbreviations. When possible, I have cited documents from the published official history, *Les Armées Françaises dans la Grande Guerre*, rather than giving the archival reference to the original. Where archives are cited, however, the location is given at the first mention in any chapter, and, where no location is given (the majority of cases), the documents are in the Army archives, the Service Historique de la Défense, in the Château de Vincennes, on the outskirts of Paris.

To avoid confusion, German and enemy army units are printed in italic. Allied armies are cited by number (in words), corps by Roman numerals, divisions by Arabic numerals, and all lower formations (regiments and so on) also by Arabic numerals.

References to Field Marshal Sir Douglas Haig's published diary may be checked in either the edition by Robert Blake (1952) or that by Gary Sheffield and John Bourne (2000). References to unpublished portions of the diary are from the typescript in The National Archives, Kew, unless the manuscript is significantly different; where this is the case, I have used the manuscript, which has been microfilmed by Adam Matthew Publications. References to the four-volume summary of the official history, *Histoire de la Guerre Mondiale*, all published in Paris by Payot in 1936–37, are cited by the authors' names and simple title *Histoire*: they are General Duffour, *Joffre et la guerre de mouvement 1914*; General Daille, *Joffre et la guerre d'usure 1915–1916*; General Hellot, *Le Commandment des généraux Nivelle et Pétain 1917*; and General Tournès, *Foch et la victoire des Alliés 1918*. All four authors served in staff positions during the war. The title *Etapes* refers to the study of 13 Division d'Infanterie, whose fortunes illustrate this work: Lt-Col. Laure and Commandant Jacottet, *Les Etapes de guerre d'une division (13e Division)* (Paris: Berger-Levrault, 1932). The title *Introduction* refers to the indispensable and highly informative introduction to the SHD's N series, covering 1872–1919: Pierre Guinard, Jean-Claude Devos, Jean Nicot, *Inventaire sommaire des Archives de la Guerre: Introduction* (Troyes: Imprimerie de la Renaissance, 1975), and available online from the SHD website.

I thank all the staff at the SHD for their unfailing welcome and precious help during my annual visits; General Bach and Colonel Guelton, for their guidance in matters military; and Dr Jim Beach, Dr Simon House and Dr André Loez, for their help in sending me part or all of their doctoral theses. I thank especially M. Gobert de Barescut, for allowing me to read his grandfather's highly interesting diary account of his war service.

For permission to quote from material they hold, I am grateful: in Paris, to the Archives nationales, the Archives diplomatiques and the Bibliothèque de l'Institut; in London, to the Trustees of the Imperial War Museum and the Trustees of the Liddell Hart Centre for Military Archives, King's College London.

Abbreviations

AEF	Afrique équatoriale française (French equatorial Africa)
AEF	American Expeditionary Forces
AFGG	*Les Armées Françaises dans la Grande Guerre*, 103 vols (Paris: Imprimerie Nationale, 1922–38), cited with tome and volume number, plus either page or annex number: thus *AFGG* 4/1, 536, refers to tome 4, volume 1, page 536.
AN	Archives nationales, Paris
AOF	Afrique occidentale française (French West Africa)
BEF	British Expeditionary Force
BNF	Bibliothèque nationale de France
CA	Corps d'armée, Army Corps
CinC	Commander-in-Chief
CS	Maréchal Fayolle, *Cahiers secrets de la Grande Guerre* (Paris: Plon 1964)
DAN	Détachement d'armée du nord (Northern Army Detachment)
DC	Division de cavalerie
DCP	Division de cavalerie à pied (dismounted cavalry)
DGCRA	Direction Générale des Communications et des Ravitaillements aux Armées (in 1918 controlled all the army's supply and transport services)
DI	Division d'infanterie
DIC	Division d'infanterie coloniale
DM	Division Marocaine
EMA	Etat-major de l'armée (Army General Staff)
GHQ	British General Headquarters
GMCC	*Guerres mondiales et conflits contemporains*
GQG	Grand Quartier Général (French headquarters)
GQGA	Foch's Allied headquarters
JMO	Journal des marches et des opérations (war diary)
LHCMA	Liddell Hart Centre for Military Archives, King's College London

NARA	National Archives and Records Administration, College Park, Maryland
NCO	non-commissioned officer
OHL	Oberste Heeresleitung (German high command)
pcdf	pauvres cons du front (poor bloody infantry)
PV	Robert A. Doughty, *Pyrrhic Victory: French Strategy and Operations in the Great War* (Cambridge, MA: The Belknap Press of Harvard University Press, 2005)
RHA	*Revue Historique des Armées* [earlier: *de l'Armée*]
RHMC	*Revue d'Histoire Moderne et Contemporaine*
RI	Régiment d'infanterie
RMF	*Revue militaire française*
SHD	Service historique de la Défense
SWC	Supreme War Council
TNA	The National Archives, Kew

Introduction

On the evening of 24 July 1914, the French war minister, Colonel Adolphe Messimy, summoned the commander-in-chief designate of the French Army, General Joseph Joffre. Messimy told him that, following the assassination in Sarajevo, Germany supported Austria-Hungary's firm stance against Serbia in the matter. That support would represent direct opposition to Russia's support for Serbia; hence France's military agreements with Russia might come into play. Joffre recorded in his memoirs that he replied to Messimy: 'Well, monsieur le ministre, if we have to make war we will do so.' It must be presumed, therefore, that Joffre believed that France could emerge victorious. This book examines the French Army, which Joffre was to use to defeat Germany, in order to evaluate how well it performed. It begins with the reforms following the disastrous Franco-Prussian war, when France was defeated and humiliated, examines the battles between 1914 and 1918, and explains how France did indeed emerge victorious to sit at the victors' table in 1919 for the signatures on the Treaty of Versailles.

The prelude to the First World War took place in North Africa. In 1911, at the height of the second Moroccan crisis, when the German gunboat *Panther* anchored off Agadir in order to protect the rights of German merchants in the North African country where French economic interests were growing, Europe feared a general war. France's then premier, Joseph Caillaux, asked Joffre what France's chances of victory were if such a war resulted from the crisis. He reminded Joffre that Napoleon Bonaparte had stated that a general should have at least a 70 per cent chance of victory before embarking on a battle, and Joffre replied that France did not possess such a margin. Caillaux ended the Moroccan crisis diplomatically, therefore, ceding a portion of the French Cameroons to Germany in return for German recognition of France's protectorate in Morocco. War had been averted for three years.

France's Army in 1914 was a relatively new institution and still evolving. After France lost the provinces of Alsace and much of Lorraine in the 1871 Treaty of Frankfurt following its defeat in the Franco-Prussian

1

war, everything had to be rebuilt. A new French Republic, the third, had to establish its authority and create a new Republican Army to meet the greatly increased power of the new German *Reich*, declared in Versailles in 1871, when the King of Prussia became Kaiser of a unified Germany. The professional army of Emperor Louis Napoleon was replaced by a republican conscript army, whose soldiers accepted compulsory military service as the male citizen's duty.

A brief discussion of the formation of this new Republican Army is followed by an operational history of the fighting between 1914 and 1918. This account examines both the high level of command, where strategy and tactics were decided, and command at lower levels, especially the divisional level where one infantry division's experience, that of 13 Infantry Division, is used as a series of narrative hooks to make more comprehensible the huge numbers involved in this, the first modern, industrial war. The book also introduces individual experiences, technological developments, military justice and military medicine to give a rounded picture of the French Army at war. The reader is directed to Robert A. Doughty's magisterial *Pyrrhic Victory* for more detail of the strategy and operations. Here, I link France's Army to the home front, through the relationship between civilian politicians and the high command, through the millions of letters exchanged and censored by the postal control commissions, and through the massive industrial mobilisation that gave the Army its weapons and munitions. I analyse the relations between France's Army and the principal Allies, at first Russia and Britain, and later the USA and Britain, because the First World War was, above all, a coalition war, and France provided moral leadership by supplying the largest army of the belligerent democracies. I examine France's Army in relation to the principal enemy, Germany, by detailing reactions to German tactics, and have carried the story into the post-war period. These three relationships – the Army and France; the Army and its Allies; the Army and its enemy – are interwoven throughout. By way of conclusion, the book ends by comparing the Army of 1914 with that of 1918, so as to highlight the changes and improvements showing the adaptability of France's Army after Joffre had accepted the prospect of war.

The image of the opening battles in 1914 is one of futile bayonet charges. Much of the fighting during 1915 is little known, as the British were not present in France in great numbers; even French historians have not examined that year's numerous battles. The 1916 battle of Verdun is well known, but not France's contribution to that year's second battle on the Somme. France's effort in 1918 is also little known, it being assumed that following 1917's mutinies, nothing more could be expected from an exhausted army. Yet, during the 1918 German offensives, the French Army came to the rescue of the British and then withstood the assaults on their own front as well, before joining the final victorious months of fighting. Whatever the percentage chance of success that Joffre believed he possessed in 1914, by 1918 it was a French general, Ferdinand Foch, made marshal of France, who accepted the German signatures on the armistice document. In the end, Joffre's confidence in the French Army had been justified. That citizen army had learned, by hard experience and at great cost, how to fight and how to emerge victorious from a modern industrial war.

Table 1 *Political and military leaders, 1914–1918*

The politicians	
President of the Republic, 1913–1920	Raymond Poincaré (1860–1934)
Présidents du conseil (premiers)	*War ministers*
June 1914–October 1915	
René Viviani	Adolphe Messimy; Alexandre Millerand
October 1915–March 1917	
Aristide Briand	General Gallieni; General Roques; Admiral Lacaze
March–September 1917	(interim); General Lyautey
Alexandre Ribot	Paul Painlevé
September–November 1917	
Paul Painlevé	Paul Painlevé
November 1917–January 1920	
Georges Clemenceau	Georges Clemenceau

The military	
Commander-in-Chief of the Allied Armies	General (Marshal) Ferdinand Foch, from 26.3.18
Commander-in-Chief, French Army	*Chief of staff*
August 1914–December 1916	
General (Marshal) Joseph Joffre	General Belin; (from 22.3.15) General Pellé
December 1916–May 1917	
General Robert Nivelle	General Pont; (from 2.5.17) General
May 1917–November 1918	Debeney
General (Marshal) Philippe	General Debeney; (from 23.12.17) General
Pétain	Anthoine; (from 5.7.18) General Buat
Army group commanders	
*GAE: from 8.1.15	General Dubail
from 31.3.16	General Franchet d'Espèrey
from 27.12.16	General de Curières de Castelnau
*GAC: from 22.6.15	General de Curières de Castelnau
from 12.12.15	General de Langle de Cary
from 2.5.17	General Pétain
from 4.5.17	General Fayolle
*GAN: from 4.10.14	General Foch
from 27.12.16	General Franchet d'Espèrey
from 10.6.18	General Maistre
*GAR: from 1.1.17 until dissolved 8.5.17	General Micheler
from 23.2.18	General Fayolle
Individual witnesses cited frequently	
Charles Delvert (1879–1940), historian	101 RI in 124 DI
Abel Ferry (1881–1918), député	166 RI
Paul Pireaud (1890–1970), agriculteur	112 RAL (régiment d'artillerie lourde)

* GAE: Eastern Army Group; GAC: Central Army Group; GAN: Northern; GAR: Reserve

Fig. 1 Four témoins whose testimony recurs throughout this book
(a) Paul Pireaud, farmer from the Dordogne, SW France, and gunner in 112 Régiment d'artillerie lourde
(b) General Emile Fayolle, commander successively of 70 DR, XXXIII Corps, Sixth Army, French Forces in Italy, Reserve Army Group
(c) Colonel Emile Herbillon, liaison officer between GQG and the government
(d) Captain Charles Delvert, 101 RI, then HQ staff Fifth and First Armies

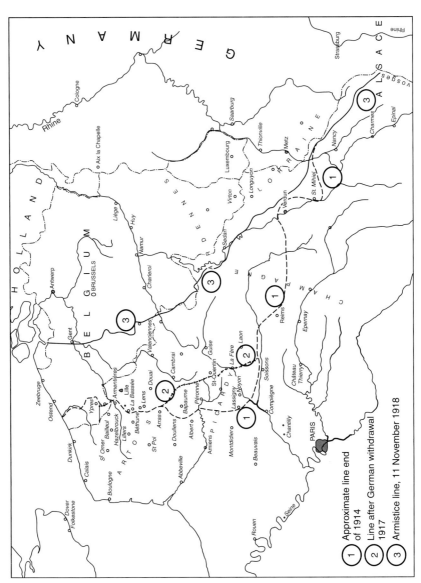

1. The Western Front, 1914–18

① Approximate line end of 1914
② Line after German withdrawal 1917
③ Armistice line, 11 November 1918

6

1 The pre-war Army

During the decades preceding the First World War, the French Army had an equivocal reputation. On the one hand, it possessed a glorious past in the campaigns of Napoleon Bonaparte that were taught in European military academies, yet, on the other, it had suffered an ignominious defeat in 1870 by the Prussian Army, while under the command of Napoleon's nephew, self-declared Emperor Napoleon III. The glorious days of the *levée en masse*, when French citizens rose to the occasion and defeated the invader at Valmy in 1792, had been replaced by the inefficient mobilisation and performance of a professional army in 1870. Then, in 1894, right-wing and incompetent officers brought down international opprobrium on the Army, to add to the earlier military defeat, when its high command accused and convicted of treason an innocent artillery officer, Captain Alfred Dreyfus, and then covered up the conspiracy.

How, then, to explain the eventual victory of the Army of 1914 that endured more than four years of battles and trench stalemate fought on French territory at appalling cost in lives and treasure? How to explain that France sat at the victors' table at war's end? This victory is one of the glories of the much maligned Third Republic.

The political background, 1870–1911

France and the French Army had been crushed totally by the Prussian Army that invaded the national territory, won a resounding victory in eastern France at Sedan on the Meuse in September 1870, and forced Louis Napoleon into exile. Political upheaval followed as Paris refused to accept defeat and rejected the idea of an armistice sought by the newly established Third Republic. In 1871 the Paris Commune managed to deny reality for some weeks, but eventually was forced to capitulate. The political fallout created cleavages between Paris and the provinces, and between left and right, that continue to this day. The Treaty of Frankfurt, which ended the state of war between France and the newly created German Empire (the second *Reich*), was signed on 28 May 1871. The treaty terms ceded the provinces of Alsace and much of Lorraine to the new power on France's eastern border, imposed a large financial indemnity, and installed German troops on French soil until such time as it was paid. The final humiliation was the crowning of Kaiser Wilhelm in the Galerie des Glaces of the Versailles palace outside Paris.

Despite the Third Republic's less than auspicious start, tremendous progress was made towards speedy recuperation and reform. The financial penalty was paid off in record time and the last German troops left France on 16 September 1873. The country's new constitutional laws had been passed earlier the same year, and the initial monarchist majority in the new bi-cameral legislature gave way gradually to the republicans. The rise of the political left was marked symbolically by the adoption in 1880 of Bastille Day (14 July) as the French national holiday.

The two great achievements of the Third French Republic, both largely due to the work of Jules Ferry, were the creation of a system of primary education and of a large colonial empire. Both had an influence on the French Army that fought in 1914–18. Ferry's Education Law of 1881 provided for free education up to the age of 13 for all boys and girls. The following year, that primary education became compulsory and 'laïque', that is non-religious. Ferry had already made provision for the training of teachers for the new schools; in 1879 he had obliged all départements to set up teacher training colleges for women, and the prestigious Ecole Normale Supérieure (founded 1831) welcomed women in Sèvres in 1881.

For Jules Ferry, the prime mover in the field of education, democracy and equal rights for all citizens were impossible without equality of education: 'the secularisation of schools and morality aims to create the unity of national spirit on a positive and uncontested basis'.[1] An historian of the French education system, Mona Ozouf, has drawn on her own experience to describe the value of schooling in creating an 'idea' of France.[2] By the time war was declared in 1914, therefore, virtually all French troops had received at least elementary education and had become literate, as the enormous volume of wartime letters sent between front and home attests. A large proportion of the 2.7 million boys attending school in 1896/97 would be mobilised in 1914.[3] The link with home and family that letters provided was invaluable in maintaining a degree of morale.

Whichever region of France the soldiers came from, they would have received the same 'idea' of France because of the unified and centralised bureaucracy already in place from Napoleonic times, and through the use of the same textbooks in all state schools. One mission of education was to unify, especially through the encouragement of patriotism. Thus textbooks in history and civics were 'of influence in keeping hatred of Germany alive'.[4] The role of the *instituteur* and, increasingly, the *institutrice* was to promote civic values, particularly since it was popularly supposed that it was their German equivalents who had won victory at Sadowa (against the Austrians) and Sedan.

The republicans who used the elementary teachers to forge anew the French 'esprit national' after 1870 included the historian Ernest Lavisse among their number. He made an important contribution to the reform of university education and was director of the nation's foremost teacher training institution, the *Ecole normale*. He also produced the school textbooks which were used in the new primary schools, including the *Manuel d'instruction civique*.[5] Another textbook, compiled by Lavisse and used widely between 1880 and 1900 when the majority of the active French Army would have been educated, presented a 'thoroughly militarist' attitude to war. It was a series of heroic stories about French soldiers, chosen from the post-1870 period. The work was in its 24th edition by 1916. Its title, *Tu seras soldat*, clearly announces its theme and Lavisse's preface explained his aim in compiling the work: 'I have desired to teach the children to love it [the army] and to prepare them to fulfil a sacred duty, that of *military service*.'[6] Lavisse wrote in 1912:

If the schoolboy does not carry with him the living memory of our national glories, if he does not know that his ancestors have fought on a thousand battlefields to unify our fatherland and to construct out of the chaos of our aging institutions the laws that made us free; if he does not become a citizen penetrated with his duties and a soldier who loves his rifle, the teacher will have wasted his time.[7]

Lavisse's emphasis on the military was reinforced by a decree promulgated in 1882 that established 'bataillons scolaires'. These extra-curricular 'school battalions' were meant to supplement the uneven provision of physical education and provided youngsters over the age of 14 with instruction on firing guns. Gymnastics clubs were also started, and in 1908 the war ministry instituted the Brevet d'Aptitude Militaire, or certificate of military training, to reward those boys who did well in such environments. The possession of the certificate usually meant a faster progression through the ranks, once its holder was conscripted. By 1913 there were 20,030 such holders, which does not constitute a large proportion of the population.[8]

Ferry's second achievement was France's colonial empire. Bismarck's post-war policy of keeping France isolated diplomatically was based on the belief that France could never be an ally, and he encouraged the

French to seek colonial expansion as a way both of distracting them from seeking any revenge for the Treaty of Frankfurt and also of creating trouble as France bumped up against Italy and Britain in Africa. In 1881 France took over Tunisia despite Italian pretensions to neighbouring Libya; in 1883 the French occupied Tonkin and Amman (both in present-day Vietnam) and added Laos in 1893 to what became the Indo-Chinese Union. A protectorate over Madagascar, off the east coast of Africa, was declared in 1885 and the island was annexed to France in 1896. A huge swathe of Africa was explored and French West Africa (AOF) and French Equatorial Africa (AEF) created south of the North African territories of Algeria and Tunisia. Egypt had to be left to the British, but most of Morocco became a French protectorate. Morocco would be a flash-point when Germany started to flex its colonial muscles, creating crises in 1905 and again in 1911.

Neither the French Army nor the war ministry was much interested in the military potential of these colonies.[9] Algeria was considered to be part of France and its three départements each sent two deputies and one senator to Paris to sit in the Assemblée nationale. The remaining colonies elected ten deputies and seven senators. The European colonists had little interest in training and arming native contingents, who might then rebel against their colonisers. It was not until after the second Morocco crisis that men such as Adolphe Messimy (war minister in 1911) and Charles Mangin (a colonial officer) began promoting the idea of large native armies.

Both Ferry's achievements – the provision of free, compulsory primary education and the creation of a colonial empire – affected the experience of French soldiers during the Great War. The fact that all (or the great majority) could read and write enabled the serving soldier to maintain the vital link with home and family and normality. France's colonies and overseas possessions supplied thousands of men, not simply as troops but more often as labour behind the lines, although this contribution was much less than its proponents had forecast pre-war. Nonetheless, France had nearly run out of men by 1918, and without colonial contingents the country would certainly have been forced to give up the fight for lack of manpower.

Questions of primary education and colonies were considered more important than the difficult task of forming a new Republican Army (despite the fact that more often than not the war minister was a military man). A presidential decree in July 1872 created the Conseil Supérieur de la Guerre (War Ministry Supreme Council). Presided over by the President of the Republic, it brought together the premier and the senior generals, along with other military and political appointees, to advise on the constitution of the army and the way in which it was employed. Reconstituted in 1888, the Council was reduced to eight members and its remit widened to include consultation over mobilisation and concentration, training and defence of the French coasts.[10] It was recognised early that conscription, rather than a professional army, was the only way to have available a large enough source of trained manpower in case of war. Besides, Germany's population was increasing at an enormous rate since the formation of the empire. Between 1870 and 1910 the German population increased by 60 per cent, and by 1914 69 million Germans outnumbered 39.8 million French.

The 1872 law on conscription imposed five years' service in the active army, followed by four in the reserves and a further eleven in the territorial army for half the eligible contingent (France could not afford to take in the whole annual contingent of 21-year-olds). A year later a law was passed mandating the Army's 'general organisation', creating permanent army corps stationed throughout the country. The aim was to enable a speedier and more efficient mobilisation in any future war, as men would know where to report. The disorderly mobilisation in 1870 had been a scandal. In 1875 a law decreed that the permanent cadre of officers should be sufficient to command double the effectives in time of war, with an army consisting of eighteen corps in metropolitan France – 144 infantry regiments, 38 artillery regiments and 70 cavalry regiments – and a further large corps, XIX Corps, in Algeria.

Previously, staff officers had formed a 'closed' staff corps, with no movement between field and staff commands, but in 1875 special courses of higher military education were established instead, open to officers from all services selected by competition. The former staff college became the Ecole Militaire Supérieure in June 1878, renamed the Ecole Supérieure de Guerre two years later. After five years' service as an officer, at least three spent in a field command, candidates were selected by examination and after two years' instruction passed out with the 'brevet d'état-major' (or psc, passed staff college), again after passing written examinations. These officers continued to belong to their service arm – infantry, cavalry, artillery, engineers – and would rotate into and out of staff positions. Finally, in 1910, after rejection of a proposal to extend the Ecole Supérieure de Guerre course by a year, the Centre des Hautes Etudes Militaires was established to give practical instruction to the 'brevetés' and a select few (such as Maxime Weygand) who had not attended the ESG. The centre's graduates were intended for army staffs in the event of war; hence the centre soon received the nickname 'school for marshals'.

Under a civilian war minister, Charles de Freycinet, who was one of the few such ministers to serve for long enough to make a difference, the moribund Conseil Supérieur de la Guerre (CSG) was re-started in May 1888 and the ministry put on a firmer footing with a decree (July 1888) fixing the constitution of the various services and technical committees that carried out the administration. Since the minister changed so frequently, it was the services and committees which kept the wheels turning, thereby gaining considerable power. Furthermore, because the army's general staff was attached to the minister, it departed when the minister changed. A further decree in May 1890 created, therefore, a separate army general staff (Etat-Major de l'Armée, or EMA). Now, instead of twelve heads of the army general staff in fourteen years, there was stability for the army, reflecting (perhaps) the Prussian/German *Grosser Generalstab*. The conscription laws were amended also. By the law of 15 July 1889, universal male service was instituted, in theory for three years, followed by seven in reserve and a further fifteen in the territorial army and its reserve – making a total of twenty-five years' obligation. However, various categories of dispensation made it easy for those with money and/or contacts to evade the three years in the active army, but the possibility of purchasing replacement was not reinstated.

These inequalities became less tolerable as republicanism took firmer hold and the growth of an urban proletariat led to more powerful trade unions and a general movement to the left in the population. In 1905 the law governing military service was changed once more, reducing to two years the time spent in the active army, but increasing the time in reserve, so that the total length of service remained twenty-five years. In addition, the obligation became (for men) universal, hence egalitarian. This reduction from three years to two in the active army was seen as the Left's revenge for the Dreyfus affair.

The affair was not the sole cause for complaint about the army, still perceived as monarchist, catholic and right-wing, not to say reactionary. Military service was disliked, even though the duty to defend one's country was accepted. Mothers did not like their sons – mostly peasant farmers whose strong arms were needed at home – living in unhealthy barracks and becoming depraved by the drinking and licentiousness in the towns. In February 1914, epidemics of flu, diphtheria, meningitis and other less specific diseases were raging in 125 out of the 367 garrisons spread all over France. At least 381 deaths from all causes were recorded between 1 and 13 February – a very large total for such a short period among an essentially young, male population (107 deaths among the 1912 class, and 145 among the 1913 class). The convocation of reserve classes for training was cancelled as a result, but they were considered to have completed their military duty nonetheless.[11]

Several currents of anti-militarism worked against the creation of a Republican Army. First, a literary current, producing humorous or dramatic novels, denounced the abuses of authority or the violence of military life; then, an older current of mistrust of military coups d'état still had life; finally, a more left-wing current believed the army to be an instrument of repression. Using the army for strike-breaking and maintenance of public order caused more dissatisfaction. The growing trade union movement was active in helping young workers to resist the 'school of vice' and of 'crime', to revolt against brutish officers, and to refuse to fire on fellow workers. Union members contributed a small amount of money to a fund, the 'Sou du Soldat', to support the fight. An Anti-militarist League was founded in 1902.[12]

Dissatisfaction grew among officers also. The reduction of military service to two years meant fewer posts for junior officers and gradually the promotion tables higher up the hierarchy became blocked. Admissions to Saint-Cyr and Saumur, the infantry and cavalry officer schools, were limited so as to reduce the pressure, and in 1905 a cadre of reserve officers was established. This encouraged 'retirement' from the active army, but younger students were accepted during the first year of military service. This had the effect of reducing the average age of the corps of reserve officers, which numbered 55,000 by 1914. Conditions for those officers who remained in the active army were not attractive. Pay was low; there were restrictions on marriage; officers could not vote; scions of military families received preferential treatment. At the end of the nineteenth century 28 per cent of general officers bore an 'aristocratic' name. It is not surprising that the 'reactionary' label stuck, especially when well-educated youngsters were choosing the better-paid life of a lawyer or doctor instead of the military.[13]

European armies had to adapt to new technological conditions. More powerful guns, smokeless powder and, above all from the French point of view, the new hydraulic brake on the standard French field gun (the famous 75) seemed to show that defensive power had increased, making offensive war more difficult and costly. The huge expansion of railway networks made moving large bodies of men and guns across country far easier and speedier. These developments were not the only vectors of change. European armies could also study foreign wars, those in South Africa, and between the Russians and Japanese in the early years of the twentieth century. These seemed to show that technology was not everything. Boer farmers could keep a professional British Army at bay, and Japanese assaults on Russian defences proved successful. Whatever the lesson derived from technology or from foreign wars, it was clear that any future conflict in Europe would require much greater planning and much greater cooperation between the war ministry and other political institutions such as the foreign and colonial ministries or the commerce ministry.

The need for such cooperation became even greater when, in 1900, responsibility for the troops garrisoning the colonies was transferred from the Navy Ministry (the troops had been counted as marines) to the Army. Consequently the Conseil Supérieur de la Défense Nationale (CSDN, Supreme Council of National Defence) was created on 3 April 1906. Its mission was to 'examine all questions requiring the cooperation of two or more ministerial departments', and to indicate to the ministers of war, the navy, and the colonies the general direction of the necessary studies for the coordination of their respective military forces. Presided over by the country's President, the council comprised the ministers of foreign affairs, finance, war, navy and colonies, with the army and navy chiefs of staff attending in a 'consultative' role. The council had a secretariat for the paperwork, and a 'committee', made up of the two chiefs of staff (army and ministry) and the director of political affairs in the foreign ministry to examine the questions to be dealt with which required agreement among the relevant ministries.[14] The CSDN was an attempt to emulate the British Committee for Imperial Defence, but it met only fifteen times between its formation and the outbreak of war.

By 1911, then, when the political climate shifted and the second and more serious Moroccan crisis began with the German gunboat *Panther* being dispatched there on 1 July, the renewal and transformation of the French body politic and its military forces had made huge progress. The Army was still viewed by many as a right-wing, aristocratic and Catholic institution, used for strike-breaking and the suppression of public disorder. Despite Dreyfus's rehabilitation in 1906, many regarded an army career with disfavour. On the other hand, the positive promotion of military values and the civic duty to defend one's country had inculcated a generation of compulsorily educated primary school children. If the barracks were still unhealthy, nevertheless the great majority of young French men accepted the need for military service.

The new Republican Army prepares for war

The second Moroccan crisis of 1911, when the *Panther* appeared off Agadir, emphasised the German threat to European peace, and gave greater urgency to the need to reform France's Army still further. The crisis brought down the ministry of Joseph Caillaux and sent Raymond

Poincaré to the premiership in 1912; also it made the war minister, Colonel Adolphe Messimy, determined to clarify the responsibilities of the high command. Fears of a military coup d'état had prevented the appointment of a single incumbent to lead France's Army in the event of war. Instead, the holder of the post of vice-president of the Conseil Supérieur de Guerre was designated Commander-in-Chief (CinC) in case of war, but he had no permanent staff. The chief of staff in the war ministry answered to the minister and dealt with the administration of the Army; he had no direct liaison with the designated CinC of the armies in the field. Messimy removed this duality by abolishing the post of vice-president of the CSG and creating that of chief of the general staff. This general officer was to be aided by two sub-chiefs, one heading the general staff in the ministry who would remain in the minister's military cabinet in any war, and the other heading the CinC's staff and dealing with mobilisation and concentration. Crucially, Messimy's successor, Alexandre Millerand, abolished the ministry post, thereby giving entire control to the designated CinC, the chief of the general staff.

This designated general was Joseph Joffre. He had not been the first choice, or even the second. Two previous candidates had declined on grounds of age or because conditions were imposed on acceptance. Joffre was a safe pair of hands. Young enough (59 years old on appointment), republican enough and a former freemason to boot, non-aristocratic (his father was a cooper), an engineer with administrative experience and a canny awareness of politics and politicians, Joffre seemed acceptable to a wide range of opinion. He was no strategist, however. He had not attended the Ecole Supérieure de Guerre and had no experience of strategic planning; rather his colonial career had involved organising fortifications. He knew his limitations, however, and insisted on appointing General Noël Edouard de Curières de Castelnau (despite his being both aristocratic and Catholic) as his deputy to supply the experience of war planning. Joffre had few original ideas of his own; rather he listened to others and took what he wanted. Nonetheless he imposed his will on the French Army indelibly in the pre-war years and during the first two years of the coming conflict.

Among those to whom he listened were a number of younger officers who soon became known as the 'young Turks'. Most of the general officers were older men, some of whom, like Joffre, had fought in the Franco-Prussian War, and they had become lethargic and even physically unfit over the forty years that followed that war. Promotion had been based on Buggins' turn or on the right connections or on being acceptable to whichever political faction was in power. A younger generation of officers was growing up, however, graduates of the Ecole Supérieure de

Guerre, intellectually aware and active in the ferment of change as they advanced up the military hierarchy.[15]

As for the conscript soldiers, there was to be a great change in the length of service. The German *Reich* had a far larger population than France and this demographic was a constant worry. Germany made changes to its military service laws in 1912, and more were announced for 1913, which increased the size of the armies that could be fielded. Since the French counted Germany as hostile, this development could not be other than a source of anxiety. Joffre's re-working of French strategic planning (discussed below) required a stronger French Army. The result was a proposal, put to the CSG in March 1913, to increase the time spent in military service in the active army from two years to three. The subsequent political fight over the bill to legislate the increase was bitter. Those on the left saw the proposition as a means of increasing the numbers of troops available for repression of dissent; those on the right sold the idea as the only method to counter a sudden German descent on French territory. The dispute revived the antagonism between those who preferred to have a smaller professional army with a well-trained militia force of reserves and those who distrusted the reserves and wanted more men under arms.

Much has been written on what became known as the Three-Year Law and what caused it to be passed. Some invoke a 'nationalist revival' after the 1911 Moroccan crisis, driven by fear of Germany; others invoke domestic concerns. They are not mutually exclusive, and most probably the foreign policy and domestic concerns reinforced each other. Gerd Krumeich, who has written extensively on the question, sees the interdependence of foreign, domestic and military politics at the root of the proposal.[16]

The bill was introduced as being a defensive measure, to provide the means to resist a sudden attack by a larger German army, but met with fierce opposition from the left. The debate continued in the press over several months between March and July, interrupted by a change of ministry, and the bill was passed in the end by 358 votes to 204. This was not a large majority for such a divisive measure, and the Three-Year Law became an important question in the electoral campaign of April 1914, especially as the same right/left split coincided with positions on the question of the imposition of income tax. Although the socialist and other left-wing parties gained seats in the election, nevertheless those who had declared themselves in favour of the new law (308 deputies) outnumbered those against or doubtful (235 and 57). The new ministry of René Viviani, which took office on 13 June 1914, might expect further attacks over the question of conscription.

As a consequence of the new law, the numbers of NCOs had to be increased to cope with the greater number of conscripts. There were 48,000 NCOs by 1914, mostly those who volunteered to sign up again after their compulsory military service, and various bonuses were put in place to ensure that sufficient men did this. Three schools to accredit such men allowed promotion to sub-lieutenant, but as the entry to the schools was competitive, those from rural backgrounds, who in the main had little or no secondary education, were disadvantaged.[17] On the other hand, the proportion of those who reached the highest rank (divisional general) and had a name denoting that they belonged to a nobility dropped from 25 per cent of such promotions in 1892 to 4.17 per cent in 1902 to nil in the years 1910–14, with slight blips (15.59 and 11.76 per cent in 1908–09).[18] The very aristocratic General de Curières de Castelnau (vicomte) was part of the 1909 blip, when he was promoted and took command of 13 DI; his successor in command of the division was the bourgeois Ferdinand Foch, promoted to divisional general in 1911.

Even before the vote on the Three-Year Law, parliament had announced that the increase in the army's numbers would be achieved by making the class of 1910, due to be released from the colours in late spring/early summer 1913, serve an extra year. This measure provoked riots in several barracks, not only in the south where resistance to Paris was endemic, but also, and crucially, in the eastern marches: Nancy, Toul, Epinal, Belfort.[19] Such unrest near the border with Germany could not be allowed to continue and the measure was revoked. Instead, after the bill became law, it was proposed to incorporate two classes in one year (the 1912 and 1913 classes). Men were registered during the year when they reached their twentieth birthday, becoming part of the class of that year, and began training the following year. Since that training began in the spring of the first year and ended in the autumn of the last year, the total time was never two (now increased to three) full years. As a result of the new law, on the outbreak of war France's active Army contained: the class of 1911, who had received two years' training; the class of 1912 with about one year's training; and the class of 1913, called up early as 20-year-olds in the latter half of 1913. The last had undergone the six months' preliminary training, but over the winter months, and could not be said to be fully trained by August 1914. The class of 1910, released in 1913, was probably more fit for purpose in August 1914 than the barely trained 1913 class. For all the arguments that the bill caused, France's Army was not much stronger in terms of numbers of fully trained men under arms than it would have been without the law.[20] The energy expended might have been used more profitably in ensuring that the younger classes of reserves had the benefit of better refresher courses and training facilities.

Indeed, training facilities all round were deficient. In 1911 there were only four military camps (and these unfinished) of more than 6,000 hectares. Increased firepower meant that the small camps created after 1871 were totally inadequate for artillery practice. Only a third of active units and a quarter of reserve units could be accommodated for exercises in coordination between artillery and infantry.[21] As for doctrine, matters were fluid. There was no single set of tactical instructions for the infantry according to which all were trained. A series of Règlements de Manoeuvre de l'Infanterie appeared in 1875, 1884, 1902 and 1904, none accepted unanimously by those in charge of applying them in training. The last pre-war Règlement was published in April 1914, hence far too late to have any effect.[22] All combatants, that final instruction read, should aim to engage the enemy closely and destroy him. 'However skilfully [the infantry] are disposed, however efficacious the support of the other arms, a successful attack always depends in the last resort on the bravery [bravoure], the energy and the persistence [opiniâtreté] of the infantry.' Instructions for the artillery confirmed its secondary role. The artillery was to support the infantry by destroying whatever was holding them up; close and constant cooperation between artillery and infantry was, therefore, essential. There was to be no artillery battle for its own sake; the sole task of the artillery was to permit the infantry attack to proceed. The role of the cavalry was to provide the high command with enemy intelligence, and to provide security for the other arms. It must be imbued with the offensive spirit and be ready to take advantage of its speed to engage the enemy with lance and sabre.[23]

Exercises and autumn manoeuvres were intended to provide the necessary practice. Reservists were supposed to attend two training sessions each year, for a total of forty days, but absenteeism was rife. Manoeuvres were intended to give the higher commands practice in working with large units, and they were attended by politicians and military attachés of foreign armies. The last pre-war autumn manoeuvre in 1913 revealed 'intolerable insufficiencies', according to Lieutenant-Colonel Weygand – two divisions becoming completely mixed up, for example. Joffre was furious and insisted on sacking several high-ranking officers.[24] General Yvon Dubail's report mentioned 'lack of decision' and 'timidity', an 'excessive desire for safety and prudence' among the chiefs, and among the ordinary soldiers a 'flabby' attitude, the result of flabby NCOs.[25] The military critic of the influential *Revue des Deux Mondes* wrote of the general agreement that many commanders were not up to the task.[26] German comments on the French manoeuvres show a remarkable similarity with Dubail's verdict. German intelligence criticised the French high command in 1908 ('exaggerated caution and limited initiative') and again in 1911 ('more careful than daring').[27]

At the operational level, Joffre had completed two documents in 1913. The operational level – where army groups, armies and army corps operate – was a new concept and Joffre's 'Règlement sur la conduite des grandes unités' was the first of its kind. The document, dated 23 October 1913, declared that the only path to success, defined as smashing the enemy's fighting forces, was through an offensive. Success required attacks pushed as far as they would go, with no second thoughts, and could only be obtained at the cost of bloody sacrifices. Any other conception should be discarded as contrary to war's very nature. The regulations on tactics ('le service en campagne'), published on 2 December 1913, continued in the same vein: only the offensive can break the will of the adversary. A defensive posture was admissible in certain circumstances, but could only contain the enemy for a limited time and could never procure success. As its most frequently cited sentence proclaims: The French Army, returning to its traditions, knows no law other than the offensive.[28] As some wit remarked, the doctrine was so offensive that even the customs officers were to act offensively.[29]

The prospective enemy

At the same time as Joffre was setting the operational and tactical methods for the French Army, he was also delimiting grand strategy. Joffre got his staff to draw up a position statement for approval by the political leaders, as a basis for this strategy. The CSG met on 18 April 1913 to discuss this position statement, upon which Joffre would base his revision of the disposition of French military forces in the event of war – what became the (in)famous Plan XVII. Drawing up such plans had begun in 1875 and they had been altered many times since, according to the prevailing diplomatic conditions. The Council unanimously accepted the document, which outlined Germany's growing military strength, and noted both the improvements in Russian mobilisation times and the British unwillingness to commit itself in writing. The document took into account the recent changes in law to the constitution of the army and proposed altering the boundaries of several military regions to create a new twenty-first region, hence a XXI Corps.[30]

However, one constraint on planning had already been put in place. It affected the disposition of the French forces along the frontiers. On 9 January 1912, the CSDN met to discuss that disposition, and to consider the states that would probably remain neutral in any conflict.

Joffre was told firmly that, while Luxembourg's neutrality might be violated without too many consequences, that of Belgium was another matter entirely. Despite the advantages to France in any conflict with Germany of a preemptive move into Belgium, the cost would be too high, for then Britain would refuse to help, and might even declare against France. Britain had not come to France's aid in 1870, and might well refuse to help in the future. This veto was confirmed by Poincaré as soon as he took over the premiership, and he never wavered. Joffre would have to draw up Plan XVII while omitting any operation involving Belgian territory, where lay the best terrain for any action against Germany. The new Alsace-Lorraine frontier was guarded by a series of forts, and to the north-east the heavily wooded and hilly Ardennes made movement difficult. A move into the Belgian plain would have been the easiest deployment.

There was no ambiguity about the perceived enemy. The Army expected no attacks from Spain or Italy or Switzerland, and Belgian neutrality was guaranteed. Nor was Austria-Hungary a likely aggressor, given the unrest in the Balkans. Russia was an ally and Britain was at least 'cordial', if uncommitted. The only possible aggressor was Germany. The German people 'thinks only of the dangers, real or imaginary that threaten it', wrote the highly respected Berlin correspondent for the *Journal de Genève*, William Martin, in 1913; a 'veritable militarist frenzy' had seized the country and 'armaments bill succeeds armaments bill, while the power of the country never seems sufficiently protected'.[31] This then was the first basis on which Plan XVII was constructed, and Joffre had the politicians' agreement that German aggression was the only contingency that required planning to counter.

The German *Reich* was more powerful than France, both demographically and economically. Germany could put a much larger army into the field than France; this was the reason for keeping a close eye on German conscription. German industry was so strong that it even held the monopoly of dyes needed for French military uniforms (and for British khaki as well). The French had a competent German-speaking military attaché in Berlin, Colonel Maurice Pellé, who was in post for the three years until summer 1912. Pellé wrote personally to Joffre in addition to his official letters to the war minister, and Joffre hastened his promotion from lieutenant-colonel to full colonel. In May 1912 Pellé wrote of the possibility of a Franco-German war because of the growing public opinion that one day or another Germany would have to 'settle accounts' with France.[32] If Pellé was able to send reports of his talks with the Kaiser or with German staff officers, he seems to have been less successful in providing accurate intelligence. Yet Joffre did receive accurate intelligence from elsewhere that was ignored or misinterpreted. Copies of German war games in 1912 and 1913 made their way to Paris, showing that in a two-front war, Germany would concentrate on wiping out France first of all. Intelligence was also received about the integration of reserve into active units and an analysis of Germany's mobilisation plan.[33] The Russian military attaché in Brussels was active in collecting intelligence about the German plans to violate Belgian neutrality.[34] On the other hand, the German Army seemed not to know the details of Plan XVII concerning the deployment of the French armies, although the new offensive spirit was certainly known from publications such as that of Grandmaison. Also published, hence freely available in Berlin, were the various French field service regulations.[35]

Joffre has been much criticised for his failure to read the German intentions correctly. The section of the general staff dealing with intelligence was its second bureau, but the bureau's forgeries and other dishonourable behaviour during the Dreyfus affair had destroyed its reputation. Moreover, there was competition and complete failure to cooperate between the two other intelligence services: that of the Quai d'Orsay, with its prowess in cryptography, and that of the Sûreté, a police organisation of the interior ministry charged with counter-espionage. The fuss over Madame Caillaux's trial for shooting dead the editor of *Le Figaro* filled the newspapers in July 1914, but more importantly warned foreign governments that the French were reading their diplomatic telegrams. Madame Caillaux had wanted to prevent the publication of her letters to her husband, written when he was married to someone else, but the editor also possessed decrypts of German telegrams, as did Caillaux himself. Although she was acquitted on the grounds of having committed only a *crime passionel* (six shots is some passion!), thereby avoiding a huge international scandal over foreign telegrams, the distraction came at a moment of great crisis when energies should have been devoted elsewhere.

The reason usually adduced to explain why Joffre felt able in July 1914 to respond to a declaration of war, when in 1911 he had declined to do so, is increased national self-confidence, leading to belief in the ability of France's Army to defend the Republic. Such an explanation seems unlikely, given Joffre's sacking of generals following manoeuvres, and given the devastating criticism aired in the Senate as late as July 1914 of France's inferiority in armaments. Part, at least, of any increase in optimism derived from the fact that Joffre felt assured of support from Russia, even if the bases of Plan XVII contained the statement that prudence dictated that British forces should not be taken into account in French planning.[36]

Russia and Britain as allies

The designation of the one enemy by whom France might be attacked was accompanied by a consideration of France's possible allies. Against this sole enemy, France could be sure of one ally, Russia, and hopeful of the other, Britain. The Franco-Russian entente reached in 1892 and 1894 broke the diplomatic isolation that Bismarck had imposed on France after the Franco-Prussian War of 1870–71. France's leaders knew that the only way France could defeat such a powerful enemy as Germany was by gaining allies, and Russia was situated ideally on the eastern frontier with Prussia in the north and on the eastern frontier with Germany's ally, Austria-Hungary, in the south. Moreover, Russia's enormous reserves of manpower could compensate for France's demographic decline. A Franco-Russian entente, or better yet a military alliance, would present Germany with two widely separated frontiers to defend, the very *Einkreisung* that Germany feared.

Yet, from its inception, the Franco-Russian entente trod a rocky path. Russia's defeat in the Russo-Japanese war (1904–05) raised doubts about the utility to France of the Russian Army. Then in 1911 France's refusal of support for Russia when Vienna annexed Bosnia-Herzegovina was reciprocated when Russia failed to support France over Germany's intervention in Morocco. That Agadir crisis led to a greater effort to strengthen the Franco-Russian entente, despite opposition from French left-wing and socialist circles, which had no wish to ally with an autocratic regime that crushed opposition. After the lawyer–politician Raymond Poincaré became France's premier in 1912, then President of the Republic the following year, ties were strengthened. Both he and Joffre were convinced that France's demographic and industrial inferiority vis-à-vis Germany could only be countered by closer ties with Russia. The original 1890s ententes had merely committed the two governments to 'take counsel' of each other on all questions that jeopardised world peace. This grew into an agreement in 1912, confirmed in 1913, that on the outbreak of war Russia would deploy at least 800,000 soldiers on the German frontier after the fifteenth day of mobilisation.[37]

The French were able to prevail in these arrangements because Russia needed French finance once Berlin closed its financial markets to Russia. French loans came, however, with iron strings attached. The money had to be devoted to building strategic railways, so that mobilisation times would be reduced, enabling large numbers of Russian troops to reach the border with Germany much more quickly. French citizens were encouraged to take up bond issues for these Russian loans by a better rate of interest than that offered on domestic loans; and possible criticism, particularly from socialists concerned about alliance with an autocratic empire, was suppressed by semi-official subsidies, funded by Russia but distributed by the Quai d'Orsay, to the French press.[38]

France's military attaché in Russia was General Pierre de Laguiche, a career artillery officer who had been in Petrograd since 1912. He spoke Russian fluently and urged Paris to send more Russian speakers. The Italian head of a military mission to Russia described him as 'very cultured', and as having gained both 'the respect and intimate friendship' of Grand-Duke Nicholas and 'great popularity' within the Russian Army.[39] Laguiche's predecessors had been sending highly detailed reports directly to the war ministry (normally a military attaché, being based in his country's embassy, would send reports to the foreign ministry). For example, General Moulin's reports on the Russo-Japanese War, sent in 1905, and on the 1906 manoeuvres, are long and well organised. The copies in the army archives contain marginalia, and so were clearly read in Paris. Moulin also reported his conversations with the British and German military attachés and with General Palitzine on the Russian and French concentration against Germany.[40] Laguiche continued to send frequent, detailed reports. On 18/31 January 1913, for example, there was a long report on Russian aviation, and in March 1914 he forwarded a comprehensive report made by his deputy, Commandant Wehrlin, on the Russian railways. By this date such information was invaluable, and Laguiche pointed out how much tact and persistence Wehrlin had used to be able to extract it. The report listed the kilometrage of new lines put into service in 1913 and 1914, which lines had been doubled, and the lengths of the various projected strategic lines. Such knowledge was an important factor in France's confidence in Russia's contribution to a future war.[41]

Manoeuvres permitted the two high commands to get to know each other a little, but were much less useful for a frank exchange of information. Joffre attended the Russian manoeuvres in 1910, accompanied by Foch and Weygand. The latter has left an interesting account of the pomp and gala dinners, but notes also Russian reticence about disclosing too much.[42] More useful were the staff talks between Joffre and his Russian counterpart General Gilinsky in the final years of peace.[43] In August 1913, when they agreed that Russia would begin offensive operations with at least 800,000 men on the fifteenth day of mobilisation, they confirmed that both France and Russia would attack into the 'heart' of Germany. The purpose was to force Germany to fight on two fronts, and once Germany was defeated, Russia would then find the operations against Austria-Hungary much easier. Joffre had been impressed during these talks by how keen the Russian officers were to learn and by the great progress in railway construction. The Tsar in turn was very pleased that Joffre had been so impressed.[44]

In Paris a general staff study of May 1914 concluded that Germany had not intended before 1913 to place any active army corps on the Russian frontier. Now, with the improved Russian railways and speed of mobilisation, Germany intended to leave two active and one reserve corps, plus a cavalry division, in the east.[45] The French strategy was beginning to pay dividends.

If the Russian alliance could now be considered as certain, it was otherwise with the British. The *entente cordiale* was signed in 1904, but no signed document committed Britain to aid France (or vice versa) in war.[46] The entente marked an end to ten centuries of traditional hostility, marked at the last by such recent events as British criticism of France over the Dreyfus affair and French criticism of Britain over the South African War. Military staff talks between the two armies began in December 1905 and were later promoted by the then Director of Military Intelligence in the War Office, Henry Wilson. Plans for the intervention of a British force on the Continent in the event of war were given an extra push during the Moroccan crisis in 1911, and invitations to annual manoeuvres and other 'jollies' marked the final years of peace. Naval cooperation was also agreed to the advantage of both France (who had slipped to fourth place behind Britain, Germany and the USA) and Britain (who needed greater security in the North Sea). The French Navy would take responsibility for the Mediterranean, although some Royal Navy vessels remained, and the British for the North Sea and French Channel and Atlantic coasts. These military and naval arrangements were confirmed in an exchange of letters between the French Ambassador in London, Paul Cambon, and the British Foreign Secretary, Sir Edward Grey. However, these letters did not commit Britain to intervene on the side of France in a European war. Moreover, the British warned very firmly that any French violation of Belgian neutrality would probably swing public opinion in Britain against any such intervention or, at the least, make it very unlikely.

It was for this very reason that Joffre made no definite provision for placing any British Expeditionary Force in the line of battle in Plan XVII. If the British came, they would extend the French left after completing their concentration on the fifteenth or sixteenth day of mobilisation. If the French could count for sure on British naval help, nevertheless the military help of the estimated 120,000 soldiers remained doubtful: 'we shall act prudently therefore', the sentence ran in the 'Bases du plan' document, 'by not taking any account of British forces in our projected operations'.[47] The fact remained, however, that by August 1914 all the detailed railway transport timetables were in place for moving six British infantry divisions and some cavalry across the Channel. This is in stark contrast to the formal alliance between France and Russia, whereby each committed to come to the other's aid, but it lacked detailed planning and knowledge of the other's strategic intentions. 'Anglo–French coordination far exceeded that established between Paris and St. Petersburg', wrote Samuel R. Williamson; it even exceeded that between Vienna and Berlin.[48]

In pre-Entente days the British Army had seemed of little value to the French, merely a colonial police force with a nice line in ceremonial. When the French military attaché arrived in London in 1904, no one in Paris 'thought that it could ever be the slightest use to us from a military point of view'. However, opinions changed as the European situation worsened, and the British system became a model for a professional army, particularly in its recruitment of native troops.[49] British opinion about the value of France's Army was provided mainly by the reports of the military correspondent of *The Times*. Three long articles appeared on the 1912 manoeuvres, and in 1913 the improvements in the use of aircraft and in motor traction for moving heavy guns were described.[50]

As they did in Russia, generals attended British and French manoeuvres. It was not simply the fact of greater proximity that made the Franco-British relationship easier, but the bubbling personality of Henry Wilson helped to create friendly cooperation. He made a point of visiting Foch, beginning during 1909 when both men were principals of their respective staff colleges, and he also made friends with General Castelnau. Wilson watched the French 1912 autumn manoeuvres and commented favourably on the infantry, although the 'cavalry was *very* ill handled'. He noted in his diary the 'outstanding things' about the manoeuvres: '(a) The ease with which these Frenchmen move, feed, and fight large masses of men; (b) The marching of the infantry'. On 14 February 1913 Wilson saw Castelnau and Joffre in the morning and in the evening dined with Foch in Huguet's house in Bourges: 'we talked till midnight'.[51]

Colonel Victor Huguet was the French military attaché in London. Like Laguiche in St Petersburg (Petrograd), Huguet sent regular detailed reports on the strength of the British Army and attended its manoeuvres. He reported in March 1911 that the six British divisions of an expeditionary corps could be mobilised, if the order was so given, and concentrated within sixteen to seventeen days, a delay that Huguet thought too long.[52] It was not only at the highest level that friendly relations were established. Exchanges and training sessions in each other's country enabled French and British officers to get to know each other. The French foresaw some serious problems, however, not all of which derived from the small size of

Britain's regular army. In a lecture in Paris in April 1913, Huguet described the British as insular and mistrustful of 'foreign' ideas. (Although the Ecole Supérieure de Guerre accepted foreign officers into its courses, no British were among their number.) The British foot soldier was less intelligent than his French equivalent, but made up for it by perseverance, tenacity and an unshakeable faith in his officers. Even after the war, a disillusioned Huguet repeated similar views about the 'Englishman', who 'drifts from day to day without looking beyond the needs of the moment'.[53]

Despite the formality of Franco-Russian relations when compared to the friendlier, if somewhat condescending, Franco-British relations, Joffre was justified in basing his strategic dispositions on sure support from Russia but only possible support from Britain.

August 1914: The mobilised army

On 7 February 1914, Joffre sent to the designated army commanders his secret instructions for the concentration of his forces.[54] His broad intention was to attack the German armies once all his forces were assembled. The only clue as to what this entailed was the brief description of 'two principal actions', the first on the right flank between the Vosges and the river Moselle, east of the fortress of Toul, and the second north of the Verdun–Metz line. Presumably Joffre wished to keep his options open and to minimise any security leak. Indeed, it must be remembered that these orders, based on the final war plan, Plan XVII, were nothing more than instructions for the concentration. They did not constitute planning for a specific offensive or offensives.

The First Army, commanded by General Yvon Dubail and comprising five corps (VII, VIII, XIII, XIV, XXI) and 6 and 8 DC (cavalry divisions), was to be deployed at the southern end of the front along the new Vosges frontier with Alsace. The first of four groups of reserve divisions was deployed to First Army's rear. Next in line and on First Army's left, General Edouard de Curières de Castelnau commanded the five corps of Second Army (IX, XV, XVI, XVIII and XX) defending the Lorraine frontier, together with a group of three reserve divisions and two cavalry divisions (2 and 10 DC). The length of front meant a lesser density of troops here than further north, because the hilly and forested terrain itself gave some protection, and the border had been provided with a series of heavily armed forts as a protection against a German incursion. These had been built immediately after the Franco-Prussian War, and consisted of two belts, from Verdun to Toul in the north and from Epinal to Belfort further south, with a gap between them intended to channel any enemy invasion. More forts were begun in the interior but were not finished, as increasing firepower seemed to reduce their value.

Next, around Verdun, Third Army, under the command of General Pierre Ruffey, comprised three corps (IV, V and VI), 7 DC and a group of three reserve divisions. Third Army covered the north-eastern sector, facing the strong German defences of the *Moselstellung* incorporating Metz and Thionville and covering (unsuccessfully as it turned out) the important iron-ore basin around Briey. It formed the liaison between the two principal offensive actions. Its role was to throw back any German incursion from the *Moselstellung* and to prepare to attack Metz.

On the left of the front, Fifth Army had a much wider sector, running as far west as the Belgian border near Hirson, but facing east towards Luxembourg and (eventually) Thionville. Fifth Army formed the left flank of the French deployment under the command of General Charles Lanrezac with five corps (I, II, III, X, XI), 4 DC and two reserve divisions. Behind Third and Fifth armies, and temporarily in second line, Joffre placed his Fourth Army so that it could move either to support operations by Third Army around Verdun or Fifth Army further west facing the Belgian and Luxembourg frontiers. It contained 9 DC and three corps (XII, XVII and the Colonial Corps). This deployment left open the whole of the Belgian frontier, north to Maubeuge and then west to the sea. If the British arrived, they would extend the French left as far as Maubeuge.

As the crisis following the assassination in Sarajevo mounted, all diplomatic attempts to avert war failed. On 1 August 1914, the Council of Ministers authorised the publication next day of the decree of general mobilisation. All military classes – the reserve, the territorials and territorial reserve – were to report to their recruitment region. On 2 August 1914, Frenchmen began arriving in orderly fashion at their specified regimental depot. Each reservist had his individual military record book, the 'livret militaire', which recorded his regiment, his service record and details of where and when to report, if mobilised. The news that mobilisation was to begin that day had percolated throughout France the previous afternoon, from Paris to the préfets of each département, then to the mayors, the gendarmes and the game-keepers. It was announced by public proclamation to the sound of beating drums, by ringing the tocsin from the churches, and by posting up the official proclamation (see Figure 2). Reporting dates were staggered to avoid overloading the railways, which were all taken immediately under military control. Once arrived and equipped, troops of the active army and those designated to join the reserve divisions grouped behind the front line armies left their regimental depot by train for their 'concentration' zone. During the

Fig. 2 Poster warning of general mobilisation for 2 August 1914

concentration period, this zone was protected by the 'covering' troops deployed along the frontier.

The men came from all walks of life and all regions of France. In south-west France, 36-year-old Louis Barthas, socialist and trade-unionist, was mobilised to his regimental depot in Narbonne despite being ill, and despite there being insufficient lodgings or uniforms for all the men.[55] In the north, Dr Gaston Top's livret informed him that he was to take the first train after 8am from his home town, and report on

Table 2 *Military rates of pay in francs*

Grade	Annual rate	Daily rate	Observations
Divisional general	28,800	80.00	Two grades of general: brigadier-general and (higher) divisional general, the army's highest rank
Lt Colonel	6,588	9.15	
Lieutenant	3,420	4.75	After 8 years in grade
Sergeant	1,224	0.72	Only paid at the daily rate, unless has
		3.40	joined up again after completion of military service
Soldat (private)		0.05	Rate unchanged since the 'one sou per day' of the Revolutionary Wars

Source: Bulletin officiel du Ministère de la Guerre, *Tarifs de solde … volume arrêté au 13 janvier* 1913 (Paris: Librairie Militaire Chapelot, 1913)

3 August to his unit 27 RAC (field artillery regiment) in Saint-Omer (Nord). He spent the first two days sorting bandages, then left on 5 August for Lille. To transport one of the three groups in his regiment, three trains were required, each with twenty-four wagons for the requisitioned horses, three for the soldiers with another for the officers, plus seventeen flat-bed carriages for the materiel.[56] In the Bordeaux area, reserve sub-lieutenant Roger Sargos, an administrator in the forestry service, anticipated the call-up and contacted his unit, 8 Bataillon de chasseurs à pied (BCP). He was told to report to Amiens on the first day of mobilisation, and there took over command of the machine-gun section of his reserve battalion. They left Amiens on the evening of 12 August to join 69 DR in Vervins, about 20 kilometres from the Belgian frontier.[57] Paul Tuffrau, graduate of the Ecole Normale Supérieure, had completed his military service in 1912 and begun teaching in Vendôme (between Orléans and Le Mans). He was on holiday, therefore, when war was declared. He was mobilised as a reserve sub-lieutenant, and joined 246 RI in command of a machine-gun section, like Sargos. He spent the days until 8 August organising his section, with its tents and horses in Paris, and then left by train, not knowing the regiment's destination.[58]

The pay for officers was considerably more than for the 'simple soldat' (see Table 2). A mobilised private, the vast majority, left his paid employment and received instead the basic pay of one 'sou' (five centimes) a day. At the wartime rate of exchange of around 25 francs to the pound, a sou is approximately a halfpenny. Regular privates, however, received 20 centimes after two years' service, 25 centimes after six and 30 centimes after ten years.

In recognition of the hardship, a law passed on 5 August 1914 provided for an allowance of 1.25 francs per day, plus an additional 50 centimes for each child under sixteen, for families whose breadwinner had been called up. Although this did not replace the average daily wage – in Paris in 1911, that was 7.24 francs, but as low as 3.72 in rural areas – it gave some large, rural families a bigger income than they had known before. The fact of these family payments made a considerable contribution to the home front's ability to continue the war, although many justified claims for the allowances were turned down in the first few months. Indeed courts martial records show that some soldiers deserted when they learned that their wives had been refused them.[59] A further contribution to household budgets of destitute families was the suspension of the requirement to pay their rent, a measure decreed ten days later.

Jean-Jacques Becker's study of public opinion as revealed by the reports of primary school teachers, who had received questionnaires from the ministry of education in which to record public reactions under various headings, shows first that mobilisation did not create a patriotic and fervent outburst of feeling. Like thunder out of a clear blue sky, the news of war came as a surprise, and first reactions were consternation, sadness and, among the women, tears. Second, Becker shows the distinct change from the day of mobilisation to the day of departure by train. Obviously emotions on departure were mixed, but appeared to reduce to the triple proposition: France did not want war; France was attacked; we will do our duty. This sentiment explains why the planned arrest of presumed trouble-makers, such as trade-unionists and other 'lefties', did not take place. Préfets had maintained lists in the so-called 'Carnets B' of such trouble-makers, but they were not needed.[60]

Table 3 shows which classes were incorporated in the ranks of the army and when. A class consists of recruits who attain their twentieth birthday in a particular year, and the class is known as the class of that year. Those of the class of 1900, then, were born in 1880. In addition to the three classes already serving in the active army, numbers were boosted by volunteers. Gaston Lefèvre – he will reappear in 1917 – volunteered after his Lorraine village was overrun and his father shot as a hostage during the German invasion. Despite being under-age, he slipped into non-occupied France and joined up in Mézières (Ardennes). Non-French citizens joined the Foreign Legion: American poet, Alan Seeger, for example, or Swiss novelist, Blaise Cendrars. There were three types of French volunteer: the so-called 'ordinary' volunteer, a young man anticipating his call-up; the second type volunteered for the duration, such men being either older, or previously exempt, or invalided

Table 3 *Incorporated in 1914*

Class	Age in 1914	Date incorporated	Percentage incorporated
1915	19	December 1914	93
1914	20	Aug-Sept 1914	91.8
1913	21	active army	⎫
1912	22	active army	⎬ 85 for classes 1909–13
1911	23	active army	⎭
1910–1896	24–38	August 1914	81 for classes 1899–1903
			82 for classes 1904–08
1895–1892	39–42	April 1915	
1891–1888	43–46	1916	

Source: Boulanger, *La France devant la conscription*, 111; Guy Pedroncini (ed.), *Histoire militaire de la France*, vol. 3, *De 1871 à 1940* (Paris: PUF, 1992), 3: 258.

out (otherwise they would have been called up along with the others of their class). The third category of 'special' volunteers came into effect only in 1915; these were men who anticipated being combed out from factory or other jobs that could be carried out by women or older men. The advantage of being a volunteer was the freedom to choose one's service. In 1914 there were 26,673 ordinary volunteers – presumably moved by patriotism as their older brothers or fathers were called up – and 45,755 volunteers for the duration.[61]

Two other sources of manpower must be mentioned. The Armée d'Afrique, mis-named, because it refers to France's nineteenth military region, Algeria and Tunisia, formed an integral part of the French Army and supplied XIX Corps for metropolitan France. Most of the French citizens in North Africa were of European descent: Italians, Maltese, Spanish, Portuguese, and a number of Alsatians, who had opted for France in 1871 and had been granted land in Algeria or Tunisia. Conscription had been extended to these provinces, since they were part of France. The colonial infantry divisions contained, therefore, a mixture of European (zouaves) and native contingents, officered by Europeans, as there was an upper bar in place for native promotions. Emir Khaled, for example, grandson of a famous Muslim leader and 'brilliant' officer graduate of Saint-Cyr, could rise no higher than 'native lieutenant'.[62] The native contingents (tirailleurs or spahi, cavalry) were frequently lumped together as 'sénégalais', although they were far from all coming from Senegal. Conscripts from mainland France might make up any shortfall in the Armée d'Afrique, and convicted men or other undesirables would be sent to special battalions within it. The XIX Corps also supplied men as volunteers for Morocco, and from 1912 native contingents of tirailleurs marocains were also raised. Various forms of inducement encouraged native troops to enrol, ranging from special enlistment bonuses to levies raised on villages or specific regions. At mobilisation and in the four months following, Algeria sent twenty-nine battalions across the Mediterranean; Tunisia sent nine; Morocco thirty-eight; and AOF three battalions of tirailleurs sénégalais. These last were the only native contingents to join combat in the early months of the war; the remainder were 'white' units.[63] Almost 50,000 men and over 10,000 horses were transported across the Mediterranean, without hitch, despite the commander of Germany's *Mittelmeerdivision*, Rear Admiral Wilhelm Souchon.[64] He was determined to strike at France's communications with North Africa so as to cut off the supply of troops to France. Forced to leave Messina (Sicily) on 2 August when Italy declared its neutrality, Souchon was steaming for the Algerian coast when he received news of the declaration of war, and on the morning of 3 August he fired the first shots in the Mediterranean. The *Goeben* bombarded Philippeville for ten minutes and the *Breslau* fired on Bône. French coastal batteries returned fire and little damage was done to either side. Being hopelessly outnumbered in the Mediterranean, the German ships ran for Constantinople, pursued (but in vain) by the Royal Navy.[65]

The second source of manpower lay in the colonial army, created to garrison the French colonies overseas, not only in Africa but also in Indo-China, in the Pacific, in Madagascar and the Antilles (Caribbean). The lower ranks were natives, because France did not have enough military to provide the necessary policing and guard duties, but the officers were French. The links between the colonies and the army in metropolitan France were very close, because officers transferred between them frequently. If regular officers wanted more excitement and better promotion prospects, rather than a dreary garrison life in France during the years of peace between 1871 and 1914, they opted for a career in the colonies. Joffre made his name in Tonkin and Timbuctoo before returning to France to a desk job. General Charles Mangin is probably the best known of the 'colonials', but there were many more. They were also looked down on somewhat by the older and more staid generals who had spent their military career in metropolitan France. The troops in the colonial army served in their colony but could be 'persuaded' to serve in France. Once again, the connection with metropolitan France was close, as three divisions of the colonial army were stationed in France and might contain French conscripts.

How did the French Army utilise the 3.5 million[66] men called to arms in 1914, of whom 1,865,000 joined combat units straight away? The structure of the five armies that Joffre deployed is shown in Table 4.

Table 4 *Basic structure of the infantry forces in an army*

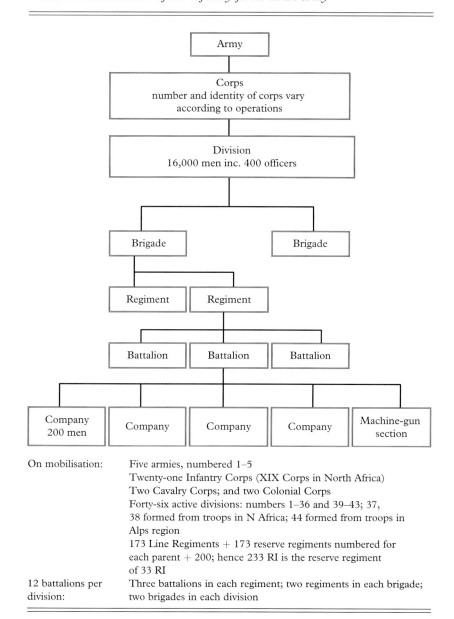

On mobilisation: Five armies, numbered 1–5
                     Twenty-one Infantry Corps (XIX Corps in North Africa)
                     Two Cavalry Corps; and two Colonial Corps
                     Forty-six active divisions: numbers 1–36 and 39–43; 37,
                     38 formed from troops in N Africa; 44 formed from troops in
                     Alps region
                     173 Line Regiments + 173 reserve regiments numbered for
                     each parent + 200; hence 233 RI is the reserve regiment
                     of 33 RI

12 battalions per   Three battalions in each regiment; two regiments in each brigade;
division: two brigades in each division

Table 5 *Divisional structure*

Service	Numbers	Percentage	Observations
Infantry	13,600	85	Armed with a Lebel rifle and bayonet each machine-gun section has two 1907-model machine guns
Artillery	1,680	10.5	Three groups of three batteries of 75mm guns (36 guns in all)
Cavalry	one squadron		Light cavalry plus cyclists
Engineers (*génie*)	one company		34 battalions expanded to give 2 per corps and 3 for the new reserve divisions
Transport (*train*)	[attached to corps]		20 squadrons (1 per corps) doubled on mobilisation to give 84 companies
Military police (*prévôté*)		4.5	
Medical service (*sanitaire*)			Group of stretcher-bearers (*brancardiers*) (GBD) (regiments had stretcher-bearers also: GBR)

Source: Guinard et al., *Introduction*, 117, 144, 169 181, 194–5.

The smallest unit containing troops of all arms, with engineers, medical staff, military police and HQ staff with all the bureaux was the division. The move from its peacetime footing increased an infantry division's size by incorporating the youngest reservists, thereby increasing (almost doubling in some cases) the number of men in a company.[67] The divisional structure is shown in Table 5.

France's total artillery resources consisted of 81 regiments, the great majority armed with the standard 75mm field gun. In August 1914, 10,650 officers and 428,000 gunners were mobilised into 1,528 batteries (excluding the fixed coastal and fortress guns) as shown in Table 6.[68]

Paul Lintier (class of 1913) provides an example of how an artillery unit operated. He was a gunner in 44 Régiment d'Artillerie de Campagne (RAC or Field Artillery Regiment), attached to IV Corps. He left Le Mans (the Corps' home depot) on 8 August, arrived north of Verdun on the evening of the following day, and marched north with the Third Army. In his journal, published posthumously in 1916, he described his gun battery. His no.1 75mm gun in 11 Battery was pulled by a team of six horses harnessed in pairs, with a similar team pulling the ammunition wagon. The personnel accompanying the gun limber and wagon were six drivers, six gunners, a corporal and a sergeant in command.[69]

The sample infantry division followed in this book, 13 DI, was one of the two allocated to XXI Corps in First Army stationed along the eastern

Table 6 *France's artillery in 1914*

Number of batteries / number of guns	Type / calibre	Comments
1043 / 4076	Field artillery (mainly 75s)	24 batteries in North Africa; another 666 guns in reserve; and another 48 adapted as anti-aircraft guns
43 / 120	Mountain guns, 65mm	13 batteries in North Africa
67 / 84 120 104	Heavy artillery: 120 short★ 120 long★ 155 short, rapid-fire	Mostly old types, hard to move, not powerful due to be replaced by the 1913 model 105mm, rapid-firing, range of 11,000 metres
375	Territorial, without transport	21 batteries in North Africa
In addition: army and corps artillery parks, stocked with outdated guns		

★ Whether a gun is classed as long or short is a function of the length of the barrel in relation to its bore (calibre). When a short-barrelled gun can be elevated at an angle of 45° or more, it is classed as a howitzer.

frontier with Germany, with the task of 'covering' or protecting the army's mobilisation. Its recruitment area was the Vosges and Alpine regions, so the men did not have far to travel to their war stations. They formed fifty-four companies of 200 men each – 10,800 infantry supported by thirty machine guns and thirty-six 75s (three groups of three batteries, each battery of four guns). The average age of the infantry was 23, and the division comprised the three classes of the active army (21- to 23-year-olds), with a strong component of reservists from classes 1910–1901, and even a few from the 1900 (34-year-olds) to 1894 (40-year-olds) classes.[70]

The French Army concentration was complete by 18 August. It had taken 4,278 trains to move everyone, and only 20 or so of them arrived late. Fourteen dedicated railway lines carried an average of 56 trains per day.[71] This was a tremendous organisational feat. The railways and their personnel all came under military control as soon as war was declared. Under the legal statute of the declaration of 'a state of siege', the army had the right to requisition what they needed, and so horses and automobiles were also made available to the military.

This then, was how the French Army stood in the hot summer of 1914, after the Serbian nationalist Gavrilo Prinkip shot and killed in Sarajevo the heir to the Austro-Hungarian throne. It was prepared to face a German attack, although would not be the first to violate Belgian neutrality. Indeed, strict orders were issued that French troops were to remain 10 kilometres behind the frontier. It counted on a Russian offensive on the fifteenth day after mobilisation, and it hoped that its friends in the British Army would arrive in time to be of help in the opening days. In 1911, Joffre had told Caillaux that France did not have the necessary 70-per-cent chance of victory in war. It is not known what percentage Joffre believed that he held three years later, but presumably it was higher than seventy.

2 1914: From the frontiers to Flanders

The opening battles: from the frontiers to the river Marne

On the evening of 2 August, Joffre warned the commanders of the covering forces that he did not intend to launch a general offensive until all his forces were assembled. He moved Fourth Army forward from its planned location to between Fifth and Third after learning that Germany had violated Luxembourg's neutrality, and he repeated the warning that troops were not to breach the 10-kilometre line behind the frontiers unless to repel any enemy incursion. There was to be no provocation; it must be Germany who declared war on France. This Germany did on 3 August. The German charge that French aircraft had bombed Nürnberg was false propaganda. Britain declared war on Germany on 4 August after the German violation of Luxembourg and Belgium swung both public opinion and the uncertain Cabinet members in favour of intervention. They had caused considerable anguish to France's ambassador in London, Paul Cambon, as they deliberated.

The Grand Quartier Général (French headquarters in the field, GQG) would operate in Vitry-le-François in the Marne département from 5 August. The fifty or so GQG officers were supervised by the major général (Joffre's chief of staff) General Emile Belin. They manned three bureaux: the first, led by Colonel Poindron, dealt with personnel and the transport and supply of materiel; the second handled intelligence under Colonel Dupont; the third, led by Colonel Pont, dealt with operations. In addition, a 'Direction de l'Arrière', the equivalent of 'lines of communication', operated the Direction des étapes et des services under General Laffon de Ladébat. The second and third bureaux received their directions from the first sub-chief of staff, General Henri Berthelot; the first and the Direction de l'Arrière came under the direction of the second sub-chief, General Deprez (soon replaced, in mid-August 1914, by Colonel Maurice Pellé, former military attaché in Berlin).[1] The *missi dominici* of Operations acted as liaison officers with the army commanders, reporting back to Joffre for good or for ill on the armies in the field. Their influence became feared and detested in equal measure. Colonel Pénelon and Major Herbillon acted as liaison officers with the President of the Republic and the government.

As intelligence reports came in concerning the enemy's intentions, Joffre issued his first 'general instruction' to the army commanders. He intended 'to seek battle with all his forces together, resting his right on the river Rhine'. He reported that there seemed to be only six corps in front of the First and Second Armies, while the main enemy forces seemed to be around Metz ready to break out westwards or perhaps southwards; 'elements' of an army of five corps were operating further north and had penetrated into Belgium. Clearly the French did not yet have an accurate picture of German intentions or of German strength. Joffre instructed First and Second Armies to attack into Lorraine, aiming for Sarrebourg and Sarrebrücken respectively, but Castelnau's two left-hand corps were to remain available for Joffre to use with Third Army if the Germans attacked out of their stronghold of Metz. Third Army was to prepare to move northwards, with Fourth Army ready to attack between the Meuse and the Argonne forest, while Fifth Army was to counter any enemy crossing of the Meuse between Mézières and Mouzon and itself to cross should the possibility arise.[2]

The main plank of Joffre's strategy was to attack at the same time as the Russians in the east. When the Russian CinC, Grand-Duke Nicholas, informed the French on 6 August that he would be ready to launch his offensive on 14 August, Joffre fixed the same date for his First and Second Armies to move into German (formerly French) Lorraine. Whilst waiting until the concentration of his armies was complete, Joffre decided to score a morale-boosting victory by sending a small force into Alsace. He believed that there were few German forces there, and the capture and return to France of some Alsatian territory would make splendid propaganda. Accordingly, despite its commander's caution, VII Corps was ordered on 7 August to advance to Altkirch, near the Swiss border, which it did easily as the Germans withdrew without fighting, and then to continue to the more important town of Mulhouse. The townspeople lined the streets and cheered their liberators, thereby showing the degree to which Germany had failed to win over the citizens of the provinces ceded in the Treaty of Frankfurt. So the boost to morale had succeeded, but the Germans counter-attacked the next day at Mulhouse and recaptured all the Alsatian territory, except for Thann. Because VII Corps was part of First Army, which Joffre planned to use in the 14 August offensive further north in Lorraine, he created the Army of Alsace, under the command of General Paul Pau, to take over the southern sector. The Alsace Army comprised VII Corps, one cavalry and two infantry

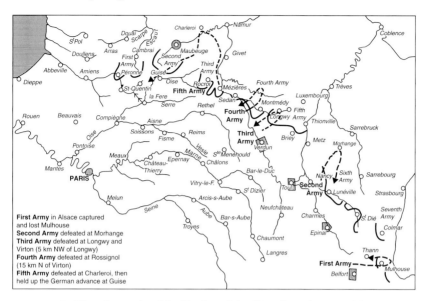

First Army in Alsace captured
and lost Mulhouse
Second Army defeated at Morhange
Third Army defeated at Longwy and
Virton (5 km NW of Longwy)
Fourth Army defeated at Rossignol
(15 km N of Virton)
Fifth Army defeated at Charleroi, then
held up the German advance at Guise

2. The aftermath of the Battles of the Frontiers, August 1914

divisions, plus the First Group of Reserve Divisions. In a move that would become familiar, he replaced the VII Corps commander because of his caution and failure to hold Mulhouse. This new unit freed General Dubail of First Army from the need to protect the southern end of the French deployment.

The drive into Lorraine on 14 August by First and Second Armies, beginning at the same time as Russian operations, was the right-hand prong of a two-step strategy, which Robert Doughty has described as Joffre's 'jab with his right' and attempt at 'a knock-out blow with his left'.[3] It was necessary to jab first, to prove to the Russians that the French would keep their word, but equally it was necessary to wait until German intentions in Belgium became clearer before attempting the knock-out. First Army was ordered to advance 60 kilometres eastward from Nancy, the capital of French Lorraine, towards Sarrebourg and Mt Donon in the Vosges mountains. The Donon commanded one of the key passes leading from the river Rhine through the mountains. Joffre ordered General Castelnau's Second Army to advance north-eastwards from Nancy, towards Morhange, taking care to protect its left flank from enemy troops debouching from the heavily fortified *Moselstellung*, the forts between Metz and Thionville (Diedenhofen) along the river Moselle. These divergent directions of attack meant that the two armies had fronts of between 70 and 80 kilometres, and the terrain was not easy. First Army had rugged mountainous terrain to cover, and Second Army faced valleys deliberately flooded by the enemy, in addition to the threat from the German forts.

The two armies made good, if cautious, progress on the first day, because the opposing forces (*Sixth Army* under Crown Prince Rupprecht of Bavaria and *Seventh* under General Josias von Heeringen) had been ordered to pull back so as to tempt the French to advance into a trap. The next day, however, 15 August, revealed how successful the German tactics were as they retreated. The more numerous German artillery caused many casualties among the advancing French, because it could send plunging fire onto French columns whose 75s had a flat trajectory and fired a less powerful shell. The German infantry also had machine guns in greater numbers. So Castelnau ordered his Second Army commanders to proceed cautiously, to position the artillery before beginning an attack, and to dig in solidly before advancing to the next position. Between 14 and 19 August, First and Second Armies made steady progress, but it became clear that counter-attacks were to be expected. On 20 August, Crown Prince Rupprecht, tired of simply letting the French advance as Moltke ordered, and having requested permission to act, counter-attacked Second Army and Heeringen's *Seventh Army* counter-attacked First Army. Although the Bavarians found General Ferdinand Foch's XX Corps too hard a nut to crack, the two other corps of Second Army were put to flight. First Army had stood its ground rather better, but, with its left flank exposed by the retreat of Second Army troops, was forced to pull back in turn. By 23 August Castelnau had collected his army on the heights around Nancy, and Dubail's men were back where they had started. It had been an expensive excursion into German territory, but the lesson had been learned: unprepared and unsupported attacks with massed infantry, whether firing their rifles or attacking with the bayonet, were too costly.

The experience of 13 DI as part of First Army's attack towards Mt Donon in the Vosges mountains was typical of these opening battles. In eight days of offensive action, 13 DI had advanced about 20 kilometres on a 20-kilometre front, and then had retreated about 30 kilometres. The action cost 2,451 casualties during the offensive and a further 3,480 during the retreat, being 21.47 per cent and 16.17 per cent of the division's effectives respectively (it had been reinforced during the course of the operation). Obviously such a casualty rate could not be sustained; the division's historians admit that it was a cruel baptism of fire. Units had been too impatient to act, with some on 14 August assaulting across open ground in the face of mortar and machine-gun fire. They had engaged too dense an infantry with too few material means against a well-prepared enemy, who covered a well-planned field of fire while using fewer men.[4]

As First and Second Armies engaged enemy troops in Lorraine, Joffre waited for further intelligence about the German armies in Belgium before issuing orders to his other armies to take the offensive. Intelligence reports suggested that the Germans intended to move deeper into Belgium than had at first been thought. Joffre was not worried by this risk to his open flank; rather he concluded that since the enemy's right was stronger than expected, his centre must be correspondingly weaker. He would launch Third and Fourth Armies into the weaker German centre, cutting off the enemy troops who had already advanced further west. He would wait, however, to allow more of those enemy troops to move across and to the north of the French front, thereby weakening the centre (so he thought) still further. In addition, he took a corps from Second Army and another from Fifth Army to strengthen General Fernand de Langle de Cary's Fourth Army for the decisive offensive. It was only on the evening of 20 August, the date of the German counter-attack in Lorraine, that Joffre issued orders for his two armies to advance north-eastwards into Belgium and Luxembourg.

Third and Fourth Armies marched, as ordered, on 21 August. They had inadequate maps and inadequate intelligence about the German troops waiting for them. Instead of hitting a weakened centre, as Joffre expected, the French were slightly out-numbered – ten German infantry corps against nine French. The next day, two of those French corps in Third Army attacked the solidly entrenched Germans at Longwy and Virton. They attacked in rain and fog and were thrown back in some disarray, suffering huge casualties. In Fourth Army, some progress was made but the Colonial Corps was cut to pieces at Rossignol. It suffered 11,648 casualties that day, and lost large amounts of materiel. Joffre's orders to continue the fight the next day could not be obeyed, because by the time that units had been re-formed and re-supplied, the Germans had driven the centre of Third Army back for 8 kilometres, and Fourth Army units withdrew piecemeal after elements of one division which had lost most of its artillery panicked and fled. Both armies were back more or less where they had started by the evening of 23 August.[5] They had fared no better than First and Second Armies in Lorraine, but they had suffered greater casualties. Indeed 22 August was France's worst day of the whole war.

The third of the frontier battles was fought by General Charles Lanrezac's Fifth Army on the left wing. It was planned as an additional offensive to the Third and Fourth Armies' action, hence was to begin on the same day. Lanrezac, however, was not happy about the situation on his front. Even before war began he sent a memorandum to GQG stating that his army needed to be deployed further west. His forces were inadequate for a march into eastern Belgium, and as it became clear that the Germans were pushing much deeper into that country, he feared that his line of march would make it impossible to cut them off. He had already requested and received permission to move one of his corps further north to Givet. This extension of his front meant that he had to guard against a German crossing of the Meuse either south of Sedan, or at Mézières, or north of Givet at Namur in Belgium. When the last of these possibilities became more and more likely as intelligence reports came in, Lanrezac urged a move westwards towards the fortified region of Maubeuge to avoid being outflanked. On 17 August the last of the forts around Liège fell to the Germans and by 20 August the Belgian Army had retired to Antwerp. So, when Fifth Army joined the offensive on 21 August, it would not be dealing with a supposedly weakened German centre, but with strong enemy forces advancing much further north and east than had been anticipated. Moreover, Fifth Army's left flank was unprotected until the British divisions came into line to extend the front.

Joffre was not as worried as Lanrezac. Fifth Army and the British only had to hold those extra German forces until his Fourth Army should have administered a stunning defeat on the Germans in the centre. Lanrezac began to shift his army further to the north on 19 August, a move that left a gap between his men and the leftmost units of Fourth Army. He entered Belgium and deployed his forces about Namur where the river Sambre runs at an acute angle into the Meuse from the south-west. His front ran, therefore, like an inverted V, with his left flank along the Sambre facing Charleroi and his right facing east along the Meuse. Upon being ordered to advance on 21 August at the same time as Third and Fourth Armies, Lanrezac replied that the British were not yet in position around Mons, hence his left would be unprotected if he moved north-wards alone. The German *Second Army* solved Lanrezac's dilemma by seizing bridges over the Sambre and repulsing all Fifth Army's attempts to recapture them. By the evening of 22 August Fifth Army's centre and left had been driven from the Sambre, and on the right, German *Third Army* had captured several bridges and was threatening to cross the Meuse in force. Lanrezac had no option but to withdraw to the south to avoid being surrounded. The Battle of Charleroi marked the third French defeat in what became known as the Battle of the Frontiers.[6]

The fourth element of that battle concerned the British who had landed in France and marched north into Belgium, where they bumped up against the advancing Germans at Mons. After hard fighting there on 23 August, the British too were compelled to retreat. From Lorraine in the east to Mons in the west, Joffre's plans had come to naught. The French commander-in-chief had lost the initiative. Clearly it would have made better strategic sense to allow the German armies to continue to advance until the French knew exactly where they were. Then the French could retain the initiative by attacking, when they were ready, enemy troops exhausted by long marches in summer heat. However, Joffre did not accept the responsibility for failure, either at the time or later in his memoirs. Officers were incompetent and some of the men had not demonstrated the necessary 'offensive qualities', Joffre informed the war minister. 'We are condemned to the defensive, based on our forts and natural obstacles in the terrain, surrendering as little as possible of our national territory', he went on. 'Our aim must be to hold on as long as possible, by trying to wear down the enemy, and to go onto the offensive again when the time comes.'[7]

GQG did not fail to appreciate the high casualty rates, and on 24 August sent a note to all armies.[8] It stated the obvious: attacks had not been carried out with 'intimate liaison' between infantry and artillery. If the infantry launched an attack on a distant objective before the artillery had done its job, excessive casualties resulted. Infantry seemed to be unaware of the 'need to organise' so as to endure. Throwing dense lines of infantry into the front line exposed them to enemy fire, halted their attack and left them at the mercy of counter-attack. A line of widely spaced tirailleurs (a skirmishing line), continually renewed and supported by artillery, should continue the fight until an assault could be launched. German cavalry was always preceded by some infantry, hence could call on infantry support if attacked. Therefore, the pursuing French cavalry ran into solidly held barrages. The note ended with the exhortation to rest the horses.

The battles of the frontiers had been expensive failures. The capture of Mulhouse was small compensation, and the town had been lost again very quickly. Yet Joffre had been justified in his reliance on his allies: French and Russian troops had attacked as agreed, and the British had arrived, although later and in fewer numbers than had been arranged in the pre-war General Staff talks. Moreover, the Great Retreat would reveal that having two such irascible commanders as Sir John French and General Charles Lanrezac in close proximity would be a problem. The choice of Joffre as CinC was also justified in the days following the disasters at the frontiers. His calm conduct of the retreat and the construction with his staff of an alternative strategy revealed that the French Army as a whole was far from defeated.

The new plan of action consisted of a fighting retreat, a transfer from east to west of as many troops as could be spared, and an offensive in the west while the right-hand armies (First, Second, Third) held their positions pivoting on fortress Verdun. The Alsace Army was dissolved and troops moved; First and Second were ordered to hold the fortress line, which Castelnau managed to do on the hills protecting Nancy. He had already halted Crown Prince Rupprecht's further southward advance after putting the French to flight. The Bavarians were aiming at the Charmes gap between the fortress lines at Toul (behind Nancy) and Epinal, and Castelnau took advantage of the Bavarian flank as they moved south. He broke up the Bavarian forces, scattering them back to the river Mortagne (whence the battle of 25–26 August took its name).[9] Third Army was driven back from Belgium, but with a new commander, General Maurice Sarrail, was able to form an arc above Verdun. Next Fourth Army, which had been strengthened with extra corps for the main attack on the German centre, was pushed much further south but was able to maintain contact with Third Army on its right. The position on its left was less secure because Fifth Army's move northwards to face the German threat and its defeat at Charleroi meant that the line between Fourth and Fifth was held very thinly. Consequently Joffre created a new army detachment, which later became Ninth Army, under General Ferdinand Foch. Of the corps commanders in the eastern armies, Foch had shown himself to be the most energetic and the most competent. Finally, Fifth Army with the BEF alongside (and tripping over each other) was forced to make a long retreat as the German *First* and *Second Armies* completed their wheel through Belgium and began to invade France from the north. Joffre was forced in turn to react to the British and French retreat because it was so disorganised. Each blamed the other for retreating without warning, thus creating an open flank, and Sir John French was threatening to withdraw much further south in order to reconstitute the BEF. Joffre ordered Lanrezac to stand, therefore, in order to slow down the German advance. The result was the confused battle of Guise on 29 August, when Fifth Army managed to hold the south bank of the river Oise. To solve the Franco-British personality clash, Joffre replaced Lanrezac with General Franchet d'Espèrey, another corps commander who had excelled in the opening battles, showing particular energy at the head of I Corps in the Guise fighting.

As the Germans came south, the refugee problems increased and the question of Paris loomed larger. Joffre decided that the government had to leave the capital, which it did, for Bordeaux, during the night of 2/3 September. Paris was transformed into a 'camp militaire retranché' and General Joseph Gallieni made its military governor. Gallieni was Joffre's designated successor, should the necessity arise, and the appointment was to lead to some clashes, since Gallieni had been Joffre's superior officer in Madagascar. Joffre grouped the miscellaneous units that he took from the eastern forces into a new Sixth Army under General Michel Maunoury.

The original plan was to concentrate this new Sixth Army on the line of the Somme with the BEF, but the enveloping German armies forestalled this, and Joffre indicated a new limit for the retreat, accepting that Fifth Army might have to descend as far south as the river Seine. From Charleroi in Belgium to the Seine is about 250 kilometres as the crow flies. By 4 September, however, army headquarters was established in Romilly-sur-Seine, although its constituent corps were deployed further north. Joffre's orders to Third, Fourth and Fifth Armies on 1 September stated that, as soon as Fifth Army had escaped the risk of enemy envelopment, the three armies would take the offensive. Meanwhile, as they retreated, they must keep in contact so as not to uncover any army's flank. He listed the southern limit of their respective retreat while insisting that there was absolutely no need to reach that line. Units of First and Second Armies in Alsace-Lorraine might be called upon to join the general offensive, as well as mobile units guarding Paris. Finally, armies should requisition vehicles if possible in order to spare the marching infantry.[10] The next day Joffre developed for all the army commanders, including Gallieni in Paris, his 'general plan of operations'. First, he meant to free the French from enemy pressure so as to enable them to reorganise and incorporate reinforcements from army depots; second, to take two corps from the eastern armies for the west and take the offensive, the left flank covered by all available cavalry; third to ask (he could not order) the British to participate by joining with Fifth Army's attack from the Seine, while the Paris garrison and Sixth Army were to attack east from Paris towards Meaux. This final element of the Marne battle was made possible by intelligence estimates of the German movements coming from two non-French sources: namely, British aviation reports and German radio intercepts. These confirmed that General Alexander von Kluck's *First Army* had turned to the south-east, bypassing Paris, and together with *Second Army* were advancing into the salient between Paris and Verdun where Joffre's U-shaped lines of retreat delimited the edges.

In the final days before the Battle of the Marne, Joffre had to reconcile several competing elements. The British had to be persuaded to participate, which task Joffre carried out in person; the German advance had to be monitored; and news of the transfer of some units to the Belgian and Russian fronts taken into account. Also Joffre had to maintain a delicate balance: exhausted retreating troops needed time to recover, yet, equally, the enemy could not be permitted to advance too far. Furthermore, Gallieni in Paris needed reassurance that the capital was not being exposed unduly to danger. On the other hand, the French had the great advantage that they were retiring on their own territory, so that transport and telephone communications became easier as the front they held shortened. The Germans, of course, were tiring rapidly, as Kluck's army had marched 500 kilometres in great heat. By early September, most of his corps were down to half strength, and almost half of the total casualties were suffering from heat exhaustion, foot sores or hunger, rather than battle wounds. Fresh reinforcements were not available, as they were for the French, because the Germans had used their reserves in the front line. By 4 September *First Army* had marched 140 kilometres beyond its railhead; more than half the motor transport and fodder wagons were out of commission. The army's 84,000 horses, pulling guns and equipment as well as soldiers, required two million pounds of fodder every day, an amount that could not be foraged along the way.[11] So, if Joffre and the seven French armies (two of the original five now with new commanders) could keep their heads, the prospects for the forthcoming battle were good.

On 4 September the date of this French counter-attack still had not been settled. Joffre asked the new Fifth Army commander whether he would be able to mount an attack the next day or the day after. Sir John French wanted assurances that his flanks would be covered, by Sixth Army on his left and by Fifth Army on his right. Despite having taken over from Lanrezac only on 3 September, d'Espèrey met Sir John's sub-chief of staff (Henry Wilson) and, after they agreed that an offensive on 6 September was possible, d'Espèrey telegraphed his reply to Joffre. Although his army was not in a 'brilliant' condition, an attack on the 6th was possible. Although Joffre and at least Berthelot on his staff would have preferred to wait a little longer, Gallieni forced the issue by ordering Sixth Army to move into position that same day, 4 September. Hence, at 22.00 on the evening of 4 September, orders were sent out for the attack to begin on the 6th. See Map 3.

The aim of the operation was to attack the German right in the salient between Paris and Verdun with Sixth Army moving east from Paris, the BEF attacking north-east, Fifth Army attacking north, supported on its right flank by the newly created Ninth Army under Foch. Foch had a double role in the centre of the French line, namely to support Fifth Army's attack on his left and to retain contact with Fourth Army on his right. That Fourth Army, along with Third around Verdun and Second and First in Lorraine and Alsace, was not to remain quiescent, for all were to pin down the German forces facing them so as to prevent any

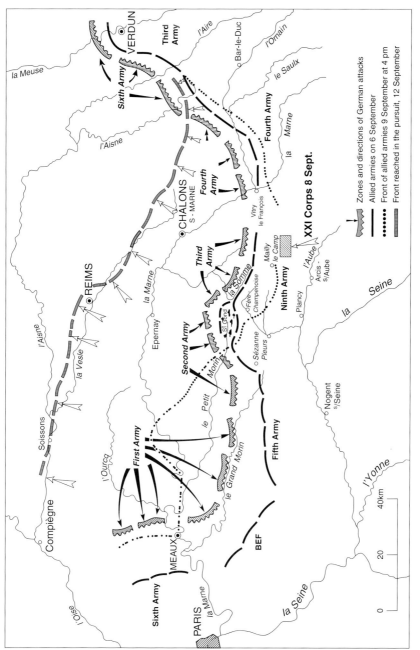

3. Battle of the Marne, September 1914

47

reinforcement of the *First* and *Second Armies* bearing the brunt of the French attack. Joffre understood the vital importance of the forthcoming battle. He sent a message to his troops:

At the moment when a battle upon which depends the safety of the country is about to begin, it is important to remind everyone that no longer is it the time to be looking backwards; every effort must be made to attack and to repel the enemy. Troops who can no longer advance must, at all costs, hold on to captured ground and be killed on the spot rather than retreat. Under current circumstances, no weakness can be tolerated.[12]

Although conventionally the Marne battle began on 6 September, the first engagement occurred the previous afternoon when Sixth Army bumped unexpectedly into German *IV Reserve Corps*. This engagement revealed Joffre's manoeuvre to the Germans and meant that Sixth Army made little overall progress during the battle, yet nevertheless it had a significant effect. Kluck shifted two of his corps on the 6th and a further two on the 7th to assist his *IV Reserve Corps*. This opened the gap between *First* and *Second Armies* through which the BEF and Fifth Army were able to advance, albeit slowly. The greatest danger to the French came in the centre, where Ninth Army managed to hold on to the marshes of St-Gond and to keep contact with Fifth Army, but the troops on Ninth Army's centre and right were beaten back and the risk of losing contact with Fourth Army became very real. If the enemy broke through Ninth Army holding the centre of the line, the remaining French armies could be rolled up on either side of the breach. By a daring shuttle of troops from his left to assist his right, Foch managed to avert the risk, but it was only the withdrawal of German *Third Army* from his front in unwilling conformity with *First* and *Second* that saved his right and centre from annihilation. After the war, when it no longer mattered, Foch admitted defeat on the Marne, but his energy and optimism had heartened GQG and politicians alike, even if his oft-cited message, 'situation excellent, I am attacking', is apocryphal.

Fourth Army faced the danger not only of a gap arising between it and Foch's Ninth Army on its left, but also between it and Third Army on its right. German attacks against Third Army meant fierce fighting around Verdun, and on the evening of 8 September Joffre authorised Sarrail to break contact with the fortress if necessary. Sarrail's men managed to hold on, however, and both Verdun and contact with Fourth Army were saved. Further east in Lorraine, Castelnau's Second Army was also hard pressed. Second Army had managed to defeat Prince Rupprecht's attacks on Nancy and the Mortagne, but the Bavarians attacked again on 5 September, causing Castelnau to warn GQG that he might have to withdraw. Joffre's transfer of divisions to the west for the counter-offensive had left Second Army with a greater number of reserve than active divisions (six out of ten) and Castelnau had little trust in their staying power. Yet, as the battle began on the Marne, it was vital that Castelnau hold on to Nancy and its strong defensive position on the heights to the north-west, the Couronné de Nancy. This Second Army managed to do, as well as assisting Sarrail and Third Army. The Bavarian *Sixth Army* was ordered to cease its attacks on Nancy as Moltke realised the danger to his troops further west. Indeed, Moltke had already transferred his *Seventh Army* to the west, which left First Army in relative calm in Alsace.

The Battle of the Marne – in truth a battle extending across most of central France from Paris to Nancy–was soon acclaimed a great victory, a 'miracle' even. It gave Joffre enormous prestige, slightly dented by an unseemly squabble over whether the glory should belong to him or to Gallieni, and enabled him to conduct operations for the rest of the year and well into 1915 with little political oversight. It was an even greater victory for French troops, who had been shocked by initial defeats on the frontiers into an immensely long retreat, and then had turned around and halted the German advance. The German *First Army*'s commander, von Kluck, paid them generous tribute. He had been surprised by the French turn-around: after retreating for ten days, 'half dead with fatigue', French soldiers had then had 'the strength to take up their rifle and attack', when the bugle sounded.[13] The US military attaché in Paris visited the Marne battlefields shortly after the fighting ceased and was impressed by the French gunners whose 'accurate' fire had had such a 'fearful effect' on the Germans. He did note also how much better quality were the German boots, knapsacks and helmets that were scatted about the battlefield, than anything the French had.[14]

Despite the constant urging of their commanders and GQG, the French troops were too exhausted to press the retreating enemy hard enough to expel him from France. Instead, once the German armies reached the northern bank of the Aisne, they dug in, and the lines solidified. The invasion of France had been stopped but the war was not over. Moltke brought the Bavarians west from Lorraine, and then lost command himself, his health and spirits broken by the strain. His replacement was the Prussian war minister, Erich von Falkenhayn. All agreed that Joffre's calm control after the defeat on the frontiers and during the retreat had been a large factor in the French Army's ability to make a new plan, to move resources to carry it out, and to do so successfully. His calm contrasts with Moltke's nervous exhaustion. A further contrast lies in the close control Joffre kept over GQG and his army generals, not fearing to sack two out five of them, whereas Moltke remained distant from the action.

To the North Sea

Although fighting continued along the whole front, in eastern France the lines did not move much either forward or back. The movement was all on the open flank in the west where both the German and the French armies each tried to envelop the other's open wing, gradually crossing the river lines towards the north, Oise, Somme and Lys. The withdrawal of Second Army from Lorraine to the open west flank left Dubail's First Army to cover the front south of Verdun alone. Together with Sarrail's Third Army, Dubail had to resist German attacks on the Meuse heights which resulted in the loss of Saint-Mihiel and Vauquois. Both these elevated positions were south of Verdun and their loss gave the enemy the power to interdict Verdun's communications, a fact which became especially critical during the 1916 German offensive against Verdun.

Next in line, Fourth Army had to counter enemy attacks in Champagne (Le Mesnil) and the Argonne (as Germans withdrew from the Aire to the Aisne), but de Langle de Cary's initiatives were hampered by having to extend his front westwards when Joffre dissolved Foch's Ninth Army. The reason for this was Joffre's wish to use Foch to coordinate the forces on the left flank, where the British and the Belgians had to be taken into account. Next, Fifth Army's role was an 'aggressive defence' in order to contain the enemy north of the Aisne, and it was involved in a series of small partial attacks and counter-attacks. Sixth Army's position after the Marne battle was north of the Aisne, but it too fought only partial engagements after failing to outflank German *First Army*.

The action was on the left flank, where Joffre had moved Castelnau and Second Army. As the fighting died down on the Aisne, where the front stabilised because the higher northern bank gave the enemy good defensive positions, Joffre reconstituted Second Army. On 19 September he gave Castelnau the task of outflanking the enemy and blocking him wherever he presented himself, so as to enable Sixth Army to continue to advance northwards. Four army corps were allocated to Second Army for this task, covered by a group of territorial divisions under the command of the 74-year-old General Brugère, a former commander-in-chief designate, who had volunteered to return to service. Castelnau lacked his army aviation which had not yet arrived from Lorraine, but GQG assured him that he faced few German forces. Castelnau pushed his troops northwards, therefore, without accurate intelligence, but soon realised that the Germans were engaging in exactly the same manoeuvre, namely attempting to envelop the open west flank. By 26 September the German right was already (and in strength) at Bapaume in the Somme département. Falkenhayn had moved his *Sixth Army* from Lorraine, so they faced Second Army once again. The colonel commanding 22 Bavarian Infantry Regiment described an action near Maricourt, just north of the Somme where in 1916 the British and French lines would join.

The battles in Lorraine had given our troops a feeling of superiority. They received an extremely rude shock when they had to accept near Maricourt that the French, even though they were from the same corps that we had brushed aside in Lorraine, had changed. They were tough, daring and self-confident. The Miracle of the Marne had so raised the morale of the French that the order to withdraw must be regarded as a crime against all things German.[15]

The continual outflanking attempts stretched Second Army's front to 100 kilometres with more and more units arriving as reinforcements. Joffre split off a detachment of troops from Second Army (it became Tenth Army) and put it under the command of General Louis de Maud'huy. So the task of outflanking the Germans fell to Maudhuy, but he had as little success as Castelnau. German troops were moving on the communications hubs of Douai and Arras, and the important manufacturing centre of Lille was also under threat. It was the dangerous situation in the north that made Joffre link the forces there by creating a provisional army group and sending Foch on 4 October to coordinate matters. Although Foch is credited with inspiring the troops to hang on around Arras, which remained in Allied hands, Lille was lost. Joffre blamed the slow British for the loss. Sir John French had requested and been granted a move from the Aisne back to northern France nearer his bases, but had not got the BEF moving quickly enough (in Joffre's view) once they arrived in their new sector. Many of Lille's citizens would suffer, in consequence, requisitions of food, housing and industrial machinery, as well as deportation for forced labour.[16]

Lille is very close to Belgium and the northern Channel ports, so the belligerent armies had almost run out of territory in which to manoeuvre. The last engagement, after which the line of trenches was completed from Switzerland to the North Sea, took place in Belgian Flanders. Foch was on hand to coordinate the three Allied armies in what became known as the 'mêlée des Flandres', and he kept in close touch with Joffre by sending personal and confidential letters most evenings. The initial phase of the fighting (16–26 October) involved the Belgian Army, which had retired southwards from Antwerp, and took place along the river Yser, between Dixmude and Nieuport on the coast. King Albert of the Belgians had wanted his troops to retreat onto French territory, but Joffre was able to persuade him to stand on the Yser. There they were supported by French marines (les fusiliers marins) around Dixmude and by French 42 DI on the coast under the command of General

Paul-François Grossetti. After desperate fighting when the Germans managed to get across the river and obtain a foothold in Dixmude, the line was secured by opening the sluice gates and allowing the land north of the river and railway to be inundated.

The fighting then moved inland to the city of Ypres. The French troops in this sector had been formed into a Belgian army detachment under the command of General Victor d'Urbal. These men and the British held an arc around Ypres, and Foch attempted to break out from the arc to ease the pressure on the Belgians on the Yser. Instead, the Germans, with strong reinforcements, made a series of heavy assaults both north and south of Ypres. The battle (First Ypres for the British, First Flanders for the French) is often regarded as a British battle in which the last of the professional army that had gone to France was destroyed. Yet the French were also present. Not only were French troops fed into line to support the besieged BEF units, but the whole battle was 'coordinated' by Foch. He had no authority over the Belgian and British armies, whose commanders-in-chief – a king and a field marshal respectively – outranked him. Instead, his coordinating role was accepted (if not welcomed) because it was imposed by his energy, personal contact and sheer bloody-minded determination to hold on to Ypres as a communications centre and final stronghold before the coast and the English Channel. Belgian and British gratitude for the role Foch played in October and November 1914 in Flanders was an important element in their acceptance of Foch's accession to supreme command during the even greater crisis in March 1918, when the Germans threatened once again to break through to the sea.

In Flanders neither Joffre nor Foch was prepared to renounce offensive operations. The best way to support the Belgians on the Yser front and the British open left flank was to continue the attempts to envelop the enemy's own open flank. However, Falkenhayn had strengthened his Flanders forces with troops freed by the fall of Antwerp, and with young German volunteers. After organising the defences of Dunkirk and posting two territorial divisions to the Poperinghe–Ypres road, Foch made plans for an offensive. Higher command still intended to attack despite the increasing ferocity and strength of the German onslaught. Sir John accepted Foch's plan for joint attacks on Roulers (by the French) and towards Courtrai (by the British) on 22/23 October. This involved a French division (17 DI, part of d'Urbal's army detachment) passing through the lines of General Douglas Haig's I Corps. Following the successful French operation which captured Zonnebeke, French divisions relieved the two British divisions of 1 Corps.[17] But operations were not entirely harmonious. The orders for 17 DI included provision for

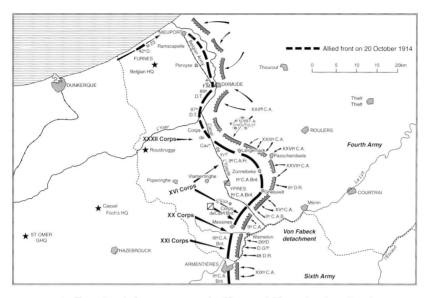

4. French reinforcements at the Yser and Ypres battles, October–
November 1914

Haig to attack the Houthulst Forest which he declined to do: 'I wired
GHQ that orders were based on an absolute misunderstanding of the
situation and that I had no intention of attacking the Foret!...[sic]'.
General d'Urbal went in person to see Haig, however, in order to 'apolo-
gise for his orders'. Personal contact was thus able to restore harmony. In
fact d'Urbal impressed Haig as a 'big smart looking polite man'.[18]

Reduced stocks of munitions and lack of reserves began to make
themselves felt. The latter problem was solved over the next few days
by taking two corps from the French Fifth and Sixth Armies (round
Epernay in the Champagne, and on the Oise, respectively) and sending
them north. Joffre said that he could not take any more units from other
sectors after that. Although the Belgians were hanging on, sheltered by
the flooding in front of the Yser and railway line, further south the
position was not eased at all. German attacks on the British lines intensified, even more as the Yser front became impossible. The heaviest pressure fell on Haig's I Corps, now in line astride the Ypres–Menin road
(Battle of Gheluvelt from 29 October). In response to that pressure and to
Sir John's request, on the evening of 29 October Foch ordered General
Conneau's Cavalry Corps to hold itself in readiness to 'respond to any
requests for support that may be made by FM French'.[19] On the 30th, it

was Haig's turn to request reinforcements. In his diary account, this is translated as being 'most anxious about the protection of our communications which ran through Ypres, as do also those of the French'.[20] Help was forthcoming once more, and the commander of IX Corps, General Dubois, sent three French battalions and a cavalry brigade directly to Haig, with their commanding officers reporting for orders at 7pm.

It is clear that Foch appreciated the gravity of the situation. The British line had given way south-east of Ypres, opening the road to St Eloi, thence to Ypres. Foch telephoned Wilson at GHQ and said that he was coming over for a conference. He arrived after midnight and Sir John was roused from his sleep. Having received confirmation that the British had absolutely no troops in reserve, Foch promised that the eight battalions of 32 DI due to arrive that morning would be sent immediately to St Eloi to support I Corps. A detachment of units from IX Corps, under General Moussy, was put directly under Haig's orders. Thus prompt action on the part of Foch meant that the line could be strengthened where it was overstretched.

Despite this help, the British were driven back still further, losing part of Messines in the morning of the 31st and Gheluvelt on the Ypres–Menin road in the afternoon. It seemed to both Sir John French and Haig that they would have to withdraw to a shorter line. The British line held by 1 Division had broken and men and guns were retiring towards Ypres. Foch intervened personally once more. Facing a field marshal with a face as 'red as a cockerel' who declared it 'impossible' to maintain the position of his I Corps, Foch argued that to retreat would cause a rout. Dismissing Sir John French's histrionic outburst that there was nothing for it but to join his men and get killed alongside them, Foch persuaded the British CinC to order Haig to remain where he was. Foch would relieve the pressure by attacking on both flanks of the hard-pressed British.[21] This was surely the right decision. There was very little room for manoeuvre between the front line and the sea, and any giving way without an organised position to fall back onto would have been bound to turn into panic and even rout. Equally, Sir John was temperamentally unsuited to maintain the calm exterior and overall control that the dangerous situation required. When Foch wrote on 31 October that the only possible course of action was to hold on, and when Sir John endorsed that decision with the comment that Haig should conform, Foch was acting promptly and efficaciously to prevent a disaster that could have left the Germans in control of Calais and wiped Belgium off the map of Europe.[22]

Although the position on Haig's right (where St Eloi was threatened) was still critical, by the evening of the 31st Gheluvelt had been retaken expeditiously by the Worcesters, and so the pressure was slightly eased there. Accordingly, d'Urbal sent a note to Haig at 6pm, indicating that agreement had been reached for the morrow that the British should hold on, whilst his IX Corps attacked on Haig's left towards Becelaere and the eight battalions of 32 DI on his right on the St Eloi–Wytschaete line towards Hollebeke.[23] These instructions were confirmed by a note from Sir John French the same evening.[24] At 11pm Foch's liaison officer arrived at Haig's HQ to discuss the St Eloi operation; and Haig also saw General Vidal, the commander of 31 DI. This frequent communication between French commanders and the British they were reinforcing made the system of feeding in reserves piecemeal work effectively.

As planned, the French attacked on both flanks of the British I Corps on 1 November, but the Germans had not finished with their own offensive. Their renewed attacks achieved the capture of Messines (from the British Cavalry Corps) and part of Wytschaete. As a result, the French cavalry under Conneau were immediately brought back from reserve to support their British counterparts and Joffre promised to send the elite XX Corps from Second Army (the corps that had defended Nancy). Foch's orders for the continuation of the battle were identical to those already issued: the British would hold on in the middle whilst the French attacked on the flanks.

However, by 2 November the German onslaughts were abating. Haig had been reinforced still further by two North African battalions of zouaves from 42 DI. This was the French division that had been supporting the Belgians who were now safe behind the flooded river, and so had less need of the French support. The XX Corps began detraining that evening. D'Urbal had insisted on protecting Haig's right flank (the more sorely pressed) by telling the XVI Corps commander that French 'honour was at stake'. XVI Corps should break the enemy's attack by 'une offensive à outrance'. Acting on the defensive would be insufficient.[25] Artillery from IX Corps on Haig's left was directed to support the XVI Corps attack, and Haig was requested to provide similar artillery support.[26] Haig seems to have been impressed, writing to his wife in praise of French officers, although his CinC was less so.[27] Sir John French had already disparaged to Lord Kitchener at the War Office the 'staff arrangements' of the French reinforcements put under Haig's command, claiming that 'they are generally late', but went on to admit that 'they have a way of their own which, when they really do begin, is very effective'.[28]

On 4 November the French thought the battle more or less ended. Joffre wanted to take back some of the reserves he had gathered together for Flanders, especially XX Corps, in case the Germans attacked elsewhere. Ammunition was also running low, as it was on the British side – and no economies could be made by sharing because of the different calibres. Haig was confident of being able to hold, even though some units were utterly exhausted. Casualties had been so heavy that Sir John French asked Foch to take over I Corps' line. This Foch was unable to do, although he promised to 'earmark a force for support to it'.[29] But the Germans had not yet finished with the battle.

On 5/6 and again on 10/11 November the Allied line suffered more violent attacks. Contre-amiral Ronarc'h commanded the French marines and Belgian troops in the Dixmude sector, and he had sited groups of machine guns to cover the approaches to the town whose capture would give the enemy an important bridgehead over the Yser and control of the railway line that passed through it. The previous German attacks on the town, between 21 and 25 October before the flooding of the river put a stop to operations, had been halted with many German casualties. By 10 November the weary French defenders of Dixmude consisted of two battalions of fusiliers marins and one sénégalais battalion (suffering considerably from the cold and wet conditions), together with one battalion of Belgian troops. All were below strength, especially the artillery units, which were down to 30 per cent of their original force.[30] So, this time, the German attack stood a much better chance of success, especially as they had obtained intelligence of the Allied defences. As a result, the massive German artillery assault forced some defenders from their positions, and when the infantry assault began at 1300 the Germans overwhelmed those who remained. Dixmude remained in German hands until September 1918, but its possession did not provide the gateway to the coast that its costly capture had been designed to achieve. The Germans took many unwounded prisoners and French machine guns, but they acknowledged the courage of the French troops. One of the volunteers in *201ResInfRgt* wrote home: 'The Frenchman showed himself to be a thoroughly courageous chap: all respect to the marines! . . . the Blacks held out in the station and would not surrender. We showed them no mercy. We broke down the door and our bayonets had plenty of bloody work to do.'[31] Several German accounts mention the presence of native soldiers. The professional soldiers of the British Army (as well as their corned beef, chocolate and brandy) gained German respect too: 'the British were better infantrymen than the French. Some had sixteen years' service and most of them eight', read one account from *105InfRgt* published in Leipzig and Freiburg newspapers.[32]

At the southern end of the Ypres salient, Conneau's cavalry attempted on 5 November to straighten out the line, where the Germans had made inroads, by retaking Messines. D'Urbal asked the British infantry to cooperate in this operation, but in the event only artillery support was forthcoming. The little progress made on the 5th was to be improved upon the following day, so the orders went.[33] On the 6th Moussy's detachment was pushed back from Zillebeke and Klein Zillebeke, thus uncovering Haig's right round Hollebeke where the British troops were 'a good deal pressed' on the 7th. Wilson went to Foch's HQ to request reinforcements but d'Urbal had already supplied three battalions and an artillery group. This was not enough, according to Haig, who 'therefore wire[d] to GHQ recommending that Foch should be here himself, in order to see suitable steps are taken to regain the necessary line of trenches to cover our communications'. British claims for relief and assistance were becoming more strident, although French requests for similar help did not always receive a sympathetic hearing. Wilson had already remarked that Sir John 'will never help if he can help it, & on the other hand he always expects the French to help him'.[34] And Haig declined to give all the help requested by 9 DI on 5 November. The French said one of its battalions had suffered very heavy losses and 'was in "the last extremes": in fact situation was serious ... Our troops been in the Trenches for the last 10 days and have also had terrible losses! But we have to stick it.'[35]

By now, as the British were merely defending and all offensive action was being undertaken by the French, a tone of superiority was creeping into Haig's diary. French morale was beginning to slip.[36] Foch was still worried about the southern face of the salient: 'Foch said he had issued a "formal order" to retake old position near Klein Zillebeke & I said too many orders had already been issued, what was wanted was execution! Foch congratulated me on action of 1st Corps.'[37] In fact, Foch now decided to use his last reserves, 11 DI of XX Corps – the unit that Joffre had wished to maintain as a general reserve, not to be used except as a last extremity. He also sacked Moussy and the commander of XVI Corps (of whom Haig had been complaining). German interrogation of prisoners seized on these negative impressions of Franco-British cooperation: 'The French complained bitterly about their Allies, the British. The French were just cannon fodder, constantly despatched into the front line by the British. The reality was that the French were the last reserves available, after the British had long since been worn out by the dreadful battles that had been going on for days.'[38]

Despite the decision to use the last French reserves, the tone on the British side was becoming querulous – no doubt a reflection of the unremitting days and nights spent under shell-fire without proper protection and along a front stretched too thinly. Haig recalled later d'Urbal's 'selfishness' during the Ypres fighting.[39] Although Joffre did send what were absolutely the last reserves available, Foch's plans to attack were thwarted by the final German onslaught against the French at St Eloi and against Haig's I Corps along the Menin Road. This final attack, parried by the Allies, marked the end of the battle. Arguments over the relief of I Corps were all that remained to mar relations. Agreement was reached on the evening of 13 November for the relief, although not without dispute. The arguments led Joffre to send a message that, if Foch and Sir John French could not hold their present position, then they would simply have to retire to a shorter line. Joffre could not send one single soldier more.[40] If Joffre was resigned to giving up territory, albeit Belgian territory, then surely he spoke the truth when he stated that he had no reserves left.

Between 16 and 31 October 1914, IX Corps from Champagne, XVI Corps from Lorraine, 38 DI from the Aisne and sixteen regiments of cavalry taken from all fronts were deployed in Flanders. Between 1 and 14 November one infantry brigade from Champagne, one infantry brigade and four battalions of chasseurs from Lorraine and two infantry regiments plus six battalions of chasseurs arrived from the Aisne – all for what is usually described as a British battle. The reduced size of the units moved to Flanders in November does not reflect a lesser willingness to help, but the reduced French capacity. In addition, guns and ammunition were becoming very short.[41] D'Urbal's army detachment alone fired 350,000 shells in the month beginning 15 October.[42] The reason for the huge consumption of shells lay in the Flanders terrain. Whereas the French 75s had been unable to dominate the battlefield in the hilly and wooded terrain during the Battles of the Frontiers, the flat ground in Flanders was ideal for their deployment and they were used intensively. Firing into assaulting enemy troops caused huge German casualties: 'at least 134,300 between 15 October and 24 November, of whom approximately 19,600 were killed. The actual figure may have been considerably greater.'[43] Joffre managed to supply sufficient shells for the guns by taking supplies from the stabilised fronts further east, but by the end of the battle crisis point had been reached, and not only among the French. The shells crisis hit all the belligerents.

Military medicine and military justice

Munitions could be replaced; men could not. France's casualty bill for the fighting in 1914 was horrendous (see Table 7). For the month of August alone, out of 1.6 million men in the field armies, a total of 206,515 were 'hors de combat'.[44] This is approximately one in eight of the men who responded to the general mobilisation call.

Table 7 *Casualties for August–November 1914*

	Total	Killed or missing	Proportion of killed and missing to total
August	206,515	128,047	More than half
September	213,444	101,482	Almost half
October	83,109	37,906	Almost half
November	78,068	32,214	41 per cent

Note: The figures for the missing must be read with care. The 'missing' were simply those who did not answer the roll call; they might be taken prisoner or evacuated as wounded or abandoned on the battlefield or blown to pieces.
Source: AFGG 1/4, 554.

The post-war record of deaths (on the battlefield or later in hospital) for the period to the end of November 1914 is 454,000.[45] The sheer scale of these numbers overwhelmed the *service de santé* not only medically but also administratively. For example, Germain Foch and Paul Bécourt, General Foch's only son and one of his two sons-in-law, were both killed in the carnage of 22 August, yet their deaths were not confirmed until February 1915 and 19 November 1914 respectively.

The medical services functioned according to regulations set up in 1910.[46] Then it had been assumed that rifle bullets would cause most wounds and that the war would be short. Central administration was run from the seventh directorate in the war ministry and within each military district there existed a further directorate and military hospitals with depots of necessary materials. Once the fighting began, the French Army's system functioned as follows. Primary medical care for wounds or illness was given by the regimental medical officer (Louis Barthas recounts how unsympathetic some of these could be). At the next level, that of the division, were to be found stretcher-bearers and sometimes an 'ambulance' – not a single vehicle as today but a treatment centre. Each corps also had its own stretcher-bearers, with eight ambulances, six hospital sections and a motorised medical section. Finally, each army had a medical chief (Médecin Inspecteur Général) in charge of the HOE (evacuation hospitals), of which there was one for each corps in the army. These hospitals were located at rail centres and could evacuate patients to the surrounding local hospitals. French territory was divided into two zones, the interior (zone de l'arrière) and the zone of the army, itself divided into forward and rear areas. The zone of the army limits varied according to the fighting and advances or retreats.

At first, all the wounded were evacuated after a preliminary first-aid bandaging, but the nature of the wounds forced a change. Instead of a

(a)

(b)

Fig. 3 (a) A camouflaged ambulance, 4 kilometres behind the front
lines at Verdun and (b) an ambulance lorry, with dog and stretcher

clean bullet wound, most men suffered from artillery fire which caused
large wounds into which dirty pieces of uniform or filthy mud had been
driven by shrapnel or other shell fragments. Evacuating to the interior
men wounded in this way caused such long delays before proper

treatment that tetanus and gangrene became real problems. On 1 August 1914 there were only five dedicated 'medical trains', able to transport 760 stretcher cases, plus another 115 trains improvised to take 45,540 such cases and 30 ordinary trains able to transport 45,000 men seated. A third of a million men were evacuated to the interior in 1914, a figure that does not include the lightly wounded or sick, who were treated in the zone of the armies.

In the face of these totally inadequate facilities, carriages normally used for transporting animals were pressed into service, and it was this practice that brought the matter to public attention. Senator Georges Clemenceau wrote a stinging editorial at the end of September in his newspaper, *L'Homme Libre*, about the filthy conditions in which wounded men were evacuated from the battlefield and the overflowing hospitals at the front. Maurice Barrès in the *Echo de Paris* joined the condemnation. The government attempted to censure the press so that such details would not be revealed to depress civilian morale. So Clemenceau's 'free' man soon became *L'Homme Enchaîné*, although Clemenceau would circulate to politicians and influential acquaintances the text of articles cut by Anastasie (the name given to the official censorship). The figures for the numbers of wounded were so high, however, that the facts about the French medical services could not be kept hidden as sons and husbands told their families of their ordeal.

In addition to wounds, the medical services had to deal with an epidemic of typhus that began in October 1914. There were 112,135 cases in the first seventeen months of war, with 10,403 deaths. Typhoid was another problem. A rich American writer, Mary Borden, had given her name to the French Red Cross in London, and was asked by its patron, the wife of the French military attaché in London, whether she would volunteer to nurse typhoid patients in Dunkirk, where there was an epidemic. Madame de la Panouse explained that the French Army's medical services had been prepared for 25,000 casualties, but 'the sick and wounded already numbered half a million'. 'English' nurses were needed, therefore, despite the Service de Santé's being unwilling to see foreign nurses in their hospitals. Borden agreed to go, but found it 'a heartbreaking business' because of the total lack of nurses and of equipment in the dilapidated casino-turned-hospital. Eventually, after writing personally to Joffre, she funded a 100-bed field-hospital that she directed personally.[47]

Obviously the sudden change from normality to military service imposed a great strain on men who had marched into Belgium and then retreated south as far as the river Marne. The strain affected not only their moral but also their physical strength, as men fell asleep on their feet. There were episodes of looting and self-mutilation. A curé near Arras witnessed the execution of a deserter who had stolen civilian clothes in order to flee, and two days later another deserter, both executions carried out in front of their fellow soldiers.[48]

The military code of justice in force in 1914 had been legislated in 1857; the Dreyfus affair had made any revision a sensitive matter. Military tribunals (conseils de guerre) to deal with offences against military law were normally convened at the divisional level. In time of war, however, officers had the right and duty to effect summary military justice by, for example, shooting men fleeing the battlefield. In addition, the declaration of a state of siege on 2 August 1914 meant that throughout the whole country, acts affecting 'state security or public order' were liable to military jurisdiction. This was a very wide theoretical net. Crimes such as spying or sabotage committed by civilians were liable to be tried in military tribunal, yet for spying there were only thirteen certain plus two more probable executions of civilians (out of twenty-four guilty verdicts) in 1914/15.[49] Trials were conducted more strictly in time of war, in that the accused's defence lawyer was not entitled to attend the interrogation of the prisoner, and the plea of 'extenuating circumstances' was only permitted in a limited number of cases.[50] Nevertheless, on 3 September, in response to cases of looting and self-mutilation, Joffre asked that courts martial, or special military tribunals, be permitted, and the decree establishing them was signed three days later. In theory this gave the commander right of life or death over all troops and the speedy trial risked judicial error, but in fact they were little used.

Executions for mutiny, especially, in 1917 have penetrated the public consciousness, along with films such as Stanley Kubrick's *Paths of Glory* (1957). Yet a sharp peak in October 1914 makes this the period with the highest monthly figure of death sentences of the whole war.[51] The average monthly total of death sentences for the three months September–December 1914 is forty (there were none in August). In October there were seventy-eight, of which fifty-five were carried out. The total number of executions in 1914 was a hundred, triple the total for 1917 (thirty-three). For the whole war, the monthly average number of executions carried out was only between seven and eight. So, in comparison, the October 1914 spike is of considerable dimensions.

Several factors may explain the spike. By October the Marne fighting was at an end and the fronts stabilised, except for the outflanking movements on the left wing ending around the Yser and Ypres. In October the numbers of voluntary mutilation increased; cavalry platoons were used to help the military police keep order in the rear areas; and it became clear that the war would not be over by Christmas.[52] Perhaps most importantly, the government's move to Bordeaux enabled the army authorities to enforce the courts martial decree more severely and with less oversight. Certainly, once the government had returned to Paris and parliamentary sittings resumed, the opposition, particularly strong from left-wing deputies, increased over the course of 1915 until the abolition of courts martial was proposed on 12 December 1915.

Even Philippe Pétain, who is usually credited with restoring the French Army to offensive health after the 1917 mutinies, did not hesitate to reduce 'mediocre' officers to the ranks and to have 'cowards' shot. General Emile Fayolle, then commanding the reserve 70 DI, noted on 5 November 1914 that Pétain, who was 'cold, calm, resolute' but very hard, admitted to having acted as a 'butcher' in the opening engagements.[53] Foch signed seven death warrants during Ninth Army's short existence.[54]

On 15 December 1914 one company of the 8 Régiment de Tirailleurs in 38 DI refused to leave the trenches and ten North African tirailleurs were chosen by lot and executed without trial by General d'Urbal, whose order was counter-signed by Foch.[55] The file on this incident, which was forwarded to GQG, reveals that the men were recently arrived from Tunisia, had been moved into the trenches immediately upon arrival, and were exhausted. Upon being ordered to move from their support trenches to the front line, the 15 Company had to be forced out by their officer's cane and then they refused to move again, despite being threatened by revolver. Some men were reported to have said 'shoot me, I'm too tired'. As punishment, the company was amalgamated with other zouave regiments so as to give the men European officers, but before that ten men were to be selected by lot and shot in front of their comrades. General Georges de Bazelaire, the divisional commander, described the refusal to obey orders as 'an act of cowardice' and 'collective treachery'. Foch decided that the regiment should be relieved if it had suffered more fatigue than others; if that were not the case, ten men were to be selected by lot and shot, if the 'leaders' could not be discovered. The army commander, General d'Urbal wanted to punish the company's colonel for not executing the men immediately, but accepted that a twenty-four-hour delay was unavoidable, because the rest of the regiment could not be brought forward to witness the execution until dark. The company was withdrawn after dark on 15 December and the lots drawn immediately. The execution was carried out the next day at 4.30pm. An order was read out in Arabic explaining the reasons for the executions, which provoked no 'incident' but seemed to have had a 'salutary effect'.[56] Nevertheless, Bazelaire reported on 25 December that the execution 'did not appear to have borne fruit', as the regiments in his division were evacuating about thirty cases of sickness or frozen feet per month.[57] It seems highly unlikely that witnessing an execution would prevent one's feet from becoming frozen. The regiment and 38 DI were relieved gradually during the course of January 1915.

The indigenous tirailleurs were beginning to obtain a reputation for panic and indiscipline. The unfortunate 8 Régiment de Tirailleurs had rioted already, before leaving Bizerta, and there were incidents in 37 DI, the other African Army division. Some tirailleurs on the Aisne front had fled in September 1914, and twelve of them had been shot. These twelve men were from 5 Régiment de Tirailleurs, based near Algiers but originally from central Algeria. Even some European North Africans were found leaving the front for various (presumably invalid) reasons during the Marne battle in September.[58] On the Oise front on 23 September 1914, General Blanc (commanding a brigade composed of 2 Rgt Zouaves and 2 Rgt Tirailleurs) shot twelve tirailleurs in person, in an attempt to stop the brigade fleeing. Four more of his tirailleurs were convicted in October of abandoning their post and two were executed.[59] On 4 November 1914 General Sarrail (Third Army) published a general order listing sixteen executions carried out during the previous month for self mutilation and desertion.[60]

It was not only other ranks who were executed. Although rare, some cases exist of officers being sentenced to death, the best known of which is probably that of sous-lieutenant Chapelant of 98 RI (25 DI in Second Army). Accused of surrender to the enemy in open field, taking thirty of his men with him, he was executed on 11 October 1914 after being condemned to death the previous day. The evidence was contradictory – certainly he gave himself up, but he was surrounded and out of ammunition; did he wave a white flag to indicate that the survivors of his machine-gun section should join him willingly or under constraint? Wounded in the leg, he was subsequently rescued and had to be carried in front of the firing squad on a stretcher, having refused the offer from a fellow officer of a revolver so that he could shoot himself and avoid the shame of the execution. There was some question of the vindictiveness of his colonel; the verdict was appealed in the 1930s. Certainly the case seems somewhat dubious, but it reflects the fears of 1914 that this new form of war might be too much for the men unless any and every seeming failure was repressed.[61]

Desertion and self-mutilation were not the only military crimes. Looting was another, and had been one of the reasons why Joffre requested the establishment of courts martial. Looting also brought home to French civilians what the war involved, just as the German atrocities did in Lorraine, northern France and Belgium. Certainly the

(a)

(b)

Fig. 4 Two groups of zouaves and tirailleurs in 1914

home front knew full well what the army was suffering. Four million letters a day were exchanged between home and front, despite censorship intended to avoid disclosure of information that might help the enemy.[62] The postal service was not working at that capacity in 1914, however. Among the many published collections of correspondence, rare is the work that does not mention the importance of receiving letters and parcels from home; the link with family and normality was crucial to the soldier's ability to keep going. Even generals suffered at times: Fayolle complained on 20 October 1914 that he had received nothing for a fortnight, and on 18 November in Flanders, a stretcher-bearer received twenty letters all at once from a batch of 116 sacks of letters that had been delayed.[63] The historian Jules Isaac wrote to his wife on 18 September: 'Your letters are my comfort always, and my joy, my only joy ... they all arrive, but irregularly.' He had just received three all at once.[64]

Sometimes letters were able to pass on information that could not be obtained in the normal way, through the press. On 5 August 1914 the law on the state of siege was promulgated; it contained a clause on 'repressing indiscretions in the press'. All information on the war, 'whatever its source, origin or nature', was to be passed by a special Bureau de la Presse in the war ministry before publication in the Paris and provincial newspapers. The sanction, which was indeed invoked, was suppression of the publication.[65] Yet censorship did not prevent the press campaign of criticism of XV and XVI Corps in Castelnau's Second Army. These two corps, raised in the south of France (hence, to some, politically suspect) were accused of breaking and fleeing when the Bavarians attacked at Morhange on 20 August.

Another link between home and front was formed by the 235 parliamentarians, 25 of them senators, who were mobilised. Most were reservists, among them many doctors, but the younger men who had been mobilised as privates caused a problem of status. A decree of 12 November 1914 enabled such parliamentarians to be promoted temporarily to sub-lieutenant. Although this caused resentment at GQG, by the time the decree came into effect Joffre had put a stop to the duality of functions. Most deputies took advantage of the offer of unlimited leave in order to carry out their parliamentary rather than their military duties.[66] There were notable exceptions: for example, Abel Ferry, André Tardieu, Paul Doumer. Ferry was unhappy about the relationship between the army and the government. 'The military are consuming the civilians', he wrote in his diary at year's end, 'they are the master in the whole of France ... parliamentarians are stymied ... there are also a few reactionaries ... clericalism dressed up in military uniform so as to make war . . . on the Republic'. As for the new war minister, Millerand, he was simply contemplating the navel – of his service directors in the ministry.[67]

The military reverses caused Viviani to rejig his ministry on 26 August so as to include a wider representation of ministers from different parties. Messimy was one of the casualties; he was replaced by Alexandre Millerand. It is clear that Messimy was temperamentally unsuited for the post of war minister and not strong enough to withstand the strain. To Abel Ferry he complained that Joffre was responsible for the 'divorce' between GQG and the troops. He blamed a failure of intelligence for the disaster at Charleroi. While admitting the 'redressement' of the Marne, he claimed that Joffre was simply indulging in partial and costly attacks. In short Joffre had no ideas, no plans.[68]

Joffre certainly had ideas about the incompetence of many of his generals. He had replaced two of the three army commanders by 3 September (Ruffey by Sarrail, and Lanrezac by Franchet d'Espèrey). By year's end, only six of the original twenty corps commanders remained in post (they were not all sacked: Foch, for example, had commanded XX Corps in August). The two corps from the south of France alongside Foch in Second Army had received a lot of bad publicity and the two generals were replaced on 31 October and 7 November respectively, once the fighting had settled down. Twenty-one infantry or cavalry division commanders remained in post.[69] When First Army was obliged to pull back from the Vosges heights as a result of Second Army's retreat after the battle at Morhange, 13 DI's commanding officer, General Bourdériat, was removed for 'lack of firmness and insufficient resistance to the fatigues of war', but he was simply too ill.[70] On the other hand, the weeding out at the top made room for the corps commander Foch, the reserve division commander Fayolle and colonels Pétain and Nivelle. Nor did Messimy have any qualms in supporting Joffre's sacking of generals, going so far as to encourage Joffre to execute immediately officers guilty of 'pusillanimity'. Messimy even invokes in his memoirs the names of six generals sent to the guillotine in 1793–94, stating that he believed that he would have done the same if France had faced the same mortal danger in 1914 as it had during the French Revolutionary Wars.[71]

In addition to sacking generals, Joffre took some lessons from the 1914 fighting, especially as regards aviation, which some had dismissed before the war as of little use. In two areas, however, the aviation service had proved its worth: in intelligence gathering, and in spotting for the artillery. It was from the air that the German turn to pass to the east of Paris was discovered, thus enabling the launching of the Battle of the Marne. This marked the cavalry's failure in one of its principal roles, the gathering of intelligence. Indeed, at GQG, Berthelot complained that it was British and not French aircraft that were the more useful.[72] On 25 September Joffre appointed Commandant Barès as head of GQG's aeronautic service. Barès wasted no time, for he had volunteered as a pilot during the Balkan Wars and knew what he wanted. On 8 October he put to the minister a plan for sixty-five squadrons (*escadrilles*) to augment the twenty-seven currently in service. These squadrons were to consist of sixteen fighter and reconnaissance aircraft to operate for an army, as required; thirty for an army corps for artillery registration; sixteen for bombing; and three for the cavalry. In a note of 10 November 1914, Joffre stated:

Aviation is not only as one might have thought formerly an instrument for reconnaissance. It has made itself, if not indispensable, at least extremely useful for directing artillery fire. It has shown in addition that by dropping powerful explosive projectiles it was able to act as an offensive arm either for long-distance missions or in liaison with other troops. Finally it has also the duty to expel and to destroy enemy aircraft.[73]

The costliest lesson of the 1914 fighting had come from the artillery. The vast expenditures of shells and the artillery's power to stop the infantry had shown that the French Army's vaunted 75mm gun was not the answer to all conditions. It had worked well in Flanders, where the terrain was flat and the enemy infantry and gun batteries within range, but the German howitzers had shown the need for guns of greater calibre, throwing a heavier shell and able to direct plunging fire, especially against enemy batteries. The French realised that it was vital to silence German batteries by counter-battery fire; it was vital also to have better observation for guns firing at greater ranges. Heavy guns were taken from naval installation and fortresses to compensate for France's inferiority in such calibres, but this was only a stop-gap measure at best. On 14 October 1914 Joffre drew up a detailed programme for using such heavy guns as France possessed, mainly old models of 90, 120 and 155mm guns, and the following month ordered that each army corps should be provided with a group of horse-drawn heavy artillery consisting of one of the available types.[74] The shell shortage was overcome by a crash programme of enrolling private firms to convert their factories to munitions production. Car manufacturers such as Citroën and Renault, for example, began producing and filling shells.

All in all, the French Army had performed creditably in the opening months of the war. Some of the credit must go to Joffre for the pre-war mobilisation planning, and even more to the ordinary soldiers who reported as required. Joffre's firm control of himself and of events enabled the Marne turn-around. In his report on the fighting around Ypres, Foch summed up the position at the end of the year as a 'negative' victory. The enemy had been prevented from carrying out his plan, but it remained to boot that enemy out of France.[75]

The US military attaché in Paris reported on 9 December 1914 that during the lull in the fighting the French were 'doing everything possible to improve the equipment and organization of their army by taking advantage of the experiences so dearly gained to remedy defects and supply deficiencies'. There was no doubt, he continued, that the current French Army was 'superior in numbers, in leadership, in equipment and in efficiency to the army that was pushed back so rapidly by the Germans last August'.[76]

Faults had been laid bare in the realms of tactics, intelligence gathering and analysis, the use of cavalry, the supply of artillery and munitions for which no industrial mobilisation had been planned, and in the medical services, where the scale of wounds caused by artillery shells had been underestimated.[77] There had been some failures of health, will and morale, among the officers as well as the troops, but Joffre had moved very quickly to repress these. The fighting revealed problems that would loom very large indeed in the coming months and years: industrial mobilisation; dealing with the numbers of refugees, prisoners of war and wounded; dealing with Allies; and above all civil–military relations. The government and parliament returned from Bordeaux for an extraordinary session on 22 December. Criticisms were being aired already about Joffre and the high command's conduct of the war. Joffre had had a free hand in 1914 with a compliant minister and no parliamentary oversight. Despite Joffre's best efforts, he would be obliged to tolerate 'interference' with France's armies in the future.

3   1915: On the offensive

In 1915 the French Army carried out a series of bloody and repetitive attacks from their own trenches against those of the entrenched enemy opposite. Attempts were made by various means to break the stalemate. These were technological (the development of new weapons) and doctrinal (the development of better tactics both in attack and in defence). Politics and diplomacy were invoked also. The politicians had returned to Paris from Bordeaux, and they attempted to impose closer control over what the army's high command was doing, thereby preventing the worst (to political eyes) military errors; diplomacy consisted essentially of bribing new members into joining the alliance. So the struggle to improve the conditions under which the war was being conducted by all, from the *poilu* in the trenches to the premier and President of the Republic, dominated the search for victory. Yet the principle on which that search for victory rested remained the offensive.

Although the winter 1914/15 had shut down most fighting, already reduced in scale for lack of munitions, Joffre was determined that the fighting should not stop altogether. There were internal domestic reasons for his decision, as well as external ones. Domestically, the government's return to the capital meant that the CinC and his staff faced parliamentary criticism over the costs to France of 1914's events, costs that were both human in the huge numbers of killed and wounded, and material in the destruction of towns and the loss of manufacturing capacity, especially the mineral resources in north-eastern France where the loss of the iron-ore deposits in the Briey basin gave Germany a crucial advantage. The new war minister, Alexandre Millerand, provided Joffre with a counterweight to criticism, since he supported Joffre and the GQG wholeheartedly. Besides, the French Army could not simply sit idly by while the enemy took French citizens as hostages or helped themselves to French coal and iron-ore deposits and machine-tools.

Externally, Joffre had to consider France's Allies. Russian calls for help could not be ignored, particularly since Russia had faithfully kept the promise to take the offensive on the fifteenth day after mobilisation, despite their mobilisation not being fully complete by that time. Joffre was well informed about Russian fears and (increasing) complaints. The French military attaché in Petrograd (General Pierre Laguiche) joined the Stavka, the Russian headquarters, and special missions, under the Russian-speaking Commandant Langlois, were despatched to report on events. The British had proved rather more difficult and Joffre had been obliged to ask for government assistance to put pressure on Sir John French through Lord Kitchener at the War Office. The British too had suffered great casualties, losing its professional army and requiring time to train and equip the volunteer recruits of Kitchener's New Armies. Moreover, the Belgian coast was a strategic concern for Britain, and the British in both France and London were planning to recapture Ostend and Zeebrugge, operations that were far from being a priority for Joffre. If he were to retain the moral leadership of the Entente to which he felt entitled, then his troops could not sit still during the winter. Moreover, Russia and Serbia needed support if they were to tie down enemy troops in the east which otherwise might be sent to France. Despite the lack of material means – which problem was being tackled, but could not be solved overnight – and despite the snowy Vosges and muddy Flanders, Joffre issued orders that operations were to continue. No open flank remained; frontal attacks would have to be undertaken. On 8 December, Joffre issued his 'Instruction générale #8': in 1915 two principal attacks were to be undertaken, in Artois and in Champagne, with five secondary supporting attacks to 'fix the enemy'.[1] Artois and Champagne flanked the German salient that pointed at Noyon, less than 100 kilometres from Paris. These two provinces presented the best terrain for offensive operations under winter conditions; further north, in French and Belgian Flanders, it was too muddy; further east around Verdun and the Vosges mountains down to the Swiss frontier, it was too cold.

On 11 December Joffre explained to Poincaré and Millerand his strategy for the coming months: a series of local actions from which he did not expect any great results as 'all the siege weapons' had not yet been acquired. He feared to wait for them, however, because there was a risk that the Germans would move troops to the Russian front if the French remained quiescent, and he feared equally that the Russians would not withstand too strong an offensive 'push'.[2] He reassured the Russians by sending a 'verbal note' via Commandant Langlois, stating that the signal to restart attacks would indeed be given in mid December, so as to tie down German troops in France and Belgium, despite the advantages of waiting a few more weeks.[3] He informed his own armies on 6 December as follows:

Whatever happens in East Prussia, the Germans will not retire [in France] until constrained and forced to it. The moment has come to force them, first of all to help the Russians by retaining on our front, by our offensive attitude, the forces there; and then because it seems necessary, after two months of relative stagnation on the greater part of the front, to react against the somewhat depressing actions of trench warfare. For these two principal reasons, it is right, moreover, to act as soon as possible.[4]

Whether the troops felt that offensive action in winter was the best antidote to 'relative stagnation' is not recorded, but the French Army had changed considerably since August 1914. The older and unfit generals had been replaced by the more energetic, and from 5 January 1915 the armies were organised into two provisional army groups (the northern under Foch; the eastern under Dubail). Joffre had already ordered each army to create its own reserve force, constituted by reducing the density of troops in the front line, and positioned near to rail centres. He had also built up a reserve under his own hand. Joffre kept a tight control over tactics and operational matters. He collected reports from his liaison officers and issued directives. This drew complaints from commanders in the field, who felt that high command ought to visit the trenches and see for themselves, and they resented the power wielded by the (often young) liaison officers.[5]

Experiments were continuing to provide better protection for the infantry with helmets and various forms of shields for trench parapets, and a response to the deadly German mortar, *Minenwerfer*, was sought. The French had suffered greatly from the heavy munitions lobbed by these weapons, and now that trenches were protected by belts of wire, a means of cutting wire by delivering a heavy explosive charge at a short distance was required. Colonel Duchêne set about experimenting with shell cases and tubes, and came up with an inelegant but effective 58mm mortar, which launched a projectile with fins to make it turn downwards. The first models were made available in April 1915, and over 1,100 had been supplied by October. A German report of that same month praised the French for having caught up, for, although the Germans began the war with *Minenwerfer* when the French had none, yet the German infantry had no fixed doctrine for their use. The French, however, began to make them with whatever came to hand, never stopped improving them and production was increasing all the time. The French had acquired 'superiority', the report concluded.[6] Nicknamed 'crapouillots', from crapaud (toad), the mortars were produced mainly in the armaments centre of Bourges in central France.

For trench warfare, particularly in sectors where opposing trenches were very close, much experimentation was carried out over the winter to

(a)

Fig. 5a The 58mm mortar (crapouillot), with its feathered projectile

develop new weapons. Some of this was bizarre: harpoons launched by catapult to pull up the enemy's wire; strings of explosive charges thrown into the wire entanglements. The Chauchat automatic rifle came out of this experimentation. At GQG Alexandre (an artillery officer in Joffre's military cabinet) was given the task of finding a useful weapon for the infantry in close fighting and got Chauchat to produce his automatic rifle for the purpose. Chauchat promised 40,000 units in a few months, saying that it would only be a load of old iron but it would fire.[7] The Americans would curse the weapon when they were equipped with it in 1917, but it lasted the war.

(b)

Fig. 5b (*cont.*) A 155mm long gun (1877 de Bange model, throwing a shell of 40–43 kilos)

The need for heavy artillery had been satisfied at first by taking guns from the forts, but as early as August 1914 Joffre demanded 100 new batteries. In July 1915 a ministerial decree ordered the creation of, first, twenty horse-drawn heavy artillery regiments, allocating the older models of gun to the various corps artilleries and the newer 155mm gun to the armies. Second, it decreed ten new regiments of tractored heavy guns using a mix of heavy howitzers and the long 155mm gun. It took some time, however, for the regiments to be equipped, as heavy guns could not be produced quickly.[8]

Secondary offensives, December 1914 to summer and autumn 1915

It must be remembered that these offensives started and stopped at various times and overlapped both each other and the principal offensives in Artois and Champagne. For clarity's sake they are treated here

Table 8 *The 1915 fighting*

Theatre / sector	Dec 1914	Jan	Feb	Mar	Apr	May	Jun	Jul	Aug	Sep	Oct	Nov	Dec 1915
Vosges / HWK	X	X		X									X
Le Linge						X		X	X	X	X		
Verdun / Saint-Mihiel	X			X									
Les Eparges				X	X								
Argonne / Vauquois		X	X	X		X							
Champagne	X	X	X	X							X	X	
Artois	X					X	X				X		
Flanders	X			X									
Dardanelles					X	X	X	X	X	X	X		
Africa / Cameroon							X				X	X	

geographically, from the south-east in the Vosges to the north-west in Flanders, but their overlapping nature must be kept in mind. See Table 8 and Map 5.

The French had seized the rocky summit of Hartmannswillerkopf (HWK) in the Vosges during their first offensive into Upper Alsace, when Mulhouse had been captured and lost again. The mountain is an outcrop of the Vosges, 956 metres high, overlooking the Alsace plain, the river Rhine and, on a clear day, the Black Forest in Germany. It stood about 5 kilometres north of the town of Thann which had remained in French hands after the Alsace offensive. Joffre wanted to secure the summit because it gave such good observation over Mulhouse and the Mulhouse–Colmar railway, which was an important supply line for the Germans. Its possession would also provide security for the French railway communications between Thann and Belfort, via Cernay. Accordingly 66 DI, using a battalion of chasseurs alpins, consolidated the French hold on the summit in an operation that began on Christmas Day. Fighting their way through thick snow (40 centimetres deep in places) and thick forests, the chasseurs alpins, known as 'blue devils' because of their dark blue berets, held on to the summit but the German positions were very close. The location in Alsace, territory ceded to Germany in the 1871 treaty, and the presence of a distinctive and distinguishable unit, caught the popular imagination. Hartmannswillerkopf, or 'le vieil Armand', became famous.

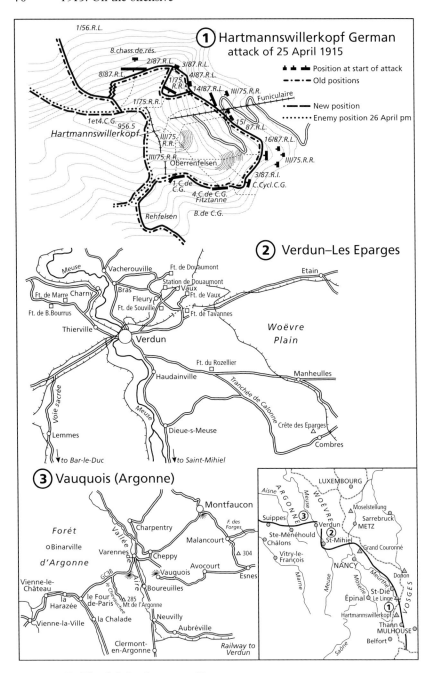

5. The fighting in eastern France

On 19 January 1915 the French lost the summit when, in fog and snow, the Germans managed to surround the troops guarding it. There followed a long series of attempts by both sides to keep possession of this important observatory. The French attacked on 6, 17 and 23 March and 152 RI managed to push the Germans off the top, capturing 400 prisoners and many guns. Naturally, the Germans counter-attacked and took back the summit on 25 April; 152 RI lost fourteen officers and 811 men, killed, wounded and captured. The rest of the year was spent in ding-dong battles with each side taking, losing and re-taking terrain, fighting in trenches at times only tens of metres apart.

The final battle of 1915 on the mountain took place in December. General Dubail, commanding the Eastern Army Group, had decided that there was an opportunity to put a halt to the constant flux, and to consolidate the French hold over the whole region by liberating Mulhouse (again). The attack on Hartmannswillerkopf was to be the 'preface' to the wider attack in Upper Alsace. The operation was given to General Serret and 66 DI who had been involved all year in the fighting. For the operation, Serret was given 250 extra guns, including two 370mm heavy mortars and other heavy guns. This density gave Serret one gun for every 13 metres of enemy front. The offensive began on 21 December after several delays, and the French gains of territory were lost again by January, when the lines returned almost to their 1 December position. The 152 RI was wiped out – 1,950 men and 48 officers killed or wounded in the two days 21–22 December – and General Serret was mortally wounded.[9] If the name of Hartmannswillerkopf became a symbol of heroism in the face of snowy mountainous terrain, the action there remains nonetheless a classic example of the minor but costly battles for observation heights that characterised 1915's fighting. Overall, the fighting between 21 December and 8 January 1916 cost France almost half the total number of effectives engaged. The French had taken some 1,700 prisoners, but the German losses in killed and wounded were significantly less.[10] At last Joffre and Dubail concluded that operations must be closed down so as to give the troops some rest, and that local operations risked drawing in more and more resources and could not be limited. Such operations ought to be avoided.[11]

About 30 kilometres further north lay another mountain-top observatory, Le Linge, another outpost of the Vosges mountains overlooking Colmar. Once again 66 DI was involved, ordered to attack the heights in support of General Pouydraguin's 47 DI. Operations in early May made insignificant advances in the face of determined German resistance, and a halt was called. In June both divisions managed to approach the mountain from the south, but their patrols warned the Germans, who strengthened their defences. French losses were heavy – almost 7,000 casualties of which almost 2,000 had died or had disappeared – but the French had tied down troops who might otherwise have gone to join those in Artois where Foch's Northern Army Group was attacking. In July more attacks were ordered, with the addition of another division, 129 DI, newly formed the previous month. Between 20 and 27 July, 129 DI managed to capture Le Linge but the Germans held neighbouring heights, so the French possession was not secure. In early August a fierce German counter-attack – 40,000 shells fell on a front of only 3 kilometres – meant that the summit changed hands several times. The Germans made further assaults using gas and flamethrowers throughout September and October, but Le Linge remained in French hands. Pouydraguin reported on 21 October that his division's position on Le Linge was 'difficult, painful and costly in men', because the enemy was so close and the terrain made constructing good defences almost impossible. Any improvement would require considerable reinforcements. This was as far as the division's commander could go in criticising the operation.[12]

Further north than the Vosges, the Saint-Mihiel 'hernia' formed a salient in the front line that cut across the river Meuse south of Verdun and interdicted the railway line into Verdun from the south. The German salient had already cost First Army, in whose Lorraine sector it lay, almost 18,000 men in the last two months of 1914. On taking command of the new Eastern Army Group, Dubail was given the task of clearing the Meuse hills by attacking the salient on both flanks and from the Woëvre plain in the salient's rear. Dubail decided to attack Les Eparges, which lies between Verdun and Saint-Mihiel, about 18 kilometres south-east of the former and about 20 north-east of the latter. The hill above Les Eparges is kidney-shaped, with a German bastion at each end (east and west), joined by a curtain wall (courtine).[13] On 17 February, 12 DI (VI Corps) launched its assault on the heights and by 27 March had managed to hold on to trenches in the east bastion and to another 60-metre-long trench situated about 80 metres in front of the jumping-off line. Fierce German counter-attacks prevented any further advance. Casualties for these meagre gains were 274 officers (84 killed) and 15,546 men (3,050 killed and 1,546 disappeared).[14] Although First Army's commander, General Pierre Roques, pressed his other army corps to attack to relieve the pressure on VI Corps on the heights of Les Eparges, little could be done because Joffre could not release enough munitions to First Army. Joffre was saving shells for the principal action in Champagne.[15]

The next assault on Les Eparges came as part of a wider operation against the whole Saint-Mihiel salient, which had the merit, at least, of saving VI Corps from having to face the concentration of enemy reserves and artillery that had accompanied the action in February–March. Joffre had told Dubail that the end of the Champagne offensive would release some troops to be used in operations 'to maintain the morale of the country and retain the initiative' in French hands. Speed was essential so as to have reached the objectives before German forces in Metz could leave the fortress to counter-attack. Dubail gave two aims for the operation: first a rapid success in freeing the Saint-Mihiel salient would provide a boost to morale and develop confidence; second the capture or, at least, putting out of action, of a large proportion of the German forces holding the Meuse heights.[16]

The artillery preparation was to have begun on 5 April, but it poured with rain on the 4th and aviation could provide no help. No progress could be made over the soaked ground, which was marshy under normal conditions, but was now covered in standing water. Repeated attacks were ordered for 6 and 7 April, but had to be stopped on Joffre's orders the next day. All hopes for a speedy surprise attack were now gone, but VI Corps managed to complete the capture of almost the whole of the Les Eparges position, fighting off two violent counter-attacks. Just as in Alsace, the Germans were not prepared to let the French retain the advantage of the observation from the heights, and they launched a powerful attack beginning on the evening of 23 April, followed the next day by a 'formidable bombardment'. They attacked the Calonne trench (west of Les Eparges), capturing 4 kilometres of the French front line and even a portion of the second. Digging in immediately, they resisted all the powerful French attempts to dislodge them. So the Eastern Army Group's Woëvre offensive closed at the end of April. The gains made by VI Corps in capturing the crest of les Eparges were more than outweighed by the loss of so much terrain. The French had taken 800 German prisoners, but in turn had suffered many casualties.

North-west of the Woëvre plain lay Verdun, whose perimeter was held by General Maurice Sarrail's Third Army. Some of Third Army's units had been involved in the Woëvre fighting, on the northern side of the Saint-Mihiel salient, and in addition Dubail had asked Sarrail to mount an operation further west at Vauquois so as to free the railway line from Sainte-Menehould into Verdun from the west, which First Army needed for the transport of its supplies. Joffre also wanted the right flank of the main Champagne operations safeguarded. Vauquois was another height (290 metres), so became yet another observatory that each side tried to deny the other. Unlike the hills at Les Eparges or Hartmannswillerkopf, the heights at Vauquois had a village on top and lay in the heavily forested Argonne region, west of Verdun. From the village, 7 kilometres to its north, the Germans were able to shell the main railway line into Verdun. Third Army had lost a good many men in November 1914 attempting to seize the hill, which was held by the German *XVI Corps*, commanded by the engineer General Bruno von Mudra. The battle for Vauquois became known as the war of mines, because so many were used.

After losing 2,400 men during January, Sarrail planned another attack for February, reinforced by combining the heavy mortars of two corps' artillery. The two divisions of General Alfred Micheler's V Corps failed completely, but as the main Champagne offensive was about to begin, Micheler sent his troops in again. After two days' heavy fighting on 28 February and 1 March, they managed to get into the village, but the Germans still held the church. Despite Dubail's appeals for reinforcements to improve on the gains, Joffre refused to commit any more resources. The ground gained was not large but the 360 German prisoners captured on 28 February came from four different divisions, which showed that V Corps had managed to tie down significant enemy forces. Between 15 January and the end of March French casualties were just over 27,000 men. The railway line into Verdun was still under fire from German shells.[17]

Throughout the summer the Germans kept the initiative in the Argonne, as von Mudra attempted to get closer to the railway line by exploding mines under French trenches before attacking. Third Army's losses in May amounted to 8,000 men. The Germans attacked again on 20 June, using four corps on a wider front than before. They used gas shells and *Minenwerfer* to destroy all the French front-line defences, and blew up blockhouses with mines. The attack fell not only on V Corps but especially heavily on XXXII Corps (General Denis Duchêne) on V Corps' left. XXXII Corps lost 4 kilometres of front-line trench on 30 June and another 3 kilometres on 2 July. In four days of fighting the corps suffered over 10,000 casualties. Joffre ordered an immediate counter-attack and supplied heavy artillery and two divisions as reinforcements, but Sarrail was unable to complete the preparations for XXXII and V Corps quickly enough. Yet another German attack on 13 July forestalled the French plans and another high point (Hill 285) was lost to the enemy. The French counter-attacked and managed to resist the Germans, but suffered thousands more casualties in the process.[18]

In less than a month, Sarrail had ceded the whole of his front line in the Argonne sector and part of the second line defences and had lost over 33,000 men. Joffre was sufficiently affected to demand a report from the Eastern Army Group commander, Dubail. As will be seen below, his report had large consequences.

Sarrail's Third Army was east of Fourth Army, who had the task of carrying out in Champagne one of the two principal 1915 attacks, discussed below. On Fourth Army's western flank was Fifth Army. Fifth, Sixth and Second Armies had been ordered to hold the passive front between the two principal attacks in the Champagne and Artois. Fifth Army's front ran from east of Reims to east of Soissons, Sixth Army's from Soissons to north of Compiègne, and from there Second Army's ran north to join Tenth Army in Artois. Hence they were not involved in the costly offensives that characterised the fighting in the Vosges, Lorraine and the Argonne. Nevertheless, they helped the two principal offensives by firing artillery barrages when requested, so as to disguise the actual front of attack. This constituted Fifth Army's only role. However, Sixth Army undertook an operation north of Soissons and the river Aisne, which led to considerable criticism. Under pressure from Joffre for action, an offensive to capture some high ground north of the Aisne was prepared. It was on the higher northern bank of the Aisne where the Germans had halted after the Marne, because the terrain was perfect for defence. At this point, the French front line also ran along the north bank. The French managed to capture Hill 132 west of the village of Crouy after fierce fighting between 8 and 11 January, but a strong German counter-attack drove them out of Crouy and back across the river, so that the French were worse off by 14 January than they had been when the operation began. The Germans pushed outposts as far as the northern riverbank. They had captured round about the same number of French (5,200 prisoners) as they had had casualties of their own (5,529).[19] The French casualties amounted to about 40 per cent of the effectives committed (12,411 killed, wounded or disappeared) and the German advance to the Aisne caused alarm at GQG and in Paris. Millerand sent a rare letter of reproach to Joffre, and Joffre threatened to resign. Joffre blamed Sixth Army's commander, General Maunoury, and Maunoury blamed Berthelot, who had taken over command of the French forces involved in the attack after leaving GQG. Berthelot and two divisional generals were sacked. Since the parliament had just reconvened (12 January) after returning from Bordeaux, emotions ran high. Berthelot's biographer described the parliamentary nervousness as 'symptomatic' of the political battles in the arena of civil–military relations that were to come.[20]

The last of the three armies holding the passive front between the two principal offensives was Second Army. It supported Foch's Artois offensive by making two subsidiary attacks in June, south of Tenth Army's front. On a 2-kilometre front, advancing 900 metres at a cost of over 10,000 casualties (1,760 killed), Castelnau's Second Army took the offensive. A second attack south of Noyon at the same time (6–16 June) made an even smaller advance for almost 8,000 casualties.[21] Second Army was then moved into the new Centre Army Group for the autumn Champagne offensive, discussed below.

The most northerly minor operation of this period took place in December 1914 in Flanders, north of both the BEF and Tenth Army's attack in Artois.[22] Eighth Army was to attack towards Werwicq on the river Lys in conjunction with the British left. The northern Ypres attacks made little headway, and the BEF made even less against Messines. Sir John French did not have his heart in the operation and impressed on his corps and divisional commanders that everybody was to 'wait for the man on his left'. Since the last man on the left was next to the French XVI Corps in Eighth Army, which made no progress, then it is not surprising that the British did not get very far either. Operations continued 'in a half-hearted way' for two more days. Foch blamed the British for the poor results obtained by the Eighth Army units, and the British (according to a report by the French Mission) refused to move until XVI Corps moved.[23]

This melancholy list of minor operations, all taking place at different times and all lacking sufficient material means for success, was recognised by some, especially those in parliament, as simply 'food for the communiqués'. Certainly Joffre had wanted to keep the troops busy, but the cost in human lives was huge. Not surprisingly, there were some minor revolts. The number of voluntary mutilations increased. In Pétain's XXXIII Corps, for example, forty such cases were judged in January 1915. Pétain wanted to shoot twenty-five of them, but in the end had them thrown over the parapet into no-man's-land with their hands tied.[24] (This incident inspired the novel and then film *A very long engagement*.) On 21 June 1915 Joffre ordered army commanders to be aware of two tactics: men bandaging their hand before shooting themselves to avoid getting powder on their skin which would betray voluntary wounding; men ingesting substances such as picric acid so as to be sent to hospital. There were twenty-three death sentences passed in 56 RI in May (all commuted) and two soldiers were executed in 16 DIC in August for deserting their post.[25] A more serious incident took place in April near Flirey, in the First Army sector where the offensive against the southern flank of the assault on the Saint-Mihiel salient was taking place. The colonel commanding 63 RI was asked to designate a battalion for an attack on 17 April, despite his regiment having suffered considerably already. In the event he chose the 'least tired', but the men of 5 Company chosen to lead the attack protested. It was not their turn, they said, and insisted that they were not refusing to do their duty but they did not want 'to get [themselves] killed uselessly on the belts of wire'. Confronted by this collective refusal to obey an order, their lieutenant picked four names out of a hat because he 'loved them all and he refused to designate some rather than some others'. Tried on 19 April, they were executed the same day. Two post-war appeals against their conviction were rejected, but in 1934 the judgement was reversed on the grounds that the men were too exhausted, in fact, to obey, and that picking their names out of a hat was unjust.[26]

The most famous case was probably that of the 'four corporals of Souain' (north of Suippes), members of a company who in March 1915 did not leave their trenches to attack as they had been ordered. The corporals were part of a reserve division (60 DR in Fourth Army), the oldest, a primary school teacher, Corporal Maupas, aged 41, having arrived on the front in Champagne in October 1914. Thirty-two of the accused were acquitted on the grounds that they had not heard the order to advance, but on 17 and 18 March the four corporals were shot, as their commanding general refused to commute the sentence. Maupas's widow mounted a press campaign after the war to get the verdict reversed, and her case was taken up by the League of the Rights of Man. In 1934 the special court set up to try the wartime verdicts that were contested acquitted the four corporals, just like the Flirey four, on the grounds that 'in wartime the sacrifice of one's life to one's duty cannot be imposed, when it exceeds the limits of human strength'.[27]

During the course of 1915 the number of death sentences pronounced was gradually reduced. Of the 496 death sentences documented by General Bach, 111 were commuted by the President of the Republic, and seventy-four men were tried in their absence, having crossed deliberately into enemy lines. Eighteen were pronounced on North Africans and nine Russian Foreign Legionaries were executed. The peak month for guilty verdicts was May (fifty-nine), and the monthly average was thirty-one death sentences. The second highest month (March) saw fifty-five death sentences (forty-five carried out). Table 8 (page 75) shows that the fighting in 1915 was heaviest in March and May. However, there is a noticeable (if fluctuating) drop over the course of the year in the number of executions actually carried out compared with the death sentences. In June and December, for example, the figures are: twenty-five out of forty-nine, and seven out of thirty-one respectively.[28] This fall reflects the parliamentary opposition to the special courts martial that had been decreed in 1914. As early as January 1915 the high command was ordered to submit all capital verdicts to the President for review. In June the practice of making a spectacle of executions with drums beating was dropped (especially in areas where civilians might witness the event), as was the trial of civilians for spying. A GQG note in March reminded commanders only to appoint qualified men as judges (of the hundred or so mobilised judges, only fourteen were used for military tribunals). In July they were reminded not to change the verdicts without a 'serious' motive.[29] These regulations indicate that some degree of abuse of procedure continued, with commanding generals urging the courts to be tougher.[30] As late as 21 October Joffre had to remind commanders that they had no right whatsoever to ignore the court's recommendation to commute a death sentence, and that the papers in such cases had to be sent to the President.[31] On 10 December 1915 parliament invited the government to put an end to the special courts martial, and Joffre did so in April the following year.

It was not only the troops who were rejecting Joffre's methods, the parliamentarians were beginning to react also. Abel Ferry, deputy for the Vosges, was a sub-lieutenant in 166 RI, and when the parliament and government retired to Bordeaux he had remained with his unit in eastern France. He had direct experience, therefore, of the fighting there in 1914 and early 1915. Ferry had already sent a letter to Poincaré in October 1914, in which he claimed that the Germans had air and artillery superiority, and that the French artillery and infantry fought separate battles – there was no liaison between the two services. He ended with a plea for more shells for the 75s and for a lot of heavy guns. The Germans 'waste their munitions but spare human lives', whereas the French saved on munitions and wasted lives.[32] The papers of war minister Alexandre Millerand contain a file of Ferry's reports on his experiences during the 1914–15 fighting. Ferry took part in the operations described above at Les Eparges, which was captured, he wrote, after three months' continuous effort and at a cost of 20–25,000 men. Was it worth it, he asked, pointing out that, excellent as the hilltop was as an observatory, there were plenty of others equally as good close by. The history of Les Eparges as of Vauquois was nothing but 'an illustration of the pernicious and bloody method used on all parts of the front. The right to carry out this or that local operation is distributed *just like possible medals and promotion would be given out.*'[33] In a letter of 21 May Ferry described a reconnaissance he had carried out in the Les Eparges sector:

A sinister, almost vertical, slope descends into the valley of 'death'. Not a single tree that a shell has not cut; as spring grows greener, the ground in Les Eparges is of a volcanic sterility. The plain is green; the Meuse heights are green, but [here] the ground is black and turned over, craters everywhere, enormous holes big enough to bury a whole squad ... the trenches are constructed of corpses, hands and feet sticking out everywhere; now you can only distinguish German from French by the boots ... the poverty of ideas in our great leaders is equalled only by the heroism and faith of all these corpses ... so much heroism so badly utilised, no other thought than to select haphazardly a place to attack.[34]

Principal operations: Champagne and Artois

The subsidiary operations just described had achieved very little and had cost a good deal. Was the prosecution of the two main offensives any better?

The terrain on the Champagne front was different from the forested, hilly ground further east and from that further west also, where proximity to Paris, and further north the industrial areas of Artois, made operations more difficult. Between Reims and the Argonne, whose western edge was delimited by the upper reaches of the river Aisne, the chalky ground was undulating. A series of small rivers ran mainly east–west across the mostly bare hillsides, scattered with managed pine plantations and sparsely populated. Apart from the marshy river banks and the sticky chalk, it was better fighting territory than elsewhere on the front. The open country and lack of natural obstacles gave the enemy less scope for building strong defences. The countryside is still bare today, and most of the pine plantations have gone.

Joffre and Fourth Army's commander, General de Langle de Cary, began a series of studies in December 1914, aiming to break through the German front in the direction of Somme-Py (see Map 6). Joffre provided extra heavy artillery and the infantry of I Corps and 10 DI, and advised de Langle not to spare the guns. He supplied unprecedented amounts of shell so that the guns could aid the infantry's progression. On 20 December, XVII Corps and I Colonial Corps set off in fine style and around Perthes-les-Hurlus got into the German front lines and beat off the counter-attacks. De Langle decided to continue attacking where his army had already gained some ground, instead of following Joffre's initial orders for moving on Somme-Py and Souain further west. On 28 and 30 December the same two corps attacked again and captured another 300 metres of enemy trench, but the appalling weather and strong German counter-attacks put a stop to any further advance. The fighting was especially violent around Perthes-les-Hurlus and the strong-point of Beauséjour, 6 or 7 kilometres further east. Between 8 and 13 January the strongpoint was captured and lost again three times. Joffre's large provision of munitions proved a mixed blessing, because the rapid conversion of French factories to produce shell, necessary to counter the shell shortage manifest as early as September 1914, had led to poor quality munitions. As a result, many of the French 75s burst their barrels because of faulty shells.

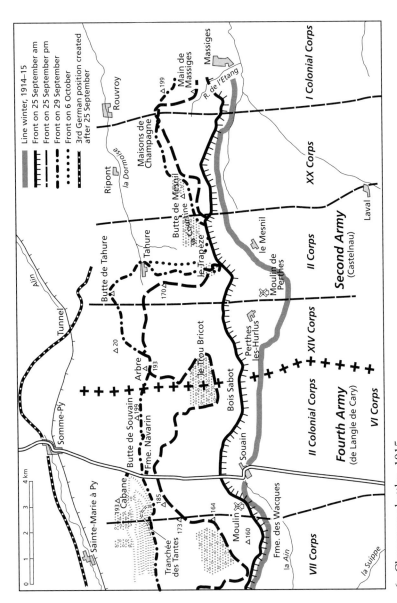

6. Champagne battles, 1915

Map legend:

Line winter, 1914–15
Front on 25 September am
Front on 25 September pm
Front on 29 September
Front on 6 October
3rd German position created after 25 September

Map labels:

Massiges
Rouvroy
Main de Massiges
R. de l'Étang
Ripont
la Dormoise
Maisons de Champagne
△199
I Colonial Corps
XX Corps
Laval
Second Army (Castelnau)
II Corps
le Mesnil
Butte de Mesnil
Courtine △
le Trapèze
Moulin de Perthes
Aisne
Tunnel
Butte de Tahure
Tahure
170
△20
Perthes-lès-Hurlus
XIV Corps
Arbre △193
le Trou Bricot
Bois Sabot
Souain
II Colonial Corps
VI Corps
Fourth Army (de Langle de Cary)
Somme-Py
Butte de Souvain
Fme. Navarin
△199
Cabane
△793
△85
Tranchée des Tantes
173 △
△164
Moulin △160
Fme. des Wacques
VII Corps
la Ain
la Suippe
Sainte-Marie à Py

0 1 2 3 4 km

De Langle drew the obvious conclusion: carefully prepared operations against 'carefully selected points', and not a wide-front massed infantry operation, were required. A methodical and minutely prepared siege, he wrote to Joffre on 13 January, was needed to deal with the enemy's second line defences, equally as solid as the first which his troops had captured. Operations now had a 'certain slowness', de Langle continued, and he intended to continue in this way. Although Joffre approved the Fourth Army commander's decision, nevertheless he advised as much speed as possible. Leaving too wide an interval between successive attacks caused greater losses than a 'general attack pushed more rapidly and vigorously'.[35] So ended the first phase of the Champagne battle, with Joffre and GQG resisting what was obvious on the ground. Rapid and vigorous attacks in winter weather and with inadequate artillery support could not be otherwise than costly.

Preparations began immediately for the second round: another main attack by XVII and I Corps in the centre, supported by the Colonial Corps in the east and XII Corps in the west. Once again, large quantities (in 1915 terms) of heavy artillery were provided – 110 heavies out of a total of 872 guns – with the addition, this time, of five squadrons of aircraft. Although the French outnumbered the Germans, the latter had modern heavy guns, twice if not three times as effective as the old French types which had been collected from coastal defences and forts. The Germans had begun to strengthen their second lines 3 kilometres in the rear, and, despite the muddy conditions, had transformed the wooded sections into mutually supporting mini-fortresses.

The second phase began badly in the early morning of 12 February, when a violent blizzard halted operations. When the general assault began four days later, it was obvious that the Germans had benefited from the early warning. Although another 4 kilometres of trench around Perthes fell into French hands, the Germans launched determined counter-attacks. At GQG Joffre became impatient. Warning de Langle not to let the conviction grow that the French could not breach enemy lines, despite powerful resources thrown at them, Joffre adopted his usual practice of changing unit commanders. He appointed General Adolphe Guillaumat to command I Corps. Also he repeated his order to de Langle to attack in the Souain sector, but once again it was around Perthes and Beauséjour that gains were being made. By 2 March the whole front line between these two points was in French hands. It had been hard fighting, Guillaumat wrote to his wife, but 'finally we have been taught the lesson by six months of hard knocks'.[36] As a result, de Langle wanted to push on to the heights of Tahure and Le Mesnil. Confusion followed the lack of consensus between GQG and Fourth Army. The former wanted action in the west of the army sector out of Souain (north of Suippes) towards Somme-Py, and the latter wanted to exploit the gains further east and attack the heights in front of them; Joffre wanted an end to repeated attacks by the same troops who were rested after each effort, and he instructed de Langle to fix the maximum width of the front to be attacked and then to feed fresh troops in so as to keep the battle going.

The final phase of the battle took place on 12–13 March, when the infantry attacks failed after an artillery preparation of three-and-a-half hours. A final assault on 16 March captured the plateau 196, well short of Tahure village and the hill behind. Some small gains had been made, but General Grossetti reported that his XVI Corps had only opened up a 'fissure' in the enemy's front. Until the fissure could be widened to become a wide breach, and until the attacking infantry could be protected from flanking enemy fire, no significant gains could be made, despite the willing sacrifices. Those sacrifices were great. The First Battle of Champagne had put over 93,000 men hors de combat.[37] Joffre reported to the minister that lack of munitions had restricted firing on other fronts while the Champagne operation was continuing. Men and shells were both being used up at an enormous rate.

GQG was not slow to draw tactical lessons from the fighting over the winter and spring. The first note for the armies, dated 2 January 1915, stated that 'position warfare' had not invalidated the principles of the French Army's offensive doctrine, but greater firepower and stronger defences meant that operations had to develop in a slower and more methodical manner. It was necessary, therefore, to prepare operations in minute detail and to use the artillery to destroy the enemy defences in order to open the way for the infantry. Simultaneous numerous attacks should be launched on as wide a front as possible. The depth of defensive positions meant that successive artillery preparations were required, as was close liaison between infantry and artillery before, during and after each attack. The events in Champagne caused a revision in April. GQG wanted an end to position warfare and a return to a war of movement to obtain a decisive victory. The aim was no longer a series of operations to nibble through successive positions, but an offensive 'to expel the enemy from the whole of his position and to defeat him without giving him time to get back on his feet'. Hence the notion of speed and continuity, and no rest between phases. All should be 'imbued with the idea of breakthrough [percée], of going beyond the first trenches captured and continuing an uninterrupted attack, without respite, night and day, until the final result'. That these are top-down instructions is obvious, yet the April instruction did stress the need for counter-battery work to suppress enemy guns during an attack and did recommend a box barrage to protect the infantry from the front and sides, as they crossed no-man's-land. On the other hand, the same pre-war density of attacking infantry was maintained: one man per running metre.[38]

As these lessons were being absorbed, set down on paper and distributed, the Artois offensive was being prepared. It was to be coordinated by Foch, using d'Urbal's Tenth Army with support from the BEF and from Belgian troops. The First Battle of Artois over the winter had achieved little, but revealed how difficult a task it was to capture the high ground north of Arras, the Vimy ridge (see Map 7). Yet Foch intended to attack there again, for the simple reason that the high ground had considerable strategic value. It overlooked the communications hub in the Douai plain and its possession would enable the French to bombard the enemy's communications. For that very same reason, the Germans would fight hard to retain the ridge.

Foch's preparations were hampered not only by the bad weather that had put a halt to the operations of First Artois, but also by the British. London was considering independent action in two areas: in Belgium to clear the Flanders coast, and in another theatre altogether, namely the Dardanelles. In addition, Kitchener was unhappy about the high costs and poor results of the fighting in France and Belgium and threatened to withhold troops. Consequently, when Foch requested a British relief of French units in order to prepare for his offensive, Sir John French refused. Joffre was so annoyed by this refusal that he postponed Foch's offensive and (in retaliation) the British went it alone at Neuve Chapelle, well north of Vimy ridge. Their three-day offensive, 10–12 March 1915, gained some ground, but at considerable cost, with well over 11,000 casualties.

Nonetheless some joint planning continued, and British agreement was obtained to relieve two French corps for the main Artois battle. The relief was complete by 20 April, but two days later the Germans intervened when they launched their assault on the northern flank of the Ypres salient by releasing chlorine gas from 5,830 cylinders dug into the ground. This was an experimental attack using the new gas weapon and it had been delayed by the necessary wait for the right wind conditions. There was no intention to make a great breakthrough, but the results were spectacular. The 6-kilometre front between Steenstraat on the Yser canal and Poelcapelle was held by troops of 45 DI and territorials of 87 DI. A heavy greenish-yellow cloud began to float across the front about a metre above the ground, progressing at 2–3 metres per second in the light wind. The German infantry wearing gas masks followed fifteen minutes later. The danger was not recognised at first, because the gas was mixed with the smoke from other shells, but as soon as the gas

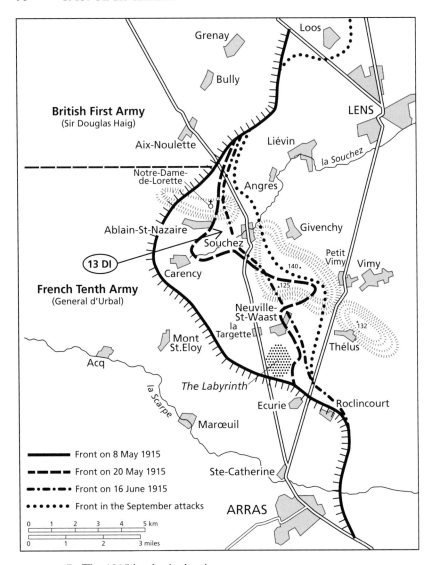

British First Army
(Sir Douglas Haig)

French Tenth Army
(General d'Urbal)

13 DI

Grenay
Loos
Bully
LENS
Aix-Noulette
Liévin
la Souchez
Notre-Dame-
de-Lorette
Angres
Ablain-St-Nazaire
Givenchy
Souchez
Petit
Vimy   Vimy
Carency
140
125
Neuville-
St-Waast
la
Mont   Targette
St.Eloy
132
Thélus
Acq
The Labyrinth
Ecurie
Roclincourt
la Scarpe
Marœuil
Ste-Catherine
ARRAS

Front on 8 May 1915
Front on 20 May 1915
Front on 16 June 1915
Front in the September attacks

0   1   2   3   4   5 km
0   1   2   3 miles

7. The 1915 battles in Artois

reached the French lines the effect was immediate. The troops streamed
away, abandoning the trenches and running towards Ypres and Poperinghe in search of breathable air. The Germans advanced 4 kilometres
and captured Langemarck, but the advance could not be exploited.
Strong resistance on both flanks of the gas cloud, Canadians on the right

and two French brigades on the left, halted the enemy. The commander of one of those brigades, Colonel Mordacq of 90 Brigade, thought that his regimental commanders were deranged when he first heard their telephone calls, but soon he saw the fleeing soldiers: 'haggard, their overcoats thrown off or opened wide, their scarves pulled off, running like madmen, directionless, shouting for water, spitting blood, some even rolling on the ground making desperate efforts to breathe'.[39]

The casualty figures are difficult to evaluate. They are certainly less than the thousands claimed for propaganda purposes in this new example of German 'barbarity'. One historian's estimate of the victims of the April 1915 attack is between 800 and 1,400 deaths for a total of between two and three thousand affected.[40] Foch reacted quickly, getting the gas analysed and primitive gas masks organised. He returned infantry and artillery that had moved south for the Artois operation back to the Ypres salient; he pressed for a counter-attack. Although some ground was retaken, finally it was recognised that to recapture the remainder of the lost ground would be too expensive and French operations there came to a halt. The British and Canadians, however, continued to suffer from German gas attacks until 23 May.

These enforced interruptions and delays to the Artois operation had allowed time to complete the detailed planning. Joffre had sufficient manpower for six corps to be allocated to the operation; artillery resources were generous: considerably more than 700 field guns, 293 heavy guns and some super-heavies, plus 10 mortars. After yet another two-day delay caused by bad weather, the infantry assault began on 9 May. The artillery had been preparing the assault by bombarding trenches and communications, so no surprise was possible. In the north of the sector, General Paul Maistre's XXI Corps (containing 13 DI) was to attack the enemy strongpoint on the hill of Notre Dame de Lorette; General Maurice Balfourier's XX Corps attacked the southern stronghold around Neuville-St-Waast; and in the centre, so protected on its flanks, General Pétain's XXXIII Corps was to make for the ridge.[41]

On 9 May the artillery began firing at 6am and four hours later the infantry assault was launched along a 20-kilometre front. In the north, XXI Corps made little progress towards Notre Dame de Lorette; in the southern sector, XX Corps managed to get into the cemetery of Neuville St Waast and recaptured the little hamlet of La Targette, but were stopped by the trenches of 'Le Labyrinthe', a very strong defensive position protecting the southern approaches to Neuville. The divisions in Pétain's XXXIII Corps did much better in the centre. Pétain had inspected his gun batteries personally, and made sure that all were well registered on their targets; moreover the infantry did not suffer from the flanking fire that prevented progress by the unfortunate corps on the flanks of the assault. Pétain's 70 DI (Fayolle) and 77 DI (Barbot) managed to take Carency and reach Givenchy, but the Division Marocaine (DM) made the greatest advance. By 11am, one hour after setting off, they had reached the ridge line (point 140). This achievement caused great excitement and made Pétain's reputation, yet it was bought too dearly and was impossible to sustain. German artillery and machine guns had no difficulty firing into such a deep but narrow salient, and took a heavy toll of French officers. The French artillery could not be re-supplied with shells in time to protect the DM, and the infantry reserves of the corps were too far away, 8 kilometres behind the front line. In the afternoon a violent German counter-attack forced the DM back from the ridge. Nevertheless they brought back some guns and some dozens of machine guns, together with 1,500 German prisoners.

Although attacks continued on subsequent days, there was no repetition of the first day's success on 9 May. The Germans were ready to counter any and all assaults as they had scrambled to bring up reserves, and the French were having problems keeping their artillery supplied with shells. Moreover the rapidly expanded programmes of shell production had led to poor quality control, and, as had happened in the Champagne attack, premature explosions were bursting gun barrels. XXXIII Corps lost twenty-four guns in this way, although it lost only four to German fire. Nevertheless, Tenth Army's commander General d'Urbal passed on to his units the urgings of Joffre and Foch, and attacks continued for several days, with small chunks nibbled from the German lines. Finally, on 15 May, Foch decided that it was pointless to continue attacking towards the ridge until a firm jumping-off line had been established and, in particular, the flanking enemy strongpoints had been silenced. As a result, time was needed to assemble the guns and munitions so as to repeat the successful bombardment of 9 May and to rest and reinforce the infantry.

Joffre had pushed for the battle to be continued with the utmost energy. This was not simply indifference to the infantry's casualties and the vast expenditures of guns and munitions, but a concern for the international situation. On the Eastern Front, a joint German-Austro-Hungarian attack in the Carpathians had resulted in a spectacular breakthrough at Gorlice–Tarnow during the week before the Artois battle. The Russians were sent reeling back, and the forces of the Central Powers would eventually re-capture the Galician fortress of Przemysl and go on to take Lemberg, the capital of Russian Poland. Joffre had to keep German forces in France occupied, both to prevent the move of any more forces to the east and also to reassure Russia that France was not standing idly by. Moreover, the negotiations with Italy over that country's joining the Entente were almost complete. It was important to show the Italians that the French could gain some victories, especially after the gas attack at Ypres, the failure of the British to make much headway in their supporting operation at Aubers Ridge, and the lack of any progress at the Dardanelles and on Gallipoli (described below). The French Army was indeed paying the price of one of the major drawbacks of fighting a coalition war.

The corps commanders refused to rush their preparations for the renewed assault on Vimy ridge, and so it was only on 16 June that reinforcements of men and munitions allowed the offensive to re-start. It had proved difficult to establish the new jumping-off line. General Charles Mangin's 5 DI (XX Corps) had managed to complete the capture of Neuville and the 'Labyrinth', but at great cost: 3,500 casualties for the capture of three 77mm guns and some machine guns. German casualties were great as well; they had fought hard to retain the village, having knocked holes through the cellars of adjoining houses to create defensive positions that had to be reduced one by one. Yet the French seemed now to be in a better position than when the campaign started on 9 May: they were slightly nearer their object-ive, the crest; the reserves were up close, ready to exploit any break-through; the new 58mm mortar was appearing; and sufficient shells had been stock-piled to enable continuous firing over several days at the same intensity as had proved effective on 9 May (over 30,000 shells), but could not then be maintained. Joffre had provided twenty infantry divisions with six more in reserve (on 9 May there had been fifteen infantry and three cavalry divisions), and 1,160 guns (1,075 on 9 May).[42] Intelligence reports showed that the French had significant numerical superiority.

Despite all these advantages, it proved impossible to make much further progress. Once again the DM did well, advancing a kilometre as far as the crest at point 119, but enemy counter-attacks took back all the gains. The French had altered their tactic so as to gain the advantage of surprise. The artillery had been firing since 10 June, but no variation was made just before the infantry assault at 12.15 on the 16th. This initial surprise was wiped out almost immediately, however, as German troops fired on all infantry movements and put many French guns out of action. Repeated French attempts over the next two days were equally fruitless and on the evening of 18 June Tenth Army's commander, d'Urbal, agreed with Foch and Joffre to call a halt to the operation.

Mangin sent in a report on the capture of Neuville-Saint-Waast. It concluded that such an operation required, first of all, the accumulation of all the necessary materiel; then the troops had to be 'inspired' with the 'firm will' to reach the objectives which should not be 'too precise' but should merely indicate 'general directions', so that advantage could be taken of opportunities that presented themselves. It was 'only the first step that counted', Mangin claimed. As for tactics, Mangin judged that 'oil stain' tactics were best. Instead of attacking the edge of a village from the open, a foothold should be gained by surprise or by mining or digging a sap, and then troops would spread like an oil stain, aided by a continuous effort to relieve the troops engaged and to supply them with munitions.[43]

Fayolle confided his thoughts on the battle to his diary. He was very proud of what his division (70 DI) achieved on the opening two days, 9–10 May, capturing 800 prisoners and fourteen machine guns. His division was on the left flank of Pétain's XXXIII Corps, attacking towards Souchez, the village in the gap between the hills of Notre Dame de Lorette and Vimy ridge itself. He had not expected much from the attack after his inspection of the trenches the previous week, predicting gloomily that the offensive would cost 20,000 men. By 13 May, impressed by the casualty lists, Fayolle had judged that Tenth Army's attack was finished. Yet Pétain ordered the completion, house-by-house, of the capture of the villages, Ablain, Souchez, then Givenchy. 'It won't lead to anything', Fayolle concluded: 'The start of winter will still find us here, the flat ground covered with the dead.' He was critical of his superior officers, of Pétain's boasting of his corps' success on 9 May, and Pétain's complaints that Foch and d'Urbal were both mad. Fayolle's own view of Foch and d'Urbal was that they took no account of the ground, and ignored the need for the indispensable 'long and meticulous preparation (reasonable jumping-off line, trench artillery, observation points for the artillery, telephone communications etc)'. Although always pessimistic, Fayolle's remarks show that he realised that his division's successes followed careful preparation and that his men failed when an operation was mounted too quickly.[44]

Foch summed up the Artois battle in a report on 1 July. The attack on 9 May had made good gains, which could not be exploited for lack of reserves. (Indeed GQG had been so excited by the possibilities that instructions were prepared for bringing in the cavalry.[45]) Yet, when the attack was re-started on 16 June, the reserves were at hand and the French fired more shells, but for all the greater chances of success the gains had been smaller. The reason was the speed of the German reaction. As early as the evening of the first day, two divisions had arrived in front of Tenth Army, with another on the 11th; by 18 June there were nine German divisions facing the French, when on 8 May there had been four.[46] Moreover, the German divisions were provided with more heavy guns, which fired more rapidly than the old French pieces; the German gunners fired without counting their shells.[47] The French had taken over 93,000 German prisoners as well as guns and machine guns, but they had suffered over 102,000 casualties themselves.[48]

Lower down the military hierarchy, 13 DI in XXI Corps had taken part in the offensive on Souchez and Notre Dame de Lorette. The division had suffered enormous casualties on 9 May. This was due to efficient German counter-battery work, which suppressed their own divisional guns, preventing them from firing accurately. Consequently, when the infantry climbed out of their trenches, the German wire was intact and, since the telephone wires had been cut, all attempts to contact the French artillery to correct their fire failed. This caused a great mass of infantry to block the communication trenches as following waves of infantry ran into the first soldiers to advance. The result was a 61 per cent casualty rate. There had been insufficient time between 9 May and the resumption of the offensive on 16 June to reconstitute 13 DI's units, and so a meagre 400–500 metres was all the gain of the second attack. The division judged that in both assaults inaccurate artillery and too great a density of infantry had been the causes of the failure to progress.[49]

When the post-war commission convened to investigate why and how the French had lost the iron and coal resources of the Briey basin in Lorraine, Joffre was asked why he had not attempted to recapture such rich territory, rather than using up so many lives in the Artois and in Champagne. He replied that he did not have the resources for such an operation in 1915; but it must be said that he did not have the necessary guns and munitions for Artois and Champagne either. French Army doctrine still sought the elusive 'percée'. After all, the Germans had shown that it was possible in the east, when they broke through the Russian front at Gorlice–Tarnow. On a much smaller scale, the DM had also broken through to the top of Vimy ridge on 9 May. Joffre reported to the war minister that German morale had been shaken by the Artois offensive, and sent him several intelligence reports and extracts from the German press to support his claim. German officers billeted in Douai, for example, had packed up their belongings, and hospitals had been emptied even of those wounded who were not transportable. Joffre's intention, therefore, was to organise for the autumn 'a general offensive comprising several powerful, simultaneous attacks'.[50] Before examining that autumn campaign, however, it is necessary to consider what the politicians were doing.

The politicians intervene, at home and abroad

The failures during the first half of 1915 had circumscribed Joffre's range of options. Parliament's withdrawal to Bordeaux in 1914 had given him a free hand, but the deputies returned to Paris and, in a special session on 22 December, voted to remain in session until the war ended. This meant that the army commissions of both houses began meeting again, forcing war minister Millerand to answer questions and respond to criticisms of the high command. The system of parliamentary commissions was a powerful means whereby deputies and senators could discuss proposed bills, air their views and demand answers of the government at a time when patriotism required silence in the open sessions of parliament. Criticism in public debate would both depress public opinion and morale and give comfort to the enemy. In law, the commissions were 'organisms constituted in each Chamber, composed of a usually restricted number of members, chosen for their presumed competence and given the task, in principle, of preparing the Chamber's work or presenting it with a report'.[51]

Even before the first parliamentary sitting on 12 January, the Deputies' Army Commission had met – they convened six times in January, and then met six or seven times per month, increasing to twelve or thirteen sittings in September–November. During 1915 the Senate Army Commission sat twenty-nine times. Georges Clemenceau was elected to the Senate Army Commission, becoming the president of its thirty-six members in November 1915. He also presided over the Foreign Affairs Commission. These two roles gave even greater power to an influential critic of the government. He had already created a storm about medical evacuations and he was convinced that the parliament should exercise solid control not only over the government but over the army as well. His frequent visits to the front informed his journalism.

An analysis of the topics of discussion in both commissions reveals that manpower, the Dardanelles and Salonika expeditions, the provision of heavy artillery and other equipment, and the right of inspection were the most frequently debated topics. The commissions did not debate from ignorance; they were well informed. Ferry's reports have already been mentioned; he wrote personally to Poincaré and Viviani and attended cabinet meetings in his role as under-secretary at the foreign affairs ministry. The liaison officer between GQG and the government, Colonel Herbillon, heard from premier Viviani in April how Ferry had warned Poincaré that the forthcoming action in the Argonne had little chance of success. Since he had been proved right, his comments were echoed in the commissions.[52] There were other sources of information: mobilised men wrote to their deputies, evading censorship by concealing notes inside their letters. Many parliamentarians were medical men and learned of the numbers evacuated to hospitals in the interior. By June, even the military officer who was head of Millerand's military cabinet was warning of the effects of the army's repeated failures to break the enemy's front, which were having a serious effect on public opinion. In the army too, letters from the front were revealing increasing pessimism, and some units were refusing to leave the trenches, as already seen, when they considered that what they were asked to do was pointless. One of XVII Corps' divisions 'had not wished' to leave the trenches at Carency (during the Artois attack). Yet GQG refused to recognise what was happening.[53]

France's shortage of artillery in the face of German superiority was a constant theme. When Viviani, Millerand and the new under-secretary of state for armaments, Albert Thomas, were summoned to the Senate Army Commission, Senator Charles Humbert complained about General Louis Baquet, the director of artillery in the war ministry. Baquet had cancelled orders for guns 'because we had too many' or stated that 'we were not making guns because we were producing shells'. Even before war was declared, Humbert had caused a stir in parliament in July 1914, about France's lack of artillery, and he continued his campaign throughout 1915. The Senate Army Commission recommended producing many more 155mm heavy guns, as they were 'indispensable', but, Humbert complained, no order was placed until October. In November he summed up the war ministry's efforts thus:

So the results of the war ministry's efforts are broken down in this way. Instead of 220 105s we only have 100; we don't have a 120 mortar, nor a gun carriage for the 155; as for the 155 mortar, everybody has one except our army. I am permitted to conclude, therefore, that such a result gives me no satisfaction whatsoever.[54]

The deputies' commission ranged more widely, discussing army clothing and the provision of gas masks as well as artillery.

Demands for more artillery could only be met by employing more people in armaments factories, but manpower was an equally burning question. It was by far the most frequently discussed matter in the Deputies' Army Commission. The cry had begun very early that some men were filling soft desk jobs in the rear, so as to make their military service easier, or even evading their duty altogether by working in factories where they were less at risk than on the front line. The hunt for the 'embusqués' or shirkers began in February 1915 when Maurice Barrès launched his 'chasse aux embusqués' in the *Echo de Paris*. Then in April, Clemenceau joined in with his 'grande embuscade nationale' in

L'Homme Enchaîné. Next the left-wing *L'Humanité* attacked ecclesiastics in October, although in general monks and priests had not attempted to evade military duty. About half of the 20,000 mobilised ecclesiastics acted as stretcher-bearers,[55] but even this task was seen as shirking by men who were even more exposed. Several shirkers' networks were discovered in Paris, however, including the 'agence Lombard' which operated between March and October 1915.[56] The enormous casualties of 1915 impelled the two commissions to seek a fairer application of the 'blood tax'.

The failure to provide for industrial mobilisation in Plan XVII – no contingency plans had been made to keep essential factories running and to replace munitions – had meant that the mass mobilisation of August 1914 had taken even those men whose training and experience were needed in the factories. Consequently they had to be taken back from the front, to the envy of those who remained. The need for manpower at the front caused Millerand to propose the early call-up of the 1917 class (they were only aged 18 in 1915), a proposal that outraged one of the members of the Deputies' Army Commission, Victor Dalbiez. He introduced a bill on 1 April 1915 to make the sharing of manpower more just by combing out the embusqués in the factories and sending them to the front line, instead of calling up 18-year-olds. His bill was amended several times in both commissions before being passed in August. Others had accepted that efficiency demanded putting the right men in the right jobs, even if this was 'unjust' in the sense that some were less at risk than others. This was a dilemma that was never solved. In the event, the Dalbiez Law did not have a great effect. Between its enactment in August 1915 and 1 January 1916, it scooped up 110,848 men, some of whom would have been gathered up in any case.[57] Two other measures resulted: first, mobilised men working in munitions factories were permitted to earn civilian rates of pay, and, second, the right to a week's leave was accorded for every four months spent at the front. Formerly leave had been a concession, not frequently allowed, but GQG realised that a period of leave was vital to soldiers' health and sanity. The leave provisions came into effect in July 1915, but could be suspended if necessary because of a forthcoming offensive.

Parliamentarians made two further improvements in conditions. Following much discussion in the Deputies' Army Commission between June and August 1915, the low rate of pay for privates was increased from five to twenty-five centimes a day. After a decree in November 1914 had recognised the need to increase the soldiers' pay, an allowance was paid to those in the 'zone of operations'. This amounted to three francs a day for officers, and 1.50 for NCOs (regular army) or one franc for those paid at a daily rate. Therefore, the right of privates to receive a pay increase could not be denied, but it was not until September 1915 that their daily rate was increased from one to five sous per day, or twenty-five centimes, back-dated to 1 July. As a second recompense, this time moral, the *croix de guerre* was instituted by a law of 8 April 1915, and awarded to those men mentioned in army and corps despatches. Over two million such medals would be awarded by war's end in recognition of the great service of many in France's Army. Napoleon Bonaparte had created the *Légion d'honneur*, but in practice this had become an honour for officers; his nephew Louis Bonaparte created the *médaille militaire* in 1852 to reward outstanding acts of bravery by NCOs and privates. It was awarded also to those general officers who had been commander-in-chief in war. The *croix de guerre* was a more 'democratic' honour within a citizen army.[58]

The commissions' activities made calls for 'contrôle' unanswerable, especially given the casualty figures and the appalling conditions of the wounded. The French word does not have the same sense as 'control' in English; rather it means inspection and supervision. The commissions wished to see for themselves how the high command of the French Army was conducting the war. Joffre, of course, was absolutely opposed to any such oversight. He refused to allow 'visitors' to the zone of the armies, extending such refusals even to the President of the Republic and his war minister. Yet, when Ferry informed Poincaré on 8 April that wounded men were drowning in mud in Woëvre trenches because they could not be moved in time, something had to be done. To prevent more such revelations, Joffre banished Ferry to the Nieuport sector on the Belgian coast, as far away from the active eastern sector as possible, but Barrès had kept up his campaign about poor medical services. This was the trigger for a measure of parliamentary control.[59] A common text was adopted on 28 July in which the deputies affirmed unanimously 'the right and the duty of Parliament to exercise its supervision ... through the intermediary of the commissions who delegate certain of their members for temporary missions ... Government has the duty to second the commissions' efforts and to ensure the complete and sincere help of the civil and military authorities'.[60]

As Dalbiez wrote in his post-war report on its work, the Army Commission stimulated the various services (war production, supplies, medical services, effectives), inspected factories, demanded explanations of the ministers, and sent some of its reports to the President of the Republic. Having noted the 'insufficient' government control of the administration of the French Army, the commission took unto itself what was a 'veritable service of inspection' of all matters concerning national defence.[61]

The government, in the form of its war minister Millerand, was obliged to accept a reduction in his powers by the creation of four under-secretaryships in his ministry. Thus armaments became Albert Thomas's responsibility (20 May), Justin Godart and Joseph Thierry took over medical service and the supply service respectively (1 July), and René Besnard military aeronautics on 14 September. Then the Viviani government fell on 29 October 1915, to be replaced by Aristide Briand, who appointed General Gallieni to the war ministry. Gallieni, Joffre's competitor, would look more favourably on parliamentary inspection of Joffre's command than Millerand had done. Also Poincaré had already attempted to bring in a more collegial form of command by attending, with Viviani and Millerand, a June meeting with Joffre and his three new army group commanders. Joffre had made permanent the two provisional groupings in the north and east under Foch and Dubail respectively, and created a third army group, that of the centre, under the command of General Castelnau. Joffre, however, was temperamentally unsuited to 'collegial' decision-making about the forthcoming autumn campaign, and insisted on retaining his autonomy when the war minister changed in October.

In foreign affairs, however, the government had greater control than the CinC. The intervention by the politicians in war-making involved the French Army in another theatre altogether. The expedition to the Dardanelles against the Ottoman Empire was of British inspiration, more specifically, that of the First Lord of the Admiralty, Winston S. Churchill. The French Army and Navy were to become involved, however, despite Joffre's firm opposition. The death of Britain's professional army in 1914 in Flanders caused many in London to query whether sending more troops to the continent was the best use of British manpower. Kitchener would even threaten, after the further casualties over the winter, not to send any more British troops to France.[62] Chancellor of the Exchequer, David Lloyd George, cabinet secretary Maurice Hankey and Churchill all came up with alternative proposals.[63] The same questions were exercising French politicians as they returned to Paris. There had always been a strong, if disparate, colonialist party that wished to reinforce and to extend French influence in the eastern Mediterranean, and Poincaré was receptive to the idea of an alternative strategy, given the stalemate in France. The Justice Minister, Aristide Briand, suggested the despatch to the east of an expeditionary force, whose arrival would compel Greece to join the Entente, thereby bringing in Bulgaria and Romania as well. Then Serbia would attack the Austro-Hungarian Empire with the help of the Slav populations. The road to Vienna along the Danube would lie open; Italy would join in; and

Germany could be attacked from the rear. The destruction of the two 'worm-eaten thrones', Austria and Turkey, would be achieved with ease.[64] Such French optimism fitted exactly with Lloyd George's fantasy that Austria-Hungary was somehow propping up Germany, so that the defeat of the former would entail that of the latter. Neither politician seemed to appreciate the difficulty (akin to herding cats) of creating a Balkan alliance to gather up the spoils of the Ottoman empire. The politicians were not alone, however, in these fancies. Both Generals Gallieni and Franchet d'Espèrey favoured an eastern expeditionary corps.

Russia's difficulties provided an impetus for looking to the east. Russian troops in the Caucasus were suffering from Turkish attacks and Petrograd demanded an offensive to relieve the pressure. Moreover, Turkey had closed the Straits, which blocked Russia's exit from the Black Sea to the Mediterranean. Yet any plan for naval action by the Royal Navy in the eastern Mediterranean would threaten French interests. First, the Franco-British naval agreements gave command in the eastern seas to the French. France's navy minister, Victor Augagneur, demanded consultation with London and the French Cabinet agreed that serious thought should be given before accepting any British plan for an expedition. Second, France had a specific interest in Ottoman Syria, Lebanon and Palestine, where for centuries France had been recognised as the protector of the Christian populations.[65] Finally, the British seemed to be taking too much interest in the port of Alexandretta, the only deep-water port at the north-eastern end of the Mediterranean and well within the French sphere of influence. To French eyes, the British already controlled Suez and should leave Alexandretta to the French, where they already had a plan to secure the area in case of the break-up of the Ottoman empire.[66]

Events now moved very quickly. Augagneur travelled to London on 26 January and accepted the idea of a Dardanelles naval expedition in return for Churchill's abandonment of the Alexandretta project. It is significant that Millerand was in London at the same time, but the war minister was kept in ignorance of the plan. Cambon wrote to Paris at Churchill's suggestion, to recommend secrecy and restriction of information to the premier, Millerand and foreign minister Delcassé. However, Augagneur and Viviani decided not to inform Millerand, on the (justified) grounds that Joffre would be annoyed to learn of the strategic initiative being taken out of his hands. Since the Conseil Supérieur de la Défense Nationale had ceased meeting on the outbreak of war, there was no higher body to oversee grand strategy in pursuit of political aims. Not only was the war ministry kept in ignorance but the French naval commander responsible for the whole Mediterranean fleet, Vice-Admiral Boué de Lapeyère, did not know of the plans either.

On 2 February Churchill sent his plan to Paris, but the chief of staff in the navy ministry was not impressed. In his view, land operations were needed before attempting to force the Straits (a view that Churchill would have done well to take into account). Moreover, he asked, what was to follow the action to force the Straits? Despite the advice of his professional staff, Augagneur agreed Churchill's plan a week later (9 February). It remained only to inform Joffre, which Briand did on 10 February in Millerand's absence. Joffre assented to what he assumed to be a purely naval operation.

On 16 February London realised that a military force would indeed have to be prepared to exploit the naval success. Two days later the French cabinet decided that the French too should contribute a division to the force. Accordingly, Millerand asked Joffre for a division but met with a refusal, so it was decided to draw troops from depots and from North Africa. General d'Amade was appointed to command what became the first division of the CEO (Corps expéditionnaire d'Orient). D'Amade had commanded the group of Territorial Divisions constituted on 19 August 1914, but he was relieved of command on 17 September, after the group's three divisions were 'lost' – their whereabouts unknown – after retiring from Amiens.[67] Joffre's decision to place such a general in command probably indicates both Joffre's lack of confidence in the whole idea of an expeditionary force at a time when the fighting in Champagne was at its height, and at the same time his taking advantage of the opportunity to push d'Amade, an unsatisfactory general, out of France. Certainly, the latter factor came into play later over the *affaire Sarrail*.

General d'Amade's instructions were to 'cooperate' with the British naval and disembarkation forces.[68] It is indicative of the poor planning that d'Amade knew neither who was in command (he thought *he* was, as being senior to General Sir William Birdwood in charge of the ANZAC troops) nor the exact purpose for which his expeditionary corps was to be used. In the event, General Sir Ian Hamilton was given overall command, an arrangement that had a knock-on effect in France. Millerand argued that the fact of placing d'Amade under the orders of a British general meant that Joffre 'ought to be recognised as supreme' in France, as a sort of quid pro quo. Millerand was 'thunderstruck', however, to learn that Sir John French's command was to be independent, whereas Joffre had been allowed 'to think from the beginning' that the British CinC 'had been instructed to act under him'. The opening of Joffre's eyes to the true relationship between the French Army and the BEF was one very minor benefit derived from the Dardanelles expedition.[69]

The naval attempt to force the Dardanelles failed miserably. Following an attempt on 19 February, another was made on 18 March during which the French battleship *Bouvet* sank after hitting a mine with the loss of almost all 600 hands. Two more French battleships were badly damaged by gunfire. Warnings followed about the risky expedient of putting troops ashore to deal with the Turkish forts, especially as the French presence had now been detected. The Turkish military attaché in Rome reported on 22 March that a French corps under d'Amade would intervene.[70] The figure he cited of about 40,000 North African troops was, however, an exaggeration.

D'Amade's force consisted of two brigades: a 'brigade métropolitaine' – one regiment from French depots (175 RI) and the second a mixed regiment of zouaves and Foreign Legion – and a 'brigade coloniale' (two regiments each containing one European and two Senegalese battalions). Hence Joffre lost no troops from his forces in France by the creation of the new corps. In addition, there was a regiment of cavalry; three groups of artillery (six batteries of the standard French artillery piece, the 75mm gun, and two batteries of 65mm mountain guns); and all the necessary administrative and medical services. In effect, the expeditionary corps comprised the equivalent of slightly more than one standard division. The corps arrived on the island of Lemnos on 18 March, but then returned to Alexandria to await developments.

Following the decision to land men on the peninsula, the corps re-embarked from Egyptian ports on 15 April and by the 21st had concentrated once again on Lemnos, ready for the invasion that began on 25 April. The French task on that day (see Map 8) was a diversionary landing on the Asiatic coast in order to distract the Turkish guns firing across the Straits and to prevent Turkish reinforcements from crossing the Straits to assist in defending the peninsula from the British troops landing there. This was the only operation to gain its objective (the village of Kum Kale) on that day, although the troops suffered heavy casualties. Two days later, on 27 April, they evacuated the Asiatic shore as planned, and joined the British on the peninsula, where they took part in the several battles for Krithia. Because they were deployed on the right of the British line at Helles, they were exposed to the fire of the Turkish guns from the Asiatic shore, and once again suffered many casualties. Despite the password, 'Entente Cordiale',[71] which was supposed to help prevent casualties from friendly fire, the British complained that the Senegalese especially were ill-disciplined and tended to run away when their European officers were killed or wounded. Such complaints were ungenerous, as the exposed positions the French were holding were regularly shelled. After all, the Turkish gunners had had generations of

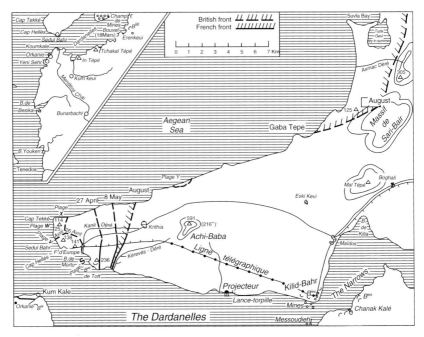

8. Dardanelles campaign, 1915

practice in firing across the Dardanelles, which are barely 5 kilometres wide at this point.

On 30 April Millerand ordered 156 DI to the Dardanelles after Kitchener had insisted that d'Amade's forces should be increased. It became the second division of the CEO, and began embarking on 2 May. This was a new division, constituted on 17 March 1915, consisting of a metropolitan brigade (176 RI and 2 Régiment de marche d'Afrique) and a colonial brigade (7 and 8 Régiment mixte colonial). As it disembarked, the first of the five attempts began with the aim of advancing up the peninsula by capturing the village of Krithia, and then the hill Achi Baba, so as to reach the Kilid Bahr plateau, level with the Narrows and opposite Chanak. All failed. General Henri Gouraud, who arrived with the second division, replaced d'Amade on 15 May. The note of 'I told you so' in Joffre's memoirs is patent: 'Wishing to extricate themselves from the impasse into which they had engaged so light-heartedly, *for the first time* the government asked me to intervene by designating a leader capable of bringing to a successful conclusion this difficult enterprise.'[72] Hamilton was pleased to be rid of the 'overwrought' French general who appealed for help constantly and whose messages were consistently pessimistic.[73]

Gouraud set about immediately improving the supply situation and the base on Lemnos, where the British ceded half the island to the French to use as supply depots and hospital facilities. Large stocks of clothing, food and munitions were kept there, so that the troops on the peninsula (where the exposed terrain made it impossible to store anything more than immediate necessities) would not be deprived in the event of a storm or other hold-up in supplies from France or Alexandria. Another base was established on the island of Tenedos to be used for aircraft and for rest and recuperation. A French naval mission used a flotilla of tugs, tow boats and barges to land 400 tonnes of supplies on the peninsula every day. The mission's triumph was to land, without any lifting gear, six heavy guns (240mm), each weighing 16 tonnes – to the admiration of the Royal Navy.[74]

The arrival of a second division with Gouraud meant that the units could be organised as a regular two-division army corps with all the usual arrangements: an artillery commander, a commander of engineers, aviation resources, heavy artillery and so on. Before Gouraud arrived, the first division had already fought the first two battles for Krithia, and by 11 May suffered 12,878 casualties among the 22,431 men landed – well over half the original contingent. Gouraud strengthened the defences of the line reached at the end of these two battles, and in a series of small operations established a good jumping-off line for the next attempt on Krithia. Even before leaving France, where he had experienced the Argonne fighting as a divisional commander in Third Army, Gouraud had demanded more artillery.

Gouraud was thinking of the bigger picture also. Again, before leaving France, he had suggested that cutting off the neck of the peninsula at Bulair, thus denying supplies to the Turks, would force them to retire. On arrival, he sent a letter to Hamilton on 18 May, only three days after taking command of the French troops, with other ideas for breaking the stalemate. He dismissed the possibility of another landing on the Asiatic coast, because it would require too many men. Instead, he suggested an attack from Gaba Tepe on the Aegean coast near the Anzacs' landing spot across the narrowest part of the peninsula in the direction of Maidos on the Dardanelles coast. The terrain would be just as difficult as that encountered at present fighting up the peninsula, but the advantages of crossing from west to east were that it was a shorter distance and the strong Turkish defences at Kilid-Bahr might then be taken from the rear.[75]

Although Hamilton thanked Gouraud for his suggestions, nothing came of them. Instead, a series of 'bite-and-hold' operations in June and July edged the Allied forces closer to Krithia. The series was successful because Gouraud knew that artillery was key: the strong Turkish defences had to be crushed before the infantry left their trenches. British and French artillery resources were combined, therefore, so that the British attacked with full support one week and the French attacked similarly the next. The casualty figures reveal that these tactics were much less costly than the fighting during and immediately after the landings. By 1 July 1915, total casualties for the corps were just over 20,000, of whom 7,581 (more than one-third) were killed or missing.[76] Yet the Allies were barely any closer to Constantinople, and the Russians had just lost Warsaw.

One of the French casualties was Gouraud himself, hit by a shell splinter as he was visiting his wounded troops, necessitating the amputation of his right arm. He was evacuated to Paris where, from his hospital bed, he continued to send letters to Millerand advocating a better strategy than simply slogging up the peninsula. His successor on Gallipoli was General Bailloud, one of the CEO's divisional commanders. Bailloud revived the Besika Bay option on the Asiatic coast. Turkish defences there were weaker and a strong Allied force could land there and march north to the Straits and capture or destroy the enemy guns on the Asiatic side, one of which had wounded Gouraud. Shutting down the guns on the Asiatic side of the Straits would take the pressure off the Allied troops on the peninsula. The British took up none of the French proposals and Hamilton used his reinforcements in a second landing from the Aegean Sea at Suvla in August. The French contribution to the landing amounted to an extension of front, relieving British troops during the night of 31 July/1 August. Then the French fought yet another engagement in the same sector as before, to provide a diversion when the Suvla and associated breakout of Anzac began on 6 August. Bailloud was very bitter. He had been kept in ignorance of the Suvla operation, and nothing had been gained by it. The Allied failure on the peninsula was now patent; Turkish defences were solid and Turkish reserves were increased by the Russian defeats which freed Turkish troops in the Caucasus. All that remained was to evacuate the peninsula. Bailloud left on 1 October, the corps having been reduced in size because of another campaign. He complained to Millerand that, despite having excellent personal relations with British commanders, such considerations counted for nothing when 'the interests or simply the prestige [of Britain] entered the equation'.[77]

That other campaign was the Sarrail 'imbroglio', also in the eastern Mediterranean, but this time in Greece, at Salonika (Thessaloniki). The fighting on the Gallipoli peninsula had been no more successful than that in France, and another political storm blew up in the summer, in addition to all the other criticisms of Joffre and the high command. The trigger was the German attack of 30 June on Third Army in the Argonne, commanded by General Maurice Sarrail, described earlier. Sarrail had considerable political support which he had been able to cultivate before the war, during the time he had been the war minister's right-hand man in 'republicanising' the French Army – a mission that involved using Freemasons and others to report on the political and religious views of officers. Sarrail had taken over command of Third Army from Ruffey before the Marne battle, and had held on to Verdun even after Joffre authorised him to break contact with the fortress if that became necessary. Sarrail maintained his contacts with deputies over the winter 1914–15 – although he was not, of course, alone in doing so – and began agitating against the high command by insinuating that Joffre and Foch might mount a military coup.[78] Then in the spring of 1915 a couple of clumsy anonymous memoranda were circulated, claiming that Sarrail would defeat the Germans while Joffre could not.[79] The CinC was unlikely to appreciate such attacks. Since the German operation against Third Army was the last in a succession of such attacks which Sarrail's troops had been unable to counter, Joffre had the ideal opportunity to get rid of a factious general.

He relieved Sarrail of his command on 22 July after he had commissioned the Eastern Army Group commander, General Dubail, to report on Sarrail's conduct. The choice of Dubail was astute, since he was regarded as another Republican general, hence could not be reproached with anti-Sarrail bias. Joffre's letter to Dubail asking him to make the report shows clearly the sort of response he wanted, and Dubail returned two, one on the purely military question and the second on the state of morale in Third Army. It was obvious that there was mistrust and dislike, with officers being decorated when they did not deserve it and being overlooked when they did. Furthermore General Denis Duchêne's XXXII Corps was part of Third Army, and Duchêne was a very difficult character also. Third Army's general staff seemed to be at loggerheads as well. Sarrail believed that he had been removed from command because a right-wing GQG did not wish a left-wing general to succeed. This is probably a smokescreen, as Sarrail admits himself that he had lost 80,000 men in eastern France for very little gain – not an achievement that could be called a 'success'. Since Sarrail published his views in a post-war memoir (in which he claimed that the Dubail report had been 'lost'), Joffre cannot be blamed for reproducing in turn in his memoirs both Dubail's damning reports.[80] Joffre transferred Third Army to Central Army Group for the forthcoming Champagne offensive, and offered Sarrail the command of the Corps Expéditionnaire d'Orient, namely the unfortunate troops on Gallipoli. Sarrail refused.

Salonika, rather than the Dardanelles and Constantinople, had always been the French focus in the east, and Aristide Briand its foremost supporter. He was Justice Minister in Viviani's government and would take over the premiership in October 1915, combining it with the foreign affairs portfolio. David Lloyd George also had preferred Salonika over the Dardanelles because he wished to attack Austria from the south.[81] He and Briand, both Celts, got on well together, and they had a long talk in the British embassy in Paris on 4 February. Briand explained his somewhat different reasons for preferring Salonika. It would be

of great advantage to France & England in a future more or less near when Russia might become too powerful, that the Balkan States should be indebted to the Western Powers as well as to Russia for their aggrandisement. An Anglo-French Expedition to the Balkans would make the peoples of Greece, Servia, Bulgaria & Roumania realize that Russia is not the only State to interest itself in the welfare of these countries. They should be so constituted as to be a barrier to Russian omnipotence & possession of Constantinople & to all the exclusive advantages which such possession would give to Russia.[82]

After much to-ing and fro-ing and political letting off steam, Sarrail was persuaded to accept an enlarged command. It was not Millerand who did the persuading, but Briand, the government's principal promoter of the eastern campaign which had no support from the military. On 3 August Millerand summoned Sarrail to the war ministry to ask what he, Sarrail, would require for his new command. Sarrail replied that he wanted to command an army, because a corps command was a demotion; he wanted independence from British command (which would require negotiation with London); and he wanted reinforcements (which Joffre promptly refused). The preparation of the autumn double offensive in France did not permit the allocation of troops to another theatre. Joffre believed that even a great success such as the capture of Constantinople would not end the war in France. What, therefore, was the point of devoting more troops (under British command) to the Dardanelles, unless simply to find a berth for a 'factious' general, namely Sarrail?[83]

Then the enemy intervened, thereby providing a solution to the Sarrail dilemma. The Allied expedition to Gallipoli had failed, but it had given the Ottomans and their German advisors a considerable shock. There was no direct land route for supplying Turkey with weapons and ammunition from Germany, so the need to entice one of the Balkan nations to join the Central Powers became urgent. Both the Entente and the Central Powers were bribing Greece, Romania and Bulgaria with territory to be taken from the defeated at war's end, but the Central Powers had the advantage of the stunning success against the Russians at

Gorlice–Tarnow, as against the Entente failures on Gallipoli and in France. The rulers of all three Balkan nations were wily and played one coalition off against the other, waiting to see which would come out on top. The Central Powers won the bidding race for Bulgaria, which signed up to them on 6 September. There was a further factor. Since Serbia's capital, Belgrade, was on the Danube, the river might become an invasion route, and Serbia had humiliated the Austro-Hungarian armies in 1914 by throwing them out of Belgrade. Falkenhayn had already suggested to the Austrians in March 1915 a joint strike against Serbia to open Danube shipping. In March they had been unwilling to allow German troops into the theatre, but the German successes against Russia and the accession of Bulgaria changed matters. A triple offensive against Serbia, under the command of the victor of Gorlice–Tarnow, General August von Mackensen, was agreed. After much argument over whose was the ultimate command authority over Mackensen, the joint offensive was launched on 5 October. The Germans drove southwards towards Belgrade, the Austro-Hungarians attacked through Bosnia-Herzegovina, and the Bulgarians attacked in the south of Serbia, cutting the railway line linking Nish to Salonika and the sea.

Bulgaria's defection to the Central Powers struck a blow at French foreign minister Delcassé's policy. He had persisted, almost alone, in attempting to outbid the Central Powers, and his failure led to his resignation. His resignation led, in turn, to the fall of Viviani's government. Yet the French could not simply abandon Serbia to its fate. Poincaré insisted on supporting Russia over any Balkans question – if France refused to help Serbia, that might destroy the Russian alliance. Moreover, Serbia had been an important pre-war purchaser of French armaments. Its army had fought valiantly in 1914, despite no military convention binding it to the Entente. Standing by Belgium in 1914 had given the Entente the moral advantage in world opinion, so it was unthinkable to forfeit that advantage by abandoning Serbia. Besides, with Greece still uncommitted, the Entente needed a base in the Balkans so long as their troops remained on Gallipoli. As for the wider theatre of the eastern Mediterranean, Britain was certain to retain control of the Suez Canal and Egypt, so France aimed to retain a hold in Greece as a counterpoise. Competition with Italy over Balkan territory combined with fear of German economic influence in the east were further powerful reasons for France to insist on the Salonika expedition.[84] Greece became a stepping-stone to France's interests in Syria and Cilicia (both parts of the Ottoman Empire).

Instead of setting out for the Dardanelles, then, Sarrail went to Salonika with instructions to 'cover the communications between Serbia and Salonika against Bulgarian attack', but to ensure that he not be cut off from Salonika. He left France on 7 October, convinced that he was being thrown out of the country, a victim of GQG and the war minister. By the time he arrived, the heavy artillery bombardment that had begun on 6 October had been followed by six assaults on the river crossings, the strongest opposite Belgrade.[85] The Serbs evacuated the city which by the morning of the 8th lay open to the enemy. On 14 October Bulgaria declared war on Serbia and began operations immediately, since mobilisation had started much earlier. The Bulgarian army was weak after the Balkan Wars, but united and strengthened by considerable hostility towards Serbia. The frontier between the two countries lay through high trackless mountain ranges down to the border with Greece, north of Salonika. Moreover, the weather was unusually misty and cold, with early snow. Nevertheless by 16 October Bulgarian troops had breached the Salonika–Nish railway (the King and government had removed to Nish at the start of war) and a few days later held a 96-kilometre stretch of the line, after capturing 2,000 prisoners. Mackensen wanted to encircle the Serbian army and destroy it, but the weather and poor roads made progress very slow. However, the fall of Nish meant that the Serbian retreat south to meet up with the Franco-British troops was cut off. The Serbian Army's retreat southwards to the sea at Salonika was blocked.

The Dardanelles expedition now merged into the Salonika expedition. The 2 DI of the Dardanelles force reclaimed its original denomination of 156 DI and began leaving Gallipoli on 1 October. There had been much havering over whether or not to evacuate Gallipoli, and the French and Kitchener were afraid of the loss of prestige with their colonial and Muslim subjects. Yet the case for evacuation was unanswerable once Kitchener had been to see for himself. The need to help Serbia by landing in Salonika enabled the transport of 156 DI, and the need to move the Senegalese who could not cope with the cold meant a further reduction in French troop numbers. At Chantilly, where the Allies met to decide the 1916 campaign, it was decided to evacuate Gallipoli altogther, and by 8 January 1916 all had departed. The French left almost 10,000 dead and missing on the peninsula, and had suffered a total of 27,049 casualties.[86]

When Sarrail arrived in Salonika, 156 DI had already begun to relieve the Serbian forces at Strumitsa guarding the railway. Two more divisions came from France. The first elements of 57 DI landed on 19 October and by the 27th occupied both banks of the Vardar river, but only after much hard fighting. The arrival in November of a newly constituted composite division from France, 122 DI, allowed for some offensive action to respond to Serbian appeals for help, but the Bulgarians had already cut the railway. All Sarrail could do was to hang on defensively. The remnants of Serbia's Army made an agonising march over snow-covered mountains into Albania, where eventually they were rescued and taken to Corfu.

Even before Sarrail had left France, the fighting there had begun again.

The Champagne and Artois double offensive

Joffre's second principal battle for 1915 was a double operation in Champagne and Artois, against both sides of the Noyon salient simultaneously. Preparations for the autumn campaign got under away almost as soon as the Artois fighting died down in June. At GQG the after-action reports on the fighting in Artois and local actions further east led to a re-consideration of strategy. Perhaps it would be better, the thinking went, not to make the principal effort on the northern flank of the enemy salient in France, where Foch was pushing to repeat his earlier attacks on the Vimy ridge. Instead, the principal effort would be made on the eastern flank, in Champagne. The northern action in Artois would tie down enemy forces and create the advantage of surprise when the main action began in Champagne.

Foch fought this thinking, arguing that in Artois there existed a tangible strategic advantage to be gained by reaching the heights of the ridge, whereas in Champagne the only aim could be to break through the enemy lines. No terrain of any strategic value existed north of the German lines in the rolling, sparsely-populated Champagne hills. Foch lost the fight, perhaps in part because Pétain argued against a repeat performance of the Artois fighting on the grounds that the enemy defences on the ridge were now too strong to attack. It is certainly true that the Germans had reacted immediately and in strength to the Allied attacks there. On 8 July Joffre announced his decision for a 'double' general offensive, in which greater resources were to be dedicated to Champagne than to Artois. Accordingly Second Army, now under Pétain's command, was taken from Foch's Northern Army Group and added to the strength of Castelnau's Centre Army Group. Castelnau declared that his aim was to rupture or (at least) push back the enemy front: 'we are seeking rupture', he stated, 'not by a methodical attack but by a surprise attack [attaque brusquée]'.[87]

The provision of sufficient materiel for this ambitious double offensive was not the only difficulty for the French. Pressure from France's two principal Allies also played a role. The experience of dealing with Sir John French and the BEF since August 1914 had convinced Joffre that some more formal command arrangement had to be agreed. Once Sir

John French began to hesitate about the conditions for joining the autumn offensive, Joffre moved. After discussion with Kitchener, Asquith reported to the King on 20 August 1915 that, although Kitchener was 'not sanguine' about the prospects for the autumn fighting, nevertheless, he was 'strongly of the opinion that we cannot, without serious & perhaps fatal injury to the Alliance, refuse the co-operation which General Joffre invites & expects'.[88]

Russia also put on some pressure.[89] The succession of disasters that followed the German breakthrough at Gorlice–Tarnow in May had led, by September, to the loss of Russian Poland. Ambassador Paléologue informed Paris about the letters from the front being received in Moscow, which complained of betrayal by the 'Germans of the interior', by their leaders, by their allies.[90] There was uncertainty also about the reasons for the removal of Grand-Duke Nicholas from command and the Tsar's assumption of personal command. Joffre could not delay an offensive in France because of the risk to the Russian alliance of doing nothing. Kitchener too understood the force of the reasoning for not refusing 'the co-operation which General Joffre invites & expects'.

The preparations for the Champagne portion of the double offensive were lengthy. In an area of poor communications, it was a huge task to organise supply for two armies (Pétain's Second and de Langle de Cary's Fourth, consisting in all of twenty-seven divisions in ten infantry corps and two cavalry corps). A standard-gauge railway, for example, had to be constructed from Sainte-Menehould north of Châlons across the rear of the battlefield, and wells sunk to provide water. In addition, the main attack was to be supported by the flanking armies, Third Army to the east, and Fifth Army to the west. Consequently, Joffre's wish to begin operations on 8 September could not be realised, and all August and most of September passed in preparations, much to the alarm of the Russians. Castelnau's plan had been approved on 25 July. On 10 September the direction of the converging attacks in Artois and Champagne was settled: Foch to aim for Frasnes-Le Quesnoy, and Castelnau for Nouvion-Sedan (on the Meuse!). The cavalry were to converge on the Scheldt (Escaut) between Valenciennes and Maubeuge, with the aim of threatening the enemy's communications between the Ardennes and Holland. (A new cavalry doctrine had been published on 18 June, describing the cavalry's role as exploitation of any success. Units should have prepared their immediate intervention in any breach in the front line, however small.[91])

A concerted effort was made to keep up morale for the forthcoming enormous French Army battles. Thirty-five divisions in Champagne and thirty in Artois (twelve of them British) were to take part, supported by

3,000 field and 2,000 heavy guns with 6.3 million and 800,000 rounds respectively. An order of the day four days before D-day on 25 September called on the soldiers to attack 'wholeheartedly, for the deliverance of the Fatherland and for the triumph of Right and Liberty!'[92] A further effort was made to keep the offensive secret, and both Second and Fourth armies moved into position well before 25 September. As a disinformation exercise, GQG ordered Pétain to go to Nancy, with the aim of giving the impression that an attack was imminent there. He was to spend two days there and do a lot of talking. Pétain was accompanied by Captain Tournès whose wife and mother-in-law were living in Nancy. His 'confidences' told to the women were bound to be repeated and picked up by German spies.[93]

The German forces opposite Castelnau's front were General Karl von Einem's *Third Army*, with a division of *Fifth Army* on its right. Their front consisted of two defensive positions between 3 and 5 kilometres apart. Although the first was observable by the French gunners, it comprised a network of trenches with their communications sometimes underground. It incorporated a series of strongpoints, such as the Butte du Mesnil or the Main de Massiges. The forested heights of the latter geographical feature were so called because the plateau (the palm of the hand) had spurs or fingers running down to the plain. The second German position took advantage of the reverse slopes beyond the rivers that crossed the front from east to west, the Py and the Dormoise. The distance and the reverse slopes made it very difficult for the French gunners to fire on this second position with any accuracy.

The infantry of the two French armies began their assault at 9.15 am on 25 September, gaining some element of surprise by there being no change in the artillery barrage before they left the trenches. Obviously the Germans knew an attack was in preparation but they did not know exactly when it would occur. Some divisions made progress: I Colonial Corps, for example, in Second Army managed to captured the fingers of the Main de Massiges, and 27 DI on the left of the army front reached the German second line. In Fourth Army it was a similar mixed story. The DM of II Colonial Corps covered itself in glory yet again by reaching the Navarin Farm (where the pompous monument to the dead of the Armies of Champagne stands today) and pressing on almost to the Butte de Souain, but was forced back. Fourth Army's left-hand corps (VII Corps) captured the entire German line to its front. Despite considerable French losses, the German front line had been broken in several places and, in the afternoon, Castelnau ordered the two army commanders to use their army reserves and press home the advantage. Joffre was delighted. He believed that exploitation of the breakthrough was possible, and in consequence put two more divisions at Castelnau's disposal and ordered Foch and Dubail to prepare to send as many munitions as they could spare to Champagne.

Despite a long period of fine weather beforehand, which had facilitated French observation over German lines, it had begun to rain during the night preceding the infantry attack. With just a few hours' respite on the morning of the 15th, it continued raining until the 28th. Now the weather prevented decent observation and so on the second and subsequent days progress slowed. The rumours that 140 RI in XIV Corps had reached a height west of Tahure, where the German second line ran, raised hopes of a breakthrough and Pétain prepared to send in his reserve corps. But it proved impossible to hold on. Fourth Army had been so battered by the first day's fighting that little progress was made, but Castelnau pressed the troops to set off early again on the 27th, as he felt sure that the German second line was 'hanging by a thread'.

During the night of 28/29 September Pétain learned the truth, that 140 RI had never occupied the ground in the German second line, and he decided to call a temporary halt and to make another methodical artillery preparation before relaunching the attack. However, Joffre insisted that the offensive continue as Fourth Army had managed to make a significant advance around the Tranchée des Tantes, about 1,500 metres west of Navarin Farm. It seemed that three brigades had already passed through the breach, and the cavalry was following. In the event, 314 Brigade (chasseurs) had made a brave dash of a few hundred metres towards the hill north of the Tranchée des Tantes, but had been driven back to their start position in disorder by machine-gun fire and gas shells. The commander of 14 DI had been ordered to 'throw all his forces into the gap, however narrow it might be'.[94] Neighbouring divisions also attempted to push through the bottleneck by night attacks in the driving rain.

All the attacking units were met by withering concentric German fire, and pushing further French units into the inferno merely increased the confusion and the casualties. After several more attempts to widen the breach during the day, Castelnau had to accept on the evening of 29 September that the rumours that the German line had been broken were false, and he suspended the attacks. The French had done well, having captured 18,000 prisoners and 130 guns, but the cost had been heavy.

In Artois, meanwhile, the third attempt to take the heights north of Arras began on the same day as the offensive opened in Champagne, 25 September. It had proved very difficult to get Sir John French to agree to extend the French front and the negotiations with Sir Douglas Haig (First Army) over the British sector around Loos required tact and patience. Castelnau had been able to issue orders to Pétain and de Langle de Cary, his two army commanders, but Foch could not do this. He kept a tight control over Tenth Army to ensure that the lessons learned from the fighting in May/June were applied, but he could only request and persuade the British First Army's commander. The start times on the morning of 15 September provide a good example of the difficulties that Foch faced.

Fearing that his munition supplies were inadequate for the battle, Haig had decided to supplement his preparatory barrage with gas and smoke shells. On the grounds that the wind blew more strongly just after daybreak, the attack was timed to begin at 5.50am. The French, however, preferred to wait to observe the effects of their artillery bombardment before launching the infantry; hence Foch decreed the start time as four hours after observation had become possible. Tenth Army's commander d'Urbal set H-hour, therefore, at 12.25pm to allow the usual early morning mist that was characteristic of late September to disperse. The British made an excellent start, capturing Loos village and moving on a further kilometre or so to the east. Consequently Haig began sending urgent messages to Tenth Army to get them to move earlier than they had planned. Although d'Urbal did, indeed, advance his launch a little, the uncoordinated attacks gave the British the perfect excuse for subsequent failures and complaints. Yet XXI Corps on the left of Tenth Army and next to the British made good progress, capturing the remains of Souchez village and La Folie farm. The corps in the centre made a little progress and the right-hand corps none at all. Foch sent messages of congratulation to Castelnau and to Haig and ordered Tenth Army artillery to support XXI Corps the next day, as theirs was the sector where most ground had been gained. Part of these gains around Souchez village had been made by 13 DI, still in XXI Corps. They engaged 14,790 men on 25 September and succeeding days, and suffered 41 per cent casualties.

It had begun raining about 1pm on 25 September, so that observation for the artillery became difficult in Artois as well as in Champagne. As a result, the French start-times became late morning or early afternoon, leading to more British complaints. Moreover, Joffre created yet more difficulty for Foch on 26 September. The good news in Champagne caused Joffre to ask him first to economise on troops so that some 'intact' divisions could be sent eastwards, and then, later that afternoon, to economise on munitions. Expenditures of shell had been so enormous that, despite earlier reassurances that stocks were plentiful, Joffre wished Foch to wind down operations in Artois, but to do so without letting the British think that they were being left to attack alone. At Castelnau's headquarters it was feared that Joffre's economy measure would free German reserves in the north to move to reinforce the Champagne front.[95]

Despite the rain, the British, and Joffre's reductions in men and munitions, Tenth Army's men managed to reach the ridge and to cling on to its western slopes, although Fayolle's XXXIII Corps was pushed off the very top. Foch offered to relieve Haig's right so as to enable the British to make further gains, but it proved impossible to make joint operations begin on the same day, let alone at the same time. Although the fighting continued until 13 October, bad weather and frayed tempers, but above all the utter weariness of the troops, prevented any further gains of territory. The political decision to send troops to Salonika to support the beleaguered Serbians put an end to the campaign in Artois.

Seventeen infantry and two cavalry divisions had been devoted to Third Artois, equipped with 420 heavy and 630 field guns. The BEF on Tenth Army's left (north) added a further twelve infantry and five cavalry divisions, supported by 110 heavy and 841 field guns. Foch had also insisted on air and naval support.[96] Opposing the joint forces were the equivalent of thirteen German divisions. Between 19 September (when the artillery preparation began) and 13 October, Tenth Army fired well over 1.4 million shells from its 75s, and a quarter of a million from its heavy guns, in addition to 63,500 shells from the old 90s that had been supplied to make up the deficiency in the heavy mobile guns that Foch kept demanding. Tenth Army had suffered 48,230 casualties, of whom 18,657 were killed or missing, which was out of all proportion to the capture of over 2,000 German prisoners, 35 machine guns and a large number of trench mortars and other materiel. The two attacks in May/ June and September/October 1915 had taken Tenth Army 5 to 6 kilo-metres up the slopes of Vimy ridge, on a front of about 9 kilometres. Fayolle's report on the autumn fighting listed uncut wire, machine guns and artillery barrages as the causes of failure. An infantry attack was only as successful as the artillery preparation, and the artillery had not sup-pressed all the German batteries.[97]

The Champagne offensive had continued also into October because of the false hopes raised by the narrow break into the German second line. High command reckoned that it was worth preparing a renewed effort before the enemy was able to bring troops back from Russia and re-organise his battered positions. Joffre had a further reason to keep the fighting going in France which was the principal theatre, he insisted to Millerand, and where the decision had to be sought. He attempted to avoid sending any troops out of France, but in vain. The politicians had decided to send troops to the east to support the Serbian Army under attack from Bulgarian troops.

So on the Champagne front a new infantry attack was launched on 6 October, after being delayed by the continuing bad weather. On the western side of the battlefields a few, hard-won gains were made but lost again. On the eastern side, XVI Corps in Pétain's Second Army managed to capture the Butte de Tahure. Castelnau realised that, without a large infusion of reinforcements, there was little point in repeating such action. It had been a successful opening to a play in several acts, but forces should have been reserved for each act, he thought. It had been a mistake to disperse resources by attacking in Artois as well, but that had been Joffre's decision.[98] On 19 October the German *Third Army* made a gas attack east of the Champagne front near the Fort de la Pompelle, one of the Reims ring of forts, and on 24 October the French attacked south-east of the Tahure heights. In both cases counter-attacks managed to regain some if not all the ground lost. The Germans also tried to take back some of the ground lost on the Main de Massiges.

Expenditure of munitions had been so enormous that the campaign could not be continued with so many casualties among the infantry and so few gains of territory. Joffre called a halt on 14 October. The casualties for the armies fighting in Champagne were horrendous: out of a total of 143,567, 43.5 per cent (62,505) had been killed or had disappeared.[99] The French Army could not sustain such a casualty rate.

Pétain's long report on the Champagne autumn offensive, with 125 pages of annexes and maps, concluded that, before undertaking in future any such costly operation and seeking the decisive battle, the enemy's forces had to be worn down 'methodically'. The first stage, wearing down the enemy, required much more heavy artillery and 'almost unlimited' munitions; the second stage, the decisive battle, should take the form of 'successive' assaults at various points, because an initial attack always cost so many casualties that it was impossible to continue it. Attacking in another sector would enable the artillery to move up in support of the troops occupying the ground captured in the first assault. To achieve the various phases of this decisive battle required the provision of more men and more materiel than the enemy possessed: 'The effort to be made is immense, the expense colossal. We must not be afraid to face the difficulties; it is not by denying that they exist that we shall overcome them.'[100]

As Pétain's staff were writing this report for him, the Belgian artist Flameng was painting Pétain's portrait. Pétain listened 'absent-mindedly' to a section of the report, and then asked whether the troops knew who commanded Second Army. Next he asked whether they knew what XXXIII Corps had done at Arras on 9 May. They must be told, Pétain insisted. Clearly, he felt that the autumn campaign in Champagne had not equalled the spring campaign in Artois, when his DM had reached the crest of Vimy ridge.[101]

As for German opinion, one of General von Einem's staff officers gave a lecture in December to the military attachés of neutral countries, and described the fighting in detail, claiming that *Third Army* had been fully aware of the forthcoming French attack. He stated that the French failure 'could not be attributed to inferiority of their troops or their material, nor to the tactical arrangements made, but to leadership which failed after the tactical break through had been actually effected on Sept. 25th'. Yet, even if an opportunity had presented itself on the first day, the means available to the French Army in 1915 were insufficient to exploit it. To attribute the French failure to the army leadership, as the lecturer did, is to consider only a part of the problem.[102]

Africa

The Dardanelles and the Balkans were not France's only overseas commitments. The first Entente victory of the war came in Africa, with the capture of the tiny German colony of Togo. With the British Gold Coast to its west and the huge resources of AOF to its east, Togo did not have any chance of survival. Its main value lay in its powerful wireless station at Kamina, which could link German ships in the Atlantic with Berlin by radio. A joint, but unplanned and uncoordinated, Anglo-French expedition ignored the German governor's attempt to declare neutrality, overcame the few hundred men of the colony's defence force, and accepted Togo's surrender on 26 August 1914. The victors divided the territory between them, an arrangement that was confirmed by the post-war League of Nations mandates. A native force of some 500 men with European officers garrisoned the French zone until war's end.[103]

Germany's other colony in west central Africa was Cameroon. Like Togo, it was bounded by British and French colonies: British Nigeria to the north-west, and French AEF to the south and east. Germany had added to Cameroon two strips of French territory, which extended the colony to the south-east, giving it access to the Congo river. This territory had been the price France paid for settlement of the Moroccan crisis in 1911, and the two strips cut across the AEF. For both territory and prestige, therefore, the local French authorities were eager to operate against Cameroon. It was a much bigger operation than the capture of Togo, and lasted through the whole of 1915 and into the following year.[104]

The governor of the AEF, Martial Merlin, was on leave in Paris when war was declared. He had made no plans for any offensive in Africa, and neither the French nor the British had up-to-date intelligence, let alone good maps. On his own initiative, the commander of the French forces in AEF, Joseph Aymérich, seized the tips of the two German salients, and prepared four columns of troops, with Belgian help, to move into Cameroon from the south. The British interest lay in a maritime blockade, to deny German shipping access to the Atlantic coast. The main port and the coast were secured by the end of 1914. Paris meanwhile had agreed that it was desirable to take back all the land ceded to Germany and, in cooperation with the British, to throw the Germans out of west Africa.

An Entente force of about 13,000 men, half of them porters, was constituted, the larger element French, including 2,000 tirailleurs. The great distance between east (where Aymérich had taken unilateral action) and west (where the main British force had taken the port) made joint action very difficult. Disease and the weather added to the difficulties. The joint expedition of May 1915 to move on Yaounde, the centre of the German defences, achieved little because of sickness and difficulties of supply. Then the rainy season intervened, and the British and French agreed in August to re-start operations after the rains ended in October in the east and in November for the west. This second action was successful, but the German defenders slipped out of Yaounde and escaped to the coast and neutral Spanish territory of Muni (Spanish Guinea).

On 23 February 1916 François Georges-Picot and Sir Charles Stracey (Colonial Office) divided the Cameroons to create a condominium (excluding the originally French portions ceded to Germany in 1911). The dividing line was drawn carelessly and across tribal lines, and the principal victims were the native inhabitants, not the Germans. The German administrators, teachers, medical teams and religious all left, thus depriving the native tribes of education and medical care. Few European soldiers had been involved in the campaign. The AEF force in October 1915, for example, consisted of 1,000 African tirailleurs, with 350 French and Belgian officers. The Cameroon expedition had been fought along colonial army lines.[105] General Aymérich became France's high commissioner in the conquered territory, to which Germany gave up all claim in the Treaty of Versailles.

The protectorate of Morocco saw no fighting, although its Resident General, Hubert Lyautey, feared for its safety when large contingents of his European forces were sent to France at the outbreak of the war. Disaffected tribes in the interior were the target of German propaganda and calls for jihad. The propaganda threat was potent, because the strongest portion of Lyautey's force was the German legionnaires, who had remained in Africa when the rest of the Foreign Legion went to

France. Four territorial regiments were sent to Morocco from the south of France, and joined the mobilised European colonists. By July 1915 Lyautey had 71,000 men at his disposal. Despite his reduced resources, he discouraged any thoughts of insurrection by insisting that France would be victorious. He maintained the usual trade fairs, and kept up road and rail construction. Except for one incident in 1914, Morocco presented no real difficulties during the war. The 1914 incident resulted in the deaths of 580 soldiers and 33 officers, and the loss of all the weapons of two battalions, when an unwise expedition against tribal warriors was undertaken near Khenifra.[106]

The end of 1915

In 1915 the French Army fought all along the front in France, and on Gallipoli. By December, three French divisions were in Salonika, and French colonial army units were finishing up the war for the German colony of Cameroon with the British. Yet little had been gained, and that at great cost. Joffre had tried to repay the debt to Russia for having mobilised and attacked within two weeks of the declaration of war by launching the autumn campaign in France, despite calls for reinforcements for Gallipoli and then for saving Serbia. The total of deaths alone (excluding the many wounded) in the French Army between August 1914 and 1 January 1915 had stood at 528,000; it had risen to 941,000 by 1 January a year later.[107]

Lessons had been learned, however. GQG recognised that sending instructions down the hierarchical chain was of little use. Instead, GQG asked for after-action reports to be sent up the chain to be consolidated and their lessons extracted. The archives in Vincennes contain, for example, for the autumn Battle of Champagne alone, five large boxes of reports from the Centre Army Group commander, through the two armies and all the corps, down to divisional level, with copied extracts from war diaries. A new artillery doctrine was distributed in November. The need for a more scientific approach was acknowledged, with detailed plans for specific phases of the artillery preparation. Certain types of gun were to be used for different purposes, and accuracy improved by using the army's topographical resources, by grading munitions to ensure greater uniformity of performance and by taking account of meteorological factors such as air pressure. The first 'aerological' corrections had been used by a group of railway guns on 9 May in Artois. Box barrages and rolling barrages were starting to be used and improved. Artillery commander, Colonel Robert Nivelle, had employed the latter tactic in the fighting in January north of Soissons.[108]

The value of camouflage had been recognised. The artist Guirand de Scevola was well connected, and knew officers such as Captain Edouard Réquin (attached to Foch's staff) and intelligence officer Colonel Cointet (attached to Second Army). In February 1915 Scevola convinced General Castelnau by several experiments that men could move around no-man's-land if wearing the camouflage that is standard nowadays. Obviously the employment of artists and theatre painters proved the worth of their work, and in August 1915, following requests for their services, the camouflage section was put on a formal footing. All 'camoufleurs' were to be attached to 13 Artillery Regiment and four sections were formed, one in Paris and one each for the three army groups. The army group commanders would receive requests for camouflage work and prioritise them; to compensate for having to travel about the front, the camoufleurs were to receive an extra 2 francs 50 per day, and to be reimbursed for expenditure on paint and so on against approved receipts.[109]

Although the shells crisis was overcome gradually during the course of 1915, the production of new guns, and especially the heavier types, was much slower. The Army Commissions of both houses raised the matter constantly. Other equipment was easier to produce quickly and in quantity. Retired supply officer Louis Auguste Adrian volunteered to rejoin the active army in August 1914, and designed the steel helmet that bears his name. The lightweight (700 grams), bluish helmets began production in April 1915, and seven million had been produced by war's end. Adrian had realised the need for head protection after seeing the shell wounds of the opening weeks. He also produced a sheepskin cape, trench boots, and metal shoulder-coverings and other, less easy-to-wear items of equipment. As the second winter of the war approached he designed a wooden, demountable and modular shed, the 'baraque Adrian', for use by troops during the 'rest' periods out of the front line. A shortage of tent canvas made him think of an alternative method of sheltering troops from the elements, and twenty factories were organised to produce the pre-cut planks and beams. The 'baraques' were used as temporary housing after the war.

A further development was beginning to take shape. Colonel J-B Estienne, an artillery officer with several inventions to his name and who played a significant role in developing the use of military aircraft for registering guns, had seen the need for 'an armoured landship able to manoeuvre over heavy ground'. The inability to move guns forward to support the infantry after its advance was the reason why initial breakthroughs could never be exploited. On 1 December 1915 he sent to GQG a design for what became the first units of the 'artillerie d'assaut' or tanks. Two weeks later Joffre authorised Estienne to 'pursue its creation with all the required speed and secrecy'.[110]

To the prospect of a second winter at war was joined the obvious fact that the constant fighting during 1915 had achieved almost nothing, and certainly had not brought the end of the war any nearer. It is not, therefore, surprising that men's spirits flagged. The historians of 13 DI record very briefly a 'momentary depression' of moral force, quickly repressed. The reason was that the fighting continued 'for too long after the moment when winning the battle could no longer be hoped for'. The division's losses had been the heaviest ever in the September fighting in Artois.[111] Incidents such as refusing to leave the trenches were recorded. Even the famed Foreign Legion, some of whose units fought with the DM and reached (briefly) the top of Vimy ridge on 9 May, caused problems. Joffre recognised the importance of morale. He had set up a postal control service to prevent 'indiscretions' about operations or the position of troops. Letters written home to family members might contain information useful to the enemy and might be easily harvested. Gradually during the course of 1915 the system was extended to cover questions of troop morale. On 4 January 1915 Joffre commissioned the officers circulating among the various postal control units of each army to examine the reports for the light they shed on morale. In July he extended the examination to correspondence sent by civilians as well as military and at the same time created permanent missions for the purpose. However, if morale reports were drawn up, none of them have survived for 1915; it was the following year that the system became generalised.[112]

The men were beginning to find their own ways of keeping up spirits. Trench newspapers began to appear, mostly based on a particular unit. French historian Stéphane Audoin-Rouzeau has listed for 1915 twenty such publications, usually roneoed and distributed free. The names echoed well-known newspapers (that is, they contained the word 'écho') – *L'Echo du Ravin*, *L'Echo de Tranchées-ville*, *L'Echo des marmites* – or they referred to guns – *Marmita*, *Le Crapouillot* – or they contained the word 'poilu' – *Le Canard poilu*, *Le Poilu déchaîné*, *Le Poilu*. Clearly 'poilu' (a nineteenth-century term, literally hairy, that is, unshaven) had already become the standard representation of the pcdf (pauvres cons du front, or poor bloody infantry). Mostly the titles indicated a humorous (or at least a cynical) orientation.

The most famous of the titles, because it is still being published, is the *Canard Enchaîné*. Canard is an interesting word, meaning an unfounded rumour but with its literal meaning of duck being a gift to cartoonists. The wordplay continues to this day. 'Enchaîné' clearly refers to Clemenceau's newspaper, *L'Homme Libre*, whose name was changed to *L'Homme Enchaîné* as a result of, and as a statement against, censorship. The *Canard Enchaîné* was not strictly a trench newspaper, but took its name from 74 RI's trench newspaper. Only a few issues appeared in September and

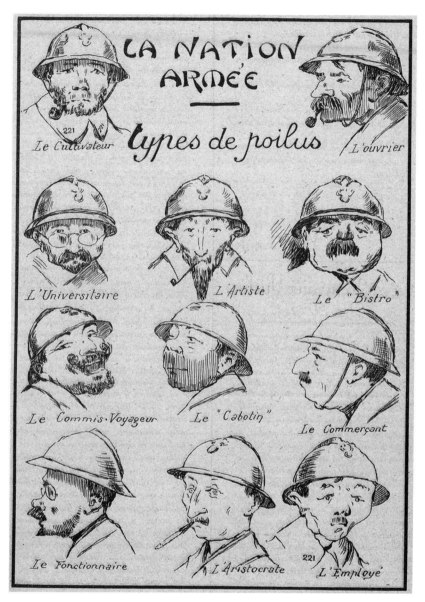

Fig. 6 The Nation in Arms: Types of 'poilus', from *L'Echo des Marmites*, 25 April 1917
From top left: farmer, workman, professor, artist, 'bistro', commercial traveller, ham actor, shopkeeper, civil servant, aristocrat, clerk

October 1915, because its editor, Maurice Maréchal, was called up. This was not strictly censorship, although a police report of 1929 gave the reason for his call-up as the humorous attacks on political and military personalities.[113] The paper began publication again, however in July 1916. The banner cartoon below the title on the front page of the first 1916 issue shows the scissors, the conventional representation of censorship (Anastasie). The scissors threaten the chained duck, which squawks 'Tu auras mes plumes, tu n'auras pas ma peau'. You may get my feathers (quills), the duck says, but you will not get my skin, or, in the colloquial sense, you will not get the better of me. The paper was read in the trenches and was available in military cooperatives. In his 1915 'presentation' of the paper, Maréchal wrote: 'Everyone knows in fact that the French press without exception since the start of the war only communicates news that is implacably true. Well, the public has had enough. The public wants false news ... [sic] as a change. It will get some.'[114] By 1917–18 it had become the second most widely diffused weekly paper in the trenches.[115]

That sense of frustration with the popular press was expressed in more formal ways also. At the end of 1915 Lieutenant Paul Tuffrau, who commanded the machine-gun section of 246 RI, was 'disgusted' by the extravagant military accounts appearing in the press. He began to write a series of anonymous articles for *Le Journal*, which had the third largest circulation of the national press. They appeared weekly throughout 1916 and 1917, with the first thirty-two of them being collected and published in book form in March 1917. Tuffrau explained his reasons for writing thus: 'I wished both to give the soldiers, whose anger I saw daily, the satisfaction of recognising that the rear was no longer unaware of their true life – and to give the homefront a more accurate notion of the misery and the grandeur of the front.'[116]

The sort of literature against which Tuffrau was writing was of the 'Debout les morts' type. In April 1915 Lieutenant Jacques Péricard wrote a tale of being surrounded by the enemy south of Saint-Mihiel, when a wounded soldier cried out 'Debout les morts!' and inspired others to rise up and repel the German soldiers. The tale was published in the staid *Journal des Débats*, but was taken up by Maurice Barrès and it appeared, embellished, in his more popular newspaper, the *Echo de Paris*. Now, not only the wounded, but the dead rose up to repel the invader. By the end of 1915, all France knew of the legend.[117] Whether all non-military readers knew that 'Debout les morts!' was the standard cry of corporals waking their recruits in the morning ('rise and shine!') is impossible to know.

Fig. 7 Detail of the Verdun milestone by Forain, *Le Figaro*,
22 March 1916

Many lessons were drawn from the unsuccessful 1915 campaigns as
Joffre solicited after-action reports from all levels of command. Since
he stated that there was no need to submit the reports through the normal
hierarchical channels, clearly Joffre hoped to receive honest appreciations
of what had gone wrong. Before putting out new instructions and doctrine, Joffre now sought the views of those in the line of fire. As a result of
the analysis of these reports, changes in doctrine were made. No longer
were 'men' to be pitted against 'materiel', for France had suffered too
many casualties already to continue in this way. As Captain Charles
Delvert remarked, it had taken GQG a very long time to come up with
such a statement of the obvious. The document, dated 8 January 1916
and entitled 'Small unit combat training', was distributed to Delvert,

Table 9 *French losses to 31 December 1915*

		Killed	Missing	Wounded	Total
France	Officers	15,984	6,053	27,472	49,509
	Men	564,784	399,973	917,785	1,882,542
Orient	Officers	313	58	475	846
	Men	9,326	4,780	14,684	28,790
Totals		590,407	410,864	960,416	1,961,687

Source: *AFGG* 3, 602.

a company commander in 124 DI in Champagne, on 21 February. 'At last! It's hard to think that it has needed eighteen months of war to conceive of this prime truth. But when will this truth penetrate the rigid [ankylosés] brains of the extraordinary superior officers that Mr Bureaucrat sends us? If it needs another eighteen months, it is very worrying.'[1]

With two million 'hors de combat' by the end of 1915, of whom well over half a million had been killed, France could not sustain such casualty rates (see Table 9).

The 1916 and 1917 classes would only provide 270,000 infantry, insufficient to replace all the combat losses. The 1916 class had been incorporated in April 1915, but Joffre decided to leave them in the interior for the time being, calling instead on the recovered wounded from older classes. The 1917 class was incorporated in January 1916. At his disposal, then, Joffre had ninety-three infantry divisions (the distinction at mobilisation between active and reserve disappeared gradually), eleven territorial and ten cavalry. These forces were to be distributed to give the greatest flexibility: the front line to be held strongly enough to prevent its rupture, with a permanent command and permanent artillery resources, but allowing for rest and training; the second line, 20–30 kilometres behind the front but deployed close to a railway line, would constitute the army group reserves, shared out behind each army in the sector; the third line of general reserves, resting, to be available quickly because also stationed close to a railway line.[2]

It was now patent that the enemy's defensive lines could not be penetrated, let alone broken right through, by a single offensive operation. None of the army and army group commanders believed in the possibility of such a breakthrough. Instead, slow and methodical, but violent and repeated, methods were to be used – what some called the 'scientific method'. Accordingly GQG issued a series of new directives, including the one that had roused Delvert. Joffre had already insisted that commanders must be more in contact with events on the front, and on

5 December an instruction on defensive tactics was issued, followed on 26 January 1916 by one on general offensives.[3] New tactics and the increasing number of new weapons meant that greater emphasis was placed on training. When Pétain's Second Army was withdrawn from Champagne at the end of 1915, Pétain was put in charge of training the divisions that were placed temporarily in reserve. Two camps were made available for practice manoeuvres and Pétain was able to train the troops according to the new directives and his experiences of the Champagne fighting.[4]

The technical arms were not neglected. As French factories began producing guns and shells in ever increasing quantities, field and heavy artillery and munitions were stockpiled for the 1916 campaign. The need to make more accurate use of the guns was recognised. Each corps was provided with an intelligence service and technical sections for detecting enemy artillery by sound-ranging and flash-spotting. The army's Geographical Service began drawing up large-scale maps upon which the location of individual batteries, derived from these new sound-ranging and other techniques, could be plotted.[5] The 'plans directeurs' were available for the battery commanders taking over a sector, and so local knowledge did not disappear as the guns were moved. Three training centres for heavy artillery were set up between December 1915 and February 1916; each army set up a centre to train young regular and the best reserve officers to act as field artillery battery commanders[6] for the twenty new horse-drawn and ten tractor-drawn heavy artillery regiments decreed in July 1915. Communications were improved between artillery and infantry, with liaison from special observation detachments, and between air and artillery as wireless was gradually installed in aircraft.

Joffre's position as de facto head of the Entente armies on the Western Front was not damaged by 1915's failures: British Prime Minister H.H. Asquith called him 'Super-Frog'.[7] Joffre still led the largest army, and his position was reinforced by the decree of 2 December 1915, making him responsible for the Balkan front as well as that of the north-east in France and Belgium. To assist with the increased responsibility, Castelnau was appointed to the new position at GQG of chef d'état-major général des armées. In addition, a new staff organisation to deal with fronts outside France was established at GQG. This was the TOE (théâtre des opérations extérieures) with similar bureaux to the principal staff establishment. The staff prepared general studies on the conduct of the war, which were discussed in the revitalised Conseil Supérieur de la Défense Nationale which began meeting again from November 1915.[8]

As 1916 progressed, however, it seemed that Joffre's only trump card as far as the politicians were concerned was his standing with the Allies, and he attempted to give greater coherence to the Allied conduct of the war. The Dardanelles and Balkans fiascos had shown beyond any doubt that such coordination was required. He had proposed a sort of inter-allied general staff or 'organe d'études permanent' to examine allied questions, to be based in Chantilly.[9] Similar ideas were circulating in London, where Albert Thomas, the under-secretary of state for munitions, and his counterpart, David Lloyd George, were discussing Franco-British cooperation in munitions. Albert Thomas even suggested that there should be 'one Munitions Ministry for both countries'. He proposed an integrated railway artillery reserve that could be used at any point along the whole front.[10] France's commerce minister, Etienne Clémentel, was pushing for greater economic cooperation with his proposal for an international conference, which took place in Paris in June 1916. The desire for greater coordination was manifested in the military conference of 8–12 December 1915, held at GQG in Chantilly to plan the campaign for 1916. All the Allies attended.

As the commander of the armies who were paying the highest price in manpower and territorial losses, Joffre had the moral authority to preside over the conference. Hence it was Joffre's outline plan which was adopted. The essential element was unity of purpose and of timing: only when all the Allies were ready would coordinated attacks take place on all fronts, so as to cause maximum disruption to the enemy. Decisive action should be sought by 'combined offensives on the Russian, Franco-British and Italian fronts, carried out with as brief a delay as possible'.[11] Joffre insisted that the British were holding 'a much shorter front, in proportion to their effectives' than the French, and that they should henceforth make a greater effort, both in France and in Salonika. He insisted also that the Allied armies remain in Salonika because of France's pledge to help Serbia.[12] Despite his earlier opposition to diverting troops from France, Joffre knew that he could not afford to alienate his political masters; if the Briand ministry fell over the question of Salonika, he would be likely to fall with it. At the ministerial meetings in Calais and Paris, which followed the military one, Britain gave up its solitary opposition to remaining in Salonika in order to support Serbia.[13]

Having reached agreement to evacuate the Gallipoli peninsula and to undertake a series of allied actions on all fronts in the summer, it remained to decide what form an attack in France should take. All the army group commanders were invited to study the possibility of operations in their respective areas, which would be at least equal in strength to the last Champagne offensive. General Dubail of the Eastern Army Group suggested an attack in Upper Alsace; Castelnau reported that only one sector in the centre, between the Argonne and Moronvillers, was susceptible to attack; and Foch of the Northern Army Group believed that an offensive was possible only on the front of the Tenth Army or on part of the front of the Sixth Army. Tenth Army might complete its occupation of Vimy ridge and attack towards Douai, or Sixth Army might aim at Chaulnes/Roye. The latter operation would suffer from the lack of any dominating high ground to occupy, whereas the possession of Vimy ridge would afford Tenth Army a great advantage.

Joffre accepted none of these suggestions, but decided to attack the nose of the German salient in one continuous operation, instead of separate attacks on the flanks as in 1915. His criteria for the 1916 campaign in France were that the front of attack should be wide (narrow breaches in the German front could not be sustained), that it should be able to be supported by artillery, and that it should be contiguous with the British. The British were to supply the manpower that the French had lost in 1915. Furthermore, now that the BEF had a new CinC, Sir Douglas Haig, and large numbers of inexperienced volunteer troops, it was important to make sure that the British conformed to French wishes. They would require leading, being slow and unimaginative. It was equally important to dispel any doubts about the French Army's firm intention to continue the war.

The main outlines of the plan of campaign were established at a meeting between Haig and Joffre on 14 February 1916. Joffre agreed to forgo the proposed partial attack in April that he had wanted, accepting Haig's and London's refusal to undertake wearing down actions before the main battle. This would be a joint 'decisive' attack astride the Somme on 1 July (assuming the Allies kept the initiative) on a front of 65–70 kilometres. Haig said that he would be able to put twenty-one divisions into the battle, or, if he took over the front currently held by Tenth Army, fourteen divisions. Foch's proposed plan (accepted by GQG on 18 February) envisaged the use of thirty-nine French divisions (in three armies) to attack from the Somme southwards as far as Lassigny (about 40 kilometres), using 764 heavy guns.[14] Although Joffre's preliminary wearing-down battle would not take place, there would be a partial attack in the Ypres–La Bassée area a week or two before the main offensive. If Russia was attacked beforehand, the date of the Allied operation would be advanced.

It was not, however, Russia that was attacked, a mere week after the Haig–Joffre agreement to fight on the Somme at the beginning of July. Falkenhayn had decided that the 1915 victories in Galicia and in Serbia meant that he could now turn his attention to the west. Britain was the main enemy, in his view, and France's Army was Britain's best sword. Falkenhayn intended to strike Britain's sword in a sector that he deemed the French Army would defend and attempt to recapture at any cost. When the British moved to support their ally, as they would be bound to do, he would strike their untrained and ill-equipped New Armies, thus bringing the war to an end. The sector Falkenhayn chose was Verdun.

Verdun

At the end of 1915 the front line in eastern France ran eastwards from Champagne before looping around the Verdun fortress southwards towards the Vosges mountains and Switzerland. This left Verdun as a pronounced salient, whose strong defences the Germans had bypassed during their invasion of 1914, but which was now in a vulnerable exposed position. Following the Franco-Prussian War of 1870–71, which brought the Franco-German frontier closer to Verdun by the cession of part of Lorraine to the new German *Reich*, the city's already naturally strong defences were strengthened further with a series of rings of forts and intermediate ouvrages. A series of forested hills rises from the river Meuse, which loops northwards through the city, the hills being crowned with the new forts. These hills are steep where they face south and west

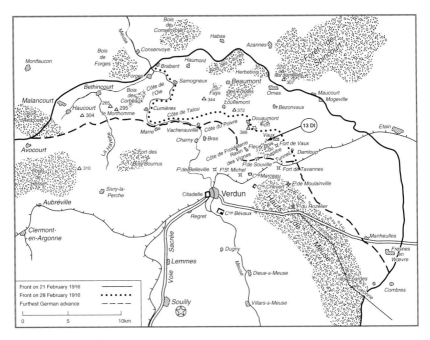

9. Verdun, 1916

towards Verdun, and fall away more gradually to the north-east whence any enemy attack might come. The river meanders so that defenders could always fire from one bank or the other on an invader using the river route.

However, the apparent value of forts for defence in modern warfare had diminished greatly. French troops holed up in Sedan and Metz in 1870 had been forced to surrender, even though Verdun had resisted, and in 1914 the Belgian forts had not withstood the German invasion. The fate of Przemysl in Galicia had confirmed the danger: the site of the Austro-Hungarian headquarters at the start of the war, the fortress had fallen briefly to the Russians after a long siege, but General Mackensen's breakthrough at Gorlice–Tarnow in May–June 1915 had led to its recapture. Joffre took from these examples the lesson that now fortresses represented a risk rather than security. Accordingly, he decided in August 1915 to change the city's status from being an autonomous 'fortified place' to the whole area becoming part of the defensive front line, known as the Région Fortifiée de Verdun (RFV).[15] Joffre had a further reason for making the change in status. Verdun's forts had contained significant numbers of heavy artillery pieces, in addition to the fixed guns in the forts' turrets. Although such artillery was mostly old or obsolescent, the French shortage of heavy guns was so acute in 1915 that the guns and their stocks of shells in the forts had been hauled away to feed the autumn campaigns in Artois and Champagne.

Instead of relying on forts as centres of resistance, several lines of trenches now needed to be constructed around the city so as to connect in an uninterrupted line with those of First Army on the right and those of Third Army on the left, now commanded by General Georges Humbert. (Third Army's former commander, Sarrail, had been banished to Salonika.) Joffre appointed an elderly artillery officer, General Frédéric Herr, to command the RFV and to oversee the construction of the new defence lines. Although Herr did his best, the work was hampered by GQG's demands for troops for the fighting in Champagne. Consequently the defensive works were not as far advanced as they ought to have been at the start of 1916. Complaints reached parliament and the new war minister, General Joseph Gallieni, who wrote in turn to Joffre to ask for assurances that the second line of defence at Verdun was complete. Joffre was furious. He replied that there was no justification for fears about Verdun's defences, and that soldiers writing about such matters to parliamentarians was an attack on military authority and the morale of all. He ended his official letter with a manuscript addition: 'I cannot permit the continuation of this state of affairs. I need the government's entire confidence. If it gives it to me, it can no longer encourage or tolerate practices which diminish the moral authority necessary to exercise my command, and without which I could not continue to bear the responsibility.'[16] This was a real shot across the new minister's bows. The credit for the Battle of the Marne was already disputed between the two generals. It was less easy, however, to counter criticism in the Deputies' Army Commission. The deputy for Meurthe-et-Moselle, Lieutenant-Colonel Driant, commanded two battalions of chasseurs at Verdun. Explaining that at the start of hostilities he had been against any parliamentary interference in the affairs of war, he went on: 'The defensive organisation is not assured at certain points. I request that a delegation of the Army Commission go to see the ground between Lunéville and Nancy, for, from what I have been told, this ground is at the mercy of a sudden German attack. You must go there and see.'[17] This was a clear statement of divergence within the French Army from the views of the high command.

On the other side of the hill, the German high command believed that the Central Powers had delivered a hard enough blow to Russia during 1915 fighting to enable them safely to neglect the Eastern Front. More-over, Serbia had been defeated in short order, and the Franco-British expedition to the Dardanelles had been a fiasco. Falkenhayn had good reason to be optimistic about the profit to be gained from striking a severe blow against the Allies in the west. German intelligence reports informed him that French manpower resources were in decline, with losses of about 70,000 men per month. At that rate, the Intelligence Section concluded, by September 1916 the French would be forced to call up even their 1918 class. If the Champagne offensive in 1915 had proved Falkenhayn wrong about France's ability and willingness to mount further campaigns, yet he still believed that the French Army was weaker than the German, despite the former's numerical superiority when combined with that of the British, which had not yet reached its peak efficiency. Moreover, intelligence reports from the front about the poor morale of French deserters encouraged him in this view.[18] Hence, in the 1916 land campaign, Falkenhayn decided to defeat France's Army, while, at sea, submarines attacked Britain's naval supremacy.

For Falkenhayn, the best way to achieve his aim was to attack at a point on the Western Front where the French would be forced, for reasons of morale, public opinion or political pressure, to counter-attack, thereby bleeding themselves white.[19] Verdun was ideal for this purpose. The French RFV salient to the front of the Imperial Crown Prince's *Fifth Army* would enable the German guns to fire into the city from three sides; the German rear areas were served by a good rail network, unlike the French railway communications, which were interdicted at Saint-Mihiel to the south and from the Argonne to the west. Moreover, the immensely strong *Moselstellung* constructed between Metz and Thionville was close by the German lines; finally, and especially, the prestige of the city would compel the French to defend it to the extent of throwing at least half of their armies into the fray (or so *Fifth Army*'s chief of staff, General von Knoblesdorf estimated).[20] Knoblesdorf's plan provided for an attack stretching from the Argonne in the north-west, across both banks of the Meuse, as far as Ornes in the north-east, but Falkenhayn cut this down as too ambitious. The attack was to be undertaken with massed artillery, and to cover only the right (east) bank of the Meuse. He promised to give *Fifth Army* an extra five corps from OHL reserve for the operation – Operation GERICHT – which was to begin early in February.

Conflict soon arose between Falkenhayn and *Fifth Army* over the aims of the proposed offensive. Knoblesdorf wanted to capture Verdun, presumably for the glory to be gained for his army and its commander, but this would interfere with Falkenhayn's objective of killing the French reserves sent to defend the city. Falkenhayn had no desire to dedicate the necessary infantry resources to capture Verdun. Rather, he wanted to retain German reserves for meeting the expected British relief attack elsewhere on the front. Some confusion may have arisen over what constituted Verdun. The citadel in the city was one thing, and the ring of outer forts was another. The capture of the ring of forts protecting the city would give the German army the high ground from which to dominate the whole area, both east and west of the Meuse. On the other hand, Falkenhayn thought that the fall of the fortress 'would not be unwelcome', and he told the Austrians that the operation could bring a decision within fourteen days. He asked *Sixth Army* in northern France to prepare an attack to 'mop up' the Entente armies after the Verdun blood-letting and the presumed British relief attack. In addition he asked *Third Army* to prepare a plan because he thought that a French counter-attack in Champagne was also possible.[21] Falkenhayn's insistence on restricting information to only the highest levels of command may have contributed to the lack of clarity about the exact aims of the Verdun operation.

With superb staff work, *Fifth Army* assembled a vast quantity of guns and shells, all camouflaged. This task was facilitated by the wooded terrain, which enabled the build-up to be concealed more easily, by the good rail network, which was improved still further, and by the atmospheric conditions, which were frequently misty in winter. Large amounts of spare parts were also stocked because of the anticipated wear on the guns. Flamethrowers and phosgene gas shells were supplied, and solid shelters built for the men. Falkenhayn's insistence on absolute secrecy, even as far as his other army commanders were concerned, helped to conceal the preparations.

Joffre was convinced that the Germans would not attack at Verdun; if they did, it would be simply a diversionary attack. The sector had been very quiet since 1914, and none of the build-up that in 1915 had accompanied preparations for an offensive had been detected. No assault trenches had been dug into no-man's-land, a sure give-away in previous operations of an impending offensive. Nonetheless intelligence reports indicated that something was afoot in the Verdun sector. Four divisions had come to France from the east, and it was known that the German authorities had already incorporated their 1917 class, although the young recruits had not yet been sent to the armies.[22] Joffre had twenty-eight French divisions in reserve, even after reinforcing the Champagne front where he believed that the main German attack would come.[23] Nevertheless, he sent his chief of staff, General Castelnau, to inspect the defences on 23 January. Driant and Castelnau were old friends, and Castelnau spent three days in Verdun. Driant told him that while the sector was completely quiet during the day, nights were lit up by rockets and the sound of lorries. Castelnau reported that the first line positions on the right bank were satisfactory, although the second position was only sketched out in some places. On the left (west) bank, however, things were much less satisfactory. There were simply not enough men to provide the labour.[24]

Falkenhayn's new way of waging war – deliberate attrition, using artillery rather than human resources – was planned to start on 12 February, but snow and rain forced a postponement until the 21st. The delay was fortunate for the French, as it gave them time to make at least a start on the improvements mandated by Castelnau following his inspection, although they were by no means complete. The delay also gave time for French intelligence to confirm the likelihood of an offensive. At 7.30am on 21 February the concealed guns opened a terrific barrage, which thirty minutes later extended along the whole of the Verdun sector front, from Avocourt in the Argonne as far as the Woëvre, well south of the citadel. The Germans used *Minenwerfer* on the front lines, and heavier calibres on the second positions. They also targeted the city and the Meuse bridges, while aircraft and Zeppelins attacked more distant targets. The Germans had air supremacy, and the few French planes sent to try to pinpoint the German batteries reported that the whole sector from the Meuse at Consenvoye to the town of Etain was an uninterrupted semi-circle of flames. The bombardment continued the whole day.

Facing this unprecedented barrage were the three French corps in the front lines. On the left bank of the Meuse, General Bazelaire's VII Corps

was responsible for the sector from Avocourt to the river, which was in
flood, and had 29 and 67 DI in the front line. Next, XXX Corps, under
the command of General Paul Chrétien, held the front on the right bank,
from the river as far as the railway line that ran from Verdun to Etain with
three divisions in line supported by some territorials: 72, 51 and 14 DI.
On XXX Corps' right, facing south and the boggy Woëvre plain, was II
Corps (General Duchêne), with three divisions in line (132, 3 and 4 DI),
again with some territorial support. The French reserves were held along
the road leading into Verdun from Bar-le-Duc in the south. They consisted of two divisions (153 and 39) and the 34 Infantry Brigade; the
troops of XX Corps had been ordered to move up as well, but they had
not yet arrived when the battle began. In addition, the Centre Army
Group had five divisions of I Corps ready to intervene if required. The
French were completely outnumbered in both infantry and artillery:
36 French versus 72 German infantry battalions, and 210 French guns
of all types versus 1,200 German ones, all deployed according to their
battery's specific purpose.

At 16.30 the German fire lifted to more distant targets and small
groups of German infantry began infiltrating the front-line French
defences, which were to have been destroyed utterly by the preliminary
bombardment. The front of the infantry assault, where 72 DI bore the
brunt since they were holding the most northerly portion of the salient,
had been treated to a box barrage. This cut off communications with the
rear, where command posts and supplies were situated, and with units on
either side. So the French units were isolated from command, from
information, and from supplies. It was to have been a German walk-
over, as the lateness of the assault indicates. The infantry was expected to
do no more than to walk across no-man's-land and to occupy before dark
the demolished trenches and shelters. However, as later wars have confirmed, the rubble of demolished defences can prove almost as effective
as intact ones. It was not a walk-over, and the shocked French defenders
were able to prevent the enemy from capturing any more than Haumont
Wood and the edges of Ville and Caures woods. The villages on the
flanks of the infantry attack – Brabant on the Meuse and Ornes in
the east – remained in French hands. The next day, 22 February, the
German infantry tried again after a further five-hour heavy bombardment. They completed the capture of Caures Wood and on the 23rd they
took what remained of the first French position, from Brabant in the west
to Herbebois in the east and then the second position as well, which was
in only a rudimentary state. The artillery bombardment had severed
communications, thereby cutting off the French defenders from information about other sectors, from supplies of ammunition and of food

and water. Since they had been cut off just as effectively from higher command, the bravery and tenacity of the groups of shattered French infantry is beyond praise.

One of the best-known examples of that bravery and tenacity is that shown by 59-year-old Colonel Emile Driant and his two battalions of chasseurs (56 and 59) in 72 DI. His criticisms of the state of Verdun's defences have been noted already. Despite their resistance in the Bois des Caures, they were overwhelmed by the weight of shell, by flamethrowers and by sheer numbers. Driant's role as a deputy and member of the Chamber's Army Commission ensured that his heroic stand would be added to the list of acusations against GQG and Joffre.[25]

As well as the infantry of XXX Corps in the direct line of assault, the French artillery on the left (west) bank of the Meuse joined the riposte. The French guns were able to pound the German positions almost at will, since Falkenhayn had excluded action on the left bank. This riposte caused the enemy to concentrate further east and infiltration began towards the strongest position on the right bank, the heights with Fort Douaumont atop. The threat to the high ground of the Hauts de Meuse caused the Centre Army Group commander, de Langle de Cary, to order the troops holding the Woëvre to pull back to the eastern edge of the hills. On 25 February the Germans captured the Côte du Poivre, one of the transverse ridges that give access to the Meuse north of Verdun, and Fort Douaumont fell, without a shot being fired. The fort was manned by a small group of territorials, since it only contained one fixed gun, a 155 which had been left simply because it could not be removed from its turret. When the order arrived to evacuate the Woëvre, the fort should have been manned again, but the order was not transmitted. The Germans were able to walk in and capture the territorials, who had been sheltering in the basement, because every time a shell had landed on the fort during the previous four days the corridors were filled with choking dust. The fort had withstood the pounding, but its few defenders could not. Naturally, the German press made a great propaganda victory out of the fort's capture.

At GQG Joffre remained calm, even after de Langle rang in person to inform him that he had ordered troops to abandon the Woëvre. Castelnau, however, was worried about the German attack. After all, he had seen the Verdun defences recently and he forced matters to a head by doing the unthinkable. Joffre was awakened during the night of 24/25 February and he acceded to Castelnau's request to go to Verdun. Castelnau believed that the situation required the high command's presence, and Joffre gave him full powers to do what he wished. So Joffre washed his hands of responsibility for the voluntary withdrawal of French troops from the Woëvre (the decision shouldered by de Langle) and for taking charge of events at Verdun. He had, however, asked General Pétain to come to GQG the next morning (25th).

When Castelnau reached Verdun, he decided that the fighting had overwhelmed Herr and de Langle. Pétain should take over with the Second Army staff that Castelnau knew to be competent, since it was not long since he had left the army, either as its direct commander or as Centre Army Group commander. He decided also that the defence of Verdun would be carried out on the right bank; the Woëvre could be evacuated but the troops were to retire no further than the Hauts de Meuse. Joffre had reassured Pétain during their brief meeting at GQG that things were not going too badly at Verdun, and Pétain left immediately for his new command, driving there through a blizzard.[26] On his arrival, Castelnau informed him of his orders to stand on the right bank. Castelnau remained for two more days in Verdun because Pétain fell ill, but measures were put in place immediately to stabilise the defence and to improve the logistical situation.

The role of General Pétain

Pétain's great contribution to the battle of Verdun lay in his organising abilities. He so arranged the defence of the RFV that the French were able to hold on to most of what remained. His mission from Joffre via Castelnau was simply to block the enemy's operation on the Verdun front.[27] In order to carry this out, he established firm doctrines for both offensive and defensive action and ensured that they were observed by all units, especially the artillery; he inspired the reorganisation of the aviation service which had been completely overwhelmed during the opening days; above all, he oversaw the logistics of the campaign by ensuring that the RFV was re-supplied and its wounded evacuated.

For offensive doctrine, Pétain issued a general order on 3 March, stating that lost ground must be counter-attacked immediately. The rest of the order, however, consisted of a list of detailed movements of two divisions into the RFV, including 13 DI who were to embark that evening to join General Balfourier's XX Corps. General Order #24 of 16 March insisted that troops must adopt an 'aggressive attitude' towards the enemy, leaving him no rest, by interrupting and destroying all his defensive works. Yet again, however, most of the order was taken up with troop movements. Clearly Pétain paid greater attention to getting defensive tactics right first of all. So he emphasised the importance of establishing liaison between units, of all units adopting the same methods, of the methodical consolidation of captured positions. His General Order

312 of 5 March set out these methods. Verdun was not a fortress, as in the past, the order began. All the individual forts and their outworks were to be considered as strongpoints within the defensive front of the sector. Hence the commander of the sector was responsible for their defence. There were to be no repeats of the loss of Douaumont. Responsibility for the city and the citadel lay with General Guillaumat, commanding I Corps.[28] The inclusion of the city itself within the defensive ring meant that, even if the Germans captured more ground, it could be claimed that Verdun was still holding.[29] The guiding defensive principle was that the front line should be *continuous*, with trenches joining up the skeleton of the forts and outworks that provided points of support for the infantry. An intermediate position ran through Bras-Froideterre, Souville, Tavannes, Moulainville. Then a 'ligne de repli' or fall-back line, jokingly called the 'panic line', was to be constructed or, at least, marked out with stakes. This encircled the city, starting, on the right bank, from the Meuse south of Fort Troyon, through Forts Le Rozellier and Moulainville, across to the left bank at Chattancourt and Avocourt and the army's western limit, where it joined Third Army.

The principal element in the defence of Verdun was heavy artillery, and most of Pétain's early orders to Second Army concerned this arm. On 1 March Duchêne had thirty-six batteries of heavy guns (plus five naval guns) at his disposal; Balfourier had nineteen, Guillaumat twenty-two and Bazelaire twenty-five heavy batteries. In addition, under army command were the city's seven batteries and eight extra heavy railway guns (200, 240 and 305mm calibres). The mission of these units was to respond to every single request for support from the infantry corps. Also they were to shell aggressively crossroads, bridges, assembly points and so on used by the enemy. The task of the field artillery and medium heavy guns (105 and 120mm) was to fire by day and night on columns of enemy troops and their supply routes. Theirs was not simply a defensive role, for both should seek out opportunities to disrupt enemy concentrations and to give the impression that an attack was imminent so that enemy machine-gun nests would be revealed as the enemy manned them and so destroyed. Each army corps was to draw up a regular daily barrage plan to bombard sensitive points and to give the French infantry confidence that it was supported and that enemy artillery did not dominate the battlefield.

To be effective the gunners needed to 'see'. The Germans had sought mastery of the air during the weeks preceding the offensive in order to hide their preparations, and in early 1916 they were well ahead of the French, who had begun the war as a world leader in aviation. They concentrated 280 aircraft around Verdun for bombing and fighter missions, four times as many as the RFV had at its disposal. Just as important as numerical superiority was Germany's technical superiority. The new Fokker E outclassed all other types of aircraft because its Maxim machine gun was synchronised with the propellor, which enabled the pilot to fire forwards. Falkenhayn's aim in his *Luftsperre* was to deprive the French gunners of all observation over German lines by shooting down the French balloons (a new tactic consisted of a dual attack, with one aircraft aiming for the balloon itself while the second destroyed the winch on the ground), by constant patrolling to block French aircraft from overflying German lines and using the new Fokkers to destroy any that got past the patrols, and by bombing French airfields to render them unusable. That at Ancemont, for example, received almost 1,200 130mm shells in just the first two days of the battle. The enemy had blinded the French artillery.

The RFV's seventy French aircraft (four squadrons) were shared thus: two were allocated to corps command, and used for observation; and two squadrons to army command, consisting of C11 aircraft for observation and the Nieuport 23 for fighting; the air services were completed by an aerial photography section and two balloon companies used for correcting artillery fire. All were completely overwhelmed by the superior German forces, although on 20 February (that is, the day before the offensive began) one French observer had managed to take some photographs showing the German preparations, and to bring down a Zeppelin.[30] GQG took immediate steps to boost the French air services. Two more French balloon companies arrived as reinforcements, along with two squadrons of aircraft immediately the battle began. On 24 February GQG sent eighteen reconnaissance squadrons, followed the next day by another fourteen formations for reconnaissance, aerial photography and directing artillery fire. So the French took immediate steps to counter German air superiority, a phrase that first appeared in 1916.

As soon as he arrived Pétain realised that he had to reverse the French disadvantage. Although he was an infantryman, Pétain knew that artillery was the key and in order to reap maximum benefit from the artillery the gunners had to be able to see. On 28 February Pétain called Commandant Tricornot de Rose from his command of air services in Fifth Army, and gave him *carte blanche* to sweep the Germans from the skies above Verdun. De Rose created the first dedicated fighter squadrons. Up until 1916, fighter aircraft had been seen as simply protection for the observers and bombers, but now de Rose created a large fighting formation, the Groupement de Combat (GC). The GC comprised several squadrons of aircraft, taken from the armies to which they were attached, and placed them under a single command (his own). The

(a)

(b)

Fig. 8 Monument to the 'Train' – the transport corps – with detail of left wing, on the Voie sacrée from Bar-le-Duc to Verdun

aim was to lift a permanent and large offensive force into the air, to threaten enemy aircraft everywhere. They were deliberately to seek out enemy aircraft and to destroy them. It was no longer to be individual combat by air aces; pilots were to act as a team. Regular patrols, using experienced pilots from other sectors, soon won back air superiority, which proved to be an important morale boost for the troops on the ground. In a further improvement resulting from the new centralised organisation, observers for the artillery regiments remained behind, instead of leaving with the gunners when their unit moved position. This left men in place who knew the terrain, instead of new personnel who did not.

The final element in constructing the unshakeable defence of Verdun was logistics, and safeguarding the supply routes into Verdun became inextricably linked with Pétain's name. The road into Verdun from Bar-le-Duc to the south became known as the Voie sacrée, sacred way, and it still bears that appellation today. However, the Voie sacrée was not the only supply route. GQG had already ordered studies to be made in autumn 1915 to plan for the necessary flow of supplies of men and materiel into the RFV and the removal of the wounded and of materiel, in case of enemy attack. Consequently a programme was put in place very quickly to upgrade the railway network. The two main lines into Verdun from the south (via Saint-Mihiel) and the west (from Reims and ultimately Paris) were unusable. The front line cut across the former because the Germans had held Saint-Mihiel since 1914; the latter was interdicted by German artillery fire at Aubréville, on the edge of the Argonne. The construction of a standard-gauge railway connecting the north of Revigny to the south of Verdun was assured on 28 February, when engineers and territorial troops were allocated to the project. A second single-line standard-gauge section of 67 kilometres was begun on 4 March linking Sommeilles Nettancourt to Dugny, just south of Verdun on the line from Saint-Mihiel. In this way the wider rail network was accessed, as from Revigny it was possible to re-join the main Paris line at Sainte-Menehould. The Sommeilles–Dugny stretch was completed in record time by two companies of the fifth regiment of engineers, and several battalions of territorials, whose men were expected each to move three cubic metres daily, and not to finish work for the day until that volume was achieved. The completion of the work gave Souilly, in whose town hall Second Army headquarters were installed, a station that operated from 26 June.

In addition to the standard-gauge lines, there was also a narrow 60cm gauge line, called 'Le Meusien', which had been upgraded during the course of 1915. Water tanks, crossing points and an extension to Dugny were all provided. However, a serious problem remained in that the stations could only handle one train at a time, and the fighting was too severe to permit the men collecting supplies to do so at regular, predictable intervals. So the forty or so wagons of supplies that a division required might be blocked in a station and be holding up other rail journeys. Consequently, storage sheds were provided along the line so that supplies could be off-loaded and stored for the divisions to collect as and when they could. Stations could then be freed for more traffic. Re-supply was standardised. The 60cm line was used only for food and forage for the horses and mules, and the standard load became 15,000 rations for the men and 4,500 for the animals. During March the logistics of supply improved, so that every night two trains carrying 100 tonnes each of shells for the 75s arrived in the Verdun munitions depot; the repair materials were removed from Verdun for use elsewhere; and at the new station at Nixéville, just west of the Voie sacrée and south of Verdun, eight trains per day could be unloaded and sent on their way.

Great as this achievement was, it was inadequate to meet all the supply needs of the soldiers fighting at Verdun. Road transport was needed also. Second Army had seven groups of trucks already in the area. Five more groups were taken from First, Fifth and Seventh Armies, making a total of 3,900 vehicles organised into 175 'sections automobiles', served by 9,000 men (of whom 300 were officers). General Herr had already banned horse traffic from the Bar-le-Duc/Verdun road, and Pétain increased the regulations governing it. For example, any truck breaking down was simply pushed off the road immediately. The system was working so efficiently that by 22 March the road was carrying 600 trucks containing materiel and 800 trucks carrying men every day. Second Army built four transverse roads as well for all traffic connecting the Revigny–Sainte-Menehould railway into the Aire river valley. So gradually an entire network of supply routes was established to fill a semi-circular area south and south-west of Verdun itself.[31]

Fighting continued, of course, all the time that the above logistics were being put in place. For example, during March, 13 DI spent sixteen days (3rd–20th) in the sector Fleury-devant-Douaumont, holding an average length of front of 2.8 kilometres, of which only a small portion was lost to the enemy. The number of combattants involved during these sixteen days amounted to 13,150, of whom 2,489 manned the eighty gun batteries (twelve 75s per kilometre each day, and 4.8 heavies each kilometre per day). The casualties during these days spent in the front line were 7,324, more than half of those engaged and amounting to 38 per cent of 13 DI's total effectives and attached units.[32]

The fighting during March and April became a slogging match, with this change: the Germans decided to attack on the left (west) bank of the

Meuse in order to silence the French guns that had been firing into their flank on the east bank. The left bank was more open and rolling than the right, and its most important feature was the ridge running from the west to the river line on a level with Douaumont on the right bank. The high points along the ridge – Hill 304, and the two summits of the Mort-Homme at 265 and 295 metres – gave excellent observation over the whole battlefield. The ridge ran down to the Bois des Corbeaux and to the village of Cumières on the Meuse. South of the Mort-Homme ridge the forts in the Bois Bourrus had equally good observation across the river to Verdun and southwards towards the remaining ring of forts.

Repeated German attacks on the Mort-Homme and, on the right bank, on Vaux village during March were rewarded only by the capture of part of Vaux. On 9 April the Germans made another fierce attack on the slopes of the Mort-Homme. Savage back-and-forth fighting all day left the French line intact, although dented in places. It was that day's fighting that inspired Pétain's famous ordre du jour, ending 'Courage, on les aura!' Clearly the French were holding on and the German attacks had failed to reproduce the brilliant capture of Fort Douaumont that was so lauded in the German press. Casualties, however, were horrendous, and Pétain tried to ensure that men did not have to stay too long in the hell of the front lines. His chief of staff, Colonel de Barescut, told Castelnau at GQG that the French were 'suffering enormously' from the bombardment on the Vaux–Douaumont front: 'After five or six days at the front, there is such nervous depression that the slightest sign of the enemy makes the troops' courage fail.' Pétain established a 'noria' system, wheeling reserves forward and men back to rest areas, but the system was deemed to be 'selfish' at GQG, because it was 'eating up the whole army'.[33]

Joffre was becoming impatient, for Pétain's constant demands for troops were beginning to interfere with the preparations for the Somme. He urged Pétain to move onto the offensive to regain what had been lost on the left bank. The only way to stop the enemy was by using the fresh troops to counter-attack, rather than to resist passively, but Pétain would not allow himself to be overruled. When Joffre visted Verdun for himself on 12 April he was impressed by the aggressive attitude that General Robert Nivelle commanding III Corps encouraged. The corps had been in sector since 2 April and three days later had carried out its orders to recapture the ground west of Douaumont. After a week's fighting, one of its divisions, Mangin's 5 DI, had cleared La Caillette Wood and the approaches to Vaux and Souville. Joffre was delighted, as was President Poincaré when he visited the sector on 18 April.[34] Accordingly, Joffre took the opportunity offered by de Langle de Cary's 67th birthday to send him into retirement and to promote Pétain to replace him in

(a)   (b)

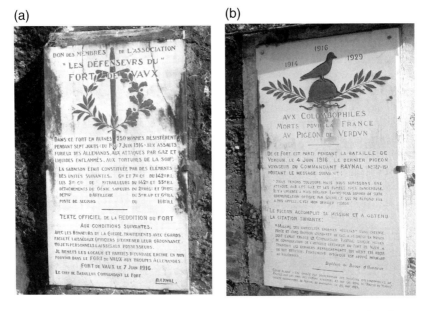

Fig. 9 (a) Monument to the defenders of Fort Vaux, surrendered
7 June 1916
(b) Monument at Fort Douaumont, Verdun, to the handlers and
their messenger pigeons used during the war

command of the Centre Army Group. General Nivelle became commander of Second Army. Pétain was very bitter and resentful; Nivelle
had only been a divisional general and corps commander since December 1915, and Pétain knew that his own so-called promotion meant that
he had been removed from the day-to-day command of Verdun, despite
having organised its defence so well. The change took effect on 1 May.

Falkenhayn had not yet done with the battle around Verdun. On the
left bank furious battles around the hill tops of the Mort-Homme led to
their changing hands several times, but by 24 May the Germans had
seized control of the observation points on Côte 304 and the Mort-
Homme. Von Gallwitz, who now commanded the sector, had used
new tactics, infiltrating around the back of the French defenders. On
the right bank, *Fifth Army* aimed for Fleury and Forts Vaux and Souville.
Possession of Souville would give the Germans a route towards the last
line of hills and forts guarding Verdun to the north. Mangin interrupted
the German preparations. Joffre wanted Douaumont recaptured to
match the enormous effect that its fall had caused and, although Nivelle
was cautious, Mangin was impatient. His 5 DI attack began well on 22

May, and some men even managed to get inside the fort. Yet the Germans were able to send in reinforcements from the north, while any French reinforcements could only reach the fort from the south over open ground. Mangin's attack failed. It proved the bloodiest action that his 5 DI saw during the whole course of the war. Casualties in the four regiments that took part amounted to 5,359, almost half of whom had been killed or had disappeared (many of them prisoners of war).[35] The artillery preparation had been insufficient.

Pétain did not remove himself from the day-to-day defence of Verdun, and he began a campaign to get the Somme offensive started earlier than planned in order to relieve the pressure. Already on 11 June, Joffre recorded Pétain's complaints about insufficient heavy artillery and his view that 'the British attack must be brought forward if we wish to save Verdun'. Even earlier, Pétain had written to Foch, who was coordinating the Franco-British preparations on the Somme, asking him not to press GQG for effectives because they were needed so badly in Verdun. GQG was using the Somme as an excuse not to give him (Pétain) the reserves he was requesting, and Foch would 'do a great service for the common cause' if he did not press GQG.[36] Pétain's campaign failed, but finally the start of the Somme on 1 July did relieve the pressure, and Falkenhayn's last offensive was on 12 July against Souville.

In September an incident that had been waiting to happen finally occurred. The railway line from Verdun to Etain passed through a tunnel to the north-east of Verdun beneath the Meuse heights. Etain was in German hands, and so the railway was not running, but it was important to deny the tunnel's use to the enemy, since it opened on the side nearer Verdun only about 10 kilometres distant from the citadel itself. Moreover, the 1.5 kilometre-long Tavannes tunnel provided a safe refuge from shelling. Consequently it was used to store equipment such as grenades, and as a first-aid post and command-post. Units were 'rested' there between turns of duty in the trenches. Captain Delvert describes the horror of the filth and smells that those inside had to endure.[37] Somehow a batch of rockets that arrived in the tunnel on 4 September caught fire, and the fire set off a store of grenades which in turn ignited the petrol in the lighting generator. The fire raged for three days and killed more than 500 men, including Colonel Florentin, the commander of 146 Brigade, and his staff.[38] Those fortunate enough to be near the western exit managed to escape, but those near the eastern exit were shelled by the enemy as soon as they emerged.

Joffre was determined to end the year with another offensive as he believed that the enemy army was incapable of withstanding both the battering on the Somme and a second attack elsewhere. Since all the heavy artillery not on the Somme was at Verdun, and it had become impossible to shift any of it because of the state of the ground, then any second attack would have to be around Verdun again. On 13 September Joffre arrived there with his instructions. A methodical artillery plan was drawn up under Second Army's commander of artillery, and the counter-battery programme began on 3 October, although the actual firing only began on 21 October. The accuracy of the shelling was demonstrated on 23 October when a violent explosion inside Fort Vaux was heard, and a fierce fire began in Fort Douaumont. That night the infantry in Mangin's group of divisions moved into position and set off in thick fog the next morning. By mid-afternoon the Moroccan regiment of 38 DI was on top of Fort Douaumont, and the tiny German garrison, all that was left after the Germans abandoned the burning fort, was captured. Joffre was leaving nothing to chance. He had gone to Nivelle's headquarters to follow the battle, and had told Mangin that morning to act audaciously and to seize the moment. However, at Centre Army Group headquarters, Pétain also kept a close eye on Verdun. He told Mangin that afternoon to consolidate his position at Douaumont and only to continue the offensive against Fort Vaux. Joffre overrode Pétain. He rang Mangin personally to order him to exploit the success as far as possible, using all possible divisions, however contrary to Pétain's 'timorous' orders such action might be.[39] Mangin obeyed his CinC and pushed his troops to a point a kilometre beyond their preliminary objective. The fighting continued the next day but, as always, the terrain made further progress very difficult. In addition the supply of munitions was faltering. By 2 November, however, the constant French shelling had driven the Germans from Fort Vaux and it was back in French hands, together with 6,000 German prisoners.[40]

This victory gave back to the French the defensive circle around Verdun itself, and Nivelle and Mangin planned yet another offensive to take advantage of what they perceived as German weakness. Although GQG staff were unwilling to risk the credit for the morale boost that the recapture of the two forts had provided, Joffre and Castelnau overrode them and approved the Verdun generals' plan for a new operation. Joffre had managed to negotiate Romania's entry into the war in August, and he wanted to show that fighting continued in France; also he wished to be able to counter with a victory the peace offer that was about to appear from the Central Powers. Once again, therefore, he visited Mangin and his divisional generals to ensure that the delays imposed by the weather did not cause cancellation, and he allocated the two further supplementary groups of heavy guns that Nivelle had requested. And, once again, Joffre overrode Pétain's instruction to withdraw the reconnaissance groups following the attack, and he ordered Mangin to leave them in place.[41] Delayed from 12 December, Mangin's attack went in finally on 15 December at ten in the morning. Eight divisions, supported by 800 guns, overran the entire zone covering the forts, recovering in under two days ground that had been lost the previous February. The five mediocre German divisions holding the sector lost 11,000 men as prisoners and a large amount of materiel. Henceforth the citadel of Verdun was safe, and the nightmare was over. Mangin's order of the day to his victorious troops was a response to the German peace note which had been published on 12 December: 'La France a répondu par la gueule de vos canons et la pointe de vos baïonettes ... Vous avez été les bons ambassadeurs de la République: elle vous en remercie.'

Verdun became the quintessential battle of the war for the French Army, partly because it lasted so long and partly because it was solely French. If Verdun was not France's 'moral boulevard' that it became later, nevertheless it has persisted in popular memory as the acme of horror and futility, and its memorial – the ossuary of Douaumont – is the principal *lieu de mémoire* of the war. Pétain ensured that Verdun would maintain its and his reputation, by presiding over many of the post-war commemorations there.

Somme

Unlike Pétain, who focused solely on events around Verdun, Joffre had to consider other fronts. He was determined to carry out the plans that had been settled with the Allies at the end of the previous year. A week before the German assault at Verdun he had agreed with Haig that the year's campaign in France would consist of a joint Franco-British attack in Picardy, to begin around 1 July on both sides of the Somme river. Joffre had no intention of allowing the enemy's assault at Verdun to derail that plan.

It had already been agreed that British troops would relieve Tenth Army in preparation for the Somme operation, and because of Verdun Joffre requested that the relief be expedited. He wrote to the Chief of the Imperial General Staff, General Sir William Robertson, in London also, asking that as many British troops as possible be sent to France, especially those currently in Egypt. Despite Haig's claims that his own intelligence suggested an enemy attack in the north, and corresponding offer to mount an attack in the north as the best way of relieving the pressure at Verdun, Joffre maintained his view that an accelerated relief of Tenth Army to allow it some rest before being sent to eastern France as reserves or reinforcements was the best help. The relief was completed by 14 March, with the new British Fourth Army, under the

(a)

(b)

(c)

Fig. 10 Louvemont, north of Verdun, before the war and today
(a) Postcard showing the mairie and the church before the war
(b) The site of the mairie
(c) One of the two tombstones that are all that remain of the church.
A chapel was rebuilt in 1932 on the site

orders of General Sir Henry Rawlinson, in line between the former Tenth Army sector (now held by the British Third Army) and the Somme.

The Chantilly agreement of December 1915 had specified that an early enemy attack against any one of the Allies would trigger an allied reponse to assist the attacked nation 'as far as resources permitted'. Accordingly, Joffre asked Cadorna in Italy whether he could mount an operation to retain the Austro-Hungarians on his front; Cadorna replied that he could do nothing before the end of May for lack of munitions. Joffre also asked Sarrail about the Salonika Front, but Sarrail, too, cited the end of May as the earliest he could launch anything more than limited local actions, as he was waiting for the Serbian troops to return from Corfu. Joffre wanted Sarrail to act politically as well so as to detach Turkey and Bulgaria, if possible, and to persuade Romania and Greece to join the Entente. With this in mind, Joffre asked the Russian CinC about sending an army to the Balkans to help in persuading the neutrals, but Alexieff seemed convinced that the Germans would make a surprise attack on his forces earlier in the year than 1 July, the agreed date for the coordinated Allied offensives. Accordingly he was planning to forestall any such enemy attack in the north, where the melting of the ice in the Riga area might permit it, and could not detach troops towards Romania and the Balkans. So this left only the British, and Joffre reiterated his request to Robertson that troops be sent from Egypt and/or Britain. On 8 March he reminded Robertson somewhat sharply that 'in this critical phase [of the war] France is entitled to expect its allies not to quibble, any more than France does, over the necessary sacrifices'. After all, with the Royal Navy ruling the waves, there was little risk in conveying British troops from Egypt to France.

At a military conference in Chantilly on 12 and 13 March, including all the Allies, the principle of coordinated attacks by all was reiterated.[42] Russia would begin the series around 15 May, with the other Allies following a fortnight later. The reconstituted Serbian troops were to be despatched to Salonika as soon as possible, and the Franco-British troops of the Army of the Orient, together with the Italians in Albania, were to keep the enemy under threat of imminent attack. Finally the blockade of the Central Powers was to be tightened as much as possible. To Robertson's question as to whether the Allies would have sufficient munitions for the coordinated offensives, Joffre replied that French production was enough to maintain their stocks despite the expenditures at Verdun. What he did not say was that, although stocks were not diminishing, neither were they increasing.[43]

As Joffre worked diplomatically to maintain the Allied strategy despite Verdun, Foch, who had not been present at the Chantilly conference, was obliged to amend his plans because of Verdun. His original plan envisaged thirty-nine French divisions taking part in the Somme campaign, but he could see that Verdun was using up resources both human and material to such an extent that his plans might be compromised.[44] He intended to capture Roye and then to cross the river Somme south of Péronne, while his left flank north of the river supported the British. On 16 March he submitted his highly detailed plan to GQG, which approved it a week later.

Foch also prepared an equally detailed set of directives for his subordinates.[45] He insisted on methodical destruction by the artillery of the enemy's successive defensive positions. Once the first such position had been taken, speed was essential, and the artillery was to be moved up quickly in order to begin its destruction of the second defensive position. Specific tasks were allocated to the various types of guns, and the number of shells required to complete that task were calculated. For example, in order to make a breach 20–25 metres wide to a depth of 25 metres in a belt of barbed wire, a battery of field artillery (that is, four 75s) had to fire from a distance of 2.5 kilometres about 600 explosive shells, more if the distance were greater. In addition, Foch sent his director of aviation to Verdun to learn from the fighting there. As a result, each of the three French armies involved in the Somme fighting received its own fighter group to protect its observer aircraft and balloons. A liaison system between the aircraft and infantry on the ground was worked out; arrangements were made to ensure that the results of photographic reconnaissance reached the artillery and infantry as quickly as possible.

As Foch feared, this detailed planning was disrupted. On 26 April Joffre wrote to him that he did not intend to invoke the *casus foederis* by asking his Allied partners to attack earlier than planned, but he was forced to reduce the resources to be allocated for the Somme campaign. Instead of thirty-nine divisions, Joffre could allow only thirty; instead of 1,700 heavy guns, Joffre could now allow 312 only. So Foch reduced the scope of his plan because he knew that he no longer had the resources to mount an attack on a front wide enough to bring a strategic result. On 22 May his resources diminished still further. Now he could count on only twenty-two divisions and 540 guns, only a fifth of which were of the most useful calibre, the short 155s. Instead of three armies aiming to cross the Somme south of Péronne, now Foch had only one, Sixth Army. He wrote to its commander, General Emile Fayolle, on 25 May to say that its main task was now to support the British action north of the Somme. Verdun had caused the downgrading of Foch's Northern Army Group from the principal to a support role.

Joffre explained his reduced plan on 21 June. The joint attack should aim to rupture the German front lines and reach the enemy's

communications hub around Maubeuge–Cambrai. The Bapaume–
Cambrai road marked the axis of progression towards the north-east,
with the British operating north of the road and the French south of it.
The French armies would have fulfilled the objective of breaking through
the enemy front if they had reached the road running south from
Bapaume, through Péronne, to Ham (see Map 10).

Foch had never wanted to attack on the Somme. He could see no
strategic territory to be won in the area, but he had worked hard to
produce the detailed plan required by his CinC. If the renewed German
attacks at Verdun had now reduced his operation to a simple support
role, he could see even less profit to be gained from the forthcoming
battle. He said so in conference on 31 May with his CinC, his premier,
the President of the Republic and Haig. However, Joffre had no intention
of renouncing his strategy, and Haig took the opportunity offered by his
army's elevation to principal role to expand his strategic horizons. Yet
events at Verdun during the month of June, as the Germans realised that
something was being prepared in Picardy, meant that Foch and Sixth
Army would have to do something. Political pressure was mounting too,
with complaints aired in the Army Commissions about the high command and about Verdun's defences, and a secret session of the Chamber
of Deputies lasted from 16 to 22 June.

In his planning Foch paid great attention to the lessons from the
Verdun fighting. He emphasised infantry tactics, the role of the artillery
and aviation. His instructions issued on 20 June and distributed down
to battalion level insisted that the infantry must be used economically.
The tactic of sending successive waves of infantry to break all resistance
by brute force must be abandoned, Foch wrote. In a modern battle, the
infantry had to be prepared to endure for a long time – Verdun had
been raging for four months already. It was vitally important, he concluded, 'only to ask [the infantry] to carry out tasks of which it [was]
capable, to exert close and methodical control'. This meant that the
infantry should be asked to occupy ground only where the artillery had
destroyed the enemy defences completely; the occupation should be
carried out only after careful reconnaissance to verify that the enemy's
defences were indeed destroyed, and 'under the constant protection of
the guns'.[46] These instructions reflected exactly the German infantry
tactics in February at Verdun: artillery destruction of French defences,
reconnaissance by officers to check the state of those defences before
the main infantry attack, and finally occupation of the ground gained by
the infantry.

The key to such infantry tactics was, in other words, the artillery. In
addition to its field artillery, Sixth Army had 528 heavy guns on 1 July,

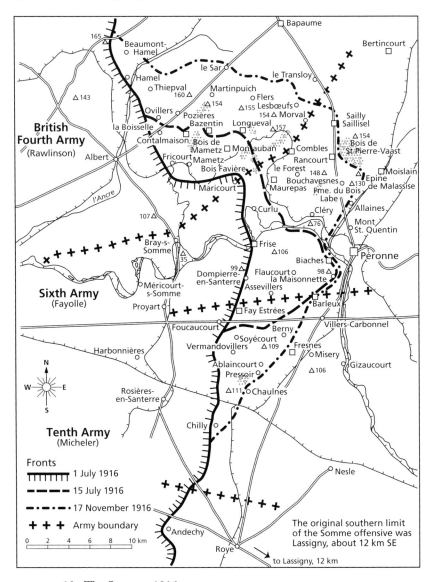

10. The Somme, 1916

more than Joffre had said earlier would be available, making a density of
one gun for every 28 metres of front. Foch allocated the heavies to the
task of counter-battery, that is the suppression of the enemy's guns. He
ordered battery commanders to check that the specific task set for their

guns had been carried out successfully. Verdun had reduced the allocation of shells for the Somme, particulary the most useful 155mm types,
and the French could not be as extravagant as the Germans had been on
21 February. Nonetheless Sixth Army outgunned the Germans on the
Somme on 1 July, the latter possessing only 184 guns of a calibre greater
than 100mm on that day.

Foch's third lesson from Verdun concerned aviation. The complete
German air superiority over the RFV in February was reversed over the
Somme. Foch's Northern Army Group had 113 fighter aircraft and three
groups of bombers (about seventy aircraft) and he paid particular attention to liaison with General Sir Hugh Trenchard, the commander of the
British Royal Flying Corps. Aircraft were to carry out reconnaissance for
the troops on the ground, observation of the fall of shell for the artillery,
and were to bomb enemy railway stations, airfields and troop assembly
areas. Foch improved the aerial reconnaissance and photographic
services.

Verdun had also proved the crucial importance of logistics. The road
network in the Somme area was poor, especially for XX Corps north of
the river. The fact that XX Corps had only started to arrive from Verdun
on 3 June and the construction of the 60cm gauge railway for bringing up
supplies was incomplete caused Fayolle's request for a postponement of
the start of the infantry attack – a delay that Haig refused to countenance
because the artillery preparation was already under way. French engineers built over 272 kilometres of railway lines, and improved the
Somme's lateral canal as a means of evacuating casualties. Road traffic
was strictly controlled, to ensure no interruptions to the flow: a lorry
every four to ten seconds along the main artery enabled 2,600 lorry-loads
to be delivered daily.[47]

At 7.30am on 1 July, at the same time as the British, XX Corps began
its assault of the German positions in the narrow sector north of the river
and in two days of fighting overran the whole first position defences at a
cost of about 800 casualties. South of the river, I Colonial Corps too
overran the German first position and by nightfall on the first day was
poised ready to attack the second position. The southernmost corps
suffered more casualties because of its place on the flank of the operation,
but like its neighbour, XXXV Corps took all its objectives in the German
front line. The opening moves were a huge success, and Joffre was
delighted.

Exploitation of this initial success proved more difficult. Joffre's attempt
to bully Haig into continuing the offensive along the whole of his front,
despite his heavy losses on 1 July, simply made the latter dig in his heels.
North of the river XX Corps was obliged to mark time until the British

troops came up in line after completing the capture of the German front position. South of the river, where the initial success had been greater than planned and German defences were weaker, there was some resentment that an opportunity for a breakthrough was being allowed to pass. For example, the cavalry of I Colonial Corps had occupied the village of Barleux, which lay beyond its objectives, but was pulled out again because of the instruction that artillery preparation had to be carried out before further infantry assaults. Furthermore, the skeleton Tenth Army was available south of the Somme, under the command of General Alfred Micheler, and the position at Verdun had eased sufficiently for Joffre to be able to send another infantry corps and a substantial reinforcement of heavy artillery. At GQG Castelnau pushed for exploitation south of the river towards Noyon, the German-occupied town closest to Paris, leaving the British to muddle along on their own (as Joffre put it) north of the river. However, neither Foch nor Fayolle was convinced of the value of such a move, for it would require moving guns and supplies and embarking on another artillery preparation. Nevertheless, I Colonial Corps continued operations for the rest of the month, suffering nearly 8,000 casualties between 15 and 21 July.[48]

What remained, therefore, was waiting for the British to catch up. It proved extremely difficult to coordinate operations so that French and British units could offer each other mutual support. If the French were ready, the British needed time to complete a relief; if the British were ready, the French failed to fire agreed barrages. Local operations, uncoordinated both among themselves and with their ally, combined with dreadful weather, removed effective control of the battle from the British and French army commanders. Complaints about the British amateurs became more frequent.

Joffre became exasperated with the lack of progress. He called Foch in to his headquarters on 31 July and insisted that only broad front and joint operations could gain success that would encourage the Italians, the Russians and, most importantly, the Romanians, whose entry to the war on the Entente side he was negotiating. When Foch returned to the north he informed Fayolle and Micheler that their role was to support the British attacks north of the river; the idea of exploitation to the south was to be abandoned. Consequently, sectors were adjusted so that Fayolle commanded only the Sixth Army units north of the river (VII, I (new), XX Corps and I Colonial Corps), while Tenth Army took over command of II and XXXV Corps, in addition to its own units, to the south. The density of Sixth Army's heavy artillery now amounted to one battery for every kilometre.[49] The easing of pressure at Verdun had allowed Joffre to devote more resources to the Somme.

Joffre's exasperation increased as the broad front joint operation that he wanted failed to materialise during August. Micheler had endless reasons to explain his lack of readiness; Sixth Army was bogged down; the British persisted in mounting small-scale local offensives in order to obtain a jumping-off point for the next big push. Haig refused to bring forward the date of this; he was waiting for the tanks. Joffre sent a carefully composed letter to Haig on 11 August, urging a return to simultaneous coordinated attacks and an end to small-scale local actions. He followed this with a sharper reminder on 25 August: it was 'incumbent' on the British to do their part in the joint endeavour after France had been suffering for six months in Verdun. He was eager to increase the effect of Romania's declaration of war (on Austria-Hungary on 27 August) and to prevent the transfer of German troops to Verdun or to Russia where Brusilov's offensive had stalled. Joffre intervened personally in conference on 27 August with Haig, Foch, Roques (the new war minister) and Poincaré, when Haig insisted he could not be ready before 15 September. That would be too late, Joffre exclaimed, because the French Army was bleeding to death. Joffre was not exaggerating. The army began to use the new 1917 class in October, and the 1918 class would be called up in April 1917; the reduction to three instead of four infantry regiments per division was proceeding. Also the war minister warned that French artillery production could not keep up with the army's demands.

Joffre had agreed to mount an offensive in the west at the same time as Romania's opening operations as a quid pro quo for the latter attacking Bulgarian forces rather than concentrating solely on the Austro-Hungarians in Transylvania. In the event the weather on the Somme caused a delay. What should have been a coordinated effort became a series of offensives spread over ten days, with Tenth Army attacking on the 4th and 5th, Sixth Army on the 12th and 13th and the British on 15 September. All the same, Tenth Army's artillery preparation, which began on 28 August, matched the Romanian advance into Transylvania. Ten infantry divisions of Tenth Army launched their assault south of the Somme at 14.00 on 4 September. The right-hand corps (X Corps under General Anthoine) reached its objectives very easily, except for the sector around Chaulnes. The divisions of XXXV Corps managed to gain some ground and took Soyécourt, but II Corps' divisions were thrown out of the German first and second positions that they had managed to capture. Little was achieved on subsequent days. Foch insisted that Micheler stop allowing small-scale local attacks, and finally, by 18 September, the remaining German strongholds in the southernmost sector of the battle-field were in French hands: Deniécourt and Vermandonvillers. German defensive tactics had improved immensely. Trench lines were abandoned in favour of shell holes which were much more difficult for the artillery to suppress. Furthermore, the new German high command of Hindenburg and Ludendorff had put an end to Falkenhayn's order to retake any lost ground at any cost. Falkenhayn had lost his position because his strategy at Verdun had failed and because Romania had been tempted to join the Entente. Consequently there was some very hard fighting before the French gains were consolidated.

North of the river Sixth Army aimed to strike due east so as to establish a strong defensive position flanked by the steep-sided Tortille stream, and then to turn northwards in conjunction with the British right flank. The first phase began on 3 September and was completed with the capture of Bouchavesnes on 12 September. Once again the German resistance was fierce and a five-day artillery battle was needed to overcome it. Relations between Fayolle and Foch became so strained that Fayolle threatened to resign. The capture of Bouchavesnes had been so costly, Fayolle stated, that he could not support the British attack that was due to begin on the 15th, by making the planned advance northwards towards Rancourt and Sailly-Saillisel, but Foch insisted. Although a few British tanks managed to get forward on the 15th, for Fayolle his troops had suffered 'useless casualties' and the day was wasted.

Nonetheless, the day was not wasted for General Estienne, France's 'father' of the tank. Although he and others deprecated the new weapon's premature use – a report of the Deputies' Army Commission stated merely that 'some village or other' had been captured – a field trial was necessary and Estienne was not slow to learn from the British experience. Reports from the head of the French Military Mission at GHQ and the French artillery liaison officer with Fourth Army soon arrived at GQG. Joffre met Estienne on 17 September and asked the armaments minister, Albert Thomas, for modifications to the French design. The reports had emphasised the tanks' vulnerability and the heat and noise that the crews had to suffer, yet also provided information about the armour-plating, the chassis, the driving gear and much else. As a result, the planned 120mm gun for the French tanks was replaced by the less powerful but more rapid-firing 75mm, since it was judged that speed was more important than firepower. In addition, Joffre asked the ministry to develop a rapid-firing or automatic 37mm gun capable of piercing armour at 1,000 metres.[50]

Despite Franco-British agreement that the campaign would continue into October and beyond, the weather took charge. Neither Fayolle nor Micheler was enthusiastic, but on 10 October, south of the river, Tenth Army began an assault on Chaulnes and then Ablaincourt and Pressoire (the site of the present-day TGV station). Battling torrential rain and fierce German counter-attacks, Tenth Army managed to hold on to their gains and the villages remained in French hands. North of the river, Sixth Army should have attacked in conjunction with Rawlinson's Fourth Army with the aim of moving north towards Sailly up the Bapaume–Péronne–Ham road (the Somme battle's objective back on 1 July). The British pulled out of the infantry operation but, with British artillery help, Sixth Army began the attack on 5 November and completed the capture of Sailly on the 12th. The Germans still held the St Pierre Waast Wood in strength, however, and prevented any further progress. So ended the Somme campaign, and Sixth Army was gradually relieved from the front line by the British extension of their own front. The huge necropolis at Rancourt, just south of St Pierre Waast Wood is proof of the price the French Army paid for the Bapaume–Péronne–Ham road.

The French Army had made an enormous effort in 1916. Although trapped at Verdun, the longest battle of the war, Joffre maintained his inter-allied plan of campaign. Indeed, August 1916 was the most 'allied' month of the war as the Russians, Italians and Romanians were all engaged in fighting as well the British and French. Joffre insisted that the Somme campaign go ahead, and by the end the French had contributed similar resources to the British. Two French armies (Sixth and Tenth, matching British Fourth and Fifth), forty-four infantry divisions in fourteen army corps (matching Britain's fifty-three divisions in eleven corps). French casualties were some 202,000, less than half those of the British, for more than half the total territorial gains made.

Exterior theatres

The French memorandum placed before the conference that decided the Allied campaign for 1916 spoke of disrupting Germany's imperial ambitions in the east as well as defeating the German and Austro-Hungarian armies. While acknowledging the defeat of the Dardanelles expedition and of the Serbian Army, Joffre claimed that on the Salonika Front it was possible to achieve something. The Allies had to be able to take advantage of any change in the Balkan situation and also to keep up the pressure on Greece. Furthermore, the Allied presence in Salonika would encourage Romania to resist German pressure, and Allied action might support any Russian operation against Bulgaria, while Serbian forces were still being evacuated from the Albanian coast. It would be dangerous to permit German submarines to use Salonika. These arguments prevailed and, despite British opposition, the Anglo-French force in Salonika was maintained in place and the base there put into a good state of defence.[51] Falkenhayn was quite happy to have the five British and four French divisions 'interned' there after his aim of chasing the Serbian Army out of Serbia had been achieved, and the Austrians had forced the capitulation of Montenegro in January 1916, after completing their invasion of the kingdom.

As the remnants of the Serbian Army reached the Adriatic coast, they were embarked, originally, for Bizerta in Tunisia, but the destination was changed for the Greek island of Corfu. Although this was an infringement of Greek neutrality, taking over the island would eliminate a German spying operation there. Also, Corfu was much nearer than Tunisia, hence the shipping requirements were less, and there was plenty of space for the French mission under General de Mondésir to reconstitute the Serbian Army, whose soldiers arrived ill and exhausted by their trek through the mountains to reach the coast. The first 2,000 arrived on Corfu on 28 January, followed by a daily average of between 4,000 and 5,000, until by 23 February, when most had arrived, there were over 133,000 men on the island. French medical personnel manned four hospitals, but there were still 3,681 deaths, mainly from pulmonary infections, during that month. It was agreed that the French would administer the base, and supply all the arms and munitions needed, and the British would help with clothing and food supplies.[52]

Joffre intended to reconstitute six twelve-battalion divisions, each armed with twenty-four machine guns, a group of 75s and two groups of mountain guns. Once reformed, the Serb divisions would be sent to Salonika to join the forces there and be deployed for training on the Khalkidiki peninsula. Between mid April and the end of May, the transfer of 135,000 Serbian soldiers to Greece was complete. They had received the new model Lebel rifle whilst on Corfu, and the horses and guns had been sent on ahead directly to Salonika. On arrival the Serbian divisions plus a Montenegrin detachment were formed into three armies, and on 17 July 1916 the first units began moving towards the front line facing Monastir (see Map 14, page 346). This was a great achievement for the French Army, collecting exhausted troops in winter and refitting and then redeploying them the following summer – especially given the events in France at the time.

As all this was happening, the German attack on Verdun prompted Joffre to order Sarrail to prepare action to tie down the German divisions in the Balkans. Sarrail produced a plan on 7 March for a major offensive by twenty-one Allied divisions, which he did not have. The recompleted Serbian divisions had not yet all arrived, and Robertson was adamant that he would send no more British. Joffre accepted that Sarrail should merely make a pretence of attacking along the Greek–Serb–Bulgarian border, so as to prevent German divisions returning to the west. With the British concentrating on preparing the Somme offensive and despite Briand's urging action in the Balkans – pressure which Joffre could not resist because of the criticism he was receiving over events at Verdun – Sarrail did little during the summer months. Then the situation changed as Romania finally agreed to join the Allies. As a condition of Romania's agreement, the Allies promised that Sarrail's Army would attack on 20 August in order to prevent Bulgarian forces from interfering with the Romanian mobilisation. In addition to the French and British divisions, Sarrail now had six Serbian and one Italian divisions, plus a Russian brigade. Joffre decided that the French in such a disparate force required a separate CinC. Accordingly, he made Sarrail the Allied CinC and appointed General Cordonnier to command the French portion of the Army of the Orient.

Far from tying down German or even Bulgarian divisions, Sarrail's army was surprised by a preemptive Bulgarian attack that began on 17 August. It overwhelmed the Serbian forces and forced the French to retire to the right bank of the river Struma. Allied counter-attacks managed to halt and to reverse the Bulgarian advance, but the Bulgarians had constructed a powerful defensive line along the Greek–Serbian frontier and across the Florina–Monastir valley. They retired behind the barbed wire and trenches of this position on 3 October. After Sarrail ordered attacks on this line to begin again, the Serbs advanced in the bend of the river Crna, as the French 17 DIC, supported by a mass of heavy artillery made a frontal attack. Beginning on 30 October, the Serbs outflanked Monastir on the east and on 19 November a Russian–French force entered the town. Blizzards put an end to any further operations. Finally, 1916 could end on a tactical success, and Sarrail's position was strengthened. This meant that the report on Sarrail and the Armée d'Orient presented by the war minister, General Roques, after visiting Salonika, was favourable. All had expected (and Joffre had hoped for) a report critical of Sarrail's dabbling in Greek politics instead of waging successful campaigns. The political situation in Greece remained complicated, however, with

Eleutherios Venizelos setting up a provisional government in Salonika favourable to the Allies, but leaving the Germanophile King Constantine on his throne.

The Romanian mobilisation, which Joffre had worked hard to combine with offensives in France and out of Salonika, did not lead to any great success.[53] As early as January 1916 the French government had sought to increase French influence by upgrading their mission in Bucharest, but Romania had resisted so as not to provoke the Central Powers. After war was declared, however, Romania requested twenty French officers to serve as 'monitors' in the Romanian Army. Joffre selected his former aide major-général, Henri Berthelot, to head the mission, after the original choice of de Langle de Cary was rejected by the French Minister, Charles de Saint Aulaire. The minister argued for an intelligent and experienced general, with tact and flexibility as well as energy, and in particular he should bear no taint of disgrace such as hung around Sarrail. Berthelot was ordered to GQG on 20 September to learn of his new appointment, just as he was in the process of moving with his XXXII Corps to the Somme, after being relieved at Verdun in mid June.

Romania's advance against Austria was blocked. Falkenhayn had arrived in the region after being removed from OHL, and he drove the Romanian army back across the frontier, inflicting heavy casualties. Meanwhile Mackensen attacked the area around the mouth of the Danube with a mixed Bulgarian-German-Turkish force and occupied Constanza, Romania's Black Sea port. By 11 November Falkenhayn was through the Transylvanian passes and Mackensen was across the Danube. Romania's capital Bucharest fell on 6 December and the country capitulated.

Berthelot had arrived in Iaşi on 15 October, and he presented an outline strategy to stabilise Romania's defences, but Falkenhayn's invasion on 11 November completed the destruction of Romania's armies. As well as entering the capital, the Central Powers occupied two-thirds of the national territory. Berthelot had remained confident and determined, as he had during the weeks before the Marne in 1914, but Romania's position at the end of 1916 resembled that of Serbia at the end of the previous year. Just as France had helped to reconstitute and re-equip the Serbian Army, so now France sent large quantities of materiel and increased the French mission to almost 400 officers and 1,000 men. By the beginning of December France had supplied some 75s (74, with another 102 under consideration) and 120 of the old 120L heavy guns. France could supply many more of these, instead of the more modern 105s that Romania had asked for, but could not supply any of the

373 howitzers also requested. Joffre asked Britain to supply these.[54] The sudden and severe Romanian defeat had placed another military burden on France. Moreover, it had repercussions on public opinion and in parliament.[55]

One final commitment for the French Army during the course of 1916 should be mentioned. This involved the colonies. A decree of 9 October 1915 had declared all indigenous men aged 18 and above were 'mobilisable'.[56] Conscription had been extended to the long-established 'Four Communes' of Senegal also in 1915,[57] and in Algeria two decrees in September 1916 generalised conscription there for indigenous French citizens. European settlers of Algeria were already covered by the 1905 conscription law, and the 5,000 conscripts of the 1916 class had already been incorporated. The new decrees raised another 25,000 from the early call-up of the 1917 class and some 12,000 volunteers (mainly indigenous) brought Algeria's 1916 contribution to the fighting to 43,000 men. In AOF, which had supplied 60,000 natives in 1915, another 50,000 were levied in 1916. Recruitment was extended to Madagascar and to New Caledonia, where formerly only French citizens of European origin had been conscripted; now recruitment was extended to the Kanak and Melanesian populations.[58] A battalion of tirailleurs du Pacifique, made up of Kanaks, left on 3 December 1916 for France. Mobilisation had been proclaimed in Indo-China on 1 April 1915, and almost 43,000 Indo-Chinese, mainly from Tonkin, fought in the trenches during 1916. These further demands on the colonies met with opposition, and revolts broke out. News of the dreadful conditions in the trenches and accounts from the wounded had filtered back home, despite attempts to keep such news from spreading alarm.

The most serious of these revolts against conscription broke out in September 1916 in the Batna area in eastern Algeria, where young men escaping from the draft were living by banditry. It took the equivalent of almost a division to suppress the trouble, but the units returned from France for the purpose were mostly tirailleurs and zouaves who could not cope with the winter conditions on the mainland. With the insurgents burning farms and sabotaging stations and railways, and the military punishing by burning villages and stealing cattle, even General Moinier in command of the force complained about methods; a debate in the Chamber of Deputies in December 1916 made much of the brutality of the repression.[59]

In addition to putting down revolts about conscription, France also had to deal with the Senussi, a puritan Islamic sect based in the Libyan desert. Germany made strong attempts to encourage the Turks and the majority Muslim African subjects of the Ottoman Empire to carry out a jihad against the two colonial powers in Africa, France and Britain. This took the form of bribing the native North African tribes to rise against their colonisers.[60] The Italians in Tripolitania were obliged to keep 30,000 men there throughout the whole war to hold onto their province that they had wrested from the Ottomans in the Italo-Turk war of 1911–12. The British too were attacked in Egypt in combination with the Turkish attack on the Suez Canal in early 1916. Then the French had to respond to attacks on the southern frontier with Tunisia in September 1915, and in the south of Algeria from March 1916 onwards – in Ouadai May–July and in Air in December.[61]

The Italians had abandoned Ghadames (near the Algerian–Tunisian– Libyan border) and Ghat (400 kilometres further south) at the end of 1914, and this exposed Tunisia's southern border to further Senussi incursions, especially as many French officers had been recalled to France. General Moinier, commanding the Army of North Africa, was obliged to reinforce the border posts and to act aggressively to repress any rebellion. He was even obliged in October 1915 to ask the war minister to return an Algerian brigade from France. The fifteen brigades supported by eight cavalry squadrons, twenty-seven artillery pieces and seven machine-gun sections managed to keep the peace over the winter 1915/16 and to deal with the several cattle raids made during 1916. However, the south of Tunisia absorbed in mid May 1916 284 officers, 12,400 men, and, by the end of the year, two squadrons of aircraft that could well have been used in France.[62]

More worrying than southern Tunisia was the southern region of Algeria, near the Sahara. On 6 March 1916 the French outpost at Djanet was attacked by a 'harka' of 500 men. They captured the post on the 24th and beat off a relieving force. General Moinier sent Lieutenant-Colonel Meynier to secure France's territory, but Meynier was ambitious (or foolhardy) and was determined to press on to Ghat in Tripolitania (abandoned by the Italians) after repossessing Djanet. With 500 men, a section of artillery and a machine-gun company, Meynier managed at the second attempt on 16 May to recapture Djanet, but the rebels escaped with their booty to Ghat.

Under strict orders not to proceed to Ghat and at the end of a supply route of 1,200 kilometres, Meynier's force attempted, nonetheless, to flush out the fighters. Naturally, the Touaregs (at the instigation of the Senussi) took the opportunity to raid the French line of communications. Meynier's column was recalled on 1 July and Djanet evacuated again on 13 July, just as the Battle of the Somme was beginning. So the reoccupation of Djanet did not last long, and the supply lines linking the network of outposts came under repeated attack.

On 12 January 1917 a temporary command of the Saharan territories was created under General Laperrine in an attempt to control the situation.[63] In the west of North Africa, in Morocco, General Hubert Lyautey had just been recalled to France as war minister.

Results of the 1916 campaign

The fighting in France during 1916 had taught the French Army some important lessons. Verdun had shown that the adage that attackers suffered many more casualties than defenders was false. In addition, on the Somme the French had attacked with many fewer losses than the British alongside. Indeed, out of the ten months of fighting at Verdun, only two *monthly* casualty figures exceeded the figure for British casualties on a single day, 1 July, on the Somme. Verdun's final total was so huge solely because of the length of the battle, and the French inflicted almost as many casualties on the Germans as they suffered themselves. French casualty statistics for 1916 as a whole were not as awful as those of the previous year, when repeated attacks in Artois and Champagne and eastern France proved so fruitless. Both Verdun and the Somme had proved that breakthrough into open country was no longer possible. At Verdun the headline-catching exploits of the enemy in the first four days were never repeated, and the 'mill on the Meuse' ground down *Fifth Army* inexorably. On the Somme, Foch's more sensible method of making the advance a step at a time, each step prepared by artillery and checked for efficacy, proved better than Joffre's and Haig's intention to break right through the German defensive positions and to bring in the cavalry to exploit the breach.

Lessons learned at Verdun were applied on the Somme. German air superiority at Verdun was countered by the second half of the year, when the Allies took back that superiority. General Estienne took important lessons from the British deployment of their tanks in September, helped by the careful reports sent by the head of the French Military Mission to the British Army. Foch was impressed by the new weapon, and realised that tanks were the best way to counter the German tactic of placing machine guns in shell holes rather than in an organised defensive line. Captured German documents were collected, translated rapidly and distributed to all concerned. Thus Sixth Army's observations on the new elastic German defence tactics were passed on, and improvements made to French flamethrowers after comparison with a better German one.[64] Unfortunately not all 'lessons' proved useful. Nivelle thought that his heavy artillery concentration that had enabled him to recapture Fort

Douaumont in October could be replicated on a bigger scale, yet his claim to have found the right method for victory in 1917 proved untenable.

Air superiority became critical in 1916. Originally it had been a means of directing artillery, but at Verdun Pétain and de Rose set up fighter groups. GQG disapproved at first and dissolved de Rose's Groupes de Combat, but changed its mind and they were reinstated on 28 March. The aeronautics sub-committee of the Army Commission played an important role here in pushing for the development of a fighter aircraft. The new Nieuport (Bébé) XI was ideal for this purpose. Production of all types of aircraft and engines took off in 1916, with production figures for engines, for example, exceeding 1,000 for every month of 1916 except February.[65] Innovation in weapons for these aircraft was important too. The Le Prieur rocket was developed to set fire to German observation balloons. Fired at close range (less than 200 metres was most effective) and lit by an electric current, the rockets were first used on 22 May by eight Nieuport XI fighters. They set alight every single German balloon on the right bank.[66]

The new tactical instructions issued at the end of 1916 attempted to bring Verdun's 'rapidity' and the Somme's 'method' into equilibrium, in order to exploit any success. Infantry were to be deployed less densely but in greater depth; cavalry troops were given greater firepower and expected to fight dismounted until the possibility of pursuit through a breach in the enemy lines appeared. The importance of better communications for transmitting intelligence was emphasised by the creation of a special service at the level of the regiment, and by improving the homing pigeon service according to the experience of Verdun and the Somme, where the birds had proved that they almost always got through (see Figure 9).[67] Finally, a new offensive doctrine was published on 16 December.[68] It pointed out that the tendency both to restrict objectives and to leave longer periods between attacks gave the enemy too much freedom to reorganise after any initial success. Speed and continuity must be sought during the preparatory period, but during the execution of an attack no limits must be placed on the exploitation of success. The role of the artillery was to destroy the enemy defences and the infantry assault was to be launched only when command took personal responsibility for ensuring that the destruction was sufficient. It was no longer the single, brutal stroke that the 1915 doctrine had recommended, rather a succession of unlimited attacks following and dependent upon the artillery's preparation. Infantry ready to seize any opportunity offered must liaise securely and rapidly with artillery prepared to move its batteries forward on request, thus avoiding delays. The document

summed up its provisions thus: hold defensive lines with the minimum
of machine guns, keeping plenty of reserves in hand; be economical
with the infantry, never launching an attack without artillery preparation; ensure close liaison between artillery and infantry, even at the
expense of slowing the action.

As for the defensive, Joffre had issued a note on the lessons of Verdun
back in March 1916, concluding in capital letters that not an inch of
ground was to be surrendered voluntarily. Even when surrounded, units
were to fight on to the last man, and the 'moral factor' was still prepon-
derant.[69] The Germans had applied this principle at Verdun under
Falkenhayn, but it was abandoned by Hindenburg and Ludendorff on
the Somme when they arrived from the Eastern front to take over high
command. It caused too many casualties.

The French suffered well over half a million casualties in the two
1916 battles.[70] Shortage of manpower had forced the French Army to
move to a three-regiment (ternary) division instead of two brigades of
two regiments each. The resultant amalgamation of active regiments in
reserve divisions and vice versa eliminated the distinction between
them. Using the infantry saved by the ternary reorganisation plus the
manpower of territorial regiments, nine new divisions were created in
1916, bringing the total number in the French Army to 107, plus seven
territorials. The ten cavalry divisions mobilised in 1914 were reduced to
seven by August 1916, and a further division was dissolved the
following year, some of their effectives joining the infantry, training as
pilots or joining the new tanks. Others fought dismounted, or in cyclist
companies, or drove motorised artillery. By 1 July 1916 the cavalry had
furnished other arms with around 3,500 officers, and 45,000 NCOs and
other ranks.[71]

The development of greater firepower compensated for the lower
infantry numbers in the ternary division. In 1916 each regiment was
supported by a company of gunners armed with eight machine guns, a
37mm gun and an 81cm mortar, in addition to new machine-gun companies attached to each battalion.[72] Thus each regiment had twenty-four
machine guns at its disposal (instead of two as in 1914). There was an
added cost to this extra firepower. It became increasingly difficult during
the course of 1916 to plan for divisions to leap-frog each other to
advance, because of the greater numbers of horse-drawn and motor
vehicles needed for transport. On the railways, thirty trains had been
required in 1914 to transport one division; in 1916 forty-two were
needed.[73]

A significant development in May 1916 was the formulation of the
Army's first heavy artillery programme. This was a late development,

given the realisation as early as August 1914 that the Army lacked heavy guns, and the delay was the source of much criticism in the parliament and in the army commissions. The programme would provide the guns for ten regiments of tractor-drawn heavy guns, each of twelve groups, and twenty regiments of horse-drawn heavies. By the end of 1916 each division had one or two batteries of the new 58mm trench mortars attached to its field artillery regiment, and two batteries of the heavy mortars (240 and 340mm) as well. The 'assault artillery' was created on 30 September 1916. This was the name given to the new tanks of whose value Estienne had convinced GQG. He became its first commander.[74]

The shells crisis of the last weeks of 1914 and early 1915 was clearly over. In the Somme and Verdun battles during September 1916, the French fired over 290,000 75mm shells and 43,000 heavy shells.[75] Now that heavy artillery was becoming more available, a training school was established in Châlons in June 1916, and it published a series of instructions on intelligence, on liaison with aviation and on the creation of topographical sections. Firing tables were drawn up to replace aerial observation and to take into account ballistic and weather conditions. At the end of the year Joffre convened a ten-man commission at GQG to study the creation of a general heavy artillery reserve.

The high command was learning from experience, but the troops also were beginning to learn lessons of their own. There had always been individual ways of refusing to obey an order or hiding to avoid being given an unwelcome duty, but the early signs of 'collective' indiscipline appeared at Verdun. The first of these occurred in March 1916 in 29 DI, when five soldiers deserted on the 11th and a week later fifteen soldiers with their sergeant abandoned their unit as it was going back into line. There were further serious incidents in May, when fifty men from 27 DI refused to return to the trenches. All the thirty-four men charged as a result of this incident were given light sentences, probably because the judges knew that earlier their regiment had suffered terrible losses in the sector to which they had been ordered to return in May. There were further incidents in 21 DI in May and June.[76] Tales of units bleating as sheep to the slaughter as they marched to the front were not easy to suppress, and Joffre attributed their spread to the press. Nonetheless, a member of Castelnau's staff used the word 'mutiny' in his diary in early June.[77] The US military attaché noted in his report of 31 May that the troops in Verdun were 'utterly worn out', not only by the physical effort but by the never-ending noise of their own and the enemy's guns. Nonetheless, he praised their 'unflinching valor'.[78]

On the Somme, which some of those who experienced both battles declared was worse than Verdun, there were incidents as well. On 4 August Fayolle seemed to despair of the best way to deal with the infantry. They would 'consent' to guard trenches only if the artillery had done all the work. He recognised that the troops were 'revolted [dégoutées] by getting themselves killed for no significant, if not decisive, result'. On 10 August Fayolle noted 'acts of indiscipline' among I Colonial Corps. He went to see Foch who dealt 'energetically' with the situation.[79] Although the subsequent court proceedings found that the strain of protracted trench fighting was the cause, nineteen men were sentenced to death for their actions (all but two of the sentences commuted by Poincaré). The corps commander, General Berdoulat, complained to GQG that the suppression of courts martial had been a mistake, because swift repression was the only way to restore discipline, but Joffre responded that there could be no re-opening of the matter: the political opposition would be too great.[80]

However, Joffre was sufficiently concerned by indiscipline to extend the responsibilities of the postal censorship commissions to the monitoring of morale. Each army had a commission censoring mail to ensure that no information that could be of use to the enemy was mentioned. On 1 December 1916, the mission's role was defined to include the provision of reports on troop morale to high command. Each mission's effectives were increased to between twenty and twenty-five members, who were to report on 'hygiene' (food, clothing, state of the trenches and so on), the war (its conduct, anti-militarist sentiments, spying), foreign affairs (relations with the Allies, opinion of the enemy) and the home front (relations with civilians, the effects of leave).[81] Their observations on such a wide range of matters would prove invaluable for gauging the Army's morale. Joffre had already sent a note to his armies on 6 October about maintaining morale and about food and hygiene in the trenches, but his mind seems to have been more on banishing 'lassitude and discouragement' than on providing decent conditions in back areas for men who were supposedly 'au repos'. The difference between the official notes put out by Joffre, which show no sign of care for the physical conditions in which the pcdf were fighting, and those that Pétain sent out in the latter half of 1917, is striking.

Civil–military relations were deteriorating as well as army morale. The army commission of both houses had been worried by the state of defences at Verdun, and the first secret session of parliament held during the war took place in June, when much criticism of the high command had been aired. The vote of confidence that the government won afterwards contained a clause about 'effective supervision' over the prosecution of the war. The deputies had won the right to parliamentary inspection for which they had been pressing. André Tardieu proposed a thirty-member commission, which was discussed during July as the Somme offensive failed to achieve a quick success. Abel Ferry was elected on 1 August by the Deputies' Army Commission as one of the commissioners delegated to carry out the supervision. He was obliged, therefore, to give up his military duties since he could not 'supervise', while in uniform, a superior officer. Henceforth Ferry devoted himself solely to the commission. It would kill him in 1918, when he was struck by a shell. In October 1916 Ferry and his colleague Albert Favre presented a report on the standard gauge and 60-centimetre-gauge railways built by the army to move men, munitions and guns quickly to where they were needed. Ferry had already made three reports on the subject, and this formal report recommended that considerably more resources be devoted to extending the network. This could have been a useful way of obtaining more steel from the armaments ministry and more workers for a task that the army agreed was necessary. Joffre, however, was furious that there should be any so-called interference with military matters. Ferry's report on effectives in November might have provided further grounds for fruitful cooperation, but by then Joffre's days were numbered.

Another secret session of the deputies was held on 21 November over the question of calling up the 1918 class, and this was followed a week later by another, during which it became clear to Briand that he would have to change the high command if he was to save his ministry. Over ten sittings complaints were aired about Salonika and about the French front. Although Briand obtained a (reduced) vote of confidence at the end of the sessions, he moved to ease Joffre out of command. Joffre had already cast off Foch, as responsible for the failure on the Somme, on the (false) excuse that he, Foch, was ill. This was not enough to save his own job, and when Joffre realised that Briand's offer of a role as the government's 'technical advisor' was an empty one, he resigned. The pill was sweetened by the grant of a marshal's baton, making Joffre the Third Republic's first marshal of France. The honour had been tarnished by the performance of Louis Napoleon's marshals during the Franco-Prussian War, and so had been in abeyance ever since. Briand also got rid of his war minister, General Roques, widely seen as Joffre's creature. Briand had been angered by Roques' favourable report on Salonika and Sarrail, which aroused much comment in the secret parliamentary sessions. General Lyautey from Morocco replaced him, as noted above.

On 15 November the Allied military leaders gathered in Chantilly, just as they had done at the end of 1915, to plan the 1917 campaign. Joffre proposed a programme that differed little from the previous year's, except for its being on a larger scale. He argued for an early start to coordinated operations to prevent any repetition of the Verdun offensive that had forestalled 1916's offensives. In France he proposed separate British and French attacks on both sides of the German salient – a repetition of 1915's strategy. Before any detailed planning could take place, he was removed from command. Joffre's replacement as CinC of the French Army was Robert Nivelle, the general who had won the final successes in the battle for Verdun.

5   General Nivelle and his 1917 offensive

The general chosen to replace Joffre is the only man with a Western Front battle named after him. Joffre had preferred Robert Nivelle to the cautious and demanding Pétain of May 1916 at Verdun, and he recommended Nivelle to Briand. Since Briand was expecting Joffre still to play a role as the government's 'technical advisor', it seemed prudent that Joffre and the new CinC should be able to work together. Furthermore, Poincaré much preferred the Joffre–Nivelle strategy of seeking the decisive battle in 1917, with the aim of capturing strategic German territory, over anything the other candidate, Pétain, might propose. Briand knew that Pétain would not work willingly with Joffre; moreover, Pétain favoured small, local actions with limited aims. Briand wanted a 'new spirit' in his rejigged cabinet and favoured Nivelle as being more likely to infuse the high command in similar manner.[1] Besides, Pétain was not acceptable politically. He had insulted Poincaré by saying 'we are neither commanded nor governed', and suggested that the head of state should act as a dictator to get things moving. When Poincaré exclaimed, 'but what about the Constitution?', Pétain replied 'bugger the Constitution'.[2] Yet his dislike of Pétain's politics was probably a less important factor in Poincaré's eyes than his wish for Nivelle's more aggressive attitude.[3] See Figure 11.

Some saw the choice of Nivelle as a risk. Pellé, who was sacked from GQG at the same time as Joffre, thought that Foch would have been a safer bet. One could put up with Foch's speechifying because of his energy, but with Nivelle it was impossible to know whether he would be as successful as CinC as he had been in his earlier command positions.[4] Nivelle's had certainly been a rapid rise from colonel of artillery at the beginning of the war. In February 1915 Nivelle had been appointed to command 61 DI, his first divisional command, then III Corps in December that same year, before taking over Second Army from Pétain at Verdun on 1 May 1916.[5] He had no experience of dealing either with politicians, or with Haig and the British, or with the staff at GQG, although he was breveté, that is, he had passed staff college

LE GÉNÉRAL NIVELLE, NIVELEUR

Fig. 11 Nivelle le niveleur, from *Le Rire rouge*, 20 January 1917
A play on words: niveler is 'to level', so Nivelle is the leveller, who will
destroy the German trenches

(in 1889). Moreover, Joffre had clearly hoped to retain some influence behind the scenes by pushing someone whose rise had been so rapid that he had not had time to create his own political following. Joffre was overheard at GQG saying that Nivelle would be a 'devoted and obedient lieutenant', and, although Nivelle lacked the 'authority to give orders to those who yesterday were his chiefs', he (Joffre) would 'cover' him with his own authority.[6] Joffre's hopes were soon dashed. Indeed, he was sent off to the USA when the Americans declared a state of war with Germany on 6 April and was thus well out of the way when Nivelle's offensive began on 16 April.

The government was in a state of flux when Nivelle took over. It had been political pressure that saw off Joffre, and the secret sessions of both houses (Chamber of Deputies and Senate) at the end of 1916 had concluded that command changes were vital following the disaster at Verdun and the disappointments on the Somme. Briand offered his resignation, but Poincaré refused to accept it as the *union sacrée* (political truce) might not withstand the effects of a change in government, following the powerful change in the military. So premier Briand juggled his ministry instead, instituting a 'comité de guerre' or inner cabinet as David Lloyd George, the new British prime minister, had done. (The French war committee achieved very little, most often meeting just before the full cabinet.) He decided to change his war minister, because Roques was judged to be too much under the influence of Joffre, despite his Salonika report which had so stunned the CinC by failing to censure Sarrail. Briand offered the job to Paul Painlevé, his education minister in the previous ministry, but Painlevé refused to serve, as he disapproved the choice of Nivelle, preferring Pétain instead. So Briand invited a new broom, General Hubert Lyautey, to serve as war minister. Since 1912 Lyautey had been Resident-General in Morocco where he had made a name for himself.

When Lyautey eventually arrived in Paris, he found a changed situation. First, Nivelle had already been appointed, the decree being signed by the acting war minister, navy minister Admiral Lacaze, without consultation. So Lyautey was faced with a *fait accompli*, made more annoying by the fact that he himself would not have selected Nivelle. Second, responsibility for armaments was removed from the war ministry in the reshuffle and vested in a new armaments ministry under the control of the Socialist Albert Thomas who had been the very successful under-secretary in the war ministry overseeing the great surges in production during 1916. The industrialist Louis Loucheur was appointed as under-secretary of state to help with this rapidly growing task. On the other hand, the decree of December 1915 that had put the Armée d'Orient under Joffre's command was rescinded and responsibility for the Salonika troops returned to the ministry.

Lyautey had hoped to compensate for his lack of political experience and absence from mainland France by relying on Joffre as the government's 'technical adviser', the fudge that had been used to ease Joffre from command. However, Joffre's recognition of that fudge and his subsequent resignation made this impossible. Next Lyautey hoped to be able to lean on the two senior generals, Foch and Castelnau, but again those hopes were blocked. Foch had no official post when Lyautey arrived, although the two men communicated with each other; Castelnau was taken out of the way by being sent to Russia as head of the French military mission to the large Allied conference to be held in Petrograd in January–February 1917. Lyautey had hoped to revive the neglected post of head of the army general staff in the ministry by appointing Castelnau to it, but he failed here too. The post was not revived until its use as a way of easing Nivelle out of command in April–May. Relations between Nivelle and Lyautey were a little strained. Lyautey knew Nivelle from Algeria, but the latter did not find his minister easy to deal with.[7]

Nivelle had to deal with more than his political masters in Paris, because he was also thrown immediately into dealings with France's Allies, in particular with Britain's new Prime Minister, David Lloyd George, who was sure that he did not want the 1917 campaign to become another Somme. Armies other than those of Britain were to do the fighting! Hence the Rome conference in January 1917, during which he tried unsuccessfully to get the Italians to undertake a campaign. Nivelle asked to speak with Lloyd George as he was returning through Paris to London, but the Prime Minister refused to discuss strategy with him unless Haig and Robertson were also present. Lloyd George thought that French generals were, on the whole, better than the British ones, and if Nivelle and the French insisted on carrying out their plan for the 1917 campaign, then there was little reason to oppose it since it gave the main role to the French Army.

Nivelle had already obtained Haig's consent to the revision of Joffre's plan, which had envisaged a repeat attack on both shoulders of the Noyon salient. Instead, Nivelle wanted a sudden and brutal attack by the French Army to destroy the enemy's forces totally by manoeuvre and battle. Instead of the BEF bearing the main brunt of the 1917 fighting, as Joffre had wished because of the dwindling French manpower resources, Haig was asked to take a supporting role by attacking in the north around Arras to draw off German reserves. Then Nivelle would deliver his crushing attack on a different part of the front. Since he did not intend to protract his offensive, as had happened on the Somme, he would be able to support Haig's Flanders operation later in the year. The Flanders mud would prevent an early start to operations, and so, if the French attack failed, there would be time to transfer French support to the BEF. Moreover, if Nivelle's assault were successful, a Flanders operation to free the Channel ports might not even be needed. The enemy would have been forced to retire.

Nivelle was perfectly confident that he had the right formula. On leaving Second Army he claimed: 'The experiment is conclusive; our method has proved itself.'[8] Haig was dragging his feet, however, over the extension of the British front to free French divisions for Nivelle's battle. This was probably the reason why Nivelle asked to speak with Lloyd George on his way through Paris. So Nivelle was invited to London to explain his ideas before the war cabinet and with Haig and Robertson in attendance. Nivelle made such a plausible case during the two meetings on 15 and 16 January that he impressed even Hankey. Haig was instructed to obey the spirit and the letter of the agreement on the forthcoming battle. The French must not be obliged to delay because of the British.[9]

Yet Haig had also been impressed with Nivelle at their first meeting, although the head of the French Military Mission to the British Army had warned Nivelle beforehand that Haig disliked subordination to the French. At first, Haig was unsure whether Joffre retained any influence, but Nivelle soon disabused him of that notion – yet another complication arising from the muddled politics of Joffre's sacking. Lloyd George's decision to back Nivelle and his plan of campaign had a huge knock-on effect for the relationship between Nivelle and the British CinC. Lloyd George used Nivelle as a way of controlling his generals, and the results were not only to poison civil–military relations in Britain for the rest of the war, but also they revealed Nivelle's lack of experience and qualifications for managing a coalition war.

The change of CinC affected GQG as well. The very name of Chantilly, where GQG had settled after the war of movement ended, had become anathema to some politicians, because it was synomous in their view with an alternative military government. It became important therefore to mark the change of command with a change of location. GQG was obliged to move to Beauvais on 10 January 1917, but Beauvais was too far north and too far distant from the proposed centre of operations, and so it was moved again on 4 April to Compiègne (about 80 kilometres north of Paris). Both moves involved shifting communications, cypher machines, mountains of paper and so on, and was a further impediment to planning the forthcoming campaign. There were personnel changes too.[10] Perhaps the most influential member of Nivelle's entourage at

GQG was Lieutenant-Colonel Eric d'Alançon. His whole military career had been spent as a staff officer; he was Nivelle's former chief of staff in 61 DI, and moved with Nivelle to Verdun in 1916. Nivelle made him head of his military cabinet. This was a new position within the GQG organisation, but reflected Pétain's use of Colonel Bernard Serrigny in a similar role. D'Alançon was seen as a somewhat shadowy, even sinister, figure, the extent of whose influence it was difficult to estimate. The mystery was not helped by the fact that he was terminally ill at this time; he died on 6 September 1917.[11]

All in all, Nivelle took over the high command at a time of great change which made his task much more difficult. At GQG the moves and personnel changes (a new chief of staff, General Pont, and some new heads of section) added to the difficulties of commanding men who had been his superiors in 1914 and 1915. Nivelle also needed to cultivate good relations with his own political masters and with British politicians and the military, whom he would require to fall in with his planning. There was no time to settle down in the job, and Nivelle planned to take the offensive on 15 February. Yet, despite his inexperience, Nivelle made a good impression at the start of his command. After Joffre, who had seemed increasingly tired and weighed down by responsibility, Nivelle was a breath of fresh air, younger and more energetic, self-confident but kindly. Liaison officer Edward Louis Spears thought he gave 'an impression of vigour, strength and energy'. Even General Guillaumat (who managed to criticise most of his colleagues) found it a pleasure to talk to Nivelle and his entourage.[12]

Nivelle's planning

The new CinC lost no time in stamping his ideas on the French Army. Nivelle re-worked the allied strategy agreed between Joffre and the Allies the previous November, and he insisted that he pick his own army group and army commanders. He offered the Eastern Army Group to Castelnau and the Northern to Franchet d'Espèrey. He left Pétain in command of the Central Army Group, but Pétain ruled himself out of contention to carry out the new plan of campaign by seeming too 'timorous' to Nivelle. In any case, it would have been difficult being in command of Pétain who had been his superior officer a few weeks previously.[13] To solve this problem, Nivelle created a Reserve Army Group that he gave to General Micheler. However, Micheler did not have the same authority as the other army group commanders, because the Reserve Army Group was a temporary expedient and Micheler's command was as 'adjoint' only, acting as army group commander 'by delegation' and solely with the

CinC's 'approval'. The choice of a relatively inexperienced general (Micheler had commanded Tenth Army on the Somme) to command the principal offensive forces was unwise. At least, Castelnau and Franchet d'Espèrey were more experienced, and even Foch might have been given the task if he had not been in such bad political odour.

In re-working the plan for the 1917 campaign in France, Nivelle had to take account of the British. The BEF had come of age on the Somme; now it consisted of over 1.59 million men, in five armies, fifty-six infantry divisions and cavalry, so it could not be ignored. Joffre's prestige as coalition leader was now gone; Nivelle would have to regain it. Despite its losses, the French was still much the larger army. It had incorporated the whole 1916 class by October that year, and the 1917 class was already under instruction. Total French effectives on the Western Front were 2,802,000 men on 1 January 1917, with a further 185,000 in the Armée d'Orient. They formed 107 infantry divisions, with a further seven territorial and seven cavalry divisions. The distinction between active and reserve divisions was long gone. The process of reducing the divisions to a ternary structure (three regiments instead of two brigades of two each) was intensified with the creation of ten new ternary divisions formed from the regiments thus abstracted. The army corps was gradually reorganised also, so as to contain normally four divisions. This was to enable the corps to endure longer in line with two of its divisions in the front line and the remaining two in reserve.[14]

On transmitting the tactical instruction of 16 December 1916, described at the end of the previous chapter, on the 'but et conditions d'une offensive d'ensemble', Nivelle wrote that, first, breakthrough to the enemy's lines as far as the main lines of his heavy gun batteries was possible in twenty-four or forty-eight hours, on condition that the operation be mounted as a single, sudden action ('d'un seul coup par attaque brusquée'). Second, the artillery preparation had to cover a zone of about 8 kilometres to include all the enemy's heavy batteries, hence modern rapid-firing and mobile guns had to be pushed as far forward as possible, and if necessary the destruction completed by the long guns. Third, the rupture must be followed immediately by a bold lateral exploitation to destroy gun batteries, to occupy the enemy's lines of communication, and to ensure the capture of enough railways to be able to re-supply themselves. Finally, a bridgehead must be established as far forward as possible to cover the concentration of troops needed to take the battle to any remaining enemy forces. In sum: breakthrough, followed by lateral exploitation – all to be carried out speedily, hence to be prepared in minute detail beforehand. Despite the fact that the 1915 battles and that on the Somme in 1916 had attempted to follow the same principles,

Nivelle seems to have convinced his political leaders (and Lloyd George) that somehow, under his command, things would be different in 1917. The fighting in October and December 1916 at Verdun had proved that the method worked. He was confident that his successsful capture of Douaumont and Vaux had given him the 'formula' for success against the German Army.

Nivelle's plan involved the BEF, and the Northern and the Reserve Army Groups. On 30 and 31 December 1916 the two army group commanders concerned received their instructions. They were to bring about 'the destruction of the principal mass of enemy forces on the Western Front, by means of a decisive battle waged against all the enemy's available forces, and followed by an intensive exploitation'. Nivelle proposed three operations, distinct in time and place, so as to force the enemy to divide his forces. The Northern Army Group (First and Third Armies under Generals Fayolle and Humbert, twenty-four infantry and two cavalry divisions) was to break the front between the Avre and Oise rivers. At worst, the Northern Army Group would hold down enemy troops; at best, the French would exploit their success to capture the enemy's lines of communication in the valleys of the Oise and the upper reaches of the Somme. North of the Northern Army Group, the British were to attack north of Bapaume as far as Arras. The Reserve Army Group was to exploit the success of the BEF and the Northern Army Group by making a violent attack, aiming to conquer right at the start the entire zone occupied by the enemy's artillery and pushing troops through the breach thus created. The main task fell to Micheler's Reserve Army Group of Fifth, Sixth and Tenth Armies, commanded respectively by Generals Mazel, Mangin and Duchêne. (See Map 11.) The fourteen divisions of Sixth Army, operating west of the Laon–Reims road, were to push towards Laon and Saint-Quentin, its right covered by Fifth Army (also of fourteen divisions) on both sides of the Aisne. At a minumum, Sixth Army's progress should free the Reims–Laon railway line for the French. The twelve divisions of Tenth Army, the army of manoeuvre, were to pass between the other two armies, and had the task of exploiting the breach towards the north and north-west with the aid of five cavalry divisions. The further aim was to reach the line Craonne–Guise, with help from the Northern Army Group attack towards Fère and Saint-Quentin, while the British continued towards Cambrai and Le Catelet. Nivelle gave 15 February as the start of operations, an impossibly early date given that a new GQG staff had to deal with a plan of campaign that had been changed entirely since the November agreements, as well as moving office twice. A certain number of secondary operations along the rest of the front down to Alsace were also foreshadowed.

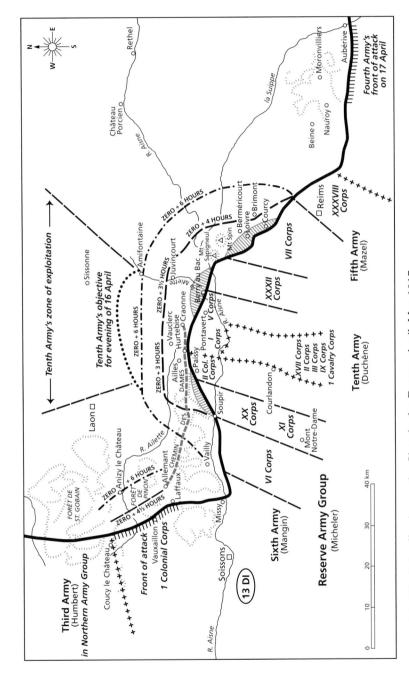

11. Nivelle's offensive on the Chemin des Dames, April–May 1917

The only way that Nivelle could collect all the divisions he needed for his ambitious plan was for the British to take over the French front from the river Somme south to the Amiens–Roye road. Nivelle wanted this relief operation to be completed by 15 January, a month before his offensive was to begin. He put into writing his ideas about the offensive, which he proposed to place before the War Cabinet in London; they would then put pressure on Haig to comply. Before leaving for London he read his note to the comité de guerre. He envisaged a three-step campaign. First, violent French and British attacks would be carried out on a wide front to rupture the enemy front at some point or, at least, to wear down a proportion of the enemy's reserves. Next, once the initial attacks had made their effect, another attack on a different part of the front would be launched between six and fourteen days later to break right through the enemy's front as far as the bulk of his artillery, *just as had been done on 15 December at Verdun* [emphasis added]. Finally exploitation both deep and lateral would take the British and French armies to wherever they wished to go: the North Sea coast, the Belgian capital, or the Meuse or the Rhine. This is cloud-cuckoo-land. Apart from Nivelle's intermediate stage – an attack on a different part of the front – this is little different from the Somme plans of the previous year. Then Haig was going to break through and roll up the enemy lines as far north as Arras; the BEF did not even reach Bapaume. One can only assume that the approval the note garnered from the comité de guerre and then in London derived from wishful rather than realistic thinking.

Although Haig had been instructed by London to comply with both the spirit and the letter of Nivelle's proposal, he used the poor state of the French railways as an excuse to delay the extension of the British front so as to free French divisions for the offensive. Certainly the French railways were under considerable strain, as the weather was particularly cold and trains were needed to move coal. Yet British demands for wagons were exaggerated. The French noted that the British were requisitioning 8,000 wagons daily to move half the number of men that the French moved using only 2,800 wagons daily. Lloyd George took the opportunity thus presented to curb Haig by plotting to subordinate him to Nivelle, but subsequent events showed that Nivelle was no match for the prime minister. Lloyd George let Paris know of his wish, via the French liaison officer at the War Office, and a conference was arranged in Calais for 26 and 27 February, ostensibly to settle the transport question.[15] The political director in the Quai d'Orsay informed Nivelle that he was to 'stand firm during the conference', 'so as to obtain command over the British'; and the liaison officer 'tried to pressure' Nivelle in the same way. Accordingly, a draft document was drawn up at GQG, dated 21

February, which Nivelle read out in a very embarrassed fashion as it became clear that the British generals had no idea what was coming. Going round and round the pudding, but not sticking in the spoon, Nivelle 'got red in the face' and 'beat about the bush'.[16] Despite Haig's outrage and Robertson's fury, Lloyd George insisted on a convention being signed that put Haig and the BEF under French direction for the duration of Nivelle's offensive. Haig would be able to appeal to London if he thought that Nivelle's instructions were imperilling his army. Lloyd George had used the French CinC for his own purposes, but unwisely Nivelle failed to capitalise. He (or his staff) began writing tactless and abrupt letters to Haig, which simply made the latter more obstinate. Nivelle complained to Briand, and Briand complained to Lloyd George. A second conference in London on 12 and 13 March produced an amended agreement. The BEF was to remain under Haig's orders; Nivelle would communicate directly with Haig and would have a British mission at GQG 'to maintain touch' between the two commanders. The arrangement was to last until the start of the battle; in cases of dispute, London reserved the right to judge whether the particular conditions fell under the agreement or not. Haig signed the convention, but added a postscript stating that the BEF should be regarded as allies, not subordinates, which upset Nivelle. This tangled negotiation took up time and energy that should have been devoted to planning and preparing the offensive.

The British were not the only difficulty. Nivelle also had to deal with meeting General Cadorna in Italy and arranging support for the Italian Army. It had become clear, after the Austro-Hungarian *Strafexpedition* of May 1916, that the Italian front was vulnerable. Neither France nor Britain could risk Italy's suffering a defeat that might induce Rome to make a separate peace. If, in that eventuality, the Austro-Hungarians reached the Adriatic, this would open that sea to German submarines which were already attacking without warning all shipping in the Mediterranean. After making a personal visit to Cadorna at the end of January, Nivelle passed the task of putting contingency planning in place into Foch's hands. It was now April and the start of his offensive was already overdue.

Russia was a further problem. It had been agreed back in November, when the 1917 plan of campaign was settled before Joffre's removal, that the Allies would gather in Petrograd, because it was so difficult for the Russians to come to Paris or London. The purpose was to energise the Russians, to reassure them that the offensive on the Western Front would tie down German forces and prevent their move east, and to encourage Russian participation in the Balkans and on the Russo-Romanian front.

Sickness and ministerial changes in Russia had delayed the conference, but it began on 29 January. Castelnau was France's delegate because Briand wanted a high-level representative so as to be sure that the Tsar and Stavka would take heed. An artillery commission also held meetings to discuss the very large Russian demands for French and British materiel. Castelnau learned that the weather would not permit operations in Russia until May, so Nivelle could not expect any diversionary action in the east at the same time as his offensive in France. After a long talk with Berthelot in Bucharest, Castelnau learned also that the Romanian Army could not be reconstituted before 15 May. On his return, Castelnau reported Russia's 'firm intention to pursue the war to the end', although Castelnau told President Poincaré that, if the value of the already weakened French Army was twenty, then the value of the Russian was only nine.[17] Officially, Castelnau reported that he was sure that Russia could hold all the German forces currently on the Eastern Front. All the same, the Russians were not able, despite all their courage, to make a decisive effort in 1917. This confirmed what a French officer had already concluded after a 44-day trip to the Russian front, namely that a serious offensive in spring 1917 was impossible. 'In a war in which everything is system and organisation', he wrote, 'I fear that the Russian soldier, simple, gentle, brave and insouciant as he is, will once again be too late to bring to operations in spring 1917 any decisive character.'[18] Yet Castelnau's return to his Eastern Army Group was followed almost immediately by the first Russian revolution, which all had hoped would come only at war's end. Then the Tsar abdicated on 15 March.

Next, the enemy took a hand. Throughout the winter came reports of a probable German withdrawal in northern France. Between the rivers Oise and Somme and in towns such as Saint-Quentin, Cambrai and Bapaume, houses were evacuated. Prisoners and refugees were being put to work on new lines of defence incorporating concrete trenches and houses on the outskirts of these towns. Signs of what was to happen did exist, therefore, but both British and French high commands found it hard to believe that the enemy would give up conquered territory without a fight. After all, France had just fought for ten months at enormous cost to retain the RFV. Why would Germany pull back unless forced to do so?

Nonetheless, by the end of February such a withdrawal had begun along the British front, but it proved impossible to follow up quickly because of enemy mines and other booby-traps. Further south, in front of the Northern Army Group, Franchet d'Espèrey was still uncertain about German intentions. The front line between Roye, Noyon and Soissons crossed the Oise, the old invasion route towards Paris. Clemenceau had printed a banner above each issue of his newpaper proclaiming 'the Germans are at Noyon'. Surely the Germans would not abandon Noyon? On 7 March Nivelle wrote that the only firm clue as to German intentions was the retreat in the north from the river Ancre in front of the British Fifth Army. There was no proof that the retreat would extend as far as the Northern Army Group's front. As further evidence emerged from prisoners and aerial observation of a huge area of fires, the German withdrawal could be denied no longer. Franchet d'Espèrey ordered his First and Third Armies next to the British to pursue, but using minimum infantry forces. On 17 March the French reoccupied Roye and the next day Noyon, but they came to a halt by the 20th along the Crozat Canal which connects the Somme and Oise rivers. Progress continued slowly until 4 April when Third Army bumped up against the outskirts of the newly constructed Hindenburg Line. It was now past the date set for the start of Nivelle's offensive. The left-hand corps of the Reserve Army Group around Soissons had also managed to re-occupy the ground abandoned by the German troops. The southern end of the Hindenburg Line was anchored on the Aisne to the east of Soissons and then ran northwards to Arras. A large salient had been straightened. This was hailed as a great victory, to be considered as a late consequence of the previous year's fighting on the Somme. Accounts in both the British and the French press described the slow Allied pursuit of the retreating Germans 'as if it were the hunt of the season, exclamation marks adorning their prose like so many view halloos'.[19] On a front of 140 kilometres, the German lines were cracking, said *Le Matin*, thus misrepresenting a skilful German withdrawal.[20]

If the German withdrawal was indeed an Allied victory, it was merely a propaganda victory. The Germans had shortened their line – something they could well afford to do since they occupied so much French territory – thereby making a great saving in the number of troops required to hold their front. As they withdrew, they poisoned wells, booby-trapped roads and buildings, and destroyed homes and farm buildings. Liaison officer E.L. Spears is eloquent on the destruction: 'It was as if Satan had poured desolation out of a gigantic watering-can, carelessly spraying some parts of the land more than others.'[21] The French seemed more upset by the wanton destruction of fruit trees, which had been cut three-quarters through and left to fall. Moreover, the Hindenburg Line was more than a line. It was a fearsome succession of very strong defensive positions running from the Belgian coast to the German frontier, eventually extending the depth of the main battle zone by 1 to 2 kilometres. Natural features such as canals and other waterways were incorporated into the defensive scheme. Named for the German CinC, the defences were begun when Hindenburg and Ludendorff were appointed to supreme command in the west. Both men had directed the war in the east until September 1916 when they replaced General Erich von Falkenhayn. On their first visit to France they were appalled by what Prince Rupprecht of Bavaria told them about the very different conditions of the fighting on the Western Front where the Battle of the Somme was in progress, and they decided that changes had to be made. Hence the decision was taken to construct what the Allies came to call the Hindenburg Line.

Now the task of the Reserve Army Group was made much more difficult because, first, the liberated German divisions could now strengthen the positions to be attacked, and, second, the Northern Army Group and British attacks could no longer be strong enough to draw those extra German divisions towards the north and away from the French front. Everything had changed, Micheler wrote to Nivelle on 22 March, and he forecast that his attack might be halted right at the start and an endless wearing-down fight ensue. Nivelle's response was to fix the date for the offensive to begin: the BEF on 8 April, followed two days later by the Northern Army Group; then Micheler's Reserve Army Group would launch their assault on 12 April, followed by Pétain's Centre Army Group the next day. His further response was to issue a directive on 4 April, re-stating his intentions. The initial phase was a *prolonged* battle to break the enemy's front and destroy his reserves; the second phase was one of exploitation in which all the Allied forces would participate. The British were to break through the Hindenburg Line in the direction of Douai and Cambrai and then capture the German defensive position from the rear, while the Northern Army Group's Third Army was attacking Saint-Quentin. The Reserve Army Group was to head for Guise (site of Fifth Army's battle during 1914's Great Retreat) and the railway junction at Hirson, while the Centre Army Group was to move north to the river Suippe and then the Aisne. This was not all. After the breakthrough, the British were to advance towards Valenciennes and Louvain in Belgium, helped by the Belgian Army and by XXXVI Corps attacking from the coast; the three French army groups were to continue in a north-easterly direction, the name of Sedan (of 1870 memory) being mentioned.[22]

Nothing had caused Nivelle to change his mind about his offensive, neither the German withdrawal, nor the delays to the start of his offensive (the original date had been 15 February), nor the difficulties with Haig. Nivelle took no account of the news that no coordinated attacks were to be made on other fronts, such as Joffre had planned. Russia, Romania and Italy were not to be relied on, and in Salonika Sarrail was delayed, so he claimed, by his Serbian and British forces. Despite all these new circumstances, surprise and speed, brutality and violence remained the watchwords. Nivelle ignored Micheler's letter about everything having changed. Although the head of the 3e Bureau, Colonel Renouard, remained convinced of the rightness of the plan despite his earlier reservations, other members of his staff were less so. Commandant Tournès thought that a British attack in Artois and a French attack in Lorraine, with the French in between, prepared in strength for the inevitable German counter-attack, was a better proposition. He put his ideas on paper, but did not tell his CinC that he thought the Reserve Army Group's planned attack was 'mad'.[23] Nivelle's stubbornness was to contribute to a great disaster.

However, Nivelle could not ignore his political masters. War minister Lyautey had provoked a scene in the Chamber on 14 March, in effect insulting the deputies, and his resignation toppled the already shaky Briand ministry. Lyautey had never believed in Nivelle's offensive, dismissing it as comic opera. He had also been talking about it to Pétain,[24] who spent the first months of 1917 sawing away at the branch upon which Nivelle was perched. Lyautey's replacement in the new Alexandre Ribot ministry that took office on 20 March was, however, a more implacable opponent of Nivelle's ideas. Despite Ribot's declaration to parliament that Nivelle had been chosen to lead the French armies to victory and had complete liberty to prepare and to direct operations, Painlevé began immediately talking to the generals involved, sometimes with and sometimes without Nivelle's being present.

Pétain's opposition to Nivelle was so patent (described as throwing a spanner in the works at every opportunity) that he felt obliged to write to Nivelle on 19 March about 'certain rumours' that had come to his ears to which the CinC should pay no attention. He, Pétain, was a 'devoted and respectful' collaborator![25] Did he guess or know that on 26 March Painlevé would declare, after talking first with Haig and then with Nivelle, that he hoped to see Pétain at the head of the French Army? Painlevé did not hide his opinion, even telling the British Liberal MP, William Cozens-Hardy (who reported it straight back to Lloyd George) that Pétain would be in charge within six weeks.[26] Spears dined with Painlevé on 13 March, before the latter even became minister, and 'heard enough to Damn [sic] Nivelle'.[27] One deputy (Henri Galli) claimed that, with Painlevé in the ministry, Nivelle would not last a fortnight.[28]

After all his informal talks, during which Painlevé clearly heard nothing but criticism of Nivelle and his offensive, a decision had to be made. Poincaré had insisted on Nivelle's appointment in preference to Pétain, and now he presided over a war council held in the presidential train at Compiègne on 6 April. As well as the relevant ministers (Thomas,

Lacaze and Painlevé) and premier Ribot, Nivelle and the four army group commanders, Franchet d'Espèrey, Micheler, Pétain and Castelnau attended. By this date, the Russian revolution was well under way, and the Americans were about to join the war. Since the political and diplomatic situation had changed so radically, was it wise to persist with an offensive in France, in which there seemed to be little confidence? As the generals took it in turn to criticise Nivelle's plan, he was put in an intolerable position. He offered his resignation, which was declined. The meeting broke up without any clear decision: Poincaré believed that the original plan with its vast strategic possibilities had been approved; Painlevé believed that the idea of a strategic offensive had been abandoned, replaced by a tactical offensive that would be halted within two days if unsuccessful. He put in writing the next day what he believed to have been 'complete agreement between the government and the CinC' that: 'it is not a question of pursuing at any cost a battle in which all our resources would be committed; rather the battle would be stopped as soon as it seemed that it would impose excessive losses on our army, likely to weaken it profoundly for insufficient and hazardous results'.[29] Painlevé explained to the parliament, in its secret session of 29 June 1917, that it would have been as easy to stop such a long-prepared offensive as it would be to stop an express train by standing in front of it. Besides, all the generals agreed that to make no offensive at all was impossible in the circumstances; and the British would not have been content to see the general to whom they had confided their army be replaced even before he had had time to prove himself, quite apart from the morale boost to the enemy by changing the French CinC yet again, so soon (less than four months) after his appointment.[30] Russia was already in turmoil, and such a change in France could only add to the uncertainty.

The offensive was, therefore, to go ahead as Nivelle had planned it. Indeed the British artillery preparation had already begun as the politicians and generals were talking in Compiègne. The front of the two attacking armies in the Reserve Army Group ran from east of Reims, above the Aisne as far as the Fort de Condé, where it turned north beyond the end of the Chemin des Dames at Laffaux, to join the Northern Army Group at Coucy-le-Château. On the right, Fifth Army's front of about 25 kilometres ran from Hurtebise Farm in the north to south of Fort Brimont (one of the ring of forts defending Reims to the north), Sapigneul and Côte 108. On the left of the Fifth Army front, I Corps (161, 1 and 2 DI with 51 DI in second line) faced north towards the Chemin des Dames and Craonne at its eastern end. Over a thousand trench artillery pieces, 860 field artillery, over a thousand heavy guns plus

Fig. 12 Painlevé and Nivelle leaving the Château of Compiègne, after the conference of 6 April 1917, in which the plans for Nivelle's offensive were criticised, but then approved

91 extra heavies supported Fifth Army's infantry. On Fifth Army's left the 15-kilometre front of Sixth Army was divided into two sections. In the eastern sector, which ran east–west from Hurtebise to Soupir, three corps (II Colonial, XX and VI Corps) were to attack towards the north and north-west. The western sector covered the ground where the front curved around northwards. The two corps in this sector (I Colonial and elements of XXXVII Corps) were to attack eastwards, the intention being to meet up with the troops from the other sector, thereby cutting off the 'elbow' in the front line. Sixth Army had available 594 trench artillery pieces, 846 field and 742 heavy guns, plus 81 heavy artillery pieces. Overall the density of guns for both armies was: one field gun every 23 metres; one heavy artillery piece every 21 metres; and one trench artillery piece every 23 metres. Although this was a greater density than on the Somme, in practice it would be less, because Nivelle aimed to break right through all the German lines. The guns had to fire on several lines, therefore, not simply the first position. Batteries had to be brought closer to the front line for this purpose and, having been spotted by the enemy, were destroyed. German gunfire also damaged the few roads in the sector, so that delivery of munitions and engineering supplies was impaired.

French intelligence identified a tripling of the number of German batteries in action between the beginning of February and the end of March.[31] It was not only the German artillery that was working efficiently. Fourteen German divisions had been identified on the front facing Fifth and Sixth Armies, double the number that had been in place in February, and another dozen were identified in the rear, ready to intervene. They had improved their defences so that three or even four defensive positions created a deep system extending to between 5 and 7 kilometres. German aircraft had mastery of the air once again, preventing the French from obtaining observation over the German lines. Moreover, from 6 April onwards, the weather was either misty or rainy or windy or snowy. Even if the Germans had not shot down French observation balloons, little useful information could have been gleaned. Nonetheless, the date for the infantry was set, after several postponements, for 16 April.[32]

One further factor weighed in the balance against the French. Since the German defenders clearly knew that an offensive was imminent, they increased their raids into French trenches to gather intelligence. On 4 April a raid captured 827 prisoners and took from the body of a sergeant in the 3 RIC (zouaves), the attack plan for his 37 DI with not only the timings for the divisional attack but also those for the VII and XXXII Corps alongside.[33]

The offensive begins

Before Nivelle's fatally compromised infantry assault began, Haig and the BEF further north had done all that had been required. The Battle of Arras began on 9 April and the Canadians gained a huge success by capturing the Vimy ridge that had eluded the French in three battles in 1915. One hundred guns, 10,000 prisoners and a 6-kilometre advance were the day's prize, and further smaller gains were made in the succeeding days. French hopes were raised, despite the meagre gains made by General Humbert's Third Army in the reduced attack of Northern Army Group. Third Army had followed the German withdrawal as far as Saint-Quentin, where the Hindenburg Line curled round the town on its hill. With a mere 252 heavy artillery pieces, of which only 80 were the more rapid-firing types, and with the poor visibility, the French gunners had little chance of firing effectively, and when they attacked on 13 April the infantry could not break through the bands of uncut wire. Third Army had simply not received the necessary resources for attacking such a strong defensive position. The resources had gone instead to the Reserve Army Group, whose assault began on the 16th, three days later.

The following account will work from east to west, beginning with Mazel's Fifth Army on the right. On that army's extreme right, next to Fourth Army, 151 DI (of XXXVIII Corps) managed to reach the embankments of the canal south-east of the village of Courcy which the Russian units in the corps had captured. The next corps in line, VII Corps (37, 14, 41 DI and one of the two Russian brigades in France) had a particularly difficult task. Its front extended for 10 kilometres, with the Germans holding the strongpoint of Fort Brimont on its hill. The plan was for 14 DI to circle around the fort to the north whilst the Russians and 14 DI were to capture the German first position and then invest the fort on the south and west sides. This involved crossing a canal (the Aisne–Marne canal) and a railway line. The 14 DI managed to do this but, once again, because the troops on its flanks had not managed to keep up with them, the division was forced to give up some of its gains to a German counter-attack. Next, XXXII Corps attacked astride the Aisne, 69 and 42 DI north of the river and 30 DI south. Here the troops made better progress and captured the first and second German positions. According to plan, five groups of tanks (eighty-two in all) arrived on the battlefield at 14.30 in order to support the attack on the third position. The German gunners had no difficulty in firing on the tanks and a good number were set on fire. The few tanks that escaped the barrage reached the German third position, but no infantry followed them. South of the river, 40 DI managed to hold on to Hill 108 on the side of Mont Sapigneul, but not the quarry beyond where the Germans' mining galeries began. V Corps deployed two divisions (9 and 10 DI, with 125 DI in reserve). The right-hand division made good progress (3 kilometres) but was unable to maintain its position because it was too far forward in relation to the troops on its flanks. Forty-eight tanks followed the infantry and advanced in columns towards the German lines north of Ville-au-Bois, 4 kilometres north-west of Berry-au-Bac on the Aisne. However, the leading tank became stuck in the first German trench, blocking the advance of the remainder, and the German artillery poured devastating and accurate fire on them from their excellent positions on the Californie plateau above Craonne. The tanks had to be abandoned, only eight able to return to base. On the left, opposite the eastern end of the Chemin des Dames, the infantry of I Corps left its trenches at 6am and managed to reach the plateaux on the ridge, but were unable to make further progress because the German defenders surged out of the deep shelters that had protected them from the artillery barrage, and they counter-attacked with machine guns. The divisions were held up on the ridge and suffered over 6,500 casualties.[34]

Fifth Army had achieved an advance of about 4 kilometres along a front of approximately the same length, but the Germans still held their formidable observatories, in particular those on the heights of Mont Sapigneul and Mont Spin south of the Aisne. If the French were to hold on to their gains, they would have to make further progress. Despite the intervention of the corps reserves on succeeding days, between 17 and 20 April no further progress was made towards capturing these two hills and Fort Brimont, although V Corps completed the capture of Ville-au-Bois and took 1,800 prisoners. On 18 April French artillery managed to defeat a German counter-attack, but the results as a whole were far from the rapid breakthrough that Nivelle had planned. Between 16 and 20 April Fifth Army captured 200 machine guns, 40 cannon and 11,000 prisoners, but the cost had been heavy: 44,253 casualties.[35]

Mangin's Sixth Army did slightly better along the western end of the Chemin des Dames. Each army corps had two divisions side-by-side for the first attack with the remaining divisions held ready to exploit any breach. On the right, II Colonial Corps suffered great losses in the opening attack, despite being very close to the ridge. Although the right-hand division (10 DI) managed to reach the crest of the ridge and move down the northern slopes, it lost most of its officers and a battalion of tirailleurs sénégalais was wiped out almost entirely. The left-hand division (15 DI) did not manage to reach Cerny on the ridge. The unfortunate North African troops were so demoralised by the cold and their losses that they were relieved on the 17th and replaced by XI Corps, who completed the capture of Hurtebise. Next in line, XX Corps, deployed two divisions, 153 DI on the right and, at 2.5 kilometres distant from the ridge, 39 DI on the left. The former managed to get into the German trenches on the ridge, but was held up by the strong resistance from a sugar factory outside Cerny (the village which 15 DI had not reached). The latter did not get as far as the ridge, but by the 18th had managed to make contact with 153 DI in front of the sugar factory which still resisted French attempts to capture it.

The sector allocated to VI Corps ran from Soupir down to the Aisne and along its south bank. The area was wooded and there were two German defensive positions before the third position on the ridge itself. Because of the difficult task facing VI Corps, the plan was to have the first day's attacking divisions (56 DI on the right and 127 DI on the left) reach an intermediate line and allow the other divisions of the corps (12 DI and 166 DI) to pass through to continue the offensive. On the right, after caturing the German first lines, 56 DI was held up by machine guns and the defenders of the trenches in the woods which the French artillery had failed to demolish. However, 127 DI managed to make some progress, capturing part of Chavonne village and Mont Sapin. The rest of the village was captured the next day, and 56 DI managed to clear the defences in the woods that had held them up by ordering another artillery barrage and only advancing at 5.30pm. During the night of 17/18 April both divisions had advanced far enough to threaten the German defenders who were pulled back to their position on the Chemin des Dames itself. This retirement enabled VI Corps to make further progress, and collect abandoned German guns and munitions. On 19 April, 127 DI got its regiment of 75s across the river and in position. By the next day, VI Corps' advance line ran between Braye and Jouy, about a kilometre south of the ridge. The 20-kilometre front of the north–south sector of Sixth Army's front was less well supplied with artillery. In addition, I Colonial Corps had only arrived on 3 April, and the planned support from Third Army to its north was to be given only after a certain advance had been made. Since the divisions had a particularly difficult task given their paucity of artillery – they had to get across a canal in the north and attack the heavily defended Laffaux windmill in the south – that advance was not achieved. By the end of the first day very few gains had been made, but the cost had been very heavy.

In summary, then, by 20 April Sixth Army had advanced along a front of about 10 kilometres between the elbow of the front at Missy-sur-Aisne and Soupir where it joined Fifth Army. Most ground had been captured in the west, with the Fort de Condé and several villages returning to French hands, but if less ground had been captured in the east, nonetheless the French now held between 3 and 4 kilometres of the Chemin des Dames from Hurtebise westwards. Sixth Army had taken 5,300 prisoners and captured 80 guns of various calibres, for 23,943 casualties.[36] Nivelle ordered Micheler on 17 April to consolidate Sixth Army's hold on the Chemin des Dames positions, while Fifth Army continued to attack. Mangin was furious, because he wanted Sixth Army's attack to continue, and he went to GQG over Micheler's head. GQG agreed with Mangin, and Sixth Army made further progress on 17 and 18 April, thus justifying his action. The disagreement between Mangin and his Army Group commander could not be resolved, however, and Nivelle settled the matter by removing Sixth Army from Micheler's control and placing it on 24 April in the Northern Army Group.

The plan had called for General Duchêne's Tenth Army to pass between Fifth and Sixth in order to exploit the breach in a north-eastwards direction.[37] By the second day Duchêne hoped that his cavalry would have reached Marle – from the river Aisne to Marle is about 45 kilometres. He was to advance his army between the other two nine or ten hours after H hour, and take over the line reached by the foremost corps. Despite a long and detailed instruction with unit boundaries and procedures for advancing between Fifth and Sixth, Tenth Army was not asked to move on 16 April because not enough progress had been made.

The original planning had not included any major operation for the Centre Army Group because of Pétain's insistence that the terrain did not permit it. However, after the German withdrawal in the north had interfered with Northern Army Group's plans, Nivelle extended the attacking front eastwards to include the centre and Fourth Army. It was to break through the enemy lines in Champagne on a front running east–west from Aubérive on the river Suippe to south of Reims, the junction with Fifth Army. Although Pétain had advised caution, Nivelle wanted just as brutal and rapid an attack as he was insisting that the Reserve Army Group's armies make. Consequently, Fourth Army's commander, General Anthoine, planned a 16-kilometre wide operation to take the Champagne hills (les monts de Champagne) to their north, with the first day's objective being a line 2 kilometres beyond the hills whose heights varied between 210 and 260 metres. Once the ground north of Reims was cleared of enemy troops, Fourth Army was to take over command of Fifth Army's two most easterly corps in order to push on towards the north-east. Fourth Army's attack was not to begin until the second day of the offensive, 17 April, in order to allow some of Fifth Army's heavy artillery to re-locate so as to support Fourth Army.

This was an ambitious plan, made more difficult by the strong enemy defences. The front had been quiet in 1916 and the chalk made the digging of deep shelters very easy. There were three enemy positions, the first consisting of three lines of trenches, the second located on the hill tops, and the third on the reverse slopes – all connected by narrow gauge railways, and with a further fall-back position along the river Suippe. Fourth Army was well supplied with artillery and firing began as early as 3 April. This gave the Germans warning of the attack and they reinforced both artillery and infantry. When the French attacked on 17 April the Germans had four divisions in line with another four in reserve; and most importantly, the number of batteries had almost doubled from the number that the French had identified on their front in March.

Progress was uneven when the attack began in rain and snow at 4.45 on the morning of 17 April. On the right (east) General Dumas' XVII Corps took some of the high ground before them, but the troops were stopped by machine guns which had been sheltered from the artillery bombardment. On the left (west) the two divisions of General Hély d'Oissel's VIII Corps got as far as the two western hills (Mont Cornillet and Mont Blond), but had to fight off strong counter-attacks. The fighting continued over the next three days, with more ground gained and 4,000 Germans captured. Yet, although the French had got a foot-hold on some of the Champagne hills, they did not hold the entire line of hills – the original German second position.

By 20 April, therefore, Nivelle's aim of rapid, brutal breakthrough had not been achieved, and where gains had been made the French were in unstable positions, held by exhausted troops requiring munitions re-supply. The medical services had been so overwhelmed that it proved impossible to establish accurate statistics for casualties, but, given the chaos, they could not have been other than great. The options were to return to their departure trenches, or to dig in and to consolidate their new positions. Nivelle chose the latter option; he did not insist on pursuing a breakthrough. This decision was taken in consultation with, and approved by, his political masters.

Indeed, the politicians had been involved closely from the beginning. Several parliamentarians had watched events from Micheler's headquarters, and also from Nivelle's. Even such critics as Clemenceau, accompanied by the new armaments minister, Louis Loucheur, watched from an observatory position.[38] Late on the first day Nivelle tried to reach Painlevé by telephone, but the minister was not available. Instead Nivelle left a message to say that he had decided to halt the attacks and to consult with the army group commanders as to future action. Ribot's view was that GQG had made yet another mistake, and the offensive was a 'real failure'. There was uproar in the parliamentary corridors, and Paris was filled with rumours. On 19 April Painlevé and Nivelle had a 'cold, correct, unfriendly' meeting for two hours in Compiègne. Painlevé's secretary thought GQG downcast and Nivelle embarrassed. The next day, however, when Nivelle spoke with Poincaré and Ribot, he seemed calm and confident. He explained that he intended to introduce Tenth Army (as had been intended for the first day) between the two other armies and to relieve the five divisions that had suffered the greatest casualties. He believed that the German losses were considerably greater than the French.[39]

Renewing the offensive

As the second phase of Nivelle's offensive began, he could not be accused of keeping the politicians in the dark. He had not insisted on forcing a breakthrough after the disappointing results of the first day, yet believed that real gains had been made, with the Germans forced to use their reserves. He could not understand, therefore, why the politicians were so unhappy. Wild rumours about the number of casualties were circulating, not helped by the complete breakdown of the medical services. Paris was becoming 'detestable' with the word 'disaster' on everyone's lips in the war ministry. Rumours of disaster reached London, and Lloyd George asked Haig why the French government was unhappy with the results of the offensive and whether they wanted to stop it.[40]

On 21 April Nivelle introduced General Duchêne's Tenth Army between Fifth and Sixth Armies with orders to take over the left-hand sector of the former's front, leaving the latter to concentrate on its southern flank facing east. Tenth Army's front ran from Berry-au-Bac to the original point of juncture between Fifth and Sixth Armies. Its instructions were to continue the battle already under way as quickly and as energetically as possible. At the same time Nivelle sent a message to Haig explaining that the French Army would soon be attacking again and that he (Haig) should take advantage of the French action. With the French holding down so many German troops, the British should be able to widen their front of attack and aim for more distant objectives.[41] Nivelle also pressed the Italians and the Russians to take advantage of the 'favourable' moment to attack. The last two urgings were in vain.

The Reserve Army Group commander was not eager to repeat the experience of 16 April. Micheler wrote to Nivelle on 21 April, asking whether limited action to consolidate the new positions on the Chemin des Dames should be undertaken first, before proceeding to an all-out attack on Fort Brimont in conjunction with Centre Army Group's Fourth Army. Micheler pointed out that Fifth Army faced determined resistance and, if it continued to push north-eastwards as directed so as to converge with Fourth Army, it risked being exposed to enemy attacks on its flanks. Moroever, Micheler had been obliged to relieve most of his exhausted units and he lacked sufficient munitions for the proposed operation. Micheler ended by asking bluntly whether Nivelle had reconsidered his instructions, and handed his letter to Nivelle personally to ensure that it could not be ignored.[42] The next day Painlevé visited Mazel and, after discussion with Nivelle and Micheler, the CinC decided to follow Micheler's more modest proposals and to delay operations until the end of the month. These modest proposals were for Fifth Army, supported by another push from Fourth, to capture Fort Brimont and the heights of Monts Spin and Sapigneul so as to relieve the German pressure on Reims; Sixth Army was to complete the occupation of the Chemin des Dames, but to wait until Tenth Army, just introduced onto the front, was ready. Sixth Army moved to Northern Army Group on 24 April, so Micheler's Reserve Army Group was reduced to two armies once again, Fifth and Tenth.

Further north, however, Haig was still buoyed by his success at Arras on 9 April; he saw no reason to suspend operations, and renewed the offensive on the BEF's front on 23 April. Nivelle reassured Haig once again the next day that the French intended to renew their offensive, but Haig continued to receive reports that the French CinC was likely to be changed. This lack of clarity forced Painlevé and Ribot to call Haig to Paris on the 26th to assure him that active operations would begin again on the French front in a week's time. Since Painlevé had already told his private secretary on 21 April that he had decided to replace Nivelle, one must conclude that these reassurances were more pious hopes than definite intentions.[43]

Although Nivelle did indeed intend to restart operations, the politicians intervened once again. In a telephone message on 23 April, Poincaré informed Nivelle of his fears that the operations were premature. Clearly Nivelle's subordinates had been bending his ear. Nivelle responded crossly that since no date had been fixed, he could not understand why the President was crediting rumours and, in any case, he could not exercise his command effectively under such conditions. Painlevé intervened also a few days later on the 29th to inform Nivelle that the government had decided to suspend the Brimont operation provisionally until the CinC could discuss the question with Pétain. Painlevé had just appointed Pétain as chief of the army general staff in his ministry. This post, the equivalent of General Robertson as Chief of the Imperial General Staff, had been in abeyance since 1914 because Joffre had filled both roles, CinC and chief of the army. Now Painlevé revived it, with the stated aim of 'ensuring a more efficacious general direction of the war, with the army general staff cooperating henceforth in the study of all the problems raised by the preparation and coordination of the ever-expanding scope of military operations'.[44] Clearly Painlevé intended to exercise greater control through the more cautious Pétain. Indeed, he wanted to replace Nivelle with Pétain as CinC, but it was felt that it was too dangerous to change CinC while operations were continuing. The revived post of chief of the army general staff was, therefore, a stop-gap measure. Painlevé appointed Fayolle, another cautious general, to replace Pétain as commander of the Centre Army Group.

The date for the start of the renewed attack was delayed several times, not least because enemy counter-attacks forced the French to undertake local operations. The Russian brigades were sent to the rear, ostensibly to be reconstituted, but the real reason will be seen below (page 207). General Mangin was removed from command of Sixth Army since he had lost the confidence of his subordinates. Nivelle requested that Mangin be made Governor-general of the AOF, but Ribot and Painlevé refused. After Mangin created a violent scene, Nivelle sent him off to see Painlevé and amended his reasons for dismissing Mangin to failing to take proper precautions as an army commander. After another shouting match, Painlevé and the cabinet confirmed Mangin's dismissal, for he was too much in the public eye and too heavily criticised, especially for the losses among the tirailleurs sénégalais, to allow him to continue in command.[45] General Paul Maistre took over command of Sixth Army. It was not until 5 May that the offensive was re-launched. By that date, however, several more stumbling-blocks had appeared.

Relations within Fifth Army were no better than Mangin's had been with his subordinates in Sixth Army. Although Nivelle had informed Painlevé that there was complete agreement in Fifth Army over the proposed operation around Reims, Mazel and his corps commanders believed that the operation would be too costly. In his new role as chief of the army general staff, Pétain sent Serrigny, the head of his military cabinet, to sound out opinion. Painlevé too sent his secretary on the same mission. Serrigny reported Mazel as saying that Nivelle was a criminal. In Pétain's estimation, the projected operations on Craonne and Fort Brimont would be 'very hazardous and very costly'.[46] Consequently, when Nivelle and Pétain met on 30 April, it was agreed that the Craonne operation would follow that on the Brimont massif, the latter operation itself divided into two phases, with an attack on the fort only following a successful first phase encircling the high ground to the north. The British ally proved to be another stumbling-block. Although the renewed British attack had gained some more ground, there was no spectacular prize such as the capture of Vimy ridge that had crowned the initial offensive on 9 April. Pétain's appointment and Nivelle's postponements worried Haig. He no longer knew who was in command, but he did know that Pétain represented a change from the offensive-minded Nivelle. Henry Wilson was opposed to any decision that brought Pétain to power, for in his view Pétain represented 'squatting'. The British had fallen in with the French plans to the extent of subordinating Haig to Nivelle; now it was time to review the relationship. Haig did not want to continue fighting in France if the French were not fighting too; he wanted to end the command arrangement and be free to move his operations to Flanders.

With the British fearful that the arrival of Pétain meant a change of policy, and the French Army in disarray, clearly a high-level conference was required to impose some order. It took place in Paris on 4–5 May 1917, with politicians and military in attendance.[47] The conference accepted that the military position had changed since the offensive began in April, but that it was vital nonetheless to continue fighting with all available resources. Both British and French military agreed that the offensive should continue, but an offensive with 'limited objectives'. Accordingly, Nivelle issued a note setting out the mission of all the French armies. Sixth (now in Northern Army Group) and Tenth were to extend their gains north from the Chemin des Dames towards the river Ailette; Fifth and Fourth were continue to seek to free Reims; in addition Second Army in the east was to prepare an operation to reduce the Saint-Mihiel salient and then move on to the Briey basin, and Third Army in the north was to aim for the Hindenburg Line between Saint-Quentin and the Oise. The note also foreshadowed action by XXXVI Corps in Dunkirk in conjunction with Belgian Army and, at the other end of the front, action in Alsace by Seventh Army.[48] On 8 May the Reserve Group of Armies was dissolved and Micheler moved to command of Fifth Army attached to Centre Army Group – the symbolic end to Nivelle's grand design for a breakthrough and exploitation. In the event, General Humbert's Third Army in the north did not carry out any operation against Saint-Quentin because it had to take over British lines as Haig regained his independence and moved to Flanders for the battle of Third Ypres.

In accordance with Nivelle's Note, the four armies fighting on the Chemin des Dames and east of Reims continued operations. On 4 May Fifth Army failed to capture the heights of Mont Spin and Mont Sapigneul, where the Germans were protected from the worst of the massive French bombardment by their deep underground shelters. Sixth Army managed to make some progress in two days of fighting on 5 and 6 May, across the northern slopes of the Chemin des Dames, but the enemy was clearly intent on fierce counter-attacks. Tenth Army, inserted between Fifth and Sixth, attacked towards Craonne and made some gains, but the little progress made by all three armies was not worth the heavy casualties suffered. East of Reims, Fourth Army continued their onslaught on the Champagne hills, and advanced 500 metres. Paul Pireaud's heavy artillery battery took part, suffering from enemy shells that dug craters 4–5 metres deep in their midst. It was 'just like Verdun', Pireaud wrote.[49] The May fighting was just as costly as the April fighting had been. By 10 May most attacks had wound down, except for Fourth Army's operation on the 20th against Mont Cornillet, in which the huge German underground shelter in the hill was bombarded with gas, and its entrances blown in, suffocating the garrison inside. French losses between 1 and 10 May were 4,200 for Fourth Army in Champagne, and 31,855 for the three armies in the Chemin des Dames sector. In all four armies, 13,690 had been killed or had disappeared.[50]

On 15 May, after some more vacillation from the politicians and a degree of obstinacy from Nivelle, who refused at first to resign, Pétain took over as France's new CinC, and Foch followed Pétain into the war ministry as chief of the army staff. Nivelle had lasted the shortest time of any of the CinCs of the belligerents, less than five months. There has been no appeal against history's verdict that Nivelle's command was a disaster. The sentence was banishment to North Africa, where he spent the rest of war, making several unavailing requests to return to France. Can anything be said in mitigation?

First of all, against the odds (weather and terrain), the French armies involved in the Second Battle of the Aisne had done well. All the forty-five fresh German divisions reported in reserve before 16 April had been engaged in the twenty-five days of fighting, some of them more than once.[51] The German official history gives the casualty figure to the end of June as 163,000, including 37,000 'missing'. These were mostly those prisoners captured by the French.[52] If the tanks had not been a great success, their employment had given useful lessons, just as the British had found on the Somme in 1916. Despite the poor performance of the medical services, the casualties were not proportionally higher than on the Somme in 1916 or in Artois in 1915. The fact that acts of 'collective indiscipline' broke out, starting in April and reaching a crisis in the last weeks of May and the first in June, has coloured judgements of Nivelle's offensive. As Lloyd George asked during the Paris conference, urging the vital importance of continuing to press Germany: 'what would our feelings be if we [the Allies] had lost 445,000 prisoners, that is to say, practically 5 divisions of fighting men, 450 guns, including some of the heaviest calibre, about 800 machine-guns, had had 36 reserve divisions put out of action, and had lost 70 square miles of territory?'.[53]

In further mitigation, it must be said that the conditions under which Nivelle was forced to exercise his command verged on the impossible. He had not asked to be made CinC, and the role of Poincaré in supporting the choice of Nivelle and maintaining that support would merit examination. Joffre had wanted Nivelle so as to be able to retain some influence, a hope that was soon dispelled. Nivelle had to deal with three ministers of war: the first (Lacaze) was only acting minister, the second (Lyautey) would not have selected Nivelle, and the third (Painlevé) interfered. He was the object of Lloyd George's scheming to rein in Haig, and he was subject to much more political control and interference than Joffre had ever had to parry. Nivelle's greatest difficulty was caused by subordinates going behind his back and complaining to ministers. Micheler, for example, had the ear of the president of the Senate, Antonin Dubost. Pétain was the most destructive. After the war council meeting of 6 April, Castelnau gave him a lift back to his headquarters. During the ride, Pétain reproached Nivelle for the 'pride that was blinding him and for certain intellectual failings'. Nivelle had never conducted more than 'small' operations, Pétain continued, and was incapable of rising to the necessary overview of the situation. Hence the 'fatal [néfaste] conception' of the battle, and Nivelle's lack of 'flexibility' rendered him incapable of responding to the new problem of the German withdrawal with a new solution.[54] Events proved Pétain's judgement to be valid, but the expression of such views reveals the profound disarray within the French Army.

Yet the weight of evidence is overwhelmingly against Nivelle. He had promised speed and surprise; he had said that poor weather did not matter, and that he had enough of the new rapid-firing 155mm guns, some of which would be carried on tracked vehicles, enabling them to move across shell-cratered ground. Above all, he had said that he would call a halt to operations after twenty-four or forty-eight hours, if breakthrough had not been achieved. He had allowed himself to be used by Lloyd George; and he had been unable to impose his authority on his subordinates. The contrast with Joffre, who sacked 168 subordinates in the first four months of the war, is stark.

As for speed, Nivelle had set 15 February as the start date, but two full months passed before the infantry assault began. As for surprise, Nivelle had been very indiscreet. The operation was the talk of London and Paris dinner tables, and the delays gave the Germans plenty of time to realise what was going to happen. Nor did Nivelle do anything about the fact that a copy of operational orders had disappeared from the body of a French soldier. As for poor weather, Nivelle claimed that he had triumphed despite the weather at Verdun in December 1916. Yet, December cold at the end of autumn is easier to bear than April snow and sleet after a long, cold winter. As for the modern 155mm guns, seventy-nine battalions of tractor-drawn guns had been created by the end of 1916, but only seventeen of these were armed with the new gun, and the organisation of the command of the artillery within the new army and army groups was deficient.[55] Finally, imposing a halt after one or two days was impossible, as it came down to a question of returning to the start position and giving up any gains, or digging in and resisting counter-attacks.

Sir William Robertson summed up thus after the war: 'I always thought his plan was ridiculous and certainly had no confidence in him as a Commander-in-chief over British troops. He was an untried man in high command at that time, and was always bragging about how he was going to destroy the Germans. No man of sense would ever brag about destroying Germans or anyone else before the event.' Again: 'Personally, I never heard of a man who was so cocksure that he could beat his enemy and that if he found he did not he would definitely stop the operations and so prevent any further losses. Even a boy at Sandhurst would have more sense than to talk rot of that kind.'[56] Franchet d'Espèrey's post-war verdict on Nivelle was that he was 'a man overtaken [dépassé] by events – he gave me the impression of a horse harnessed to a cart that is too heavy, incapable of holding it back on too steep a slope'.[57] The German historiography of the battle does not examine Nivelle's role; rather it emphasises the success of the new elastic defence in depth, which gave the German troops retirement positions on the Aisne, just as the Hindenburg Line provided the same protection further north.[58]

Charles Delvert, who had witnessed the first day as a liaison officer, pointed out how different were the conditions at Verdun at the end of 1916, where Nivelle claimed to have found the 'method' for victory, and those on the Chemin des Dames. Around the Verdun forts, the ground had been so churned up by the eight months of shelling since February 1916 that it was impossible to construct a proper trench, let alone a deep defensive position. Nivelle's attack trenches there were only 3–4 kilometres distant from their objectives. Yet the Chemin des Dames had been quiet since 1914, so was well defended; the chalk permitted the construction of tunnels and shelters; wire could be fixed firmly. Moreover, the enemy had found the answer to massive preliminary artillery bombardments: pull back to the second position and wait for the exhausted attackers there.[59] Although Nivelle, Mangin and Mazel were sacked as a result of the failed offensive, it was the pauvres cons du front, the poor bloody infantry, who paid the greatest price. See Figure 13.

(a)

(b)   (c)

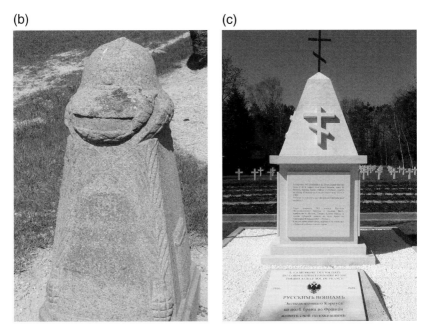

Fig. 13 (a) and (b) Monument to the 'heroes and martyrs' of the Aisne offensives, April 1917
(c) The memorial to the Russian Expeditionary Force that fought in France

Mutinies

Although Pétain and Poincaré both used it at the time for lack of any better, the word 'mutiny' is too strong for the incidents of collective indiscipline that occurred in May and June 1917, following Nivelle's failed offensive. The various incidents were so disparate in type, extent and duration that it has proved hard to define precisely what constituted the 1917 'mutiny'. Does a group of drunken soldiers shouting 'down with war!' count as mutiny? Or reading pacifist tracts handed out in the Gare de l'Est in Paris while passing through the capital on the way home on leave? Or one or two soldiers slipping away into the woods whilst moving up the front lines and then rejoining their units a few days later, claiming to have lost their way? What is the minimum number of men required for a mutiny, as opposed to the offence of refusing to obey an order? If 300 men are shouting that they will not move into the trenches the next day but are calmed by their officers, is this mutiny? Moreover, written sources are uneven: about a quarter of the military justice files of French Army units have not survived; unit war diaries are inconsistent when reporting such incidents; some incidents are known only through soldiers' accounts written post-war. These difficulties over definition and source material explain why it is impossible to give an accurate figure of the numbers involved, and why historians have offered differing figures. The official history gives 170 incidents (of which 51 were committed by a 'few men only', revealing uncertainty over whether a 'few men' could constitute a mutiny), whereas the acknowledged historian of the mutinies and the first to examine the phenomenon in depth, Guy Pedroncini, cites 250 incidents. That the official history would under-report is understandable, but recent research revises the number of incidents downwards. Denis Rolland mentions 200 (but only 163 of them known 'with certainty') and André Loez brings the number down to 108, by weighting the documentary evidence. Similarly, if the number of divisions involved is considered, the official history gives 54, Pedroncini 68, Rolland 78 and Loez 60, which is to say, nevertheless, a good half of all French divisions at the time. The numbers involved may have been between 25,000 and 30,000 or much more, between 59,000 and 88,000.[60]

The greatest number of incidents (five) occurred in 77 DI, but they took place over a very short time period, 1–5 June 1917.[61] Until 20 May the division had been a unit of the Northern Army Group and had taken part in the slow pursuit of the Germans as they retired to the Hindenburg Line. Then the division had been withdrawn on 20 May, transferred to Sixth Army, and had been supposedly resting for ten days. This had not necessarily been very restful, however. Some rest areas were within range of enemy guns, and all were most uncomfortable, with accommodation in ruined farm buildings, wooden baraques, in tents or even without any shelter at all. Nevertheless, the division made a good impression when they were reviewed by its commander, General Guillemot, on 30 May. Since Verdun the previous year the men had had no long rest period, whereas they knew that divisions in rear areas had got their leave on time. Consequently, during the course of May, men of 159 RI stated that they would not return to the trenches unless the leave position improved; 60 BCP made similar complaints. On 31 May, 150 men of the latter regiment demanded leave, but their officers managed to calm things down. The next day, 1 June, the order came to return to the front line, and the men demanded to see their families before risking their lives again. That evening 60 BCP again refused to return to the trenches without a period of leave beforehand, but they remained calm. About 400 of them walked in columns to neighbouring villages to attempt to drum up support, but they agreed to return to their quarters. Next morning some 250–300 men left their guns behind and dispersed into nearby woods, stating that they would not return fire if fired upon. The remainder of the regiment, however, refused to join the revolt and they left in trucks in the afternoon. The commander of I Cavalry Corps ordered his troops to surround the men in the woods, but agreed not to use force when 60 BCP's commander said that the men had grenades. He was able to persuade the men to return to their duty.

Another regiment in the same division, 57 BCP, also demanded leave before returning to the trenches, and on 2 June about 150 of the chasseurs refused to obey orders. During the night the men were disarmed and arrested. Some officers obviously sympathised with their men, and it seems that no junior officers were harmed during these incidents. Indeed, General Guillemot 'reintegrated' 57 BCP, but the Sixth Army commander, now General Maistre, insisted that these men should be arrested like the others. Shortly thereafter, about 100 men of 97 RI abandoned their cantonment and dispersed, but gave themselves up on 5 June. Men of 159 RI were also complaining about lack of leave, and on 4 June a squad left its battalion when going up to the line to relieve their comrades.

Military tribunals (conseils de guerre) tried the men. Table 10 shows the extent of the trials in 77 DI, and the sentences passed. The greatest number of convictions in this division was for 57 BCP. Pedroncini points out that fully 104 of these convicted men had no previous conviction; 101 were unmarried; the largest single profession was 'cultivateur' (29); and they came from at least 38 different départements. So little linked these men other than their temporary burst of anger.

Our 13 DI was not free of incidents of indiscipline. After being withdrawn from the Somme in 1916, the division alternated rest and

Table 10 *Trials of men in 77 Division d'Infanterie*

Regiment	Charges	Sentence	Observations
60 BCP	18 in total:		death sentences:
	15 refusal to obey	death	9 overturned on appeal;
	an order		4 commuted; 2 carried out
	3 desertion	detention	1 for 20 years; 2 for 10 years each
159 RI	11 desertion	detention	1 man 6 years; 9 men five years;
			1 ten years
			(sentence suspended in 6 cases)
61 BCP	11 desertion (8 plus	hard labour	1 man 20 years; 2 men 15 years;
	conspiracy to desert)		rest 5–10 years
			3 suspended sentences
57 BCP	122 in total:		
	48 refusal to obey	23 death	death sentences: 22 overturned;
	63 conspiracy to desert	rest hard labour	1 pardoned
	11 desertion		
97 RI	8 (abandoning post in	3 death, the rest	mitigating circumstances
	front of the enemy)	hard labour (5–7	accepted in the 5 not sentenced
		years)	to death

training periods between 20 January and 29 May, hence it missed the
April fighting on the Chemin des Dames. Then it was moved to Dommiers, a village south-west of Soissons. During the evening of 30 May a
'certain number' of men from the two chasseur regiments attempted to
hold a meeting near Dommiers cemetery in order to discuss the rebel-
lions in other units. Officers intervened and the men dispersed, but next
evening they managed to hold their meeting on Dommiers firing range.
About 100 men, from all four regiments (20 BCP, 21 BCP, 21 RI, 109
RI) attended, as did some others from 43 and 6 DI. Three of the
chasseurs read an appeal from mutineers of other corps for 13 DI to join
them; then all debated whether to agree to attack. The majority said that
they would 'hold the sector' but not attack; a minority refused even to
hold the sector. All agreed to meet again the next day, 1 June. There were
none of the usual complaints about lack of leave or unfair allocation of
rest periods; this was a more serious incident in that men were voting
whether to attack, just as the Russian brigades had done before 16 April.
On the other hand, the commander of the divisional infantry, Colonel
Michel, reported that the number of protestors was very small, describing
the majority of the men as 'healthy'. He decided to allow the meeting to
take place on 1 June, so as not to let the 'gangrene' fester by covering it
up, and General Bouillon agreed. Sûreté agents dressed in military
uniform and reliable soldiers were ordered to attend to keep an eye on

proceedings. The three chasseurs who had read out the appeal were arrested, tried and condemned to death for inciting soldiers to armed rebellion. Two were executed on 10 June; the third had his sentence commuted to hard labour in perpetuity. (He was amnestied on 24 December 1920.) The men were aged 21, 30 and 38, and came from Loiret, Marne and the 8th arrondissement in Paris. They had different jobs, thus reflecting the same variety as in all mutinies.[62]

A third regiment in 13 DI, 109 RI, also became involved. During the night of 1/2 June, groups from 17 RI came to 109 RI's quarters and roisted them from their tents. Two more waves of 400–500 men from 17 RI came through during the night. Most of those in 109 RI, who were forced to disperse, returned but about ten left voluntarily, armed. The commander of 17 RI tried to blame 109 RI for debauching his men. One of 109 RI captains reported that it was useless to use force to repress such an incident, but high command should live closer to the men. Higher command did not like this of course: XXI Corps commander General Pont, Nivelle's former chief of staff, rejected the report as superficial (containing 'des choses inconsidérées'). The division's court martial punished the ten who joined the mutiny severely, by ordering three death sentences (two men were reprieved, but Corporal Lefèvre was executed), and prison sentences for the remainder. Pedroncini suggests that the reason for such severity was the fact that the rest of 109 RI did not mutiny, so these men might have become ringleaders in any future incidents. Yet Julien Weber, a priest coopted onto the court martial, hints that the ten who were tried were simply those who had been caught when the others slipped quietly back to their bivouacs.[63]

The fate of Corporal Gaston Lefèvre is particularly poignant. He was born in Morfontaine (Meurthe et Moselle) in 1897, and his village lay in the path of the German invasion in 1914. The names of thirteen civilian victims (out of a population of 344) are recorded on the village war memorial. One of the thirteen was his 58-year-old father, Jean-Baptiste Lefèvre, cantonnier (road-mender), who was shot at point-blank range in the street in front of his home, and one of his sons. Another son, Gaston's elder brother Alphonse, was killed at the front in December 1914. Although under-age and living under German occupation, Gaston crossed the enemy lines and volunteered for military service. Convicted on 9 June 1917 as a mutineer, he was executed in Soissons on the 16th at 4.30 in the morning, despite his appeal for clemency being taken up by the deputy for Nancy, Louis Marin. In 2011 the town council of Morfontaine agreed unanimously that Gaston Lefèvre's name should be added to the war memorial, so joining those of his father and brother.[64] (See Figure 14.)

Fig. 14 Corporal Gaston Lefèvre's name added to the war memorial in Morfontaine (Meurthe-et-Moselle) to join those of his father and brother, 11 November 2011

As this brief account of some of the recorded incidents reveals, there was little to link the men who became involved enough to be brought before military justice. Perhaps pre-war experience of trade-union action could be assumed to be a unifying factor. However, André Loez's analysis of the sociology of the mutineers confirms Pedroncini's comments cited above. Loez discovered that the men were not predominantly factory workers, combed out from the home front. He compared all the trials held throughout the entire year of 1917 in six divisions, four in which mutinies occurred and two where no such incidents were recorded. Although the results cannot stand for the entire French army, nonetheless they permit distinctions to be made between men who were tried for mutiny and men who were tried for the usual run of military 'crimes': drunkenness, looting, insulting an officer, and so on. He found that the proportion of those tried who had a previous criminal record (civilian or military) was almost the same: indeed, 62.2 per cent of mutineers and 63.9 per cent of 'non-mutineers' had no previous record at all. The mutineers were younger (average age 25.4 as against 28 years) and fully half of them had not been conscripted in 1914, but later. Similarly, the proportion of married men among the mutineers was 21.8 per cent (30.1 per cent among non-mutineers), of whom 13.9 per cent had children (as against 21.2 per cent of non-mutineers). From these figures it may be deduced that older, steadier men with family responsibilities, and older, steadier men who had been in the war since 1914, adopting coping mechanisms upon seeing friends and brothers killed alongside them, were less likely to appear before military courts for acts of mutiny than younger men without family responsibilities. Loez also found that mutineers were more likely to be urbanites than countrymen, more likely to come from the Paris region than non-mutineers, and, surprisingly, less likely to be miners or similar workers than non-mutineers. Out of more than 400 mutineers in Loez's sample, there were only 14 factory workers and 9 miners, both categories assumed to be more militant than others in the national workforce.[65]

What drove these very different men to risk a firing squad rather than risking their life in the trenches? The usual reason given is 'lassitude'. The war had gone on for so long that morale collapsed. Yet neither the failed 1915 Champagne operations nor incidents noted in 1916 – bleating, for example, on moving into the front lines – had led to mutiny, and a year later on the same Chemin des Dames the German military offensive did not lead to mass desertions. The difference in 1917 lay in the raised expectations. If the lowly privates in the trenches did not understand how Nivelle's strategic ideas differed from those of Joffre, yet they knew that Joffre had not achieved victory and that his replacement was very confident that *he* had the key. The press had portrayed the German withdrawal to the Hindenburg Line as an Allied victory whereas, in fact, it signalled a greater German understanding of defensive principles, freed German divisions for use elsewhere, and penetration of the 'line' proved an extremely difficult task at war's end. Then the British opening moves in the offensive on 9 April had won a great prize. Foch's northern armies had failed thrice to capture the heights of Vimy ridge in 1914–15, but in 1917 the Canadians pulled it off. For the French, on the other hand, disappointment and depression followed, when it became clear by 20 April that their offensive had failed. Mangin's boast that he would sleep in Laon on the night of 16/17 April was proved hollow.

So historians have adopted the conclusion that the wave of indiscipline was a purely military matter, because the incidents were related spatially and temporally to the Chemin des Dames offensive that began on 16 April, but by the 20th had clearly failed. Yet no incidents were recorded in the front lines; all took place in rear areas. Moreover, those divisions showing the greatest number of incidents – the 77 and 13 DI discussed above – had not been in the fighting on 16 April. So the spatial connection to the Chemin des Dames is not solid; nor is the temporal connection. General Pétain's appointment is often represented as having had the purpose of healing the army. He was the commander who cared for his men and refused to permit further pointless offensives. Yet his appointment on 15 May was *followed* by the crisis of the last days of May and early June. Rather, Pétain's appointment marked the fact of Nivelle's removal, thereby confirming publicly the failure of the offensive. Furthermore, Pétain had agreed during the conference in Paris with the British that offensives would continue. Indeed, the French were forced to continue in order to consolidate their gains on the ridge, because to return to their start lines would be an impossible admission of defeat, probably causing even greater displays of indiscipline.

The crisis of discipline was connected temporally to other events as well as Nivelle's offensive. Briand's government fell in March, so there was political uncertainty. On 6 April the USA declared war, but the immediate effect was not a morale boost but rather, as the army's morale reports indicate, a fear that the war would drag on even longer as there could be no instant infusion of American troops in the trenches. There were strikes and industrial unrest in Paris and in other French towns. The most significant event in the weeks leading up to the start of the offensive was the first Russian revolution and the abdication of the Tsar. This news became known very quickly and was received very favourably. Clemenceau's editorials in his newspaper *L'Homme Enchaîné* during March had pointed up the parallels with the French nation's rising in 1789. The Russian brigades, who attacked on the right flank and fought very well, sustaining many casualties in the attempts to advance to Fort Brimont, had greeted the news of the revolution and abdication with several incidents of unrest. Once the order arrived from Petrograd to elect soldiers' soviets, on the very day, 16 April, of the start of the offensive, the French high command swiftly removed the Russians from the front, eventually quarantining them in central France where later they mounted a large May Day demonstration, and then had a proper mutiny.[66] Their example could not have been lost on their French comrades. So the crisis in the army was linked to the political effervescence all around.

That the political situation played an integral role in the crisis is seen in the political demands that many of the mutineers made. The attempts to storm trains so as to reach the capital and their political representatives, and the letters written to deputies, show that the men's aims were an end to the war.[67] Peace offers were in the air, from the German peace note at the end of 1916 rejected by the Allies, to the forthcoming conference of Socialists in Stockholm, where neutrals and belligerents were expected to revise war aims. Some elements of the French press advocated pacifism, although the scandal of French journalists and even a deputy receiving German subventions to promote such ideas did not break until later in 1917. However, the press and the pacifist tracts handed out to soldiers at railway stations increased the political ferment.

The soldiers' grievances were not only political. Another common demand was the restoration of leave. Nivelle had reduced all leave on 21 March, as usual, but the repeated postponements left those men who had remained in position for the original February date feeling unfairly penalised. A long GQG report of 30 May analysed the leave problem, recognising that 'in such a long war' leave was 'an absolute necessity, an indispensable moral comfort'. In September Pétain increased leave from seven to ten days every four months, with travel time added on.[68]

A further element lay in the conditions on the home front. It is well known that the link with home and family, sustained by letters and periods of leave, was vital for the fighting men. The winter of 1916/17 had been exceptionally hard, and it had been impossible to transport enough coal for factories to continue production and for homes to be heated, since the railways were being used to prepare the offensive and the canals were frozen because it was so cold. Prices continued to rise and some items became so scarce that rationing had to be introduced. Sugar, for example, was rationed from March 1917, and coal from September. Men and women working in war industries were being paid higher wages and suffered a much lower risk of death or injury than the men in the trenches. Resentment against 'embusqués', those with safe jobs far away from danger, was still rife. If soldiers were fighting for their homes and families, but the war meant that there was not enough money or food for them, then why continue to fight?

There was a wave of strikes in the spring of 1917. In Paris it began with female workers in the clothing industry, and spread to building and transport workers. Production in factories doing war work was so threatened that compulsory arbitration was introduced. The call for a strike on May Day was obeyed, and cries of 'Down with war!' and 'Long live peace!' were heard at demonstrations. About 100,000 workers in Paris, the great majority of them women, and 5,000 women workers in a Toulouse gunpowder factory were on strike over the May–June 1917 period. If the discontent was mainly economic, the reports on home front morale from the prefects of about half France's départements showed a decline. This decline was particularly worrying in the towns which had become large production centres for war materiel.[69] The soldiers were not alone, then, in their protests.

To return to matters purely military, the postal control showed much resentment that leave was attributed unfairly and that some units spent much more time in the front line than others. Also, many of the complaints concerned the number of men killed and injured by French shells – 'friendly fire'. Artillery–infantry liaison was very poor in the Chemin des Dames offensive, and, at 100 metres every three minutes, the pace of the rolling barrage was set at far too rapid a rate. Nivelle had used this new tactic at Verdun, but it was much more difficult to control over a wide area, especially where troops were attacking uphill – and it is about 5 kilometres from the river Aisne up to the crest. Anyone who has stood on the narrow ridge of the Chemin des Dames and looked south, down towards the former French lines, will appreciate that maintaining a pace of 100 metres every three minutes would be hard enough, even without carrying a heavy pack and being fired on by enemy machine guns.

Therefore, when Pétain took over the command of the French Army on the Western Front on 15 May, he was faced with an acute crisis demanding immediate measures. Those measures combined carrot and stick, with longer-term improvements in training to follow. The most urgent response had to be repression. The situation could not be allowed to continue. Although Pétain's reputation is as the healer of a sick army, he was a strict disciplinarian. In earlier years Fayolle had noted examples of Pétain's firmness. Although many death sentences were commuted, as seen above, the number of executions carried out was small. Pétain requested the reinstatement of courts martial on 7 June, demanding immediate execution after the pronouncement of a death sentence. Poincaré temporarily gave up his right to grant mercy to convicted men sentenced to death. Decimation did not take place, although the selection methods of so-called leaders of the indiscipline were at times dubious. When Spears was writing his book, *Prelude to Victory* about events in 1917, he asked Painlevé for help, and Painlevé sent him a dossier with the details of 1917's verdicts for 'collective indiscipline': 112 death sentences of which 25 were carried out, and 345 other convictions.[70] This accords with other sources, which give 26 (Rolland), 24 (*AFGG*) and 27 (Pedroncini).[71] Indeed, it would have been pointless executing too many men – they were needed to fight the enemy. Nonetheless, an unverified number of 'undesirables' were shipped out to various French colonies, their removal and fate being kept from their comrades, who no doubt thought that those removed had been executed. The courts martial were held speedily and sentences carried out within a few days. Painlevé found his duty of reviewing the death sentences very hard. Very soon he rescinded the permission for immediate execution.

In further repressive measures, the press was forbidden to mention the trials, and action was taken against the distribution of pacifist tracts. Trench newspapers were required to send copies to GQG, but this demand was not always met.[72] Drunkenness was reduced by holding back some of the combat and long-service bonuses, not allowing soldiers to have so much money in their pockets, and controlling more closely the amount of wine being delivered to village shops and bars.

The role of both junior and senior officers in dealing with events bears examination. Clearly some junior officers sympathised with their men's demands, which was not surprising since they lived with their men. Losses in junior officers had been very high, and many of their replacements lacked a natural sense of authority, or had been promoted from the ranks and found it hard to command their former comrades. Others tried to hide what had happened by not reporting such events to higher authority. Pétain issued instructions on 8 June that officers were to be firm in repressing all acts of indiscipline.[73] He would 'cover with his authority' all those who showed energy and initiative in so doing, but inertia would be counted as complicity. The higher ranks were, however, noticeably absent during the crisis. Corps and divisional generals, and army and army group commanders, kept away from the hotspots until it was safe to appear before the men again, for it would have led to even more disruption if the stones occasionally thrown at colonels and junior officers were aimed at general officers. Those senior officers nevertheless had their opinions, and they tallied closely. They agreed that the trouble came from the interior, Paris in particular, where revolutionary ideas were being spread by German money. The three army group commanders, Castelnau, Fayolle and Franchet d'Espèrey blamed factors outside the army for the troubles. Divisional commanders, on the other hand, saw the complaints about leave and the unequal lengths of time spent in attack sectors as contributory factors.[74]

Pétain's carrot took the form of acceding to the principal demand that arrears of leave should be made up and granted more equitably. Pedroncini praises Pétain for having been the only senior commander to advocate this step. The others believed that mutinous troops should be isolated from the interior, not permitted to rejoin their families. Yet, once offensive operations ceased, regular leave had to be re-started, because parliament had made it a legal requirement. Moreover, granting leave removed some of the trouble-makers from the zone of the armies. The reports on morale sent in by the departmental préfets show that men on leave caused trouble in their home towns. Hence, as the army generals complained that pacifist agitation and publications on the home front were affecting morale in the army, the reverse could also be the case. Pétain recommended that a quarter of a unit's effectives might be allowed to go on leave at any one time, when circumstances permitted. For corps and divisions withdrawn from the line and sent to the rear to be reconstituted, the proportion could be allowed to reach 50 per cent.[75]

If trouble-makers were to be allowed to travel to their homes on leave, it was important to improve conditions which might give rise to more trouble. Travel conditions were notoriously bad for soldiers travelling home on leave. Leave trains had the lowest priority and this meant that sometimes whole days could be spent on a station platform as troop trains and wagons full of shells went through. Indeed, until Pétain's reform in September, some men spent so long travelling from home and returning to their units that they hardly had any time at home. So Pétain organised better facilities on stations – refreshment and rest rooms. Also he ordered 400,000 beds for the rest areas. It is an eloquent criticism of lack of care that almost three years had passed before such a basic measure was taken. Pétain also did something about the appalling food that was produced for the men. Training was provided for cooks; fresh fruit and vegetables were supplied; and a central organisation created in each army to ensure that the divisional cooperatives were stocked with a range of food for the men to buy, instead of alcohol.[76]

Soldiers had more money in their pockets, because earlier in March parliament had voted credits to pay for two allowances to add to the basic pay, which remained at 0.25 francs per day for privates. Pay rises had been awarded for professional army officers in 1916, when differential pay rates for generals were introduced according to responsibility – division, corps, army or army group command. Now, an allowance of a franc a day for each day spent in the firing line, 'l'engagement direct dans le combat', was paid to all junior officers, corporals and privates, whether foreign-born, native-born or French. In addition, a long-service allowance was paid those who had served two years beyond their legal obligation – in effect, all survivors of classes older than that of 1913. This was at the rate of 0.20 francs per day (0.60 for corporals and 1 franc for junior officers), and reflected the long-service allowance already paid to the professional army. Both these extra allowances, the 'indemnité de combat' and the 'haute-paye de guerre', were paid half in cash and half in saving stamps. The stamps were affixed to a 'carnet de pécule' and paid out in cash on demobilisation or to the next-of-kin in case of death.[77] In May 1917 Paul Pireaud wrote to his wife that he was receiving 1.45 francs per day, 0.85 centimes in cash and the rest in stamps for the pécule.[78]

Pétain sought more literary means to improve morale, and asked the writers on his staff to investigate such topics as the measures adopted during the Revolutionary Wars to deal with insurrection. He decided to write and publish five articles, under his own name, on why France was fighting, as a form of conversation with the French Army. Only the first was ever published because it raised such fears among the politicians that Pétain, the improvised journalist, might become too popular.[79] The article, 'Pourquoi nous nous battons', appeared on 27 June 1917 in the *Bulletin des Armées*. Pétain's statement of why France was fighting was reproduced the same day in the majority of daily newspapers. Nowadays it is easy to read between the lines and to see how Pétain was responding to the most loudly stated grievances. He began by stating that 'we' were fighting because Germany had attacked and France's aims were to expel the invader and to ensure that there could be no repeat. It would be a crime to betray 'our dead and our children', and a bad peace would be worse than the present war. The essential conditions for the fight were 'tenacity' and 'discipline', and Pétain wished to explain 'as a friend', convinced that France's soldiers would understand and would continue to do their duty, 'all their duty'. It is easy to see why the government would not like Pétain's statement. War aims were the province of government, not the military, and references to continuing to do one's duty verged on revealing that some men were not. Pétain had never worried about trespassing on politicians' prerogatives, however.

Germany had started the war [Pétain continued] and had violated Belgian neutrality. Those who claimed that the Allies were 'mad to continue this war' forget that they did not start it. Despite defeats on the Marne and the Yser, Germany still sought to gain from the peace, as its offer of December 1916 revealed. France was not so foolish as to agree to an armistice and to give Germany the time spent in negotiation to re-group and attack again later. German socialists, who claimed that Germany sought no territorial conquests, still refused to disavow their government.

Here Pétain met head-on the claims of some mutineers that there was no point continuing the war; that Germany had offered peace terms; and that the international Socialist conference that was to take place in Stockholm should be supported. He ended the article thus:

But Germany has by no means renounced its plan to destroy and to dominate. // It willed the war to achieve them; alone in Europe it prepared war; it wanted it and caused it, making it unpardonable by its actions and atrocious by its methods; by holding on, without having the loyalty to admit it, to its exorbitant claims, Germany alone is the obstacle to peace ... all we ourselves do is to defend ourselves in the name of Liberty and to save our existence.[80]

Herbillon thought the statement well thought out and full of common sense, and that in general the public approved it. Although ministers feared that it might raise a polemic in the press, Herbillon believed that what Pétain had said deserved to be said.[81] How many soldiers bothered to read it is, of course, impossible to know.

The crisis period was over by the end of June, although isolated incidents continued to occur until January 1918, none of which involved large numbers of men. So the carrot and the stick proved effective. Leonard V. Smith contends that the mutinies led to a re-negotiation of the relationship between military authorities and citizen-soldiers of the Republic, which enabled the war to continue. André Loez argues that the mutinies petered out because there was nowhere for soldiers to desert to (unlike for German soldiers in 1918, or unlike the vast expanses of Russia), and there was no political or social organisation to cover them. Whichever explanation one accepts, the fact remains that the war continued. Whether the pcdf accepted war (consent) or refused war but were forced to continue (constraint), the war would continue for more than another year. Did the men accept to continue because Pétain promised no more costly offensives – giving the credit to Pétain – or were there no more costly offensives because the men refused to undertake them? Some credit is given to this latter possibility by the request made on 3 June by Sixth Army's new commander, General Maistre. He asked for a postponement in the planned offensive, because of the real risk of the men refusing to leave the trenches. Maistre was sure that the 'effervescence of indiscipline' was passing, but that equally time was needed to 'stabilise' matters. His Northern Army Group commander, Franchet d'Espèrey, seconded this request: the fresh divisions supplied to Sixth Army for the proposed attack were in a 'bad moral state', and an offensive in such conditions would lead only to the deaths of those good elements unaffected by the bad.[82]

One final matter requires attention before leaving this question of the crisis of indiscipline. Many have wondered how the German Army failed to discover what was happening and failed to take advantage of a position so serious that there were said to be only two reliable divisions between Soissons and Paris, although other fronts were trouble-free.[83] The Germans did not remain in complete ignorance, however. Lacking a network of agents in France and Britain, their main source of intelligence came from statements from prisoners and from letters and other documents found on wounded and killed French soldiers. Disaffected French prisoners would not trouble to hide their complaints. The raw intelligence was collected and submitted to OHL, and thirty-nine reports for May and June 1917 from the intelligence officers of the individual German armies are extant, mostly from *Seventh Army*, which had borne the brunt of the attacks.[84] The first, dated even earlier, 29 April, concerns four French companies which refused to attack, and so recognised the indiscipline very quickly. The reports mentioned placards with slogans such as 'we'll get into position but we won't attack' (18 DI), and 'we'll stand on the firestep, but we won't fire' (4 DI). One report on the latter division, dated 5 May, even stated that a French captain had committed suicide because his company refused to advance. Another French officer (156 RI) threatened to abandon his battalion's position if his exhausted troops were not relieved, noted a report of 1 June. The same intelligence officer recorded five days later the removal of 5 DI because the men refused to return to the front line. The strikes in Paris were reported by a German agent in Switzerland as having 'an air of revolution'. So, as common-sense suggests, the German Army did not remain in ignorance of the mutinies.[85]

However, the raw data were collated and presented to OHL for the first time only on 26 June, almost two months after the first report. The compilation noted that the main centre of disturbances was on the Chemin des Dames, and other sectors of the front remained quiet. It identified disturbances in ten divisions and the specific regiments involved, including 77 and 13 DI, described above. Although reporting that French troops were 'bargaining' over whether to stay or to move into position, and that some troops had been executed for refusing, yet the conclusion was that the situation of the French Army was 'worrying, but certainly not dramatic'. The report of 30 June, however, was stronger. It identified twenty-eight troubled divisions and the work of pacifist propagandists, but still doubted whether the French Army's operational capabilities were affected. By this date the crisis had passed and the number of incidents was declining, so it was too late to start preparations for a serious offensive. In any case the Germans were making very strong counter-attacks on the heights that the French had captured. These counter-attacks may have been stronger because of knowing that the defenders facing them were mutinous, but the Germans probably would have counter-attacked in any case because they had lost such good observatories over the French lines, observatories from which the French now profited. Moreover, Germany's strategy for 1917 had been agreed already, and that strategy was to remain on the defensive in the west as the submarine offensive did its work.[86] As is well known, intelligence is usually interpreted to fit pre-existing attitudes, but the Germans were already on the alert for the British attack further north. Preparations for Third Ypres could not be hidden, and the opening moves in the battle at Messines had already taken place before the first compilation of raw data reached OHL. When Spears was researching his *Prelude to Victory*, he contacted not only the principal French players but also a German colonel, late of 6th Dragoons. Colonel Martin had been stationed at the time between Reims and Laon and agreed that they should have been more suspicious of the quiet, but the German reserves were being 'sucked into the whirlpool of Flanders' and so they 'kept pretty quiet' themselves. In fact the Nivelle offensive had kept *Seventh Army* 'hanging by [its] teeth'. However, he continued, OHL did receive reports of what was happening 'on the French side'.[87]

There were further reasons not to react too openly to the news of the French mutinies. During the offensive the French and British together had captured over 50,000 German prisoners.[88] The same lassitude that afflicted the French troops was evident among the German troops too. A postal control report from *Fifth Army* stated on 12 July 1917 that 'everyone wishes an end to the war as soon as possible' – a sentiment very similar to those being expressed in the French reports.[89] The state of morale on the German front made Ludendorff wary of giving too much prominence to the strikes and demonstrations in French cities. He asked that the German press not report such events.[90] In order to counteract demands for a negotiated peace, OHL set up a programme of propaganda, the *Vaterländische Unterricht*, from mid-September.[91] So OHL was aware of the French Army's difficulties, if not their full extent, but was unable to take advantage because Germany was beginning to face similar problems of its own.

There is extant a report of riots and absence without leave among soldiers near the French border in Karlsruhe at the end of February 1917. The men had been promised leave, but instead were ordered to embark for the front. The report of what happened as the men prepared to march out of barracks is remarkably similar – except for the absence of drunkenness – to many of those written about French battalions a few months later. For that reason, it is worth quoting at length.

The men were grumbling openly while lining up and did not hide that they were moving very slowly on purpose. They scorned the company commander who was hurrying them along ... They demanded furlough and pushed their rifles on the ground ... somebody shouted out loud: 'First group halt! We don't want to go to the front lines!' Then the whole platoon came to a stop ... the march to the railway station was a complete mess. The men were laughing and hooting and were shouting to the civilians who came along ... most of the men refused to go on to the platform. Some of them threw their rifles and knapsacks on the road ... They also refused when they had to board the train ... Six men did not enter the train again at all but let it depart without them. They were subsequently arrested. The riots continued during the train ride and particularly at the stations.[92]

Clearly, revolt was in the air in May/June 1917.

Autopsy of a disaster

Nivelle's offensive and its aftermath had a huge impact, and not only on the troops. Secret sessions of both houses of parliament debated the affair, and both army commissions produced reports. Nivelle himself was sent on leave with the rank (and salary) of an army group commander. At the end of his leave Pétain stated that he had no army group for him to command, and Nivelle was shunted off to Algeria where he spent the rest of the war in command of the troops there. In September 1918 Lloyd George requested a photograph, which Nivelle sent and asked for one of the Prime Minister in return.[93] In the index entries to Lloyd George's *War Memoirs*, Nivelle appears with the sub-heading 'unfortunate as Generalissimo'. The man who was responsible for placing Haig under the command of a French general, whom he had helped to over-promote, could not go beyond 'unfortunate'. Nivelle was not even invited to the victory parade on 14 July 1919, despite his strong letter of protest. He had to be content with presiding over the victory celebrations in Algeria. He died in 1924, but passions had cooled by 1931 when his ashes were removed to the governor's crypt in the Invalides along with those of fifteen other marshals, generals and admirals.

The political pressure on Painlevé in the army commissions and in parliament forced him to agree to an enquiry into the offensive. Under the presidency of the elderly General Brugère, the Commission of Enquiry was 'to study the conditions in which the offensive of 16–23 April took place in the valley of the Aisne and to determine the role of the general officers who exercised command'.[94] Brugère was a former military governor of Paris and former generalissimo, and his two co-commissioners were Generals Foch and Gouraud. The law stated that any such commission must consist of generals who had commanded at least an army corps and obviously, in this case, it was better if they had not been involved in the offensive. Foch had returned to centre-stage when he replaced Pétain as chief of the army staff in May; Gouraud had commanded the French Expeditionary Force on Gallipoli where he had been severely wounded, and he replaced Anthoine in command of Fourth Army, when Anthoine moved to Flanders with First Army (see next chapter).

The three generals met for the first time on 22 August.[95] Their role was simply to examine what had happened, not to suggest sanctions against any of the commanding generals. They decided to hear testimony only from Nivelle himself, from Micheler as army group commander and from the two army commanders involved, Mazel and Mangin. They wished also to obtain written testimony from those who had attended the war council of 6 April at GQG in Compiègne, at which no official minutes were taken. Thus they recognised the importance of the political element in the offensive, although this was not in their remit. Foch summed up the war council and the relationship between the military and politicians neatly: the government sought the light but its eyes remained closed.[96]

In a series of twelve sittings, from several of which Foch was unavoidably absent as his duties of chief of the army general staff took him away, the generals read their statements and answered questions, but there was no calling of witnesses or confrontation when two accounts differed. Foch and Gouraud, as serving officers, did not agree with the retired president of the commission, who clearly wanted a stronger condemnation of Nivelle and his plan. In the end, Brugère wrote in a private letter to Painlevé that Nivelle 'had not been up to' the high command with which he had been entrusted. The report itself, however, neither blamed not criticised Nivelle, for anything could happen in war, and it was impossible to state with certainty that his aims could not have been achieved. Indeed, the Second Battle of the Aisne could not be called a military defeat, the commission concluded, considering the numbers of German prisoners and materiel captured and the fewer casualties than in Champagne in 1915. Painlevé thought the commission's report was 'rose water'. Although supposedly confidential, it did not take long for copies to circulate, and press polemics to follow.

Painlevé's role is murky. The war council on 6 April, ten days before the offensive began, took no responsible decision, merely refusing Nivelle's resignation. Then the commission of enquiry was a ploy to escape political criticism, and had no teeth to impose sanctions. There was no logic to the start and end dates, 16 and 23 April, imposed on the commission, since they covered neither the preparation nor the continuation of the battle. Pétain's role was also discreditable, in that he requested an appearance before the commission, which had not intended to hear him, when he repeated all the criticisms of the offensive that were well known already. He claimed to have told Painlevé on 1 April that 'the attack in question had no chance of success and would only end in pointless losses'.[97] This proceeding reveals how deeply wounded the French Army was in 1917, not only the poilus but the high command as well, and how low civil–military relations had sunk.

Pétain's own views on what he called 'A Crisis of Morale in the French Nation at War', were used as the basis for the account in the official history.[98] The symptoms were seen at first in a 'pacifist propaganda campaign', which the government failed to suppress and the press encouraged, by reporting all the strikes and revealing military preparations. Then the leave question, poor food and drunkenness, and a defeatist attitude resulting from the repeated failures to win a victory, made matters worse. Unable to resist a criticism of Nivelle, Pétain referred next to the 'risky obsession with rapid results' and 'fantastic strategic over-confidence' that Nivelle displayed, that the politicians agreed at first to support, but then undermined in the War Council on 6 April. Pétain's final factor in the crisis was the relaxation of military justice, which had abolished the courts martial and reintroduced the right of appeal against a death sentence.

It is a pity that what remain from Nivelle's offensive, the Second Battle of the Aisne, are only his name and the mutinies. Nivelle boasted that he had the method and he became the perfect example of hubris. In short, his brief period of command was a disaster. However, his offensive was not a total failure for the French Army. Among the 163,000 German casualties noted above, 28,815 were prisoners of the French by 10 May, with Sixth taking over 10,000 and Fifth Army over 11,000. The French had captured 187 guns, 465 machine guns and 149 *Minenwerfer*.[99] They stood by then along most of the Chemin des Dames, and in October 1917, as the next chapter will show, they threw the Germans back from the northern slopes of the ridge as well. Charles Delvert witnessed the fighting in May and June. The offensive had been stopped and defeated

on 16 April, the first day, Delvert wrote later.[100] High command should
have realised this, but:

The bloody errors of 1915 began again. There was not a single poilu in the war so
far – officer or private – who did not judge them as such. They completed the
frustration of spirits already sickened by the events of the 16th. The troops had
been unable in fact to accept that, after two-and-a-half years of war, they should
be massacred uselessly in a worse conceived and above all worse prepared affair
than all those in which they had participated already. That at least is what they
declared. And we were grieved to witness the following June the poor courageous
men of 133 RI among others – the 'Lions' who carried Loivre so bravely despite
the German machine guns – die at the hands of a firing squad. That was the
epilogue of the offensive of 16 April.

6   Restoring the Army

Doctrine, training, weapons

Pétain's successful handling of the French Army after the mutinies following Nivelle's failed offensive (see Chapter 5) has obscured Pétain's other significant achievements in improving its organisation. If his appointment did not arouse great enthusiasm amongst his colleagues – 'the most acceptable' of the possibilities, wrote Guillaumat[1] – yet he had the necessary qualities to restore the French Army. Pétain's strength was his sense of order and organisation, and he imposed his views about training, doctrine and materiel provision upon a reorganised GQG staff. It is important to note, in this respect, that Pétain was an infantry officer, hence likely to be more in tune with the pcdf, unlike his two predecessors, Joffre an engineer and Nivelle an artillery officer. (Joffre's GQG in 1915, for example, had four artillery officers and three engineers in the senior positions.) Colonel Pétain began the war as a brigade commander, moving quickly through the various levels of command, from division to corps to army and army group. Although he had spent time as a lecturer in the Ecole Supérieure de Guerre, his experience was of active command in the field, rather than as a staff officer. He believed that training was important, as well as liaison between infantry and artillery and between aviation and artillery, and he imposed that belief on the French Army.

He wasted no time in issuing his first directive on 19 May. It opened with these words: 'The balance of opposing forces [on the Western Front] does not admit at the moment any idea of breaking through the front and following up with a strategic exploitation.' Rather, the enemy's forces had to be worn down, while the French Army suffered minimal losses. Seeking distant objectives meant diluting the artillery fire to cover the depth of terrain and making surprise impossible; it risked producing only 'insignificant' results. Pétain had a double authority for this statement. First, the British and French, politicians and military, had agreed their policy in Paris on 5 May, when Robertson read out the results of the discussion with Haig, Pétain and Nivelle. While accepting the need to continue offensive operations, the April plan was 'no longer operative'. 'It is no longer', the unanimous statement continued, 'a question of aiming at breaking through the enemy's front and aiming at distant objectives. It is now a question of wearing down and exhausting the enemy's resistance, and if and when this is achieved to exploit it to the fullest extent possible ... We are all of the opinion that our object can be obtained by relentlessly attacking with limited objectives, while making the fullest use of our artillery. By this means we hope to gain our ends with the minimum loss possible.'[2] Second, Pétain had prepared his directive following his study of the plans and operational orders for Nivelle's offensive, and he had presented it to the comité de guerre.[3] He had approval, therefore, from both his British ally and also from his political masters.

Directive #1 was distributed only to army and army group commanders. Therefore it cannot be held to have convinced soldiers that they would not be compelled to fight in the same old, wasteful ways, thus 'healing' the French Army. It distilled what Pétain considered to be the lessons of the Aisne offensive. Future attacks were to be economical in men but to use the greatest possible artillery resources. Attacks should aim at a succession of different sectors, and should be mounted as rapidly as possible so as to tie down the enemy's reserves. Mobility and readiness

Fig. 15 Pétain checks on conditions for the soldiers in the rear areas. He was the only wartime Commander-in-Chief to be an infantry officer

to employ all resources meant preparing the front with appropriate transport and defensive arrangements, while not forgetting that the enemy might use his reserves to attack wherever he wished. Preparing the front for offensive operations would help in its defence also.[4]

A few days later Pétain went in person to explain his thinking to the Central and Eastern Army Groups. He stated that there would be no 'gladiator divisions' (specially trained storm troops), but all divisions would share offensives, periods of rest and of holding trenches. General Guillaumat (Second Army) asked that army corps be returned to their organic composition after being stripped of forces for Nivelle's offensives, and Pétain agreed to do this. General Anthoine (Fourth Army) pointed out that lack of training had been the cause of the failure of some recent attacks, whereas well-trained troops had gained better results. Pétain agreed here as well. Finally, along the quiet fronts, east of the Moselle, Pétain advised that the second defensive lines were too close to the first; they should be sited 4 to 5 kilometres back.[5]

On 28 May Pétain confirmed his intentions to War Minister Painlevé, repeating that experience and reason both proved that breakthrough was impossible, given the current equilibrium of forces. Wearing down the enemy, without wearing down the French Army at the same time, was his aim, but certain consequences followed. Firepower was increasing continuously, hence the French needed more artillery of their own, not only to neutralise the extended depth of the enemy's, but also to gain surprise by not having to move guns from one sector to another, thereby signalling an intention to attack. Guns of varying calibres, mortars and tanks, in greater numbers than planned in the current programmes, were vital if a future French attack was to succeed against the enemy's increased firepower. Railway equipment, light railways and roads were equally vital, as was mastery of the air.[6] In short, Pétain wanted more, lots more, of everything.

He reorganised the high command to conform more closely to the improvements that he wished to make. He retained Generals Franchet d'Espèrey and Castelnau in command of the Northern and Eastern Army Groups respectively, and appointed Fayolle to succeed him in command of the Centre Army Group. The mocking acronyms for these army groups remained valid, therefore, in two of the three. The Northern (Groupe des Armées du Nord, or GAN) was said to stand for Groupe des Animaux Nuisibles (of dangerous animals), because of Franchet d'Espèrey's tendency to dash into things rather than discussing them; the Centre Army Group (GAE) was the Groupe des Armées de l'Eglise (of the church), because of Castelnau's clerical reputation, despite the fact that two of his aides were Protestant. The Central Army Group, before Pétain's promotion, was the Groupe des Augures Constipés,

Table 11 *Pétain's GQG*

Commander in Chief: Général Philippe Pétain				
Major Général: Général Eugène Debeney				
A-MG (General Poindron)	A-MG (General de Barescut)	A-MG (Colonel Duval)	Special services (Colonel Zoppf)	A-MG (General Raguenau)
1er bureau	2e bureau (Colonel Cointet) and cartography	Air service	Intelligence, including traffic control, military police postal control political affairs	4e bureau, covering a: supply
Personnel	3e bureau (Colonel Zeller)	Telegraphy	Relations with civil authorities	b: transport (except air)
GQG command Mail services	Relations with Allied officers	All liaisons, inc pigeons	Information [moved to Pétain's cabinet in July] Encryption and code-breaking	c: services

Note: A-MG: aide-major général, sub chief-of-staff

where the staff, 'professing the quintessence of strategy and tactics', were no more forthcoming than their chief, Pétain.[7]

Pétain made changes, however, at GQG, although he kept General Eugène Debeney as chief of staff. Debeney had replaced Nivelle's chief of staff (General Pont) on 2 May as part of the government-imposed changes following the failed offensive. Debeney, an infantry officer, had begun the war in a staff job, but since then had commanded a division (twice) and a corps (twice) at Verdun and on the Somme. He had been in command of Seventh Army in Alsace when called to GQG as chief of staff. He had long known Pétain and approved his nomination to CinC.[8] Pétain did change, however, the responsibilities of the various sub chiefs of staff, and these were finalised, as shown in Table 11, on 4 July.[9]

One of the most significant changes was the creation on 23 May of a new 'training section', to be headed by Colonel Emile Laure. It became part of the 3e Bureau (operations).[10] Laure had been 13 DI's chief of staff, and before that a battalion commander in 43 DI, until he was wounded in May 1915 in Artois. Laure was chosen precisely because he was new blood, never having served in a large staff. The training section's role was to 'follow all questions concerning the tactical preparation of the combat arms' by visiting the front and the training schools. It was to solicit the opinions and wishes of those in the fighting line and to prepare training texts, so that new developments could be disseminated throughout the whole army. An artillery officer and an engineer were appointed to the training section, and constant liaison established with the cavalry and with General Estienne in charge of the tanks. Aviation was the only area that was not covered, but Pétain had created a special 'service aéronautique' within the third aide major-general's remit. Training schools and course content were standardised across armies and army groups; courses were set up for specialists in, for example, telephony, machine guns or tanks; the training of artillery officers was emphasised especially; and Laure spent much time going from army to army and school to school, disseminating information and collecting opinions. A long directive issued on 20 June explained how the training was to be organised at all levels, and established schools for training the instructors themselves. Further instructions concentrated on liaison, especially between artillery and infantry. Aerial observation was important also, and liaison between tanks and artillery. On 1 July a note came out about the exercises that the infantry should practise to familiarise themselves with the tanks.[11]

By way of example, the study centre for artillery established in June 1917 was organised with lists of staff and materiel. Each course was to last two weeks, followed by a six-day 'stage' on a firing range, chosen according to the students' speciality. The study centre for engineers was set up in July. Its purpose was to disseminate information about the best methods and tools. The courses consisted of lectures and discussion of the lessons learned about the effects of artillery fire, the use of aerial photography, the war of mines, heavy construction such as bridges, the organisation of camps and the provision of electricity. These were followed by practical map exercises on setting up supply lines for an attack, or strengthening defensive organisations. The thirty attendees on each course were to include artillery and infantry officers, so that the engineers would know exactly what they required.[12]

Pétain's action in these matters makes a contrast with the French Army's first CinC. Joffre had concerned himself solely with the conduct of operations. He was not opposed to change – for example, he supported Estienne and his tank proposals – but obviously he did not consider it part of his role to carry through any change himself, nor did he have any direct contact with troops. Pétain, on the other hand, was an infantry officer, who had come up through the ranks of command. He delegated more responsibility to his army and army group commanders, in order to leave himself more time for visiting the front and listening to junior officers. He obliged staff officers to spend time at the front, and liaison officers to explain the reasoning behind instructions.[13]

Table 12 *Production of selected artillery in 1917*

Model of gun	Numbers available 1 August 1917	Observations
Trench artillery		
58mm	2,130	A slight reduction on same date 1916 (2,390)
340	30	New heavy mortar first introduced in 1917
Field artillery		
75	5,890	In August 1916, 4,260; in August 1915, 3,240; in August 1914, 4,050
105	327	August 1916, 105
155 (8 old models)	2,255	The most numerous (943) is the 1877 model 155 long, with which the French started the war (1,392 units)
220	193	Becoming obsolete: 329 in 1916; 286 in 1915; 331 in 1914
New rapid fire:		
Schneider 220	39	
100 mm	48	New in 1917
Heavy artillery (modern)		
155 (5 models)	988	First appeared in 1916 (102 units)
220 TR mortar	40	New in 1917. TR, tire rapide [quick firing]
280 mortar	30	August 1916, 15
extra heavies	331	None in 1914; 78 in August 1915; 223 in August 1916

Source: Statistical tables in *AFGG* 11, 567–8.

All this training required the formulation of new doctrines for both big and small units. To carry out this work, under the aegis of the new training section, Pétain established a 'commission de refonte', headed by a corps commander and containing representatives from all arms and from GQG. Laure acted as its secretary. A preliminary doctrine was drawn up and tested in the La Malmaison battle (see below), where it proved its worth. For the smaller units, such as machine-gun sections, study groups were formed; British and German documentation was studied; suggestions circulated and soundings taken. All this was an enormous methodical and intellectual exercise in rebuilding the whole French Army as the war reached its third anniversary.[14]

Training was not enough by itself. The troops had to have new weapons and plenty of them. Industrial mobilisation was now well under way. Tables 12 and 13 detail the equipment that the French Army had at its disposal by 1 August 1917.

Pétain was a firm advocate of aviation, and on 2 August 1917 he appointed Colonel Duval to take charge of aviation services at GQG as an aide major-général. Duval worked very cordially with Daniel Vincent,

Table 13 *Shell production and smaller weapons in 1917*

Type	Maximum production	Observations
75mm shell	175,000	1 August 1917: maximum *daily* production of unfilled shell
155mm shells	52,000	September: maximum daily rate
220mm shells	6,700	October: maximum daily rate. Also 171,000 imported during 1917
Machine guns	312,652	Units produced in 1917 (7,637 in 1915; 27,033 in 1916)
Light machine guns	133,417	Units produced in 1917 (55,363 in 1916)
Rifles	almost 2.5m	By Dec 1917 (2.14m in 1916)

Source: AFGG 11, 569.

appointed undersecretary of state in Ribot's government on 20 March.[15] An aviator himself (second lieutenant, observer) and long-time chairman of the Aeronautics Budget committee, Vincent was well placed to act. He consulted directly with manufacturers and obtained raw materials, forcing them to use their capacity to the full. He stopped the production of obsolete models, and reduced the number of models under construction, thereby increasing production greatly. Most unusually, the programme set up on 2 March for the production of 2,665 aircraft was almost complete by 1 August when 2,335 aircraft were in service. Duval and Vincent agreed a further programme of 2,870 aircraft on 6 September. Although a squabble between Painlevé and Vincent meant that the latter was 'promoted' to education minister when Painlevé became premier on 12 September, production continued to rise. Duval was able to work just as productively with Vincent's successor, Jacques-Louis Dumesnil. During the course of 1917 production of aircraft rose from 846 in January to 1,225 in March, and from 1,278 in September to 1,576 in December, for a total of 14,915 aircraft. However, it was in the numbers and the quality of French aero engines, especially rotary engines, where France dominated. In 1917 France produced 23,092 aero engines, with production almost doubling over the twelve months, from 1,579 in January to 2,715 in December.[16] The most serious problem was not production but the need to keep up the technical progress.

The aviation sub-committee of the Deputies' Army Commission was very active.[17] It prodded the minister frequently about how far behind Germany the French lagged. A report at the end of 1917 pointed out the reasons. First, the Germans were now flying only in groups, and the French did not have enough aircraft to be able to match the tactic.

Second, the Germans had two- or three-seater aircraft with powerful engines that allowed them to fly higher. As a consequence, the gunner did not have to fly the aircraft and could see much further. Finally, low-level night-time bombing missions were wreaking havoc with French airfields, and the French could find no effective response other than reprisal bombing of German cities. In the face of greater German technical progress, the commission demanded that more powerful two-seater aircraft be built. It had been hoped that when the USA joined the war in April, aircraft production would receive a great boost from the 'almost unlimited reservoir of men and materiel'. These hopes were disappointed as the US air service had no combat aircraft at all, and only fifty-five obsolete training aircraft; neither trained pilots nor completed aircraft arrived in France in significant numbers. The Commission had proposed an allied aviation programme also, but nothing came of this idea in 1917.[18] Nevertheless, the work done in 1917 helped to give France the edge in 1918. Indeed, three new models came into service in the latter half of 1917: the Spad 13 fighter, armed with two machine guns, able to fly at 220 kilometres an hour and up to a height of 2,000 metres; a reconnaissance aircraft, the Breguet BR 14 A2, armed with two or three machine guns; and the Breguet bomber BR 14 B2, with a 300-kilo bombload, and able to fly at an altitude of 5,800 metres.[19]

As well as aviation, Pétain wished to promote the use of tanks. Although their performance on 16 April had been very disappointing, lessons were absorbed immediately and their second appearance on the Chemin des Dames battlefield in May was better organised. Yet the biggest problem remained technical: breakdowns were never less than a quarter of the fleet. Again, the need for better liaison with the infantry and for a more mobile and more reliable tank was patent. Fortunately General Estienne was already thinking of new developments. In July 1916 he had met the car manufacturer Louis Renault, and they discussed building a 'char mitrailleur' or machine-gun tank. Estienne had seen the tanks that the British were putting through trials, and he knew that firms such as Schneider at Le Creusot were having difficulty obtaining raw materials and labour. In November 1916 this firm was producing tanks at the rate of only one a day, and had completed twenty-six, of which fourteen had been delivered, with a further twenty-three being assembled.[20] Estienne believed that a smaller (and cheaper) tank was better suited to France's production capabilities. Accordingly he contacted Renault again and they agreed a prototype small tank, whose mock-up appeared in January 1917, followed by trials that began on 22 February. Estienne had convinced Joffre of the value of a small tank, and Joffre recommended to Albert Thomas that a hundred be ordered. The Armaments Minister, however, was not persuaded and authorised only the prototype; then Nivelle replaced Joffre. Nivelle was not convinced either, preferring to use tractored vehicles for carrying artillery forward. Estienne's persistence prevailed over ministry disapproval and, following the trials, an order for 2,000 light Renault tanks was placed on 9 March. Officers who had experienced the tank offensive on 16 April were invited to the official trials on 21–22 April.

The advent of Pétain as CinC ensured that Estienne's ideas would be followed, for in 1914, when Pétain commanded 6 DI, Estienne had commanded that division's field artillery regiment. In September 1917 Pétain increased to 3,000 the order for the new tanks. If he was not literally waiting for the 'tanks and the Yanks', nonetheless he wanted the new weapon. The light Renault FT was highly successful. At 6.5 metric tonnes in weight, it could be transported on a lorry, which increased mobility enormously. It had a 360 degree turret so that the gunner could fire all round. The engine was at the rear, which decreased the risk of fire that had so demoralised the witnesses on 16 April. Intensive training, incorporating the answers to questionnaires sent out after every exercise, gave greater confidence in the new weapon's ability to deal with German anti-tank tactics. Bridging materials were supplied to counter the increased width of German trenches. Pigeons were used to give better liaison between tanks and infantry, and eventually four tanks were fitted with wireless.[21] Despite continued opposition from the Armaments Ministry – they used the tallest and fattest officers they could find for the trials in an attempt to prove that the tanks were too small – production continued and the Renault FT came into its own on 18 July 1918.

The entry of the USA into the war meant that supplies of steel would be assured, so long as enough shipping escaped the submarine to transport it across the Atlantic. And, after seeing the British tanks in England and in action on the Somme, Estienne believed that light tanks could compensate for the deficiency in their own 'colossal armoured warships' by swapping light for heavy tanks with the British.[22] Once again, however, little came of the scheme.

Pétain's appointment as CinC marked the opportunity, as Michel Goya points out, to create 'a useful relationship between headquarters, the generals and the troops'. Instead of being centralised within the high command at GQG, as in 1914, control over doctrine slipped down the chain to the generals, and its evolution in practice even further to combat troops. Pétain set in place an organisation that combined these three elements of the army, creating a 'modern and coherent' process.[23]

The 'batailles de redressement'

The purpose of better training and better equipment was to be able to win a military victory, which is always the best way to restore an army's morale. According to the chief of the 3e Bureau, Colonel Zeller, Pétain asked his staff to prepare three operations to be undertaken before the winter, in order to show the world that French soldiers remained capable of attacking. All three should be mounted under two essential conditions: they should have strictly limited objectives; and those carrying them out should be given all the resources they ask for: men, munitions, materiel. The point of imposing these conditions was to restore the confidence of the army in itself and of the nation in its army.[24] In the event, the series of limited operations – of 'redressement' or recovery – did prove successful.

Pétain's changes and improvements were tested in two solely French operations carried out in significant sectors: Verdun where Pétain remained convinced that he had saved the fortress, and the Chemin des Dames where it was necessary to consolidate the French gains and, more importantly, to remove the stain of failure. These two battles would confirm the validity of Pétain's cautious methods over the rapidity and violence of Nivelle's. In addition, Pétain contributed to two British battles: Third Ypres, where French First Army fought alongside Gough's Fifth Army; and Cambrai, when at first Haig refused Pétain's offer of troops, but later changed his mind. These will be treated in chronological order according to their start date, but the action in Flanders continued from 31 July to the end of November, hence coincided with the others.

Flanders

The first of the three French victories of 1917 came in Flanders, north of Ypres. Haig's gaze had been on Flanders and the Belgian ports for a long time. It had been part of the agreement with Nivelle back in January that, should the French offensive not yield the expected results, then the British would be freed to act further north. The French would cooperate by taking over some of the British front in the Somme area. As early as 17 April, the second day of the offensive, Robertson had seen that the Calais agreement subordinating Haig to Nivelle's plans was a dead letter because the offensive had failed. He wanted its annulment so as 'to secure British interests'.[25] Haig had met Pétain during the Paris conference on 4 and 5 May, but they do not seem to have had any private conversation. There the generals had agreed, and the politicians concurred, that it was vital to keep hitting the enemy, but with limited objectives and using artillery rather than infantry. Haig had sent his plans for Flanders to GQG on 5 May, but received no reply to his questions about any French contribution. This was because the manoeuvring, which had already started to replace Nivelle by Pétain, was not yet complete. Haig was left not knowing who was in command. Henry Wilson had been Nivelle's British liaison officer at GQG, and he subjected Haig to a sustained campaign of denigration of Pétain. So it was a pleasant surprise when Haig met Pétain on 18 May, and found him 'so quiet for a Frenchman'. Pétain's travelling to speak with Haig in private was one of his first acts as CinC, and he confirmed French participation in Haig's planned campaign, as well as preparations for three other French offensives (of which only two took place).

Pétain's agreement to supply six French divisions for Flanders may seem surprising. Pétain must have known what Wilson had been saying about him, and got rid of him from GQG as soon as he arrived. So Pétain may have wished to prove Wilson wrong. There had only been a few incidents of collective disobedience by this date – crisis point was reached later – hence divisions could be offered to Haig without any risk. Nevertheless the British were beginning to suspect that all was not well with the French Army, and so Pétain may have thought also to reassure Haig that he had offensive capacity to spare. Finally, he had been warned by Nivelle that the British wanted to take control in Belgium, where a strategic success would give Britain a larger say in the affairs of the Entente. Of course, Pétain did not wish the French Army to be excluded from military action that might have such a decisive influence.[26]

The worsening crisis of morale meant that the first of the three proposed French offensives (on the Chemin des Dames) could not now take place. Therefore Pétain sent Debeney to see Haig on 2 June to explain matters. The soldiers had to be given the leave owed them, as an 'absolute necessity for the conservation of morale'. Artillery and aviation support would be forthcoming, however, so that the BEF would not be left to face the enemy alone, and Debeney confirmed the despatch of the six divisions promised for Flanders.[27] Haig did not seem to be too perturbed by the news.

During a conference on 7 June, Pétain and Haig, together with the Belgian chief of staff, General Ruquoy, signed a joint 'protocol' specifying the terms of the agreement they had reached for the Flanders offensive. The French units were placed under Haig's command, effective from 16 June – compensation for the previous Haig–Nivelle arrangement? – with any remaining points to be settled by Haig. Just as in the Calais agreement, it was specified that, if operations in Flanders ceased, the French units would be relieved, part by the British and part by the Belgians. Perhaps to Haig's surprise after all the criticisms of the new

French CinC that he had heard, Haig found Pétain 'most anxious to help in every way, and thoroughly businesslike'.[28] The aim was to clear the Belgian coast, the British acting out of Ypres, the Belgians to join in later. The following day, 8 June, the British preliminary moves began at Messines.

The six divisions that Pétain allocated to Flanders were: two divisions (29 and 133) of XXXVI Corps, commanded by General Nollet, and four divisions of General Lacapelle's I Corps (1, 2, 51, 162), all under the command of General Paul Anthoine and combined as First French Army. Anthoine had been in command of Fourth Army in Pétain's Centre Group for the Aisne campaign, so Pétain knew and trusted him. I Corps had been mauled at Craonne on 16 and 17 April, but most of its regiments had been raised originally in northern France, including Pétain's own former command, 33 RI from Arras, so might be less resistant to being moved there than troops from other regions of France. They had not been involved in any mutinous incidents, having been withdrawn from the front on 21 April, after which they remained at rest or under instruction until 20 June, when they began moving to Belgium. As for XXXVI Corps, it had been stationed on the coast, protecting Dunkirk, since its constitution in May 1915. For this reason, it too had escaped the mutinies apart from a couple of incidents of drunkenness (entirely understandable) on 14 July. Any charge that Pétain unloaded mutinous regiments to Flanders in order to remove bad influences is without foundation.

Anthoine arrived in the sector on 12 June and set up his headquarters at Rexpoede four days later. His army's task was to protect the northern left flank of General Gough's Fifth Army, acting as a pivot around Boesinghe. Once the first phase of the operation was complete and both British and French had broken out of the Ypres salient to occupy the higher ground all around, the Belgian Army was to join the exploitation northwards towards the coast. The infantry assault was planned for 25 July, which meant that Anthoine had approximately one month in which to reconnoitre and prepare the marshy ground ready for the artillery to begin its work. In front of the French ran the flooded canal connecting Ypres and the Yser, with streams running into the canal from the Houthulst forest, occupied in force by the Germans and still in part inaccessible today because of unexploded ordinance.

Lengthy preparations were required for this assault, since roads, railways and clean water all had to be provided. Because of the short time frame, Haig lent 7,000 labourers to Anthoine to complete the work in time. The artillery preparations were meticulous, doubtless because Anthoine was himself an artillery officer. At his disposal Anthoine had

60 batteries of 75s (240 guns), 277 trench artillery pieces (mainly the 58mm mortar), and for heavy artillery 176 short guns (howitzers and mortars) and 136 long-barrelled guns for counter-battery work. In addition, Anthoine had 64 extra heavies, 22 of them of 305 calibre or greater, to deal with the enemy's communications and solid *Blockhausen*. This accumulation amounted to 893 guns for a front of barely 7 kilometres, or one gun every 2.5 metres, if all aligned instead of being staged in depth.[29] These powerful resources were assisted by three fighter aircraft groups, including the famous Cigognes squadron and their equally famous pilots, Georges Guynemer and René Fonck, two bomber squadrons and three squadrons of observation aircraft for the artillery, plus seven observation balloons.[30]

The four divisions of I Corps arrived in Flanders between 25 June and 10 July, and two of them took over the front between Boesinghe and Nordschoote, with the battalion of territorials holding the flooded northern sector of the front. The enemy had reinforced his front in the expectation of a large offensive, and by mid-July ten German divisions awaited the attack with a further seven or eight in the rear. In addition, the German divisions battered at Messines would become available as well, once they were reconstituted. German aviation resources had also been strengthened because aerial photography had confirmed the preparations for an attack. Over eighty German air units were concentrated gradually in Flanders.[31]

The artillery preparation began on 15 July. It consisted of three phases: destruction of enemy batteries; destruction of enemy defences to be carried out in parallel with counter-battery work and interdiction; finally, the immediate preparation of the infantry attack. In the second phase the principal targets were command posts, telephone exchanges and observatories, and relief and re-supply columns were to be interdicted with as great a rate of fire as possible. In the third and final phase, the firing cadence was to be increased only very gradually, so as to retain an element of surprise over the exact hour of the infantry assault. The artillery did its work so effectively that the two defence lines nearest to the canal had been completely levelled and some French advance groups were able to cross the canal by 26 July, enabling the engineers to begin installing the bridges for the main body of the infantry.

On 21 July Anthoine requested a delay in launching the infantry assault. This is attributed sometimes to French foot-dragging or to difficulties because of the mutinies, but was purely because the weather had prevented proper observation of the damage wrought by the artillery. Haig granted the delay without any difficulty. Anthoine ensured that the repeated delays (from 25 to 28 July, and again to the 31st) did not leave the men in the front trenches not knowing what was going on, as had happened on the Chemin des Dames. Therefore he relieved the two French divisions in line for the first assault, returning them in time for the new date of 31 July.

The infantry's role was to cover the British left flank, and the objective was the line of the Steenbeek between Blankaart lake and the northern edge of Houthulst forest. The objective could not be reached in one go, so the assault was to be carried out in stages. The first aimed to capture the first two enemy lines on the eastern side of the canal and to get into position to attack the third. The second phase was to organise this position ready to attack as quickly as possible without repositioning the artillery. The capture of the enemy's third line would give possession of all the ground south of the Martjevaart/Saint Jansbeek waterway, including the spit of land between it and the canal just south of Nordschoote. The artillery barrage was fixed at a rate of 90 metres every four minutes, a considerably slower rate of advance than in the Aisne. Ninety metres was the nearest round-figure equivalent of 100 yards, it having been decided to use the imperial measurement. To synchronise more exactly, the French gunners were to pause from time to time to make sure that they did not get ahead of their British neighbours.[32]

The preparation had been so meticulous that the front detachments had been able to cross the canal even before the rest of the infantry began their assault at 4.25 on the morning of 31 July, and so they reached their objectives easily. French counter-battery fire neutralised the enemy guns, and the French were able to maintain contact with the British on their right. It was not until 4pm that the German guns were able to riposte. As the infantry progressed they saw how the artillery had destroyed the enemy defences and so could appreciate the contrast with their experience on 16 April before Craonne. Then, said Sergeant Werquin from Arras of 201 RI (1 DI) of the class of 1915, 'it was a real joy for the old poilus; never had we seen such artillery work; never had the Boche been battered [maté] to this point'.[33] Although the casualties in the two divisions had been very light – 1,300 men killed, wounded and disappeared on 31 July[34] – both were relieved on 5 August. The rain that had begun in the evening of 31 July had continued more or less unbroken, making conditions very exhausting as the ground became a series of muddy lakes.

There were only three days in August when no rain fell at all and the total for that month (127mm) was almost double the average. The heaviest rainfall had occurred between 1 and 4 August, during the French infantry action.[35] The bad weather meant that the next phase of the operation could not start before 16 August. The artillery preparation required fine weather for observation, but I Corps managed to make minor gains here and there, establishing themselves in the ruins of several farms. The aim of the next phase was to reach the line of the Saint-Jansbeek, crossing over the Steenbeek on the right where the French and British lines joined. This Anthoine's men achieved. As they set off on 16 August, Pétain was decorating the men of 1 and 51 DI who had carried out the first assault on 31 July. After being rested, between 18 and 22 August they relieved the two divisions who had carried out the attack. Pétain's instructions stated that Anthoine should see to the well-being of the troops and the maintenance of morale, and this Anthoine did.[36] Indeed Anthoine arranged for trucks to convey the men to the coast to bathe in the sea during the few fine spells of weather in August.

For the rest of August and all September, the French had to mark time. Although Gough's Fifth Army's left had kept level with the French, the right had not done so well, because the high ground of the Gheluvelt plateau was still in German hands. From this high ground, the German artillery bombarded the British below. Until it was captured, there could be no question of breaking out of the salient, still less of heading towards the coast. Consequently it was not until October that Haig decided to make another combined Franco-British effort. The two divisions of XXXVI Corps, under the command of General Nollet, had taken over the French front on 15 September, so that I Corps could be rested and undergo further instruction. The front was now so well established where the wide Saint-Jansbeek river gave protection that fewer infantry were needed to hold it. The French artillery kept up their counter-battery work, as roads were repaired, bridges built and duckboards laid.

It is important to emphasise at this point, before the renewal of the assault towards Passchendaele in October, that one claim in the British official history of the Battle of Third Ypres is completely false. Supposedly, Pétain 'begged' Haig to continue the offensive in Flanders so as to protect his own French troops. On the contrary, it was Haig who badly wanted the French to make a supporting attack on the Aisne. On 29 September, the French Mission at GHQ sent a telegram to GQG, describing Haig's insistence that the La Malmaison attack (described below) should begin before 5 October. Haig needed the French to pin down enemy troops on the Aisne and to draw enemy reserves away from Flanders.[37] Anthoine too urged Pétain to help the British attack, but Pétain refused to act on the Aisne before he was ready. Instead he promised a two-day heavy bombardment whenever Haig wanted it. 'History will doubtless show', Haig remarked sourly in his diary, 'that the French are not playing the game!'[38]

Haig planned to get the British onto the Passchendaele ridge as the French pushed northwards towards the Houthulst forest and Clercken ridge. Again Anthoine broke the operation down into four logical phases. If successful, these would extend the exploitation to the north and bring in the Belgian troops whose cooperation depended on the progress made by the British and French. He had fewer guns than on 31 July for two reasons: Pétain was preparing for another operation on the Chemin des Dames; and the politicians had decided that guns were to be sent to Italy (both described below). Nevertheless, 623 guns of all calibres supported the operation: 45 batteries of the 75s; 34 batteries of the 155 howitzers; and 59 batteries of various calibres of heavy guns.

The first phase was completed successfully on 9 October behind a rolling barrage advancing 100 metres every six and then every eight minutes, and liaison was established with the British on their right and the Belgians on their left. The operation cost 423 casualties, but captured 537 prisoners (including 13 officers and 54 subalterns).[39] The weather now intervened once more, and it was not until 27 October that the subsequent phases could begin. Then, thanks to the good visibility on the best day for two months, French counter-battery work neutralised the German guns, and French aircraft swept the skies and machine-gunned columns of enemy reinforcements. The French artillery had twenty-five guns to every German one, and German batteries only managed to fire off five or six shells before their position was recognised and the guns neutralised.[40] By the end of the Third Battle of Flanders, the French and Belgians held a line running from the south of Lake Blankaert to the southern edge of Houthulst forest, and the Yser river had been cleared of the enemy. The operation out of Dixmude and the landing on the coast had not been possible, but the ring of high ground around the Ypres salient was now in Allied hands, with the Canadians taking Passchendaele village. First Army left Flanders, its headquarters moving to Toul in eastern France, and XXXVI Corps resumed its station on the coast at Dunkirk.

First Army had captured 1,500 prisoners including 30 officers, 43 guns, some 100 machine guns and other weapons. The army's six divisions had faced thirteen German divisions. In three months of fighting First Army had fired between six and seven million tons of shell of all calibres, for a cost of 8,527 casualties, of whom 1,625 were killed.[41] Compared with earlier casualty figures, these are very small. One of those killed was the flying ace Guynemer, killed on 11 September. His body was never found.

Pétain had made two visits to the Flanders sector. Following his August visit mentioned earlier, he appeared again on 6 October, just before the action was about to re-start. He brought a cheque for 1,000 francs (about £40) for the colonel of each of the regiments mentioned in army orders, to be distributed to men going on leave, or as the colonel decided. Clearly an extraordinary effort was being made to make the poilus feel that they were cared for; equally clearly the incidents of collective indiscipline that were over by October had impressed the high command with the urgent need to improve the dreadful conditions under which the pcdf were obliged to fight. As I and XXXVI Corps left Flanders in December, their morale was very high, although the postal control revealed disgust with the political treachery described in the press. In the first week of October, Minister of the Interior, Louis Malvy, was accused of having sold the plans for the Chemin des Dames offensive to the Germans, and a deputy, Victor Turmel, was arrested on suspicion of dealing with the enemy. Then, even such a personage as a former premier, Joseph Caillaux, had his parliamentary immunity revoked, and was arrested in January 1918. As one soldier of 110 RI wrote: 'terrestrial mud in front, moral mud in the rear; glorious mud and shameful mud'.[42]

Verdun

The second 'bataille de redressement' took place around Verdun. During the German retirement to the Hindenburg Line in March, Nivelle had asked Pétain to prepare an operation for Second Army to replace his main offensive, in case the German retreat made it impossible to carry it out. So Pétain studied a double operation to take place simultaneously, the first to take back the heights of Mort Homme and Hill 304 on the west bank, and the second to pinch out the Saint-Mihiel salient. The first would enable French guns to dominate the right bank of the Meuse once again and free the railway station at Verdun from German bombardment; the second would enable the French to move eastwards towards the important Briey basin with its iron-ore deposits that had been under German occupation since August 1914. In the event, the German retirement did not force Nivelle to change his plans, but the studies for an operation to disengage Verdun continued. Thus, when Pétain became CinC, the plans existed already. This was one of the three offensives that he had told Haig about in May, and its date was set for 15 July. However, the fierce German counter-attacks on the Chemin des Dames, and the need to spare the troops, forced a postponement.[43]

The attraction of an operation to free Verdun is obvious: Pétain had been 'sickened' when Joffre replaced him by Nivelle as commander of Second Army on 29 April 1916.[44] Pétain believed that *he* was the saviour of Verdun, and so a successful recapture of lost ground there would be a mixture of revenge and vindication.[45] However, the news that an offensive was to be undertaken at Verdun was not popular among the men, and there were more mutinous acts. A hundred or so from the several regiments in 25 DI refused to go into the front lines just before the offensive was due to begin, of whom forty-seven were tried.[46] Guillaumat (now commanding Second Army) even had to try a lieutenant-colonel for abandoning his post. He was sentenced to lose rank and given a five-year suspended prison sentence.[47] There could be no failure, therefore, either from the point of view of the men's morale and confidence in the high command's methods, or for Pétain's personal prestige.

The attack was planned for both sides of the Meuse.[48] On a 9-kilometre front on the left bank, XIII and XVI Corps each consisting of four divisions, two in line and two in reserve, were to advance 3 kilometres, so as to re-take Hill 304 and Mort-Homme together with the Côte de l'Oie. On the right bank XV and XXXII Corps were to advance 3 kilometres so as to remain level with the troops on the left bank. This would mean taking the Côte du Talou and hills 344 and 326 and the Bois des Caurières. The road and 60cm railway networks were improved so that each corps had at least one branch of the 60cm railway and a 6-metre-wide stone road for supplying its batteries with munitions. This involved laying 34 kilometres of new roadway. For their attack, the four corps had 1,280 field guns, 1,520 heavy artillery pieces, both short and long, and 80 extra heavies. The hilly, wooded terrain made it very difficult to get trench artillery in place, and only 268 pieces were provided. So many shells were supplied that the weary troops were unable to use them all. The sixteen squadrons to protect the observation aircraft and balloons were inadequate, however, mainly because there was insufficient space for airfields in the hills, and German aviation had an easier task in destroying material, as aircraft were crowded together on the ground.

The front between the Aisne and the Moselle was held by von Gallwitz's *Fifth Army*. The Germans had had more than a year since May 1916 to strengthen their defensive positions around Verdun. On the left bank of the Meuse, the immensely strong position of Montfaucon in the Ardennes was only 6 kilometres distant (the Americans would find its capture very difficult in 1918), and the Germans had dug tunnels, one of them a kilometre long, from the front line on Mort-Homme to the rear, so that they could deploy troops in complete safety. On the right bank, four defensive positions had been constructed, the fourth occupying the old front lines of February 1916. The French had identified 380 German batteries on the front of attack, which were making great use of the new mustard gas shells first used at Ypres. The gas persisted in the soil for several days. The Germans were aware of the lengthy French preparations and attacked several times in an attempt to disrupt them. This led to a series of attacks and counter-attacks to recapture lost ground until the Central Army Group commander, Fayolle, ordered that counter-attacks should cease in cases where the cost in munitions and men was disproportionate to the disputed ground. Any lost ground could be recaptured during the general offensive.

The artillery preparation began on 11 August, followed two days later by destruction fire. This had to be prolonged because bad weather forced a postponement of the infantry attack until the 20th. On the left bank gas shells impeded the assembly of the four divisions (25, 26 and DM, 31 DI), but they made good progress and captured all their objectives except for Hill 304. This feature had very steep sides to the north and south which made the maintenance of a rolling barrage very difficult once the troops reached the crest, so it was decided to encircle the hill on the east and west before taking possession. This was completed easily on 24 August and the few remaining German defenders taken prisoner. Already on 20 August, 31 DI had captured 1,000 men and an entire regimental staff who had been trapped in the tunnels under Mort-Homme after the French heavy mortars had destroyed their entrances. The total haul of prisoners captured by the two divisions of XVI Corps was 3,800 from three different German divisions; thirty-five German guns had been destroyed. The DM captured an entire German battery and blew up its guns.

On the right bank of the Meuse, XV Corps had a particularly difficult task as its objectives lay beyond a sort of no-man's-land, the Côte de Talou, which extended for 3 kilometres. Despite this and despite a fierce enemy artillery barrage during the night as the troops assembled, they reached all their objectives except for part of a trench running between the two hills (hills 344 and 326). They completed the capture of Samog-neux village the next day, helped by the fact that the DM on the left bank was already in possession of the Côte de l'Oie. The right-hand corps, XXXII Corps, took the greatest number of casualties. Although it reached its objectives, a line through the woods, the enemy trenches were very close to the new position and German guns still occupied the heights between the villages of Bezonvaux and Ornes. Consequently the high command decided to mount a further attack to improve the French position, and this took place on 8 September. Troops in the centre and on the left reached their objectives, but the right-hand regiment suffered considerable casualties when German troops counter-attacked from the ravines leading down onto the Woëvre plain which was full of enemy artillery. During these operations in August and September the four corps of Second Army captured 11,000 prisoners, XXXII Corps alone bagging 100 German officers. The French casualties amounted to well over 14,000, almost a third of them (4,470) killed or disappeared.[49]

The enemy made many counter-attacks in September and October, especially on the right bank where they seemed determined to take back the high ground observatories they had lost. Fayolle noted in his report on operations that the objectives set on the right bank were badly chosen, because they were too close to high ground still held by the enemy. This meant that the enemy positions overlooked the French ones, so that the retention of the ground gained proved more expensive in casualties than the original capture. The captures on the left bank had included a wide band of ground in front of the heights, hence had been retained more easily. Finally, the position on the right bank was settled for the winter. On 25 November, in appalling weather conditions and after a very heavy artillery preparation of five hours – eighteen groups of field, twenty-four groups of heavy, and nine groups of trench artillery, for a front of 4 kilometres – the men of 128 DI on the left and 37 DI on the right created a covering zone for the new French positions by capturing a line of enemy concrete shelters, blowing them up, then returning to their own lines. Yet, despite the hard fighting from 20 August until the end of November, the extended battle on the right bank did not give rise to any of the incidents of indiscipline that had followed Nivelle's offensive.

Once again reports from the corps commanders, from Guillaumat and from army group commander Fayolle, were sent to GQG.[50] The comparison with the same sector, the right bank of the Meuse, and same period a year previously, autumn 1916, is inevitable. Nivelle's 1916 recapture of Fort Douaumont led to his appointment as CinC to succeed Joffre; now, under Pétain as CinC, the Germans had been pushed back to their February 1916 lines, and the French had taken the Mort-Homme on the left bank as well.

Fayolle deserves credit for ensuring that the artillery was positioned as close as possible to the infantry. He instructed the infantry not to rush in a 'brutal and mechanical way', as had been ordered on 16 April, but to take a series of coordinated steps, with pauses factored in between phases. Some officers, Fayolle continued, believe that a pause in operations destroys the infantry's 'élan'; yet what 'breaks their élan are intact belts of wire and machine guns firing. Besides, it is less a question of speed than of safety and a minimum of losses.'[51] It was also Fayolle's policy to keep the divisions with the task of leading any assault in the same position long enough for them to become thoroughly familiar with the terrain. Then the second-line divisions with the task of supporting them took over the front line for a week to give the attacking units some rest, with the result that when the latter were returned to the line by lorry, their support units behind also knew the terrain.[52] Anthoine had used the same system of temporary relief for attacking troops in Flanders.

The Verdun operation had lasted into November, but the almost complete success of 20 August made the headlines. Poincaré came to the Verdun citadel on 29 August to decorate Pétain with the Grand' Croix of the Légion d'honneur, and Pétain thanked the President 'effusively'. In his speech Poincaré addressed his words to the CinC: 'Ever since the day when you were called to re-establish our military position before Verdun, the world's attention has been fixed on this glorious city ... The whole of humanity has understood that, on the great and tragic part being played out on both banks of the Meuse, depended the liberty of the people and the future of civilisation.'[53] Yet, if within Second Army there were no recorded incidents of indiscipline, morale was not great. The losses suffered, the new German gas shells and the inferiority of French aviation were frequent themes of the more than 22,000 letters read in twelve regiments of Second Army at the beginning of October.[54] Despite the speeches, therefore, and despite Pétain's connection to the city, the Verdun fighting should be counted the least successful of the three French battles in the latter half of 1917.

La Malmaison

The third of Pétain's limited objective, local actions was on the Chemin des Dames itself. It would show Nivelle how it should be done, and it would complete the capture of one of the objectives of 16 April. This should have been the first of the three, but the indiscipline of May and June had to be quelled before operations could start; then, the heavy artillery devoted to the Verdun attack had to be returned – a distance of approximately 150 kilometres. It was the operation that Haig urged Pétain to begin on 6 October, so as to ease the situation in Flanders, when Pétain refused to be hurried.

General Maistre's Sixth Army operational order for the offensive gave as its aim the *limited objective* of occupying the plateau of the Malmaison fort and Ange Gardien as far north as the foot of its northern slopes, that is to say as far as the river Ailette and the Oise–Aisne canal. The purpose of this occupation was to provide observation over the Ailette and enable flanking fire into the remaining enemy positions on the Chemin des Dames ridge; to deprive the enemy of observation over the French positions in the Aisne river valley; and finally to push the enemy's artillery back beyond the Ailette. Three army corps were allocated: XI on the right, XXI in the centre and XIV on the left. Pétain ordered that Sixth Army should receive all the guns that it wanted. The total amounted to:

768 field guns (75s); 590 short heavy artillery pieces ranging in calibre from 155 to 280; 316 long heavy artillery pieces, more than half of them being 155s; 102 extra heavies of calibres from 155 to 400; and 232 trench artillery pieces. Three fighter groups of aircraft plus two squadrons and an observation balloon for the extra heavy artillery were joined by fourteen squadrons and twelve balloons for each of the three corps involved. Sixty-three tanks were to be used again, but, it was hoped, more successfully by acting on the lessons of April/May.

The good road and 60cm Decauville railway network allowed the French to position huge quantities of guns and munitions, which arrived daily throughout the month of September. Because a good many ravines ran through the high ground at right angles to the ridge, the terrain enabled all the batteries to be protected along the 10-kilometre front. The artillery preparation was to last four days but was extended because of the poor visibility that interfered with aerial observation. Although the enemy was well aware that an offensive was coming – French intelligence discovered three new divisions ready to intervene, and sixty-four new German batteries, bringing the total to 180 – the French concentrated on interdiction fire, aimed at stopping all enemy movement. This countered the German build-up to some extent. Groups of moppers-up were organised, some armed with flamethrowers, to deal with the enemy's many underground shelters. Finally, because it was learned that the Germans had discovered the hour of the infantry assault, this was brought forward one hour.

The assault began at 5.15 on the morning of 23 October whilst it was still dark. On the right, despite a heavy enemy bombardment of the departure trenches, XI Corps reached its objectives and captured the fort of La Malmaison. The two remaining corps also reached their first and second objectives, although the divisions on the flanks were repulsed (67 DI of XXXIX Corps on the right and 129 DI on the left). Machine-gun nests were silenced either by the tanks or the moppers-up, but the technical deficiencies of the tanks were revealed once more. Of the sixty-three tanks available, only twenty-nine moved beyond the front line and fifteen others broke down as soon as they had reached the enemy's first position. Although helped by the misty conditions, which, on the other hand, hindered the aircraft, the tanks did not have good visibility and several tank commanders were killed when they lifted their head out of the turret in order to see where they were going. The churned-up terrain hindered those tanks that did manage to get forward, and the experience confirmed Estienne's view that a smaller, lighter tank was required. The next day the French firmed their hold on the Malmaison plateau and pushed out patrols to the north. As a result, on 25 October the order was

Fig. 16 The remains of the fort of La Malmaison, north of the Chemin des Dames

given to move through the Pinon forest on the left, and on the right to capture Pargny-Filain, the Chapelle Sainte-Berthe, and Filain the next day. On the entire front of the Sixth Army the enemy had been thrown back across the Ailette, and the battle was terminated.

The booty was considerable: 11,500 prisoners including 240 officers; 200 guns and 220 mortars; 720 machine guns. French casualties were comparatively light. The right-hand corps had suffered the most, but XIV Corps took only 2,500 and XXI Corps 1,600 casualties. The army total for the three days of operation was less than 14,000 killed, wounded and missing, a figure to be compared with the almost 20,000 British killed on a single day, the first day of the Somme the previous year. Over the following days, Tenth Army further east kept up heavy artillery fire on the remaining enemy lines, with the result that by 2 November the Germans had evacuated all their positions on the Chemin des Dames. The victory at La Malmaison itself had led to a considerable further success.

In the middle of the deployment, 13 DI took part as one of XXI Corps' constituent units. It is worth examining here the role and achievements of 13 DI in detail, because La Malmaison represents an early example of the all-arms battle that would be repeated on a larger scale in July 1918, when Foch's counter-attacks ended the German offensives.[55] After being withdrawn from the Somme, the division spent the winter in eastern France being trained in the methods that were supposed to incorporate the lessons of 1916. This meant training in how to break through two German positions and then to exploit the breach. In 1915 and 1916 the French attacks had always managed to capture the first German position but had been halted on the second. Now the division was studying how to exploit success and to manoeuvre in open ground. The division had lost one of its four regiments (17 RI) when it became ternary. In 1917 it comprised 21 and 109 RI with the third regiment made up of two battalions of chasseurs. The divisional artillery consisted of three groups of field artillery (62 RAC). They arrived in the Château-Thierry region from Belfort on 15 and 16 April, ready for Fayolle to deploy them in First Army to exploit the anticipated breakthrough. There they marked time until 18 May when the entire XXI Corps was transferred to Soissons and to General Maistre's Sixth Army. (The collective disobedience during this time was described in the previous chapter.) There was apprehension about returning to the front, not to exploit success as they had been led to hope, but to endure more fighting. Criminal 'meneurs' tried to foment revolt, but the officers soon managed to restore their authority.

In early June the division took over the front at Laffaux, extending for about 4.5 kilometres. The hill of Laffaux with its windmill made an elbow in the line and had no proper defences because of the fierce fighting following 16 April. Nonetheless, apart from a few minor skirmishes, the division saw no action between its arrival and the end of August. On 5 September, following twelve days' rest, the division returned to the Laffaux sector and was employed in preparing the La Malmaison offensive.

The German defensive positions in front of 13 DI were very strong, because of the right-angled elbow in the line. South of the Laon–Soissons road, the east–west section of the German front line met the new Hindenburg Line positions running north-west, thus creating the strongly reinforced elbow that enabled the Germans to fire in enfilade on 13 DI's attacking troops. The first enemy position consisted of three lines of trench 200–300 metres apart, wired irregularly; the second had two lines of trenches with many shelters in the first and the second situated on a reverse slope, both protected by a 5-metre-deep belt of wire. Between the two positions were sited numerous machine-gun nests and the many caves and quarries provided shelter for reserves. Then, beyond the second position lay most of the artillery emplacements. The river Ailette and parallel canal lay about 6 kilometres to 13 DI's north, but it would be downhill to the river after capturing the plateau of La Malmaison/L'Ange Gardien. A modern and very large guardian angel overlooks the busy Soissons–Laon road today.

Preparations were meticulous. The staffs were rested and fully conversant with the task they had to carry out. They were provided with maps and aerial photographs, they traced out their route on large-scale maps, and they practised. The infantry rehearsed the attack using mock-ups of the terrain. The artillery positions were all prepared by July, and the division was supported by the greatest density of guns it would ever enjoy: one gun for every 5 metres of front. The men moved into position during the three nights preceding the attack. The rolling barrage was set at a rate of two minutes per 100 metres for the first 200 metres, slowing to three minutes per 100 metres thereafter. The density was twenty rounds a minute. After a short halt on the intermediate objective, the troops should reach their first objective, a line running east–west 1 kilometre north of the Vaurains Farm. Engineers to get the position into a defensible state and machine-gun sections to protect the flanks of the assault troops against enemy enfilade fire were to remain on the first objective. Meanwhile the support battalions of the attacking regiments would carry out the new tactic of passing through the lines and continue the progression towards the second objective, a line a kilometre north of Vaudesson, four hours after the initial assault. The rolling barrage for the renewed assault would begin at a rate of three minutes per 100 metres, reducing to six minutes. In order to maintain contact with the flanking divisions, two pauses were timetabled, with the barrage standing still 200 metres in front of the troops.

To give even more support, two groups of machine guns were provided, one of twelve and the other of twenty guns, and four batteries of three Schneider tanks. One tank battery was to help clear the ravine west of Vaurains, whilst the other three were to join the attack troops on the first position one hour after H-hour to ward off any counter-attacks. One aircraft was to follow the infantry's progress and another aircraft to keep close liaison with the command. A series of signals and flares was established so that the infantry could indicate where they were held up whenever a delay occurred of more than ten minutes. Also two groupings of artillery were to fire fixed barrages on any point where the aviation indicated a gathering of enemy troops, and in front of the second object-ive once that was reached.

Helped by the tanks when they were held up by machine guns, all units of 13 DI had reached their objectives by midday on 23 October, or soon thereafter. The night was spent in reinforcing their positions. On 24 October reconnaissance patrols reported that there were few troops in front of the division, but it proved impossible to move up the guns because the ground was so chewed up. Consequently the move onto the line of the Ailette was ordered for the next day, 25th, with XIV Corps on the division's left providing the artillery barrage and the whole of 13 DI moving forward. By 4pm some units had reached the river and the remainder reached it that night. Although orders were received on 26 October to attempt a crossing, this proved impossible and command let it be known that since all objectives had been reached, the operation was ended. The division's 1,108 casualties represented a mere 6.8 per cent of the effectives engaged.

It had not been an offensive, rather a huge artillery operation, wrote the authors of 13 DI's history. Yet there were lessons for the infantry too. They had learned the value of the tactic of resting the attacking troops just before the infantry assault, and of the refusal to set objectives that could not be retained once captured – there was no question of pushing down to the marshy valley of the Ailette once the objectives on the ridge had been taken. The commission working at GQG on the new tactical doctrine had produced a draft version just before the offensive began, as well as working on the 1918 campaign. La Malmaison confirmed the new doctrine and Pétain signed it off on 31 October. Its main principles were: first, wearing down the enemy's forces; second, offensive fronts to be prepared well in advance so as to be able to keep feeding the battle; surprise to be sought by varying attacks; and attacking elsewhere rather than exploiting a local success. At GQG they felt that La Malmaison had vindicated their work.[56]

Cambrai

Despite his profuse thanks to Pétain for the sterling work that Anthoine's First Army had done in Flanders, Haig was unwilling to allow any French participation or share of glory in his Battle of Cambrai. Just as Haig mounted a rapid limited-objective attack at the end of 1916, at Beaumont-Hamel, to provide a quick victory after the generally unsuccessful Somme campaign, so he repeated the exercise in November 1917. His stock was now very low, both with politicians and the press, the latter having been previously strongly supportive; both the establishment of the Supreme War Council (see below) and Lloyd George's strong words in its support had been a blow to Haig's pride. A surprise artillery attack on the Hindenburg Line near Cambrai, supported by the tanks that had been unable to operate in the muddy conditions in Flanders, might give Haig's reputation a boost. Such, at first, proved the case. Third Army made a stunning advance on the first day, 20 November, but the assault soon faltered and an equally stunning German counter-attack on the 30th took back almost all the British gains. Surprise had been achieved because there had been no artillery preparation at all to give away the fact of an impending offensive. Also, the secret had been well kept, although Haig did inform Pétain, who offered an army detachment of two infantry and two cavalry divisions under General Degoutte to help in the exploitation phase.

Although a British battle, Cambrai is added here because of Pétain's offer to provide this sizable army detachment to assist in the exploitation. Improvements in GQG efficiency meant that on the night of 19/20 November, when Pétain asked for several divisions to be moved to act as reserves for Haig, the transport was complete by the following afternoon.[57] The French took up a position near Péronne, just south of the Cambrai sector, but Haig informed Degoutte on 25 November that they could be stood down. However, after the French began leaving the area and the German counter-attack began, Haig requested French assistance. Pétain understood how violent the counter-attack was and he halted Degoutte's departure, sending two further divisions (129 and 154 DI) and the headquarters staff of XIV Corps to the area. The French remained there until 16 December, for Haig to use if necessary.[58]

From the French point of view, the most important result of Cambrai was that it gave Haig a reason to delay taking over the front of the French Third Army, as he had agreed. Instead, he stated that the BEF needed rest and training after the effort of Flanders and Cambrai, and he offered to complete the relief of just two French divisions by the end of December. Some cynical French whispered that Cambrai had been mounted for the purpose of delaying the relief – unlikely, but no doubt an added benefit from the British point of view. The French did gain one advantage, however, in receiving spectacular confirmation from Haig's offensive of the benefits of surprise. Debeney circulated a note dated 27 November to army and army group commanders, and to army schools, pointing out that the enemy would doubtless draw the same conclusions after the complete surprise of the Cambrai attack. Since it was impossible to prevent a rupture of the front when surprise and massive resources are used, it was therefore vital to ensure that defensive positions be able to contain any breach. Well-placed reserves should prevent enemy exploitation in depth, but to ensure against *lateral* exploitation, a system of positions parallel to the front was insufficient. A network of cross trenches (*bretelles*) should be organised to compartmentalise the ground, taking advantage of natural features such as water lines. Debeney required all commanders to supply by 15 December a map showing their defensive arrangements and to set up immediately a programme of labour to complete the necessary work.[59]

Haig's initial rejection of Pétain's generous offers of help for Cambrai, after demanding French help in October and more troops from Britain, reinforces the 'suspicion' of Haig's biographer that 'one of the main goals of the Cambrai operation was to boost Haig's and the British army's prestige, and that Haig had no wish to share any glory available with another commander-in-chief and another army'.[60] Indeed, in Paris, Clemenceau's military advisor remained 'sceptical' about why the operation had been mounted at all.[61] (Clemenceau had taken over as premier from Painlevé on 16 November.) So Pétain receives no credit for his willingness to contribute to another offensive operation in 1917. The British official history disparages Pétain's offer, claiming that the French troops merely disrupted British supply arrangements.[62] Haig was so dismissive as to write to Robertson on 25 November, that is after the start of Cambrai but before the German counter-attack, that the British were 'now the only one of the Allied Armies capable of carrying out a vigorous offensive, and that our power to do so must depend on the extent to which our resources are concentrated in France'.[63] This failed Franco-British cooperation was a harbinger of the further failure, described below, to reach a common strategy for the 1918 campaign.

The results of Pétain's offensives, and lessons learned

The vindication of the work of the 'commission de refonte' at GQG on recasting the instruction on large unit offensives has been noted already. It replaced the previous December's 'Instruction sur l'action offensive des grandes unités'. The new instruction recommended seeking surprise, either strategically by launching a sudden attack on ground where the enemy could not quickly bring up reserves, or tactically by keeping the enemy ignorant of the exact time and place of an anticipated attack and submerging the enemy with the speed of execution. It also recommended neutralisation of the enemy's batteries and observation points, rather than their destruction, as a means of increasing surprise. Technical progress in sound-ranging and flash-spotting and the increase in production of rapid-firing models of guns both meant that preparation could be reduced to a minimum. The 'normal' objective of an infantry attack was to be determined by the range of its supporting artillery. This eliminated the programmed waiting periods for artillery to be repositioned; now objectives were limited to the range of the artillery. The attacking unit was no longer the army corps, but the division which was to attack on a front of 1,200 metres in a square formation. This was formed by placing the division's three regiments in line along the front (400 metres each) and placing each regiment's three battalions in line, one behind the other. This allowed the 'passage des lignes', in which units were being trained to pass the second and third battalions through the first as each intermediate objective was reached. This had worked successfully in Flanders and for 13 DI at La Malmaison. Such tactics should enable a division to capture between 2 and 3 kilometres of terrain in each attack. Now a corps was supplied with four instead of two divisions, so that it could keep two divisions in line with two in reserve, thus enabling a regular rotation for rest and training purposes.[64] This is Pétain at his methodical best. His contribution to the defence of Verdun in 1916 had been just such a careful organisation of his resources; now he repeated the exercise on a grander scale. Method replaced Nivelle's rapidity, but successive methodically prepared attacks were to be launched as rapidly as possible with air superiority, which Pétain considered to be vital. These ideas resemble those that Foch would impose in 1918.

This instruction was followed on 22 December by the famous Directive #4 on the defensive battle.[65] The German withdrawal to the immensely strong Hindenburg Line in March–April had shown the value of giving up terrain for a position of great depth containing several lines. Then, at Cambrai, the British had proved that surprise could defeat front-line defences with relative ease, as the Germans had also proved at Riga in September 1917. If the French defences were not to be overrun by such tactics, then defensive principles needed changing. The now confirmed Russian defection made that change even more urgent as German divisions returned from the east to France.

The directive's two basic principles were defence in depth and the exploitation of intelligence about the enemy's intentions. Command was to establish several different plans to cover various hypotheses about possible enemy attacks. The most important factor in the new instruction lay in the method of conducting the defensive battle. It was the role of high command to define a second defensive position, the 'line of resistance', which was to be retained at all costs. When faced with a very powerful attack, the high command might decide to give battle only on the second position. This was to be sited between 6 and 8 kilometres to the rear of the first, depending on the terrain. In such a case, no reinforcements were to be sent to the defenders of the first position, who were nevertheless to put up as strong a defence as possible in order to give the second position troops time to organise. The CinC's general reserve could be sent to reinforce the army under attack or else to launch an attack elsewhere.

Only after the Entente had regained numerical superiority over the German Army, that is, when sufficient American troops had joined the front, could they return to the offensive which alone could guarantee victory. (Note that Pétain has not renounced the offensive altogether.)

Pétain urged the completion of improvements to defensive positions as a matter of urgency, especially in 'sensitive' areas, but the work on preparing for an offensive should continue albeit as a second priority. Each army group commander was to provide by 25 December a clear and precise programme of the work necessary to meet these requirements. Equally, each army group commander must understand that the CinC's ability to take the offensive when an opportunity presented itself depended on the value of the preparations for an offensive already made and on the combat value of the troops. This was to be maintained by small local actions such as raids to gather intelligence, by taking care not to respond to feints or threats of attack which the enemy was bound to employ, and, finally, by training and care to keep the troops in the best physical and moral condition possible. The army group commanders were to ensure this last in person.

Pétain's ideas met with resistance because they accepted the likelihood that some ground would be given up in the event of an enemy attack. Therefore he embarked on a round of visits to the armies to explain that giving up ground did not imply a defeat, as some commanders feared, but provided rather the opportunity to win a defensive victory by forcing the enemy to manoeuvre. As a result of these visits and the criticisms he heard during them, Pétain prepared with great care an instruction, issued on 24 January 1918, on how the principles of his Directive #4 were to be applied.[66] Instead of a 'front' or a line, Pétain substituted the idea of a 'zone', and he introduced the concept of a 'champ de bataille d'armée', changing the army's sphere of action from a position to an entire battlefield where movement was possible – 'the organised ground on which the army's mission is to halt and to defeat the enemy'. The distance between the enemy's front and the line of resistance constituted the 'margin of security' 'covered' by the troops in the front, nearest the enemy. Reinforcements could either support the 'covering troops', or mount counter-attacks, or occupy the 'position of resistance'.[67]

These provisions were somewhat idealistic, taking little account of practical difficulties. Apart from the unwillingness of generals to give up ground after three years of striving to expel the enemy, especially where this ground had been won at huge expense, such as Verdun or the Chemin des Dames, there were other problems. There was a shortage of labour to construct the new second positions further back and to replace all the shelters for troops and battery positions that had been constructed in the front line, especially on fronts which had been static for some time. Furthermore, the specified distance between front and second positions, 6 to 8 kilometres, imposed a considerable burden of liaison and movement between them. Finally, how could a series of limited objective

Table 14 *Decline in effectives*

Mobilised men, 1000s			Detached for war work, 1000s				
Date	Zone of Armies	Zone of Interior	Factories	Agriculture	Public services	Mines/ navigation	Suspended callup
1.1.17	2,987	1,542	515	—	357	65	64
1.7.17	3,005	1,507	559	130	349	75	70
1.1.18	2,898	1,525	534	307	352	110	123
Totals							
1.1.17		4,529			1,001		
1.7.17		4,512			1,183		
1.1.18		4,423			1,426		

Adapted from Hellot, *Histoire*, 306, annex 3.

actions lead to 'dislocation' of the enemy's front? The 31 October instruction 'raise[d] to the level of a system' that which should have remained merely a 'temporary expedient'.[68] If the infantry had no experience of large operations and lost confidence in them, how could they know when to pass on to the offensive and stop relying on the artillery to do all the work?

In addition to circulating the new instructions for the offensive and the defensive in the light of 1917's battles, Pétain also needed to build up his reserves to the level he believed necessary, namely forty divisions. Over the twelve months from 1 January 1917 to 1 January 1918, the numbers of mobilised men declined steadily. The decree calling up the class of 1918 had already been passed in March 1917, and the men were incorporated in November. The call-up of the class of 1919 would be passed in parliament on 2 January 1918. If the numbers in the class of 1919 showed a slight increase over the previous year, the class of 1920 would supply 3,775 fewer effectives.[69] Table 14 shows the decline in effectives during the course of 1917. The largest variation lies in the territorial divisions which were all disbanded except for four, which became active divisions, and another one used for the defence of Paris. These older territorials were needed to work on the land. The cumulative effects of loss of agricultural workers and shipping losses due to the submarine war left France so short of food by autumn 1917 that ration cards for bread were issued. Foch's wife remarked on their distribution on 8 October 1917.

Although the French Army's losses in the latter half of 1917 were the lightest of the war, nevertheless 189,300 soldiers lost their lives on the battlefield or in hospital between 1 January 1917 and 1 January 1918. On the other hand, Pétain did have extra native contingents available. For example, the Bataillon mixte du Pacifique served with 72 DI in Champagne from August to October 1917. The battalion consisted of four companies of Kanak (raised in Nouméa) and Tahitian tirailleurs. Pétain attempted to make up the deficit by amalgamating US troops with French units, but General Pershing would have none of it.[70] The need for French instructors was accepted, however, and 332 specialists crossed to the USA in October 1917, to join the 24 who had been there since May. In France, the first US Division was twinned with 47 DI and extra instructors added to the division's general staff. In September, 18 DI replaced 47 DI, and the next month 69 DI was brought into the scheme as two more American divisions arrived.[71] Pétain had the charge, therefore, of providing officers for instructing US troops, but was not permitted to combine the trained troops with depleted French units.

The USA had joined the war back in April, but by December the numbers of fully trained American troops in the four US divisions in France were minuscule. The general total of 144,871 for 28 December 1917, calculated by the French Military Mission to the AEF, included 99,525 combatants, 35,874 service troops (administrative, engineers, medical and so on), but 9,472 of the total were British or French interpreters, liaison officers and instructors.[72] Indeed, as already noted, the principal effect of the American declaration of war had been negative. The letters of the mutinous soldiers in June and July revealed the general view that another belligerent merely meant the war's prolongation. Furthermore, Pétain complained that giving new weapons to US soldiers meant that his own armies were less well armed.[73]

So, in the armies in the field, on the lines of communication, in training establishments and administrative establishments, Pétain had 188,000 fewer men at the end of 1917 than had been available at its start, the equivalent of more than eleven 1914-sized divisions. The total number of divisions had not diminished, however, because of the change to a single divisional infantry of three regiments from the two brigades each of two regiments that had begun the war. This change to the ternary was almost complete by the end of 1917, in a total of 113 divisions; 39 regiments had been suppressed, nearly all of them reserve regiments.[74] These 113 divisions had fewer men, but were much better armed. Beginning in December 1917, regiments were supplied progressively with Stokes mortars.

In September 1917 Pétain reorganised the combat section to reflect the increased firepower. In principle, each regiment of about 3,400 men had twelve companies (four for each of the regiment's three battalions,

Table 15 *The combat section from September 1917*

			No. of men
Section commander + 1 sergeant			2
1st half-section	commanded by a sergeant		1
	1 squad	1 corporal; 8 grenadiers/riflemen	9
	2 squad	1 corporal; 2 riflemen; 2/3 pourvoyeurs [carriers]; 3/4 VB grenadiers	9
2nd half-section	commanded by a sergeant		1
	3 squad	1 corporal; 2 riflemen; 3/4 VB grenadiers; 1/2 pourvoyeurs	9
	4 squad	1 corporal; 8 grenadiers/riflemen	9
		Total of 40 men per section	

Table adapted from Guinard et al., *Introduction*, 131. VB stands for Vivier-Bessière, the names of the two designers who built a grenade launcher to slip on to the end a rifle.

plus a machine-gun section) (see Tables 4 and 15). In August 1916 the number of men per company had dropped to 194 and three machine guns (two in 1914) were allocated to each machine-gun company.[75] Each company of 194 men comprised four sections. The much wider range of weaponry meant that, instead of a line of riflemen placed a regulation distance apart and controlled from on high, the troops became specialised and forced to work more independently as a team, where a particular weapon required more than one man to carry it and its munitions. Each section thus became, in Michel Goya's words, a 'tactical cell'.[76]

The final disposition of this new combat section followed months of trial and error. The first project, drawn up in May 1917, was sent to the Northern Army Group, which disseminated it down to regimental level. After ten days it returned, fully annotated, to GQG, and a revised document was issued on 18 July, which also incorporated British experience of the organisation. After trial within a selected company in a large number of different corps, the results were collated during August and the new organisation adopted on 10 September.[77]

In addition to these personal and trench weapons, the increasing artillery resources tabulated at the start of this chapter meant that divisions were being allocated even greater firepower. During the course of 1917 almost every division received a group of short 155s, and a battery of twelve 58mm trench artillery. The number of regiments of tractor-drawn heavy guns was doubled in October 1917.[78] The best illustration of the increased firepower is seen in Table 16 comparing the three 'batailles de redressement'.

Table 16 *Density of guns*

	Flanders	Verdun	La Malmaison
Front of attack (km)	4	18	10
Men per km	33,750	23,333	31,200
Batteries per km	38	34	40
Guns (field and heavy) per km	141	125	170
Number of field guns engaged	218	948	732
Number of heavy guns engaged	238	1308	976
Percentage of total resources	4.2% field	18.5% field	14.3% field
in guns (Western Front)	9.6% heavy	36.2% heavy	27% heavy

Source: Hellot, *Histoire*, 221; *AFGG 5/2*, appendice II, p. 1281.

Pétain valued the weapon of intelligence as well, and great improvements were made to France's army intelligence during 1917. Strategic photo reconnaissance became the self-appointed task of Commandant Paul-Louis Weiller. An artillery officer, he began the war doing aerial spotting for his gunners, taking photographs with his own camera. After realising that his photographs did not correspond with the 50-year-old maps, he worked out a system of updating maps from aerial photography, and the Army Geographical Service adopted his system. Weiller obtained his pilot's licence in August 1915, and developed a camera lens with the enormous focal length of 1.5 metres that enabled highly detailed prints to be made of the ground below. He spent the whole of 1917 perfecting his system of flying systematically over an area to record changes.[79] It paid huge dividends in 1918 and Foch was highly appreciative of his work. The teams of train-spotters, who reported German troop movements, were now well organised. The Third Army's intelligence service was the first to describe in detail the various sections of the Hindenburg Line, and First Army's reports on the German defences in Flanders informed a document on the construction of defensive positions, issued in September 1917. Studies of German tactics were drawn up and disseminated. The German success at Riga, for example, was the subject of a long study, eventually printed and distributed widely. The 2e bureau of each army began to work more closely with its 3e operations bureau, which led to far better documentation as the intelligence gathered by the former fed into the operational documents issued by the latter. This was yet another of Pétain's organisational improvements, symbolised by his placing both bureaux at GQG under one aide-major général, General de Barescut.[80]

Other fronts intrude

Pétain's urgent need for reinforcements for his diminishing effectives, in the form of British relief or of American amalgamation, was made sharper by the French commitments on other fronts. Russia had been the key to France's willingness to go to war in 1914, but the Bolsheviks asked for an armistice on 27 November 1917. Attempts to prop up the ailing Russians meant that masses of French-supplied weapons and munitions still lay on Russian docksides. Equipping the slowly arriving Americans was also a very large commitment. In addition to supplying its own armies with modern artillery, France had commitments to Romania, Serbia/Salonika, and a new commitment in Palestine.

Although the French suppressed thirty-nine regiments in 1917, two new ones of tirailleurs were created, one of them for the Détachement Français de Palestine.[81] For this same small grouping was created also a Légion d'Orient comprising mainly Armenian and Syrian elements. Given the constraints of falling effectives in France, it might seem strange that yet another commitment from France's colonial army would be undertaken outside the metropolis. The reason for this lay in French fears for the post-war Middle East settlement. As British forces approached the Christian Holy Places in Palestine at the end of 1917, the French feared a takeover, as seemed to have happened with the Muslim holy place in Mecca, where the British appeared to have appropriated the credit for the Arab revolt. Then, Baghdad was captured in March, and Beersheba on 31 October. It seemed that the British were taking over the whole Middle East.

The question of Syria and France's long-standing interests in the Ottoman Empire had been the reason for French participation in the failed Dardanelles expedition in 1915. Palestine and Lebanon formed part of a greater Syria, what the French called 'la Syrie intégrale'. When it became clear that the Ottoman Empire would be broken up at war's end, despite France's preference for its retention, Britain and France negotiated a division of the spoils in 1916, the Sykes–Picot agreement, which left Palestine as a 'brown zone', or grey area, whose final disposition was to be settled later. The Arab revolt against Turkish rule and the advance of British troops towards Jerusalem made the French fear Britain's pretentions in the Middle East. This fear was exacerbated at the end of 1916 when David Lloyd George became Prime Minister. He was determined to 'grab' Palestine and not allow the 'Atheistic French' to get their hands on the Holy Places.[82]

The British push into Palestine and Syria was not the only threat to French interests in the Middle East. In addition to taking over the Arab revolt, the arrival of Feisal's Bedouin in Aqaba in August 1917 became a British achievement also, and attributed to one British colonel at that. In accordance, therefore, with the policy of not allowing the British to get away with snatching another stretch of territory as they had supposedly snatched Egypt, the French sent a mission to Sherif Hussein. Colonel T.E. Lawrence's mission is the one known today, but the French mission under Lieutenant-Colonel Edouard Brémond was just as important, although Lawrence is reported to have 'hated' the Frenchman.

France had very large Muslim populations of its own in North Africa. With the publication in June 1916 in London of an official note announcing the Arab revolt, the French had to act. They sent two missions, one political and Brémond's military one. Brémond installed his mission in Jeddah in September, and supervised the journey of 600 pilgrims to Mecca in October. Paris saw the political value of supporting the Arab revolt and, equally, of alleviating the loss of income because of the naval blockade of the Arabian coast, which prevented the arrival of pilgrims by sea just as the state of war prevented overland arrivals. Facilitating a pilgrimage would give the French prestige with their own Muslim subjects and political clout with Arabs in general.

In November they supplied artillery (mountain guns) to the Sherif Hussein, who was in difficulties against the Ottoman troops. French North African Muslim troops operated with the Arab forces in the guerrilla war against Turkish railways, and they trained Arab guerrillas to use the new automatic rifle.[83] Captain Rosario Pisani came from Morocco to command the artillery and engineers. Feisal, one of the Sherif's sons, so appreciated his services that he asked Pisani to accompany him to Paris for the treaty negotiations in 1919, much to Lawrence's annoyance. The 200 French-supplied troops were Moroccan, Algerian or Tunisian; the junior officers were Arabic-speaking volunteers, mostly born in North Africa; and the twelve officers were French specialists.

This, then, is the background to the formation of the Détachement française de Palestine (DFP). On 15 May 1917, the DFP consisted of 2,238 officers and men, commanded by Lieutenant-Colonel de Piépape, former chief of staff in the Dardanelles in 1915. It was a tiny force in comparison with the British. Yet its presence during the entry into Jerusalem in December 1917, recounted in Chapter 9, was a vital marker for the retention of France's influence within the collapsing Ottoman empire, and for the continued role for France's colonial army, 'la Coloniale'.

France also had commitments in eastern Europe: Russia, the Romanian Army, and the Serbian Army as part of the Salonika force. By

February 1917, some 400 French officers and 1,000 men had been sent to the French military mission in Romania, headed by experienced French general, Henri Berthelot, to act as advisors and instructors. By the summer of 1917, the Romanians had redeemed the previous year's defeat by creating ten fully equipped divisions and five more needing only guns. Although Paris was unwilling at first to provide modern weapons and aircraft, Berthelot's persistence prevailed. The transport through Russia to Romania was the major difficulty. Berthelot also demanded medical personnel to deal with the insanitary conditions that made the typhus epidemics so much worse. Eventually 100 French medics were working in the country. As Russia descended into revolution and disarray, Romania became an important focus for propping up the Eastern Front. The revived Romanian Army repaid the French investment by defeating the Central Powers' attempt to capture Moldavia and knock them out of the war. The enemy attack that began on 6 August under the command of von Mackensen (the hero of Gorlice–Tarnow in 1915) was resisted so strongly that by the end of August the Central Powers decided to give up the attempt. The American General Hugh Scott visited Romania in 1917 and remarked that the Romanian Army had 'the benefit of the services of a brilliant French commander as instructor, General Berthelot, aided by 400 French officers'. In the opinion of his biographer, without Berthelot's 'resolute defense of the autonomy of Romania and her army it is quite likely both would have been engulfed in the Russian Revolution'.[84] The *monthly* deliveries required to sustain the Romanian Army by November 1917 are shown in Table 17.

Table 17 *Monthly supplies of selected materials to Romania*

Personal weapons and mg munitions	2,000 rifles
	14,500 belts of ammunition for Hotchkiss machine guns other rifle and revolver cartridges
Infantry materiel	200,000 grenades
	39,800 rockets (signalling, lighting and so on)
Artillery materiel	10 barrels of 75s
	brakes/gun carriages
Munitions for French-type artillery	31,600 shells for 120s
	13,800 shells for 155s
	3,000 mortar shells for 58s
Munitions for Romanian-type artillery	38,400 shell cases for 105s
	6,200 shells for 120s
	25,200 shells for 150s
Fused rockets	7,400

Source: Fournitures aux pays alliés 1915–1917, 24 November 1917, 10N 72.

As well as Romania, the Serbian troops were equipped as part of the Armée d'Orient, in accordance with Sarrail's decisions. Hence it is not possible to give precise figures for the weapons and munitions supplied to the Serbian Army. After Sarrail's May offensive, which was meant to support Nivelle's operation in France but achieved little, he undertook no further significant action. In one of his four French divisions, there was serious unrest caused mainly by the question of leave, as in France. At the end of June, men had gone to the port to embark for a period of leave, but there were insufficient boats and they were returned to the front. The subsequent indiscipline was entirely understandable, as General Grossetti, their commander, recognised when submitting his report.[85] Obviously, the French could supply no more troops since they were dealing with the mutinies in France after Nivelle's offensive. The British insisted on removing some of their own, one division going to Palestine. The Russians were equally unable to contribute extra resources to the Balkans. After lengthy wrangling over Salonika during all the Allied conferences in the latter half of 1917, when little more than agreement to talk again was ever achieved, the British finally got their wish to have Sarrail removed. When Clemenceau became premier he had no interest in retaining Sarrail, not having been involved in all the politicking and back-stage deals that had gone on, and he simply informed the general that he was recalled. Sarrail went into retirement, and General Adolphe Guillaumat replaced him. Guillaumat had been in command of Second Army in the Centre Army Group since December 1916 when Nivelle became CinC.

Events in Russia descended into chaos. Alexandr Kerensky, the only Socialist minister in the provisional government, appointed minister of war in May, was determined that Russia should continue the war. The offensive that bears his name began on 1 July on the front in Galicia, but discipline had broken down. Although the Russian armies faced weak Austro-Hungarian forces and were equipped with large quantities of mainly French-supplied guns, when the Austro-Hungarians, reinforced with German units, counter-attacked, the Russians simply 'voted with their feet'. Since the ultimate authority, the Tsar, had departed – Nicholas and his family were executed in Ekaterinburg on 16 July – and since the Bolsheviks were promising redistribution of land, the Russian soldier simply walked home so as not to miss out in the redistribution. A Bolshevik revolt in Petrograd was quashed, although Lenin managed to escape to Finland to fight another day. Recriminations over the failed offensive led to further disorder, so that by the end of July it was clear that little more in the way of military support could be expected along the Eastern Front.

Major Langlois sent in a long report on conditions in Russia, dated 20 July 1917, to Painlevé and to Pétain.[86] The demise of the tsarist regime was no loss, Langlois stated, although the lack of military discipline and anti-allied propaganda were worrying. It was vital for France to retain Russian 'loyalty' and to keep Russia in the war. The form of any Russian military operation was unimportant, but France had to play an active role in reorganising the Russian army immediately. 'We must keep Russia on our side at all cost until the end of the war. This is a condition not only for military victory, but also for France's postwar economic renaissance.' Langlois was advocating yet another charge on the French Army at a time when Pétain was coping with reductions in effectives and wavering morale at home.

The politicians were worried too. In conference in Paris on 25–26 July, the Allies discussed what to do in case Russia defected, thereby freeing German divisions for transfer to the French front. Following the advice of their military, they agreed that political, economic and military support had to be given, with Britain concentrating on Russia's navy, the USA reorganising Russian railways (by providing rolling stock and technical expertise) and France providing support to the army. The French were to increase the size of their mission so that officers could be placed in all the Russian higher commands, with the head of mission based in Petrograd in the war ministry.[87] Foch lost no time in producing a document on the 28th on French action in Russia, which was accepted by the comité de guerre two days later. In order to give urgently needed support to the Russian war ministry to counter the German-inspired 'extremists', Foch proposed a powerful mission to repeat the same improvements that Berthelot had achieved in Romania. A 'high military personality' was to gain influence rapidly by his experience and authority so as to 'guide' the Russian war minister in 'reconstituting' the army. French officers based at Russian headquarters would represent the head of mission, passing on his views and reporting back on the views and intentions of the Russian high command. A certain number of French officers based in each Russian army were to offer 'technical advice' and by their example show Russian officers how to apply 'modern' discipline. Foch proposed supplying technical experts: cartographers, grenadiers, wireless operators and so on.[88] He had already prepared details of the composition of the mission, and in early August appointed General Albert Niessel as its head. Niessel was a highly experienced corps commander; he had fought alongside the British on the Somme in 1916 and on the Chemin des Dames in 1917; he was a Russian-speaking officer with experience in the country. He did not want to leave his IX Corps, but Foch insisted.[89] Langlois became his chief of staff. Clearly Foch appreciated the urgency of the situation in Russia and acted rapidly to counter it, but he was optimistic that the situation could be retrieved. Pétain meanwhile, at the same comité de guerre meeting that approved Foch's proposals for Russia, urged that the Russian troops in France should be returned home as soon as possible to avoid their revolutionary ways influencing French troops.[90] The mission sent to Russia consisted of 250 officers and 500 other ranks[91] – a large drain of experienced and well-qualified manpower.

Things got no better, however. Niessel reported on 1 October that the problem was not simply a question of military organisation, but that an energetic effort to counter Bolshevik propaganda was required. The Allies had to defeat the slogan of 'no annexations, no indemnities' and present the case for continuing the war. The question was now 'strictly political'.[92] The German offensive of 1 September against Riga, its capture and subsequent threat to Petrograd itself had proved that the disintegration of the Russian army had passed the point of no return. The French mission reported the offensive as a 'débâcle' and Pétain told the comité de guerre on 3 September that there was nothing more to be hoped for from the Russian army. Furthermore, he thought that as many as forty German divisions could be moved to France, through Switzer-land if necessary.[93] The army general staff produced a memorandum detailing a possible peace treaty using Russian territory as a means of compensating the Central Powers for ceding Alsace-Lorraine to France, along with a myriad of other territorial arrangements.[94] Small wonder, therefore, that Pétain's note to Haig of 16 October about the plan of campaign for 1918 envisaged Russia's making a separate peace. Russia had been the *sine qua non* for going to war in 1914, and now it seemed that the only possible strategy in 1918 without Russia was to remain on the defensive.

The news from Riga, when German forces crashed into the town and threatened Petrograd, was widely discussed in the press. The army's report on morale of 22 September stated that there was no greater cause of depression than the Russian situation. Both military and civilian opinion reflected irritation and exasperation. Postal control reports spoke of recriminations from all classes of society.[95] Then came the news of the Bolshevik seizure of power in Petrograd. On 7 November (25 October in the Julian calendar in use in Russia), as the Allies were meeting in Rapallo to set up the Supreme War Council for the future conduct of the war, Lenin took over from the discredited Kerensky with the aim of taking Russia out of the war. He asked Germany for an armistice on 27 November. The Russian defection was one of the primary factors 'among the elements of demoralisation' in the French Army at year's end. Morale reports pointed to the conviction that the struggle would be prolonged by Russia's actions, and to the 'fear, craftily exploited in the German press and accepted by ours, of having to make greater efforts, to suffer great assaults hard to bear'. The 'dream of a rest over the winter with plentiful periods of leave that many soldiers had built up' was destroyed.[96] In Italy, Paul Pireaud threatened to 'sign up for an extra six-month stint at the end of the war to give the Russians a good thrashing'.[97]

Italy and Caporetto

One further military commitment to a theatre outside France had to be made before the end of 1917. Events much further south overshadowed the Chemin des Dames where La Malmaison had been a resounding success and, together with Flanders and Verdun, had completed the restoration of confidence that Pétain sought to inspire in the French Army. The offensive against La Malmaison began on 23 October and ended three days later, but on 24 October a mixed German and Austro-Hungarian force attacked the Italian Army's eastern flank on the Isonzo river in north-east Italy. The ensuing disaster has been known ever since as Caporetto, and because of it, the success at La Malmaison is often overlooked in general histories of the war.

Lloyd George had tried at the Rome conference in January 1917 to make the Italian front the principal theatre of the 1917 campaign, but had failed – Nivelle's offensive was the result. Nevertheless, the Italians had attacked on the Isonzo in May as part of the whole Allied effort – French, Russian and Italian. In the tenth and eleventh battles on the Isonzo the Italians had inflicted so much damage on the Austro-Hungarians that Vienna accepted what had long been resisted. Kaiser Karl knew that his empire could not withstand further great losses, and asked the German high command for help to mount an offensive to deal with the Italian threat. Although he hesitated at first, Ludendorff agreed to supply a German army not only to prop up Germany's ailing ally, but to prevent any further Austrian attempts to make a separate peace. The Germans certainly knew about the 'Austrian option' being contemplated in Paris, and Baron Lancken of the German government of Belgium kept Berlin informed about possible talks with Aristide Briand, France's former premier.

Ludendorff appointed General Otto von Below, the victor of Riga against the demoralised Russian forces, to the command of a new *Fourteenth Army*, with the Bavarian Alpine expert General Krafft von Dellmensingen as his chief of staff. The aircraft and heavy artillery that had created the success before Riga were transported south to the Julian Alps where they joined seven German and eight Austro-Hungarian infantry divisions. In the early morning fog of 24 October these troops advanced on Caporetto, supported by gas and mortar fire and preceded by a powerful rolling barrage. The Italian Second Army was routed and driven back westwards as far as the Piave river after three days of continuous pressure from the German and Austro-Hungarian forces. This river was the last major obstacle to the east of the Venetian lagoon. If the Venetian plain lay open to the enemy, the Austrians could sweep down from the Trentino region and threaten Italy's main industrial centres of Turin and Milan. By 10 November, the Italians had lost more than a quarter of a million men taken prisoner, as well as over 10,000 killed and over 30,000 wounded. Nearly half their artillery had been abandoned or destroyed. Taking a leaf out of the French Army's book, the Italian CinC, General Luigi Cadorna, blamed his government for failing to suppress pacifist and defeatist propaganda.

Such a huge Italian defeat affected France. If the Italians were knocked out of the war, Austro-Hungarian troops would be freed to relieve German divisions on the Russian front, where armistice talks would soon begin in any case. Thus German divisions would be freed in turn to return to the west, where they would reverse the numerical superiority that the Allies had enjoyed in 1916 and 1917. Moreover, if the Austro-Hungarians were not required on the collapsing Russian front, they could easily move through the Alps against France's south-eastern border and invade, thereby opening another French front and threatening the important industrial centres around Lyon and Saint-Etienne. It was vital to support the Italians against both eventualities.

Foch, chief of the French army staff in Paris, reacted immediately. Before taking up his position, Foch had spent the early months of 1917 making arrangements with Cadorna to send French support to Italy if needed. He had also been instrumental in setting up 'Plan H' ('H' for Helvetia), a defensive plan to guard the Swiss frontier against any violation of Switzerland's neutrality. In addition he had been involved in the negotiations over sending British and French guns to Italy. This was Lloyd George's idea when it became clear that Haig's Flanders offensive had bogged down. So Foch was completely au fait with the situation in Italy and was prepared to act.

On 26 October he informed Cadorna and Robertson in London that French troops were ready to march, if required, in accordance with the agreed support plans. Although London was less keen to help, Foch argued that it was in the Allied interest to support Italy both morally and materially. As the war minister's representative, he ordered Pétain to put the relief plan into action by sending four French divisions, an army headquarters staff and heavy artillery across the Alps. The move should begin on 28 October, employing twenty-six (rising to forty) trains daily. It is to the credit of the efficient railway transport arrangements already in place that the move could begin on that date, only twenty-four hours after the decision was taken to send troops.

The despatch of these French units to Italy caused a breach between Foch and the French CinC, Pétain, which was to widen as the fighting in 1917 came to an end and planning for the 1918 campaign began. The division of responsibilities between the CinC and the chief of the army staff in the war ministry had never been delimited satisfactorily. Pétain and Foch were very different characters and it would have been surprising had they been able work together in harness. Although war minister (and briefly premier) Painlevé claimed that there was never any dispute between the two generals, their respective spheres of activity had been separate between May and the end of October: Pétain dealt with difficulties in the army and organised the three offensives described above, while Foch's role had been more diplomatic and international. He had been working closely with his counterpart in London, Robertson, over the problems of Greece and what to do about Russia and the Middle East. Italy, however, provided a spark to the latent dissension between the prudent Pétain and the fiery Foch.[98]

In a meeting with Painlevé, Pétain insisted that he would go himself to Italy and command the French troops there. Foch lost his temper and demanded the command for himself. Foch won the argument, because Painlevé and Lloyd George were planning to create an Allied general staff as a step towards placing the supreme command into the hands of a single general. Since the main front was in France and France still had the largest army on the Western Front, that general would have to be French. Furthermore, since Foch was the only French general with experience of dealing with the second largest army, the BEF, he was the logical choice. Lloyd George knew him from the Allied conferences of 1917 and was prepared to support Foch's nomination.

Foch arrived in Italy on 30 October, beating Robertson by a day. Foch impressed Cadorna with his bustle and energy, and he is generally credited with having restored spirits in the Italian high command. Credit must be given to the Italians themselves, however, for their stand on the Piave and their rapid restoration of fighting capabilities. The British and French politicians soon followed their generals and in the seaside town of Rapallo created the Supreme War Council (SWC). The goal was better coordination of the Allied effort on the Western Front through a council made up of two members (the premier and one other minister) of the governments of Britain, France and Italy, advised by a permanent military representative from each country. The council's mission was 'to watch over the general conduct of the war' and to report its progress to each government. Although each national CinC retained command of his own armies, war plans were to be submitted to the council for possible amendment. On the grounds that a national chief of staff should not occupy a position on the SWC, Lloyd George appointed Henry Wilson as the British representative in order to sideline Robertson, whose advice he did not like. In theory, therefore, Foch too was ruled out, but he was already in Italy and so remained there for a few weeks with Wilson after the politicians returned home. The Italians appointed Cadorna as their military representative, compensation for his sacking after the disgrace of Caporetto. The new Italian CinC was General Armando Diaz.

The French XXXI Corps of two divisions (64 and 65 DI) plus two unattached divisions (46 and 47) disembarked their infantry and artillery in Italy on 6 November, followed five days later by the two divisions (23 and 24 DI) of XII Corps. The force's artillery consisted of six groups of mountain guns (65mm); seven groups of 145 and 155mm long guns; four groups of 155 short guns. Tenth Army commander, General Denis Duchêne, took command of the expeditionary force (the Forces Françaises en Italie, or FFI). Foch and Wilson visited every part of the Italian front, and had a regular morning discussion with Diaz over when and where to place the French and British reinforcements. After signing a protocol on these matters Wilson returned to the War Office in London on 16 November and Foch asked for Fayolle to come to Italy to replace him. It was judged that Duchêne had too difficult a task in combining command of his army with relations with the Italian command, and so Fayolle was delegated for the latter task. Certainly Duchêne was not the most diplomatic of generals – did Pétain choose him precisely for this reason? Clemenceau described him to the Senate Army Commission as 'difficult to live with', because he treated his equals in an intolerable fashion, and refused to obey his superior, Fayolle.[99] Duchêne returned to France and took over Sixth Army on 11 December. Foch remained in Italy for a few days more to oversee the insertion of the Allied troops. After talking with Fayolle, in whom he had complete confidence, and after leaving an encouraging letter for Diaz, Foch returned to France on 23 November to great acclaim for having 'saved' Italy. Fayolle was glad to see the back of him. 'Good riddance', he recorded in his diary.[100]

Although being sent to Italy was somewhat less dangerous than being sent to the Chemin des Dames, yet fighting on foreign soil caused real difficulties for the French soldiers. Leave was less frequent (every six instead of four months) and the postal service less efficient. Sometimes even stationery for the vital letters home was hard to obtain. More importantly, morale was less easy to sustain. Fighting to defend one's home was one thing, but fighting for such an unreliable ally as Italy was quite another. The postal control picked up such comments as: 'It's always us who pay', and 'it's truly ridiculous to go and get yourself killed for people who don't even defend themselves'.[101]

In November, Paul Pireaud's artillery regiment was sent to Italy where French artillery resources were needed because of the loss of such large numbers of Italian heavy guns. Despite the wine ('better than at home', Pireaud remarked), the troops complained about lack of enough warm clothing for the mountains. Yet he judged 'that from the point of view of danger we will be better off here than in France because everyone believes that the Boches are going to unleash an offensive on the French front with the troops that have become available following the armistice with Russia'. He was furious when the leave policy was improved to be equivalent to that operative in France, but applied only to support, not front-line, troops:

Bunch of shirkers bunch of bastards it's high time that the Boches sent some bombs in their direction. How is it possible to make such laws those who are chasing girls in Vicenza and Montebello and Verona will have leave every four months while those [of us] who are chasing the Austrians we only get to go home every six months. The infantry troops who are going into the trenches these days, that's really going to raise their morale it's shameful nonetheless to think that they are trying to favor those who get to sleep in beds to the detriment of those who are bedded down in the snow and sleep only one night out of three. Anyway, I still love you very much but morale is really low.[102]

During the first days of December two French and two British divisions relieved Italian divisions of the Fourth Army facing the German *Fourteenth Army*. The line ran from the Piave at Nervesa to a couple of kilometres west of the Monte Tomba on the river Brenta whose summit was in enemy hands, giving good observation over the Allied lines. Consequently General Maistre, Duchêne's replacement, ordered an assault on the mountain by 47 DI on 30 December. The lessons about careful artillery preparation and meticulous liaison between artillery and infantry that had been learned from operations in Flanders, Verdun and La Malmaison were again in evidence, and the Austrian division holding the heights was pushed back 1,800 metres, leaving behind 500 dead, 1,500 prisoners, 63 machine guns and 8 artillery pieces in 47 DI's hands. The French division suffered 54 killed and 205 wounded. The snow prevented any further action that year.

Troops were not the only aid that France supplied. It was agreed to send 150,000 rifles with 25m cartridges, 2,000 machine guns (later increased to 3,500), 300 75s complete with gun carriage and 300,000 shells, and 175 guns of 120 and 155 calibre with shells. These were on their way by early January. France also agreed to send 100 Nieuport aircraft. The British also sent materiel to replace all that had been lost in the retreat after Caporetto. The rest of the winter was spent in training in the schools that the French set up and in exchanges of officers, so that Allies and Italians got to know each other and each other's methods.[103] Fayolle was able to report to Paris at the end of the year that the Italians had recovered sufficiently so that there was no need to send more troops or to fear a repeat of Caporetto. It was not only the weather that shut down the fighting at the beginning of 1918. The Austrians showed no aggressive spirit and the German divisions were removed gradually. During the course of January, French intelligence recognised their departure and by the 16th knew that General von Below was in Laon (north of the Chemin des Dames) and that four of his original seven German divisions were also in France. In his planning for 1918, however, Pétain could count on six fewer divisions and their artillery because they were in Italy, where most remained until the end of the war.

Events in Italy coincided with the fall of Painlevé's ministry over a petty vote of confidence. The creation, in cooperation with Lloyd George, of the SWC was Painlevé's last achievement. Poincaré turned to the only politician left who could command enough support to form a government, Georges Clemenceau, the 'Tiger', France's final wartime premier. The planning for 1918 would be carried out under Clemenceau's leadership. He left no doubt that he would remain firm in defence of France to the 'last quarter hour'. Before the Chamber of Deputies he proclaimed his single-minded purpose, 'la guerre intégrale' [nothing but war] and his identical domestic and foreign policies: 'je fais la guerre'.[104] Clemenceau was very different from Painlevé, who had supported Pétain fully in his actions as commander of the French Army; but tigerish Clemenceau was less likely to support a purely defensive strategy.

Planning the 1918 campaign

Pétain had accomplished his first task as CinC of the French Army with great success. He had restored its offensive strength and had proved in Flanders, in Verdun and at La Malmaison on the Chemin des Dames that French armies could engage battle and defeat the enemy. He had ensured that the lessons derived from these successes be documented and taught in training camps, and he had had offensive and defensive doctrines drawn up for future action.

Yet future action, in 1918, was constrained by military considerations (the available effectives), diplomatic factors (Allies and Allied bodies), and by internal French domestic factors (mainly political). The return of German divisions from the Eastern Front was the most critical of the military constraints on Pétain's freedom of action in 1918. French Army numbers were declining inexorably, and not even another law, the Loi Mourier, passed in 1917 with the aim of combing out more men from shirkers' jobs in the interior, could make much difference.[105] In any case, Pétain wanted the production of munitions factories in ever greater amounts. Italy consumed more French soldiers, and the slowly arriving Americans were untrained and unequipped. Little help could be expected from the British, who, as selfish as ever, were delaying the promised extension of their front.

France's diplomatic situation had changed completely during the course of the year. Russia was out – indeed there was talk of the Bolsheviks repudiating their debts, many of them owed to France – and the USA was in, but only as an associated, not an allied, power. In addition to this turnaround, the British and French premiers had created a Supreme War Council, with military advisors. It and they were likely to intervene in any decision-making process. Moreover, General Foch was an important player in this forum. Despite Pétain's desire to take command there himself, Foch was already in Italy when the SWC was created, and had acted as France's military representative on the Council during his time there. When Lloyd George insisted that he would not allow a country's military representative to have a dual role as his own army's chief of general staff as well as on the SWC, Foch's chief of staff, General Maxime Weygand, was sent to the SWC in Foch's place. There was unlikely to be any divergence of views between Foch and Weygand.

The third constraint on Pétain's planning of the 1918 campaign was domestic. His strategic views were far from meeting with acceptance from politicians and other generals. The Army General Staff in Paris insisted that an offensive would be necessary in the end, but there was no plan from the 'defensive' Pétain and his entourage.[106] The French Army's first CinC, Joffre, had criticised Pétain's Verdun offensive as being all very well in itself but insufficient to win a war. Joffre agreed with Foch that a succession of small-scale attacks with limited aims created a bad impression.[107] Former war minister, Alexandre Millerand, regretted that no French offensive was planned to meet the imminent danger from Germany, and declared that Pétain would always say that he could not take the offensive, because he did not in fact wish to do so.[108] Other politicians too were becoming impatient. The presidents of both the Senate and the Chamber of Deputies asked to attend the 12 December meeting of the comité de guerre. General Micheler had been sending complaints to his political 'friend', Antonin Dubost, the president of the Senate. The comité de guerre had a long discussion of the advantages and disadvantages of 'partial offensives', and Pétain threatened to resign. Although Poincaré and Clemenceau immediately expressed their confidence in him, nevertheless a week later Clemenceau was complaining to Poincaré that Pétain was 'too negative, too timid'. 'You heard him the other day', said Clemenceau, 'We were asking him "Will you be able to hold?" He didn't reply: "I shall hold, on these conditions". He replied: "I shall not be able to hold unless … [sic] That's our man to a T.'[109]

Despite all these constraints, Pétain was sure in his own mind about the required strategy. There was to be no repeat of April 1917, no big offensive to finish the war. Instead, he would employ the Verdun and La Malmaison formula: a series of limited-objective offensives, well supported by artillery and costing as few losses to the infantry as possible – then an offensive in eastern France, in Alsace or Lorraine, to capture some German (formerly French) territory that could be used as a bargaining counter in any peace negotiations. (Despite Pedroncini's emphasis on the Lorraine option, there is no indication at this early date that Pétain intended to carry out a large operation there.)[110] He was determined to husband France's dwindling manpower reserves and not to contemplate decisive action to end the war until the Americans had arrived in force, and had been trained and equipped. In order to hold on until the latter half of 1918, Pétain needed the British to take over a greater proportion of the front in France so that he could maintain a strategic reserve of forty divisions, the number he considered to be the minimum.

Pétain presented these ideas to Haig in mid October,[111] a few days before the La Malmaison operation but well before the end of the fighting in Flanders. The two men met in Amiens on 18 October, when Pétain handed over in person a note with his ideas. On the hypothesis that Russia would make peace and leave the war, Pétain foresaw only a defensive posture, with a 'rational' sharing of forces according to manpower and a concentration of reserves at the point where an enemy attack was likely. Alternatively, should Russia remain a belligerent, Pétain proposed four attacks – two around Reims (Moronvilliers and Brimont); Saint-Mihiel in conjunction with the Americans; then the principal attack aiming north-east of Reims combining with a British attack from Saint-Quentin towards Bohain (18 kilometres further to the north-east). There is no mention of territorial bargaining chips in this document. Pétain left a copy of his note with Haig, who promised to respond the next day and 'putting his hand familiarly on [Pétain's] shoulder, said "we will always be in agreement"'.

A copy of Pétain's note was forwarded the next day to London with GHQ's comments, in which Pétain's views, as the British understood them, were fleshed out. The French CinC expected as many as fifty German divisions might move to France if Russia left the war. This was why the British had to take over more line so that he could build up a reserve force capable of meeting that threat. Pétain wanted relief as far as the southern edge of Saint Gobain forest, a front presently held by five French infantry and two cavalry divisions. He preferred that the British not attack in Flanders again, but left that decision to Haig (presumably knowing that the British CinC would go his own way in any case). Haig interpreted Pétain's views as 'anxiety', and claimed that 'the vigorous prosecution of our offensive would ... be the wisest military policy', as it would be 'unsound' to leave the initiative to the enemy.[112] Haig still intended to continue Third Ypres in Flanders and to re-start operations there in 1918 after winter forced a temporary halt. He wrote to Pétain on the 19th, after giving 'careful thought' to the request to extend the British line, stating that he was unable 'to agree that the best use of the British forces is to extend them on a defensive line to the detriment of the offensive which they have proved their ability to carry out and from the success of which such great results may reasonably be expected to follow'.

Pétain and his staff knew from their meeting with Haig that there was no hope of getting British relief for some of the French front, because Haig made it abundantly clear that he wished to continue the Flanders battle, even into 1918.[113] So Pétain and Haig had completely divergent views on the strategy for 1918. What is more, Haig had a very low opinion of what the French Army might be able to achieve in future. He told the War Cabinet in London of his doubts that the French could stand 'a resolute and continued offensive on the part of the Enemy' for very long.[114]

The solution to such failure to agree was supreme command – a general with the authority to act could have imposed a common strategy on the Western Front. Pétain had been trying to take supreme command into his own hands for some time. His chief of staff, Debeney, produced a scheme for coalition command on 16 October 1917; his chef de cabinet, Serrigny, had prepared various notes on the need for unity of command, going back to October 1916. Serrigny's ideas for a 'rational organisation of the coalition', dated 10 November 1917, even appeared in the press.[115] When Pétain lost the battle over retaining control of the French divisions sent to Italy, he tried again. He proposed dividing the Western Front, giving command of all the troops in the northern half to Haig, while he commanded the remainder of the front as far as the Adriatic.

This idea got no further than the war cabinet in London.[116] Next he prepared a note for his own comité de guerre on 18 November[117] in which he emphasised the need to move reserves speedily in a crisis, such as the Russian defection freeing German divisions would soon provoke. Ad hoc agreements to help were barely acceptable in normal times but could be fatal in an emergency. In the present circumstances, he concluded, unified command in the hands of a single chief appointed by the Allied governments was needed even more than in the past. Instead of getting supreme command into his own hands, however, Pétain had to accept the hands of the SWC – not to mention the rumours that Joffre would return as supreme commander once enough Americans had arrived in France.[118]

Although the military representatives in the SWC had agreed with Pétain that the Russian defection meant that the Allies had to stand on the defensive in the west, Foch was agitating for an offensive plan to be produced, and Lloyd George was trying to get support for a policy of knocking Turkey out of the war. Neither of these came to fruition, but the SWC proposed an allied general reserve. The politicians decided that it would be a good idea to create such a reserve so as to be ready to respond to the anticipated German offensive, wherever it occurred. An Executive War Board under Foch's presidency was created to set it up. Neither Pétain nor Haig was interested in giving up some of his own scarce manpower resources to create the reserve which Foch had set at thirty divisions. Although the Italians agreed to supply six of the seven divisions requested, and Pétain reluctantly admitted he could supply another eight, Haig managed to delay matters long enough for the whole scheme to fall through.[119] Pétain was furious at what he took to be Foch's attempt to impose his own plan for 1918 by collecting Allied divisions. GQG's first response to Foch's letter from the Executive War Board had to be toned down, because it was too 'brutal'.[120]

By now, it was February 1918. Pétain and Haig agreed a scheme of mutual support to resist the expected German offensive. They had already agreed privately the extent of the British takeover of 30 kilometres of the French front down to the river Oise, without reference to the SWC to whom the decision had been referred. Then, on 21 and 22 February 1918, the details of the mutual support scheme were settled, with precise details as to which units would move where in different eventualities. Neither the British nor the French knew where the offensive would occur, but they *did* know that it would indeed come, and come in March. On 1 March, French intelligence reported 179 German divisions on the Western Front, and gave the varying statements of German prisoners captured on 23 February. They mentioned Cambrai, Flanders, Alsace and the area between Reims and the Argonne. In other words, they gave no clue as to where the main offensive would take place.[121]

So, thanks to Pétain's actions, the French Army was rested, better trained and better equipped when Ludendorff's spring offensives began on 21 March than it had been a year earlier. Fayolle had returned from Italy to take command of the reconstituted Reserve Army Group of divisions that Pétain had refused to hand over to inter-allied control as part of a general reserve. Pétain had planned for a series of limited offensives, with perhaps the possibility of capturing some territory in Alsace or Lorraine as a bargaining chip, or even of undertaking a break-through with American help in the latter half of the year. The work on implementing Directive #4 was far from complete, so that the new ideas of an elastic defence in depth had not percolated throughout the entire army, and especially not where commanders disagreed with the whole principle. Had Pétain done enough to keep the French Army intact for another year?

Certainly he seemed to have gained the confidence of the ordinary soldier. Captain Delvert copied this letter from one such in First Army in Flanders because it seemed to Delvert that it expressed the views of many. He had read the letter as part of his duties in the postal control commission on 27 October 1917.

I have today's newspaper which is celebrating our fine victory on the Aisne [La Malmaison on the Chemin des Dames]: it is very important, especially from the point of view of the new positions it gives us. That Chemin-des-Dames was terrible. It was the monster that was devouring our regiments. It seems that frequently a company which had gone up in the morning with an effective of 150 men came back down in the evening with 50–60 men ... And yet we could not abandon it. The position was too important for any future advance ... *I assure you that the troops will have great confidence in Pétain.* Since he has become CinC we have to our credit Verdun, Flanders, the Aisne, and if I judge by what I have seen here, with very much reduced casualties. In sum, the war is transformed; we need more gunners than infantry; the artillery destroys everything and some infantry companies go forward without their rifles and with just a few grenades to occupy the positions.[122]

7   1918: German offensives

The anticipated blow fell on 21 March when Ludendorff threw down his last card in his gamble to win the war before the British could transport, and the French train and equip, enough American troops in France to trump the numerical advantage that the Germans currently possessed. Following the armistice with Russia, forty-four German divisions had transferred to the Western Front. Although these now contained fewer men than an Allied division, some of them had been specially trained in the tactics that had won decisive victories at Riga and Caporetto. At least 188 German divisions faced 163 Allied infantry divisions in France: 58 British, 99 French, and 6 American. In addition the Allies had 12 Belgian divisions, the French and British divisions in Italy and the cavalry divisions. Of the 6 US divisions, however, 2 were still disembarking and none of the others was ready to fight. The French had armed the Americans: by 15 March the total supplied amounted to 156 batteries of 75s, 35 batteries of short 155s and 5 groups of the modern extra heavies, plus 2,894 machine guns and 12,864 automatic rifles.[1]

Two offensives against the British front

The last intelligence before the Germans attacked reported 108 enemy divisions on the front, with 74 in reserve, whose whereabouts were known in about two-thirds of cases. The only enemy activity that the French had noted was two trench raids (coups de main) around Reims and Verdun; otherwise 20 March had been 'a calm day overall'.[2] Pétain believed that the German offensive was about to begin, as did General Cox, the new head of intelligence at GHQ. Pétain's head of intelligence, Colonel Cointet, agreed with Cox on the two most likely areas of attack: the rivers Scarpe and Oise, and also in Champagne. They disagreed, however, on the relative weight of the attacks, Cox judging that the French sector would see the main action, because the political situation in France was less stable. Cointet believed, on the other hand, that the

British would bear the brunt of the attack.[3] Whichever assessment was correct, there was no joint planning to resist the enemy offensive. The only Franco-British arrangement concerned the use of reserves for support in case of emergency, and this had only been made because Haig and Pétain wished to avoid dealing with the SWC and supplying divisions for a general reserve.

In order to give each other mutual support against a powerful offensive by these numerically superior German divisions, the British and French headquarters had agreed a detailed programme to counter likely German attack plans. When Gough's Fifth Army relieved the French Third, the latter went into reserve, leaving just a headquarters staff. If the main German offensive was engaged on its front, Third Army would be reconstituted and intervene either by relieving some Fifth Army units, or by placing French units under British command. Alternatively, it could form a stop line behind the British, or preferably mount a counter-attack. All the transport and supply arrangements were settled on 21 February for French troops to concentrate in one of three possible sectors to meet the expected German offensive. For these tasks, Third Army was given five infantry divisions, a cavalry corps, three regiments of heavy artillery, ten squadrons of aircraft and a large artillery park. On 22 February a similar scheme was settled whereby the British would relieve Sixth Army or mount a counter-offensive should the Germans attack the French front.[4] General Fayolle was ordered back from Italy, where the military situation had stabilised, and given command of the reconstituted Reserve Army Group ready to take charge either of the riposte to a German violation of Swiss neutrality or of the response to a German offensive in France.

Ludendorff's aim was to punch a hole in the Allied front and to see what might transpire, or, more specifically, after punching the hole, to roll up the British against the sea, destroy their armies, and then turn on the French. His March offensive ran from the river Scarpe in the north around Arras to the junction of the French and British armies on the river Oise – a distance of 103 kilometres. See Map 12. Impeccable German staff work had assembled a formidable array of guns and aircraft without allowing either the French or the British to find out exactly where the blow was to fall. On the first day of Operation MICHAEL, 21 March 1918, the Germans fired over three million rounds which mostly fell on two British armies, General Byng's Third and General Gough's Fifth. With fewer than half the men and guns of the enemy, the British fell back in disarray. The Germans advanced 5 kilometres that day, repeating the advance the next day, and making an amazing 16-kilometre advance on the 23rd, when they reached Ham and Péronne.

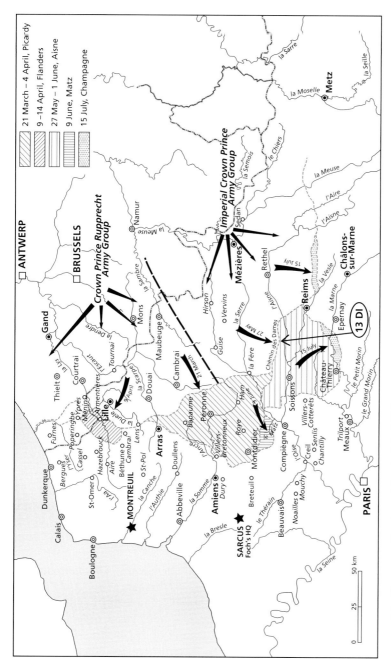

12. German offensives, March–July 1918

Just before midnight on that first day, Pétain alerted three divisions of General Pellé's V Corps to the danger, whilst Haig was writing in his diary that the day's results were 'highly creditable to the British troops'. When early next morning Haig received a clearer impression of the effects of the German attacks, he invoked the agreed provisions for mutual help. By the afternoon of the second day, three French divisions had arrived by road and one of them, 125 DI was already in action. On 23 March, when the Germans made their greatest advance, Pétain and Haig met to discuss the situation. Haig asked for twenty French divisions to be moved to the Amiens area, but Pétain claimed to have replied sharply that it was a question of 'military honour', that Haig should order his troops to stand and be killed. He, Pétain, could only take over up to Péronne if the British held from Péronne to Ham. In short, Barescut recorded, it was a 'cordial' meeting, but 'very clear and peremptory [très net et tranchant]'. Haig appears to have missed the rebuke, for his own diary record mentions only that Pétain was 'most anxious to do all he can'.[5]

Pétain was already worried that the British were retiring too far and too fast. Indeed, at GQG the staff judged that Fifth Army no longer existed.[6] Nonetheless Pétain reactivated the Reserve Army Group and placed Fayolle in command of its two armies, First and Third, together with the remnants of British Fifth Army. Fayolle's command covered the whole area between the former Franco-British junction as far as Péronne on the bend of the Somme. Seven French divisions arrived during the course of 23 March, three by road and four by rail. First Army was now commanded by General Debeney who had taken over from Anthoine after the end of the Flanders battle. It consisted on 26 March of three divisions (133, 166 and 4 DC) joined by 163 DI on the 29th. Third Army, still commanded by General Humbert, consisted of Pellé's V Corps and VI Corps, the latter being swapped to First Army. However, V Corps was a large unit, with five infantry divisions (including the 125 DI which had already joined the fighting on 22 March) and one cavalry division. Third Army grew with the addition of XVIII Corps on 26 March, XXX and XXXV corps the next day, and on the 29th XXXIII Corps.

Crisis point was reached on 24 March. Pétain told Clemenceau that Haig was retiring northwards towards the Channel ports. If Haig continued thus, refusing to reach out to the helping hand that Pétain was extending to the British armies, then they both faced defeat, and this result, so Pétain believed, would be the fault of the British. He saw Haig again late that evening, when Haig repeated his request for a large French force to come to his aid. The account of this meeting in the British official history follows Haig's own, in which he describes the French CinC as being 'very much upset, almost unbalanced, and very anxious'. This post hoc description, as well as being unlikely – Pétain was too proud to appear 'very anxious' – accords neither with Haig's contemporaneous account, nor with that of the British head of the British military mission to GQG, who was present, nor with Barescut who noted in his diary that Pétain had cheered Haig up.[7] According to Barescut, the interview between the two CinCs was cordial, but precise and definite. He reported Pétain as asking Haig to 'hold on at all cost'.[8] The French could only take over the front as far as Péronne if the British continued to hold north from Péronne. By now, however, the Germans were across the Somme and crossing the old Somme battlefield.

Haig's later claims that Pétain said that he had orders to cover Paris rather than maintain contact with the British, and that he (Haig) was so concerned by this that he sent a telegram to London asking for a member of the government to come to France, are both false. The insulting tone of the phantom telegram, allegedly asking for some 'determined general who would fight', reflects in all probability Haig's dislike of Pétain's tone when insisting that the British hold on.[9] That Pétain did speak firmly to Haig, warning him that the French Army could not continue stretching out its left hand indefinitely, is confirmed by what Pétain told Clive a few weeks later. Pétain said that he had had the whole of France to retire into, but that Haig would be very badly placed, with his back to sea, if he continued to withdraw.[10] Haig was indeed thinking of retiring to the Channel ports, against the policy that had been in place from the start that it was more important to keep contact with the French than to hold on to those ports. As Barescut acknowledged, Pétain was less likely to insist with Haig than was the energetic Foch.

The next day, 25 March, the difference between Pétain and Foch became more marked. Lord Milner had arrived in France, despatched by Lloyd George with full powers to act on the government's behalf. The Chief of the Imperial General Staff, Henry Wilson, also arrived in France, leaving London after having received telephone calls from both Foch and GHQ. Eight more French divisions arrived in Fifth Army's sector, two arriving by road and six by rail. Three more would arrive by road the next day, another seven on the 27th, and a further four on the 28th. The British complained that they arrived without guns and munitions, but this was unavoidable in the circumstances – would they have preferred to wait for the French guns to arrive? Nonetheless small units were thrown into the gaps in the line immediately they reached the front. Many commentators saw the parallel with what had happened at Ypres in 1914, when units were similarly thrown into line pell-mell.

So Pétain did far more than he had promised in the mutual support arrangements. On 25 March it became clear to French intelligence from interrogations of prisoners that enemy units had been moved away from the Champagne area, hence that German action there had merely been a feint. Cointet informed Pétain of this mid afternoon, and Fourth Army in Champagne confirmed GQG's interpretation, whereupon Pétain ordered two more reserve divisions (38 and 77 DI) from Epernay (Champagne) to the Somme.[11]

The British and French military and political leaders spent 25 March in discussions and agreed that all should meet the next day to decide what to do. At that next meeting, in the Doullens town hall, Foch was appointed to coordinate the Allied armies in France. Foch's wife wrote this account in her diary after he arrived home late that night.

In light of the events of these last few days, unity of command is more necessary than ever ... Poincaré understood that it was indispensable and supported Ferdinand ... discussions, talks ... then the British arrived, talked on one side ... an hour later all gathered around a big table and it was there decided and resolved that the French and British governments give General Foch the task of ensuring the coordination of all the Allied forces in the west. About time! We have lost two precious days, said Ferdinand ... 'Pray to God that it is not too late.' In fact, the situation is serious, the British have abandoned the line of the Somme. 'It's disgraceful', says Ferdinand – Field Marshal Haig was saying that he could not move away from his bases and General Pétain was alleging that his army had to cover Paris, that he could not scatter it, and that between the two of them a breach was opening to let the Boches through ... Field Marshal Haig said to Ferdinand: 'It's Ypres all over again.' 'Let us hope', he replied, 'that it ends the same way.'[12]

The reaction within the army to Foch's appointment was mostly positive, although not unanimous. In Salonica, Guillaumat judged Foch to be 'anarchic and impulsive', but knew now from his own experience of inter-allied command that it would require more than Foch's nomination to restore the situation.[13] Yet Poincaré's liaison officer responded to the President's feeling of having done a good day's work by saying that in all military spheres there would be 'a feeling of relief and confidence'.[14] Pershing's officer at GQG reported 'evident pride and satisfaction' at Foch's appointment.[15] At GQG there was relief. Barescut had already canvassed Weygand on 23 March to do all he could to get Foch put in charge: 'General Foch's personality is indisputably the one needed for this designation.' Cointet thought that Foch's characteristic energy on taking command showed 'mastery of events', and in Humbert's Third Army the staff had been impressed by Foch's sureness of touch and precision of views.[16] There was never any question that Pétain might be given the Allied command. His chief of staff, General Anthoine, was saying on 27 March that the war was lost and that no time should be wasted before making peace.[17]

Pétain's order to the Reserve Army Group had been that the British Fifth Army hold on the Somme, and French Third Army from Montdidier to the Oise. If retirement became necessary, Fifth Army was to retire to a line along the river Avre between Amiens and Montdidier, while Third retired on a line from Noyon to Roye. This disposition would create an intact line between the British forces north of Amiens, through Fifth Army between Amiens and Montdider, then through Third to the Oise, to join up with the rest of the French Army.[18] Barescut, however, thought that such a big withdrawal to the Oise–Montdidier line was very risky.[19] Once Foch began his 'coordination', however, ideas changed. He insisted that not another metre of ground should be ceded. Fayolle complained that he was pulled between the two men: according to Foch 'Amiens must be covered. Order of importance: 1) Amiens, 2) Noyon. Pétain calls me on the telephone this morning and says: 1) Noyon, 2) Amiens. The day before yesterday, "Use the Oise as cover." Besides he has no plan.'[20]

At first the poilus were proud of their contribution to stopping the enemy and especially proud that the new Allied generalissimo should be a French general.[21] The morale report for the second fortnight of March on the armies not involved in the fighting claimed that, far from being downcast, the troops were 'stimulated' by the German offensive. In particular, the German big guns firing on Paris provoked real anger, and not only amongst those who had friends and relatives living or working there.[22] The military governor of Paris confirmed the 'confidence' of its citizens in the protective measures put in place, and he spoke of the 'greatest calm' among those who had remained in the capital and had not fled the bombing and shelling.[23]

Ludendorff's MICHAEL offensive had run out of steam by the end of the month and he put a halt to it on 5 April. Foch's energetic and ofttimes resented pep talks had inspired commanders to patch up the holes in the front where and when they appeared, and the enemy was forced to suspend operations because of its own supply problems. The successful Allied resistance had proved the wisdom of appointing a supreme commander. Moreover, Pétain had done far more to supply troops than had been arranged in the pre-war mutual support agreement, and French troops had fought hard to mend the breach in the Allied front. Between 21 and 31 March the French suffered 37,278 wounded and 20,175 killed or missing, the proportion of killed to wounded indicating

Fig. 17 One Allied and three French Commanders-in-Chief
(a) Joseph Joffre (1852–1931) (b) Ferdinand Foch (1859–1929)
(c) Robert Nivelle (1856–1924) (d) Philippe Pétain (1856–1951)

that the French were fighting hard.[24] The post-war comment of Sir Herbert Lawrence, Haig's chief of staff in March 1918, is most unjust:

Even with Foch's good will, he had great difficulty in getting them [the French] to do anything and the utmost he succeeded in doing at the time was to put four divisions behind the Arras front where they did nothing but interfere with our lines of communication.[25]

Rather, Fayolle's summary is to be preferred: Foch supplied the plan, Pétain the means, and Fayolle himself the execution. The French Army's contribution to stopping the MICHAEL offensive was to take back the front between Somme and Oise that Fifth Army had occupied and lost, and to resist the German attacks there; also to constitute the Reserve Army Group with Fayolle who knew the area and the British from the Somme battle in 1916 and to supply a number of divisions as reserves.

Clearly the end of the fighting in Picardy on the Somme did not mean the end of the battle. Ludendorff's next target, as the Allies realised, and soon had confirmed, was the British front once again, this time further north in Flanders. This second blow was to have been much stronger, but MICHAEL had cost too much and so GEORG became GEORGETTE. Nonetheless Prince Rupprecht's *Sixth Army* carried out an initially successful attack along the line of the Flanders hills, aiming to reach the important rail junction at Hazebrouck, thence to Calais and the sea.

By the time that GEORGETTE began on 9 April, the Allied response to the German offensives was well in place. Foch had moved to confirm his role by asking for greater powers. He had been appointed to coordinate, but he had no resources of his own and it was vital to plan for the future. Moreover, only the British and French had signed the Doullens agreement. Clemenceau invited Lloyd George to discuss the matter, and on 3 April in Beauvais they were joined by Generals John J. Pershing and Tasker H. Bliss, the American CinC and the American representative on the SWC. There, all agreed to entrust Foch with 'the strategic direction of military operations'. Later, on 14 April and after further discussion, Foch was permitted to use the title 'Général en chef des armées alliées'. Foch had set the main plan of defence in March: plug the holes and defend Amiens. He appreciated the vital necessity of retaining the rail communications east of Amiens, which Ludendorff appeared not to have considered important, and which Pétain had been prepared to forgo by suggesting a line of resistance further south. Also Foch recognised clearly the need to build up a 'masse de manoeuvre' to counter-attack, but that was not yet possible, because French troops were being used to bolster the British front and because American manpower resources were too limited.

The movement of French reserves north to Flanders constitutes the second factor in the Allied response to the German spring offensives. On 7 April, Foch ordered Pétain, as the Beauvais agreement now gave him the authority to do, to send three cavalry and four infantry divisions to the west of Amiens, ready to intervene northwards in support of the British or southwards if the French were attacked. The cavalry divisions had not been available on 21 March, because they were being used to police worker unrest in industrial centres in central and southern France. The unrest having died down because the workers recognised the emergency, the cavalry was able to return to strictly military duties. Foch's order stripped the French front from the river Oise to Switzerland, leaving a mere forty-six French plus three American divisions holding quiet sectors to man the line with a further twelve divisions in reserve.

Despite the unified command and the movement of French reserves to the north, the second German offensive smashed the Portuguese divisions of First Army and then broke through the Second Army front in Flanders. Armentières and Messines were lost, and Haig issued his famous 'backs to the wall' order of the day. By 12 April the Germans were within 6 kilometres of Hazebrouck and were beginning to threaten Bailleul and the high ground of the Flanders hills. By 15 April Foch had moved the four divisions of his Tenth Army that had been withdrawn from Italy, together with all its artillery and aviation, to sectors north of the Somme ready to intervene if necessary. These units joined those that had already been moved, and their administration was assured by the creation of the DAN (Détachement d'armée du nord) under the command of General de Mitry. The DAN's three cavalry and nine infantry divisions came under Foch's orders on 19 April, so they were no longer available to Pétain as reserves.

On 24 April the Germans renewed their GEORGETTE attacks. South of the Flanders sector, *Second Army* launched an attack against Villers-Bretonneux, with the aim of securing a base so that the artillery and more forces could attack Amiens. Villers-Bretonneux is situated on high ground, on the old Roman road that runs due east from the city to south of Péronne, dominating Amiens and more importantly within artillery range of the railway junction at Longueau to its east. The three-corps attack, employing ten divisions in the front line with another four in the second, supported by 1,208 guns, 710 aircraft and 13 tanks, began at 04.45 German time (French time is an hour earlier) on 24 April, with the infantry going in at 07.15. This was the area of the junction between the French First Army and the remnants of the British Fifth, now re-named the Fourth and commanded by General Sir Henry Rawlinson. German prisoners had warned that an offensive was imminent, and the junction was well supported. The four divisions of XX Corps were established solidly to the west of Amiens; the British 18 Division lay behind British Fourth Army's right-hand corps; and two French divisions (DM and 37 DI) were echelonned behind the left-hand French corps.

As usual, the initial German rush was successful and Villers-Bretonneux and the portion of Hangard Wood held by the British were captured. The loss of Villers-Bretonneux could not be allowed, and so Foch ordered immediate counter-attacks. Although an Australian brigade sent up for that purpose failed to re-take the village, at least it stopped the Germans making any further progress. The pressure on the French front was felt further south, in Hangard village, Thennes and north-west of Castel. Furious fighting lasted all day, but the Allied front did not break. Haig recognised, as did Foch, that Villers-Bretonneux must be recaptured and he allocated more British resources for that purpose. Accordingly, at 18.30 that evening he asked Foch to order French First Army to relieve his right-hand corps. After moving more French units into the area the next day, and preparing a counter-attack to be made by the DM in conjunction with the British, it proved impossible to begin the recapture of Villers-Bretonneux immediately, so it was on the morning of 26 April that the joint attack began. With the DM operating between Villers-Bretonneux and Hangard Wood which the British were to capture, 131 DI further south was to recapture Hangard village. The DM covered itself with glory yet again, making most progress and taking over from the exhausted British battalions in Hangard Wood. The Germans made no further infantry assaults after 27 April and Foch ordered Fayolle's Reserve Army Group to take over the whole sector between Villers-Bretonneux and the Avre river, keeping contact with the Australians on their left. Also, Foch ordered the preparations to be continued for an attack to push back the enemy even further from the Allied rail communications, but the German attack further north on Mt Kemmel that began on 25 April consumed French resources yet again. The German attack had made no appreciable gains; Amiens was no closer; no French troops had been diverted, although the Australians had been moved into line and had recaptured Villers-Bretonneux; and the cost was high. German casualties were 8,000, and OHL ordered a halt to operations on 26 April.[26] If the attack on Villers-Bretonneux was meant as a diversion from Flanders further north it had failed.[27]

Before the Flanders attack on Mt Kemmel began, however, Pétain had sounded the alarm. He wrote a long letter to Foch on 24 April complaining that the British were 'reducing their effort' by suppressing nine divisions because of lack of reinforcements to make up their losses, while 1.4 million mobilised men remained behind in Britain. On the other hand, by 27 March he, Pétain, had committed twenty-seven divisions, either engaged in fighting or moving into the battle zone. Now, almost a month later, forty-seven French divisions were in the former British sector, either supporting British troops or having relieved them. In exchange, the British had supplied four worn-out divisions to be built up again in a quiet sector of the French front. Pétain could not understand this inequality: 'an incomprehensible error, at the very least'. No fresh troops were available to respond to any German attack that might occur on the French front. Pétain ended by stating forcefully that France would fight tomorrow on the British and perhaps Belgian fronts, later on the French front, just as French troops had fought on the Italian front – but France wished 'to be certain that the British Army and British Empire, like the French Army and France, are determined to make *the maximum effort*'.[28]

In light of these figures, Pétain's anguish is understandable. French intelligence still had not learned the location of forty-eight of the sixty-nine enemy reserve divisions on the Western Front, so the German armies remained capable of striking a powerful blow in one or more other sectors.[29] Yet it was more important to prevent the separation of the British and French armies, because that would enable the Germans to deal with each in turn. As Allied commander, Foch was looking at the whole picture; Pétain was thinking solely of the French front and building a head of steam about 'perfidious Albion'. Fayolle, however, was less worried, writing in his diary of Pétain's pessimism and even going so far as to prophesy that Pétain would not finish the war as CinC.[30] Pétain's own operations bureau was beginning to criticise him and his chief of staff General Anthoine.[31] As for Foch, he was pleased that relations with the British seemed to be improving, and that the junction between Belgians, British and French was assured. Although the position around Villers-Bretonneux was 'hot' for a while, he wrote to his wife, he was sure that the British would come through and by 25 April he believed the situation to be stabilised. He had seen Pétain on the 24th, the date of the latter's letter just cited, but he claimed that they were in agreement because '*I decide* and shoulder the responsibility'.[32]

The fighting in Flanders was more serious than the attack around Villers-Bretonneux. This was the final German attack of their second offensive, an attempt to break through to the coast. As a result of the fighting at the start of GEORGETTE on 9 April, General Plumer had been forced to pull back his Second Army in order to shorten his front, thereby abandoning the Passchendaele salient that had been won at such awful cost the previous year. Foch insisted that the rest of the Ypres salient be retained, and he placed the DAN under Plumer's command. To the south of Ypres and protecting the Channel ports lies a chain of low hills, dignified by the name 'mont' only because the surrounding land is so flat. The highest, most easterly of these hills is Mt Kemmel which was strongly fortified and whose summit provided excellent observation. It had been in Allied hands since 1914. The British IX Corps was completely exhausted, and 28 DI took over the defensive lines on Mt Kemmel on 18 April, with 34 DI moving into position on its right the following night and 133 DI in contact with the British line. German intelligence noted their presence on 22 April.[33]

Indications that the Germans were preparing to attack Kemmel had come from prisoners as early as 20 April, as well as from increased aviation sorties and road building, and the radio silence which confirmed the prisoner statements. During the evening of 24 April, 28 DI learned from captured prisoners that a powerful gas attack was to begin early next morning. The French also knew the location of some of the main enemy batteries and that the elite Bavarian *Alpine Corps* had arrived opposite the French. Although thus forewarned, 28 DI was very weak. It had already lost twenty-five officers and 1,024 men by the evening of 24 April and was in a difficult position by next morning. The division had been ordered to advance the French lines 500–1,000 metres to the east of Mt Kemmel. The French artillery barrages pounded the objectives, but the infantry only managed to advance a short distance. Uninformed, the gunners maintained their barrage, leaving a band of some 300–800 metres unbombarded, from which the Germans did not neglect to profit.

Following their usual careful planning the German bombardment on 25 April was highly effective. It began with gas shells in order to neutralise the front lines, and the flanking sectors were drenched with gas to prevent re-supply and to disrupt preparations for any counter-attack. Warned just after midnight of the gas attack to begin at 4am, 28 DI had no time to prepare for the violent bombardment that instead began earlier, at 2.30. Then, at 5.30, the *Minenwerfer* came into action, followed shortly thereafter by the infantry using flamethrowers. The brief but very heavy bombardment was worse than before Verdun in 1916, some French declared. This assault completely overwhelmed the French defenders who also suffered harrassment from machine guns firing from aircraft that had control of the skies. The Germans broke through and overran 28 DI in short order, splitting the French and British troops and penetrating around the hill from the north. Seventy minutes later, units of the *Alpine Corps* were in position on the summit of Mt Kemmel.[34] It was another spectacular, albeit limited, success for gas warfare. Yet the German breakthrough had been so successful that the infantry ran into their own gas and, having swept over the summit just after 8am and then down the other side, they halted until the artillery could be moved up ready for the next objective. This was the road running west from Ypres, via Vlamertinghe to Poperinghe. The delay enabled the Allies to fill the 6-kilometre gap in their front. On 26 April, Foch ordered up more French artillery units and, the next day, three more divisions (168, 42, 121). This was enough to parry the renewed German attacks on each day between 26 and 29 April, when Ludendorff finally called a halt to GEORGETTE. The stiff Allied resistance, the knowledge that French troops had been moved in large numbers to Flanders, and the fear of a French attack developing on the Somme combined to force OHL's hand.[35] Mt Kemmel remained in German hands almost until the end of the war, but to little effect; it was abandoned in the last weeks of the war during the general retirement. The Germans had been unable to capture any other of the Flanders hills, and Ypres and the Channel ports survived, although the coal mines around Bruay were within range of German guns. The remnants of the unfortunate 28 DI were withdrawn on 30 April and returned to Pétain's command.

At GHQ it was believed that the French had simply run away. Haig was scathing: 'The French have lost Kemmel – a position of extraordinary strength. How they managed it I don't know.'[36] Although a degree of *Schadenfreude* and relief that the disasters were, finally, not all British is understandable, yet Haig's comment in his post-war account is grotesque: 'between 21st March and 15th April, the French did practically nothing and took no part in the fighting'; and when, finally, French troops took over the Kemmel sector, 'these French troops lost one of the strongest positions on our front and practically made no effort to re-take it'.[37] One British artillery officer commented post-war that 'the French gunners had run like hares!', and another British officer remarked: 'We had been told that the French would hold the hill at all costs.' However he admitted: 'Certainly the bombardment was intense and as concentrated as any I had experienced.'[38]

Yet the evidence is clear that the German artillery barrages before launching the infantry attack on Kemmel were stupendous. They prevented the re-supply of the defenders with munitions.[39] And, for the French, it was another case of having to fill a gap in the line caused by a British retreat. Captain Henri Desagneaux arrived in the north with his unit on 14 April. The French inhabitants were pleased to see French troops, as they had lost confidence in the British. Relations between British and French troops were tense, Desagneaux claimed: roads were lined with enormous British camps, but the men were doing nothing except polish horse brasses and spruce up harnesses.[40] When extracts from the French translation of Haig's diary and papers were published in

1964, French readers were outraged. The British had run away at Kemmel 'like rabbits', one writer claimed.[41] The Army's report on morale for the first two weeks of May reflected, of course, the hard fighting. The pride in coming to the rescue had become 'great physical fatigue' resulting from the 'implacable character of the struggle', the great length of time in line in active sectors, and the losses. Some units of the DAN had begun expressing a desire for relief 'with a certain vehemence', leading the report writer to conclude that they had been truly 'overworked'.[42]

Despite Haig's unjustified scorn, the fighting for Kemmel hill had been fierce. The French memorial on the hill is an ossuary with the remains of 5,294 men, of whom only 57 are identified by name. As for the casualties of 28 DI, who had defended the hill, they were 4,183 men and 106 officers for 25 April alone, bringing the division's total casualties for that day plus the preceding nine days to 5,248 men and 131 officers. As their commanding general reported, the men were extremely tired but there had been no signs of large numbers having abandoned the battlefield. The division now consisted of no more than ten companies of men.[43] The enemy was unable to make any further progress because German casualties were great also, *Fourth Army*'s battalions being reduced to 200–300 men, instead of 750–800.[44] The Germans had planned to push the Allied line back as far as the Ypres–Poperinghe line in the initial onslaught, supported by a huge artillery barrage which included guns as large as 42cm calibre.[45] The telephone log for 29 April reveals that Lossberg, *Fourth Army*'s chief of staff, told Ludendorff at 12.20 and again at 21.35 that the enemy's artillery was powerful, disposed in depth and well sited. There were also many machine-gun nests.[46] Ludendorff closed GEORGETTE down on 1 May.

Ludendorff's fears of a French counter-attack on the Somme, mentioned above as a factor in his decision to suspend GEORGETTE, were not unfounded. Foch was eager to mount a counter-offensive, even though for the moment the Allies were desperately plugging holes. A detailed study was made at GQG for an operation to free Amiens, but the plan had to be postponed because too many resources had gone to Flanders.[47] Foch was not prepared to launch an offensive without the necessary means. Preparations continued nonetheless, and by the end of May Fayolle was almost ready with an operation to free Montdidier first and then Amiens. Fayolle believed that such an operation could provide a much-needed morale boost without costing too much in troops. Foch's directive for the operation arrived on 21 May, but Pétain was waiting to criticise Fayolle's plan, so the latter thought. There was constant disagreement between Foch and Pétain, Fayolle wrote, with Foch always wanting to attack but Pétain unwilling. Both were right, Fayolle concluded. What was needed was to 'combine them to make one single man, a true complete leader'.[48]

MICHAEL and GEORGETTE had both failed. The French and British Armies had not been separated, nor had Ypres fallen, opening the way to the coast. The French Army's contribution to the successful defence had been the despatch of large numbers of troops to stop up the gaps during MICHAEL. Then, during GEORGETTE, the French had not relieved British divisions but had been inserted behind the BEF, ready to intervene if necessary. In addition, French troops had fought to defend Villers-Bretonneux, and had taken over the front on Mt Kemmel, being successful in the first endeavour but failing to retain the high ground in the second. Nevertheless, German artillery still threatened the vital Paris–Amiens railway, forcing the Allies to use longer routes with smaller throughput, and the equally vital coal mines around Bruay. Although the British losses were much more severe, French casualties in March and April amounted to 92,000; forty-one French divisions had taken part in the fighting; the French front was now 97 kilometres longer, and French reserves were greatly depleted. On 1 May, between the Oise and the North Sea, they amounted to twenty-four divisions, plus two cavalry divisions requiring reconstitution. For the rest of the front, from the Oise to Switzerland, there were sixteen divisions (only seven of them fresh) and three cavalry divisions. Yet French intelligence estimated the number of German divisions on the same date, 1 May, at 206, that is to say twenty-four more than on 20 March. The whereabouts of forty-nine of them were unknown.[49] As Hindenburg put it post-war: 'Twice England had been saved by France at a moment of extreme crisis.'[50]

The repercussions on the French Army

From the point of view of the French troops who had not been transferred north and who remained between the Oise and Switzerland, the most significant result of the two German spring offensives was the fact that the French Army were now stretched very thinly. Each division had to man a much wider front and had fewer or no reserves behind it in case of emergency. On 7 May Pétain sent to Foch a table showing the current situation of the French Army. Its front had grown from 530 kilometres on 20 March to 655 kilometres: it had taken back 30 kilometres on the left bank of the Oise that the British had abandoned, and the Reserve Army Group and the DAN held another 80 and 20 kilometres respectively, with twenty-four divisions in line (including one US division) and a further eighteen in reserve, six of whom were still moving between sectors. The Eastern and Northern Army Groups were left with forty-six divisions in line (including three US divisions) and fifteen in reserve. Of these fifteen, two were Italian and not yet ready for the front, and one British. More British were due to arrive under the *roulement* scheme, but all were among the most severely tested in the recent fighting. (Roulement, or rotation, was intended to place tired British divisions in a quiet French sector in order to recuperate.) Furthermore, among the twelve French divisions in reserve, only three had not been in the fighting – one of them being 13 DI – and the two most battered divisions from the Mt Kemmel battle (28 and 154 DI) would be fit for nothing for several weeks. Although the front from the Oise to Switzerland was quiet, the Verdun sector was fairly active, requiring frequent reliefs of the troops there. Pétain concluded that the French armies had 'reached their limit'; the British would have to manage in the north; French depots were empty of troops until July.[51] He foreshadowed the dissolution of units since Clemenceau as war minister had refused his reiterated request for a further 200,000 men to make up the deficit.[52] The class of 1919 had been called up in April 1918, and 229,215 men incorporated, 75 per cent of the total.[53]

The task of increasing Allied manpower fell to Foch and Clemenceau. Both embarked on a long and acrimonious series of discussions to extract more British and American troops.[54] The French were convinced that more than a million British soldiers in uniform were to be found in the UK, not all of whom could possibly be required for Home Defence. Foch insisted with Haig, and Clemenceau likewise with Lloyd George, that depleted British divisions should not be suppressed but filled up again with some of those million-plus men. Foch also insisted that the 'B' men – those previously declared unfit for overseas service – should not be formed into separate divisions, creating a two-tier organisation of units fit only to hold quiet sectors but not to fight. He won that argument.

The second source of manpower lay across the Atlantic and there were equally acrimonious debates over transport and deployment of the inexperienced and mainly untrained doughboys. Pétain had argued unsuccessfully for amalgamation over the winter, although on 28 March Pershing had loudly trumpeted his offer to engage all his infantry, artillery and aviation: 'all that we have are yours; use them as you wish … the American people will be proud to take part in the greatest battle of history'.[55] Agreements were made, and argued over, to transport American infantry and machine-gunners only, leaving behind administrative troops until the emergency had ended. Lloyd George believed that the new arrivals should join the British since they were transported in British ships for the most part; the French believed rather that the British were pulling a fast one and that they themselves had priority, as they were training and equipping them. Moreover, the task of training the Americans was an added burden, as US infantry regiments were attached to French divisions for intensive training before being returned to their American divisions. On 1 May Pétain issued a note on training to army and army group commanders, insisting on the need for tact and diligence in this task.[56] Barescut had to warn Pétain himself about tact, saying that there should be no request for US troops to join French units, nor should there be any talk of 'instruction'. Rather the talk should be of a future American sector.[57]

A third source of manpower lay in France's empire. Mangin's 'force noire' had not become a very powerful force thus far, but the manpower deficits were becoming too pronounced to forgo this source. Mangin was not without political influence as he had contacts among deputies, who were also members of the Chamber's army commission, and he knew Clemenceau. After being sacked after the 1917 Chemin des Dames battle, Mangin had established enough contact with Clemenceau in Paris that the new premier and war minister gave him another command in December. In a report that he gave to Clemenceau the same month, Mangin claimed that 70,000 natives could be raised from Africa as part of a force of 'colonial contingents' of over a third of a million plus a further quarter of a million labourers.[58] Clemenceau claimed not to be a French imperialist, but metropolitan France was in dire need of manpower. Accordingly he charged the black African deputy, Blaise Diagne, as 'Commissioner of the Republic' to undertake a recruitment mission to his constituency in Senegal. There was resistance from the colonies to this, because recruitment would remove their source of cheap manpower, but Clemenceau was not interested in such arguments and even promised Diagne that some improvement in the 'social condition' of native Africans might follow the war. Diagne arrived in Dakar on 18 February 1918 with an imposing 350-strong entourage. By all accounts, he enjoyed a great propaganda success, but the numbers were less impressive. Although a first levy raised 63,000 men in French West Africa and 14,000 in French Equatorial Africa, there were many medical problems, and the influenza epidemic reached West Africa in September. By November, 50,000 men had reached France or Algeria, some of them volunteers attesting to the successful propaganda, but this was too late, of course, for Pétain in May.[59]

Conscription had been extended to indigenous French citizens in Algeria, which was part of France, in 1916. The conscripts and voluntary engagements of 1918 were almost 50,000 of which 13,942 were engagements. However, many of the conscripts were tubercular or otherwise unfit because of famine conditions over the 1917/18 winter, and few served in France. In addition, Algerian labour was recruited and a monthly average of 3,422 men crossed the Mediterranean between January and April 1918. This was a much lower figure than the previous year but reflects the rarity of shipping to transport the men.[60] Morocco provided 10,000 men, Madagascar 4,000 and Indo-China 6,000 during the course of 1918, but once again, by the time these men had been trained, the crisis had passed and they did not serve in France.[61] In 1917 a second recruitment round in New Caledonia had produced 390 Kanak natives who arrived in France in early 1918. They brought to 948 the total native contingent embarked (in all 1,137 enlisted in the two recruitment rounds), being 10.8 per cent of the total adult male Kanak population.[62]

There was help also from the Italians. They had returned four of the French divisions sent to Italy after Caporetto in 1917, and in April 1918 they supplied an Italian corps of two divisions, under the command of General Alberico Albricci. The II Italian Corps relieved a French corps in the Argonne in mid May. In addition, 60,000 Italian labourers were provided for digging defensive lines behind the French front. American troops were moving into front-line and active sectors, rather than simply relieving quiet sectors to free up French divisions. The first American action, well supported by French command and French artillery, was at Cantigny at the end of May.

Meanwhile Pétain had to ensure that the French divisions that remained under his control were prepared for the new infiltration tactics used by the Germans. He reminded his army and army group commanders that the offensives had shown the vital necessity of keeping up training in small unit actions during rest periods. Most lower level commanders knew only trench warfare and were finding it difficult to adapt to the new conditions. Artillery officers were not used to having to come into action rapidly, and infantry officers were unable to manoeuvre in depth. Pétain urged that general officers should supervise training so as to enable their men to regain 'flexibility and mobility' and to develop as much as possible the ability to manoeuvre. Training was now more important than ever.[63] Lessons were drawn from the recent fighting: issue orders rather than make plans for immediate counter-attacks; teach men to operate in flexible groups, using the terrain and encircling strongpoints rather than attacking head on; there should be strict liaison between infantry and tanks, which were useless operating on their own.[64] On 23 April Pétain asked the army commanders involved in the March–April fighting to prepare a report on the fighting, with details about the artillery, aviation, tanks and enemy manoeuvres, to be provided as quickly as possible with a note about the lessons learned from the action.[65] A note about the German use of tanks at Villers-Bretonneux was circulated on 8 May to all armies with the purpose of pointing out to the infantry the areas vulnerable to attack. Wooden models of tanks were to be constructed for instructing the troops.[66] Other practical details also received attention. The maps used by British and French gunners were marked up differently, but sound-ranging units, for example, needed to be able to communicate intelligence about enemy batteries. A conference was convened in Paris with a view to standardising 'plans directeurs'.[67] Pétain requested that funds be set aside so that rewards could be given for prisoner captures. With the thinning of troop densities in the front line it was becoming more difficult to take any prisoners in trench raids, yet the intelligence gained thereby was invaluable. Clemenceau granted the request, providing 50,000 francs for each of the ten armies.[68]

During this period between German offensives, Pétain took one further step which had a significant effect. He had always seen eye to eye with the man he appointed to head the aviation services at GQG in September 1917, Colonel Duval. Pétain wanted a 'mass' of aviation to support the ground battle, for the French air service had done very well in helping the British to resist MICHAEL. Although German aircraft had reconnoitred the ground before the assault and reported troops moving up to the artillery, the French had gained air superiority by 24 March. They flew hundreds of sorties between 22 and 26 March, day and night, bombing railways, bridges, munitions depots and supply convoys. They machine-gunned enemy troops on the ground and shot down German observation balloons. Although the British and French together lost more aircraft (189) than the Germans did (65) between 21 and 26 March, the Allies had greater reserves.[69] Currently, however, resources were spread around the armies, but a battle was not necessarily confined to one single army sector. Pétain wanted mastery of the air, with French bombers destroying railway stations, assembly points and so on in the enemy rear, thereby forcing German fighters to come out to be destroyed in turn. Then French observation aircraft could spot at liberty for the artillery. Duval had worked the previous year to standardise aircraft types, helped by the under-secretaries Vincent and his successor Dumesnil. On 14 May Pétain issued the order creating the Division aérienne (Air Division), under Duval's command. It consisted of four groupings, each named for its commander: the first contained two wings (Escadres 1 and 12); the second, three fighter and two bomber groups; the third, one wing (Escadre 11); the last, two bomber groups, one of which was Italian. Duval retained his role as head of aviation at GQG in addition to this new command, in which he reported to the Reserve Army Group's commander, Fayolle, whose chief of staff he had been briefly. A few days later, however, Pétain took control himself. (As comparison, the Royal Air Force had been created on 1 April 1918.)

Although some army and group commanders disliked losing control of their own aviation resources – but not Fayolle, who realised how important the 'principle of mass' was to aviation[70] – Duval created a force that more than justified its existence in July, as will be seen in the next chapter. He argued against using the Air Division as a strategic bombing force, as the British wished to use their Independent Air Force under Sir Hugh Trenchard. What was the point of bombing Cologne, Duval asked, if the war was lost in France? Instead he drew up a doctrine that replaced individual action by massed groups with the aim of destroying the enemy's aviation.[71] Having trained together, the French pilots would create the mass and the concentration that Pétain and Duval wanted. The experience in Flanders confirmed Duval in his decision. The DAN's aviation service reported how German aircraft had massed for the attack on Mt Kemmel, machine-gunning trenches and gun batteries, and then had returned to its normal tactic of smaller patrols over a wider front.[72]

There was one 'fly in the ointment' during all these changes and improvements within the French Army: relations between Pétain and Foch. There is ample evidence that the two men were in complete disagreement over strategy. Foch urged the preparation of a counter-offensive, whilst Pétain resisted. 'We must be economical, if we wish to last out, and not throw ourselves into a mad adventure', Pétain told the liaison officer with the government.[73] Yet he kept insisting that he was on good terms with Foch – as he had insisted to Nivelle – although this did not stop him from complaining to Poincaré about Foch's throwing troops in Flanders into 'unthinking, badly prepared attacks'.[74] Matters came to a head over Fayolle's preparation of the Amiens offensive that Foch had been attempting to launch so as to liberate the Paris–Amiens railway. On 15 May all met at Fayolle's headquarters, and Foch laid out his views about how the offensives, that the Allied armies should be preparing without delay, were to be 'envisaged'.[75] Clearly annoyed, Pétain wrote to Foch the next day, stating that the Allied CinC's comments 'constituted only a discussion at the tactical level'. He requested, therefore, a 'written directive' with Foch's 'strategic idea', so that he would have 'a basis for the definitive instructions to be given to General Fayolle'.[76] This was clearly a shot across Foch's bows, telling him to leave tactics alone and restrict himself to strategy. It must be admitted that Foch did interfere in matters tactical, but this might be forgiven in the two crises of March and April. Pétain was sufficiently annoyed to threaten resignation but Barescut managed to dissuade him from such an extreme step.[77]

As the arguments raged at the highest levels over obtaining more British and American manpower and between Foch and Pétain over the planning for a counter-offensive, the whereabouts of many of the German reserve divisions remained unknown. From 30 April the 2e Bureau's daily intelligence reports recorded an unchanging figure of 206 German divisions on the Western Front. The number of those divisions in reserve in the rear varied between a low of sixty-two on 4 May and eighty-two on the 17th. On the eve of the next German offensive, 26 May, French intelligence recorded eighty such divisions, the whereabouts of only thirty-five of them being known. More worryingly still, sixty-two of those divisions were considered to be 'fresh'.[78] The raw numbers did not give a true story, because the March and April offensives had greatly depleted the infantry within those divisions. Nevertheless, it was divisions that the intelligence reports counted. Pershing's liaison officer, Major Paul H. Clark, was told on 20 May that GQG had no idea where the next offensive was to strike.[79] (The fact that Pétain re-started the training school for staff officers at Melun indicates perhaps that GQG did not expect an attack on the French front.)[80] Foch insisted that another attack on the junction of French and British troops in the north was entirely possible, indeed was likely, since that was where the greatest profit could be gained by separating the two armies or by reaching the Channel ports. Pétain remained concerned, however, for his thinly manned front that stretched from the Oise to Switzerland.

Three offensives against the French front

The failure of both MICHAEL and GEORGETTE imposed on OHL certain conclusions. First, they realised that Foch had been correct to move the bulk of the French reserves into northern France because thereby he had halted the German advances. Second, Foch intended to hold northern France at all costs, but this meant that he had too few resources to mount a strong counter-attack. Third, in order to retain the initiative, the German armies had to attack again before the arrival of American troops gave Foch greater resources. Finally, that German attack had to draw French reserves from the north before the British could be finished off. This meant, in consequence, an attack further east. General von Boehn's *Seventh Army* was ordered to prepare an operation, code-named BLÜCHER, using units pulled from the eastern army groups. It could not have such a wide front as MICHAEL or GEORGETTE, given the longer German front now created in northern France and the losses already sustained. Nor could it take place too far east since the aim was to disrupt the Allied troops opposite Army Group Crown Prince Rupprecht, in order to renew the attacks against the British. The Germans selected the Chemin des Dames sector whence they had been dislodged the previous year. Supporting attacks on both flanks were to threaten Reims and prevent a French attack out of Montdidier.[81]

Although ideally positioned to obtain the main objective – to force the Allies to remove French reserves from northern France – yet the terrain chosen for BLÜCHER was difficult for the attacker. The geographic features, river valleys and intermediate ridges, all ran east–west. The road and rail communications did the same, but the Germans would be attacking from north to south. Thus rivers had to be crossed, the Ailette, the Aisne and the Vesle, and the ridges in between climbed. Ludendorff had sufficient sense to refuse all requests to widen the attack, but on the other hand he expanded the first day objectives several times during the planning.

Equally, the geography should have made the task of defending the Chemin des Dames sector slightly easier. General Denis Duchêne's Sixth Army had been holding the heights of the narrow ridge since the French pushed the Germans off and down into the valley of the Ailette after the the Battle of La Malmaison in October 1917. According to Pétain's directives on defence, Duchêne should have held the Chemin des Dames itself as an outpost line, with the position of principal resistance several kilometres to the south, along the Aisne river. Duchêne had good reasons not to follow the prescription. The Chemin des Dames ridge was very strong, with good observation north and south. To prepare to abandon the ridge line in favour of a much lower position in the rear did not appear sensible. Equally as important, the ridge had been won at enormous cost, after the armies had been driven in 1917 to refuse to continue attacking. The morale effect of abandoning it, on both military and civilian opinion, would be incalculable. Despite reminders from his army group commander, Franchet d'Espèrey, and from Pétain himself, Duchêne maintained his view that the Sixth Army's principal line of resistance should lie along the Chemin des Dames ridge itself.

Sixth Army's front extended from the river Oise in the west to the outskirts of Reims, 90 kilometres further east. Eleven divisions, eight French and three recovering British, held the front backed up by some territorials and twenty-seven machine-gun companies. Each division was responsible for a wider front than usual, with 21 DI in the centre holding 11.5 km of front line. Pétain had his twelve-division reserve deployed fairly close behind Sixth Army, and four of these were under Duchêne's control. Two of the four, however, had barely recovered from the fighting in Picardy and Flanders. Two German prisoners captured on 26 May confirmed the earlier indications that an attack was about to take place, early next morning, on the Chemin des Dames. Consequently Pétain alerted Sixth Army's reserve divisions, and Franchet d'Espèrey ordered his 1 Cavalry Corps to move up. Duchêne alerted his divisions at 7pm and ordered the artillery to fire all night on crossroads and assembly points, although not to begin counter-battery fire until the German guns opened up. The infantry in the front line had seen no indications of any attack, however, as the superb German staff-work had hidden its preparations. Nor had French aviation seen any signs of a forthcoming offensive.

Suddenly, at 1am on 27 May, one of Colonel Bruchmüller's orchestrated bombardments began on a 43-kilometre-wide front and to a depth of 10 to 12 kilometres. Unlike in Flanders, where ypérite, a form of mustard gas, had been used, the Germans fired mostly 'blue cross' gas shells, but in very large proportions: only 20 per cent of shells used against French batteries were explosive; the remainder were 70 per cent 'blue cross' and 10 per cent 'green cross'.[82] The blue cross shells contained an arsenic-based powder which attacked the upper respiratory system, causing sneezing and vomiting. This made the sufferer remove his gas mask, so that the volatile and highly toxic gas in the green cross shell could do its work. The deluge of gas neutralised the French batteries which, it will be remembered, had been ordered to wait for the Germans to open fire before responding. The result was catastrophic. Gas was used also in the *Feuerwalze*, the supporting barrage for the infantry assault (two-fifths gas, three-fifths explosive), which indicates how well the German gunners had mastered the technique of firing gas shells accurately. Mustard gas was only used to suppress flanking attacks, thus leaving the main front of attack clear of the most persistent type of gas. With almost as many *batteries* as the British and French had guns, and with 3,080 gas projector tubes and 1,233 trench mortars, the Germans achieved the greatest superiority of tubes – 3.7 to 1, or a tube every 9–10 metres – of any First World War battle. Some captured tanks and approximately 500 aircraft completed the German offensive power of the twenty-nine infantry divisions devoted to BLÜCHER. Three million shells were fired on the first day, from guns that were calibrated in rear areas beforehand, by measuring the muzzle velocity of individual guns and applying mathematical formulae for the specific weather conditions on the day. Accordingly no warning was given by batteries registering their guns, and the barrage began in darkness. Besides, with such a high proportion of gas shells, pinpoint accuracy was not required.[83]

The results of such overwhelming firepower were not surprising, although the force of the assault came as a huge shock to the French. The German infantry attack began a mere two hours and forty minutes later, just before dawn. Elements of the leading corps reached the top of the Chemin des Dames ridge an hour later; between 9 and 10am the Germans were along the Aisne. By 11am the Germans were across the Aisne and the Aisne–Marne canal, and by 8pm the first units had reached the Vesle, which river several units in *Seventh Army*'s centre crossed two hours later. They had progressed so far and so fast that the French had no time to evacuate their guns from the north bank of the Aisne, and more significantly, Duchêne's order to blow up the Aisne bridges arrived only after the Germans were already across the river.

The Germans continued their progression the next day, 28 May. Despite having reached their objectives for the whole battle, namely the heights south of the Vesle, they were ordered to continue. Ludendorff decided to exploit the success rather than stick to the original plan of attracting French reserves so as to be able to launch operation HAGEN in the north against the British. So by nightfall the Germans had entered Soissons and had made a further 10 kilometres' ground south of the Vesle. Sixth Army had been pushed out of all its organised positions, and had nothing but open country at its back. The next day the Germans continued to push through the 25–30 kilometre gap in the centre and by evening had almost reached the Marne, a river they had last seen in 1914. The only bright spot was the French resistance around Reims which had faltered but did not break.

By now, however, the French had managed to get their defensive act together. Duchêne had thrown his reserves piecemeal into the fighting early on the first day, and they had been swallowed up to no purpose. Pétain and Franchet d'Espèrey organised General Micheler's Fifth Army of ten infantry and three cavalry divisions to join the battle. Two of their units arrived on the first day and were engaged, with three more arriving on the 28th and a further three the next day. In addition, on 28 May, Pétain took two divisions from the Eastern Army Group and another eight from Fayolle's Reserve Army Group, and these units arrived gradually between 30 May and 1 June.[84] That same day, 28 May, Pétain saw Foch, who remained confident that the attack was a diversion – as indeed it was so intended – and had told Clemenceau so. That day's intelligence assessment stated that Crown Prince Rupprecht still had more reserves (forty-one divisions) available than the armies of the Imperial Crown Prince on the Aisne (twenty-four). Indeed, with twenty-four *fresh* divisions, as many as the Imperial Crown Prince's *total*, Rupprecht presented a much greater danger. Pétain announced the necessary measures to halt the enemy in a directive issued late that evening: the two flanks of the enemy breach were to be held strongly, that in the east backed by the Montagne de Reims where Fifth Army came into line between the Fourth around Reims and the battered Sixth, and in the west by holding the plateaux to the north and south of Soissons. Two American divisions began moving on 30 May towards Château Thierry to reinforce the French at the bottom of the bulge.[85]

Although Pétain and GQG had organised the best defence possible, holding the edges of the breach so as to channel the enemy onslaught, they remained pessimistic. The Germans did reach the Marne on 30 May. Also they attacked the two 'moles', or flanks of the salient, capturing the plateau north of Soissons and pressing Fifth Army very strongly around Reims. Yet the German advance had been so pronounced that re-supply was becoming a serious problem for them. Ludendorff knew that he needed the railway line between Soissons and Reims because the north–south communications were inadequate. Although the Germans held Soissons, the French still held Reims, and without Reims the line could not be used. Ludendorff ordered *First Army* to help the *Seventh* to capture Reims. So GQG feared for Reims in the east and for the roads to Paris via the Marne and the Oise.

There was no question whatsoever of evacuating Paris, as had happened in 1914. Parliament would not permit the government to leave, nor had Poincaré any desire so to do. Clemenceau stalked the corridors defending Foch and Pétain against the flying rumours and criticisms. Guillaumat was brought back from Salonika in case a replacement was required for either general. On the other hand, there was some question of abandoning eastern France. On 30 May Pétain asked Castelnau to draw up a statement of what needed to be done, in the case of a forced withdrawal, to maintain contact with the Northern Army group. Castelnau responded that, since he had no reserves whatsoever, he would be forced to withdraw if he was attacked, so as to regroup and manoeuvre to 'contain the enemy whilst waiting for better times'.[86] The next day, Franchet d'Espèrey ordered Fifth Army to evacuate Reims in order to retain some reserves for keeping the front intact to the Marne, but Fifth Army ignored the order. On 1 June Pétain instructed Fifth Army to resist where they were, with officers using violence against their own men, if necessary.[87]

What about the troops? By the end of the offensive the Germans had captured 600 guns and some 50,000 prisoners.[88] Although the rapid German advance over areas that some units knew well had produced a 'painful' effect on the men, morale remained 'excellent' or 'very good' in 36 per cent of reports from the commanders of 946 units that the postal control commission studied. A further 62 per cent reported 'good' or 'satisfactory' morale, the remaining 2 per cent not offering an opinion.[89] The men had attributed the German success on the Somme in March to the British Army's 'inexperience' and so they had not been adversely affected, but they had been 'surprised' by the loss in May of positions that many knew personally to have been strong defensive ground. The sight of refugees and fears for families in the invaded areas had been depressing, but confidence returned once resistance had stiffened. The arrival of young, eager Americans had been an 'essential element' in the restoration of confidence, together with the knowledge that the enemy had paid dearly for the Chemin des Dames offensive without gaining any 'decisive' objective.

One of the units thrown into the fray on 27 May was 13 DI. The division was one of the few to have escaped the fighting in March and April. After the victory at La Malmaison in 1917, the division had spent the winter in the Vosges; on 24 May it began its move westwards by train to join Sixth Army's reserves, concentrating around Ville-en-Tardenois. By the evening of 26 May its artillery and engineers had arrived and the division was complete, ready to undergo a period of training. That night, however, the staff were warned to be ready to move into action and the men could hear the start of the German bombardment, some of them even being affected by the gas that was fired. By 9.30am on the morning of 27 May the divisional artillery had set off to join the left of the British IX Corps and the division's commander, now General Martin de Bouillon, went to make contact with the British. Already the original point of junction had been moved, and the infantry began marching early afternoon ignorant of the situation in front of them. After spending the night in woods, they found their centre under strong enemy attack and their left completely uncovered. The division managed a fighting retreat over the next few days, and inflicted numerous casualties. As Ludendorff recognised: 'the resistance of this division cost the life and health of numerous German soldiers', he wrote in an intelligence report on 10 June. The nine days during which 13 DI was engaged cost the division 2,825 casualties of its own.[90]

Foch moved his headquarters to be nearer GQG, and on 31 May met Haig and, later the same afternoon, Pétain, Duchêne and Clemenceau. After two hours' discussion they agreed that the worst was over and that their intelligence service had provided them with enough information to understand the German plan. Foch had been pressing Cointet for intelligence of Rupprecht's divisions, and it was now possible to confirm that any new German divisions would have to be transferred to the Marne from the north.[91] After 1 June the tide turned. Crown Prince Rupprecht was informed that HAGEN could not start before mid-July, when the whole point of BLÜCHER had been to enable the northern attack to begin promptly around 1 July, and Crown Prince Wilhelm learned that *First Army*'s attack against Reims had stalled. Although Ludendorff continued to issue operational orders, and some progress was made against the French north and south of the Villers-Cotterêts forest, by 4 and 5 June the battle had ceased. It was decided to concentrate on preparing operation GNEISENAU. The French had committed thirty-seven divisions to stopping the German advance, and losses had been severe. During the German offensive, 27 May–5 June, the French armies suffered 98,160 casualties, of whom almost 30,000 were wounded, and 68,890 had been killed, had disappeared or been taken prisoner.[92]

The search for the guilty, for those responsible for the débâcle, began immediately. The parliamentarians had received a considerable fright, and Clemenceau was spending his time at the front and in the various army headquarters, and so unable to calm the calls for Duchêne and even Pétain to be sacked. Barescut noted an anti-Pétain cabal; the Paris gun, 'Big Bertha', began firing again. Then Clemenceau had to spend the three days 1–3 June in meetings of the SWC in Versailles with more bad-tempered exchanges about manpower, both British and American.

The Army Commission of the Chamber of Deputies charged Abel Ferry with producing a report on the 'rupture' of the French front, or what soon became known as the 'surprise' of 27 May. Its official title was the Third Battle of the Aisne. Ferry wrote first of the long-term causes: the lack of sufficient men because of all the expensive offensives undertaken in past years in France and in the Balkans, and the failure of the intelligence services to pinpoint the German reserves as effectively as the Germans pinpointed the Allied ones. He pointed out the strength of Allied positions, given the terrain. The reason for putting the tired British divisions on the Aisne was precisely because the front was considered invulnerable. How then had the Germans managed to break through so comprehensively, creating the French Caporetto or the French equivalent of the British 21 March? Ferry's assessment, dated 17 July and acknowledged to be provisional until all the reports were in, laid the blame, except for the long-term factors, on the shoulders of the Sixth Army commander, General Denis Duchêne. It was his decision to ignore Pétain's instructions about resisting on the second line of defence, and he had placed most of his manpower in the first line with orders to hold it. The British had protested against this decision and had been ignored as well. Then he had sent forward his reserves from the intermediate position, and they had been swallowed up, having achieved nothing. Finally, he had failed to order the destruction of the Aisne bridges in time, so that the Germans had been able to bring up their artillery and progress still further towards the Marne.[93] Duchêne was certainly guilty of over-confidence (even arrogance?) in overriding his superior's instructions and over-estimating the strength of his army's positions. Equally his brutal nature cannot have helped matters. Ferry called him a 'sort of bad-mouthed, uncontrolled brute', and recounted how meals in the mess were silent because his staff would not speak to him. Duchêne used to leave the silent dinner table, telling his staff: 'Sirs, to your kennels'. Castelnau's staff in 1914 had held similar opinions about Duchêne.[94]

Duchêne did not bear the sole responsibility. The army group commander, General Franchet d'Espèrey, tolerated Duchêne's refusal to follow Directive #4, as did Pétain. Duchêne complained that he had been left to cope alone on 27 May, and that Franchet d'Espèrey had not been near his command post. Yet all communications had been cut, which made control of the battle impossible. The order to evacuate Reims had come from Franchet d'Espèrey. In his post-war report on operations in 1918, Pétain claimed that the only sanction he could have imposed on Duchêne was to have relieved him of his command and, since an offensive was imminent, such an action would have been too dangerous. Yet Duchêne had been in command of Sixth Army since December 1917 and in sector since then. Moreover, it was only very close to 27 May that the offensive was suspected. Pedroncini suggests that Pétain did not want to cause conflict with Foch since the offensive-minded Duchêne was more in tune with Foch's ideas than with his commander-in-chief's. It is more likely that Pétain recoiled from dealing firmly with Duchêne because the latter was such an unpleasant character. Pétain himself was convinced that the fundamental reason for the German success was that the Allied front was held too thinly. The events of March and April, he told Clemenceau, had imposed new and heavy charges on the French armies, with the inevitable result that the divisions on the Chemin des Dames were too stretched, even for the naturally strong defences of the sector.[95] Without saying so directly, Pétain laid the blame on the British for giving way in March and April, and on Foch for keeping French troops behind the British fronts.

This leads to the question of Foch's responsibility for the breakthrough. In Paris he was blamed for keeping French troops in the north, and only releasing them drop by drop. Clemenceau had to defend both Foch and Pétain in parliament and before the two army commissions. Yet, unlike Pétain, Foch was looking at the whole Western Front. He got the Belgians to extend their front in Flanders so that divisions could be released from the DAN. He resisted the British insistence that Crown

Prince Rupprecht still had fresh divisions.[96] His British liaison officer thought Haig happy to accept Foch's authority when it was a question of saving the British Army in March, but he and especially his chief of staff, General Herbert Lawrence, were less happy to go to the aid of the French Army in May. It was only when intelligence revealed that five German divisions had moved from Rupprecht to Wilhelm that Foch began to insist on taking away Tenth Army and units from the DAN, leaving the British to create their own reserve and to prepare to supply more British divisions. As a result, Haig appealed to London, as the Beauvais agreement permitted him to do, on the grounds that Foch's orders put the British Army at risk. That ploy failed when Milner and Wilson went over to France and confirmed Foch's authority.

The French Army's intelligence service had failed to give a timely warning. It was only a few days before the German offensive began that it became clear that the Chemin des Dames was indeed the principal target, rather than being a diversion or disinformation. Yet, in Foch's defence, it has to be said that he had read the German intentions correctly. Despite all the criticisms from politicians and military of his decision to keep French reserves in the north, it was undoubtedly more important to prevent the separation of the British and French armies, and to safeguard the port and railway communications there, than it was to allow the enemy to advance in Champagne. Foch knew that there was no strategic advantage to be gained by progressing southwards from the Aisne and, assuming that Ludendorff knew this as well, judged the greater threat to lie in the north. Ludendorff allowed himself to be tempted by the breakthrough on the Aisne into removing materiel and divisions from Rupprecht's armies, with the result that HAGEN had to be postponed and was never carried out. In contrast, Foch maintained fixity of purpose in the face of all the criticisms, and was proved correct. His British liaison officer at Allied headquarters said that he had never admired Foch more than in the crisis days at the end of May 1918.[97]

Sanctions were imposed. The commanders of XI Corps and 157 DI, and also Duchêne and Franchet d'Espèrey lost their jobs. General Degoutte replaced Duchêne in Sixth Army; General Maistre took over from Franchet d'Espèrey and the army group renamed Centre Army Group. Pétain had defended Duchêne, saying that he had insufficient men for defending his front because of the costs to the French Army of defending the British front in March and April, but was overruled.[98] Pétain also lost his chief of staff, Anthoine. Although not directly responsible for the failure on the Chemin des Dames, Anthoine had made too many public, pessimistic statements, and Foch took the opportunity to get rid of him. He appointed General Edmond Buat to GQG in his place.

Clemenceau asked Pétain for a succinct report on 12 June. He instituted an enquiry into events as a means of quieting the politicians, some of whom were asking why there was no legal procedure to charge generals with incompetence, especially since lower levels were liable to trial by military tribunal. He set up a three-member commission on 25 July, like the one that Foch had sat on in 1917 about events in the same sector, with the two presidents of the Senate and Deputies' army commissions and General Guillaumat in his capacity as Military Governor of Paris. Guillaumat had been recalled from Salonika during the crisis days as the only possible replacement for either Foch or Pétain, and Franchet d'Espèrey was banished there as his replacement. The commission's purpose was to investigate 'in particular' whether any general officers had committed any 'serious error' during their command. It began its work on 30 July, but Guillaumat stated that they would only consider events at the level of Sixth Army command and below. Clemenceau confirmed this decision later, thus preventing any discussion of the role of either Pétain or Foch. The commissioners held six meetings before the end of September, but were held up by the rapid flow of events as the war came to an end. It must have seemed that their work had become irrelevant when the Armistice was signed. Nonetheless, they sent out questionnaires to the generals concerned in December 1918, and reported eventually that the cause of the collapse was the overwhelming enemy superiority of men and materiel, compounded by the 'excessive' length of front held by Sixth Army and the lack of general reserves. This lack was due to high command's judgement that no more terrain could be ceded in the north, whereas a retreat could be accepted and repaired elsewhere.[99] Clearly, this was a fair assessment, but before Clemenceau had even set up the commission the next two German offensives had begun.

The first of these, operation GNEISENAU, was launched on the western side of BLÜCHER. Ludendorff's failure to stick to his original plan had given the Germans a huge salient to defend and insufficient means of supplying the troops holding it. The western mole of the salient contained the thick woods around Villers-Cotterêts where the French could mass preparatory to a counter-attack, and Ludendorff needed some space to the west to free the area around Soissons and its railway line to Reims. Moreover, a successful attack to the west would eliminate the ground between the bulge around Montdidier created in March/April and the new Champagne salient. Thus Ludendorff could straighten out his front, hence free up some forces. However, conditions were less favourable than in May. The nights were shorter, leaving less time for the accumulation of men and materiel, and there was less cover than there had been north of the Ailette. The operation had been planned for some time as a supporting attack for BLÜCHER, but BLÜCHER's failure meant a couple of days' postponement for GNEISENAU. The direction of the attack was towards the river Matz (which gave its name to the battle), pivoting on Montdidier, thence towards the Montdidier–Compiègne line. Compiègne lies on the Oise, and that river has long been the main invasion route to Paris. Although Ludendorff had no intention of getting mixed up in a siege of Paris, a threat to the capital could only increase the nervousness of its citizens and politicians.

This time the French knew the attack was coming. In the line of fire was General Humbert's Third Army, one of the two armies in Fayolle's Reserve Army Group. It held the front between the Oise and Montdidier with seven divisions. Ever since taking over the front at the end of the March/April fighting, Third Army had been preparing the counter-attack that Foch wanted, but now that it faced an attack itself and now that resistance on the first defence lines had been proved dangerous even when those lines were as strong as those on the Chemin des Dames, the situation had changed. Consequently, from the beginning of June, Pétain ordered Humbert to halt studies of the offensive and to prepare the line of resistance in front of the army's second position, which had scarcely been sketched out. Fayolle kept a close watch on Humbert and the progress of the defences, especially since army corps commanders were not entirely convinced, as Duchêne had not been, that abandoning the first position was necessary.[100] Fayolle's action is a clear example of learning from experience.

Pétain had accumulated what reserves he could to resist the forthcoming German offensive. He inserted Tenth Army between the Third and the battered Sixth to ensure the defence of the western mole of the German salient. He grouped the three divisions that Foch had agreed to release from the DAN and the three divisions released from the Eastern Army Group when five barely trained American divisions took over their quiet sector, together with the Reserve Army Group's own five remaining reserve, to make an eleven-division reserve force ready to intervene to support Third Army. The two French cavalry corps were pulled out of the Champagne fighting and ordered to re-group behind Third Army as well. Foch too did his best to get British divisions out of Haig, but Haig was unwilling to accept that the German preparations were more than an attempt at deception, such as had happened in March. He believed that 'serious attacks' were to be expected in the north and that the bulk of the German reserves remained on Rupprecht's front.[101] As noted above, finally Haig appealed to London but was told to conform to Foch's orders. The French intelligence reports between 1 and 8 June fluctuated between fifty-nine and sixty-four for the numbers of German reserve divisions. The majority of these were considered fresh, and the whereabouts of fewer than half were known.[102] So both the British and French CinCs were obliged to juggle resources as best they could, while Foch had to deal with complaints from both. As Barescut put it, 'we are walking a tightrope'.[103]

The German attack was launched on 9 June following the same principles that had brought success on 27 May: an early morning artillery barrage, fired in the dark because unregistered (1.4 million shells were fired of which a third were gas); the infantry assault a short time after the three-and-a-half-hour barrage, at 4.20am. This time, however, there was no surprise, and the French intelligence service made up for its previous failure. French aerial observers had spotted the build-up and German deserters gave away the date and the time of the offensive. Moreover, in late May the Mont Valérien listening post, in western Paris, picked up a German radio transmission which Captain Painvin was able to decipher very quickly. It ordered the German units north-west of Compiègne to press on with their preparations. This gave the French the location of the next offensive in good time, but the radio message was treated with some suspicion because it was the only time during the war that only a single listening post had picked up a radio transmission. Normally several posts heard it.[104]

Once again, the German infantry did break through Third Army's front because of the weight of guns and men (thirteen divisions), but it was not a rout. The French fell back and the enemy reached the Matz, but Humbert had not packed the front lines as Duchêne had done, and he ordered the French guns to begin firing before the expected German barrage. Although the Germans began firing ten minutes earlier than the prisoners had announced, which reduced the efficacy of Humbert's counter-barrage by reducing its length, it was enough to disrupt the start of the infantry assault. Nevertheless, by 11am the enemy occupied about 12 kilometres of the French second line – there simply had not been enough time or labourers to create Pétain's elastic defence in depth.

On the second day, 10 June, the Germans managed to progress a little further, reaching the northern bank of the Oise, but the French had enough guns and aircraft to prevent their advancing any closer to Compiègne. That evening Foch arrived at Fayolle's HQ and supported Mangin's request to mount a counter-attack. Mangin had not had an active command since being sacked in 1917, but was a corps commander in reserve in First Army. If speed was vital, as it was, then Mangin was energetic enough to carry out the task. He was given command of XXXV Corps, with five of the fresh reserve divisions (although Pétain refused to allow him to use the fifth), and 163 Schneider and Saint-Chamond tanks.[105] Despite having little time to assemble his forces, Mangin, pushed by Foch, was ready by 11am the next day, 11 June. With no preliminary artillery preparation to give warning of attack, and behind a dense rolling barrage, Mangin's forces surprised the Germans and progressed between 1 and 4 kilometres along a 7-kilometre front. Despite Mangin's success in capturing 1,000 prisoners and ten guns, the result of surprise and the tanks, Foch and Pétain knew that the German forces were still too strong and they called a halt on 12 June. Unlike Ludendorff, they were not tempted to bite off more than they could chew. Although two more German offensives were launched against the northern edge of Villers-Cotterêts forest and against Reims, neither made much headway. Effectively, the fighting in the Champagne area was over. According to the commander of a machine-gun company in one of Mangin's divisions, the French soldier now realised that he was not destined simply to receive repeated enemy blows, but was capable of giving them.[106]

The cost to France's armies of operations BLÜCHER and GNEISENAU had been very heavy. Between 27 May and 16 June French casualties (killed, missing, prisoners and wounded) amounted to 139,160, and 212 guns had been lost, most put out of action before being abandoned.[107] Yet again deputies and senators were highly critical of both Pétain and Foch, and again Clemenceau was obliged to defend them both. The postal control commissions reported great pride in having stopped the German offensive and having 'barred the road to Paris', but the men knew they had suffered heavy losses in doing so. The 'dominant note' in Tenth Army's correspondence was fatigue, so the commission reported on 16 June.[108] Third Army was in a similar state. Physical fatigue, coupled with influenza and the effects of gas shelling had depressed the men already in May, an effect accentuated by the fighting in June. Leave had been stopped during the fighting and was re-instated at the end of June, although granted only sparingly. Given what had happened in 1917, this situation had to be monitored. Although calls for revolt were rare, some letters were seized by the censors for opinions such as this one:

Clemenceau has decided to fight on to the last man! It's true that he doesn't count as a man, he's a brute without soul or conscience ... everyone has had more than enough, especially with the leave situation.[109]

The only bright spot was the arrival of the Americans. Although opinion had been hostile at first – the 'Sammies' were only prolonging the war, pushing up prices by spending too freely and having a great time with

French women – the entry of American troops into the front line had had a good effect. The two American divisions that had held the bottom of the Marne pocket and fought in Belleau Wood had impressed by their youth, their enthusiasm and their spirit.

A sense of renewed confidence enabled the French Army to prepare for the next onslaught. They had helped to stem the first two German offensives, and had withstood the second two, with Mangin's counter-offensive on the Matz compensating for the 'surprise' on the Chemin des Dames. A further component of the increased confidence lay in the ability of all the Allies to replace their lost materiel. The Allies had defeated the German submarine, so that ships were delivering supplies of raw materials for French factories as well as bringing American soldiers across the Atlantic. Although the fighting had diminished the Army's stocks of munitions, factory outputs were recovering from the strikes of May and would deliver in July some of their highest monthly figures. The production record for aircraft engines was set in July (4,490), and in the same month output of aircraft (2,622) was second, by 280 units, only to the August 1918 figure.[110] Twelve battalions of light Renault tanks had been formed by 22 June, and another three by 20 July.[111] Also in May, French production of ypérite (mustard gas) began after several months of experimentation. By the armistice, the three private firms employed in the production of the gas had supplied 1,937 tonnes of it, enough to fill 2.5 million shells.[112]

Although the full complement of the 1916 programme of heavy artillery was never produced, yet by 1 July 1918 every division now had one battalion of 155mm howitzers (1,260 pieces in all) and every army corps had one or two battalions of 105s plus one battalion of 155s, all of the guns being horse-drawn. The General Artillery Reserve, created in early 1917 under the command of General Buat, was at the disposal of the CinC, so could be used wherever it was needed rather than being allocated to any specific army. More importantly it was mobile. The Reserve manned 327 heavy guns (some of them naval guns and/or mounted on boats), and a tractor-drawn division of heavy guns, consisting of forty battalions of howitzers (441 guns) and forty battalions armed mainly with the most useful heavy gun, the 155mm (480 guns).[113] The newest version of this gun, the GPF or Grande Puissance Filloux, was produced in the government arsenal at Puteaux and under contract by Renault. It provided 35° of elevation and could traverse through 60° without being moved. It threw a 43-kilo shell a distance of 16 kilometres.[114] The French Army would have had considerably more of these 155 GPF, if it had not been for supplying the Americans: 224 long 155s and 762 short 155 howitzers over the period of American fighting.[115]

Even the old 75s were still available: there were 4,824 75s in all armies on 1 July 1918. As General Herr summed up the position, on 1 July 1918 the French artillery now had 'a rational organisation', 'a large proportion of modern, rapid-firing long-range guns', and its personnel had received a high standard of training. They had been forced to leave their gun pits and re-learn the art of manoeuvre, whilst relying even more on techniques such as sound-ranging for opening fire without warning.[116] It was ready for the next battle.

Disagreements between Pétain and Foch continued, over two matters in particular. Pétain believed that the British should no longer require French support on the northern front, because they had had two months of relative peace in which to reorganise; consequently he wanted French Army troops returned to his command. Second, Pétain refused to distribute to his armies Foch's note about German tactics and the best way to counter-attack. Foch brought the disputes to a head by reporting Pétain's refusal to Clemenceau. Clemenceau convened the comité de guerre on 26 June to discuss the situation, and he and the committee agreed unanimously to support Foch over Pétain. Furthermore they decreed that, while foreign CinCs had the right of appeal to their government, according to the April Beauvais accord, such a right was unnecessary for a French general. Henceforth Pétain would have to obey Foch's orders.[117]

In contrast to the now greater clarity of the relationship between Allied and French commanders, the German high command found itself in a cleft stick. It had to deploy troops to hold a much longer front, while still insisting that the main goal was to attack and defeat the British in the north. Yet the Marne salient had to be supplied or abandoned, and the latter option was inconceivable. In order to supply the salient, Reims had to be captured, and so another offensive was planned against the French front. It was to be a pincer attack, with *Seventh Army* driving into the salient, across the Marne and then turning eastwards towards Epernay where it would join *First Army* whose troops were to reach the town by advancing around the eastern flank of Reims. Reims itself was not to be attacked frontally, but cut off by the two German armies joining up south of the town and capturing its defences in the hilly and wooded Montagne de Reims. As usual, Ludendorff increased the scale and objectives of the double attack, which in turn increased the time needed for preparation. *Third Army* was to advance in Champagne as far south as Châlons on the river Marne to protect the Marne crossings for the neighbouring armies and, perhaps, to make a great success out of what was originally an operation to free communications to supply the Marne salient. Furthermore, the Germans were running out of guns as industry had been unable to keep up with the wear and tear suffered during the intensive combat operations. They also lacked lorries and petrol to move men and materiel. The replacement manpower for the huge numbers killed and wounded in the four offensives was of much lower quality than the specially trained *Stosstruppen* of March. These were men combed out from the home front or more comfortable billets in rear areas, or they were returned prisoners of war from the Russian front 'infected' with Bolshevism, or they were industrial workers sent to the front as a punishment for striking. Such men could not be expected to do as well as those who had made such spectacular progress against the British in March or against the French in May. Nevertheless the forces arrayed against the French were substantial: twenty attacking divisions in *First* and *Seventh Armies*, with another seven in *Third Army* protecting the eastern flank of the offensive; then, another twenty-one divisions in the three armies' second and third lines; about 900 aircraft; 6,353 guns plus over 2,000 trench mortars.[118] All this amounted to a front of about 110 kilometres, with troops suffering badly from the influenza epidemic.

The greatest disadvantage for the Germans was that all surprise had been forfeited, because the Allies knew when and where the next offensive was to come. Air reconnaissance and prisoner interrogations confirmed the French in their belief that a new German offensive was being prepared, but this time, they were ready: 'a defensive battle was never waged under more favourable conditions', Gouraud told his Fourth Army. Moreover, a German officer captured on 13 July was carrying a copy of his attack orders, and the next day a French trench raid captured twenty-seven German soldiers, one of whom gave away the date and time of the attack.[119] Besides, the French had learned how to cope successfully with the German offensives, as their counter-attack on the Matz had shown. Once again Pétain insisted that he needed more reserves. Five American divisions were taken from the British divisions where they were being trained and sent to quiet sectors in the east so as to free French divisions. The DAN was returned from Picardy to Pétain's control and became Ninth Army from 6 July. (Ninth Army had been dissolved after the Battle of the Marne in 1914, when its then commander, Foch, became Joffre's adjoint.)

Now that intelligence on the extent of the forthcoming operation had become clear, Foch knew that it would be impossible for the Germans to launch another attack quickly on the British, and so he felt justified in asking Haig for some British divisions. The final disposition of French forces was thus: the three armies in General Maistre's Centre Army Group deployed, in Fourth Army, fourteen divisions (thirteen French and one American) in the front line or in reserve; Fifth Army had eleven such divisions, two of them Italian; and Sixth Army had eight, two of them American. These divisions were ordered to halt the German offensive. Ninth Army formed the general reserve with another eight infantry and three cavalry divisions, together with General Godley's British XXII Corps with two divisions and a further two due to arrive. General Fayolle's Reserve Army Group had the task of mounting the counterattack, with the left flank of Sixth Army and Tenth Army (now commanded by the promoted Mangin), a total of twenty-four infantry (four of them American) and three cavalry divisions supported by 2,000 guns and 520 tanks. The rest of the front, from the Argonne to Switzerland and from north of the Oise to Belgium, had been stripped almost entirely of French troops. Some fifteen American divisions were undergoing instruction, and the British and Belgians retained some twenty or so of their own divisions. The French CinC of the Allied armies intended to strike back with all the forces at his disposal.

First, however, the next German offensive, MARNESCHUTZ, had to be resisted. On the right of the German action, Gouraud's Fourth Army, east of Reims, was ready. After their succesful trench raid they knew the start time of the German artillery barrage (ten minutes after midnight on 15 July), and they opened fire themselves forty minutes earlier so as to disrupt the enemy's preparations. The infantry assault began at 4.30am behind a dense rolling barrage, but the French defenders in the lightly held front trenches had warned the main body of troops behind them, using messenger pigeons and the telephone lines which had been buried deeply enough to withstand the shelling. Held up by the French front defenders, the first and second German waves became mixed up, and they lost the protection of their rolling barrage, because they could not keep up with it. By the time that the German infantry reached the main French position of resistance, the French gunners were mowing them down in the open, as well as the German gunners attempting to advance their batteries to support them. French pilots reported that the disorder in the enemy camp was so great that there was unlikely to be any further attack the next day.[120] So it proved. For Rudolf Binding, 16 July was 'the most disheartening day of the war'. The French 'had put up no resistance in front; they had neither infantry nor artillery in this forward battle-zone ... Our guns bombarded empty trenches; our gas-shells gassed empty artillery positions; only in little hidden folds of the ground, sparsely distributed, lay machine-gun posts, like lice in the seams and folds of a garment, to give the attacking force a warm reception.'[121] Nine experienced German divisions plus their reserves had taken part in the attack, but the French did not need to engage their own reserves, because the success was complete.

West of Reims, in the Château Thierry/Marne salient, the Germans did much better. Despite the French artillery's counter-preparation which interfered greatly with the units attempting to bridge the Marne, by midday Fifth and Sixth Armies had been pushed back beyond their position of resistance and the Italian II Corps was struggling in the Ardre valley. Fifth Army suffered large losses that day, and by evening the Germans had made a shallow bridgehead south of the Marne along a front of about 14 kilometres. General Maurice Pellé's V Corps in Fifth Army had been outnumbered two to one, and his report asked for two of his divisions to be relieved immediately, because of their great losses. One of his regiments in 8 DI (317 RI) had been wiped out completely, as it had been manning the forward posts.[122] Sixth Army, however, had suffered mainly on its right where it was in contact with the Fifth, and its artillery, supported by bombing raids by the Air Division, was able to punish the German sappers trying to construct and maintain more bridges and gangplanks across the Marne. On 15 July, the Air Division flew 723 sorties, shot down 24 enemy aircraft and dropped 46 tonnes of bombs. A captured German message called the bombardment a 'veritable hell'.[123]

One of Sixth Army's divisions, 125 DI, was normally deployed in V Corps in Fifth Army, and its commander wrote to Pellé, V Corps, with an account of the German assault on his division and on Sixth Army. His division had been in the thick of it, he wrote, the third heavy fight in four months. Casualties were even greater than in the fighting of 9 June on the Matz, but his men 'had the definite impression that this offensive was a resounding defeat for the Boche'. All were hoping to take part in a general offensive against the enemy, but first 'we need time for training . . . we will come out of this testing time victorious, however hard our losses (275 officers and 10,500 other ranks in less than four months)'.[124]

The next day, 16 July, Pétain supplied two more divisions to Berthelot's Fifth Army, which was enough to prevent the Germans making much more progress. In addition he inserted Ninth Army between Fifth and Sixth Armies to strengthen the point of junction and to leave the latter responsible only for the north bank of the Marne, where Degoutte was planning a strong counter-offensive to throw the Germans back into the river. De Mitry's Ninth Army was to take care of the German bridgehead south of the river, and that evening the German Crown Prince ordered all attacks there to cease. With the attack halted on the eastern side of Reims also, the only German objective left was to capture the city from the south, and orders were issued for 17 July to push along the Marne's northern bank. Even this limited objective proved impossible. British and French aircraft and French artillery had destroyed 70 per cent of the German bridging trains and *Seventh Army* was ordered to go onto the defensive. The bridgehead south of the Marne was to be evacuated, and Germany's fifth and last offensive had been blocked.

Gouraud's successful defence of Reims has been lauded as the optimal example of Pétain's Fourth Directive instruction – the principle of elastic defence in depth. It has been compared to Fifth Army's difficulties south-west of Reims, and the distinction drawn between the defensive Pétain and the offensive-minded Foch/Berthelot. Professor Pedroncini wrote: 'The defensive battle of 15 July, won almost immediately on Fourth Army's front, no longer allowed any doubt about the efficacy of the tactical methods laid out in Directive #4. The battle confirmed with facts General Pétain's ideas.'[125] Yet to compare the situation of the two French armies on 15 July is to compare apples with oranges. Fourth Army had been occupying its Champagne sector since 1914, and Gouraud had commanded it for a year following his return to service after being wounded on Gallipoli, and then again from mid June 1917. On the other hand, Fifth Army had been pushed into its sector south-west of Reims after the 'surprise' on the Chemin des Dames, less than two months earlier, in order to prevent the separation of Fourth and Sixth armies. Consequently it had occupied for about seven weeks ground not fought over since 1914, and its previous commander, General Micheler, had been purged when heads rolled after that German offensive. His replacement, General Buat, was transferred to GQG after only four weeks to replace General Anthoine, judged too 'pessimistic'. General Berthelot replaced Buat on 5 July, just ten days before the German assault; he had been in Romania since October 1916, and then in June 1918 had been sent on a mission to the USA. Furthermore, Fifth Army's attention had been concentrated on preparing the counter-attack on both sides of the Château Thierry salient, and its role only became a defensive one when it was confirmed that the next German assault would be large and would come on both sides of Reims. In other words, Fourth Army knew the terrain, Fifth Army did not; Fourth Army had been commanded by the same general for a long time, Fifth Army had had three commanders in two months; Fourth Army had intelligence from trench raids, and Fifth Army's role had changed from attack to defence shortly before MARNESCHUTZ began.

By now, mid-July, France had borne the brunt of the five German offensives. After sending forty-seven divisions to support the British front during the first two, it had received, by comparison, minimal British and American support in resisting the last three. The fighting during the period March–July 1918 cost the French army almost 400,000 casualties, of whom 187,749 had been killed or had disappeared, many of them taken prisoner.[126] All five offensives had been resisted successfully, however, and American manpower was finally arriving in great numbers. Pétain summed up his post-war account of 1918's defensive battle thus:

Since 21 March, alone of the Allied armies, [the French Army] had taken part in all the great battles which the enemy delivered despairingly to decide the outcome of the war. It had raced to the battle in Picardy with thirty-four divisions; it had sent eighteen divisions into Flanders; on the Aisne it had had to engage forty divisions, and then seventeen between Montdidier and Noyon a few days later. Finally, from 15 July, it fought in Champagne a gigantic battle with all its available forces, more than fifty-seven divisions; so, without ceasing, with no relief, in March, in April, in May, in June, then in July, it had led the struggle.[127]

It was time to take back the initiative.

8   The path to victory

Foch had decided to unify the defensive and offensive battles. Even before MARNESCHUTZ began, he was planning the counter-offensive. Mangin's small-scale counter-attack after Germany's June offensive on the Matz had shown that the French Army was still capable of winning a victory. Despite the 'surprise' on the Chemin des Dames in May, Foch had confidence in French intelligence reports, and he was seeing GQG's head of intelligence, Colonel Cointet, regularly. On 17 July Ludendorff was told that it would take several days before operations could re-start to cut off Reims, which town's railway station was still badly needed, and then he set off for Rupprecht's headquarters to continue the planning for Operation HAGEN against the British lines. By the evening, however, the German lines were in a state of chaos and the *Seventh Army* units south of the river were ordered to return to the north bank as French artillery and aircraft fire was destroying almost all the pontoon bridges. Now the French Army was ready to retaliate.[1]

The 18 July counter-attack

Mangin believed that conditions around Soissons were favourable for a counter-attack, and on 8 July Pétain approved his proposal as a good riposte to the expected German attack. Mangin had taken over command of Tenth Army on 10 June and two of his five army corps (XX and XXX Corps) had been making small local gains ever since along his east-facing front between the Oise and the Savières, a small tributary of the Ourcq. These advances gave excellent jumping-off positions north and south of the heavily wooded forest of Villers-Cotterêts, which would provide equally excellent cover. A surprise attack was, therefore, perfectly possible. Mangin was confident that these successful local attacks proved his troops capable of bigger things, for the numbers of prisoners captured during them pointed to a serious diminution of the enemy's offensive capability. His army group commander, Fayolle, endorsed Mangin's views, while warning that the infantry and artillery resources that Mangin was demanding would be dependent upon availability after the German offensive.

Next to Tenth Army, Sixth Army commanded by General Degoutte held the front between the Ourcq and the Marne. On 8 July Degoutte reported that his army would be able to capture the high ground between the two rivers, thus enabling his right-hand units to cross the Marne. On receipt of this good news, Foch and Pétain met the next day and agreed that Fifth Army (General Berthelot) should also participate in the attack on the right flank of the Marne salient, between Dormans and Prunay (close to the Fort de la Pompelle, one of the ring of forts protecting Reims to the south-east). Foch ordered that the Tenth and Fifth Army attacks be simultaneous, so that the added pressure of Sixth Army between them would create very difficult conditions for the German withdrawal.

As intelligence continued to show that the next German offensive was to be a very large assault in the Marne salient, Foch knew that the British front was correspondingly safe for the moment. He asked Haig to send four British divisions grouped as a corps command to the Vitry-le-François area, and to alert a further four divisions in case they were needed. Pétain asked Foch to request from the British 'a more complete participation in the charges that for three-and-a-half months had been weighing on [his] armies'. Pétain hoped for either three British divisions or an attack by the British on their front.[2]

On the same day as this request to Foch, 12 July, Pétain issued his instructions to the two army group commanders involved, and also his Directive #5, which was to be distributed down to divisional level. The three armies were to make a sudden assault at dawn after a short, but intense, artillery preparation, with the aim of crossing back over the Marne and putting such pressure on the flanks as to force the evacuation of the salient as far as Fère-en-Tardenois. The date and exact time were not yet decided. Obviously, they depended on the expected German offensive. In his directive, Pétain pointed to the need to take the offensive, and he wished the troops to be 'oriented' towards 'simple, audacious and rapid' methods of attack. Secrecy, surprise and speed were essential, followed by deep and far-reaching exploitation. (These words recall those of Nivelle about his 1917 offensive!) Maintaining secrecy was a question of 'honour' for unit commanders, and surprise was to be achieved by using a large proportion of smoke and gas shells just before the initial assault. Every tactical success was to be exploited as far as possible.[3] On 14 July, the day before the German assault began, Pétain instructed Tenth Army to be ready to launch its attack on the 18th, four days later.

Mangin issued his battle orders that same day, 14 July. After breaking through the German front, Tenth Army was to keep going eastwards, without stopping, towards Fère-en-Tardenois in the centre of the German salient. The tasks and the resources of each corps were clearly set out. The infantry attack, accompanied by tanks, was to be launched without any artillery preparation, progressing behind a dense rolling barrage and protected by the heavy howitzers, that suppressed the German batteries. Mangin left the two divisions of XVIII Corps and the two of I Corps to cover his flank north of the Aisne. The attacking front in the centre was held lightly by XX Corps (11 DI and DM) and XI Corps (48 and 128 DI), but additional troops were organised among the trees of the forest of Villers-Cotterêts, hidden from aerial observation by the enemy. These consisted of three infantry divisions (19, 38, 153 DI) and XXX Corps, which was to be introduced between the two corps holding the front line. Mangin also had at his disposal a reserve of eight divisions, including 1 and 2 US DI, and the cavalry of II Cavalry Corps. The 501 Tank Regiment was brought by rail, and four regiments of heavy artillery from GQG reserve put at the disposal of the Reserve Army Group, all of whose artillery would support Tenth Army. Fayolle insisted that Tenth Army concentrate solely on driving east towards Fère-en-Tardenois, and not become embroiled in subsidiary actions such as an attack on Soissons. So, as the German offensive began on the 15th, Mangin and Tenth Army knew exactly what they were to do and how to do it; they were beginning to concentrate men and materiel for the action.

On that first morning of the German offensive, however, Pétain caused a temporary hiatus, when he suspended preparations. He had been so impressed by the German crossing of the Marne that he judged it too risky to continue concentrating reserves for the counter-attack due on the 18th. He decided at 10am to retain use of his reserves for defence rather than for the planned offensive. Foch heard of this order at Fayolle's headquarters at midday, and he cancelled it immediately. No longer did Pétain have any right of appeal against Foch's decision. Pétain's order to suspend preparations affected II Cavalry Corps, which was returned to GQG control, and the artillery of 2 US DI, but movement restarted a couple of hours later for the cavalry and at nightfall for the guns. Concentration was completed during the dark over the next forty-eight hours. A severe storm made movement difficult during the night of 17/18 July, but had the beneficent side effect of blinding the enemy's aviation and covering the noise of the tanks as they assembled. On completion, Tenth Army's resources for a front of 25 kilometres amounted to four army corps (sixteen divisions), one cavalry corps of three divisions, 1,545 guns, 346 tanks and 581 aircraft[4] – a considerable achievement within a very short time span for officers and men who had been fighting without much break since 21 March.

Tenth Army was not alone in its attack. On its right, Degoutte's Sixth Army comprised three infantry corps including General Hunter Liggett's I US Corps; this made ten divisions in all, including two American. Supported by 588 guns, 147 tanks and 562 aircraft, Sixth Army was instructed to devote its left to Mangin's attack whilst using its right-hand units to join the defensive battle against the German assault. Degoutte's divisions between the Ourcq and the Marne were to cooperate with Tenth Army as Mangin's offensive progressed, but the German advance on 15 July in the pocket south of the Marne reduced Degoutte's ability to join the offensive. However, success in blocking further German progress changed the situation yet again. Pétain introduced Ninth Army between Sixth and the heavily pressed Fifth Army, and placed Degoutte's right-hand divisions under its command, thereby freeing Degoutte from the need to deal with the defensive and allowing him to concentrate on cooperating with Mangin's offensive. His orders were sent out at 11pm on 16 July.

Ninth Army was the reconstituted DAN, which had returned from Flanders and was under the command of General de Mitry. On 17 July at 8am, it moved up to Sixth Army's right, taking over the mixed-up units of III and XXXVIII corps that had been part of the latter army's defence of the Marne. De Mitry's first task was to reorganise his troops and throw the enemy back across the river, and so, when Pétain's order arrived that evening for the offensive to begin on the morrow, he was able to carry out little more than local actions. The army was ready, however, for action on the 19th with its ten divisions, of which two had required reconstituting, 644 guns, 90 light tanks and 182 aircraft.

The original planning for the counter-offensive had included Fifth Army on the eastern flank of the pocket, but it had been so battered by the German offensive that it was still involved in the defensive battle and could only offer one division (2 DIC with its fifty-four field and seventy-two heavy guns and twenty aircraft) and an artillery barrage to support the offensive. Indeed Fifth Army's II Italian Corps had suffered so many casualties that its relief by General Alexander Godley's British XXII Corps became necessary. Upon the speed of that relief would depend the ability of the rest of Fifth Army to join the offensive. As for Fourth Army east of Reims, its infantry reserves were taken to join Tenth Army.

In summary, then, Foch and Pétain had at their disposal for the attack on the German salient fifty infantry and six cavalry divisions, whereas the Imperial Crown Prince had fifty infantry divisions, but these had just suffered a defeat, the failure of MARNESCHUTZ. Of course, reserves could be brought from Crown Prince Rupprecht's forces, but Ludendorff still intended to use them in operation HAGEN. France's slight numerical advantage was increased by the excellent road and rail communications in the sector, especially given the enemy's lack of them to supply their own troops in the salient. What is particularly impressive about the line up of the Allied forces – and they were indeed Allied in character, with American, British and (soon to be relieved) Italian troops engaged, as well as the French – is not only the number of tanks and aircraft available (about 1,000 tanks and 1,701 planes), but also the speed with which the operation was mounted. Granted a counter-offensive had been planned for some time, but the exact conditions under which it would take place were changing daily between 15 and 18 July.

As well as being an inter-allied battle, Foch's July counter-offensive was notable as the first large-scale combined arms battle. As the new Renault tanks came off the production line, the assault or special artillery (as the tanks were known generically) was structured differently. From 8 May onwards, eight regiments, numbered from 501, were created gradually, a ninth formed in November 1918. Five of them were ready by 20 July. Each regiment comprised a grouping of three or four units (each of sixteen tanks) of the older and heavier Schneider or St Chamond tanks, and three battalions of light tanks. Each light battalion had three companies, each of twenty-five tanks.[5] In theory, each division had a battalion of light tanks, thus providing each of the division's three infantry regiments with a company of tanks – when all were in working order. For the Marne offensive, however, all the French Army's tanks were collected together, except for 502 RAS (Régiment d'artillerie spéciale) which was attached to Fourth Army and 503 RAS to Sixth. The remainder, 520 tanks, were allocated to Mangin's Tenth. It was intended to be a great and unpleasant surprise for the enemy.

The operation merged the defensive battle against MARNESCHUTZ-REIMS and the counter-offensive into one great action, later named the Second Battle of the Marne. The battleground resembled a huge sack with the river Marne across the bottom where the enemy had enlarged the salient by crossing the river. Tenth Army's attack into the left or west side of the salient would drive into the rear of the enemy's lines, cutting them off from the communications passing through Soissons. Sixth Army was to extend Tenth Army's front down to the river at Château Thierry. From there, Ninth Army was still defending the bottom of the salient, but its counter-offensive was to throw the Germans back across the river. Fifth Army took on the right or east side of the salient. Its task was the hardest because it had been badly mauled, and the terrain along the Ardre valley was difficult. Like its neighbour, Fifth Army had to complete the defensive battle before moving on to the offensive. East of Reims, Fourth Army's infantry was not involved, but its artillery harassed the Germans in order to support the main offensive.

Facing Tenth Army were *Ninth Army* to the north and, in the salient, *Seventh Army*. The latter had sixteen divisions, ten in the front line, but only two of them fully combat-ready. There had not been time to replace the casualties of the three days' fighting during their offensive, and the influenza epidemic was severe – over a third of a million cases in the German Armies on the whole Western Front in July.[6] Already some of *Seventh Army*'s artillery had started moving for the attack on Reims on 17 July, thus depriving the Germans of support when Mangin launched his assault. Although Ludendorff immediately ordered one division from OHL's reserve to help *Seventh Army*, his other support measures – the despatch from Flanders of two of Prince Rupprecht's attack divisions, and halting the transport of all the resources moving north for HAGEN – could not have any immediate effect.[7] Consequently Mangin alone had greatly superior forces, in both men and materiel, and the French Sixth, Ninth, Fifth and Fourth Armies added to his superiority. Yet the intelligence reports for both 16 and 17 July still gave the number of German divisions in the west as 207, with 64 (62 on the 17th) in reserve, the whereabouts of fewer than half of these latter being known.[8]

At 4.35 on the morning of 18 July, just half an hour before sunrise, the 2,100 guns of Tenth and Sixth armies opened fire simultaneously. There was no artillery preparation. Behind a thick smoke and shell barrage, eighteen first-line divisions left the protection of the forest of Villers-Cotterêts and advanced eastwards, with the tanks close on their heels dealing with centres of German resistance. East of Reims, Fourth Army had already begun its artillery barrage, and at 5am the guns along the Marne and on the Montagne de Reims joined in as well. So the whole salient from Soissons down to Château Thierry, along the Marne and up to Reims was now under fire, leaving the Imperial Crown Prince ignorant of where the infantry assault was to come. Once the early morning fog cleared, the Air Division was able to fly unmolested and report the whereabouts of the French infantry, thus enabling the tanks to be directed where they were needed. Tenth Army had achieved complete surprise, despite the Germans having learned from prisoners that the attack was planned. The war diary of Crown Prince Wilhelm's Army Group cited the 'strong' force that Foch had 'assembled with the greatest rapidity and under absolute secrecy ... About 5: 30 AM [German time is an hour later], a heavy drum fire started along the front from the Aisne to the Marne, followed immediately by the infantry attack, supported by numerous low-flying planes and tanks in masses hitherto unknown.'[9] By evening, Tenth Army's centre had advanced 9 kilometres and Sixth Army alongside 5 kilometres. Progress on the fronts of Ninth and Fifth armies had been much less, but they were both still reorganising themselves to become an attacking instead of a defending force.

Pétain went to see Mangin during the course of the day at his observation tower in the forest (see Figure 18) and congratulated him on his success. When the fevered and impatient Mangin asked for reinforcements to exploit his success, Pétain's face 'became an icy mask' and he told Mangin to make do with what he had. Fayolle noted that evening how 'very restrictive' Pétain was, but Fayolle too seemed not very optimistic about the possibilities of further advances.[10]

The offensive continued the next day to exploit the first day's successes, although the great advantage of surprise was, of course, no longer a factor. Further progress was made against the German salient, but Ninth and Fifth Armies were still not ready to take the offensive. Pétain and Foch discussed the situation that morning, and Foch put in writing his understanding of what they had agreed: the offensive must aim to destroy the enemy forces south of the Aisne and the Vesle; the greatest energy and rapidity must be deployed to take maximum advantage of the surprise; Tenth and Sixth armies must continue their attacks in the direction of Fère-en-Tardenois, in the centre of the salient. As soon as possible, Ninth Army was to push the enemy back across the Marne, and Fifth Army was to advance up the Ardre valley to Ville-en-Tardenois, 20 kilometres east of Fère. Clearly the original plan for the attacks on the flanks both to reach Fère, thereby trapping the German forces remaining in the salient, was no longer possible, given the German success against Fifth Army during MARNESCHUTZ. Although Pétain passed on Foch's instructions, he was not happy about them. He told Buat that he had countersigned them because he did not want to cause a conflict with Foch. All he could do, Pétain continued, was to make clear that such 'impracticable' orders did not come from him.[11]

Mangin's orders to his corps commanders on the evening of 19 July read simply 'Tomorrow, continuation of the attack, same objectives'. In Fifth Army, Berthelot realised that he could move onto the offensive sooner than he had thought possible by inserting the two British divisions of XXII Corps into the line and passing them through the weary Italian II Corps rather than operating a standard relief. They were to attack up the Ardre valley in the direction of Fismes, where the Ardre runs into the Vesle. This meant that the British were, in their corps commander's words, 'hustled in, in a great hurry', without their artillery, but Godley could see that 'in the circumstances' this was the right decision and 'justified by the event'.[12] As for Ninth Army, its orders were changed

Fig. 18 The monument showing General Mangin's high observatory in the Villers-Cotterêts forest during the 18 July 1918 successful counter-attack

slightly because indications pointed to a German withdrawal across the Marne. Consequently, Ninth Army should not be content with clearing the south bank of the Marne but should attempt to force a passage across onto the north bank. By dawn on 20 July, therefore, all the armies in the Reserve and Centre Army Groups were ready to attack. The Air Division put one of its brigades at the disposition of Tenth Army, and the RAF's 9th Brigade supported the Sixth. The remaining aircraft were to carry out reconnaissance missions, concentrating especially on the movement of troops using the road and rail communications into Soissons from the Meuse further north and from Crown Prince Rupprecht's Army Group in Picardy.[13]

Further progress was made that day, 20 July, with the aerial reports indicating large movements of enemy troops retreating north. Sixth Army threatened to encircle Château Thierry on both east and west, and so the Germans evacuated the town during the night of 20/21 July. This enabled Sixth Army with the Americans to cross the Marne, but German resistance was stiffening. Tenth Army and the Americans in XX Corps were held up in front of Buzancy. Mangin relieved his four most 'fatigued' divisions by four fresh ones, including two British divisions (51 and 34 Divisions) that Haig had released grudgingly. Progress slowed, however, and on 22 and 23 July no notable advances were made, although Ninth Army had managed to force its way across the Marne. If the aim of trapping German forces within the salient had not been achieved because of the disciplined German withdrawal, nonetheless the French, with their American, British and Italian divisions alongside, had taken back the initiative. Ludendorff cancelled HAGEN on the evening of 20 July, although at first Haig did not realise this.[14] Indeed, British intelligence continued to stress the large numbers of enemy troops opposite the British front, and Second Army around Ypres refused to accept that HAGEN had been cancelled.[15] By 23 July, however, Haig's growing optimism about the BEF's ability to withstand any further German assault had grown into a decision that it was time for the British to act.[16]

Lieutenant Herbert Sulzbach, an artillery officer in the 63 (Frankfurt) Field Artillery Regiment, won the Iron Cross, First Class, during the Villers-Cotterêts fighting just described. His diary entry for 21 July reveals the cost of that honour.

I don't know the word indicating the difference in degree required to describe the wholly crazy artillery fire which the French turn on for the attack in the morning. The word 'hell' expresses something tender and peaceful compared with what is starting here and now. I have really had enough experience of barrage in offensives, both our own and the enemy's. It's as though all the barrages one had ever known had been combined to rattle down on us now. At 6 a.m. I do observation for my batteries at the command post, but you can hardly keep going in this massed fire, you can hardly see anything because of the smoke, you have to keep throwing yourself flat on the ground, and you can't understand why you haven't been hit. I don't see how the French have managed *this* – first bringing our offensive of 15 July to an unsuccessful halt, and then, completely unobserved by us, preparing and carrying out an attack on a huge scale with such quantities of troops and equipment. The Americans must be very strongly represented here, especially with artillery and infantry. It is also a fact that in the War, and because of it, the French have grown hugely in strength, energy and morale; they have got tough and developed very considerable endurance.[17]

The Americans *were* represented, although not 'strongly', and the artillery they used was supplied by France.

In order to retain the initiative, Foch had already started to plan for the next stage. As early as the afternoon of 21 July he had issued a general directive, emphasising the need to prepare to act further north where the Germans might attempt to block them. While continuing the current successful operation, Foch insisted, exhausted divisions had to be pulled out of line and reconstituted, creating reserve forces behind the front. German reserve divisions had been reduced from the sixty-two estimated on 17 July, the eve of Foch's counter-offensive, to forty-two on 24 July, although more than half of these were still located behind Crown Prince Rupprecht's front in the north. A further favourable effect of the fighting for the Allies was the reduction of numbers of men in German battalions to 880, down by 100 from the 21 March figure.[18] Several practical measures were undertaken or begun. British troops were returned to Haig's command, and arrangements made to create the First US Army. On 20 July Foch asked Clemenceau to call up the 1920 class immediately, so that training could begin in October. Troops would then be ready for combat in 1919, in what Foch expected to be the 'decisive' year of the war.[19] Finally, talks began about creating a centralised transport and supply organisation at Foch's Allied headquarters, the Direction Générale des Communications et des Ravitaillements aux Armées. Such an organisation would permit greater efficiency and rapidity in moving men and materiel, as required, around the entire Western Front.[20]

The 24 July memorandum and plans

On 24 July Foch called to his headquarters the national CinCs. They were now three, Pétain, Haig and Pershing, because Foch had agreed on 10 July, before the final offensive and counter-offensive, that he would permit the creation of an independent US Army. That decision had been vindicated by the contribution of the five US divisions that had taken part in the recent fighting and the other divisions who had taken over and extended the gains. Tenth Army's postal control reported such sentiments as this: 'Opinions on the Americans continue to be more favourable ... not only are they good mates, solid men, courageous and intrepid soldiers, they are "marvellous", "splendid", "sublime". There is great enthusiasm.'[21]

This meeting was the only such occasion, before the talks about armistice conditions in October, when the national CinCs conferred formally. Foch had his chief of staff prepare a memorandum which was read out and given to Haig and Pershing in translation. It stated Foch's views plainly: it was time to move onto the attack as the series of German offensives had failed and as increasing American manpower began to tip the balance in favour of the Allies. Moreover the Allies had superiority in tanks and aircraft, and guns were arriving from the armaments factories in great numbers. Clearly Foch wished to retain the initiative, now that the Allies had gained moral ascendancy over the enemy.

He proposed three operations to free up railway communications before contemplating a more general offensive. The first, in the centre, involved the French and aimed to liberate the rail connection between Paris and eastern France in the Champagne area. In other words it was a continuation of the current fighting to clear the Germans out of the Marne salient completely and push them back behind the Aisne. The second, in the north, involved the British and the French and aimed at clearing the Paris–Amiens railway. This was the operation in Picardy that Foch had been waiting to launch ever since April and that Fayolle had been preparing while negotiating between Pétain and Foch. If rapid results were achieved in this operation, action even further north might be possible to eliminate the threat to France's coal mines in the Bruay area. The third, in the east, involved the Americans and their new army and aimed to clear the eastern end of the rail connection to Paris and remove the threat to Verdun by reducing the Saint-Mihiel salient that the Germans had held since 1914.[22] The three commanders reacted differently. Pershing was delighted. His bases were in eastern France and he had had in mind an operation against Saint-Mihiel from the start. Haig had already reached a more optimistic frame of mind, believing that the BEF could now undertake offensive operations, and he and Foch reached agreement before the meeting even started that his Fourth Army with French First Army support would carry out the Amiens plan. Pétain was less enthusiastic. He was concerned that he had lost so many resources, both human and materiel, and he asked for time to consider the possibilities.

The first operation in central France was simply a continuation of the Champagne fighting currently underway, and the meeting of the CinCs did not interrupt the operations in the Marne pocket. As they conferred on 24 July, Sixth Army continued to follow *Seventh Army*'s withdrawal, and an attack the next day coordinated between Sixth and Tenth Armies freed Oulchy-le-Château and Oulchy-la-Ville, enabling the French to fire along the Ourcq valley in enfilade. After the next German staged withdrawal, these two armies and Fifth Army also advanced until they all bumped up against the German line running through Fère and Ville-en-Tardenois. Ludendorff had accepted the German Crown Prince's arguments that they had to evacuate the pocket and get behind the Aisne/Vesle river barriers, but only after withdrawing as much materiel as possible. This meant that the German resistance stiffened considerably, until each stage of the withdrawal was complete. By 3 August the enemy was solidly established on a shorter front behind a strong water line, although Tenth Army had achieved one more success when it broke through the German lines on 1 August and recaptured Grand-Rozoy. The principal objective had been won: the railway line between Paris and Nancy through Château Thierry and Epernay was now free from the threat of German guns.

At 110,000 over nineteen days, German casualties were heavy and largely irreplaceable. OHL had committed seventy-three divisions, thirteen of which had been transferred from Crown Prince Rupprecht's forces, hence putting an end to HAGEN.[23] French intelligence estimated the number of German reserve divisions at only fifty on 30 July, although this figure crept back upwards to the sixties during the first fortnight in August.[24] Between 15 and 31 July, the five French armies in the attack (Fourth, Fifth, Sixth and Tenth; Ninth Army was withdrawn on 24 July) captured 14,728 German prisoners, with over 12,000 more captured by the Americans, British and Italians. Between 15 July and 5 August, the French armies with their Allied contingents captured 612 guns, 221 mortars and 3,330 machine guns, also liberating 181 and 393 of their own guns and machine guns respectively.[25] Fourth Army to the east of Reims had been supporting the main attacking forces, but still suffered 9,087 casualties (6,842 killed or disappeared) between 16 July and 5 August. The total figures for Fifth, Sixth, Ninth and Tenth Armies for the same period are 95,165 (24,899 killed or disappeared).[26]

Pétain was worried about losses in tanks and reduced stocks of shells but, above all, about the human losses. He presented Foch with a situation report on the French Army on 31 July. Despite the reinforcements he had received, his deficit had grown to 120,000 men. Since there were insufficient in the depots to make this good, Pétain drew the obvious conclusion that France was 'at the very end' of its effort. He had not one single 'fresh' division in reserve, and divisions were remaining in sector for long periods. His armies were losing the US divisions to Pershing for the US First Army and Saint-Mihiel; he was to supply four divisions to Debeney for the French First Army in Picardy. Pétain believed the situation so serious that he asked Foch to reconsider the French contribution to the forthcoming American and British operations. Yet Foch was concerned to keep up numbers in the French Army. When he had asked Clemenceau to call up the 1920 class, he ended his letter: 'The stronger we are, the sooner we shall be victorious, the better we shall be heard.'[27]

Therefore, Foch pressed on with the second of his proposed operations. He urged Haig to advance the start date of the Amiens attack by two days, from 10 to 8 August, to enable the French in Champagne to rest and re-group before attempting to cross the Vesle and the Aisne. On the evening of 6 August, Maistre and Fayolle were instructed to place their armies on the defensive, although Mangin was still, typically, full of fight. The approach to his new headquarters was lined by captured guns.[28] So the Germans were given a respite of only two days between the end of operations in Champagne and the start of operations in Picardy. Foch had returned the British XXII Corps to Haig's command so that the British could make the earlier start.

Planning to free the Paris–Amiens railway had fallen into abeyance because of the three German offensives against the French front in May, June and July. Yet Haig too understood the importance of pushing the enemy away from Amiens, and so the groundwork had already been done for the operation before Foch listed it as one of the Allies' objectives in his 24 July memorandum. After their meeting that day, Haig wrote in his diary that they had agreed 'to proceed with the operations east of Amiens *as soon as possible*. Rawlinson and Debeney are meeting today, if necessary to coordinate their plans.' As the Army Group commander in the sector, Fayolle leaned more to Foch's ideas about the offensive than to Pétain's caution. Picardy had been quiet since the two German offensives in March and April, and so the omens were good for an attack to follow speedily the expulsion of the enemy from the Marne salient.

More good omens had appeared. The Australian Corps had undertaken a minor operation on 4 July to straighten out their line in front of Hamel village, and they had reported low morale among the German defenders and poor defences. They made an overwhelming attack, infantry, artillery and tanks all liaising closely, killed or wounded a thousand of the enemy, and took another thousand prisoner, at relatively little cost to themselves. The medical condition of these prisoners showed how hard the influenza epidemic had hit. Other local operations carried out by the French were also successful, and so confirmed weaker German defences. First Army attacked west of Avre on 23 July, for example, and captured three villages, almost 2,000 prisoners and some guns.[29] However, these local operations caused bad feeling between Debeney and Rawlinson, the two army commanders. Rawlinson was highly critical: he heard that Debeney was 'in a great fright', and he thought it 'very unsatisfactory to have a man like Debeney to work with'. He was 'not altogether satisfied' that Debeney was 'doing things properly' in preparing the successful 23 July attack, but admitted that First Army 'seem to have done very well and my Tanks helped them considerably'.[30] But Rawlinson seems to be making no allowance for what First Army had done in March/April, nor for the fact that First Army's advances after 18 July were the result of following up the German withdrawal after the French counter-offensive, for which all Debeney's reserves had been removed. Furthermore, Rawlinson was probably remembering the frustrations of cooperating with the French during the last offensive he had commanded in 1916, which was in the same area, the Somme, with the French alongside.

The general outlines of the Amiens/Montdidier operation were set out when Haig and Foch met the two army commanders, their chiefs of staff and General J.P. Du Cane, Foch's British liaison officer, on 2 August. Debeney and Rawlinson had already agreed the boundaries between the two armies, although the latter was unhappy at the prospect of the French and British fighting alongside each other. He would have preferred the French to pinch out the German salient by attacking northwards from Montdidier, but Foch insisted that two separate attacks were not strong enough, and he wished to combine their strength. Rawlinson 'strongly deprecated the employment of two armies side-by-side', but admitted that Foch had the right, as generalissimo, to insist.[31] Also Foch had placed First Army under Haig's command for the operation.[32] This decision enabled Foch to flatter Haig – he sent him a personal letter via his chief of staff with the news – and (perhaps) removed Debeney from Pétain's control. There would be no countermanding of preparations as had happened with Mangin and Tenth Army on 15 July. Pétain was not invited to the meeting when Haig and Foch discussed the operation and disposition of the First Army.[33] Indeed, GQG knew little of what was being planned.

First Army's forces throughout July had been merely its three organic corps (IX, X and XXXI Corps), its reserve divisions having been taken for the Marne defensive then offensive operations. By 26 July Pétain had supplied four more divisions for the Amiens/Montdidier operation and on 31 July, XXXVI Corps was transferred to Debeney's command because it was already deployed behind First Army's new front, although it remained in reserve. On 8 August itself, II Colonial Corps was also put under Debeney's command. Rawlinson's Fourth Army was to attack along both banks of the Somme on an 18-kilometre front from the Ancre south to the river Luce, a muddy tributary of the Avre, the Australian and Canadian Corps spearheading the attack with their large, rested divisions. First Army extended the attack for 34 kilometres south from the Luce with, from north to south, the three divisions of XXXI Corps, the two divisions of IX Corps, the three divisions of X Corps, and the two divisions of XXXV Corps. There were no reserves behind the two central corps, but the two outer corps carrying out the principal action had two and one divisions behind them respectively. Considerable artillery forces compensated for the reduced infantry resources. Supporting the infantry were approximately 1,624 guns, 90 light tanks and over 1,000 aircraft, including the 600 of the Air Division, which were put under First Army command.

On First Army's right, General Humbert, whose Third Army had borne the brunt of the fourth German offensive on the Matz, was ready by 10 August to extend the action with his two corps in the general direction of the north-east as soon as the First Army's progress made this possible. (At GQG the staff thought that Foch was 'exaggerating' and aiming too far.[34]) On First Army's left were the Canadians. The French were fortunate here, in that the right-hand Canadian unit was General Raymond Brutinel's Independent Canadian Force of armoured cars with machine guns – the two Canadian Motor Machine Gun Brigades. Brutinel was a Frenchman who had emigrated to Canada, but was permitted to serve with the Canadians rather than returning to join the French Army. Having made his fortune in Canada, he had offered to raise privately a unit of motorised machine guns.[35] Naturally he spoke both French and English and was able to liaise directly with the left-hand French division, 42 DI commanded by General Deville. Facing First Army was the point of junction between two German armies, *Second* and *Eighteenth*, with a total of thirty divisions, of which ten were in reserve, but the whereabouts of only six of them were known to the Allies. However, the poor road and rail communications into the Montdidier salient were well known, hence it would be impossible for the Germans to bring up large numbers of reserves with great rapidity. The retreat from the Marne had pulled the Germans back from the Montdidier salient as well, so that there only remained some German outposts west of the Avre.

On 6 August Haig informed his two army commanders that the attack would begin on the 8th, and on 7 August Rawlinson and Debeney agreed the hour of 4.20am. At that time the British Fourth Army would begin without warning the rolling barrage for the infantry and the tanks; First Army's left corps, XXXI, would begin at 5.05am, hoping that the slightly later start would maintain the surprise. His XXXV Corps on the southern flank was to join in on the second day, depending upon results, and Fayolle ordered Third Army to prepare to attack on the third day, 10 August. Sequencing the attacks would keep the enemy off balance. Fayolle was aiming already at a much wider extension of the battle, to capture not only the whole Montdidier area but also the hilly country (called 'little Switzerland') further east, including the high ground around Boulogne la Grasse, about 8 kilometres east-south-east of Montdidier. The Air Division was to carry out day and night bombing on targets such as stations and other assembly points, and on the 8th itself to destroy enemy balloons. Only two battalions of light tanks were available after the losses on the Marne.[36]

The later start of XXXI Corps obviously did surprise the enemy who was already dealing with the advance of the Canadian Corps, and the French were able to make good progress. Next IX Corps came into action at 8.20am, crossing the Avre despite a strong reaction from German machine guns. After a short pause, both corps continued their progression in the afternoon. By the end of the day, so much ground had been gained that the operation's main objective, freeing the Amiens–Paris railway, had been achieved. If the Canadians had advanced 10 kilometres, 2 more than the French alongside, nevertheless, by the evening of 9 August, First Army had captured 7,000 prisoners. A few days later, on 11 August, the armaments minister, Loucheur, was able to inform Foch that output from the coalmines in Bruay had returned to pre-April offensive levels. Both objectives of Foch's plan for the northern offensive were achieved.[37]

The gains made on 8 August were indeed greater than had been hoped. Haig went to see Debeney that afternoon, and found him 'pleased with himself' at the day's success, despite three battalions of colonial infantry having 'bolted' before a German machine gun. Haig's claim in the amended version of his diary – that he found First Army's commander 'much distressed and almost in tears' because of it – is ungenerous to say the least. Although it had become fixed in British minds that France's colonial infantry was unreliable, there is no sign in the war diary account of 15 DIC of IX Corps (the only colonial infantry in First Army) that it had failed to carry out orders. Rather, it had carried them out successfully. The corps was withdrawn at the end of the second day, having achieved all its objectives.[38]

Debeney's orders for his right-flank corps to attack on 9 August were already issued. For IX and XXXI Corps, the orders were to press on.

Foch was delighted with the progress and sent two messages to Debeney on 9 August to be sure to keep going, 'with drums beating', and capture Roye, so that not only could Third Army join the offensive as planned, but Tenth Army as well. Foch's extravagant language was probably the result of his new status. On 5 August Clemenceau had read out to him the decree making him a marshal of France, the Third Republic's second such honour, Joffre's being the first. By evening on the 9th, First Army encircled Montdidier and its fall became a matter of hours. During the night of 9/10 August *Eighteenth Army* withdrew to the north of Roye.

That evening Fayolle decided that conditions were good enough to launch the planned Third Army offensive next day. Also he made provision for its extension, should the Germans decide to retreat behind the Canal du Nord instead of resisting the French action. In this eventuality Fayolle ordered Third Army's right-hand corps and Tenth Army's left-hand corps to make a joint advance to push the enemy back to the Oise so as to be able to capture from the rear the high ground between Noyon and Chauny. Fayolle also ordered Mangin's Tenth Army to prepare an offensive using the remainder of his army between the Oise and the Aisne. The aim of this latter operation was to push the enemy back behind the Ailette as well as the Oise and, by capturing the high ground between the two rivers, force him to abandon his new defence lines behind the Aisne and the Vesle. Fayolle allocated the Air Division to Humbert, who ordered his two corps (XXXIV and XV) to attack at 4.20 next morning.

On the third day of the offensive, 10 August, both First and Third Armies attacked. First Army's X and XXXV Corps encircled Montdidier and captured the town, which had been completely destroyed, but by the afternoon were held up in the old 1916 Somme defences. On the left the progress of XXXI Corps was also halted by midday. Third Army repeated the British tactic of 8 August: an infantry attack at 4.20am with no prior artillery preparation. It made a 12-kilometre advance, and captured 2–3,000 prisoners.[39] By evening the army's left rested on Boulogne-la-Grasse in liaison with First Army, and its right on Mareuil and Elincourt. Foch was delighted, of course, and tried to make Haig bring in his own Third Army with the aim of reaching Bapaume and Péronne on the Somme. Foch proposed that Fourth British and First Armies should now make for the Somme between Péronne and Ham, and Haig's orders for the next day reflected Foch's wishes. At GQG the day's events came as 'superb news'. Barescut thought that they had won the 'finest victory since the first Battle of the Marne' and that the Germans 'in despair' would have to get behind the Somme or even the Hindenburg Line. He went on leave the next day since he no longer had any work to do at GQG: 'when one is successful, everything is easy'.[40]

It was less easy for the troops on the ground. Not only were the British and French attackers becoming very tired, but the Germans had scrambled a response and were making a determined stand, putting their machine guns to good use. The Allies had made such good progress that their own gunners no longer knew with certainty where the German batteries were located, hence were unable to suppress enemy fire as efficiently as they had on 8 August. The gains made by First and Third Armies on 11 August were small. Nevertheless their success in pushing back the German rearguards meant that the west flank of the enemy's positions behind the Aisne and Vesle were becoming uncovered, so it was time for Tenth Army to come into action. Mangin had requested twenty-nine divisions in order to complete his army's mission – 'megalomania', Fayolle called it – and told his troops: 'No more topographical objectives, but *directions* . . . it is time to shake off the mud of the trenches'.[41] Fayolle ordered the transfer of XVIII Corps from Third Army's right to become the left flank of the Tenth, while the rest of Tenth Army was to echelon its forces along a north–south axis linking up with the French positions around Soissons. The army would then be in a position to attack eastwards into German defence lines. Mangin responded that he would be ready by 15 August.

Foch intervened once more. It was vital, he wrote, to take advantage of the deep advances made by the First and British Fourth Armies by extending the battle on the flanks. Thus he approved Tenth Army's plan, but he had less success with the British. The commander of the Canadian Corps had convinced Rawlinson, who then convinced Haig, that the German defences now facing them were too strong simply to press on to the Somme river line as Foch wanted and as had been planned for the 15th, the same date as Mangin's moves. After a frosty meeting, during which Haig claimed to have told Foch 'quite straightly' that he, Haig, was responsible to his government for the British troops under his command, and not the generalissimo, Foch accepted that the British Third Army would attack in its turn, further north towards Bapaume.[42] He replied equally clearly ['nettement'] that he expected the British Third Army's attack to begin very soon, thereby rendering Fourth Army's task in reaching the line of the Somme easier.[43] Each Third Army, British and French, now had the task of extending the battle on both flanks.

First Army's role now changed. Instead of its forming part of a Franco-British push, Foch returned command of its forces to Fayolle in Reserve Army Group so that the remaining operations linked First and Third with Mangin's Tenth Army (in Centre Army Group). In addition, Foch's decision to permit the formation of an independent American army meant that First Army lost guns to equip it. Fayolle was instructed to send forty-five batteries of field and thirty batteries of heavy artillery as well as six groups of extra heavies to the Woëvre in eastern France where the First US Army was forming.[44]

Foch intended now that the three French armies should aim to clear the entire Noyon–Lassigny region, preparing ultimately to push on to the Roye–Chauny–Soissons area. He urged, again, that no time be wasted and pressed Pétain and Haig to be ready for concerted action on 20 August. After a series of small, local actions which enabled Tenth Army to advance its artillery into position on high ground, the general attack began at 7.20am on 20 August. By evening Tenth Army had advanced 4 kilometres, taken 8,000 prisoners and captured 100 guns. The Imperial Crown Prince's *Ninth Army* was expecting to be attacked, but the high number of prisoners indicates a half-hearted resistance. Ludendorff ordered *Ninth Army* to pull its right behind the Oise during the night 20/21 August, and the following night its centre behind the Ailette. Tenth Army continued its advance over the next three days, reaching the banks of these two rivers and enabling Third Army to reach Lassigny. With the British Third Army (pressed by Haig in the face of some resistance from its commander, General Byng) reaching the outskirts of Bapaume, the area between the Oise and the Somme became easier for First Army and British Fourth Army and they continued their attacks towards Chaulnes and Roye. By the end of the month Bapaume, Combles, Roye, Noyon and Péronne were in Allied hands and the German *Second* and *Eighteenth Armies* had been pushed back to the Hindenburg Line. Further east, *Ninth Army* was hanging on to the junction north-east of Soissons, where the north–south section of the Hindenburg Line joined the west–east section. However, Tenth Army had got across the Chauny–Soissons road in places and so was well placed to attack the Hindenburg Line itself. It had been a stunning success, and Ludendorff decided to pull all his armies back behind the Hindenburg Line, which freed Mont Kemmel and ensured the safety of the northern coalmines. Therefore, all Foch's aims for the northern operation outlined in his 24 July memorandum had been achieved.

The three French armies involved between 8 and 30 August in what was named the Third Battle of Picardy captured 633 German officers, 30,820 other ranks, and 890 guns. French intelligence estimates of German reserves showed that the sixty-eight German divisions identified on 10 August had been reduced by the 30th to forty-four. The presence of an Austrian division in the Verdun region, whose arrival was confirmed on 29 August, gave further evidence of the decline in German strength. The cost of the Allied victory for those three armies was over 85,000 casualties, but a significant proportion of these (80 per cent) were (merely) wounded. The reason for the higher proportion of wounded probably lies in the fact that the Germans were using their machine guns to defend their positions because the Allied counter-battery work had suppressed the German guns so efficiently. A machine-gun bullet caused a less lethal wound than a shell splinter. The remaining French armies also captured some German prisoners and guns and suffered 14,310 casualties.[45]

As for the French First Army, whose performance is given such little credit in the English-language historiography, between 15 July and 31 August it captured 13,236 prisoners (including 308 officers), 319 guns, 237 *Minenwerfer*, 2,613 machine guns and a mass of munitions and vehicles. Its casualties in August alone were 1,023 killed and 5,960 wounded. Indeed, the French opinion of the British Fourth Army's performance was not uncritical. The head of the French military mission at GHQ sent in a report on 13 August on British operations on the Somme. He concluded that, as early as 9 August, the British high command had been 'haunted' by the fear of creating a salient with insufficient protection on its left, as had happened at Cambrai the previous year. By the 10th, the high command had decided to limit the execution of the orders to attack that it issued in conformity with Foch's instructions. Rawlinson in particular seemed to lack the same ardour for operations beyond the original plans, being very slow to exploit new opportunities.[46]

First Army's postal censors noted that the fatigue and slowing advance had caused a slight diminution in 'ardour' but 'morale remains overall very good'.[47] A French stretcher-bearer asked himself in his diary on 17 August what the troops thought of the current operations. They approved, he answered himself:

Morale is intact. Despite the physical misery (our regiments, who have been in line for two months, are covered in fleas) and legitimate impatience to take some leave, the *poilus* are chanting victory. There's good reason to: 76,000 prisoners and 1700 guns since 18 July. We had never known such a result. And the coming days still have some happy surprises for us![48]

Even before the Picardy battle began and as the Champagne battle continued, Foch began preparing for the third element listed in his 24 July memorandum, the Saint-Mihiel operation. After acceding on 10 July to Pershing's request for an autonomous army, Foch contemplated giving the Americans the task of clearing the Paris–Avricourt railway, by reducing the Saint-Mihiel salient which jutted across the Meuse below Verdun. Avricourt was the eastern limit of the French railway system after losing part of Lorraine to the German *Reich* in the

Fig. 19 Foch, as supreme commander, holding a French and a British
soldier in his hands, *Le Rire Rouge*, 24 August 1918
'For victory, what was needed? A single chief and two hands which
are not unaware of each other' [and the right hand knowing what the left
hand is doing].

post Franco-Prussian War settlement. On 4 August Foch saw Pershing and asked him to constitute his army in the Saint-Mihiel sector, despite the fact that all his divisions with experience of combat were in the Aisne sector, where it had been the original intention to base it. The same day he saw Pétain and his chief of staff, and urged on Pétain the need to hasten the American preparations so that the operation could be launched before the end of the month, because the weather would be too bad after mid September. The Woëvre plain, north-east of the salient, is very marshy once autumn rains begin. According to Buat, both Foch and Pétain would have preferred that the Americans continue to operate between the Oise and Aisne rivers, but this would have been a 'very risky' operation for an army that was not yet really an army. Saint-Mihiel, however, could safely be left to them since they knew the terrain and had been studying such an operation ever since the previous year.[49]

Pershing retrieved his American divisions from the French sector where they were no longer needed and, to Haig's disgust, most but not all of his divisions serving with the BEF. Next he put in to GQG a long list of requirement for guns, tanks and aviation. On 16 August Foch approved Pétain's plan for a significant operation involving fourteen American and ten French divisions. The Champagne and Somme successes justified a large-scale affair. By the end of the month, however, Foch's views had changed. Now he had a better idea of what the fighting in the Champagne and in Picardy had achieved. The Germans had been pushed back to their main line of defence, the various portions of the *Hindenburgstellung*, and it was now time to undertake the larger general offensive that he had foreshadowed in his 24 July memorandum. French railway communications had been freed, and the line interdicted at Saint-Mihiel mattered less, now that the line through the Champagne from Paris to Nancy was clear. Converging attacks towards the Meuse at Mézières would be a much more profitable operation, because the principal German railway rocade, the one that carried most supplies to the armies in northern France and Belgium, could be attacked there. The capture of Mézières, where there was only a narrow corridor along the river valley with the high ground of the Ardennes to the north, would interrupt German supply lines and even allow the Allies to shell the second rocade that was within range at this point. Accordingly, Foch wrote a note to Pershing on 30 August explaining all this, and asking him to reduce the scope of Saint-Mihiel in favour of a joint Franco-American operation in the Argonne and Champagne, west of the Meuse.

Pershing was furious. He assumed that the French were trying to prevent him from winning a purely American victory. Although nearly half the units and virtually all the armaments were French, it was indeed an American operation, under US First Army command. He was 'mad as a hornet', Pershing's liaison officer with Foch wrote in his diary. With Pétain's help, a compromise was reached on 2 September. Saint-Mihiel was to be reduced and the Americans would prepare to join Fourth and Fifth Armies in what the Americans later called the Meuse–Argonne campaign.[50] It was agreed that a smaller attack, in both effectives and time, would begin against Saint-Mihiel on 10 September, with the reduced aim of cutting the salient along its base line and reaching Vigneulles in the centre, well short of the main German defence position. Then a larger force of 12–14 US divisions would be transferred north for joint action with Fourth Army to begin between 20 and 25 September.

The final Saint-Mihiel plan involved eight US and four French divisions. On the north flank of the salient two US divisions were to attack, with support from a secondary attack by 15 DIC out of Les Eparges, where there had been bloody fighting in 1915. It is noteworthy that 15 DIC was the unit which Haig had reported bolting on 8 August in the Amiens/Montdidier attack, but the division was now back in line after being rested and undergoing training between 10 August and 5 September. The principal attack was against the south face of the salient, where all the units were American. On the 'nose' of the salient and connecting the two flank attacks, II Colonial Corps had all three of its divisions in the front line (2 DCP, 26 and 39 DI). This corps was part of Second Army in the Verdun sector, under the command of General Hirschauer, but placed under Pershing's command for the operation. Hirschauer was annoyed at being deprived of the action, but Pétain had explained that his role was to 'organise' the 'affair' and then 'pass it over' to Pershing at the right time.[51]

It was not possible to start on the planned date of 10 September, and Pétain complained to Foch that the Americans were talking too much, so that secrecy could not be maintained. Nevertheless, after a four-hour artillery preparation on 12 September, the southern principal attack began at 5am and had reached Thiaucourt by the afternoon, as the Germans did not put up much resistance. They had known that the attack was coming, and had already decided to withdraw from the salient. The secondary attack began at 8am with the French division (15 DIC) in the centre, and it too made good progress, capturing Les Eparges, which it occupied until 15 October – three years after the fruitless attacks of 1915. The orders of II Colonial Corps were to hold down any enemy reserves and to accompany the American troops, only attacking in earnest if the latter did advance. Consequently the French took ground north of Saint-Mihiel village and the village of Apremont. More progress was made next day, and the two arms of the pincer joined up, creating by

4pm a continuous line across the salient, through Vigneulles, Haudmont to the Meuse hills. Meanwhile, II Colonial Corps cleared Saint-Mihiel of remaining German troops and advanced in turn to Vigneulles. This completed the objectives of the operation. During the two weeks 7–21 September, when the only action was the Saint-Mihiel operation, Second Army captured 3,572 prisoners for a loss of 773 casualties of whom 165 were killed or had disappeared.[52] It was now time to turn to preparation of the Meuse–Argonne operation.

Pershing was delighted with the results and praised Foch's energy. He showed Foch and Weygand around the area on 20 September: '[Foch] seemed in excellent spirits and most delighted with the operation.'[53] Foch believed, however, that more could have been done to capture German men and materiel; Hirschauer noted that it was necessary to follow up the retreating Germans 'boldly'. Yet this was another boost to Allied morale. The French contribution had been more than the four infantry divisions: over 3,000 guns (some manned by French gunners, and two corps artillery staffs provided because the Americans only had one trained staff);[54] 267 French tanks (almost half manned by French crews); the entire Air Division (600 aircraft); and the British bombing force commanded by General Trenchard. All the motor transport and all the shells that the Americans used came from the French.

The French Army's report on morale noted how the continued Allied successes were maintaining confidence among the troops. Those in Second Army who had taken part in the Saint-Mihiel offensive under American command commented how the new army had carried out a test run that was a master stroke. Two points in particular had struck the Second Army troops: the ease of their advance with high numbers of prisoners captured, and the relatively low number of casualties. They noted also the superiority of French aviation.[55] The tactic of massing resources in the Air Division, thereby enabling a large concentration at a single point very quickly, was proving successful. The Air Division's 600 aircraft joined American, Belgian, Italian and Portuguese aircraft for a total of 1,481, under the command of US General William ('Billy') Mitchell.[56] It must be said, however, that by this date, German losses in aircraft and fighter pilots were very high; they lost over a quarter of their combat aircraft between March and November 1918. Also, Germany was running out of fuel: in September a maximum per diem allowance of 250 litres for an observation squadron and 150 litres for pursuit and attack squadrons reduced their effectiveness.[57]

Foch's change of plan about Saint-Mihiel that had so annoyed Pershing was caused by the realisation that the large 'general offensive' that he had foreshadowed in his 24 July memorandum was perhaps possible, since the Allied railway communications had been freed before the onset of bad weather. Having regained control of his own communications, Foch intended to attack the enemy's. Whilst maintaining the pressure by extending the battlefront and allowing the enemy no rest, Foch wanted the Allied armies to move up to the Hindenburg Line behind which Ludendorff hoped to stand. With all the terrain regained in the two salients that the earlier German offensives had created, the Allies now had a shorter line to hold. As a consequence, Pétain was able to withdraw Third and Sixth Armies, recovering their artillery and aviation resources and allowing divisions to be rested before the general offensive. This left First and Tenth Armies in Fayolle's Reserve Army Group, Fourth and Fifth Armies in Maistre's Central Army Group with the small forces of Second Army holding Verdun. Castelnau's Eastern Army Group covered the entire eastern frontier with only the smaller Seventh and Eighth Armies.

The general offensive: 'tout le monde à la bataille'

A comparison of Foch's directive for future operations of 3 September with Pétain's memorandum of the 8th on the 'Battle of 1919' illustrates clearly the differences between the former as the Allied CinC and the latter, the French CinC.[58] Foch is brief: while the British continue the pressure in the north and the French in the centre, the US Army will free the Paris–Avricourt railway (that is, the Saint-Mihiel salient) no later than 10 September, and then begin an offensive 'as strong and as violent as possible' in the direction of Mézières, covered by French Fourth Army on its left. Foch then lists the intermediate stages of the progress towards Mézières in the general offensive which was to begin around 20–25 September. This is short, precise and to the point. Pétain's memorandum five days later fills thirty-five printed pages, and must have taken his staff weeks to prepare. It contains a 'study' of the 'decisive' battle of 1919, consisting of a 'preliminary offensive' along a 90-kilometre front followed by a 'decisive offensive' on a 30-kilometre front, together with six long annexes listing the current and anticipated resources in manpower, guns, aircraft, tanks and tactics. It proposes a continuation of the previous four years of fighting, namely attrition of the enemy forces before launching the decisive attack. It talks of the 'intellectual preparation' of the high command, 'intensive training' for the troops, 'completion of artillery and aviation programmes', and greater development of tanks, but fails to mention where or when the 1919 battles were to take place. In fact, it reads like a staff college paper. Pétain admits that in 1919 the enemy will 'no doubt be established behind a strongly fortified front, abundantly supplied with anti-tank defences, and covered by a deep outpost zone or water lines'. The document is Pétain at his careful and organised best, but that sentence reveals a man prepared to allow the Germans to establish the strong defensive position he describes, whereas Foch intended to strike while they were weak, and to strike at the precise point where they were weakest. Had Pétain been in supreme command, no armistice could have been signed in 1918, let alone at Rethondes on 11 November.

The strategic position was excellent for the launch of Foch's general offensive. Imminent collapses in Macedonia and the Middle East, reports of Austria-Hungary's peace note and civilian disorder in Germany, intelligence reports that Germany's total of divisions on the Western Front had dropped below 200 for the first time, all bolstered Foch's intention to keep the pressure on firmly.[59] His thinking during August and September had centred on the idea that extending the battle-front laterally, as he had insisted with Debeney and Haig, should have the aim of converging, not excentric, attacks. Foch knew that the weakest point in the German rail network supplying the armies in France and Belgium lay in the narrow corridor between the high ground of the Argonne and the Ardennes where the river Meuse runs west and then turns north into Belgium. Through the town of Mézières on the Meuse ran the busiest German supply line. Breaking through the Hindenburg Line and capturing Mézières would trap the enemy between the North Sea and the Meuse, and cut off the troops in Lorraine and the Vosges. It would force him to use the inadequate roads through the hilly and inhospitable Ardennes to evacuate his armies.

Foch followed his 3 September directive with more notes and visits to the three national commanders to ensure that his intentions were understood. Every note that flowed from his GQGA contained the word 'speed' or 'without delay', or something similar. A Belgian operation was added to the others, with the aim of capturing Bruges and cutting off the German armies from the sea, and then the area north of the river Lys as far as the Dutch border. Foch envisaged a tri-national force to incorporate the Belgians, who were eager to engage in liberating their country. He urged First Army to support the British, and Tenth Army to support the central French armies, but it was from the Franco-American mass on the right that he expected the greatest results. On 23 September Foch settled the dates of the series of attacks: the Franco-American in the Meuse–Argonne would begin on the 26th; then the next day the British First and Third Armies would set off for Cambrai; on the 28th it was the turn of the Flanders Army Group under the nominal command of King Albert, with General Degoutte as his French chief of staff directing operations; finally, on the 29th, the fourth successive day, the Fourth

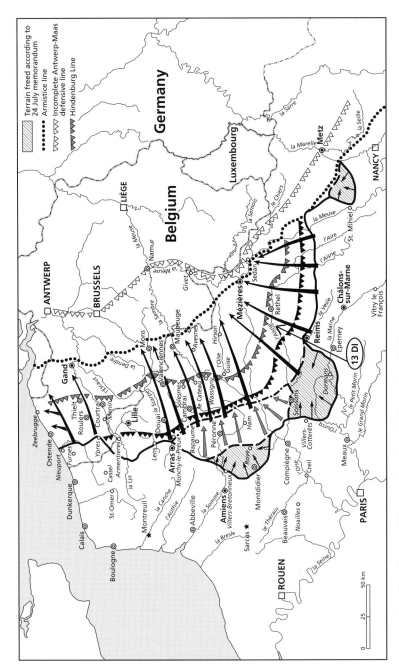

13. The Battle of France, 24 July–11 November 1918

Terrain freed according to 24 July memorandum
Armistice line
Incomplete Antwerp-Maas defensive line
Hindenburg Line

Germany

Luxembourg

Belgium

ANTWERP

BRUSSELS

LIÈGE

Namur

Metz

NANCY

la Sarre

la Seille

la Marelle

St. Mihiel

la Meuse

l'Aire

l'Aisne

Sedan

Mézières

Rethel

Reims

Châlons-sur-Marne

Vitry le François

Epernay

la Marne

la Vesle

13 DI

Dormans

le Petit Morin

le Grand Morin

l'Ourcq

Soissons

Villers-Cotterêts

Meaux

Creil

Compiègne

PARIS

Beauvais

Noailles

le Thérain

Montdidier

Royel

Amiens

Villers-Bretonneux

Sarcus

la Bresle

la Seine

ROUEN

la Somme

Abbeville

Montreuil

la Canche

l'Authie

Arras

Monchy-le-Preux

Lens

Douai

la Scarpe

Cambrai

Bapaume

Péronne

Ham

l'Oise

Guise

Wassigny

le Cateau

Solesmes

Valenciennes

la sambre

Maubeuge

Avesnes

Hirson

Mons

la Dendre

Lille

Armentières

la Lys

Menin

Courtrai

Roulers

Thielt

Gand

l'Escaut

l'Yser

Ypres

Furnes

Nieuport

Ostende

Zeebrugge

Dunkerque

Cassel

St-Omer

Calais

Boulogne

0   25   50 km

338

British and First French would set off together, as on 8 August, towards Busigny. The Germans did not know what to expect. With the Allies continuing to push towards the Hindenburg Line and the Saint-Mihiel operation occurring during the days of preparation, it was impossible for Ludendorff to know where the next blow was to fall.

It fell at 5.25 in the morning of 26 September. General Gouraud's Fourth Army, in liaison with the US First Army, began their assault between the river Suippe and the western edge of the Argonne. Since Foch hoped that the double-strength US divisions in this right-hand attack would make the most progress, Pétain had taken resources from Fayolle's Reserve Army Group to strengthen Fourth Army. Therefore Gouraud had significant resources for the battle: in the west the four infantry divisions of IV Corps anchored the army's left flank, a further six corps (II, IX, XI, XIV, XXI and XXXVIII each increased to three or four divisions) comprised the attacking force of twenty-seven divisions. In addition, Gouraud had at his disposal the three divisions of I Cavalry Corps, and four more infantry divisions in reserve, including the 2 US Division and, eventually, 36 US Division. To support these infantry resources Gouraud had asked for forty-eight regiments of field artillery (75mm guns), seventy-two groups of the most useful calibre of heavy artillery (155mm short guns), as well as trench artillery. His demands were considered excessive, given the need for speed and secrecy in assembling men and materiel, and General Maistre, his Central Army Group commander, believed that the resources already supplied were adequate.[60] These amounted to 2,766 guns in all, of which 1,326, or almost half, were heavies. Available on the opening day of the attack were 51 heavy Schneider tanks and 225 light Renault tanks, with another 90 light and 234 St Chamond heavy tanks in reserve. In addition, Gouraud had his army's aviation resources with a fighter group and observer squadrons for directing the heavy artillery fire.[61] Given this weight of fire, Fourth Army made good progress on the first day as the German *First* and *Third Armies* abandoned their forward positions. It soon became clear, however, that the enemy intended to hold its main defensive line, and progress slowed. Nevertheless the strongpoints of the Main de Massiges, the Buttes du Mesnil/Tahure, Souain and Navarin – where French armies had attacked repeatedly in 1915 – were captured on the first day, and the next day the centre made most progress, reaching the Py river at Sommepy.

Under Pétain's overall control, Fourth Army's role was to cover the US First Army. Pétain had strengthened the Americans with two French corps, XVII Corps (18 DI and 10 and 15 DIC), and II Colonial Corps, now containing 2 DCP, 39 DI and US 79 Division. The US First Army's artillery was all French and some of the batteries were served by French gunners; in addition 189 Renault tanks (47 of them manned by French crews) supported the attack. The Americans had struggled to transport their forces from Saint-Mihiel in time, but set off, as planned, five minutes after the French.

By the end of the second day the Americans had stalled and by the end of the month had halted, less because of the enemy's resistance than because of the Americans' 'difficulties in moving and supplying their troops', as Pétain reported to Foch. Foch's solution was to withdraw some American divisions from the overcrowded tangle of the Argonne, and place them in Second Army. This was General Hirschauer's army, holding the passive Verdun sector. Placing Second Army between Fourth and US First Armies would extend the latter's front of attack eastwards to the line of the Meuse. Pershing was outraged at this further attempt, as he saw it, to take away American divisions from his command in order to fill out French units, and refused point blank. Foch insisted, therefore, that the American assault begin again and, more importantly, not stop. This it did on 4 October.

Fourth Army meanwhile had not had any easier a task, but by 1 October it had breached the last German defensive position, and so was poised to capture from the rear the Champagne hills still in German hands. By 3 October Fourth Army troops had captured 18,000 prisoners and more than 200 guns. Their success had enabled Fifth Army on their left flank to join the battle, driving northwards from Reims to the Aisne. Between 30 September and 3 October, Fifth Army pushed the Germans back beyond Berry-au-Bac, where in 1917 the French tanks in their first battle had been destroyed. On Fifth Army's left, Tenth Army increased the pressure between 8 and 15 October, sending the German Crown Prince's entire army group back behind the Hindenburg Line, protected by the formidable river barrier of the Aisne. In twenty days of battle the French had reoccupied La Fère and Laon, freed Reims and conquered the Champagne hills. Yet Foch was disappointed because the American portion of the Franco-American attack had not met his hopes and expectations.

The second of the series of rolling attacks was carried out by the British First and Third Armies, starting on 27 September, the day after the Franco-Americans. Two days later, led by the Canadian Corps again, they had reached the outskirts of Cambrai and broken the Hindenburg Line. Then, on 28 September, it was the turn of the Flanders Army Group. Degoutte's requests for troops and materiel had so exasperated Buat at GQG that he was driven to 'regret at times' that the Allied CinC was a Frenchman.[62] Yet Foch insisted that the Belgians should receive significant resources to enable them to make a whole-hearted effort in the joint battle. Pétain claimed to have handed all possible tanks to the Americans, and had none left for Flanders, although he was able to supply the mustard gas shells that Degoutte had requested.[63] The Flanders Amy Group consisted of the Belgian Army, British Second Army commanded by General Plumer, already in Flanders, and Degoutte's three divisions of VII Corps and three cavalry divisions in II Cavalry Corps. The Flanders front was not strongly defended because Ludendorff had taken troops to reinforce Cambrai, threatened by the previous day's attack, and so the Allies had an easier task when they set off at 5.30 on the morning of 28 September after a three-hour artillery barrage. On a front of 25 kilometres stretching from the south of Dixmude to the south of Ypres, the Belgians in the north, the British in the south around Ypres and the French following in reserve made good progress and helped to force the Germans to make yet another wide retreat.[64] In two days the British and Belgians had taken back Messines, Wytschaete and Dixmude, almost the whole line of the Flanders hills, and had captured 9,000 prisoners and 200 guns. Foch released VII Corps to Degoutte on 2 October. By the next day, despite the cratered terrain and poor weather, the Flanders Army Group had advanced 14 kilometres, almost to Roulers. However, a halt was now needed to re-group and bring the new French infantry units and their artillery into line. It would be 14 October before the attack could be re-started.

The last of the series of rolling offensives, by British Fourth and French First Armies, began as intended on 29 September. The British broke through the Hindenburg Line, as the other British armies had done two days earlier further north. Debeney's role was to support the British by attacking south of Saint-Quentin, which the French occupied on 3 October. General Rawlinson's Fourth Army had made much better progress, widening the breach in the Hindenburg Line and advancing beyond, and his diary is full of complaints about Debeney hanging back and not keeping up with the British. Debeney's Army Group commander Fayolle also noted that he was limiting himself to following the British right flank, and mounting operations 'like a clock-maker'.[65] Yet his army had been stripped of artillery for the Americans and of troops for Fourth Army, because Foch gave greater weight to the Meuse–Argonne attack. The four corps of First Army had only two divisions each, except for three in XXXVI Corps, and the army had captured more than 5,000 prisoners when Saint-Quentin was liberated.

Despite Foch's bustling between headquarters, pushing everyone into even greater efforts, it was clear that all the armies needed a breather by mid October. Foch had sent a highly critical letter to Pétain on

4 October, claiming that Fourth Army's gains, 'no doubt' honourable, were less than could have been expected. Clearly driven by impatience and not tact, he urged Pétain to instruct all his army commanders to be more energetic and more inspiring. Buat complained that Foch 'had never been able to take account of what is and what is not possible'.[66] Yet, by 15 October the US First and the Centre and Reserve Army Groups had reached the *Hunding* position in the *Hindenburgstellung*, where the river lines (Aisne, Serre, Oise) constituted formidable barriers. The British were already east of *Hunding*, approaching Douai and Le Cateau, and were less than 10 kilometres from Lille. In Flanders the British had arrived on the right bank of the Lys, the French had captured Roulers, and the Belgians stood before Thourout. The principle of sequenced heavy blows on different parts of the front had proved its worth.

It was not simply on the Western Front that Foch directed operations. Strictly speaking, Foch had only the right to 'coordinate' operations in Italy, not to 'direct' them, as he could on the rest of the Western Front. However, this had not stopped him from urging the Italian CinC, General Armando Diaz, to attack, especially during the German spring offensives when relief was needed badly. Although some of the French divisions that had been sent to Italy after Caporetto in 1917 had returned to France because of the 1918 crisis, there remained two divisions of XII Corps. General Jean César Graziani commanded these two divisions, and the FFI (Forces Françaises en Italie) took part in the Italian defeat of the last Austro-Hungarian offensive on the river Piave in June. In this two-day offensive, the French captured 324 prisoners, including eight officers, who were unanimous in stating that they had suffered heavily from French artillery fire. French losses were 130 killed and 307 wounded.[67] Paul Pireaud was annoyed that the Italian high command claimed the victory as revenge for Caporetto without mentioning the French or the British contribution: 'The French greatly deserve the title of the finest soldiers in the world[,] no one can do anything to touch them.'[68]

Now Foch tried to get Diaz to take part in the general offensive, especially since morale was so low in the Austro-Hungarian forces. Over the summer there had been little action, and for the French troops there was the advantage of knowing that they were not involved in the hard fighting in France – Pireaud enjoyed lounging in the sun – but tempered by concern for their families. Foch continued to urge action and Diaz continued to find excuses. By October, however, it became clear to Diaz and, more importantly, to the politicians in Rome that, if they did not take the offensive soon, they risked being ignored at the peace conference. American, British and French successes meant that the war could not last much longer. On 4 October Austria-Hungary contacted President Woodrow Wilson about an armistice. Accordingly, Diaz proposed to break out across the Piave as far as Vittorio Veneto, to separate the two Austrian armies, and then to push north into the mountains. He created two new armies, one under the British CinC, Lord Cavan, and the other (Twelfth Army) under Graziani. In addition to his French 23 DI, three Italian divisions were deployed to his army; his 24 DI joined Italian Sixth Army. In all, Diaz collected 4,750 guns, 600 of them the heavy mortars ideal for mountain fighting, and a plentiful supply of shells.[69]

Weather delayed the start of the operation, because heavy rain had caused the Piave to flood. It was on 27 October that Graziani's troops began the crossing and made a bridgehead on the opposite bank. The next day, they managed to complete a pontoon bridge and attacked north, capturing the heights, with 23 DI taking insignificant losses. They captured 700 prisoners and 18 guns. On 29 October the victory became plain. By that evening 23 DI had captured 1,800 prisoners and a large number of guns. The Austrians had now retreated so far that by 31 October they appeared to have evacuated the Asiago plateau altogether and to be blowing up ammunition dumps. That evening, therefore, 24 DI in the Italian Sixth Army was ordered to occupy the plateau, which they achieved easily, capturing 200 prisoners. General Odry, 24 DI's commander, was keen to take advantage and ordered his troops to press on next day.

The French had contributed to the Italian victory, and Pireaud was able to write home to his wife that the FFI were not shirkers, as some press articles had implied.[70] Indeed, the victory had been so great that the armistice requested by the Austrians was signed at Villa Giusti on 3 November, and the Austro-Hungarian empire fell apart. Yet it was May 1919 before Pireaud returned to France to be demobilised, because only the older classes could be liberated during the wait for the completion of the treaty negotiations.

The French contribution during the last months of the war, beginning on 18 July, when at last the Allies went onto the offensive, is generally overlooked in English-language accounts. After playing the principal role in the Marne counter-offensive, the French Army played only supporting roles, but they were significant ones. The British official history is dismissive of First Army's part in the battles of Amiens–Montdidier, yet 42 DI was not far behind the Canadians and, more importantly, Third Army extended the battle a mere two days after it began, with Tenth Army extending it still further on 29 August. Third Army's entry into the battle had been planned and agreed before 8 August, but Haig had to be pushed to speak to his own British Third Army about extending the northern flank. It was, therefore, only on the 21st that the British Third Army began the Battle of Albert, whereas the French Third Army had gone into action on 10 August. Meanwhile the French finished clearing the Marne salient, pushing the enemy troops back beyond the river lines where they had begun in May. At the same time, First Army was giving up artillery to provide the AEF with the means to fight Saint-Mihiel, a battle in which four French infantry divisions took part and for which all the equipment needed was supplied from French sources. Then Fourth Army moved north towards Mézières alongside the Americans in the Argonne.

The liberated civilian populations seemed overwhelmed by the fast-moving events. President Poincaré visited Saint-Quentin on 17 October with his liaison officer Colonel Herbillon. The town had suffered terribly, Herbillon remarked, and the inhabitants insisted on telling stories of the sufferings they had endured. On 22 October Clemenceau made the last of his wartime visits to the front, and was received by General Mangin in Laon. Although the town and cathedral had not suffered damage, the population was 'cold', showed no enthusiasm, and seemed 'completely anaesthetised' by the experience of occupation with frequent visits from the Kaiser.[71]

The postal control records make clear how utterly weary the French Army was as well by the end of October. Casualty figures were just as high in these later offensive operations as they had been in the scrambled defence earlier in the year. Morale was certainly higher in victory than in defeat, yet, for many in Third Army, casualties were so high and fatigue so overwhelming that 'the advance no longer seems a powerful enough comfort'. In First Army the censors noted that the men were 'visibly depressed by an excess of physical fatigue'. In Sixth Army, 'fatigue is extreme and rest demanded by all'.[72] From 1 May until October 1918, 13 DI were engaged during 134 days or 73 per cent of the time. They suffered over 6,600 casualties during that period.[73] The French Army would not be able to continue at the same pace for very long. Fortunately, they did not have to do so.

9 Armistices and demobilisation

The Central Powers disintegrate

Just as Foch's general offensive was about to begin on the Western Front, events in Macedonia gave even greater reason for hope in a quicker than anticipated end to the war. The Allied armies in Macedonia numbered over half a million at the beginning of 1918, but by 14 September their strength had been increased by the arrival of Greek divisions. Greece had joined the war on 2 July 1917 after the removal of King Constantine, and a large French military mission, headed by General Braquet, the military attaché in Athens, had helped to put the Greek Army onto a war footing. Sarrail's replacement as Allied CinC in Salonika, General Guillaumat, had been recalled to Paris as a precaution, because he was the only possible successor to either Foch or Pétain, should the aftermath of the German May 1918 offensive on the Chemin des Dames demand sackings, as had happened in 1917 after the French offensive there. General Franchet d'Espèrey, former commander of the Northern Army Group, replaced Guillaumat in Salonika. Franchet d'Espèrey had 670,000 men under his orders in twenty-eight divisions: four British (some of the earlier strength had been transferred to the Middle East), nine Greek, one Italian, six Serbian and the French cavalry brigade plus eight French infantry divisions commanded by General Henrys. As well as constituting the largest contingent, the French Army had also armed the Greek and Serbian contingents. The British official history of the Macedonian campaign praises the French for their work, which 'cannot be too highly estimated'. After the Serbian and Romanian armies, the Greek 'was the third East European Army of which France had undertaken the reorganization in the course of the war, in every case with striking success'.[1]

Allied forces were superior in number, as the new Greek divisions had tipped the balance, and had more modern artillery and aviation than the enemy facing them, who were mainly Bulgarian, and showing signs of wishing to leave the war. Given this superiority, it would help the armies

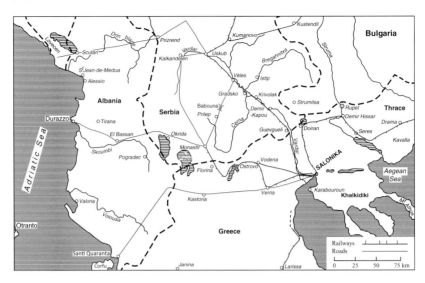

14. The Salonika Front

fighting in France if the Allied armies based in Salonika could crush the Bulgarians and so force the Central Powers to send aid in the form of troops taken from the French and Italian fronts. Before his recall to France in June, Guillaumat had carried out several coups de main, in which captured prisoners confirmed the Bulgarians' poor morale. As the Serbians wished to take the offensive to win back their country, he was preparing a wider offensive operation to profit from these advantages. When he put his ideas to Clemenceau back in Paris, Clemenceau ordered Franchet d'Espèrey to prepare a general offensive for the autumn. He did not consult his Allies about this decision, and Lloyd George was furious. The British view was that the Turks were the main enemy, and that Bulgaria could be detached diplomatically. The contrary opinion pointed to Bulgaria's essential position as the link and pipeline for supplies between Germany and the Ottoman Empire, since, with the defeat of Bulgaria, the Turks could not continue in the war.

After some hard words in the Supreme War Council, which requested a report (favourable in the event) from the military representatives, Franchet d'Espèrey's plan, sent to Paris in July, was approved and on 10 September Clemenceau authorised its execution. Franchet d'Espèrey wasted no further time and began his bombardment of the Bulgarian positions at 7am on the 14th. With complete mastery of the skies and superiority in numbers of guns (566 against 158), two French and one Serbian infantry division launched their assault the next day and put the

Bulgarian divisions to flight. During the next two days the Serbians pressed on through the mountains, widening the breach and opening the way to the Vardar valley, where the German and Bulgarian forces joined hands and where their depots and munition dumps were situated. The Armée d'Orient, meanwhile, attacked the German *Eleventh Army* and forced it to retreat to cover Uskub and the upper Vardar, for, if the French could reach Uskub first, they would cut the German forces off from their weakening Bulgarian ally. Accordingly, Franchet d'Espèrey sent his cavalry brigade through the high mountains on the western side of the Vardar valley. After a very difficult ride along tracks in mountainous terrain, in places 2,000 metres high, the cavalry reached Uskub on 29 September, surprising the garrison and cutting the Bulgarians' line of retreat. A brigade of French infantry reached Uskub the next day. The Serbians had already reached Veles on the 27th, and the British defeated the Bulgarian *First Army*, pushing it back across the border into Bulgaria at Strumitsa. The Bulgarians had already requested an armistice on 26 September, but Franchet d'Espèrey refused to halt operations until plenipotentiaries arrived and accepted the conditions that would be presented to them. They duly arrived in Salonika on the 28th and signed the next day. By the terms of the agreement, Bulgaria evacuated all Greek and Serbian territory, handed over all guns and military equipment, and permitted the Allies to use all railways. The men of German *Eleventh Army* were to lay down their arms and consider themselves prisoners of war. The Bulgarian parliament ratified the armistice on 2 October. This was all excellent news as Foch launched his general offensive in the West.

Upon first hearing that the Allies had broken the front in Macedonia, Ludendorff created an Austro-Hungarian/German army group. He supplied it with five Austrian divisions, one taken from the Italian front, and five German divisions. Four of these had been returning to France from the east and were diverted to Serbia, and the fifth was made up of the remains of the élite Bavarian *Alpine Corps* that had taken Mt Kemmel back in April. They were concentrated in the area of Nish and along the Danube and Save rivers, and Ludendorff hoped that they would be enough to prevent any Allied incursion into Austria-Hungary from the south. So the Allied victory in Macedonia had succeeded in diverting Ludendorff's attention and some (albeit weak) German divisions that otherwise would have arrived in France. Ludendorff feared, as a further consequence, that taking German divisions from the Ukraine to prop up the Macedonian front would weaken defences against Bolshevism.[2]

Clemenceau acted immediately upon hearing the news of Franchet d'Espèrey's success, and he called General Berthelot to Paris. Berthelot had headed the French military mission to Romania in 1916, sent there after the country's declaration of war. The mission was withdrawn in March 1918 after Russia's defection, and then the treaty between the Central Powers and the Ukraine made Romania's position impossible. He had organised the rebuilding of Romania's Army during 1917, and was able to render one last service before he left. He suggested to Paris that a joint Allied statement be made, recognising that Romania had always done its duty by the alliance, acknowledging the force that had impelled Romania to an odious peace, and offering to consider the imposed peace treaty null and void, once general peace negotiations were under way. Both Paris and London agreed to Berthelot's suggestion.

Back in France, Berthelot took over command of Fifth Army on 5 July 1918, and was not pleased to hear Clemenceau's orders, given to him on 1 October, just as victory was beckoning. Berthelot learned that he was to go first to Salonika, there to create an 'Army of the Danube', thence to cross through defeated Bulgaria and to revitalise the Romanian Army once again, now that Bulgaria was out of the war. Similarly, Franchet d'Espèrey was not pleased by the arrival in Salonika of another French general whose forces were to depend on his Armée d'Orient for their logistics but who reported directly to Paris. Berthelot left Paris on 8 October and arrived in Salonika a few days later. He urged Romania's king and premier to rejoin the war at once or risk failing to obtain its national aspirations at the peace table. As for himself, he wished to make a 'sensational entry' at the head of his army and so to 'pass into Romanian posterity'.[3] Austria's capitulation prevented that, but Romania did indeed rejoin the Entente, just in time, on 10 November. Only a token force from Berthelot's Army of the Danube, consisting of 30 DI, 16 DIC and elements of 76 DI, with two groups of 155s and three squadrons of aircraft,[4] had crossed the Danube by then, but he continued his advance towards Bucharest. On 15 November, after a 'festive' crossing of the Danube by the rest of his army, he was received 'with open arms' by the citizens of Giurgiu, who named streets of their city after him and the two French soldiers who had died during the river-crossing.[5]

After the Bulgarian armistice came the Turkish one. The ill-will that had dogged Franco-British relations over the Salonika expedition was present also in the Middle East, and especially in the final Palestine campaign against the Ottoman empire. Lloyd George wrote to his 'dear friend', former armaments minister, Albert Thomas, now out of government, to congratulate him on the results of the Salonika campaign, reminding him of the days in December 1915 when they had combined to persuade the British Cabinet not to abandon it. Without that intervention, he wrote, the Austrians would have (*not* might have!) occupied Salonika, Greece would have become a German 'satrap', and today's great wound in the flank of the Central Powers leading to their ruin would not have occurred.[6]

Lloyd George's hypocrisy is all the more egregious because he had been removing troops from Salonika for the Middle East for some time; moreover, he had raised a fuss in the SWC over Clemenceau's order to undertake operations in Salonika. Lloyd George's interest lay not in Greece but in the Middle East, in Palestine and Mesopotamia. Yet France could not allow him a free hand in the Middle East because of its own claims to Syria and Lebanon. Therefore, when the front against the Turks in Palestine stabilised in mid 1917, the French Army created a 'Palestine detachment', the Détachement d'armée de Palestine or DFP (see Chapter 6). It consisted of a battalion of volunteer territorials from 115 Territorial Infantry Regiment based in France, two battalions of native tirailleurs from Bizerta, and an ambulance, joined by a squadron of native cavalry (spahis) in June.[7]

When Allenby captured Gaza in November 1917 and began the Palestine campaign, the 2,800 men of the DFP moved towards Jaffa on the coast, where the French Navy was supporting the campaign. The diplomatic agreement, negotiated by Mark Sykes and François Georges-Picot, had divided up the Ottoman Middle East between Britain, France and Russia, with Palestine accorded an international status because of the Holy Places. Lloyd George was determined, however, as shown in Chapter 6, not to allow the French to control Palestine. It took a determined effort on Georges-Picot's part to get Allenby to allow a French detachment to join the formal entry into Jerusalem in December 1917 alongside the British and Australians. Then Allenby refused to permit Georges-Picot to set up a civilian administration, maintaining that he was the sole military authority. Instead, the French forces occupied the railway line between Jerusalem and Jaffa. Although in Paris Clemenceau's military advisor Mordacq claimed that the 'French contingent had particularly distinguished itself during this brilliant offensive', it has to be admitted that the DFP's presence was for show.[8]

Yet the French had contributed to the Middle East theatre in another way. Lawrence has taken all the glory for the hit and run tactics and raiding by the Sherifian forces along the railway from Aqaba northwards. The French contributed men and guns to this harassment of the Turkish lines of communication. For example, a raid on the railway line south of Ma'an was described in a report sent to Paris on 21 October 1917. With the intention of blowing up a train travelling south, eleven men left Aqaba in the evening of 26 September. They were Colonel T.E. Lawrence with two 'hommes de confiance', Captain Rosario Pisani and two tirailleurs serving the machine guns, three Syrians, and two servants. On 30 September they collected about eighty Bedouin with fifty or so camels, and on 6 October a train was spotted moving slowly:

> Major Lawrence is a hundred metres away from the line and will explode the mine; the two machine guns are in place; I have the task of charging the train with the Bedouin. We are 150 metres from the line. The train arrives at 8 o'clock and passes over the mine which explodes, destroying completely the locomotive and the first carriage.

After a twenty-five-minute gunfight, the pillage began, and the Bedouin took a huge booty in foodstuffs. Lawrence and Pisani took six survivors prisoner, including four officers; about fifty other Turks had been killed.[9]

In the opening months of 1918 progress slowed. Georges Clemenceau had become France's final wartime premier on 17 November 1917, but he was not particularly interested in the Middle East, believing that the war could only be won in France. Yet the French needed to keep an eye on what the British were doing there, as an increase of British troops in the Middle East meant fewer for the fronts in France and in Salonika. Indeed, the front in France compelled a halt to the British advance from Jerusalem into Syria, because Allenby was forced to return two divisions to Haig in early April to help resist the German offensives.

This was only a temporary halt, however. After having been snubbed over Jerusalem, the French needed to maintain their military presence in the region (see Map 15). Consequently, as it became obvious that Allenby's British forces were about to advance once more into Syria, the French Palestine Detachment, now Palestine and Syria (DFPS), prepared to participate. The Légion d'Orient, consisting of Armenian and Syrian volunteers assembled and trained on Cyprus, joined the detachment, which consisted by 1 May 1918 of 7,378 French officers and men, led by Lieutenant-Colonel de Piépape, who had been a chief of staff on Gallipoli in 1915. This was a tiny force in comparison with the nearly one-third of a million British and Empire troops, and the DFPS had little in the way of weapons and transport. Nevertheless, France could not let Allenby have a free hand in Syria, especially since the recruitment campaigns among expatriate Syrians in France and the USA had raised disappointingly few men. Indeed, France feared that this disaffection among Syrians was the result of seeing the great number of British forces and deducing that France was too exhausted to help free them from the Turkish overlords.[10]

Accordingly it was agreed to reinforce the DFPS by adding the battery of 80mm field artillery from the French military mission based at Port Saïd and, from France, a battery of 65s, two companies of machine-gunners, a squadron of aircraft, and a force of cavalry amounting to one

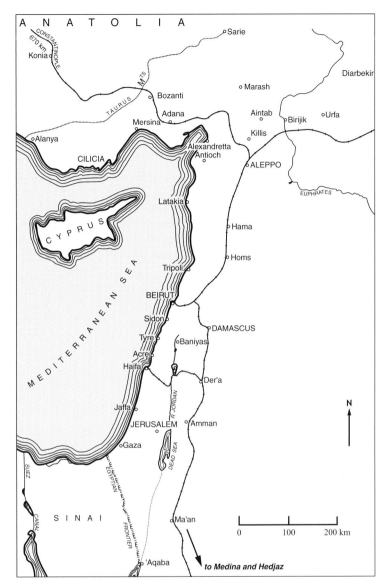

15. Palestine campaign

division. It was believed that the prestige of the North African units would be of great profit in an area where cavalry could indeed make a contribution. Georges-Picot attempted to bring a European battalion from the Western Front, but his request was refused. Unfortunately, in

July the ship bringing from Marseille another battery of field artillery and horses from France, with the spahis, who embarked at Bizerta, was sunk by a German submarine before reaching Port Saïd, and the aviation resources did not arrive in time to be used. Nonetheless, French troops liberated Palestine and Syria alongside the British.[11]

Pisani's French detachment remained with Lawrence and the Sherifian army, which had the task of tying down the Turkish *Fourth Army* as Allenby advanced. The French provided two sections of 65mm mountain guns, a machine-gun section and an engineering section, for a total of 140 men.[12] After concentrating on 12 September, the mixed Arab-British-French force took Der'a and destroyed sections of the railway. When the force turned west to join up with Allenby's troops, they came across about 8,000 men, elements of the Turkish *Fourth Army*, retreating in good order. Pisani's artillery was so effective that the enemy continued its retreat without trying to defeat the numerically inferior Allied forces. Doubtless the Turks thought that they were dealing with a much larger force than was, in fact, the case. On 28 September the Allied detachment joined up with the British cavalry in Der'a. French cavalry units joined the Australian mounted troops in forcing the river Jordan and encircling the Damascus defences from the north. They entered Damascus in solemn procession with the British on 2 October. On 9 October a mixed detachment – elements of the chasseurs d'Afrique, the territorial battalion and the Syrian company of the Légion d'Orient – arrived by sea in Beirut, and Piépape was appointed military governor of the town. On 14 October he was named military governor of the western zone, comprising the Mediterranean coastal strip from Alexandretta to Acre and Mount Lebanon.[13] At this point Paris decided that it was time to make more of an impression and a general officer, General Hamelin, was appointed to direct military affairs in the sector with Piépape as his adjoint. Hamelin had been in the army general staff in the war ministry dealing with African and East Mediterranean affairs. Next, Paris insisted that the French should occupy Alexandretta, and a force prepared to land by sea. Because of the mines laid in the approaches to the port, it was decided to wait for the British to conquer Aleppo and clear the Turks out of Alexandretta before attempting to land. The Turkish signature on the armistice document on 30 October put an end to operations.[14]

On the grounds that the French held the naval command in the eastern Mediterranean, Clemenceau complained about British high-handedness in negotiating the armistice alone with the Turks; yet, since Franchet d'Espèrey had acted alone in negotiating the Bulgarian armistice, this was not much of an argument. At the time the Turkish armistice was signed, Lloyd George was in Paris to discuss Germany's request for its own armistice. He complained that Britain had done all the work in the Middle East and suffered many casualties, whereas nobody else 'had contributed anything more than a handful of black troops to the expedition in Palestine'. And those troops had only acted as 'policemen to see that we did not steal the Holy Sepulchre! When, however, it came to signing an armistice, all this fuss was made.'[15] The fuss died down, of course, because events on the Western Front were moving to their conclusion.

Western Front

At German headquarters in Spa, the launch of Foch's general Allied offensive and the news of Bulgaria's collapse caused Ludendorff to inform OHL staff that, to avoid the double 'catastrophe' of an Allied breakthrough forcing the German armies back to the Rhine and a revolution at home, an armistice was necessary. He wanted a halt to the fighting based upon President Woodrow Wilson's Fourteen Points. He expected such an armistice to contain easier terms than Britain and France would demand, but he was prepared to go on fighting if their demands were too exorbitant. On the night of 3/4 October the new German government of Prince Max of Baden sent a note via Switzerland to Washington asking for a general armistice on land, on water and in the air, and for the USA to restore peace. French intelligence picked up the telegraphic message before it reached Washington.

Even if armistice terms had been signed by both Bulgaria and Turkey putting an end to fighting, Foch was not prepared to call a halt in France and Belgium, despite Germany's message to the US President. Although all the Allied offensives had slowed around the time of Germany's request, Foch kept up the pressure and, after a week to ten days of reforming and re-supplying the armies, the general offensive re-started in the second half of October. On the 10th he had re-stated his intentions in the light of the armistice talks, which as yet concerned only President Wilson and the German government. Of the three sectors where the Allies were attacking – in Belgium, around Solesmes/Wassigny and in the Meuse–Argonne – the British in the centre were making the greatest progress. Hence Foch wished to exploit success by combining the Belgian and British operations so as to free Lille and to push north-east between the Sambre and Scheldt (Escaut) rivers towards Mons – at last, the name of a Belgian town was appearing in operational orders. In order to allow the BEF to change to this more northerly direction, First Army was to take over the front up to Wassigny and to overrun the line of the river Serre. Foch strengthened the northern forces still further by detaching two US divisions from Pershing and sending them to reinforce the Flanders Army Group. He also appointed General de Boissoudy to command the French units there, now designated Sixth Army. This freed Degoutte from the task of commanding the French portion of the army group, enabling him to concentrate on his role as chief of staff under King Albert's nominal command of the four-nation troops. As for the Americans and Gouraud's Fourth Army in the Meuse–Argonne, Foch had already rowed with Pershing about the continuation of the battle. Now, as more and more American infantry arrived in France and Pershing constituted a second US Army, activated on 12 October, Foch granted Pershing's request to be treated as a national commander, like Haig and King Albert, rather than as the commander of a single army under Pétain's command. From 16 October Pershing was to receive his orders directly from Foch and not through Pétain as before, although naturally Pershing and Pétain would need to keep in close contact where the joint action of Fourth and US First Armies was concerned. This move was probably Foch's stick and carrot approach to dealing with the obstinate American CinC. The threat to ask Washington for a replacement was thinly veiled[16] – Clemenceau was furious with Foch for not so requesting – and Pershing's pride at his 'promotion' to equal status with other national commanders might make him more amenable to French direction, which would have greater weight coming from Foch, who was more forceful than Pétain.

In Flanders the French units of Sixth Army joined the front line and, with the British and Belgian armies alongside, restarted operations on 14 October. The next day they reached Courtrai and Menin, and Ludendorff authorised Crown Prince Rupprecht to abandon the coast and retreat behind the *Hermann* position. The Allied armies followed closely, reaching Thourout on the 16th and the next day Ostend. On 20 October King Albert entered Bruges and the left wing of his army now extended as far as the Dutch frontier. As already noted, constitutionally the King was head of Belgium's Army and never came under French command, but in effect it was Degoutte who commanded the successful liberation of Belgian territory. He managed to keep on good terms with the King, who had been appalled at the number of Belgian casualties and miffed by the liberated Belgian citizens' enthusiastic welcome to French troops. Degoutte had no part in the row between Haig and Foch over the return to the BEF of the British Second Army in the Flanders Army Group, which marred the last few days of the group's existence.[17] The Belgian, British and French armies captured 18,500 prisoners in the last two weeks of October, 5,200 of them taken by the French, together with large quantities of guns and machine guns.[18]

Germany's *Hermannstellung* ran along the Scheldt to Valenciennes, thence to Le Cateau, but Haig's Fourth Army was already in Le Cateau, having captured it on 17 October. By the 24th, British Fourth and Third Armies were knocking at the doors of Landrecies, Le Quesnoy and Valenciennes. These gains enabled the remaining British armies to get forward, and to liberate between 17 and 21 October the industrial Lille–Roubaix–Tourcoing area and its inhabitants. So, in the north, it was an uninterrupted series of victories.

In the centre, between the Oise and the Aisne, the French armies set off again slightly later, on 17 October. During September Debeney's First Army had had the dual task of keeping its left-hand units up with the British, and on its right enabling the capture of the German lines in the rear. In the process it had suffered 5,428 casualties killed and wounded, by far the greatest proportion of them in XXXI and XXXVI Corps. Only XV Corps had significant resources in heavy artillery.[19] During early October Fayolle had urged Debeney to provide better support for the British, but again Debeney repeated that he needed more men and more guns.[20] First Army was coming to the end of its operational strength by the time fighting re-started.

On 17 October, in liaison with the British, First Army attacked on both sides of the Oise, capturing part of Mont d'Origny after house-to-house fighting. Their 1,400 prisoners declared that they had received orders to resist at all costs. The next day the prisoner haul amounted to approximately 3,000 and a large number of machine guns was also captured. North of the Oise, First Army kept up with the British, and south of the river it followed the retreating Germans, but an unusually high water level prevented the troops from crossing the river.[21] After the third day of hard fighting, First Army's left was in contact with the British along the Oise and the Sambre–Oise canal; the army's right was on the heels of the retreating Germans who abandoned the line of the river Serre. This enabled Tenth Army to join the pursuit. The section of the *Hunding-stellung* that linked the two waterways was one of the most formidable of the system: it was protected by strong belts of wire, and the Germans put up a fierce, obstinate resistance for several days.[22] XX Corps reinforced First Army on 18 October, but its original organic divisions, 11 and 39 DI, had gone to Flanders and to II Colonial Corps in US First Army respectively. The French Army's traditional linkages were loosening. Now XX Corps consisted of 153 and 168 DI, whose number indicates that they were originally reserve infantry divisions. Placed on the left of Hély d'Oissel's VIII Corps, XX and VIII Corps attacked the

Hundingstellung on 20 October. It took some very hard fighting between 24 and 26 October to reduce the defences, but with a fresh division (47 DI) well supplied with artillery and tanks, this was achieved and the enemy began to withdraw on the 27th, leaving 3,700 prisoners in First Army's hands, with twenty-four guns and a large number of machine guns. Fayolle's orders were to continue to press the enemy without respite, in the general direction of Guise and La Capelle. On its left the army was to prepare to cross the Oise and the Sambre–Oise canal in conjunction with the British, and on its right to join with Tenth Army in breaking the enemy position on the Serre.[23] Because the strong enemy resistance continued, Debeney decided that a concerted preparation was required in order to get forward. This was postponed several times, and on 31 October Fayolle ordered First Army to halt the right-hand operations against the Serre defences and to concentrate on the left in conjunction with the British.[24] Fayolle commented that Debeney, who was 'puffed up with pride' on the 28th, was 'less proud than usual' by the last day of the month because of the repeated delays. Since 17 October when operations re-started in earnest, First Army had captured more than 7,000 prisoners and a considerable amount of materiel, including 1,200 machine guns and over 200 artillery pieces, and had advanced about 30 kilometres on the right, although less on the left.[25] Debeney's army had made considerable progress, and Fayolle's somewhat ungenerous comments may derive from the fact that on 30 October he discussed armistice terms with Foch.[26]

Tenth Army had been confined to a passive role since the start of the general offensive on 26 September. It was to follow the retreating enemy and ensure that it maintained contact with First Army on its left and Fifth Army on its right. Simply maintaining a continuous front would cause the Chemin des Dames to fall by itself as they advanced.[27] Fayolle reiterated these orders on 12 October. Because of its passive role, Fayolle had taken divisions from Mangin's command, leaving him only ten: two in reserves and two each in XVI, XVIII, XXXV and II Italian Corps.[28] The impatient Mangin was not satisfied with simply maintaining the continuity of the line, especially in a sector, the Aisne, where he had been disgraced in 1917. In his post-war account he admitted that his mission had been continuity but that he had never stopped attacking.[29] Laon, where Mangin had said he would sleep on the night of 16/17 April 1917, was freed at last on 12 October.

On 16 October Tenth Army had also reached the *Hundingstellung*. The Germans were defending this section just as obstinately as the section before First Army, and Tenth Army had enormous difficulty in getting across the Serre and the marshy areas around the river. Helped by First

Army's advance on 26 October, XVI Corps managed to capture one of the Serre bridges, but the next day Pétain withdrew Mangin and his army staff. Fayolle believed that Mangin had been removed because he (Mangin) did not know how to run a battle and he annoyed everybody, especially his XVI Corps who claimed that they had been pushed into attacking with no thought of what was possible.[30] Although Fayolle appears not to have been informed of it, Mangin and his staff were moved for a different reason. They were to go to Lorraine for a new offensive that Pétain had long had in mind, ever since becoming CinC in 1917. General Humbert and his Third Army staff took over Tenth Army's corps and its front of attack, with instructions to break the line of the Serre in conjunction with First Army.[31] Debeney, however, had to postpone the start of concerted action because First Army was stuck around Guise.

Meanwhile, in Champagne, Fourth Army had reached the line of the river Aisne and held almost all the southern bank by 15 October. The Americans alongside had managed to clear the Argonne forest and were in touch with Fourth Army. It was a hard slogging match to dislodge the enemy from the northern bank, where the Germans had halted in 1914 after the First Battle of the Marne. They had held the terrain to the north of the river ever since, because the higher northern bank gave the Germans excellent observation over the French on the other side. So the battle slowed, and Fourth Army was hampered still further by the need to evacuate more than 27,000 men during the month of October, most of them for influenza.[32] This high number probably reflects the proximity to the Americans who were arriving from the USA, many already infected with the virus. Foch intervened and instructed the French to aim north-eastwards, not attempting to cross the Aisne frontally but taking advantage of the bend in the river to progress towards Le Chesne, thereby 'unblocking' the line of the Aisne from the east.[33] Gouraud agreed with Pershing that it would take a few days to integrate the new resources offered by Centre Army Group for this operation, namely the entire army group's artillery resources, and more tanks and aviation. It was agreed that US First Army would re-start operations on 1 November with Fourth Army following suit the next day. As a sign of how far Fourth Army had advanced since 26 August, army headquarters moved on 29 October from Suippes, south-east of Reims, 25 kilometres further north.

As the French armies moved further and further north, Foch was discussing armistice terms. As early as 8 October he had laid out his minimum conditions to the Allied leaders meeting in Paris. These conditions met two criteria: first, the Germans should not be able to re-start hostilities if the armistice broke down or if Germany simply used it as a breathing space to incorporate the 1920 class and re-stock weaponry; second, the Germans should be held to ransom for the payment of reparations by being obliged to evacuate some German territory, namely the left bank of the Rhine, which the Allies would occupy, along with bridgeheads on the right bank. The British thought Foch's terms too harsh, but, after Ludendorff resigned on 26 October and the next day the German government accepted President Wilson's note directing them to seek the Allied terms from Foch, these already seemed less harsh because of October's military successes. Meeting on 25 October with Pétain, Haig and Pershing (General Gillain was unable to attend for the Belgians), Foch was not inclined to accept Haig's wish for easier terms. Pétain, on the other hand, was even harsher. He suggested that the Allies should hold the entire right bank of the Rhine from Switzerland to the Dutch frontier to a depth of 20 to 30 kilometres; he demanded more railway materiel – 5,000 locomotives and 10,000 wagons – than Foch had proposed collecting; and he would put a three-day limit on Germany's evacuation of the occupied territories, to ensure that the enemy would be forced to abandon much heavy materiel. Pétain showed no signs here of begging Foch not to sign a premature armistice, a claim that he made in the 1920s and 1930s with the hindsight derived from the threat from Hitler.

The next day, 26 October, Foch summarised the discussion and submitted a final draft of the military terms, essentially his own military terms, to be presented to Germany in the event that they did indeed request an armistice. Foch knew both that the Allied armies were tired and also that the Germans in the front lines were still putting up a stiff resistance, yet he was not prepared to call a halt to operations. Having the wild beast at bay was not the moment to stop; rather the blows should be redoubled, Foch claimed; 'nothing gives wings to an army like victory'.[34] Hence the fighting continued.

On 1 November the US First Army with Fourth Army alongside advanced several kilometres closer to the Meuse at Sedan and Mézières. Their progress continued the next day, as the Flanders Army Group reached the outskirts of Ghent and the British reached Valenciennes. On 3 November the Austrians signed their armistice in Italy and hostilities ceased the next day. On 5 November the Germans began a wide retreat between the Scheldt and the Meuse, destroying railway tracks and bridges, blowing up roads and booby-trapping buildings as they went. The concentric action had reduced the length of front that the four French armies (from right to left, Fourth, Fifth, Third, First) had to man: from 130 kilometres on 5 November to only 75 kilometres. Because he wanted to take some US divisions for the Lorraine offensive, Foch arranged for Fourth Army to extend its front.[35] Pétain warned his army group commanders to reduce the density of troops in the front line because of the increasing difficulties of re-supply. Not only were the French now a long way from their railheads, but the Germans were destroying roads and bridges as they retreated.

On the evening of 7 November Debeney's First Army had the pleasure of receiving at their forward outpost line a German delegation requesting passage so as to meet Foch. Yet it was still not the end. On 8 November Fourth Army reached the line of the Meuse, and First Army was held up along the Hirson–Avesnes rocade. The next day, however, First Army crossed the frontier into Belgium, Fifth Army reached Charleville, and Fourth Army, Mézières. The Flanders Army Group reached the Scheldt.

An offensive in Lorraine

Foch's strategy of a series of concentric offensives was working splendidly, but at GQG the operations bureau was contemplating an alternative solution to ending the war. In a series of studies made during August, Pétain's staff developed a different sort of operation from those Foch had laid down in his 24 July memorandum. Instead of continuing to pursue the retreating Germans, they suggested that it would be better to attack as far away as possible from the current sectors, in an area that would threaten the enemy's communications, and provide political bargaining chips. In other words, they were studying Pétain's Lorraine idea, preliminary plans for which existed already.[36] It is notable that these study papers were thinking solely of the French front and took no account of the mass of enemy reserve divisions known to be deployed further north. Rather, it was a 'point of honour' that the French Army should deliver the decisive blow.[37] At GQG there was an awareness of the need for a French victory, not only because France's efforts were being overlooked as British and American Allies were capturing the glory of victory, but also because within France itself Foch seemed to be gathering all the credit. Pétain's comment in his feeble old age reveals a depth of resentment: 'If a military leader won the war, it was me, only me.'[38]

On 7 September, after two of Foch's three operations to free France's railway communications had been completed successfully, Pétain ordered his Eastern Army Group commander, General Castelnau, to make any changes necessary in his Lorraine front to enable the deployment, within no more than six months, of thirty attacking divisions on a 60-kilometre front. Castelnau submitted his proposal on 24 September for an operation to be undertaken by Eighth Army. It was based on surprise and aimed at breaking out into open country between Metz and the area of the lakes where, in August 1914, Castelnau and his

Second Army had advanced to Morhange. After a visit to Castelnau's headquarters on 20 September, Foch had proposed adding some US divisions to Eighth Army to strengthen the assault, but his directive of 10 October, in which he gave the direction of advance to his attacking armies, took no account of an operation in the east.

The continuing successes gained by Foch's general offensive encouraged GQG's 3e Bureau to make further studies of the possibilities in Lorraine and, by 18 October, the operation had increased to an attack east of Metz using twenty-five divisions. The next day Pétain ordered Castelnau to be ready to launch the attack within three weeks, and Foch approved this on 20 October. Foch believed that the Franco-American armies would soon reach the Sedan–Mézières stretch of the Meuse where the principal German rocade ran, and so deprive the German forces in Lorraine of contact with the main body of the German Army. This advantage, if exploited quickly, should give the Lorraine offensive a greater chance of success.[39]

The extra divisions for it came from Tenth Army, which was moved from the Champagne sector. A week later Pétain set the date of 15 November for the start of the operation. He also requested that Foch supply ten to twelve US divisions, but Foch replied that no more than five could be sent. Pershing was hardly likely to agree even to that number. Foch also asked that, even if the reinforcements had not all arrived, the operation begin sooner than 15 November, since the Supreme War Council was now discussing armistice terms. Also he ordered that Tenth Army be given the main role, rather than Eighth Army. Obviously Foch expected more aggressive action from Mangin and his experienced Tenth Army than from General Gérard, whose front had been quiet for so long.

It was now too late, however, for any such action. Castelnau had agreed to advance the date by twenty-four hours to 14 November, but by then the Germans had signed. Mangin was furious. Castelnau too believed that the Lorraine offensive could have routed the enemy, but accepted that its abandonment spared many lives: 'let us hope', he wrote to his son Louis, 'that it will not have unfortunate repercussions on the "future"'.[40] Pétain's post-war report on the 1918 campaign admitted that important fortresses had been won undamaged without his offensive:

Driven to certain, irreparable disaster, the enemy capitulates ... they abandon Alsace-Lorraine to us without fighting ... they hand over intact the fortified places of Metz and Strasbourg, which for forty-eight years they had held to be the symbol of their invincibility.[41]

When Fayolle visited Metz in January 1919, he marvelled at the strength of the fortified city, saying that it was a 'miracle' that it should have fallen to the French without having to strike a blow.[42]

Much has been made of the lost opportunity in Lorraine, especially by Pétain, on the grounds that a premature armistice robbed the French of a military victory there, and led to the Second World War. This judgement assumes that a victory in Lorraine was on offer – Pétain was unlikely to be as energetic in pushing the enterprise forward as Foch, say, would be – and it is a judgement made with hindsight, as the Hitlerian threat became ever more manifest. General Anthoine, Pétain's chief of the general staff until June, when Foch sacked him, went so far as to claim on 11 November 1940 – on the first anniversary of the 1918 armistice since the fall of France – that Lloyd George and Clemenceau had cooked up the armistice between them and that Sir Henry Wilson influenced Foch to accept the deal.[43] The idea that Foch would have been thus influenced is so far-fetched as to be laughable. Several factors show conclusively that the chances of a great success in Lorraine were very limited. Certainly the French had great numerical superiority there, and the German troops on the ground were older and had seen little action since 1914. Nonetheless, the Germans were already beginning to evacuate Metz and would have operated the same scheme of destruction of vital infrastructure as was occurring in the rest of France. Winter was approaching, and the days were shortening. Moreover, even if the French and Americans reached Metz and the important rail junction of Longuyon 70 kilometres beyond, it was still a further 200 to the Rhine.

Yet the principal factor to take into account in judging a possible Lorraine offensive is the transport system, and it was almost entirely worn out. The railway authorities informed GQG that it would take twenty-one days to transport seven divisions to Lorraine, given the state of wagons, locomotives and the lines. Previously two or three divisions had been transported daily.[44] Although Foch's headquarters now controlled transportation through its command of the railways, the head of the DGCRA warned that breaking-point was near. Metaphorically he declared that the rope was being stretched very thin, as all demands for moves during the general offensive were met. By the end of October, the rope had broken.[45] The supply of horses for pulling the guns was also becoming critical.[46] Paul Clark was told on 17 October by the head of the DGCRA as he moved to take up his post in Foch's headquarters: 'I realize somewhat the hard task before me – our movements are so rapid these days and the communications in the territory in which we are now operating are so largely destroyed that – that [sic] the solution of the problems will tax me to the utmost.'[47]

The experience of Daniel Halévy illustrates the difficulties. He had been an interpreter with the AEF in Lorraine, but returned to 25 DI that was to join Mangin's Tenth Army. Halévy left Chantilly near Paris on

4 November and disembarked from his fifty-carriage train after forty-two hours. The train had crawled at an average speed of 15 kilometres an hour with frequent lengthy stops.[48] In 1922 Weygand asked whether the Lorraine offensive could have been supplied, given the difficult progress through a 'zone of destruction'. He was informed that enough supplies, albeit in reduced volumes, could only be moved up to 40–50 kilometres beyond the railheads for about sixty French divisions. Of course, British and American divisions also had to be transported and supplied.[49] Such limitations would have ruled out any far-reaching exploitation in Lorraine.

The relative value of all these factors might be open to individual judgement, but the indisputable fact remains that when Germany signed Foch's armistice document, the Rhinelands and bridgeheads on the east bank were handed over to the French and Allied armies without the need to fire another shot, drop another bomb or fire another gas shell. In the eleven days of the November fighting, when First and Fourth Armies were only following a retreating enemy, there were 5,000 deaths in the French Army as a whole, not counting wounded casualties. Given Mangin's character, it is unlikely that his Tenth Army would have suffered fewer casualties in fighting for Metz and Longuyon. Foch always insisted post-war that his principal reason for agreeing to grant an armistice was to avoid further bloodshed. Moreover, apart from the 'uselessness [inutilité]' of killing men for nothing, Foch said soon after the war, a pursuit of the Germans 'en pleine débâcle' would have provoked in the French Army 'une pagaïe fâcheuse et préjudiciable'.[50] The armistice terms were harsh, and they obtained for France both a guarantee that Germany could not re-start operations and a foothold on German territory, as a pledge for the payment of reparations.

Pétain's planned operation in Lorraine would have involved twenty-five divisions. The experience of just one division in the last week of the war shows the scale of the problems that he would have faced if the operation had gone ahead. After leaving Fourth Army and a week's rest, 13 DI joined Fifth Army.[51] On 1 November the division moved into the front line north-west of Château-Porcien as part of XIII Corps. Guillaumat now commanded Fifth Army, taking over after Berthelot was sent back to Romania. He realised that a German withdrawal was likely and ordered deep 'coups de main' as reconnaissance missions. On 5 November, 13 DI was alerted for one such mission. As the field and heavy artillery began a heavy barrage to stop any enemy counter-battery work, the infantry moved forward and discovered that there was nothing in front of them. Progress continued in like manner over the next two days, in the face of some German machine-gun fire, but hampered more by the huge shell holes in the forests which hindered re-supply of munitions. The action on 8 November resembled nothing more than a pre-war manoeuvre with enemy fire rather than blanks. The division was ordered to form a single column, with an avant-garde composed of two battalions of 21 RI ahead. The divisional cavalry preceded the avant-garde, and managed to prevent the enemy from wreaking more destruction. On 9 November, 13 DI acted as avant-garde for the whole of XIII Corps, and the same disposition of troops was ordered as for the previous day. The pursuit continued, but on the 10th it proved very difficult for the artillery to keep up because the enemy had destroyed the bridges over the river Sormonne. The cavalry protected the infantry as they crossed over improvised bridges, but by the end of the afternoon the artillery was too far behind to support them. Bringing up food and munitions was now a bigger problem than enemy resistance, as the roads too had been cut in several places. Because the supply columns were being forced to go back as far as Grandchamp to load up, the idea of dropping supplies by aircraft was discussed. This modern tactic was not needed, however, as 13 DI received the news about the armistice at 3.30 on the morning of the 11th and halted in the area of Belval.

After helping to break through the *Hundingstellung* in October, 13 DI had followed up the enemy on a 4.5-kilometre-wide front between 6 and 11 November over the amazing distance of 45 kilometres, for losses described as 'insignificant'. In the wooded terrain, which was all but impenetrable because of the shelling, thus rendering the tanks unusable, the infantry had been forced to defend themselves using their own 37 mm guns and Stokes mortars. The problem of moving the batteries of 75s forward and supplying munitions was almost insoluble. If batteries moved individually, as and when it became possible, liaison with the infantry who had moved on was difficult; if they waited until all could move together, other advancing infantry was deprived of support for a period. The advance made the transmission of reports and orders from headquarters more difficult. It was often late at night that the liaison officers reached divisional headquarters to report on the line reached, hence early morning before orders for the day were sent back in the dark over forest tracks to the distant front line. Furthermore, air reconnaissance was becoming more difficult as the terrain was new for the pilots, airfields were far back and the weather was mostly bad with low cloud.

Surely, if Germany had not signed on the morning of 11 November, a halt would have had to be called. Even re-supplied by air, 13 DI could not have continued advancing at the rate of 45 kilometres a week for any longer. The retreating enemy forces were causing too much destruction of the communications infrastructure in terrain that was already very difficult. Pétain's divisions in Lorraine would have faced the same logistical problems, even if the retiring enemy put up no resistance whatsoever.

The Lorraine offensive was not the only operation under consideration in the last days of the war in the west. On 3 November Foch met in Paris with Generals Bliss and di Robilant, the American and Italian Permanent Military Representatives at the Supreme War Council, and General Sir Henry Wilson for the British. Hence it was not a regularly constituted SWC meeting. They discussed using the Allied troops freed by Austria's cessation of hostilities to attack Germany itself. They proposed a concentric attack on Munich, the capital of Bavaria, using an army group composed of three armies. The first, consisting of ten divisions of Italian mountain troops, would concentrate around Innsbruck for an attack on Munich from the south. Calculating the road and rail capacity between Trent and Innsbruck, they estimated that it would take 22 days to complete the concentration in Austria. The second and third armies, each consisting of ten to fifteen divisions, including the British and French divisions currently in Italy, would attack from the west after concentrating around Salzburg. Three railway lines with a capacity of fifty-six trains per day would permit concentration within 30 to 35 days, although it was admitted that shortage of coal might interfere with these calculations. The army group was to be commanded by an Italian general officer, under 'the strategic direction' of the Allied CinC on the Western Front. A resolution to give effect to these arrangements was drawn up to be submitted to the SWC, but the German capitulation intervened. Nonetheless, the designated Italian commander, General Badoglio, maintained the concentration of troops around Innsbruck and wrote to Foch on 13 November that light infantry and cyclist units were to be held ready to intervene in Bavaria, 'if intervention were necessary', not the full-scale operation that had been envisaged but 'rather as intimidation'.[52]

Crossing the Meuse

One of the last engagements of the war was Fourth Army's crossing of the Meuse between Vrigne-Meuse and Sedan by 163 DI in XIV Corps. Among Fourth Army's corps commanders, it seems to have been a race for the glory of reaching the northern bank of the river. On 9 November, despite violent machine-gun barrages, IX Corps managed to get some units into Sedan where they freed several thousand civilians. On their left, 61 DI (XI Corps) crossed the Meuse and entered Mézières, where there were 50,000 French civilians to be liberated. As for XIV Corps and

163 DI, the corps occupied Dom-le-Mesnil, on the river between Sedan and Mézières, but found that the whole area before them had been flooded by the destruction of the locks and dams. When the XIV Corps commander learned at 13.30 that XI Corps had already entered Mézières, he ordered his own 163 DI to cross the river at Vrigne-Meuse. This action would figure in the last official communiqué of the war.

Commanded for more than a year by General Boichut, 163 DI had reached the Meuse on 8 November. It had been transferred to XIV Corps on 29 October and, after crossing the river Aisne, had marched in the rain and the cold to reach the Meuse on the the evening of the 8th. The next day Fourth Army's orders for the 10th were to keep close watch on the enemy, to seek any opportunity to cross the river and establish a bridgehead, so that communications and equipment could be brought up to make a forced crossing. General Marjoulet, XIV Corps' commander, had already gone further than these cautious orders, and at 4.30pm had ordered 163 DI to cross the river and make for Vrigne-Meuse. The operation was to be carried out quickly, without stopping at nightfall. Boichut attempted to win a delay for his weary division, but Marjoulet insisted that the crossing must be made that night: 'the enemy is hesitating about signing the armistice. They think they are safe behind the Meuse. We must act audaciously to strike a blow against the enemy's morale.' Marjoulet told him to drive a line of trucks into the river, as a bridge, if necessary.

This expedient was not needed, because in front of one of 163 DI's regiments were the remains of a dam and several locks that the Germans had destroyed. A thick mist enabled the men to lay planks across the gaps undetected, although the night was bitterly cold. By 8.15 on the morning of 10 November, 415 RI of 163 DI had crossed the Meuse and set up telephone communications with the south bank. Once the mist lifted, they were sitting ducks for German machine-gunners who held the heights north of the river, overlooking the railway, which still runs along the north bank of the Meuse. The enemy was bound to defend this vital railway line, and the important marshalling yards at Lumes, north of Flize, where 1,200 full wagons were waiting to be sent back to Germany. Moreover, the French artillery could not support the men on the northern bank as their whereabouts were not known exactly, and, furthermore, the villages were full of French civilians. Nevertheless, the fragile bridgehead managed to hold on until evening along the line of the railway. During the night of 10/11 November the engineers worked to build rafts and gangways across the river so as to re-supply the position. The enemy, meanwhile, was bombarding Mézières with gas shells and incendiary bombs, setting fire to the hospital, which had to be evacuated. That evening, however, listening posts had picked up the message from the German government to their plenipotentiaries that they should sign the armistice agreement.

On 11 November the Germans continued to shell Mézières, but at 11am, on the north bank of the Meuse, Private Delalucque of 415 RI sounded the 'Cessez le feu', followed by 'Levez-vous, Garde à vous' and 'Au Drapeau'. The last soldier to be killed in the sector was 40-year-old Private First Class Augustin Trébuchon, Croix de Guerre, killed by a bullet in the head at 10.50. During the three days 9–11 November of the Meuse crossing and the establishment of the bridgehead, 163 DI suffered 96 killed and 198 wounded, two-thirds of these casualties in the single regiment that got across the Meuse.[53] At the headquarters of 163 DI in Dom-le-Mesnil, the division's chaplain recorded the moment when the armistice came into effect:

On the north bank of the Meuse the battalions waited, watchful, guns in their hands, in their hastily dug shallow trenches for the hands of the clock to mark the hour of the end of the nightmare. The nightmare carried on as though nothing new had happened. Shells crashed into the ground, the machinegun rattled out its song of death ... 10.45 a round of 150s lands on Dom-le-Mesnil. 10.57 machineguns are firing on both sides. 11 o'clock down at the far end of the gangway an invisible bugle sounds the ceasefire.[54]

The position on 11 November 1918 and the march to the Rhine

The armistice conditions which the German plenipotentiaries accepted by their signatures early in the morning of 11 November were essentially Foch's own military terms. The document contained thirty-four clauses. They related to naval conditions, East Africa and Germany's eastern borders, but the important military clauses that affected the French Army were contained in the first eleven. Foch ensured that there should be no opportunity for Germany to begin hostilities again. German forces were obliged to evacuate within fifteen days the Allied territory they occupied, the left bank of the Rhine and three bridgeheads on the right bank; they were to cease all destructive measures and reveal the whereabouts of mines, poisoned wells and so on; and they were to surrender 5,000 guns, 25,000 machine guns, 3,000 *Minenwerfer* and 1,700 aircraft. Foch was under no illusions about Germany's capacity to replace weaponry, but his transport clauses would surely prevent any further German offensive. Within thirty-one days, 500 locomotives and 15,000 wagons were to be handed over in good working order, together with spare parts; the railway network in Alsace and Lorraine was to be handed over in the same time frame, together with its coal supplies, materiel and personnel; and 5,000 lorries were also to be delivered in good condition within 36 days. If the German Army wished to re-invade, it would have to do so on foot.

As Foch presented these terms to the Germans for signature, the French armies were still in line. At the Armistice the French Army in the Balkans had helped to liberate Albania and Serbia and stood along 100 kilometres of the Danube; in Romania where a French general had already done sterling service in training and equipping the Romanian forces, the Army of the Danube stood ready to cross the Danube; in the Middle East French troops were on board ship off Beirut and Alexandretta waiting to disembark; in Italy French General Graziani was preparing to invade Bavaria. The earlier Austrian armistice, signed on 3 November in Italy, had opened the possibility of an invasion of southern Germany. On the Western Front, General Boissoudy's Sixth Army in Flanders had crossed the Scheldt and moved a good distance eastwards from the river. First Army was on Belgian territory at Chimay, alongside the British Fourth, and this despite Rawlinson's complaints that the French would not keep up. On First Army's right, Third Army had replaced Mangin's Tenth and had crossed the vital Hirson–Mézières railway, cutting off Germany's essential supply line. Next, in touch with Mézières, Fifth Army was in Charleville on the Meuse, and Fourth Army had sent units across the river, near Sedan, redeeming the fiasco of 1870. Finally, Tenth Army had been transferred to Castelnau's Eastern Army Group and was almost ready to take the offensive with the Eighth Army that had been guarding the quiet Vosges sector since 1914.

The two armies in the centre that did most of the attacking between July and November, and more especially during the general offensive that began on 26 September, were First Army alongside the British and Fourth Army alongside the Americans. First Army had advanced more than 150 kilometres since 8 August, taking more than 32,000 prisoners and capturing 4,500 machine guns, 500 artillery pieces and 507 *Minenwerfer*.[55] Fourth Army advanced 35 kilometres in the war's last six days alone, capturing more than 5,000 prisoners. The French Army as a whole on the Western Front captured well over 130,000 prisoners and more than 2,000 guns.[56] Over 2.5 million French soldiers were serving on the Western Front, the largest Allied contingent, with a further 41,000 in Italy; 191,000 in Serbia, Bulgaria, Romania; 6,000 in Asiatic Turkey – making around 2,800,000 in total.[57]

These 2.8 million troops still had work to do. By the terms of the armistice, Germany was to evacuate within fifteen days the occupied territories in Alsace-Lorraine, Belgium, France and Luxembourg. The French Army's first task was, therefore, to ensure that the evacuation was

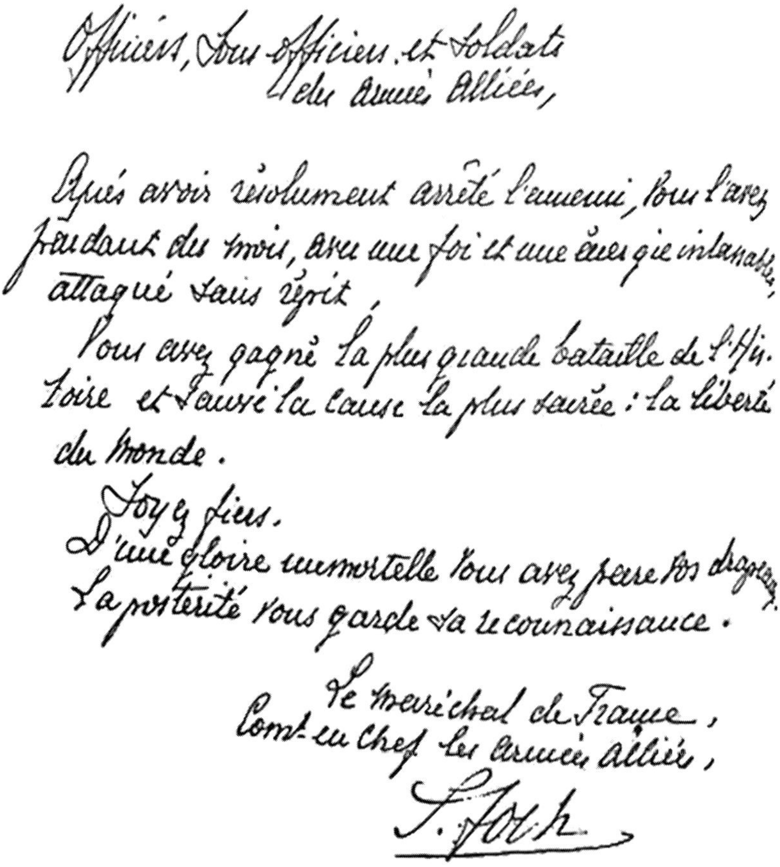

Officiers, Sous-Officiers et Soldats
des Armées Alliées,

Après avoir résolument arrêté l'ennemi, vous l'avez
pendant des mois, avec une foi et une énergie inlassables,
attaqué sans répit,
Vous avez gagné la plus grande bataille de l'Histoire et sauvé la cause la plus sacrée : la liberté
du Monde.
Soyez fiers.
D'une gloire immortelle vous avez paré vos drapeaux.
La postérité vous garde sa reconnaissance.

Le Maréchal de France,
Comt en Chef les Armées Alliées,
F. Foch

Fig. 20 Marshal Foch's 'order of the day', 12 November 1918, to all ranks of the Allied armies
'After having halted the enemy resolutely, you attacked him for months with unwearying faith and energy, and without respite. You have won the greatest battle in History and saved the most sacred cause: the liberty of the world. Be proud. You have covered your standards with immortal glory. May posterity be always grateful.'

carried out and to reoccupy national territory. The successive lines to be reached by certain dates formed part of the armistice agreement. On 17 November the Allied armies were to advance from the point they had reached on 11 November. Hence, they were accorded five days' rest, clear of marching. The march to the Rhine was to begin on the sixteenth and be completed by the twenty-eighth day following 11 November. The German bad faith as regards booby-traps and handing over railway materiel meant that the French had to be cautious. Several 'incidents' involving the handover of materiel, or even criminal actions, had caused Foch to order that the enemy had to be followed, but not so closely as to risk any military action.

The Eastern Army Group, deprived of its chance of glory in the cancelled Lorraine operation could move, finally, from its fixed defences. Renamed the Castelnau Army Group, it now comprised Second Army, reduced to headquarters only and returned to Nancy, where it began the war, and Gouraud's Fourth Army, that had carried out the Meuse campaign with the Americans. Seventh Army remained in the Vosges where it helped with the continuing training of US troops. Castelnau's divisions entered Alsace on 17 November to a delirious reception, and reached Colmar on the Rhine on the 22nd, where Castelnau installed his headquarters. He was the only general, of the five who commanded an army in August 1914, still to hold a command position.

The Reserve Army Group moved from northern France to the eastern frontier. Renamed the Fayolle Army Group, it took over Eighth and Tenth Armies, with headquarters at Sarrebourg. The eighteen infantry and three cavalry divisions of these two armies followed 10 kilometres behind the retreating enemy troops into the German Rhinelands, reaching the Rhine on 9 December. Triumphal entries were made into Strasbourg and Metz, in the recovered provinces of Alsace and Lorraine, with Pétain receiving his marshal's baton in Metz. He joined Joffre and Foch as France's third marshal. By 17 December the Allied armies were installed in the Rhineland, with the French occupying the most northerly of the three bridgeheads conceded in the armistice. A fourth bridgehead in Kehl, opposite Strasbourg, was added in February 1919.

General Maistre's Centre Army Group comprised First, Fifth and Sixth Armies, with headquarters near Châlons. The Flanders Army Group was dissolved on 18 November, and General Boissoudy, who had commanded the French Sixth Army within the group, moved to Nancy to command Second Army, whose previous commander, General Hirschauer, became military governor of Strasbourg. 13 DI remained in XXI Corps in Fifth Army as a second-line unit.

From Salonika, Franchet d'Espèrey moved his headquarters to Belgrade. His French troops had been hit badly by the influenza epidemic and by the onset of cold winter weather. Troop numbers dropped by 23,000 because of sickness and leave over the two months November–December. The three regiments of 122 DI joined the force occupying Turkey, one of them guarding the railway in Constantinople. Because of heavy snow, Nish and Sofia could not be supplied from Salonika, and so the railway from Constantinople became the vital supply line for the Armée d'Orient. The remaining troops of Franchet d'Espèrey's force were instructed to keep up the pursuit of the German *Eleventh Army*, commanded by Feld Marschall August von Mackensen. It had been occupying Romania, and, under the terms of the Austrian armistice, was given fifteen days to evacuate Romania, Hungary and Austria. However, German troops were still lingering in Hungary in early December, despite the Armistice Commission's orders that Hungary intern them. Indeed large quantities of materiel were passing through Hungary, returning to Germany. Mackensen demanded that full facilities be accorded his army units, travelling in trains passing through Austria and Bavaria, thus avoiding the new Czechoslovakia. Eventually the Entente ordered that the Hungarian authorities should arrest Mackensen, and he was handed over to the French, who interned him until 26 November 1919. One of the Armée d'Orient's regiments, 227 RI, guarded him during March, doubtless as a reward for the regiment's two mentions in despatches during the September fighting.[58] The Allied armies in the east had the task of maintaining order in Hungary and the Balkan countries until peace was signed.

In the Middle East, the French detachment occupied Alexandretta on 12 November and the area around Adana at the end of December. By early 1919 French and British troops were in full occupation of the former Ottoman provinces, up to the Cilician border. On 10 January the disparate French elements in the Hedjaz, Egypt, Palestine, Syria and Armenia were combined in the 'troupes françaises du Levant', and reinforced from mainland France. Then troubles began over the control of Syria, with the new King Feisal expecting to rule from Damascus over the whole area; they continued into the peace treaty negotiations.

Demobilisation

An armistice is not peace. The tasks just outlined had to be completed to ensure that no resumption of hostilities could occur, yet France's Army was very tired. The 'profound joy' that the French Army's postal control commission reported on 29 November 1918, based on an analysis of 101,788 letters, was tempered by some 'lassitude'. This was caused by the difficult physical conditions in some parts of the line, fatigue from the long marches in the last days of fighting, and impatience to return to a normal life. The frequent moves had made feeding the troops and delivering letters difficult, and the rain did not help. The older classes were finding the return to a regime of exercises and firm discipline hard to bear. On the other hand, the length of leave periods had been increased, although leave was still not allowed for Algeria and for the Lille area, only recently liberated after four years of enemy occupation. There was some consolation in the warm welcome for their liberators from the civilian populations, whether in Belgium or in Alsace and Lorraine. The armistice had been received with great joy but not excessive enthusiasm, the commissioners reported, with the most profound feeling being one of deliverance. Although some had not expected the end to come so quickly, the pursuit of the last weeks had convinced them that they had defeated the enemy militarily. Some German soldiers had attempted to fraternise, but had not been welcomed, especially when the French prisoners of war began returning 'in a deplorable state'. By far the most frequent topic mentioned in the letters (almost 20,000 mentions) was that of demobilisation. The older classes thought that they should be liberated immediately.[59]

Daniel Halévy had written to his mother on 8 November that he was expecting to do 'great things' after a few more days of waiting for Pétain's Lorraine offensive to begin. Yet he already had the sense that something would intervene to stop the operation: 'The professionals are sad, they did not truly think that it had to come to an end, and they are not the only ones. People are saying "It's finished!" with as much amazement as joy, they are like poor people who have won the lottery, and do not know what to do with the money.'[60] Indeed, the announcement of the signing of the Armistice provoked a number of conflicting responses.

How many times had we dreamed of this blessed day that so many will not have seen, how many times had we scanned and searched the mysterious future, the star of safety, the ever invisible lighthouse in the dark night. And now the day, forever immortal, had arrived! Our hearts could not hold this happiness, this joy that crushed us, and we stood there looking at each other silent and stupid. But we were called back to reality by calls of 'Fall in!' and the whistles of the day's adjutants calling us to drill as usual.[61]

Relief at having survived, incredulity that the end had come at last and, above all, a fierce desire to return home to family, to 'normality', dominated thoughts. Yet, as Barthas reveals, the end did not come immediately. France's Army now had to administer a state of war until a peace treaty was signed, but at the same time to manage millions of men who had nothing to do except wait, and that increasingly impatiently.

On 6 December Clemenceau appointed Louis Deschamps, a républicain de gauche, as under-secretary of state for demobilisation within the war ministry. In the Chamber of Deputies the victory speeches were interspersed with calls by those seeking to know what arrangements were to be made for demobilisation. Deschamps argued that no laws should be passed for the time being, since the country was still at war and about 900,000 older men were already scheduled for demobilisation. By the end of the year the class of 1891 – that is, those men who had reached their 47th birthday – and all older classes had been released. Deschamps' argument that it would be foolish to compromise the huge sacrifices of more than four years by a few weeks' impatience was accepted, and on 13 December the Chamber passed unanimously a resolution expressing confidence in the government to apply the principle of equality by releasing classes of men by age, with exceptions being made for those with heavy family responsibilities.[62]

In January 1919 another five classes (1892–96) were demobilised, and a further five (1897–1901) the following month. In March the classes of 1902–05 and in April those of 1906–09 were released.[63] All these men had been reservists in 1914. They returned to the depot in their original military region where they had left the clothes and belongings with which they had arrived for mobilisation. Naturally, with all the changes of affectation, men did not always return to their departure depots, or they no longer fitted the clothes they had left behind, or (frequently) time and rodents had damaged or destroyed what they had left. Accordingly they were issued with a suite of clothing including underwear and a 'demob' suit named after the under-secretary of state for pensions, Léon Abrami. Demand outstripped supply and so suits were made of dyed fabric originally intended for army uniforms, and all were cut to the same pattern. Shoes in the most popular sizes ran short. If the demobilised men did not want the clothing, as most did not, they were given instead a derisory 52 francs.[64] Their 'carnet de pécule', showing the sums that had been retained from their combat allowances and paid out in stamps, was redeemed at the same time. The system had been established in order to ensure that soldiers had access to money on demobilisation. These procedures and accompanying paperwork exasperated men who longed only to reach home. They had marked time whilst waiting to be released, not knowing the exact date when that would come, as earlier classes had to be cleared before their turn came, and they vented their discontent on the trains that transported them. The bill to return administration of the railways to pre-war conditions, provided that they gave absolute priority to military and economic needs, had been introduced in February 1919.[65] In May 1919 a monthly average of 13,000 broken carriage windows and 400 train doors was reported.[66]

In theory, on arriving home, the men had fifteen days during which to reclaim the employment that they had had in 1914. Of course, some men returned to villages flattened by the war or to find that their wives had disappeared or been punished for 'horizontal collaboration'. Agricultural workers could slip back into work, but in towns it was more difficult. Frequently, in the joy of reaching home, men simply forgot to send to their former employer the formal letter, with which they had been issued, in order to reclaim their job within the fifteen-day deadline. In other cases, the firm no longer existed, or the employer had been obliged to fill the position to remain in business. Then there was competition from those who had been demobilised earlier (the majority of them disabled, hence with a claim to an employer's goodwill), or from those being laid off from munitions factories whose products were no longer needed, or from returned prisoners of war.

Demobilisation was even more difficult for the Salonika troops, who felt abandoned by the Fatherland. Official news of the armistice on the Western Front only reached them days later, and Paris wanted to bring an end to Bolshevism – 'encircle' it and 'bring about its fall', Clemenceau told Franchet d'Espèrey on 27 October. Very few men volunteered to continue the war; they wished simply to go home, despite the very difficult journey through Greek transit camps, to Taranto in Italy and then a four-and-a-half-day train journey to France.[67]

One of the armistice articles stated that all Allied prisoners of war were to be released immediately. Most of the French prisoners were in Germany and as early as two months after the armistice, many had already returned to France, some by train through Switzerland, some by sea and the majority handed over to the nearest French Army unit. A certain Captain Charles de Gaulle had been a prisoner of war in Germany since being captured at Verdun in May 1916. His last prison was the Wülzburg fortress near Weissenberg in eastern Bavaria. Somehow he reached the Swiss frontier by 1 December and was in Lyon two days later. In Switzerland he had been awarded a train ticket (third class) to return to France, but borrowed the money to upgrade to second class, as third class was beneath his dignity as an officer. Details of his journey are scanty, perhaps because of a degree of shame at not having participated in the victory, and because he made it under his own steam, rather than as part of an organised repatriation.[68] Except for those too ill or too badly wounded to be moved, or a few isolated cases, all French prisoners that Germany admitted to holding had been returned by 16 January 1919 – over half a million. This was a tremendous achievement, presided over by a special mission in Berlin headed by General Dupont, formerly of the French intelligence service. Some mothers and wives, who had pinned their hopes on the survival of their sons and husbands, refused to accept that more were not hidden, but the fact had to be accepted that 38,963 men had died in captivity, many as late as 1918 because of the influenza epidemic.[69] In February 1922 the government accorded those men who had died in captivity the *mention* 'mort pour la France', a legal designation which gave them the same status and rights as those killed in combat. In 1921 the Ministry of Pensions decided to repatriate the bodies and return them to those families who claimed them. This task was completed between 1923 and 1926. Barely 500 bodies remain in Germany today, although a monument/ossuary in present-day Poland contains the remains of 1,333 French soldiers.[70] A necropolis was constructed specially in Sarrebourg (Moselle) to receive the unclaimed bodies, and a monument 'la Captivité' erected in the centre of the cemetery. Some 4,000 other French prisoners of war died in France, but in the départements occupied by the Germans, and others died in German field hospitals, many in Alsace.

German prisoners of war in France, however, were retained as a pledge against a resumption of hostilities. Their presence added to the difficulties of the job market, as they were being used for reconstruction. General Anthoine, last met when he was sacked as Pétain's chief of staff, was administering the scheme, under which, unfortunately, it was cheaper for employers to use prisoner labour than to employ the demobilised veterans.

A halt was called to demobilisation in April 1919. Both Foch and President Poincaré were concerned that men were being released too quickly. The treaty negotiations, begun in January, were nowhere near completion, and Germany was showing signs of refusal to accept defeat. Indeed, refusal to sign any peace treaty seemed a possibility. Deschamps told the Senate Army Commission on 28 May 1919 that the Rhine Army would not be eligible for demobilisation; it was to consist of nine infantry and two cavalry divisions. In June 1919, as fears increased that Germany would still refuse to accept the treaty, Mangin's Tenth Army was brought up to fourteen divisions. Even after the treaty had been signed on 28 June, Deschamps admitted to the Senate Army Commission on 3 July, that it would not be possible to reinforce the occupying forces any further once all classes except those of 1918 and 1919 had been demobbed, which was due by October.[71] The 1918 class was to be demobilised in June 1920, because being called up in 1917 they had completed their three years, and the 1919 class (called up in 1918, but not all incorporated) was to be demobilised in March 1921.

Therefore, no more classes were released after April until August 1919, after Germany had signed, when the classes 1910–14 were demobilised, thus releasing all those who had served in the active army for the entire war and before. Those of the class of 1911 who had survived had given eight years' service. The entire demobilisation process was complete by November. An official end to hostilities was decreed on

24 October 1919, which meant that all laws and regulations enacted for the duration of the war became redundant on that date.

Although demobilisation by classes, with the oldest being released first, was the most equitable method – but men with six living children were released irrespective of age – the process was disruptive. Apart from the uncertainty of not knowing the exact date of release, the removal of older men from squads or companies who had fought and died together broke the bonds of comradeship that had sustained them. Regiments were dissolved as they lost officers, and companies were amalgamated. All these factors added to discontent and impatience and, from the high command's point of view, made the men left in the French Army less efficient, were there to be a resumption of hostilities. The men in Eighth and Tenth Armies garrisoning the Rhinelands were particularly bitter, seeing the demobilised Germans walking about with their wives and girlfriends on their arm, whilst they, the victors, had to mount guard.[72]

The halt to demobilisation between April and August 1919 was the result of a real fear that Germany might not sign the peace treaty. The German delegates had been called to Versailles and were shocked at what they saw as the severity of the terms. Clemenceau told Poincaré on 21 April that he was becoming more and more sure that Germany would not accept the treaty and that 'il faudra remarcher' – they would have to march again.[73] At GQG a study was made of the resistance that Germany could offer to an Allied invasion. It concluded that adding together the remnants of the old army with the volunteers for the new *Reichswehr* army, there could be 425,000 men to resist such an Allied invasion.[74] When the German delegation presented a long list of counter-proposals in June, the fears increased. Clemenceau, Lloyd George, President Woodrow Wilson and Baron Sonnino (for Italy) called Foch in for a meeting about what could be done to force the Germans to sign.[75] Foch pointed out that now he had eighteen French divisions. With another ten British, five American and six Belgian divisions, his Allied armies could deal with the German forces, but would have to deal with a large hostile population as well. In November 1918, he remarked, he had 198 such divisions, but the politicians did not seem to understand that what Foch could have done then, or even a couple of months ago, was not what he could achieve with partially demobilised armies on 15 June 1919. Fortunately neither an invasion of Germany from the Rhine bridgeheads, nor the planned invasion of Bavaria, was required.

10   From 1914 to 1919: Aux armes, citoyens!

France's Army through the years of war

In August 1914 Joffre's stated intention was to take the offensive once all his armies had assembled. Despite some claims to the contrary, the French Army's 'doctrine of the offensive' did not imply a belief that sufficient offensive spirit could carry a soldier in his red trousers and armed with a bayonet into the enemy's lines, where he could pluck a laurel wreath from an enemy gun. Unfortunately, however, too many insufficiently trained men, led by unfit or incompetent commanders, attempted to mount infantry charges, unsupported by artillery and lacking intelligence about the enemy's whereabouts and strength. Yet, fortunately, enough sense of the offensive survived the slaughter of the Battles of the Frontiers to enable the French to retreat far enough to turn around and halt the invasion on the Marne, much to German surprise. In 1915 the French Army began to think about methods, and how to break out from the static trenches and through the enemy's front line. The thinking was mainly top-down at first, but gradually ideas began to percolate upwards as well, and by the end of 1915 GQG was soliciting detailed after-action reports in order to learn lessons. The aim remained breakthrough, but this proved elusive as the belligerents matched ever greater volumes of shell. The two Western Front battles of 1916 showed that, even when the front lines were breached, the depth of the defensive positions meant strategic failure. One answer was the 'scientific method', in which lengths and depths of front were assessed and the numbers of shells necessary to shatter defences were calculated, but this method was no more successful on the Somme than the enemy offensive had been at Verdun. There the Germans had concentrated an immense weight of artillery against a limited objective, but the French defenders managed to hold on. Nivelle's successful counter-stroke at Verdun in October 1916 gave him the top job in 1917, but then his attempt to duplicate his tactical success on a strategic scale failed utterly, achieving neither surprise, nor speed, nor overwhelming superiority of firepower. His failure led men to cry 'halt'.

Nivelle's successor, Pétain, led the French Army through the months of indiscipline. In France, under Painlevé as war minister, demands for delayed leave were answered, political instability was calmed, and industrial unrest among France's women as well as men workers was repressed. In Russia, however, the result of political effervescence was revolution and abdication. Pétain showed the army that victories could be won – in Flanders, at Verdun and at La Malmaison on the Chemin des Dames. These were won with a literally crushing weight of shell. At La Malmaison 80,000 tonnes of munitions were collected before the battle, and each metre of ground under attack received 7 tonnes of shell. This was a density ten times greater than during the 1915 Champagne offensive, and remained a record until 1943.[1] It was calculated that if all the guns and limbers on the La Malmaison front had been aligned, instead of arrayed in depth, they would have stood axle to axle.[2]

Such expensive offensive methods could not be sustained, and Pétain concentrated on the defensive until such time as depleted French and British manpower resources could be supplemented by the arriving Americans. By 1918 his defensive methods were beginning to be accepted, but only after considerable resistance from other generals, not always overcome. More importantly, however, Pétain's insistence on training and instruction began to pay dividends. In July 1918, with Foch in command to seize the strategic moment, the French Army was able to fight on the Marne a classic inter-arms battle, combining infantry, artillery, tanks and aircraft. The Army gave France its sword and buckler – Foch and Pétain – and in combination the two generals gave France the victory.

It was not these two professional soldiers alone but the immense national citizens' army that won it. From the start date in August 1914 to 1 January 1919, 8,410,000 men were mobilised, 195,000 of them officers, many promoted during the course of the war, and 7,740,000 other ranks. In addition, 260,000 natives from North Africa (that is, Algeria and Tunisia) and 215,000 other colonial natives also served. The total number of killed and disappeared cannot be estimated exactly, as detailed records were not made at first, and some of the disappeared in fact returned as released prisoners of war. Furthermore, an unknown number died of their wounds or as a result of their war service later than June 1919, when the parliamentary report on casualties was drawn up. The figure of 1,383,000 dead and missing must not, therefore, be treated as an exact number recording each and every soldier – but its magnitude almost defies belief.[3]

Those who survived, however damaged in mind or body, had shown that a citizens' army could adapt and improve as necessary. Although the enemy adapted also to the conditions on the Western Front, French flexibility won out because by 1918 they had the weapons necessary for victory. At different times technology gave both sides the edge; the air war, when mastery of the skies depended on the technical specifications of the aircraft, provides a good example. Mastery belonged to the Allies and to the enemy at different times, ending finally with the Allies.[4]

As this brief summary shows, the Army of August 1914 was a very different organisation by 1918. It began the war with five numbered armies, and ended it with 102 divisions in nine (First to Eighth and Tenth, the Ninth having been dissolved), plus the Armée d'Orient, the Armée du Danube, the force (mainly territorial) under the command of the Paris military governor, the two divisions of the FFI in Italy, and the units in the Middle East that became the Troupes françaises du Levant in January 1919. The proportion of infantry within the army had dropped from 71.8 per cent of total effectives to 50.4 per cent in 1918; those in the artillery almost doubled from 18.1 per cent to 35.7 per cent; the engineers increased as well from 4.9 to 6.9 per cent; the cavalry was not much altered (from 4.8 per cent to 4 per cent), but many in the cavalry served dismounted or transferred to tanks or aviation. Before the war the Army's 'service automobile' had fewer than 200 officers, but more than 650 by December 1914 and 2,800 by 1918.[5] In 1918 the few remaining divisions still consisting of two brigades of two regiments each were reduced to a single Infanterie Divisionnaire of three regiments like the others; 63 DI became the Polish Division; thirty-three regiments were dissolved, all of them reserve units except for one, recently formed, colonial regiment. The effective strength of a company was reduced from the theoretical 194 to 175 in October 1918.[6]

Pay had quintupled from the miserly 'sou', or five centimes, of August 1914 to 0.25 francs per day for an ordinary soldier, but was supplemented by long-service and combat allowances. If the war had gone on longer, Clemenceau was proposing to increase the basic rate to 0.75 centimes, only half of the increase being paid in cash. The Army Commissions were pressing for a franc per day, but, as late as October 1918, it was feared that the war might continue into 1919, making such a large increase very expensive. Besides, Pétain argued that the men would only spend the extra money on alcohol.[7]

If the proportion of cavalry effectives remained fairly constant, nevertheless the changes in the two corps of cavalry were, of course, enormous. By 1 July 1916 the cavalry had already lost 3,500 officers and 45,000 other ranks to the infantry, the artillery and aviation. Three cavalry divisions were dissolved in 1916 and another the next year. Regiments of dismounted cavalry were created, one per division, and eventually in

January 1918 two whole divisions of dismounted cavalry (DCP or Division de cavalerie à pied) were formed. The remaining mounted regiments were gradually armed with increasing numbers of machine guns. The most significant change was the provision of motorised guns (37mm) and machine guns. This enabled the cavalry to move quickly – more quickly than infantry – to points wherever necessary, and to arrive ready-armed.[8] Each of the two Cavalry Corps had about 100 such vehicles.[9]

The need for mobility and speed, reflected in these changes to the cavalry, meant a greatly increased role for the engineers. They, the Génie, were responsible for preparing and equipping the battlefield with shelters, observation posts and so on; for establishing/re-establishing communications; for destroying or repairing roads, bridges; supplying water and electricity to the battlefield; and building and maintaining barracks and hospitals in the rear. On mobilisation in 1914, the thirty-four battalions of the Génie, with a further two in North Africa, expanded to provide a company of sappers per division, two more for each corps, and for each reserve division three newly created companies, consisting of one sapper, one for bridges and one for depots.[10] Numbers expanded as the number of divisions and corps increased, and by war's end the Génie was organised as follows: each division had a commander for the divisional engineers who made up two companies of sappers (220 men and four officers), one depot company, a detachment of telegraphists and a section of 'projecteurs de campagne', contraptions which shone a concentrated light where needed. Each corps had a corps engineer commander in charge of two companies of sappers and a company of telegraphists. Each army had a general with a staff and a director of services, with a variable number and differing types of companies, including electricians and radio operators. Five supplementary services increased in importance during the course of the war: water, which required the digging of wells and installation of pumps; woods (to manage the forestry resources of each sector); electricity to provide light in the shelters; and camps and cantonments. The fifth, highly important, service was roads – the most famous example being the Voie sacrée leading to Verdun, but this is only one example among many similar ones.[11]

The intelligence services improved greatly during the war years.[12] In 1914 Berthelot had complained that intelligence about the whereabouts of the German right wing was provided by British airmen, and that French cavalry had failed in this role. French cryptanalysts were among the best in the world. Chapter 7 showed how Painvin's swift decipherment of a German telegram, in recently upgraded code, enabled the French to know where the offensive against Humbert's Third Army on the Matz was to fall. Air and photo reconnaissance improved, as did aircraft and cameras, and the intelligence they provided allowed maps to be updated and enemy movements spotted. The 'Groupe de canevas de tir d'armées' (GCTA), part of the army's Service géographique, produced the plans directeurs for the artillery. In 1917 the GCTA had two special trains which followed the troops on operations so as to be able to produce new up-to-date maps as quickly as possible.[13] Although the surprise German offensive on the Chemin des Dames in May 1918 represented a failure by French intelligence, the destruction of a large network of its agents just beforehand was a large factor in the failure. Foch's orders to overfly the same areas, day after day, enabled all changes in the enemy dispositions thereafter to be tracked, and there was no repeat intelligence failure.

The French had an advantage in the matter of intelligence agents and train spotters. Because northern France and French-speaking Belgium and Luxembourg were under enemy occupation, this meant that a disaffected population could provide a pool of potential agents. Hence the French Army had 40 networks with 650 agents to provide intelligence about German trains and movements of troops. The German Army could not match this since, apart from a small area in Alsace, nowhere did the Allies occupy German territory. One of the most successful networks covered the important rail junction in Luxembourg, where Madame Rischard and her husband supplied information via cleverly coded messages in an agricultural newspaper, sent through the ordinary mail. On Foch's recommendation, Madame Rischard was introduced into the Légion d'Honneur in 1919, and awarded the Croix de Guerre avec Palme.[14] Furthermore, the Allies could share intelligence, even when sharing troops or guns was impossible or simply unwelcome. An allied bureau had been set up in late 1914 in Folkestone to coordinate the information coming from Belgium especially, and also to monitor cross-Channel traffic. Another allied bureau was established in Paris in 1915 to monitor mail, visas and censorship. An unidentified 'German military critic' judged after the Armistice that the German defeat was 'due in large part to the particularly brilliant intelligence services of our adversaries. Foch was informed constantly and correctly about the number of German reserve divisions, on their distribution and combat value, and even on the intentions of the high command.'[15]

One of the greatest improvements seen between 1914 and 1918 was in the medical services but, it must be admitted, from a very low base. Returning fit men to the fighting as quickly as possible was vital – despite the paradox of needing to patch men up to be returned to be wounded again, or killed – hence the topic receives extended treatment here.

As the war of movement ended and trench fighting became the norm, the weight of medical resources moved away from the corps down to the divisional level, although the corps retained toxicology laboratories and eventually a special ambulance ('ambulance Z') for patients who had been gassed. The groups of divisional stretcher-bearers were reinforced gradually to include a dentist and seven pharmacists (there were none in 1914), and the number of stretcher-bearers in each division increased from 132 men in 1914 to 177 by December 1917.[16] These increased resources came with increased civilian control following the scandals of 1914 that had been widely reported in the press. In January 1915 a civilian commission of parliamentarians and medical authorities was established to supervise the war ministry's 7th Directorate, which ran the French Army's medical services. Then, on 1 July 1915, Justin Godart was appointed under-secretary of state for the medical service, removing it from direct control by the war minister. Although a lawyer and not a medical man, Godart proved a highly efficient minister, able to work with both military and medical personnel. He remained in post for almost three years, an unusually long period for Third Republic ministries, and was succeeded in February 1918 by Louis Mourier.[17]

In the field, as it became apparent that the majority of wounds were not caused by bullets, but by grenades, shrapnel or shell splinters, the system of evacuating the wounded to the interior had to be changed. Such wounds quickly became infected, and delay in treatment could be fatal: it was the slow evacuation of the wounded in filthy trains that had caused the outcry in 1914. Hospitals were built, therefore, close to large railway stations as near the front as possible, often housed in the new pre-fabricated baraques Adrian. The journey of a wounded man followed, thereafter, three stages. First, the regimental first-aid post was respon-sible for applying a preliminary dressing, and sending the man, either on foot or by stretcher, to the second stage. This second stage was the divisional ambulance, located 10–12 kilometres behind the front lines. The ambulance was not a vehicle, but a medical unit, containing a mobile surgical unit (auto-chir) with four operating tables for those too badly wounded to be moved further (see Figure 3 in Chapter 2). The third stage was the hospital – hôpital d'opérations et d'évacuations (HOE) – which contained 3,000 to 4,000 beds. In principle, there was one HOE for every corps.[18]

At GQG the medical services were run by a 'direction générale du service de santé', attached to the lines of communication. This arrange-ment made liaison difficult between the operations staff, who naturally wished to remain discreet about forthcoming attacks, and the medical services responsible for dealing with their aftermath. In February 1917, however, a change was made – yet another complication for the new CinC Nivelle preparing his offensive – and the 'directorate' was replaced by a 'Bureau Santé', whose director was the under-secretary of state, Godart. He was not permitted to correspond with the medical men in the individual armies, however, and a confusion of responsibilities contributed to the new scandal of the medical failures during Nivelle's offensive on the Chemin des Dames.

The breakdown of the system in April 1917 was due to several factors. The six corps originally intended for the offensive on the Chemin des Dames each had their regulation HOE, but when another two corps were added to the order of battle, two more had to be provided. Accordingly, GQG made plans for 4,000 beds, for the use of Sixth Army, to be provided in Laon and Anizy – behind the German lines, hence dependent upon a successful breakthrough, which did not, of course, occur. Also Godart arranged for hospitals in Orléans (about 200 kilometres distant from the battlefield) to act as HOEs. Then, the baraques ordered in January for the planned HOEs were delayed, first by slow production in the factories, then by transport problems due to freezing weather followed by a thaw. Godart blamed GQG for lack of proper arrangements; GQG blamed the engineers for not constructing the baraques in time; the Génie blamed the transport corps for not delivering them. The HOE at Prouilly (10 kilometres from Fismes) was particularly affected. Out of the twenty-four planned baraques for the installation, only sixteen had been erected by 16 April. The deficit was made up by using the baraques housing the very engineers who were putting them up. The wounded placed in one of these were left for several days without treatment, because they had been forgotten.[19]

Numbers were the problem. Nivelle's offensive was so huge that it is doubtful whether any medical services could have coped. There were simply insufficient doctors, surgeons and nurses in the whole of France. The Prouilly HOE, for example, treated 1,499 severely wounded men over the three days 16–18 April in its two autos-chirs, with its seventeen surgical teams working twelve-hour shifts. Since an operation lasted on average one hour, only 533 men were operated on during those three days.[20] More surgeons would have been needed to operate on all of them, but GQG's request for a 50 per cent increase in medical personnel had received the response that such an increase was impossible. Triage broke down completely, so that trains were filled with lightly wounded or, worse, in some cases, were occupied forcibly by them instead of by those requiring urgent evacuation. Moreover, the regulating station for evacuations was in Fère-en-Tardenois. There was no telephone communication between that station and the HOE that wished to request a train to evacuate the wounded; and the line through the station was single-track, with munitions and troops moving to the front given priority over the wounded being moved to the rear.[21]

Since the civilians invited to observe the first day's operations on 16 April had seen all the wounded flooding back to the ambulances, there was no hiding the medical disaster. The army commissions demanded explanations of Godart. He acted by creating by decree on 11 May 1917 a 'médecin-chef' in each army, corps and division headquarters, who would work closely with the CinC so that the medical arrangements would be made in tandem with drawing up operational orders. Now the medical services had a staff and equal authority with other arms, such as the artillery. Also, a medical officer was deployed to each regulating station to supervise the passage of all medical trains. He had the authority to decide who would travel and where the trains would be directed.[22]

The failure of the medical services during Nivelle's 1917 offensive had caused a great scandal, but lessons were learned and improvements made.[23] Pétain's 'defence in depth' and constitution of reserves had been applied to the medical services as well. In the first half of 1918, these changes resulted in the reduction to one of the two divisional ambulances (because divisions moved frequently) and the maintenance of two corps ambulances, one for surgical and the other for medical cases, including the gassed, each holding 250 beds. Also, two lines of 'primary' HOEs were provided, reduced to about 500 beds for wounded who could not be moved, and another 1,000 beds for giving first aid to enable the wounded to be evacuated. There were also two innovations. The lightly wounded and not seriously ill were evacuated to the interior, as in 1914, to be returned to their units after treatment; and so-called 'secondary' HOEs were created well away from the front lines (at a distance of about ten to twelve hours by rail). These secondary installations could deal with thousands of cases and were sited so as to be able to receive complete trainloads of wounded at any one time. Because of improved triage near the front, the wounded could be moved a greater distance for surgery and treatment. The system of secondary establishments where the majority of cases could be treated depended completely upon the railway facilities: fast railway lines, and a series of 'medical regulating stations' where the wounded were checked and all those whose condition would be worsened by further travelling removed from the trains.

The functioning of the medical services in the Chemin des Dames sector in 1918 shows how far the system had improved since the 1917 disaster described above. For the German offensive expected in July and for Foch's counter-offensive, medical resources in central France were expanded by taking them from the Eastern Army Group and from the

DAN, which was in the process of being transferred from Flanders to the Marne and so not using its own medical services. Tenth Army was directed to send half its wounded to Third Army medical units, which in their turn were augmented by some of First Army's resources in Picardy where the front was quiet. Fourth, Fifth and Sixth Armies were allocated extra medical trains, and barges were organised along the Seine, Marne and Oise. Regulating stations had the authority to divert trains from the Central Army Group's lines of communication to other secondary HOEs.

On 15 July, when the German offensive began, Fourth Army held the Reims sector. As already described, it operated a successful withdrawal from the front line, and so its hospitals were pulled back, leaving only triage facilities placed on communication lines. Extra vehicles (600 cars and 15 lorries per army corps) were provided to cope with the extra distance to the surgical units. German bombardment rendered the hospital at Châlons unusable and its staff was shared out among other installations. Given the success of Fourth Army's elastic defence, fighting had died down by the second day, and so Fourth Army facilities were devoted to the badly pressed Fifth Army, next in line. In fifteen days of fighting, Fourth Army's medical units dealt with 12,694 wounded, 3,009 ill and 2,296 gassed patients; 5,866 wounded were operated upon and 6,828 were evacuated without surgical intervention. Of the more than 16,000 soldiers evacuated, 11,000 remained on the lines of communication (using 43 medical trains) and 5,000 (in 19 trains) were evacuated to the interior.

Fifth Army was in a much less favourable position. Because it had been driven back by the German offensive, it could not use its forward medical units, and in addition the rail communications were worse in its sector. Some of its wounded were treated by Fourth Army, and buses, lorries and cars were provided to take patients away from the triage and first aid posts. In the fifteen days of fighting 18,500 wounded, 2,796 ill and 4,500 gassed men passed through Fifth Army's medical units, and the thirty-six teams of surgeons operated on over 3,000 wounded. British and Italian units were fighting in Fifth Army also, and the French helped out in their medical units.

Sixth Army, with a US Corps, held the bottom of the Marne salient. The army had nineteen triage ambulances, one for each division, or surgical grouping (one per corps), comprising in all 1,450 beds. Four HOEs further in the rear brought up to 5,600 the number of available beds. Two good roads connected to the rail centres at Meaux and Coulommiers, and the canal at Meaux was also used for evacuations. During the battle 15,279 wounded and sick men passed through Sixth

Army's medical services; 3,400 were evacuated by water, mostly to be operated upon in Paris hospitals; and forty-eight French and eighteen American medical trains passed through its regulating station of Le Bourget.

Tenth Army's mission was, of course, the counter-offensive. It had a line of surgical ambulances to treat those wounded too seriously to be moved (about fifty beds), placed 10–15 kilometres behind the front line. Next there was an 'advanced grouping' of triage ambulances, which acted also as embarkation centres for the medical trains. Finally two HOEs operated in the second line, together with a civilian hospital centre of 1,000 beds. Tenth Army also used Third Army's facilities. The use of two types of unit near the front, the surgical ambulances and the triage/embarkation units proved its worth in the advance that Tenth Army made. It enabled the battlefield to be cleared of the wounded quickly. In an advance, an army could not rely on a good rail service, which was vital in other cases. Through the regulating station at Le Bourget there passed 24,210 wounded, 1,587 ill and 4,520 gassed soldiers of Tenth Army, which sent another 4,600 men to Third Army medical facilities.

In global terms, over 96,000 cases were treated in the medical units belonging to the armies involved in the fighting in July 1918. More than two-thirds were transferred immediately to the more distant secondary HOEs, but all these were treated within acceptable delays. These totals are similar to those of the second half of April on the Aisne in 1917, but in 1918 the medical service 'operated to general satisfaction'.[24] Mortality rates for those who passed through the system were 5.5 per cent of those wounded treated in army units, 0.62 per cent of those treated on the lines of communication and 0.18 per cent in hospitals further back – which indicates an efficient triage system. The low percentage of wound infection showed that evacuation of most men to the secondary HOEs was acceptable.

This account makes clear how vital the liaison between medical and transport personnel was in managing an efficient, and life-saving, medical service during military operations. Although coping with medical trains passing through the regulating stations complicated the task of the railway directors, yet the presence of medical staff in those stations ensured that during the intense fighting of the latter half of July properly constituted trains arrived at their destination without delay, and sometimes sooner than had been thought possible.

At the end of July, however, another matter needed attention from the medical services. There had been 11,000 cases of influenza in the French Army that month, and there were 12,000 more in August, accompanied by a quadrupling of deaths attributable to the disease or the pulmonary infections that it caused. The peak came in October, with 117,161 cases (9,049 deaths). More than a third of France's Navy came down with flu, and the Army at Salonika had about 42,000 cases as well. With soldiers moving from depots to the front as reinforcements, and going on leave or returning, it was impossible to halt the spread. Civilians were affected too, to the extent that influenza became a notifiable disease. In Paris, during the single week 20–26 October 1918, 1,473 deaths were attributed to influenza, being almost half the total deaths recorded there that week. It was April 1919 before the epidemic was halted.[25]

Turning now from the men to their equipment, the French Army underwent great changes in this respect too, during the course of the war. The red trousers became the less visible 'bleu horizon'. A steel helmet, the 'casque Adrian' and steel baraques Adrian were produced. Unfortunately the idea of providing iron bedsteads for the soldiers nominally 'at rest' did not occur to the high command until Pétain became CinC. The French Army had 164 motorised vehicles in 1914, and requisitioned private cars; by 1918 there were 98,000. In 1914, a mere 2,000 telephone sets meant that commanders were scrounging them in the villages through which they passed, or sending orders to Switzerland, but there were 200,000 in use by 1918. It is the same story with radio sets: 50 in 1914, and in 1918 28,000.[26] The development of effective gas masks was, however, much speedier. From the simple cotton pad held against the nose and mouth, produced immediately in 1915 after the first German gas attack at Ypres, a daily average of 30,000 pads was produced between August 1915 and February 1916. Between July 1915 and April 1916, 12 million protective glasses were produced; in February 1916 production began of a complete mask that covered the whole head – 25.9 million were completed by war's end. All belligerents took effective measures to protect the troops from the effects of gas, which explains the low casualty figures. The gas weapon's greatest use was to neutralise, not to kill, and to cause discomfort by the need to wear the protective mask for long periods.[27]

In 1914 the infantry's personal weapon was an already obsolete Lebel rifle (1886 model, modified 1893), with its 55cm-long bayonet which made the whole weapon almost the height of a man.[28] As the eight cartridges were fired off, the reducing weight altered the rifle's centre of gravity, affecting its aim. The 1914 pattern Hotchkiss heavy machine gun was not much better than the older models also in use. For every 400 men equipped with the Lebel rifle, there was one machine-gunner. By the end of 1917 the ratio had dropped to one machine-gunner for every five men. This ratio led to the creation of combat sections, commanded by a sergeant, in which men had a specific role, such as in protecting the machine-gunner, or carrying the ammunition. The presence of these combat sections permitted greater flexibility than did 1914's rigid lines of riflemen. Other trench weapons that accompanied the infantry as they attacked were mortars and 37mm guns. Regiments were supplied with up to six mortars and three 37mm guns each. The infantry had grenades (over two million available in the Armée de l'Orient alone) in addition to automatic rifles and machine guns – on 1 November 1918 there were even more Lewis machine guns in the interior ready to be issued (66,293) than with the armies in the field (58,806).[29] An average of between two and three million grenades a month were leaving French munitions factories between August and October 1918.

As for all belligerents, the greatest changes occurred in the artillery arm, especially in the provision of heavy guns. The belief that the French 75mm gun could do all that was required disappeared during the 1914 Battles of the Frontiers. The growth in artillery was spectacular, both in numbers of men in the army and in production figures. The artillery consisted of 26,000 officers and 1,093,000 men by 1918, almost triple the 1914 effectives when the 900,000 or so mobilised men working in munitions factories are included.[30] During the war more than 27,000 75s and 3,000 short 155s were built, with 210 million and 32 million rounds respectively. By the end of hostilities 1.7 million engineers and workers were involved in munitions production.

The experience of 13 DI brings these numbers down to something more easily comprehensible. Michel Goya has allocated values to the various categories of weapon – for example, a heavy artillery piece is worth 150; a tank, 200; a 75mm gun, 100; a machine gun 30; a rifle 1, and so on. In this way, he has calculated that 13 DI's firepower increased from 610 in the opening battles of August 1914 to 11,540 in 1916 on the Somme, and to 31,550 at La Malmaison in 1917 on the Chemin des Dames, then dropping to 12,070 in September and October 1918.[31] Thus the firepower in 1917 was over 50 times greater than in 1914. The decrease in the 1918 figure shows both the massive and unrepeatable allocation in weapons that Pétain made for La Malmaison, and the exhaustion of the last few weeks of the war.

Table 18 shows the numbers of the various types of artillery available in 1914 and in 1918. The blanks indicate that the calibre of weapon was not produced in 1914, and show therefore the greater variety of gun available by war's end.

The newest weapon was the tank. General Estienne had realised very early on that a method of crossing the fire-swept no-man's-land was needed, and developed his ideas with support from Joffre during 1916.

(a)

(b)

Fig. 21 (a) A heavy gun under construction, with its camouflage paint
already applied. The figure seated on top reveals the scale
(b) A Renault FT tank, with camouflage paint

Table 18 *Comparison of artillery 1914 and 1918*

Type	Numbers in 1914	Numbers in 1918
65mm mountain	120	112
75mm	4,746	4,968
105mm long	–	576
145 & 155 GPF	–	480
155 short	104	1,980
155 long	–	720
220 mortar	–	324
280 mortar	–	117
Extra heavies	–	327
Trench artillery	–	1,600
Anti-aircraft guns	48	900

Note: The numbers refer only to the guns in France; they exclude those being built or being repaired or kept in arsenals, hence the figures for the end of November, rather than 11 November as above, are slightly greater. More than 27,000 75s were produced during the war (the small increase in November 1918 shows how many were lost) and 3,000 short 155s.
Source: Frédéric Guelton, *L'Armée française en 1918* (Saint-Cloud: 14–18 editions, n.d.), 47; Guinard et al., *Introduction*, 157.

He took advantage of the lessons learned during the British trials on the Somme, and had 256 tanks on hand for Nivelle's 1917 offensive on the Chemin des Dames. These heavy machines proved a disappointment, although there were still around 100 of them left by war's end. Estienne had absorbed once again the lessons of the 1917 fighting, and he worked with the car manufacturer, Louis Renault, to develop a light tank that could be produced more quickly and more cheaply. These only began to appear in small numbers in February 1918, but by the time of the July counter-offensive, there were enough for the massive intervention that proved so effective in supporting General Mangin's Tenth Army infantry. By 1 October 1918, 2,653 light tanks had been delivered – a remarkable effort by French armaments workers.[32] Women formed a large proportion of the extra workers taken on by Renault in the months April–October 1918, the record coming in April, when 44 per cent of new workers were women. The percentage of women workers at the main Renault factory outside Paris was a tiny 3.82 per cent in January 1914, and rose to 31.63 per cent in the spring of 1918.[33] At the same time as producing tanks, Renault workers were filling shells (4.14 per cent of total French production of shells), building 12,510 aircraft engines (15.46 per cent of the total French production), and 256 tractors/tracked vehicles.[34]

Renault was not the only manufacturer producing aircraft engines. Total French production rose from 40 in August 1914 to 374 in December and to well over 4,000 in each of the three months June–August 1918. The wartime total was 92,386, of which a quarter was ceded to the Allies: 12,000 to the British, 5,750 to the Russians, 4,800 to the Americans, and the remainder to the Italian, Romanian and Belgian armies. The output of finished aircraft rose from 50 in August 1914 to over 2,000 for each of the months April–October 1918, when supplies of the necessary raw materials were arriving. Here too women made up a third of the workers. Once again a number of finished aircraft (18 per cent of the total of 52,146) were ceded to the Allies, most (3,330) going to the Americans.[35]

The assured supply of aircraft enabled Pétain to create the Air Division which did such good work in the final victorious battles that were described in Chapter 8. Military aviation on the outbreak of war had only an observer role, using two groups of aircraft (150–160 aircraft in total) and one group of balloons. In 1916 its role increased with the creation of day and night bomber units and fighter aircraft. Joffre and his chief of aviation Barès had laid the groundwork by promoting the air arm, but it was the availability of large numbers of aircraft that made the Air Division possible. Pétain's head of the air service, Colonel Duval, reduced the types of aircraft being produced, and by March 1918 was able to combine squadrons (nominally of 15 aircraft each) of bombers and of fighters into wings of between 160 and 180 aircraft. Then, when the Air Division was formed, he created two brigades, each with a bomber and a fighter wing. The bombers were not to be used for strategic bombing, as the British preferred, but were employed in attacking enemy assembly points and protecting the observation aircraft of the armies as they spotted for the artillery. Duval had ordered the construction of a whole series of airfields along the length of the front, so that aircraft could land as necessary and be used where needed. Once again, mobility provided flexibility and rapidity.

The principle of concentrating a specific resource, air power, in one organisation, under the control of one man, rather than spreading resources throughout the entire army, was a significant development, and it was applied to the artillery as well. Once the race to produce more and better heavy guns was well under way, GQG decided to retain control in the CinC's hands, giving him a mass of artillery that could be directed where necessary. On 7 January 1917, a Réserve générale d'artillerie lourde (RGAL) was created, under the command of General Edmond Buat, to administer the French Army's heavy and extra-heavy artillery. Just before he was removed from command in December 1916,

Joffre had established a ten-man commission, presided over by General Guillaumat, to draw up a new artillery doctrine for the heavy guns that France had lacked at the start of the war.[36] Nivelle continued to support the concept. Mostly such artillery consisted of the heavy guns taken from forts and naval installations, but during the course of 1916 the short and long-barrelled 155s had started to leave the foundries in Le Creusot and St Chamond. It had been intended to make the heavy artillery mobile by mounting the guns on barges served by naval personnel, on railway wagons or on trucks. To achieve the necessary manoeuvrability, Buat had his own staff, a special centre in the main camp (Mailly, in Champagne), dedicated railway lines, depots and schools for mechanics and chauffeurs.[37] As well as the artillery training school that Pétain had set up in 1916 in Châlons, two further schools opened in Amiens and Toul, east of Nancy. The Fontainebleau school, where a special course to prepare young officers to command a battery of field artillery was established, produced 10,000 officer cadets and second lieutenants for the artillery in 1917. From August 1917 a monthly bulletin was published to spread new tactical and technical ideas and methods as widely as possible.

The RGAL consisted of three sections: the extra-heavy guns already in service; the ten regiments (numbered 81–90) whose guns were pulled by tractors; and the guns served by naval personnel. Its commander controlled training and supervised the technical improvements that needed to be made. Unfortunately, command of the horse-drawn guns remained under GQG control or that of the unit using them, which made training and the incorporation of lessons from the fighting less efficient. Accordingly, in January 1918 the reserve became simply the general artillery reserve and all types of artillery were attached to it.[38] Every gun not allocated to an army or an army corps was placed in the reserve in order to provide strategic mobility. The Reserve had two motorised corps, one of heavy artillery drawn by tractors (260 batteries, 14,000 vehicles), and one of regiments of field artillery (75s) pulled by lorry or other vehicle. These motorised regiments of field artillery had begun to be formed at the end of 1916 because of the shortage of horses. Since they proved successful, forty new regiments of 'artillerie portée' were proposed (thirty-seven of them created by 1918). By war's end a quarter of all the approximately 580 batteries were pulled or carried by a motor of some sort.[39]

This assembly of a mass artillery under GQG control, and mobile enough to be moved quickly, was an important adaptation to the needs of the 1918 battlefield, where speed was required to punch holes in different parts of the front in succession. Improved techniques, such as grading shell, allowing for meteorological conditions, laying guns from the map rather than by direct observation of the fall of shell, all meant that the guns could be used immediately they arrived and did not require several hours of range-finding. The assembly of a large mass of aircraft in the Air Division under GQG control and allocated to any army that required it at a certain time fulfilled the same purpose.

The aim of using masses of aircraft and of heavy artillery, organised as just described, could only be achieved if the means to move them were available, just as sufficient transport for the medical services was vital. In 1914 Joffre could not have fought the Marne battle without access to the rail network, which brought troops from eastern France to fight the enemy armies, who had marched on foot from the German frontier through Belgium. By the final weeks of the war, however, railway transport was at breaking point. This made it impossible to move divisions quickly to Lorraine for Pétain's planned offensive there, as shown in Chapter 9.

Horses were still important. On 1 July 1914 the French Army had 190,000 horses on its books, augmented by year's end by another 740,000 horses and mules requisitioned (as the declaration of the state of war permitted) from civilians. An average of 30,000 or so new animals was required monthly thereafter, most of them purchased in other countries. Feeding such numbers as well as supplying the AEF with horses to pull the guns that the French supplied were constant problems.[40] After the war those remaining were sold off and mostly supplied as meat. It was much easier to provide a motorised vehicle, and, in a phrase attributed to several authors, victory came on a flood of petrol.

Each of the twenty infantry corps in France in 1914 had its own transport corps, *le train*. In October 1916 each division was allocated a transport section with its own horses, carts and 129 men commanded by three officers. These numbers were reduced in October 1918 to only sixty horses or mules and sixty-four men in all. This decrease was because of the shortage of horses and the subsequent growth in motor transport. From 6,000 in 1914, the French Army had 43,000 vehicles in 1917, and 45,000 in 1918 plus another 25,000 or so devoted to the transportation needs of the artillery and aviation services. The number of drivers and mechanics increased ten-fold, to 110,000 men by war's end.[41] The German Army was handicapped by being unable to match the Allied resources in motor transport. The British controlled virtually the whole world supply of rubber for tyres, and the petroleum resources of the Middle East; the USA, which supplied two-thirds of the world's oil consumption, was on the Entente side. France had been a world leader in car production, and could easily transform factories to build armoured cars and lorries, as well as importing them from the USA. The French

Army and its equipment were moved by train and lorry; hence there was no repeat in 1918 of 1914's long retreat on foot.

Lorries ran from railheads to the front where roads permitted, but trains were needed for the longer haul of heavy materiel. The British and the Americans built and maintained railways in their sectors – they reverted to France after the war – but the arrival of the Americans placed an even greater strain on the rail system. This forced a degree of Allied cooperation, resulting in the formation in July 1917 of an Interallied Transport Committee in Paris, to deal with the common use of rolling stock and technical expertise. After the creation of the Supreme War Council and after Foch's appointment to supreme command, another Inter-Allied Transportation Council was established in Versailles. The return to a war of movement after July 1918 put increased strain on the rail system, especially as troops of different nationalities were moved about the front. The final fix, imposed only in October 1918, was the creation at Foch's headquarters of the Direction Générale des Communications et des Ravitaillements aux Armées (DGCRA), under a French director, General Payot.

During the war there was always conflict between the Army's rail needs and France's economic life. In the zone of the armies, control of the rail system was held by the army, whereas the civilian transport minister controlled the zone of the interior. Military control was seen as incompetent, and, beginning in 1916, there were frequent complaints in parliament. In July 1918 control was returned to the civilians, in the person of Albert Claveille, transport minister. Priority was given, however, to military needs, and a director-general of military transport answered directly to the war minister, and premier, Clemenceau. With Foch and Clemenceau working together, the DGCRA and the director of military transport had effective control over all rail and canal transport in France. If the war had continued into 1919, Allied control in the hands effectively of one man in supreme command would have given the Allies a huge advantage over the retreating German armies.[42]

From all these changes between 1914 and 1918, it is clear that France's army had been forced to adapt quickly to the world's first international, modern, industrial war. Unlike the British, it did not have the luxury of time to train and equip forces, because the country had been invaded; its mineral-rich areas were occupied and their citizens deported for forced labour or turned into refugees. The relative importance of the infantry declined as French casualties mounted, and the cavalry reduced in size even more, but the technical arms (air, artillery, engineering, radio telegraphy, tanks) grew and profoundly affected the conduct of operations. Armies were no longer made up of armed men, but of arms, mostly mechanically driven, served by men. The initial failures of the combination soldier–Lebel bayonet–75mm gun led to the production of new weapons and specialisations that destroyed old certainties. The creation of the RGAL removed the heavy artillery from divisions and corps and detached it from trench artillery. The combat section wielding a heavy machine gun was an infantry unit, but could equally well be considered as an artillery unit. The relationship between tanks and infantry was still evolving in November 1918. Aviation was gradually being detached, as the separate existence of the Air Division showed the way to a separate arm, as had happened in Britain. All these evolutions meant that the French Army of 1914 had changed more profoundly by November 1918 than the BEF or the AEF did from a later start.[43]

The French Army and France, its Allies and Germany

The French soldier remained a citizen, as the letters to his parliamentary representative revealed, especially during the 1917 mutinies. The presence in almost all the 36,000 French communes of a memorial to their children 'morts pour la France' or to their 'glorious dead' united the poilu, his family and the Republic, beyond the politics of right or left.[44] The Republic had been victorious, and the army had provided that victory. Pre-war popular attitudes were suspicious of reactionary generals on white horses. By war's end, these were replaced by a shared sense of sacrifice, although embusqués were still resented. After all, generals had lost sons too: Foch lost his only son and one of his two sons-in-law on 22 August 1914; Castelnau lost three sons and a fourth spent years as a prisoner of war. Generals d'Amade and Pouydraguin lost sons. When Colonel Renouard, former head of operations in GQG, died in 1918, two of his brothers had already been killed in action.[45] Politicians also lost sons; Louis Barthou, responsible for piloting the Three-Year Law through parliament, lost his only son in 1914, and Senator Paul Doumer, future president of the republic, lost four sons. Seventeen deputies were killed in action, one of them a duke, another a miner. This acceptance of the role of the military within the Republic continues today with the military parades on each 14 July throughout France. When the Green candidate in the 2012 presidential campaign, Eva Joly, suggested that a show of military force was not a suitable way to celebrate a country's national day, there was an immediate outcry. Indeed, the victory of 1918 presented no risk of a military coup, such as Franco's in Spain or the rise of Mussolini in Italy; certainly neither Foch nor Pétain would have considered for a moment such a course of action. They had had enough of politics and politicians.

The war united France in other ways too. Men from different French regions spoke different dialects, and some native colonial troops spoke no French at all. Even men from different areas of the same region could not necessarily understand each other. Historian Marc Bloch recorded the arrival of reinforcements from the 'four corners of Brittany', who could neither understand each other nor make themselves understood. One of them, unable to explain what ailed him, died one evening.[46] The end of regional recruitment and the mixing of units exposed men to a much wider experience of their country's diversity. Colonial troops learned that there were entities larger than a clan or tribe, and took back that concept to their home villages, together with experiences such as factory work.

The monuments to the dead of the Franco-Prussian War are few in number, usually decided on private initiative and erected up to thirty years after the event.[47] The Great War was different. A law of 25 October 1919 provided for a small state subvention for towns and villages who wished to commemorate and glorify those killed for France during the Great War. The great majority of monuments were inaugurated before the end of 1922, most of them consisting of an unadorned stele erected in a prominent position: the village square, next to the church or the mairie. Often, in small villages, these sites are next to each other. Given the date of the armistice, close to All Souls' day on 2 November, it was easy to combine religious and civic ceremonies around the monument, and many parish churches contain plaques listing those parishioners whose names also appear on the monument outside. Armistice Day is still a public holiday today, despite attempts to have the commemoration moved to the nearest Sunday so as to keep everyone working.

The huge participation by France's male population in fighting the war until victory did not lead to acceptance of the three-year commitment to military service that had passed into law in 1913, despite the fact that the proportion of 'insoumis', those who refused to serve by escaping into Spain or by other means, was so low. The new Chamber of Deputies, elected in November 1919, called the Chamber 'bleu horizon' because of the large number of veterans, acted on their belief that reservists had proved their worth, and so a long period of compulsory military service was not required. Pétain agreed.[48] By the laws of 1 April 1923 and 31 March 1928 the duration of active service was reduced to eighteen months and then to a year, although the time spent in the reserves was increased so that the total 'impôt du sang' remained at twenty-eight years. In order to avoid the riots that had accompanied the extension to three years in 1913, the government was accorded the right to maintain contingents under arms when the international situation demanded it. Furthermore, as the very low birth rates of the war years began to affect

Fig. 22 The war memorials in (a) Vorges (Aisne) showing a poilu, and (b) in Broussy-le-Grand (Marme), showing the plain stele type, both placed among the houses.
(c) An ossuary in the Soizy-aux-Bois (Marne) French military cemetery, with 1,282 names
(d) Part of the Suippes Farm French military cemetery with Muslim headstones.

the size of the contingents twenty years later, the classes of the 'hollow years' were obliged to remain for a second year under arms. The proportion of 'insoumis' between 1914 and 1922 never exceeded 2.5 per cent (the rate in December 1915) and decreased continuously thereafter. Once the new 1923 law came into force the rate fell considerably to 0.5 per cent.[49] Universality and equality were the watchwords, and conscription became a vector of national cohesion. The sons of foreigners who served in the French Army were naturalised by a law of 3 July 1917. Military service for the reclaimed citizens of Alsace and Lorraine became a means of integration and assimilation.[50] Military conscription ended formally in France only in 2001.

The figure of 1,383,000 killed and missing has been cited already. Of course, these were not the only casualties of service in the French Army.[51] In 1920 there were 600,000 widows, 760,000 orphans and 650,000 elderly who had lost their breadwinner. Then there were those disabled by their war service. Clemenceau told parliament: 'ils ont des droits sur nous' – the wounded and disabled were owed something by the grateful nation. It has proved even more difficult to find a true figure for these men than for those killed, and it was only as a result of the need to calculate monetary figures for the budget that an attempt was made to count them. In discussion of the pensions law in early 1919, it was stated that 1.9 million pensions needed to be paid; this figure had dropped to 1.5 million the following year; in 1922, 1,117,874 disability pensions were being paid to ex-servicemen.

The rates were not ungenerous. The pensions law promulgated on 31 March 1919 awarded 2,500 francs to a private with a 100 per cent disability, plus 300 francs for each dependant child and 400 francs for each elderly dependant; widows received 800 francs. Medical care was provided free of charge. By way of comparison, a woman typist might earn 1,800 francs a year, rising to 3,600 by the end of her career; a miner in 1919 earned over 3,000 francs.[52] 'Germany will pay' was the cry, but no agreement on reparations was achieved before the Treaty of Versailles was signed. Two other measures should be mentioned. The phrase that appears on all war graves, 'mort pour la France', is a legal designation, recorded on a death certificate and applied by the army, in cases of death in action or military hospital, or claimed by the family. It ensures the right of dependants to a pension. The official register is maintained today, updated as families discover old records and as duplicates are removed.[53] The second measure was the establishment, by a law of 27 July 1917, of the statute of 'pupille de la nation' or ward of court, similar in effect to the official 'mort pour la France'. This legal status gave a child, who was not necessarily orphan of both parents, the right to moral and sometimes material help from the state. It covered mainly those children born between 1904 and 1914, and it remained in effect until the child reached 21 years of age.[54]

During the debate on the pensions law, the associations of disabled veterans, organised already during the course of the war, had lobbied in support of their interests. Post-war more associations were formed of veterans, who in the main did not join the disabled groups. The groups met for practical and material support for their members, rather than for left-wing political agitation (as some feared) or for attempts to recreate the 'brotherhood' of the trenches. They were active in reforming the code of military justice, or in specific specialist questions. The facially disfigured, for example, had their own association from 1921. In a time of great unemployment it was even more difficult for the 10–15,000 of such men to find work, and the association fought hard for four years to obtain the right to compensation. A large subscription was opened in 1925 to create a 'home' for those unable to work, opened in 1927 by Gaston Doumergue, then President of the Republic.[55]

Mutual support, both practical and emotional, was particularly necessary. In the seventy-seven non-invaded départements, the number of marriages in 1913 was 247,999 but only 75,200 in 1918. The estimated number of children who would have been born but for the war was 1.6 million, and the divorce rate more than doubled from pre-war's 561 per 10,000 marriages to 1,235 in 1920.[56] Even when French veterans were able to return to their former job or found other work, financial difficulties loomed. Tax demands had been suspended during the war but soon resurfaced. A tax demand after paying the blood tax, 'l'impôt du sang', for more than four years was too much, and the government was obliged to place a moratorium on such demands in March 1919. Payment of rent, too, had been suspended in August 1914, as families lost their bread-winner to the army and so were unable to pay. The government also acted quickly in the matter of pensions. By a law of 22 March 1919 a gratuity of 250 francs was to be paid to each man, plus an additional allowance of 15 to 20 francs per month of service at the front. The full amount could be taken in the form of a one-year treasury bond; alternatively, the 250 francs could be taken in cash, with the remainder being received in monthly payments of 100 francs. This was not enough to live on, but, of course, Germany would pay.

Civil–military relations had been transformed during the course of the war. The government had effectively abdicated its right of control during the opening weeks as crisis followed crisis. With the President and the government exiled in Bordeaux, France's victory in September 1914 in the first Marne battle gave Joffre an initially impregnable position as 'saviour of the Marne'. Then, as CinC of the largest Allied army in the West, he became de facto generalissimo until British forces grew. With the unswerving support of the war minister, Alexandre Millerand, Joffre insisted on his right to act as he saw fit and to exclude politicians from the zone of the armies. Yet the casualty lists began to outweigh Joffre's usefulness as the only Frenchman to whom the British would listen, and senators and deputies began to make their views heard. They insisted on an expedition to the eastern Mediterranean as an alternative to the Western Front, and they criticised the high command in secret sessions and in the Army Commissions of both houses. They imposed on Joffre their right to inspect the troops and to report on medical matters, on the condition of barracks, on the state of railway communications, and much more besides.

The deputies in particular, being on average younger than senators, knew at first hand what conditions prevailed. At the beginning of February 1915 there were 235 parliamentarians on the army's rolls, including 25 senators.[57] They were mostly the older territorials, and many of them were doctors, appointed to hospitals near their homes, hence close to their constituents. The disadvantage from the military point of view of such a collection of politicians in their midst was obvious, and GQG resented the temporary rank that was given to deputies who would otherwise have been simple privates, and resented the leave granted to return to Paris for parliamentary sittings. Eventually Joffre accorded parliamentarians the option to take 'unlimited' leave so as to remain in Paris for their parliamentary duties. A further disadvantage in GQG's eyes was the political links that were facilitated between generals and politicians, the presence on Foch's staff of André Tardieu being a prime example.

Abel Ferry, deputy and an under-secretary in the Foreign Office in 1914, was a fierce critic and prominent in the fight to establish parliamentary control of the army. Until July 1916 he continued to move back and forth between Paris and the front, finally giving up the uniform. As one of the commissioners inspecting in the Aisne the working of a new model of automatic rifle, Ferry was mortally wounded by a shell on 8 September 1918, and two other officers with him were also killed by the same shell. One of these, Gaston Dumesnil, was deputy for Angers and had volunteered for military duty in 1914, giving up the unlimited leave option that Ferry had chosen in 1916.[58] For those parliamentarians who had no personal experience, their constituents, the *poilus*, wrote to them, as was their right as citizens of the Republic. In the archives of the Deputies' Army Commission are to be found 329 letters written, or transmitted by other deputies, to the commission between April and

November 1917. A quarter came from civilians (wives or parents) and the rest (246 letters) from military personnel, mainly NCOs and officers; they sought 'justice and equity'.[59]

Relations between the army, as represented by the high command, and the government deteriorated further in 1917, when the poor choice of Nivelle to succeed Joffre was contested. Appointed by one government under Briand but disavowed by its successor under Ribot, Nivelle was placed in the impossible position of mounting a battle in which his minister had no faith. Painlevé cut the ground from under him by consulting with subordinate officers and subjecting the CinC to an embarrassing war council in which resignation was offered but refused. In the end, the *poilus* paid the price for these lamentable proceedings. Painlevé's dual appointment of Pétain and Foch provided stability for the rest of the year and the three men managed to work together to restore the French Army, to maintain France's diplomatic role within the Entente, and to boost the industrial mobilisation that produced the vast numbers of tanks, guns and aircraft that won the war in 1918.

Finally, civil–military relations took another turn when Clemenceau came to power, with his many years' experience of journalistic and political thuggery. Acting as both premier and war minister, he imposed a sort of Jacobin rule that worked effectively with both the poilus and the high command. He made innumerable visits himself to the trenches, waving his stick at the enemy trenches. On one such visit to the front around Reims on 5–6 July 1918, a group of poilus presented a bouquet of dusty flowers to the premier. He was so overcome by emotion that the bouquet remained thereafter on the mantelpiece in his Paris flat and was buried with him.[60] The army commissions lost much of their influence in the last year of the war because Clemenceau simply shut the parliament out. He supported both Foch and Pétain when parliament would have censured them following the German 'surprise' offensive on the Chemin des Dames in May 1918. Finally he became 'père la victoire', and insisted on negotiating the peace treaty without interference either from the parliament or from Foch. The Army's leaders were not permitted to influence the peace. Yet, when Clemenceau was persuaded to stand for President of the Republic as Poincaré's term came to an end in 1920, the centre-right majority in the new Chamber of Deputies did not want him. The Republican caucus met before the official vote – under the constitution the President was elected by the two houses, Senate and Chamber of Deputies acting together as the Assemblée Nationale – and voted for another candidate. Deeply wounded, Clemenceau withdrew from public life.

The veteran generals of France's Army continued to serve, however. Clemenceau's opponent in the treaty negotiations, Marshal Foch, remained Allied CinC of the occupation forces, and as marshal of France sat on the Conseil Supérieur de la Guerre. Pétain remained CinC of the French Army, and was elevated to marshal immediately after the armistice. Fayolle, Franchet d'Espèrey and Lyautey were also thus honoured in 1921 (and, posthumously, Gallieni and Maunoury), but not Castelnau. The inter-ministerial Conseil Supérieur de Défense Nationale was revived, but met only twice in 1920 and twice again in 1921. In their discussion of the recruitment question, Foch pointed out that the Three-Year Law of 1913 had provided 'a numerous, but insufficiently armed' army.[61] He had learned the lesson that in a twentieth-century war materiel was at least as important as men. The reduced size of the post-war army meant that there were far too many officers. Those promoted during the war to an acting rank were obliged to re-enlist, if they so wished, at their substantive, not temporary, rank. Retirement age for general officers was lowered, and pay rises were inadequate to keep pace with the cost of living. As a result, the officer corps was not rejuvenated, and, as always happens when cuts are made, it was the young and energetic, able to find employment elsewhere, who left the army.

In summary, in 1919 the relationship between France and its Army could not have been closer. France's Army was carved, literally, on war memorials all over France; the huge military cemeteries, and many hundreds of smaller ones, that cover acres of northern and eastern France reveal how so many Frenchmen accepted conscription to fight in its ranks. Even Alfred Dreyfus volunteered, despite being almost 55 in August 1914, and served until war's end, although never at the front. Unwilling to obey every order, as 1917's mutinies proved, nevertheless at times of crisis the French Army stood firm. The soldiers' parents, wives and sisters worked in the factories that produced the guns and munitions. Their political leaders found a way of working with the Army's leaders by the last year of the war, after the pendulum had swung too far the military's way in the person of Joffre and too far the politician's way in the person of Nivelle. Clemenceau and Foch would quarrel bitterly in 1919 and beyond, but in 1918 they made a formidable team. Perhaps the words, written in 1916, of officer cadet Louis Mairet, wounded on the Somme in 1916 and killed on the Chemin des Dames on 16 April 1917, might stand as an epitaph for many of the poilus of France's Army:

The soldier of 1916 does not fight for Alsace, or to ruin Germany or for the fatherland. He fights out of decency, out of habit and necessity. He fights because he can do no other. Then he fights because, after the initial enthusiasm, after the discouragement of the first winter, resignation came with the second. What we hoped was only a passing state of affairs ... has become stability, stable in its very instability. We have swapped home for a shelter, family for combat comrades. We have adapted our life to poverty [misère], just as once we did to well-being. We have adapted our feelings to daily events, and found equilibrium in lack of equilibrium. We no longer even imagine that things could change. We don't see ourselves returning home. We still hope for it; we don't count on it.[62]

Even the Socialist Louis Barthas expressed similar sentiments of resignation at almost the same time, in 1916, and in the same place, the Somme:

It was not the flame of patriotism that inspired this spirit of sacrifice, it was only a spirit of bravado so as not to seem more cowardly than one's neighbour, then a presumption of confidence in one's own star, for some the secret and futile ambition for a decoration or a promotion, finally, for the mass of soldiers, the uselessness of recrimination against an implacable fate.[63]

The relationship between France and the Allies changed as well, but for the worse. France began the war with two principal allies, Britain and Russia, along with support from Belgium, and ended it with Britain, but without Russia, and with two new ones, Italy and the USA. Romania, Greece and Serbia were allies too, but required as much help as they gave support. Russia had been the cornerstone of France's pre-war policy, because, without the Russian steamroller's weight in the east, France could not have accepted war in the west. British help could not be counted upon and, in any case, the small British Army would make but a small addition to France's own military forces. The French Army kept a very close watch on events in Russia with regular lengthy reports and various missions, both political and military. Russia's defection was resented, and Foch attempted in vain to rally the flagging eastern front. When this failed, Foch became as anti-Bolshevist as Winston Churchill. A French division under General Berthelot was sent to help combat the Bolsheviks in southern Russia, but had to withdraw from Odessa, and, after a revolt on board ship in the Black Sea, returned to France.

The French Army equipped the Americans, and shipped huge amounts of materiel to Russia. In all, 7,000 guns, 10,600 aircraft, 25,000 aircraft engines and 400 tanks went from France to the various Allies.[64] France's Army contributed also to keeping the smaller Entente allies in the war. General Berthelot's military mission to Romania played a vital role in restoring the country's army after the crushing defeat of 1916, and Berthelot was welcomed back to the country in November 1918, just in time to get the Romanians to rejoin the Entente before the armistice was signed. France sent arms to Belgium and to Italy, and created Polish and Czech divisions with former Austro-Hungarian prisoners of war who had defected to the Entente. In addition to weapons and other materiel, France also sent a sizeable contingent to Italy after

Caporetto and French divisions took part along with British divisions in the final victorious battle at Vittorio Veneto.

Russia's replacement as principal ally was Britain, and it was with the British that the French Army fought most of the Western Front battles, with the notable exception of Verdun. It was a rocky relationship, as ten centuries of mainly hostile relations made inevitable. At first, Britain's small professional army merely extended the French left, but this was the critical sector. The scramble on the Marne and return northwards to the North Sea and Ypres left Joffre demanding more and Sir John French digging in his heels. Foch's coordination of Belgian, British and French forces in the first battle of Ypres gave him credit when crisis came again in March 1918. Then relations were strained by repeated French calls for a greater British effort, amid complaints that the British were treating the war as a sport and calling time after a few days' fighting. When Haig replaced Sir John French as CinC in December 1915, he was already convinced that the French Army was finished, remarking with great condescension: 'a large percentage of men now in the ranks of the French Army are middle aged fathers of families, who are not so keen upon advancing under fire to the attack as the younger men earlier in the campaign'.[65] He certainly used the excuse of fears for French Army morale in 1917 as justification for his own decisions. Thus, in 1918, according to British historiography, the French did nothing and the BEF did all the fighting. As Henry Wilson put it, 'The French are not fighting at all & the Americans don't know how so all falls to us.'[66] This was simply the mirror image of French complaints in 1914 and 1915: the British were always slow, always late. The theme was now Rawlinson's complaint that Debeney's First Army was always hanging back, always waiting for the British to get forward before moving themselves. The British official historian goes so far as to state that the reason for the late decision in 1918 to prepare the Lorraine offensive was 'the policy of leaving the fighting to the British and the Americans'.[67]

It was the treaty negotiations that finally broke the strained Franco-British alliance. As Lloyd George retorted, when Clemenceau reproached him for Britain's hostility after war's end, 'was that not always our traditional policy?' France's demand for a secure eastern border with Germany was replaced by a temporary occupation of the Rhineland. While Foch raged against this arrangement, Clemenceau accepted it in return for a military guarantee from both Britain and the USA that they would come to France's aid in the event of further German aggression. When the US Senate failed to ratify the treaty – the military guarantee that had been signed at the same time was not even submitted to a Senate vote – Lloyd George also wriggled out of the commitment. He had probably foreseen what would happen. Yet France had been so weakened by the war that any break with Britain became inconceivable. The experience of 1914–18 meant that in 1939 the coalition machinery, including the Supreme War Council and unity of command, was set up immediately, instead of waiting for over three years.

As for the USA, France had supplied most of the AEF's weapons and had tried to make its CinC follow the French lead. The French Army had supplied instructors and interpreters, but General Pershing preferred his own methods. Relations with Pershing and the American armies were complicated: respect for the New World's youth and enthusiasm was mixed with exasperation that the CinC of those young and enthusiastic doughboys would not accept the lessons of experience gained the hard way. Foch was sufficiently aware to accept what he knew he could not change, despite Clemenceau's urging to demand Pershing's replacement. After the armistice and during the treaty negotiations, President Wilson refused to tour the ravaged French towns, and the doughboys simply wanted to go home. The American military representative on the SWC even felt compelled to ask, when it was feared that Germany might not sign, whether American soldiers would consent to fight again. After they had spent time as occupation troops in Germany, many would return to the USA with a greater respect for the Germans than for the French.[68]

The French Army had weathered the blow to the alliance when Russia defected, even though the revolution and political unrest were factors in the mutinies of May/June 1917. If relations between the British and French were never close, they managed at least to end the war on the same side, but the Middle East settlements would prove a source of future conflict. The war in Italy and the French contribution to the fighting there have been forgotten. Furthermore, the role of the USA as the world's arsenal in the Second World War has clouded the fact that France supplied the American Army with its equipment in the first one. Indeed, the supply of professional expertise (as military missions) and quantities of weapons to Russia and to the smaller allies, Belgium, Greece, Romania and Serbia is yet another forgotten French achievement.

If the relationships between the nation and the army and between France and its allies had been changed profoundly by the war, the relationship with the principal enemy, Germany, was unchanged. As early as January 1919 the General Staff of the Army felt the need to publish *Pourquoi l'Allemagne a capitulé*, translated into English and published at the same time as *Why Germany Capitulated on 11 November 1918*. It appeared the same month in German translation as *Der Irrtum des Marschalls Foch*. The German title (*Foch's error*) itself illustrates why the 68-page brochure had to be produced. The preface explained that the German Army was marching back across the Rhine, and being greeted as 'undefeated' returning troops. The brochure's purpose was, therefore, to show the 'true' state of the German troops, with an account of the operations from 15 July to 11 November 1918, an evaluation of the condition of the German Army on the latter date, and extracts from German documents showing the state of discipline and morale therein.

Although German troops were evacuating French and Belgian territory according to the armistice terms, they were falling behind in delivering the guns and railway materiel that those terms stipulated. The armistice signed on 11 November had been for thirty-six days, and already, by the time of its first renewal on 18 December 1918, the Germans were in arrears – by 9,000 heavy guns, 7,000 machine guns, almost 1,000 aircraft – and, especially important in case of a resumption of hostilities, only 208 of the agreed 5,000 locomotives had been handed over.[69] This bad faith did not augur well for the future, and presaged the sinking of the German fleet in Scapa Flow, just as the peace treaty was about to be signed. Then, Germany defaulted on its reparations payments and left France to pay pensions and to re-build devastated areas, on top of its own war debts.

The Rhine frontier had been the minimum guarantee of France's security; much of the country, from its president downwards, had supported Foch's arguments for making Germany's western frontier the river barrier. Woodrow Wilson and Lloyd George had not permitted this, and occupation of German territory was limited to the left bank and the bridgeheads conceded in the armistice document. General Fayolle made a ceremonial entrance into Mayence/Mainz, with Mangin and Gouraud, but was struck by the 'order, prosperity and richness' of a country which did not present the 'picture of a defeated people'. On 16 June, days before the signing of the Treaty of Versailles, he believed that the German government was delaying in order to save face and to be able to claim that the treaty had been forced upon them. They would sign on the last possible day, Fayolle concluded, because they only had a 5 per cent chance of success if they re-started the war. 'So they will sign', he wrote in his diary, 'but they will not carry out its terms.'[70]

Fayolle's fears for France's future security were shared by many. Foch worried that France's widows might have to suffer the loss of their sons also in a future war with Germany. The Army's intelligence bureau believed that a sudden German attack was possible, given Germany's refusal to accept defeat and its consequences. Despite ending the war with more aircraft and tanks than any other power, and with the prestige of victory, France's Army was still afraid of their neighbour, whose army returned to Germany's unravaged industrial infrastructure. The *Revue Militaire Française* published many translations of German operational studies, and the French 'watch on the Rhine' kept the German question to the forefront of military thinking. Over 100,000 French soldiers were engaged in this occupation. In this, France's colonial troops gave valuable service in the occupation force. Demobilisation left the Army short of men, but the use of natives led to great German resentment. Those native troops who had volunteered during the war signed up for the duration of the war plus two years. The last North African troops left the Rhine in 1925.

The French Army's efforts during the First World War had been stupendous. It had conscripted a larger proportion of its adult male population than Britain or Germany, a figure made possible by the nation's acceptance, by a very large majority, of the need to defend the homeland and expel the invader. The Army had imposed a huge industrial effort on the country, which rose to the challenge; industrial output reached great heights. It was also the French Army which supplied the general, Ferdinand Foch, whose strategic vision and ability to learn from past mistakes matched his skill in dealing with allies and politicians alike, and who seized the opportunity presented in July 1918 to begin the march to victory. The Army had proved remarkably resilient, even as men died and numbers grew. After turning around from a long retreat to stop the German invasion on the Marne in 1914, it resisted for ten months at Verdun in 1916, recovered from the disastrous offensive of 1917 and its subsequent mutinies, and went to the aid of the beleaguered BEF in March and April 1918. If the British have believed ever since that the French Army did little to contribute to the fighting between August and November 1918, this was because, by these final months, the French were on their last legs.

Of course, allies were needed for the final victory: British manpower as well as British ships and British coal; and the infusion of American youth and strength. If Mangin's *force noire* had proved an illusion, nevertheless the contribution of the labour of Africans, Antillais, Indo-Chinese, Malgaches, Kanaks and Pacific Islanders was most valuable. The French Army's prestige never stood so high again as it did for a few short years after the victory parade in Paris on 14 July 1919. Anthony Adamthwaite sums up its position thus: 'In 1919 French arms and prestige appeared supreme: an army of 900,000, 2,500 tanks, the largest air force in the world . . . *poilus* were deployed in Europe, north Africa and the Middle East; Paris was the world's diplomatic capital.'[71] Yet, as Britain reverted to its preferred traditional policy of seeking a continental balance in Europe by accepting Germany as a customer, and as the USA withdrew into isolationism, France's Army stood on the Rhine lacking the Russian (now Soviet) bulwark in the east and facing 'hatred more inveterate than ever and unextinguished national anger'. Thus did Charles de Gaulle end his last lecture to his prisoner-of-war camp companions.[72]

Arc de triomphe

On 28 June 1919 the German plenipotentiaries drove through the gate and crossed the courtyard of the palace of Versailles, their route flanked by French cavalry in dress uniform. They signed the peace treaty in the Galerie des Glaces, where over a generation earlier the Kaiser's grandfather had had himself crowned after the Franco-Prussian war. That defeat had now been avenged, but neither the supreme Allied commander nor the commander-in-chief of the French Army was present at the signing ceremony. The Army was represented not by its high command, but by some mutilated French soldiers who were seated close to the signing table so that the Germans could see them.

Less than three weeks later, on 14 July, the annual Bastille Day procession became the victory parade, and Foch, Pétain and Fayolle arrived from the Rhineland for the ceremonies. A large cenotaph was constructed to stand beneath the Arc de Triomphe, then to be moved the night before the parade began. The aviation service was eager to fly both over and through the Arc in tribute to the soldiers, but fears for the safety of the enormous crowds negated that proposal. Difficulties were caused by Clemenceau's insistence that Marshal Joffre should take part as the victor of the Marne. Joffre's staff, if not Joffre himself, believed that a press campaign had forced Clemenceau's hand. The invitation was delivered by hand to Joffre in his hotel in central France.[73] Next, Foch appears to have been displeased by having to share the limelight, when Clemenceau specified that Joffre would ride on Foch's left in the procession. Joffre wished to have his staff ride behind him, but Foch refused on the grounds that Joffre did not have a staff. At this Joffre thumped the table hard enough to break it and asked Weygand to settle matters. With his usual tact, Weygand indicated that he had no objection to General Belin, who had been Joffre's chief of staff at GQG in 1914, riding alongside him.[74]

There were more problems with the make-up of the procession and the cenotaph. The detachment from the Foreign Legion had not been able to arrive in time, and so some veteran legionnaires had to be rounded up as representatives; the territorials arrived in time but with 'lamentable' uniform and equipment that had to be replaced. During the night of

Fig. 23 The victory parade, 14 July 1919. The cenotaph is on the right of the photograph.
Foch and Joffre led the parade behind the 'mutilés', followed by the national contingents.

13/14 July, the citizenry invaded the seating prepared for the dignitaries – perhaps a symbolic reprise of the storming of the Bastille – and the cavalry had to be roused to help the police expel the invaders. Then the enormous cenotaph that had been placed beneath the Arc de Triomphe, which was to be moved during the night so that the parade could pass, became stuck. A special carriage, adapted from one designed to transport a heavy gun, had been built to move it, and eventually the French Army's engineers, using as much brute force as technical skill, managed to heave the cenotaph into its designated place by 6am.[75] It had been constructed by the army's camouflage section, but its artistic style offended some sensibilities, despite its classical columns and four draped female allegorical figures. It was called 'pagan', 'anti-aesthetic and anti-democratic', even 'boche'.[76]

At the head of the parade came mutilated and wounded poilus in their wheelchairs, then Foch and Joffre, then Pétain leading the French Army units. One of 13 DI's regiments, 21 RI, came from Langres in eastern

France to take part. Next appeared the Allied contingents in alphabetical order, which put the Americans first. Haig had declined the invitation initially, but was prevailed upon to attend. The Italian General Diaz was unable to be present. Fayolle saw Foch and Pétain on the Place de la République after the parade, the former striking a 'ridiculous pose' with his baton.[77] The royal blue velvet on the baton is very worn, as may be seen today in the Musée de l'Armée in the Invalides, and it is very probable that an exuberant Foch would have swung or twirled the baton many times. Joffre seemed old and worn down; he was crumbling, 'il croulait de vétusté', wrote journalist Louise Weiss.[78]

As the parade was being prepared and taking place, the parliamentarians were discussing the negotiated treaties. A commission was established to consider the clauses and took months to recommend ratification. They insisted that Clemenceau appear before them to explain why Foch's wish to garrison the west bank of the Rhine as a guarantee that reparations would be paid had been watered down. Eventually, however, the Chamber ratified the treaty on 2 October 1919 by 372 votes to 58, with 74 abstentions; and on 24 October an official end to hostilities was decreed. The treaty came into effect in January 1920.

On the first Armistice Day after that date, 11 November 1920, the final public ceremony of the war took place.[79] A young soldier, Auguste Thin of the Class of 1919 – he was the youngest of those who had volunteered in 1918 – selected one of the eight coffins brought to a casemate in the citadel of Verdun from eight different battlefield sectors. Taken to Paris, the coffin remained during the night of 10/11 November in the Place Denfert-Rochereau, by the Lion de Belfort. Denfert-Rochereau, the defender of Belfort, was one of the few heroes of the Franco-Prussian War, and so the square named after him linked this victim of the war of 1914–18 to the previous Franco-German conflict. On 11 November, accompanied by a symbolic bereaved family and, as on 14 July 1919, by some *mutilés de guerre*, the coffin was carried to the Pantheon, thence to the Arc de Triomphe. The coffin was buried beneath the Arc the following January, and on 11 November 1923 the eternal flame was lit for the first time. The internment is marked with the inscription: 'Ici repose un soldat français mort pour la France 1914–1918.'

Notes

CHAPTER I

1 Antoine Prost, *L'Enseignement en France 1800–1967* (Paris: Armand Colin, 1968), 196.

2 Mona Ozouf, *L'Ecole de la France* (Paris: Gallimard, 1984). See especially the 'Présentation', 21–2.

3 Figures (2,783,000) calculated from the table in Prost, *L'Enseignment*, 218. They include boys in both state and private (religious and non-religious) schools. The number of girls in education at the same time was 2,749,000.

4 E.M. Carroll, *French Public Opinion and Foreign Affairs* (London: Frank Cass & Co. Ltd, 1931), 5.

5 Pierre Nora, 'Ernest Lavisse: son rôle dans la formation du sentiment national', *Revue historique*, 228 (July/December 1968): 73–106. Lavisse's influence is confirmed by his being chosen to head the post-war committee charged with determining the extent of German war guilt and with recommending reparations.

6 Général E. Lavisse, *'Tu seras soldat'. Histoire d'un soldat français* (Paris: Colin, 24th edn, 1916). Presumably the military rank is honorary for the occasion. The description (and translation) comes from Carlton J.H. Hayes, *France: A nation of patriots* (New York: Columbia University Press, 1930), 365.

7 Cited in Charles Sowerwine, *France since 1870: Culture, politics and society* (Basingstoke: Palgrave, 2001), 53.

8 See Rachel Chrastil, *Organizing for War: France 1870–1914* (Baton Rouge, LA: Louisiana State University Press, 2010), 117–20.

9 Christopher Andrew and A.S. Kanya-Forstner, *France Overseas: The Great War and the climax of French imperial expansion* (London: Thames and Hudson, 1981), 13.

10 CSG, Notice historique, 1N 1.

11 Les épidémies dans les garnisons en février et mars 1914, carton 3096–1, Archives du service de santé, Val-de-Grâce, Paris.

12 William Serman and Jean-Paul Bertaud, *Nouvelle histoire militaire de la France 1789–1919* (Paris: Fayard, 1998), 605–8.

13 Ibid., 561–71.

14 Historique du CSDN, 2N 1.

15 See Michel Goya, *La Chair et l'acier* (Paris: Tallandier, 2004), 56–67.

16 Gerd Krumeich, *Armaments and Politics in France on the Eve of the First World War* (Leamington Spa: Berg, 1984).

17 Serman and Bertaud, *Histoire militaire*, 561–3.

18 Walter S. Barge, The Generals of the Republic: The corporate personality of high military rank in France, 1889–1914 (PhD thesis, University of North Carolina at Chapel Hill, 1982), 10 (Table 1–1).

19 Serman and Bertaud, *Histoire militaire*, 553. Events in south-west France, in the barracks at Rodez, almost became mutiny.

20 Jean-Jacques Becker, 'Les "Trois Ans" et les débuts de la première guerre mondiale', *GMCC* 145 (1987), 7–26.

21 Goya, *La Chair et l'acier*, 126–7.

22 Ibid., 112.

23 Guinard et al., *Introduction*, 60.

24 Général Weygand, *Mémoires: Idéal vécu* (Paris: Flammarion, 1953), 62–3.

25 Observations . . . inspections au cours de ses inspections en 1913, n.d. [before 28 November 1913], 1N 13.

26 Yves Gras, *Castelnau ou l'art de commander* (Paris: Denoël, 1990), 135–6.

27 Cited in Robert T. Foley, 'German intelligence assessments of France before the Great War', *Journal of Intelligence History* 5 (2005), 8–9.

28 Guinard et al., *Introduction*, 59; for more detail, see Doughty, *PV*, 25–8.

29 F. Gambiez and M. Suire, *Histoire de la première guerre mondiale: Crépuscule sur l'Europe* (Paris: Fayard, 1968), 173.

30 CSG, 18 April 1913, 1N 11.

31 William Martin, in *La Crise Politique de l'Allemagne Contemporaine* (1913), cited in Michael E. Nolan, *The Inverted Mirror: Mythologizing the enemy in France and Germany, 1898–1914* (New York/Oxford: Berghahn Books, 2005), 87.

32 Pellé to Joffre, 26 May 1912, in Jean Le Chatelier (ed.), Le Général Maurice Pellé (1863–1924), 2 vols (1985, typescript in Library, Ministère de la Défense, Paris), 1: 62. Pellé's letter of the same date to Millerand is only slightly less dramatic: reprinted in *Documents diplomatiques français*, 3rd series [*DDF*], vol. 3: document 45.

33 Doughty, *PV*, 42.

34 A. Anders, 'Les Relations entre la Russie et la France (période d'avant guerre)', in *Les Alliés contre la Russie* (trans. from Russian, Paris: André Delpeuch, 1926), 50–1.

35 Terence Zuber, *Inventing the Schlieffen Plan: German war planning 1871–1914* (Oxford University Press, 2002), 256–8.

36 *AFGG* 1/1, 19.

37 Procès-verbal de l'entretien du 13 juillet 1912 entre les chefs d'état-major des armées française et russe, in *DDF* 3: document 200; and Procès-verbal des entretiens du mois d'août 1913 entre les chefs d'état-major des armées française et russe, *DDF* 8: document 79.

38 See D.N. Collins, 'The Franco-Russian Alliance and Russian railways', *Historical Journal* 16: 4 (1973), 777–88; René Girault, 'Sur quelques aspects financiers de l'alliance franco-russe', *RHMC* 8: 1 (1961), 67–76; D.W. Spring, 'Russia and the Franco-Russian Alliance: Dependence or interdependence?', *Slavonic and East European Review* 66: 4 (1988), 564–92.

39 Generale Maurizio Marsengo, *Eroi senza Luce: Una missione militare in Russia durante la Guerra Mondiale* (Torino: Unione Tipografico-Editrice Torinese, 1935-XIII).

40 Reports of 27 June 1905, 20 August, 14 December 1906, 7N 1477.

41 Laguiche reports of 14/27 February, 1914, 18/31 January, 15/28 March 1914, 7N 1478.

42 Weygand, *Idéal vécu*, pt 1, ch. 4.

43 Most of the protocols have been published in the official *Documents diplomatiques français*.

44 Delcassé to Pichon, 21 August 1913, *DDF*, 8: document 62.

45 Louis Garros, 'En marge de l'alliance franco-russe 1902–1914', *RHA* 6/1 (1950), 29–43. The study is cited at pp. 40–2, but not its location in the archives.

46 John Keiger, 'Crossed wires, 1904–14', in Robert Tombs and Emile Chabal (eds), *Britain and France in two World Wars* (London: Bloomsbury, 2013), 29–46.

47 *AFGG* 1/1, 19.

48 Samuel R. Williamson Jr, *The Politics of Grand Strategy: Britain and France prepare for war, 1904–1914* (London: The Ashfield Press, 1990, pb edn), 316.

49 Huguet, *Britain and the War: A French indictment* (trans., London: Cassell, 1928), 3, 4.

50 *The Times*, 28 September, 2 and 9 October 1912; 15 and 17 September 1913.

51 Wilson diary entries, cited in Major-General Sir C.E. Callwell, *Field Marshal Sir Henry Wilson Bart., G.C.B., D.S.O. His life and diaries*, 2 vols (London: Cassell, 1927), 1: 116–17, 123.

52 William Philpott, 'Plus qu'un simple soldat: La France et la perspective d'un soutien militaire britannique avant 1914', *RHA* 264 (2011), 32–40, at p. 36. See also his 'The Making of the Military Entente, 1904–1914: France, the British Army, and the Prospect of War', *English Historical Review* 128: 534 (2013), 1155–85.

53 Huguet's lecture, 13 April 1913, described in Patricia E. Prestwich, French Attitudes Towards Britain, 1911–1914 (PhD thesis, Stanford University, 1973), 299–300; Huguet, *Britain and the War*, 10.

54 Directives pour la concentration, *AFGG* 1/1, annex 8.

55 Louis Barthas, *Les Cahiers de guerre de Louis Barthas, tonnelier (1914–1919)* (Paris: François Maspero, 1978), 14–15.

56 Cited in Damien Baldin and Emmanuel Saint-Fuscien, *Charleroi 21–23 août 1914* (Paris: Tallandier, 2012), 27–9.

57 Roger Sargos, *Témoignage, 1914–1918: D'un officier forestier*, 3 vols (Bordeaux: Imprimerie Delmas, 1966–67), 1: 17–18.

58 Paul Tuffrau, *1914–1918 Quatre années sur le front: Carnets d'un combattant* (Paris: Imago, 1998), 29–31.

59 Jean-Jacques Becker, *The Great War and the French People* (New York: St Martin's Press, 1986), 17–21; Martha Hanna, *Your Death would be Mine: Paul and Marie Pireaud in the Great War* (Cambridge, MA: Harvard University Press, 2006), 53–7.

60 Jean-Jacques Becker, '"That's the death knell of our boys ..."', in Patrick Fridenson (ed.), *The French Home Front 1914–1918* (Providence, RI/Oxford:

Berg, 1992), 17–36; idem, *Le Carnet B* (Paris: Klincksieck, 1973); Michael S. Neiberg, *Dance of the Furies: Europe and the outbreak of World War I* (Cambridge, MA: Belknap Press of Harvard University Press, 2011).

61 Philippe Boulanger, *La France devant la conscription: Géographie historique d'une institution républicaine 1914–1922* (Paris: Economica, 2001), 128–40; Jules Maurin, 'Les Français engagés volontaires de la Grande Guerre', in Hubert Heyriès and Jean-François Muracciole (eds), *Le Soldat volontaire en Europe au XXe siècle* (Montpellier: Presses universitaires de la Méditerranée, 2007), 101.

62 Gilbert Meynier, 'L'émir Khaled, acteur et témoin de la Grande Guerre', in Gérard Canini (ed.), *Mémoire de la Grande Guerre* (Nancy: PUN, 1989), 249–63.

63 Jaccques Frémeaux, *Les Colonies dans la Grande Guerre: Combats et épreuves des peuples d'outre-mer* (Saint-Cloud: SOTECA 14–18 Editions, 2006), 26–50.

64 Philippe Masson, *Histoire de l'armée française de 1914 à nos jours* (Paris: Perrin, 2002), 32.

65 Paul G. Halpern, *A Naval History of World War I* (London: UCL Press, 1994), 51–2.

66 Serman, *Nouvelle Histoire Militaire*, 720, gives 3,580,000 men.

67 Guinard et al., *Introduction*, 119.

68 Frédéric Guelton, *L'Armée française en 1918* (Saint-Cloud: 14–18 Editions, n.d.), 39. See also Anthony Clayton, *Paths of Glory: The French Army 1914–18* (London: Cassell, 2003), 207–8.

69 Paul Lintier, *My Seventy-Five: Journal of a French gunner (August–September 1914)* (London: Peter Davies, 1929 [1917]), 8.

70 Laure and Jacottet, *Etapes*, 20–2.

71 Hew Strachan, *To Arms* (Oxford University Press, 2001), 206.

CHAPTER 2

1 Commandant Muller, *Joffre et la Marne* (Paris: G. Crès, 1931), 35; Roy A. Prete, *Strategy and Command: The Anglo–French coalition on the Western Front, 1914* (Montreal/Kingston: McGill/Queen's University Press, 2009), 53–4; R. Alexandre, *Avec Joffre d'Agadir à Verdun: Souvenirs 1911–1916* (Paris: Berger-Levrault, 1932), 120–2.

2 Instruction #1, 8 August 1914, *AFGG* 1/1, annex 103.

3 Doughty, *PV*, 57.

4 Laure and Jacottet, *Etapes*, 20, 23.

5 On the fighting see Simon J. House, The Battle of the Ardennes, 22 August 1914 (PhD thesis, King's College London, 2012). House argues that the French had the opportunity (unexploited) to score a tactical defeat over the enemy.

6 Damien Baldin and Emmanuel Saint-Fuscien, *Charleroi 21–23 août 1914* (Paris: Tallandier, 2012).

7 Joffre to War Minister, 24 August 1914, *AFGG* 1/2, annex 149.

8 Note for the armies, 24 August 1914, ibid., annex 158.

9 Elizabeth Greenhalgh, *Foch in Command: The forging of a First World War general* (Cambridge University Press, 2011), 19–20; Duffour, *Histoire*, 187–8.

10 *AFGG*, 1/2, annex 1792.

11 Holger Herwig, *The Marne, 1914: The opening of World War I and the battle that changed the world* (New York: Random House, 2009), 219. For more detail of the logistical difficulties facing the German armies, see Martin van Creveld, *Supplying War: Logistics from Wallenstein to Patton* (Cambridge University Press, 1977), 122–8.

12 *AFGG* 1/2, annex 2641.

13 Cited in Herwig, *Marne*, 311.

14 Major Spencer Cosby, 'Visit to Battle Fields', 16 September 1914, and report #5, 24 September 1914, RG 165, M1024, reel 215, NARA.

15 Oberst Otto Schulz, cited in Jack Sheldon, *The German Army on the Somme 1914–1916* (Barnsley: Pen & Sword, 2005), 34.

16 See Helen McPhail, *The Long Silence: Civilian life under the German occupation of northern France, 1914–1918* (London/New York: I.B. Tauris, 2001).

17 *AFGG* 1/4, annex 3267.

18 Haig diary, 23 October 1914, acc. 3155/96, National Library of Scotland.

19 *AFGG* 1/4, annex 3497.

20 Haig diary, 30 October 1914.

21 *AFGG* 1/4, annex 3640.

22 'Note remise au maréchal French', 31 October 1914, with endorsment, *AFGG* 1/4, annex 3636.

23 Ibid., annex 3669.

24 Ibid., annex 3683.

25 Ibid., annex 3759.

26 Ibid., annex 3760.

27 Letter, Haig to Lady Haig, 3 November 1914, acc. 3155, National Library of Scotland.

28 Letter, Sir John French to Kitchener, 31 October 1914, PRO 30/57/49, TNA.

29 Wilson diary, 4 November 1914, Wilson mss, DS/Misc/80, Imperial War Museum, London.

30 Jack Sheldon, *The German Army at Ypres and the Battle for Flanders* (Barnsley: Pen & Sword Military, 2010), 216.

31 Ibid., 220.

32 Ibid., 247.

33 *AFGG* 1/4, annex 3921.

34 Wilson diary, 2 November 1914.

35 Haig diary, 5 November 1914.

36 *AFGG* 1/4, 380.

37 Haig diary, 8 November 1914.

38 Sheldon, *German Army at Ypres*, 362.

39 Haig diary, 18 April 1915: 'the same selfish d'Urbal as I had found him in the fighting before Ypres last autumn'.

40 Telephone message, 17 November 1914, 17N 338 Coopération Franco–Britannique et Interalliée, [d]1.

41 *AFGG* 1/4, 396–7.

42 Ibid., 556.

43 Ian F.W. Beckett, *Ypres: The first battle, 1914* (Harlow: Pearson Education, 2004), 176.

44 *AFGG* 1/2, 825.

45 Guinard et al., *Introduction*, 213.

46 Unless stated otherwise, the details of the French Army's medical service are taken from ibid., 193–201.

47 Mary Borden Spears, *Journey down a Blind Alley* (London: Hutchinson & Co, 1946), 8.

48 Cited in Vincent Suard, 'La Justice militaire française et la peine de mort au début de la Première Guerre Mondiale', *RHMC* 41: 1 (1994), 136–53, here p. 136.

49 Ibid., 146.

50 Pierre Renouvin, *Les formes de gouvernement de guerre* (Paris/New Haven: PUF/Yale University Press, 1925), 33–8.

51 Suard, 'La Justice militaire'.

52 Ibid., 150.

53 Fayolle, *CS*, 52. At this time (5 November 1914) Fayolle commanded 70 DI in Pétain's XXXIII Corps.

54 Jean-Christophe Notin, *Foch* (Paris: Perrin, 2008), 126.

55 Gilbert Meynier, 'Pour l'exemple : un sur dix! Les décimations en 1914', *Politique Aujourd'hui* (January–February 1976), 55–70. Meynier is wrong to call the executions 'decimation': ten men were shot, not one in ten of the company (which at full establishment should contain 200–250 men).

56 Pièces relatives à un acte d'indiscipline devant l'ennemi au 8e tirailleurs, 16N 194/3.

57 Meynier, 'Pour l'exemple', 69.

58 Ibid.

59 André Bach, *Fusillés pour l'exemple 1914–1915* (Paris: Tallandier, 2003), 390/1.

60 Suard, 'Justice militaire', 143.

61 Bach, *Fusillés pour l'exemple*, 379–83.

62 Martha Hanna, *Your Death would be Mine: Paul and Marie Pireaud in the Great War* (Cambridge, MA: Harvard University Press, 2006), 9.

63 Fayolle, *CS*, 47; André Kahn, *Journal de guerre d'un juif patriote* (Paris: Jean-Claude Simoën, 1978), 60.

64 Jules Isaac, *Historien dans la Grande Guerre: Lettres et carnets 1914-1917* (Paris: Armand Colin, 2004), 52.

65 Renouvin, *Formes de Gouvernement*, 39; Fabienne Bock, *Un Parlementarisme de guerre 1914–1919* (Paris: Belin, 2002), 78–80.

66 Bock, *Parlementarisme de guerre*, 59–69.

67 Abel Ferry, *Carnets secrets 1914–1918* (Paris: Grasset, 2005), 65 (entry for 30 December 1914).

68 Ibid., 63 (entry for 24 December 1914).

69 The 162 sackings are listed in Pierre Rocolle, *L'Hécatombe des généraux* (Paris: Lavauzelle, 1980), 262.

70 Ibid., 95.

71 Général Messimy, *Souvenirs* (Paris: Plon, 1937), 350–1.

72 Berthelot diary, 10 September 1914, Henri Berthelot papers, Hoover Institution Archives, Stanford, CA.

73 Patrick Facon, 'Aperçus sur la doctrine d'emploi de l'aéronautique militaire française (1914–1918)', *RHA* 1988/3, 81–3.
74 General Herr, translated as 'Field artillery: past, present and future', in *Field Artillery Journal* XVII: 3 (1927), 221–46, here pp. 244–5. See also Michel Goya, *La Chair et l'acier: L'Invention de la guerre moderne* (Paris: Tallandier, 2004), 186–91.
75 See Greenhalgh, *Foch in Command*, 70, 90.
76 Major Spencer Cosby, report #7, 9 December 1914, RG 165, M1024, reel 215, NARA.
77 Général Maître, 'Evolution des idées sur l'emploi de l'artillerie pendant la guerre', *RMF* (1924), 201–13.

CHAPTER 3

1 *AFGG* 2, annex 280.
2 Raymond Poincaré, *Au Service de la France: Neuf années de souvenirs*, 11 vols (Paris: Plon, 1928–74), 5: 500–1.
3 Note verbale for Grand-Duke Nicolas, 16 December 1914, *AFGG* 2, annex 365.
4 Daille, *Histoire*, 78–9.
5 Doughty, *PV*, 122–4.
6 General Fleck, cited in Colonel Duchêne, 'Comment naquit l'artillerie de tranchée française', *RMF* (January 1925), 107–24, here p. 124; Pierre Waline, 'Pour que les "crapouillots" de l'artillerie de tranchée de 1914–1918 ne soient pas oubliés', *RHA* 1977/3, 51–63.
7 Général R. Alexandre, *Avec Joffre d'Agadir à Verdun* (Paris: Berger-Levrault, 1932), 182.
8 Guinard et al., *Introduction*, 147.
9 Preface to G. Goes, *Hartmannswillerkopf* (Paris: Payot, 1934), 7–8; Frédéric Guelton, 'Le vieil Armand', *14–18: le Magazine de la Grande Guerre* 34 (2006), 6–19; *AFGG* 3, 676–88.
10 *AFGG* 3, 687.
11 Etude au sujet des opérations dans les Vosges, 4 January 1916, ibid., annex 3234.
12 Pouydraguin to Seventh Army, 21 October 1915, ibid., annex 2997.
13 Maurice Genevoix wrote an account of his experience there in his eponymous book (published 1923).
14 Daille, *Histoire*, 95; *AFGG* 2, 501.
15 *AFGG* 2, 493.
16 Ibid., 527–8.
17 Daille, *Histoire*, 92–4.
18 Duchêne's long report in *AFGG* 3, annex 875.
19 Mark Humphries and John Maker (eds), *Germany's Western Front: 1915* (Waterloo, ON: Wilfrid Laurier University Press, 2010), 31; Berthelot's report in *AFGG* 2, annex 623.
20 Glenn E. Torrey, 'L'Affaire de Soissons', *War in History* 4: 4 (1997), 398–410, here p. 410.

21 Doughty, *PV*, 165.
22 See Elizabeth Greenhalgh, *Foch in Command: The forging of a First World War general* (Cambridge University Press, 2011), 76–9.
23 Telegram, Huguet to Joffre, 16 December 1914, *AFGG* 2, annex 367.
24 Fayolle, *CS*, 79 (entry for 22 January 1915). Fayolle wondered where strong character ended and 'ferocity, savagery' began, which is an interesting comment about the man who 'healed' the French Army in 1917.
25 Vincent Suard, 'La Justice militaire française et la peine de mort au début de la Première Guerre Mondiale', *RHMC* 41: 1 (1994), 136–53, here p. 148. See also the many cases in André Bach, *Fusillés pour l'exemple 1914–1915* (Paris: Tallandier, 2003), chs 13 and 14.
26 Pedroncini, 'Cours martiales', 399–401; Bach, *Fusillés*, 546–8.
27 Bach, *Fusillés*, 536–46; Guy Pedroncini, 'La Justice militaire et l'affaire des quatre caporaux de Souain', *RHA* 1973/2, 55–69.
28 Bach, *Fusillés*, 521–2.
29 Maïté Ferret-Lesne, 'Les conseils de guerre spéciaux (1914–1932), *RHA* 1998/3, 49–58, here p. 52.
30 Suard, 'La Justice militaire française', 147.
31 Circular, Joffre to commanding generals, 21 October 1915, in Millerand papers, 470AP/36, AN.
32 Letter to the President of the Republic, 13 October 1914, reproduced in Abel Ferry, *La Guerre vue d'en haut et d'en bas* (Paris: Grasset, 1920), 17–19.
33 Notes du 13 avril 1915, and Premier mémoire sur les opérations en Voëvre [sic] 5 au 16 avril, in dossiers IV and III, Millerand papers, 470AP/14. The second document was distributed to the members of the Viviani cabinet on 5 July 1915, and reproduced in Ferry, *Guerre vue*, 32–6. Original emphasis.
34 Extract of a letter, no addressee, 21 May 1915, in folder 'IV Eparges', ibid.
35 Letters 13 and 15 January1915, *AFGG* 2, annexes 607, 630.
36 Paul Guillaumat (ed.), *Correspondance de guerre du Général Guillaumat 1914–1919* (Paris: L'Harmattan, 2006), 52 (letter of 1 March 1915).
37 *AFGG* 2, 481.
38 See the analysis of these two instructions in Colonel Lucas, *L'Evolution des idées tactiques en France et en Allemagne pendant la guerre de 1914–1918* (4th edn, Paris: Berger-Levrault, 1932), 55–65.
39 Olivier Lepick, *La Grande Guerre chimique 1914–1918* (Paris: PUF, 1998), 77–81, here p. 79. Mordacq became the head of Clemenceau's military cabinet when the latter became premier at the end of 1917.
40 Ibid., 81.
41 For a recent study of this battle, based on the author's doctoral thesis, see Jonathan Krause, *Early Trench Tactics in the French Army: The second battle of Artois, May–June 1915* (Farnham: Ashgate, 2013).
42 Daille, *Histoire*, 123.
43 Conclusions tirées de l'attaque du village de Neuville St Waast par la 5e Division (Général Mangin) du 26 Mai au 10 Juin 1915, 23 June 1915, 16N 1964. Mangin also provided a 25-folio 'historique' and a further 16-folio collection of 'récits' of the capture of the village: ibid.

44 Fayolle, *CS*, 99, 104, 106, 107, 111, 113 (entries for 30 April, 13, 18, 24 May, 13, 17 June 1915).

45 Daille, *Histoire*, 124.

46 Foch to Joffre, 1 July 1915, and Foch's handwritten note of same date, *AFGG* 3, annexes 818, 819.

47 Foch to Joffre, 8 August 1915, ibid., annex 1152.

48 Daille, *Histoire*, 123–4.

49 Laure and Jacottet, *Etapes*, ch. 3.

50 Joffre to Millerand, 23 August 1915, *AFGG* 3, annex 1233.

51 Fabienne Bock, *Un Parlementarisme de guerre 1914–1919* (Paris: Belin, 2002), 123.

52 Colonel E. Herbillon, *Du Général en chef au gouvernement: Souvenirs d'un officier de liaison pendant la guerre mondiale*, 2 vols (Paris: Tallandier, 1930), 1: 143 (entry for 15 April 1915).

53 Buat, 'Note pour le ministre', 18 June 1915, Millerand papers, 470AP/14.

54 Session of 19 November 1915, 69S–2, fo. 3413, Archives du Sénat, Paris.

55 Xavier Boniface, *L'Aumônerie militaire française (1914–1962)* (Paris: Editions du Cerf, 2001), 70.

56 Charles Ridel, 'La chasse aux embusqués', *L'Histoire* 325 (November 2007), 38–45.

57 John Horne, '"*L'Impôt du sang*": Republican rhetoric and industrial warfare in France, 1914–18', *Social History* 14: 2 (1989), 201–23.

58 See the discussion in the Deputies Army Commission on 2, 30 June, 28 July, 6, 13 August, 30 September 1915, C7494, AN.

59 See J.C. King, *Generals and Politicans: Conflict between France's high command, parliament and government, 1914–1918* (Berkeley/Los Angeles: University of California Press, 1951), ch. 3; Bock, *Parlementarisme*, 129–35.

60 Cited in Michel Baumont, 'Abel Ferry et les étapes du contrôle aux armées, 1914–1918', *RHMC* 15: 1 (1968), 162–208, here p. 180.

61 Dalbiez report cited in Bock, *Parlementarisme*, 133–4.

62 In a conversation with the Belgian premier on 16 February 1915: see Greenhalgh, *Foch in Command*, 101.

63 George H. Cassar, *The French and the Dardanelles: A study of failure in the conduct of war* (London: George Allen & Unwin Ltd, 1971), ch. 3.

64 Georges Suarez, *Briand: Sa vie, son oeuvre, avec son journal et de nombreux documents inédits*, 5 vols (Paris: Plon, 1938–41), 3: 87.

65 See Christopher M. Andrew and A.S. Kanya-Forstner, *France Overseas: The Great War and the climax of French imperial expansion* (London: Thames and Hudson, 1981), 44–54.

66 Cassar, *French and the Dardanelles*, 74–5, note 15.

67 The artillery commander in one of the group's three territorial divisions was Colonel Emile Mayer, author of *Nos Chefs de 1914* (Paris: Stock, 1930). Mayer's chapter on d'Amade gives ample indication of his unsuitability for high command, despite his passage through the Ecole Supérieure de Guerre. See pp. 201–46.

68 Millerand, Order concerning the mission of the Corps Expéditionnaire de l'Orient, 2 March 1915, *AFGG* 8/1, annex 17.

69 For the command relationship see Elizabeth Greenhalgh, *Victory Through Coalition: Britain and France during the First World War* (Cambridge University Press, 2005), 25–8, citing from a letter of Lord Esher to Sir John French.

70 Tim Travers, *Gallipoli 1915* (Stroud: Tempus, 2001), 39.

71 Ibid., 180.

72 *The Memoirs of Marshal Joffre*, 2 vols (London: Geoffrey Bles, 1932), 2: 370.

73 Hamilton to Kitchener, 5 May 1915, cited in Cassar, *French and the Dardanelles*, 122.

74 Commandant Desmazes, 'Les Débarquements alliés aux Dardanelles', *RMF* (April 1926), 73–4.

75 Letter, Gouraud to Hamilton, 18 May 1915, *AFGG* 8/1, annex 201. A large portion of another Gouraud letter laying out the reasons for an alternative strategy is reproduced in Sir Ian Hamilton, *Gallipoli Diary*, 2 vols (London: Edward Arnold, 1920), 1: 295–301.

76 Table of losses, *AFGG* 8/1, 549.

77 Bailloud to Millerand, 1 October 1915, with 2 enclosures, Millerand papers, 470AP/6.

78 Jan Karl Tanenbaum, *General Maurice Sarrail 1856–1929: The French Army and Left-Wing Politics* (Chapel Hill, NC: University of North Carolina Press, 1974), 53.

79 King, *Generals and Politicians*, 68–9.

80 Joffre's letter to Dubail and Dubail's two reports exist in the Millerand papers, 470AP/15; they do not appear in *AFGG*. Sarrail memoirs in *Revue Politique et parlementaire* 107 (1921), 161–80 and 399–417; 108 (1921), 81–104 and 221–47; in the English translation of Joffre's memoirs they appear in an appendix.

81 John Grigg, *Lloyd George: From peace to war 1912–1916* (London: HarperCollins, pb edn, 1997), 202–6.

82 Memorandum by Lord Bertie, 5 February 1915, Bertie papers, add. mss 63,036, fo. 78, British Library.

83 Joffre to Millerand, 29 July 1915, Millerand papers, 470AP/16, [d] Dardanelles II; Poincaré, *Au Service*, 7: 35–8.

84 See David Dutton, *The Politics of Diplomacy: Britain and France in the Balkans in the First World War* (London/New York: I.B. Tauris, 1998), ch. 6.

85 For details of the invasion, see C.E.J. Fryer, *The Destruction of Serbia in 1915* (New York: Columbia University Press, 1997).

86 *AFGG* 8/1, 126, n. 1 (where the arithmetic is astray).

87 Meeting of Army Group commanders, 11 July 1915, *AFGG* 3, annex 1150.

88 Asquith to King, 20 August 1915, CAB 37/133, TNA.

89 Nick Lloyd, 'Lord Kitchener and "the Russian News": Reconsidering the Origins of the Battle of Loos', *Defence Studies* 5: 3 (2005), 346–65.

90 See Paléologue to MAE, 7 September 1915, Série Guerre A, P01056, Archives diplomatiques, Paris.

91 Daille, *Histoire*, 179.

92 *AFGG* 3, 285.

93 Général Serrigny, *Trente ans avec Pétain* (Paris: Plon, 1959), 38.

94 Daille, *Histoire*, 195.

95 Jacquand Souvenirs, 27 September 915, Castelnau papers, fo. 800, 1K795/36.
96 Greenhalgh, *Foch in Command*, 130–1.
97 Fayolle, Observations on the recent attacks, 30 November 1915, 16N 1976.
98 Yves Gras, *Castelnau ou l'art de commander* (Paris: Denoël, 1990), 252.
99 *AFGG* 3, 540.
100 Report on the operations of Second Army in Champagne and the lessons to be drawn, 1 November 1915, *AFGG* 3, annex 3042.
101 Jacquand Souvenirs, 10 November 1915, Castelnau papers, 1K 795/36.
102 Colonel J.M. Kuhn [US military attaché in Berlin], 'Notes on the French Offensive in the Champagne in September 1915', 5 January 1916, RG 165, M1024, reel 216, NARA.
103 *AFGG* 9/2, 833–41; Hew Strachan, *To Arms* (Oxford University Press, 2001), 505–9. Strachan's chapter on Africa, published as a separate volume, has good maps: *The First World War in Africa* (Oxford University Press, 2004), 15, 26.
104 *AFGG* 9/2 is devoted almost entirely to the Cameroon campaign. See also Marc Michel, 'Le Cameroun allemand aurait-il pu rester unifié? Français et Britanniques dans la conquête du Cameroun (1914–1916)', *GMCC* 168 (1992), 13–29.
105 Jacques Frémeaux, *Les Colonies dans la Grande Guerre: Combats et épreuves des peuples d'outre-mer* (Saint-Cloud: SOTECA 14–18 editions, 2006), 125.
106 Ibid., 126.
107 Guinard et al., *Introduction*, 213.
108 Général Maître, 'Evolution des idées sur l'emploi de l'artillerie pendant la guerre', *RMF* (1924), 209; Denis Rolland, *Nivelle: L'inconnu du Chemin des Dames* (Paris: Imago, 2012), 52.
109 Elizabeth Kahn Baldewicz, Les Camoufleurs: The mobilization of art and the artist in wartime France (PhD thesis, University of California, Los Angeles, 1980), 29–34; 1er Bureau, Note, 14 August 1915, *AFGG* 3, annex 1171.
110 Historique général de l'AS, 16N 2121.
111 Laure and Jacottet, *Etapes*, 99.
112 The historian of the postal control records has found no trace of any 1915 reports: Jean-Noël Jeanneney, 'Les Archives des commissions de contrôle postal aux armées (1916–1918)', *RHMC* 15 (1968), 209–33, here p. 211.
113 Douglas Allen, *War, Memory, and the Politics of Humor: The Canard Enchaîné and World War I* (Berkeley, CA: University of California Press, 2002), 24.
114 Cited in Jean-Jacques Becker, 'Les débuts du *Canard Enchaîné*', *L'Histoire* 28 (1980), 81–2.
115 Benjamin Gilles, *Lectures de poilus: Livres et journaux dans les tranchées, 1914–1918* (Paris: Editions Autrement, 2013), 310.
116 Paul Tuffrau, *1914–1918 Quatre années sur le front: Carnets d'un combattant* (Paris: Imago, 1998), 14.
117 Leonard V. Smith, Stéphane Audoin-Rouzeau and Annette Becker, *France and the Great War 1914–1918* (Cambridge University Press, 2003), 55–6.

CHAPTER 4

1 Charles Delvert, *Carnets d'un fantassin: Massiges, 1916, Verdun* (Paris: Editions du Mémorial, 1981), 56.

2 Daille, *Histoire*, 238–9.

3 Ibid., 234.

4 Bernard Serrigny, *Trente ans avec Pétain* (Paris: Plon, 1959), 43.

5 Michel Goya, *La Chair et l'acier: L'Invention de la guerre moderne (1914–1918)* (Paris: Tallandier, 2004), 290–1.

6 Général Herr, 'Field artillery: past, present, and future', translated in *Field Artillery Journal* 17: 4 (1927), 329–58, here p. 337.

7 Letter, Asquith to Sylvia Henley, 28 October 1915, MSS Eng. Lit, c.542/2/396–99, Bodleian Library, Oxford.

8 Guinard et al., *Introduction*, 69. See General R. Alexandre, *Avec Joffre d'Agadir à Verdun: Souvenirs 1911–1916* (Paris: Berger-Levrault, 1932).

9 Joffre to Millerand, 12 October 1915, with the text of the invitation to the Allied conference at Chantilly, *AFGG* 4/1, annex 26.

10 Conférence interalliée de Londres, October 1915, 7N 1263.

11 *AFGG* 3, 631. The minutes of the conference and the conclusions reached are in *AFGG* 4/1, annexes 46, 47, 49. There is a copy of the conference conclusions (I.C. 5), in French, in CAB 28/1, TNA.

12 *AFGG* 3, 637, 636. *AFGG* 4/1, appendix 50. For the political, diplomatic and economic imperatives behind the French desire for post-war dominance in the Near East, see D.J. Dutton, 'The Balkan campaign and French war aims in the Great War', *English Historical Review*, 94: 370 (January 1979), 97–113.

13 For the Calais conference see David J. Dutton, 'The Calais Conference of December 1915', *The Historical Journal* 21: 1 (1978), 143–56. Dutton calls Britain's capitulation to the dictates of French domestic politics a 'travest[y] of international diplomacy' (p. 156).

14 Foch to Joffre, 2 February 1916; Joffre to Foch, 18 February 1916: both in *AFGG* 4/1, annexes 151, 288.

15 Doughty, *PV*, 256–7.

16 The two communications, 16 and 18 December 1915, are reproduced in *Les Carnets de Gallieni* (Paris: Albin Michel, 1932), 234–7.

17 The full speech is in the minutes for 1 December 1915, C7494, AN, and a short extract in Abel Ferry, *Carnets secrets 1914–1918* (Paris: Grasset, 2005), 169–70 (entry for 17 December 1915).

18 Robert T. Foley, *German Strategy and the Path to Verdun: Erich von Falkenhayn and the development of attrition, 1870–1916* (Cambridge University Press, 2005), 183–5, 187; Holger Afflerbach, *Falkenhayn: Politisches Denken und Handeln im Kaiserreich* (Munich: R. Oldenbourg, 1994), 353–9.

19 Foley, *German Strategy*, 189, for the first use of *verbluten* (bleeding white) in Falkenhayn's planning, although he did use similar words in his pre-war correspondence: Afflerbach, *Falkenhayn*, 363–4.

20 Foley, *German Strategy*, 190, n. 39.

21 Ibid., 196–8, 202.

22 *AFGG* 3, 703.

23 Ibid., 702, 705.

24 Yves Gras, *Castelnau ou l'art de commander 1851–1944* (Paris: Denoël, 1990), 281–2.

25 See Alistair Horne's vivid account in *The Price of Glory: Verdun 1916* (London: Macmillan, 1962), ch. 7.

26 Serrigny, *Trente ans*, 46; Maréchal Pétain, *La Bataille de Verdun* (Paris: Payot, 1929), 45.

27 Instruction, 25 February, 16h, *AFGG* 4/1, annex 683.

28 Ibid., annex 1027.

29 Serrigny, *Trente Ans*, 64.

30 Gaëtan Sciacco, 'La bataille aérienne de Verdun', in Claude Carlier and Guy Pedroncini (eds), *1916: L'émergence des armes nouvelles dans la Grande Guerre* (Paris: Economica, 1997); Alain Morizon, 'L'Aviation française de 1916', *RHA* 1966/3, 40–52; Louis Chagnon, '1916 ou l'année de rupture en matière de l'utilisation de l'armée aérienne', *RHA* 242 (2006), 37–47.

31 Allain Bernède, *Verdun 1916: Le point de vue français* (Le Mans: Editions Cénomane, 2002), 128.

32 Jacottet and Laure, *Etapes*, 335–9.

33 Barescut's opinion of state of troops on 4 April cited in Daille, *Histoire*, 346; de Bary memoirs, 25 April 1916, Castelnau papers, 1K 795/36, fo. 1240.

34 Denis Rolland, *Nivelle: L'inconnu du Chemin des Dames* (Paris: Imago, 2012), 63.

35 Leonard V. Smith, *Between Mutiny and Obedience: The Case of the French Fifth Infantry Division during World War I* (Princeton University Press, 1994), 144.

36 Guy Pedroncini (ed.), *Journal de marche de Joffre (1916–1919)* (Vincennes: Service historique de l'Armée de Terre, 1990), 12 (entry for 11 June 1916); Pétain to Foch, 8 May 1916, Foch papers, 414AP/2, AN.

37 Delvert, *Carnets*, 142–6. See also Horne, *Price of Glory*, 305–7.

38 Pierre Miquel, *Mourir à Verdun* (Paris: Tallandier, 1995), 273–4.

39 Pedroncini (ed.), *Journal de marche de Joffre*, 146–7 (entry for 24 October 1916).

40 Daille, *Histoire*, 436.

41 Pedroncini (ed.), *Journal de marche de Joffre*, 168 (entry for 26 November 1916).

42 *AFGG* 4/1, annex 1212.

43 Ibid., 562.

44 Foch carnets, 23 March 1916, 1K 129/10.

45 La Bataille Offensive, 20 April 1916, *AFGG* 4/2, annex 2.

46 Elizabeth Greenhalgh, *Foch in Command: The forging of a First World War general* (Cambridge University Press, 2011), 168–9.

47 Rémy Porte, *La Direction des Services Automobiles et la Motorisation des Armées Françaises (1914–1919): Vues au travers de l'action du Commandant Doumenc* (Paris: Lavauzelle, 2004), 186–90.

48 Doughty, *PV*, 295.

49 Daille, *Histoire*, 412.

50 Elizabeth Greenhalgh, 'Technology development in coalition: The case of the First World War tank', *International History Review*, 22: 4 (2000), 806–36, here pp. 813–14.

51 *AFGG* 4/1, annexes 46, 49.
52 Frédéric Le Moal, *La Serbie du martyre à la victoire 1914–1918* (Saint-Cloud: SOTECA Editions 14–18, 2008), 96–108.
53 This account of the French mission to Romania is based on Glenn E. Torrey, *Henri Mathias Berthelot: Soldier of France, Defender of Romania* (Iaşi/Oxford/ Portland, OR: Center for Romanian Studies, 2000), ch. 5.
54 Joffre to Robertson, 5 December 1916, *AFGG* 5/1, annex 225.
55 Joffre telegram to head of French Mission at Russian HQ, 25 November 1916, ibid., annex 168.
56 Chantal Antier, 'Le recrutement dans l'empire colonial français, 1914–1918', *GMCC* 230 (2008), 26.
57 Christopher Andrew and A.S. Kanya-Forstner, 'France, Africa, and the First World War', *Journal of African History* 19: 1 (1978), 11–23, here p. 17.
58 Jacques Frémeaux, *Les Colonies dans la Grande Guerre: Combats et épreuves des peuples d'outre-mer* (Saint-Cloud: SOTECA 14–18 editions, 2006), 64.
59 Frémeaux, *Colonies*, 251–2, Anthony Clayton, *France, Soldiers and Africa* (London: Brassey's, 1988), 101–2.
60 See Hew Strachan, *To Arms* (Oxford University Press, 2001), 729–54.
61 *AFGG* 9/2, 845.
62 Ibid., 849.
63 Ibid., 854.
64 Doughty, *PV*, 296.
65 Charles Christienne and Simone Pesquiès-Courbier, 'L'effort de guerre français dans le domaine aéronautique en 1914–1916', in Gérard Canini (ed.), *Les Fronts Invisibles Nourrir, Fournir, Soigner* (Paris: PUN, 1984), 239–42. In 1916, 7,459 aircraft and 16,785 engines were built.
66 Sciacco, 'Bataille aérienne'.
67 *AFGG* 4/3, 74–5; Colonel Lucas, *L'Evolution des idées tactiques en France et en Allemagne pendant la guerre de 1914–1918* (4th edn, Paris: Berger-Levrault, 1932), 159–65.
68 But et conditions d'une action offensive d'ensemble, 16 December 1916, discussed in Lucas, *Evolution*, 161–5.
69 Joffre, Note relative aux enseignements à tirer des affaires de Verdun, 30 March 1916, *AFGG* 4/1, annex 1603.
70 See Doughty, *PV*, 309–10. In all, 579,978 casualties, of which 334,800 were killed.
71 Ibid., 139.
72 Ibid., 103.
73 Ibid., 123, 263.
74 Ibid., 148, 150, 165.
75 *AFGG* 11, appendices 49, 50.
76 Guy Pedroncini, 'Le moral de l'armée française en 1916', in *Verdun 1916: Actes du colloque international sur la bataille de Verdun, 6–7–8 juin 1975* (Verdun: Association Nationale du Souvenir de la Bataille de Verdun, 1976), 159–73.
77 Diary, de Bary, 5 June 1916, Castelnau papers, 1K 795/39, fo. 478.
78 Lt-Col. Spencer Cosby, report #2927, 31 May 1916, RG 165, M1024, reel 216, NARA.

79 Fayolle, *CS*, 171–3 (entries for 4, 6, 10 August 1916).

80 William Philpott, *Bloody Victory: The sacrifice on the Somme and the making of the twentieth century* (London: Little, Brown, 2009), 256; Guy Pedroncini (ed.), *Journal de marche de Joffre (1916–1918)* (Vincennes: Service historique de l'Armée de Terre, 1990), 88 (entry for 14 August 1916).

81 Jean Noël Jeanneney, 'Les archives des commissions de contrôle postal aux armées (1916–1918)', *RHMC* 15 (1968), 209–33.

CHAPTER 5

1 Georges Suarez, *Briand: Sa vie, son oeuvre, avec son journal et de nombreux documents inédits*, 5 vols (Paris: Tallandier, 1938–41), 4: 68–9. See also Denis Rolland, *Nivelle: L'inconnu du Chemin des Dames* (Paris: Imago, 2012), 81–4.

2 Abel Ferry, *Carnets secrets 1914–1918* (Paris: Grasset, 2005), 227 (entry for 1 May 1917); Général Serrigny, *Trente ans avec Pétain* (Paris Plon, 1959), 82.

3 Georges-Henri Soutou, 'Poincaré, Painlevé et l'offensive Nivelle', in Jean-Claude Allain (ed.), *Des Etoiles et des croix: Mélanges offerts à Guy Pedroncini* (Paris: Economica, 1995), 91. Soutou goes so far as to opine that Nivelle's offensive could just as well bear Poincaré's name.

4 Rolland, *Nivelle*, 81–4; Jean-Christophe Notin, *Foch* (Paris: Perrin, 2008), 242–3.

5 For his career 1914–16, see Rolland, *Nivelle*, ch. 2.

6 Ibid., 82.

7 Ibid., 89–90.

8 Doughty *PV*, 324–5.

9 David R. Woodward, *Lloyd George and the Generals* (Newark, DE: University of Delaware Press, 1983), 143.

10 Rolland, *Nivelle*, 92–9.

11 E.L. Spears, *Prelude to Victory* (London: Jonathan Cape, 1930), 130–1.

12 Ibid., 31; Paul Guillaumat (ed.), *Correspondance de guerre du Général Guillaumat, 1914–1919* (Paris: L'Harmattan, 2006), 175 (letter to wife, 8 January 1917).

13 Rolland, *Nivelle*, 88. Rolland states that the usually accepted view – that Pétain refused the command – is mistaken.

14 Hellot, *Histoire*, 27.

15 Woodward, *Lloyd George*, 138–49. Also Elizabeth Greenhalgh, *Victory through Coalition: Britain and France during the First World War* (Cambridge University Press, 2005), 138–48.

16 Lord Hankey, *The Supreme Command 1914–1918* (London: Hutchinson, 1961), 2: 615–16.

17 Yves Gras, *Castelnau ou l'art de commander 1851–1944* (Paris: Denoël, 1990), 347.

18 Colonel Rampont, Report on the Russian Army, November 1916, 7N 758.

19 Spears, *Prelude*, 251.

20 *Le Matin*, 20 March 1917, p. 1.

21 Spears, *Prelude*, 223.

22 *AFGG* 5/1, annex 1167. Added emphasis. The idea of 24–48 hours seems to have disappeared.

23 Tournès diary, 20 March 1917, 1K 860/3.
24 Pierre Miquel, *Le Chemin des Dames* (Paris: Perrin, 1997), 45, 50; J.C. King, *Generals and Politicians: Conflict between France's high command, parliament and government, 1914–1918* (Berkeley/Los Angeles, CA: University of California Press, 1951), 145.
25 Tournès diary, 22 February 1917; Rolland, *Nivelle*, 131.
26 Helbronner diary, 26 March 1917, Painlevé papers 313AP/122, AN; Cozens-Hardy to Lloyd George, 17 June 1918, with account of Nivelle's offensive, Lloyd George papers, F/52/2/7, Parliamentary Record Office, London.
27 Spears diary, 13 March 1917, SPRS 5/16, Churchill Archives Centre, Cambridge.
28 Cited in Rolland, *Nivelle*, 141.
29 Painlevé's letter reproduced *in toto* in A. Ribot, *Journal de Alexandre Ribot et correspondances inédites, 1914–1922* (Paris: Plon, 1936), 78–9, note.
30 Comité secret du 29 juin 1917, séances du 2, 4 juillet, *Journal Officiel, Débats parlementaires: Chambre des députés*, 30 June 1922, 365, 391.
31 Charles Delvert, 'L'Offensive du 16 avril 1917: déposition d'un témoin', *La Revue de Paris*, 1 May 1920, 64–102, here p. 82.
32 Hellot, *Histoire*, 117–22; Doughty, *PV*, 345–9.
33 Delvert, 'L'Offensive', 84.
34 On the tanks in Nivelle's offensive see Tim Gale, *The French Army's Tank Force and Armoured Warfare in the Great War* (Farnham: Ashgate, 2013), ch. 2.
35 Abel Ferry, *La Guerre vue d'en haut et d'en bas* (Paris: Grasset, 1920), 264. The figures relate to the period 16–20 April 1917. Official figures cover a slightly longer period, 15–25 April 1917: 47,871 total casualties, of which 6,097 were killed, 11,726 disappeared, 29,238 wounded: *AFGG* 5/1, annex 1917.
36 Ibid. *AFGG* figures slightly less: 20,029.
37 Instruction, 1 April 1917, *AFGG* 5/1, annex 1127.
38 Louis Loucheur, *Carnets secrets 1908–1932* (Brussels: Brepol, 1962), 41.
39 Helbronner diary, 19 April 1917; Raymond Poincaré, *Au Service de la France: Neuf années de souvenirs*, 11 vols (Paris: Plon, 1928–74), 9: 118 (entry for 20 April 1917).
40 Colonel E. Herbillon, *Du Général en chef au gouvernement: Souvenirs d'un officier de liaison pendant la guerre mondiale*, 2 vols (Paris: Tallandier, 1930), 2: 65–9 (entries for 19, 21, 23 April 1917).
41 Note for General Wilson [to be conveyed to Haig], 21 April 1917, 16N 1686.
42 Reproduced in Paul Painlevé, *Comment j'ai nommé Foch et Pétain* (Paris: Félix Alcan, 1924), 380.
43 Helbronner diary, 21 April 1917.
44 *AFGG* 5/1, 713.
45 Helbronner diary, 27 April 1917. Painlevé, *Foch et Pétain*, 94–100. Painlevé would have given Mangin a front command later, but Foch and Pétain refused to allow it. He offered Mangin a corps, which Mangin refused, but later accepted.
46 Helbronner diary, 27 April 1917; Serrigny, *Trente ans*, 124.

47 Summary of the Proceedings of the Anglo-French Conference held at Paris on May 4 and 5 [1917], IC 21, CAB 28/2, TNA.

48 Mission of the different armies, 5 May 1917, *AFGG* 5/1, annex 1837.

49 Martha Hanna, *Your Death would be Mine: Paul and Marie Pireaud in the Great War* (Cambridge, MA: Harvard University Press, 2006), 207–8.

50 Denis Rolland, 'La question des pertes sur le Chemin des Dames', *Mémoires de la Fédération des sociétés d'histoire et d'archéologie de l'Aisne* 55 (2010), 441–60, here p. 451.

51 *AFGG* 5/1, 783.

52 Reichsarchiv, *Der Weltkrieg 1914 bis 1918*, Bd. 12 (Berlin: Mittler und Sohn, 1939), 410.

53 Anglo-French Conference, 4–5 May 1917, IC 21, p. 3, CAB 28/2. These figures are somewhat exaggerated. Presumably, therefore, Lloyd George was including the territory recovered by the German Army's voluntary withdrawal to the Hindenburg Line.

54 Pétain's words cited in Gras, *Castelnau*, 354.

55 Général Herr, *L'Artillerie: Ce qu'elle a été, ce qu'elle est, et ce qu'elle doit être* (Paris: Berger-Levrault, 1923), 67–8.

56 Robertson to Spears, 22 July and 14 November 1932, Spears papers, SPRS 2/3/96–7, LHCMA. Robertson was responding to questions from Spears, who was writing his *Prelude to Victory*.

57 Letter, Franchet d'Espèrey to Spears, 29 January 1932, SPRS 2/3/12, LHCMA.

58 Benjamin Ziemann, 'Le Chemin des Dames dans l'historiographie allemande', in Nicolas Offenstadt (ed.), *Le Chemin des Dames: De l'événement à la mémoire* (Paris: Stock, 2004), 341–9.

59 Delvert, 'L'Offensive', 68.

60 The lower figures are from Leonard V. Smith, Stéphane Audoin-Rouzeau and Annette Becker, *France and the Great War 1914–1918* (Cambridge University Press, 2003), 122, but citing no source; the higher figures are from Denis Rolland, *La Grève des tranchées: Les mutineries de 1917* (Paris: Imago, 2005), 374.

61 The details of the events that took place in 77 DI are taken from Guy Pedroncini, *Les Mutineries de 1917* (Paris: PUF, 1967), 142–9.

62 Ibid., 163–6. Rolland gives a full account of these incidents in *La Grève des tranchées*, 182–97.

63 Jean Julien Weber, *Sur les pentes du Golgotha. Un prêtre dans les tranchées* (Strasbourg: la Nuée bleue, 2001), 174.

64 Denis Rolland, 'Affaire Gaston Lefèvre: Quelques lettres de trop?', and Damien Becquart, 'Le premier 11 novembre du caporal Gaston Lefèvre', *La Lettre du Chemin des Dames* 24 (2012), 38–42.

65 André Loez, 'Si cette putain de guerre pouvait finir': Histoire et sociologie des mutins de 1917 (PhD thesis, University Paul Valéry, Montpellier III, 2009), 393–405.

66 Jamie H. Cockfield, *With Snow on their Boots: The tragic odyssey of the Russian Expeditionary Force in France during World War I* (New York: St Martin's Press, 1998), 120, 124–5.

67 Leonard V. Smith emphasises that soldiers were citizens, and presents the mutinies as the re-negotiation of relations of authority: *Betweeen Mutiny and Obedience: The case of the Fifth Infantry Division during World War I* (Princeton University Press, 1994).
68 Report, 30 May 1917, *AFGG* 5/2, annex 372; Pedroncini, *Mutineries*, 236.
69 Jean-Jacques Becker, *The Great War and the French People* (New York: St Martin's Press, 1986), chs 14, 15.
70 Spears papers, 2/5/6, dossier #1, LHCMA.
71 Rolland lists their names and family circumstances, *Grève*, 383.
72 Stéphane Audoin-Rouzeau, *Men at War: National sentiment and trench journalism in France during the First World War* (Providence, RI/Oxford: Berg, 1992), 22.
73 CinC to all authorities, 8 June 1917, *AFGG* 5/2, annex 459.
74 See the summary of opinion given in Pedroncini, *Mutineries*, 281–301.
75 *AFGG* 5/2, 201.
76 Pedroncini, *Mutineries*, 242.
77 War Ministry, 'Hautes-payes de guerre, Indemnités de combat, Pécules', 19 April 1917. Poincaré had signed the decree bringing these measures into effect the previous day. The combat allowance was increased again to 3 francs per day in 1918: GQG, 1er Bureau, 24 July 1918, 7N 448. One-third was paid in cash and two-thirds in saving stamps.
78 Hanna, *Your Death would be Mine*, 218.
79 Jean de Pierrefeu, *G.Q.G. Secteur 1: Trois ans au Grand Quartier Général*, 2 vols (Paris: Edition Française Illustrée, 1920), 2: 36–7. Pierrefeu states that the writer Louis Madelin provided some preparatory notes.
80 Transcribed from *Echo de Paris*, 27 June 1917.
81 Herbillon, *Souvenirs*, 2: 106 (entry for 27 June 1917).
82 Maistre to Northern Army Group, 3 June 1917, with Franchet d'Espèrey addendum, 4 June 1917, *AFGG* 5/2, annex 412.
83 Painlevé, *Foch et Pétain*, 143.
84 Berichte der Nachrichtenoffiziere der Armeen über die Stimmung im französischen Heere nach dem Zusammenbruch der französischen Frühjahrsoffensive, 1937, RH 61/656, Bundesarchiv/Militärarchiv, Freiburg i.B. The document was compiled for the Reichsarchiv's official history, *Der Weltkrieg*.
85 Markus Pöhlmann, 'Une occasion manquée? Les mutineries de 1917 dans la stratégie et l'historiographie allemande', in André Loez and Nicolas Mariot (eds), *Obéir/désobéir: Les mutineries de 1917 en perspective* (Paris, La Découverte, 2008), 385–98.
86 Markus Pöhlmann, 'German Intelligence at War, 1914–1918', *Journal of Intelligence History* 5: 2 (2005), 25–54, here p. 41.
87 Letters, Lieutenant-Colonel Alexander G. Martin, to Spears, 23 November, 24 December 1931, Spears papers, 2/3/74–75, LHCMA.
88 Rolland, *Nivelle*, 226.
89 Cited in Alexander Watson, *Enduring the Great War: Combat, morale and collapse in the German and British armies, 1914–1918* (Cambridge University Press, 2008), 168.
90 Pöhlmann, 'Une occasion manquée?', 391.

91 Watson, *Enduring*, 81.
92 Generalkommando, *XIV Korps*, 2 May 1917, reporting on events of 28 February, cited in English in Bernd Ulrich and Benjamin Ziemann (eds), *German Soldiers in the Great War: Letters and Eyewitness Accounts* (Barnsley: Pen & Sword, 2010), 152–3.
93 Nivelle to Lloyd George, 6 September 1918, and Lloyd George to Nivelle, 25 September 1918, both letters in the Lloyd George papers, F/50/3/20 and 23, Parliamentary Records Office, London.
94 See Denis Rolland, 'Ni responsables, ni coupables: La Commission Brugère', in Offenstadt (ed.), *Le Chemin des Dames*, 249–52.
95 The commission papers are in 5N 255.
96 Session of 22 August 1917, ibid., fo. 6.
97 Session of 10 September 1917, ibid., fo. 36.
98 Pétain gave the text of his report, dated 1926, to General Spears, because he believed that an English translation would be received more calmly than publication in France. Spears intended to include it in a second volume to follow his *Prelude to Victory*, but the Second World War intervened. It was published in 1966 in his *Two Men Who Saved France* (London: Eyre & Spottiswoode). It appeared in French the same year as *La Crise morale et militaire de 1917* (Paris: Nouvelles Editions Latines).
99 *AFGG* 5/1, 782–3.
100 Delvert, 'L'Offensive', 102.

CHAPTER 6

1 Paul Guillaumat (ed.), *Correspondance de guerre du Général Guillaumat, 1914–1919* (Paris: L'Harmattan, 2006), 209 (letter to wife of 17 May 1917).
2 Summary of the proceedings of the Anglo-French conference held at Paris on May 4 and 5, IC 21, CAB 28/2, TNA.
3 *AFGG* 5/2, 85.
4 GQG, Directive #1, 19 May 1917, ibid., annex 235.
5 Questions traitées par le général Pétain dans son voyage aux G.A.C. et G.A.E. (24 et 25 mai 1917), ibid., annex 309.
6 Note en réponse au télégramme … du ministre de la Guerre, 28 May 1917, ibid., annex 349.
7 Zeller memoirs, fos. 135–6, in Castelnau papers, 1K 795/39. Franchet d'Espèrey's English nickname reflects the same qualities: 'desperate Frankie'.
8 Général Debeney, *La Guerre et les hommes: Réflexions d'après-guerre* (Paris: Plon, 1937), 22.
9 *AFGG* 5/2, annex 630.
10 Commandant Laure, *Au 3ème Bureau du Troisième G.Q.G.* (Paris: Plon, 1921), 15–21. Laure is one of the author's of the study of 13 DI cited throughout this book. Michel Goya, *La Chair et l'acier: L'invention de la guerre moderne (1914–1918)* (Paris: Tallandier, 2004), 238.
11 See Guy Pedroncini, *Pétain Général en Chef 1917–1918* (Paris: PUF, 1974), 78–83.
12 Note pour les groupes d'armées et les armées sur l'organisation d'un Centre d'Etudes d'Artillerie, 9 June 1917; Note pour les groupes d'armées et les

armées sur l'organisation d'un Centre d'Etudes du Génie, 14 July 1917, both in 16N 2088.

13 Goya, *La Chair et l'acier*, 236.

14 Ibid., 240–1; Laure, *3ème Bureau*, 32–49.

15 Charles Christienne and Pierre Lissarague, *A History of French Military Aviation* (Washington, DC: Smithsonian Institution Press, 1986), 142.

16 Ibid., 148.

17 The minutes are in C7502, AN.

18 Note on the technical value of our military aviation, 23 November 1917, ibid.; d'Aubigny [president of the aeronautics sub-commission], letter to the minister, 19 April 1917, C7498; d'Aubigny report, 28 March 1917, C7502, AN.

19 Charles Christienne and Simone Pesquiès-Courbier, 'L'effort de guerre français dans le domaine aéronautique en 1914–1918' in Gérard Canini (ed.), *Les Fronts invisibles: Nourrir, fournir, soigner* (Presses universitaires de Nancy, 1984), 233–46, here p. 243.

20 Sous/secrétaire d'Etat, 'Note pour M. Roques [War Minister]', 23 November 1916, 16N 2121. Completed orders of the St Chamond tanks were even fewer in number. Of four available on 26 November, three had broken down: GHQ, AS, 'Renseignements au sujet du 1er Groupe d'A.S. au Camp de Cercottes', 26 November 1916.

21 Goya, *La Chair et l'acier*, 348–9.

22 Estienne to Commander-in-Chief, 27 November 1916, 16N 2121.

23 Goya, *La Chair et l'acier*, 269–70.

24 Zeller, 'Pétain', fo. 145, 1K 172/8.

25 David R. Woodward, *Field Marshal Sir William Robertson: Chief of the Imperial General Staff in the Great War* (Westport, CT: Praeger, 1998), 107.

26 This point is developed at length in Pedroncini, *Pétain, général en chef*, 120–1.

27 Résumé de l'entrevue du 2 juin à Bavincourt entre le Major Général et le Maréchal Haig, 3 June 1917, Benson mss, B/1/107, LHCMA; and *AFGG* 5/2, annex 407. See J.P. Harris, *Douglas Haig and the First World War* (Cambridge University Press, 2008), 330–1.

28 Haig diary, 7 June 1917.

29 Charles Delvert, *Les Opérations de la 1re Armée dans les Flandres (Juillet–Novembre 1917)* (Paris: Fournier, 1920), 26; *AFGG* 5/2, 624–7. Delvert was on the staff of First Army during the battle.

30 Hellot, *Histoire*, 220–1.

31 E.W. von Hoeppner, *Germany's War in the Air* (Nashville, TN: Battery Press, 1994 [German original 1921]), 110.

32 Instruction générale #11, 6 July 1917, *AFGG* 5/2, annex 652.

33 Delvert, *Flandres*, 111.

34 Hellot, *Histoire*, 227; Delvert, *Flandres*, 120, gives 1050.

35 Robin Prior and Trevor Wilson, *Passchendaele: The untold story* (New Haven/London: Yale University Press, 1996), 97: 40.7mm during 1–4 August.

36 Delvert, *Flandres*, 151.

37 *AFGG* 5/2, annex 1129.

38 Haig diary, 29 September 1917.

39 Delvert, *Flandres*, 172.

40 Ibid., 194.
41 Ibid., 196.
42 Ibid., 166–9, 197–8.
43 Pedroncini, *Pétain général en chef*, 92.
44 Rolland, *Nivelle*, 65.
45 Pedroncini, *Pétain général en chef*, 90, writes of Verdun that its 'name and the successes of 1916 were a stimulant'.
46 Guy Pedroncini, *Les Mutineries de 1917* (Paris: PUF, 1967), 173–4. He cites minor incidents in 4, 20, 31 and 69 DI also.
47 Guillaumat, *Correspondance*, 224 (letter of 22 July 1917).
48 Hellot, *Histoire*, 188–93.
49 Pedroncini, *Pétain général en chef*, 97.
50 Analysed in ibid., 97–100. The reports are all in 16N 1993.
51 *AFGG* 5/2, annex 801. Report dated 24 July 1917.
52 Enseignements tirés des opérations d'août 1917 à Verdun, 26 November 1917, 16N 1993.
53 Raymond Poincaré, *Au Service de la France: Neuf années de souvenirs*, 11 vols (Paris: Plon, 1928–74), 9: 259, 254–5 (entries for 29 and 25 August 1917).
54 Rapport sur l'état moral des armées, 11 October 1917, 16N 1485/1.
55 Unless stated otherwise, all the detail for this section comes from Laure and Jacottet, *Etapes*, ch. 5.
56 Laure, *3ème Bureau*, 40–9. Laure was 13 DI's former chief of staff.
57 Buat's preface praises the French transport service's 'ingeniosity': ibid., iv.
58 *AFGG* 6/1, 137–42.
59 Note pour les généraux commandant les groupes d'armées et les armées, 27 November 1917, ibid., annex 120.
60 Harris, *Haig*, 408.
61 Général Mordacq, *Le Ministère Clemenceau: Journal d'un témoin*, 4 vols (Paris: Plon, 1930–31), 1: 96. Mordacq wrote that they were told that it was a diversionary action to help the Italians.
62 Wilfrid Miles, *Military Operations: France and Belgium 1917*, 3 vols (London: HMSO, 1948), 3: 222.
63 Haig to Robertson, 25 November 1917, Robertson papers, 7/7/68, LHCMA.
64 Hellot, *Histoire*, 292–4; Doughty, *PV*, 424–8; Pedroncini, *Pétain général en chef*, 212–20. The instruction is to be found in 16N 1689.
65 Directive #4 pour les groupes d'armées et les armées, *AFGG* 6/1, annex 202.
66 Instruction pour l'application de la Directive #4, *AFGG* 6/1, annex 288.
67 Pedroncini analyses the various corrections that Pétain made to the wording of this document: *Pétain général en chef*, 217–19.
68 Colonel Lucas, *L'Evolution des idées tactiques en France et en Allemagne pendant la guerre de 1914–1918* (4th edn, Paris: Berger-Levrault, 1932), 208, 222–3.
69 Guinard et al., *Introduction*, 205; Philippe Boulanger, *La France devant la conscription: Géographie historique d'une institution républicaine 1914–1922* (Paris: Economica, 2001), 59, 345: annex 9.
70 See Robert B. Bruce, *A Fraternity of Arms: America and France in the Great War* (Lawrence, KS: University Press of Kansas, 2003), ch. 5; André Kaspi,

Le Temps des Américains 1917–1918 (Paris: Publications de la Sorbonne, 1976), ch. 8.

71 Kaspi, *Le Temps des Américains*, 109, 112.

72 Figures based on table in ibid., 194.

73 Cessions de matériels français aux États-Unis, 25 October 1917, *AFGG* 6/1, annex 21.

74 Guinard et al., *Introduction*, 124.

75 Ibid., 148.

76 Goya, *La Chair et l'acier*, 381–2.

77 Ibid., 381–2, 240–1.

78 Guinard et al., *Introduction*, 148, 150.

79 Christienne and Lissarague, *History of French Military Aviation*, 181. Weiller died in 1993.

80 See Olivier Lahaie, Renseignement et services de renseignement en France pendant la guerre de 1914–1918 (PhD thesis: Université de Paris IV, Sorbonne, 2005), 630–54.

81 Guinard et al., *Introduction*, 124.

82 Memorandum GT 372, CAB 24/9, TNA. He told the British ambassador in Paris: 'We shall be there by conquest, and shall remain.'

83 *AFGG* 9/1, ch. XI. On the hadj pilgrimage see Général Brémond, *Le Hedjaz dans la guerre mondiale* (Paris: Payot, 1931), ch. IV.

84 Cited in Torrey, *Berthelot*, 199, 203.

85 Général Sarrail, *Mon Commandement en Orient*, ed. Rémy Porte (Saint-Cloud: SOTECA 14–18 editions, 2012), 319, n. 3.

86 Copy of 9th Langlois report, 20 July 1917, in Albert Thomas papers, 94AP/181, AN.

87 Suggestions for support to be given to Russia in order to prevent a possible defection, GT 1531, CAB 24/21.

88 Foch, Note sur l'action de la France en Russie, 28 July 1917, 16N 3019.

89 Général Niessel, *Le Triomphe des Bolchéviks et la paix de Brest-Litovsk: Souvenirs 1917–1918* (Paris: Plon, 1940), ii.

90 Poincaré, *Au Service*, 9: 218 (entry for 30 July 1917).

91 Ioanni Sinanoglou, France looks Eastward: Perspectives and policies in Russia, 1914–1918 (PhD thesis, Columbia University, 1974), 253, n. 25.

92 Ibid., 213; Albert Thomas papers, 94AP/186; Niessel, *Triomphe des Bolchéviks*, 12.

93 Poincaré, *Au Service*, 9: 267 (entry for 3 September 1917).

94 EMA, 3e Bureau Avant, Note au sujet de l'attitude qu'il convient d'adopter à l'égard de la Russie, 11 October 1917, 16N 3021.

95 Jean Nicot and Philippe Schillinger, 'L'Opinion face à la guerre: l'influence de la révolution russe d'après les archives du contrôle postal', *Actes du 97e Congrès national des sociétés savantes* (Nantes, 1972), 451–71, here pp. 462–3.

96 Jean Nicot, *Les Poilus ont la parole: Lettres du front: 1917–1918* (Paris: Editions Complexe, 1998), 166.

97 Martha Hanna, *Your Death would be Mine: Paul and Marie Pireaud in the Great War* (Cambridge, MA: Harvard University Press, 2006), 236 (letter of 23 December 1917).

98 For more on this topic see, Greenhalgh, *Foch in Command*, 246–9. Paul Painlevé, *Comment j'ai nommé Foch et Pétain: La politique de guerre, le commandement unique interallié* (Paris: Félix Alcan, 1924), 128.

99 Audition, Senate Army Commission, 14 December 1917, S69–6, fo. 9141, Archives du Sénat, Paris.

100 Fayolle, *CS*, 246.

101 Hanna, *Your Death would be Mine*, 237; Nicot, *Les Poilus ont la parole*, 78.

102 Hanna, *Your Death would be Mine*, 228–40 (letters of 23 December 1917 and 7 February 1918).

103 *AFGG*, 6/1, 117–23.

104 Clemenceau's speeches, 20 November 1917, 8 March 1918, in Georges Clemenceau, *Discours de guerre* (Paris: PUF, 1968), 130, 172.

105 John Horne shows that the 'net benefit' to front-line effectives, after taking into account the return to the homefront of older mobilised classes, may have been as little as 15,000 men by 1 February 1918: '"*L'Impôt du sang*": Republican rhetoric and industrial warfare in France, 1914–18', *Social History* 14: 2 (1989), 210–23, here p. 215.

106 Herbillon, *Souvenirs*, 2: 183 (entry for 21 December 1917).

107 'Conversation du 6 octobre 1917 avec le général Foch', Guy Pedroncini (ed.), *Journal de marche de Joffre (1916–1918)* (Vincennes: Service historique de l'Armée de Terre, 1990), 229.

108 Herbillon, *Souvenirs*, 2: 173 (entry for 28 November 1917).

109 Poincaré, *Au Service*, 9: 413, 420 (entries for 13 and 19 December 1917).

110 Pedroncini, *Pétain général en chef*, 111–12; See also Doughty, *PV*, 392; and Jean-Baptiste Duroselle, *La Grande Guerre des Français: L'Incompréhensible* (Paris: Perrin, 1994), 408–13.

111 Note sur le plan de campagne de 1918, 17 October 1917, *AFGG* 6.1, annex 13; copy in WO 158/24.

112 Ibid. See also Haig's diary account of his meeting with Pétain, 18 October 1917.

113 Barescut diary, 18 October 1917.

114 Haig diary, 7 January 1918.

115 Debeney, Organisation du commandement de la Coalition, Fonds Clemenceau, 6N 54; Serrigny, letter, 26 October 1916, 1K 61; Serrigny, *Trente Ans*, 156.

116 War Cabinet 263, 2 November 1917, CAB 23/4; Pedroncini, *Pétain général en chef*, 242.

117 *AFGG* 6/1, annex 86.

118 Mordacq, *Ministère Clemenceau*, 1: 102; Herbillon, *Souvenirs*, 2: 158, 170 (entries for 30 October, 24 November 1917).

119 On the Allied General Reserve Scheme, see Greenhalgh, *Foch in Command*, 287–91; David F. Trask, *The United States in the Supreme War Council: American War Aims and Inter-Allied Strategy, 1917–1918* (Middletown, CT: Wesleyan University Press, 1961), 54–62.

120 Barescut diary, 9 and 10 February 1918. The chief of staff, now General Anthoine, had written the original 'brutal' response.

121 Intelligence report #1352, 1 March 1918, *AFGG* 6/1, annex 412.

122 Delvert, *Flandres*, 198. Original emphasis.

CHAPTER 7

1 Tournès, *Histoire*, 51.
2 Compte-rendu de renseignements #1371, 20 March 1918, *AFGG* 6/1, annex 482.
3 Cointet, 'Cahier 1918', 1K/87, fos. 2–3.
4 *AFGG* 6/1, 86–91.
5 Barescut diary, 24 March 1918; Haig diary, 23 March 1918.
6 Barescut diary, 23 March 1918.
7 Clive diary, 24 March 1918, CAB 45/201, TNA: 'Pétain was content with what the F.M. is doing and said when coming away "I shall sleep better tonight than I have done for many nights".' Barescut diary, 25 March 1918.
8 Barescut diary, 25 March 1918.
9 No trace of the telegram has been found. See Elizabeth Greenhalgh, 'Myth and memory: Sir Douglas Haig and the imposition of Allied unified command in March 1918', *Journal of Military History* 68: 2 (2004), 771–820.
10 Clive notebooks, 18 April 1918, CAB 45/201, TNA.
11 Cointet, 'Cahier 1918', fo. 17, 1K/87.
12 Mme Foch diary, 27 March 1918, 414AP/13, AN.
13 Paul Guillaumat (ed.), *Correspondance de guerre du Général Guillaumat 1914–1919* (Paris: L'Harmattan, 2006), 305 (letter of 4 April 1918).
14 Colonel E. Herbillon, *Du Général en chef au gouvernement: Souvenirs d'un officier de liaison pendant la guerre mondiale*, 2 vols (Paris: Tallandier, 1930), 2: 235.
15 Clark report #23, 28 March 1918, Clark mss, Library of Congress.
16 Cointet, 'Cahier 1918', fos. 30, 26.
17 This is hearsay, but credible, evidence via Barescut: ibid., fo. 32.
18 Pedroncini uses a long exposition of this deployment to refute the argument that Pétain had accepted as inevitable the break between British and French forces: Guy Pedroncini, *Pétain général en chef 1917–1918* (Paris: PUF, 1974), 302–13.
19 Barescut diary, 24 March 1918.
20 Fayolle, *CS*, 263 (entry for 27 March 1918).
21 Comments taken from the XXXVI Corps postal control records, in 36 CA Commission de contrôle de Dunkerque: Rapport d'ensemble du 22 mars au 4 avril 1918, 16N 1390.
22 Renseignements sur les corps de troupe d'après le contrôle postal, 6 April 1918, 16N 1485.
23 General Dubail to Clemenceau, 8 May 1918, 16N 1536.
24 *AFGG* 6/2, 552.
25 Letter, Lawrence to Edmonds, 21 May 1928 (in correspondence about the British official history), CAB 45/177, TNA.
26 David T. Zabecki, *The German 1918 Offensives: A case study in the operational level of war* (London/New York: Routledge, 2006), 196.
27 Reichsarchiv, *Der Weltkrieg*, vol. 14 (Berlin: Mittler und Sohn, 1944), 289, 310.
28 Pétain to Foch, 24 April 1918, *AFGG* 6/1, annex 1906. Original emphasis.
29 2e Bureau, Compte-rendu de renseignements #1407, 25 April 1918, *AFGG* 6/1, annex 1941.

30 Fayolle, *CS*, 271–2 (entries for 18 and 30 April 1918).

31 Clark report #51, 22 April 1918, Pershing papers, RG 200, NARA.

32 Letters, Foch to Mme Foch, 20, 22, 23, 24, 25 April 1918, vol. 45, Fonds photographique, BNF. Original emphasis.

33 Zabecki, *German 1918 Offensives*, 195 citing *Sixth Army* intelligence reports.

34 Sir James E. Edmonds, *Military Operations France and Belgium: 1918*, 2 vols (London: Macmillan, 1935), 2: 410–13.

35 Zabecki, *German 1918 Offensives*, 198.

36 Esher diary, 27 April 1918, ESHR 2/21, Churchill Archives Centre, Cambridge; letter, Haig to Lady Haig, 25 April 1918, Haig mss. acc. 3155, no. 150, National Library of Scotland.

37 'Notes on the Operations on Western Front after Sir D. Haig became Commander in Chief 1915', 30 January 1920, Haig mss, acc. 3155, no. 213a, fo. 63.

38 Brigadier-General W.P. Monkhouse to official historian, 2 April 1933, CAB 45/124; Dr T.D. Shiels to same, 5 February 1933, CAB 45/125.

39 *AFGG* 6/1, 498.

40 Henri Desagneaux, *Journal de guerre 14–18* (Paris: Denoël, 1971), 194, 196.

41 *Le Nouvel Candide*, 26–27 February 1964.

42 Note sur le moral des troupes, 15 May 1918, 16N 1485.

43 General Madelin to commander II Cavalry Corps, 26 April 1918, *AFGG* 6/1, annex 2018.

44 *Fourth Army* war diary, 28 April 1918, in René Tournès and Henry Berthemet, *La Bataille des Flandres d'après le journal de marche et les archives de la IVe Armée Allemande* (Paris: Charles Lavauzelle, 1925), 355.

45 Fritz von Lossberg, *Meine Tätigkeit im Weltkriege* (Berlin: Mittler, 1939), 339.

46 Tournès, *Bataille des Flandres*, 381, 384–5.

47 Etude au sujet d'une action offensive pour dégager Amiens, 28 April 1918, 16N 1714.

48 Fayolle, *CS*, 274 (entries for 19 and 21 May 1918).

49 *AFGG* 6/1, 522–4.

50 Marshal von Hindenburg, *Out of my Life* (London: Cassell, 1920), 357.

51 Pétain to Foch, letter with table, 7 May 1918, *AFGG* 6/2, annex 124.

52 Pétain to Foch, 12 May 1918, ibid., annex 160.

53 Philippe Boulanger, *La France devant la conscription: Géographie historique d'une institution républicaine 1914–1922* (Paris: Economica, 2001), 111.

54 For details of this acrimonious debate, see Greenhalgh, 'David Lloyd George, Georges Clemenceau and the 1918 manpower crisis', *Historical Journal* 50: 2 (2007), 397–421.

55 John J. Pershing, *My Experiences in the World War*, 2 vols (New York: Frederick A. Stokes Company, 1931), 1: 365.

56 *AFGG* 6/2, annex 79, where details of numbers involved and content of the training are given.

57 Barescut diary, 13 May 1918.

58 Marc Michel, 'Colonisation et défense nationale: Le général Mangin et la force noire', *GMCC* 145 (1987), 34.

59 Marc Michel, *Les Africains et la Grande Guerre* (Paris: Karthala, 2003), ch. 4.

60 Gilbert Meynier, *L'Algérie révélée: La guerre de 1914–1918 et le premier quart du XXe siècle* (Geneva: Droz, 1981), 404, 411.

61 Jacques Frémeaux, *Les Colonies dans la Grande Guerre: Combats et épreuves des peuples d'outre-mer* (Saint-Cloud: SOTECA 14–18 Editions, 2006), 65–6.

62 Adrian Muckle, 'Kanak experiences of WWI: New Caledonia's *Tirailleurs*, Auxiliaries and "Rebels"', *History Compass* 6: 5 (2008), 1326–54, here p. 1329.

63 Note pour les généraux commandant les groupes d'armées, 5 and 13 May 1918, *AFGG* 6/2, annexes 109, 175.

64 Note au sujet de la manoeuvre en terrain libre, 9 April 1918, 16N 1694.

65 Note, 23 April 1918, 16N 1695.

66 Note pour les armées, 8 May 1918, ibid.

67 Report, 13 May 1918, ibid.

68 Letter, Pétain to Clemenceau, 4 May 1918, *AFGG* 6/2, annex 98.

69 E. von Hoeppner, *Germany's War in the Air* (Nashville, TN: Battery Press, 1994), 149–50; Résumé of air operations 22–26 March 1918 inclusive, 28 March 1918, *AFGG* 6/1, annex 966; Martin Kitchen, *The German Offensives of 1918* (Stroud: Tempus, 2001), 88.

70 Fayolle, *CS*, 274 (entry for 21 May 1918).

71 Patrick Facon, '1918, ou l'emploi en masse de l'aviation', *RHA* 1998/3, 89–98.

72 Intelligence on the action of enemy aircraft on the DAN front, 30 April 1918, *AFGG* 6/1, annex 2104.

73 Herbillon, *Souvenirs*, 2: 254 (entry for 6 May 1918).

74 Poincaré, *Au Service*, 10: 169 (entry for 12 May 1918).

75 GQGA, JMO, 15 May 1918, 26N 1. Fayolle in his *CS* does not refer to the meeting.

76 Pétain to Foch, 16 May 1918, *AFGG* 6/2, annex 197. Pétain signed himself 'votre bien dévoué'.

77 Barescut diary, 13, 15 May 1918.

78 Run of reports in GQGA records:15N 5.

79 Report #77, 20 May 1918, Pershing papers, RG 200. Another officer at GQG told Clark two days earlier that there was 'no evidence' about where the Germans would strike next. His personal view was that it would be around Amiens: report #75, 18 May 1918, ibid.

80 Pétain to Paris commander and Cavalry Corps, 17 May 1918, 16N 1696. The courses were to re-start 'in a few days'.

81 See Zabecki, *German 1918 Offensives*, 209–12.

82 Olivier Lepick, *La Grande Guerre chimique 1914–1918* (Paris: PUF, 1998), 251.

83 Zabecki, *German 1918 Offensives*, 216–18.

84 Details in *AFGG* 6/2, 137–8.

85 2e Bureau, Presumed Situation, 28 May 1918, ibid., annex 511; GQG, Directive générale, 28 May 1918, ibid., annex 540.

86 Yves Gras, *Castelnau ou l'art de commander* (Paris: Denoël, 1990), 376.

87 *AFGG* 6/2, annexes 898, 989, 966. Pedroncini, *Pétain général en chef*, 376.

88 Zabecki, *German 1918 Offensives*, 226.

89 GQG, Appréciation des chefs de corps sur le moral des troupes d'après les comptes-rendus concernant 946 unités pour la période du 15 Mai au 15 Juin 1918, 30 June 1918, 16N 1486.

90 Laure and Jacottet, *Etapes*, 185. Ludendorff's report is reproduced in Olivier Lahaie, Renseignement et services de renseignement en France pendant la guerre de 1914–1918 (PhD thesis: Université de Paris IV, Sorbonne, 2005), annex 138.

91 Cointet diary, 'Cahier 1918', fo. 72.

92 *AFGG* 6/2, 260. In addition the British suffered 28,679 and the Americans 474 between 26 May and 5 June.

93 'Rupture du front français le 27 mai 1918 au Chemin des Dames', 17 July 1918, extracts reproduced in Abel Ferry, *La Guerre vue d'en bas et d'en haut* (Paris: Grasset, 1920), 297–322.

94 Abel Ferry, *Carnets secrets 1914–1918* (Paris: Grasset, 2005), 300, 303–4.

95 Pétain to Clemenceau, 13 June 1918, *AFGG* 6/2, annex 1517.

96 Jim Beach, *Haig's Intelligence: GHQ and the German Army, 1916–1918* (Cambridge University Press, 2013), 296–8.

97 Lt-General Sir John DuCane, *Marshal Foch* (privately printed, 1920), 37.

98 Pétain to Clemenceau, 13 June 1918, *AFGG* 6/2, annex 1517.

99 The documentation and the report are in 5N 256 and 257.

100 Tournès, *Histoire*, 141.

101 Beach, *Haig's Intelligence*, 298.

102 15N 5. Cointet states (fo. 89) that the 2e Bureau estimated that Rupprecht had forty-six reserve divisions on 8 June, of which twenty-six, more than half, were fresh.

103 Barescut diary, 7 June 1918.

104 'Souvenirs du Général Cartier', *Revue des Transmissions* 87 (November–December 1959), 19–20. Painvin's own account of his breaking the new German code is in *Revue des travaux de l'Académie de Sciences Morales et Politiques* (2nd semester, 1968), 45–63.

105 Fayolle, *CS*, 283 (entry for 11 June 1918); Capitaine Dutil, *Les Chars d'assaut: Leur création et leur rôle pendant la guerre 1915–1918* (Paris: Berger-Levrault, 1919), 153.

106 Pierre Paul, 'La Contre-Offensive Mangin de Méry-Courcelles (11 Juin 1918)', *RHA* 1968/4, 42–50, here p. 50.

107 Tournès, *Histoire*, 146.

108 Jean Nicot, *Les Poilus ont la parole: Lettres du front: 1917–1918* (Paris: Editions Complexe, 1998), 419.

109 Ibid., 420, 426.

110 Charles Christienne and Simone Pesquiès-Courbier, 'L'effort de guerre français dans le domaine de l'aéronautique en 1914–1918', in Gérard Canini (ed.), *Les Fronts invisibles: Nourrir, fournir, soigner* (Nancy: PUN, 1984), 239–40.

111 Guinard et al., *Introduction*, 168.

112 Lepick, *Grande guerre chimique*, 227.

113 Général Herr, *L'Artillerie: Ce qu'elle a été, ce qu'elle est, et ce qu'elle doit être* (Paris: Berger-Levrault, 1923), 125–6.

114 Ian V. Hogg, *Allied Artillery of World War One* (Marlborough: The Crowood Press, 1998), 94–9. Lieutenant Colonel Filloux was responsible for several important modifications to French guns during the course of the war.

115 André Kaspi, *Le Temps des Américains: Le concours américain à la France en 1917–1918* (Paris: Publications de la Sorbonne, 1976), 244.

116 Herr, *L'Artillerie*, 124–9.

117 For more on this decision and the Foch–Pétain relationship, see Green-halgh, *Foch in Command*, 373–4. Barescut makes no mention of it, but records Foch tearing a strip off Pétain earlier: diary, 19 June 1918.

118 Zabecki, *German 1918 Offensives*, 258–9.

119 Michael S. Neiberg, *The Second Battle of the Marne* (Bloomington, IN: Indiana University Press, 2008), 94; F.A. Paoli, 'Le Coup de Main du 366e R.I. 14 juillet 1918', *RHA* 1968/4, 51–60.

120 Fourth Army Report on Battle of 15 July, Gouraud papers, PA-AP 339, vol. 34, Archives diplomatiques, Paris.

121 Rudolf Binding, *A Fatalist at War* (London: George Allen & Unwin, 1929), 234.

122 V Corps report, 16 July 1918, *AFGG* 6/2, annex 2265.

123 E. Petit, 'L'Aviation française en 1918', *RHA* 1968/4, 159–69, here p. 164.

124 General Diébold to General Pellé, 19 July 1918, Pellé papers, ms 4432, Bibliothèque de l'Institut, Paris.

125 Pedroncini, *Pétain général en chef*, 404.

126 Pertes des armées françaises, *AFGG* 6/2, 552.

127 Rapport du maréchal commandant en chef les Armées françaises du Nord et du Nord-Est sur les Opérations en 1918: La Campagne défensive, part 6: 'La Bataille de Champagne', 77.

CHAPTER 8

1 For a recent study of the battle, see Michael S. Neiberg, *The Second Battle of the Marne* (Bloomington, IN: Indiana University Press, 2008). For the use of the tanks, see Tim Gale, *The French Army's Tank Force and Armoured Warfare in the Great War* (Farnham: Ashgate, 2013), ch. 8.

2 Pétain to Foch, 12 July 1918, *AFGG* 7/1, annex 17.

3 Instruction for Reserve and Centre Army Group commanders, 12 July 1918, ibid., annex 18; Directive #5, 12 July 1918, ibid., annex 19.

4 Ibid., 55.

5 Guinard et al., *Introduction*, 163–8.

6 'Die Grippeerkrankungen bei der Truppe', Reichswehrministerium, *Sanitäts-bericht über das deutsche Heer*, 3 vols (Berlin: Mittler und Sohn, 1934), 3: 122. In all, 374,524 cases.

7 David T. Zabecki, *The German 1918 Offensives: A case study in the operational level of war* (London/New York: Routledge, 2006), 265–7.

8 Intelligence reports, GQGA 2e Bureau, 15N 5.

9 War Diary, Army Group German Crown Prince, 18 July 1916, in *The German Offensive of July 15, 1918 (Marne source book)* (Fort Leavenworth, KS: The General Service Schools Press, 1923), 621, doc. 444.

10 Commandant Laure, *Au 3ème Bureau du Troisième G.Q.G.* (Paris: Plon, 1921), 180; Fayolle, *CS*, 289–90 (entry for 18 July 1918). Laure was present with Mangin during the conversation with Pétain.

11 Instruction, 19 July 1918, *AFGG* 7/1, annex 157; Buat diary, 19 July 1918, ms 5391, Bibliothèque de l'Institut, Paris.

12 Godley to Wigram, for the King, 27 July 1918, Godley papers, I, fos. 84–5, LHCMA.

13 Operational Order #92, for 20 July 1918, *AFGG* 7/1, annex 176.

14 Zabecki, *German 1918 Offensives*, 305.

15 Jim Beach, *Haig's Intelligence: GHQ and the German Army, 1916–1918* (Cambridge University Press, 2013), 301.

16 Haig diary, 23 July 1918.

17 Herbert Sulzbach, *With the German Guns: Four years on the Western Front, 1914–1918* (London: Cooper, 1973), 206.

18 *AFGG* 7/1, annex 281.

19 Ibid., annex 178.

20 See Elizabeth Greenhalgh, *Victory Through Coalition: Britain and France during the First World War* (Cambridge University Press, 2005), 230–2; ead., *Foch in Command: The forging of a First World War general* (Cambridge University Press, 2011), 446–92.

21 Cited in Jean Nicot, *Les Poilus ont la parole: Lettres du front: 1917–1918* (Paris: Editions Complexe, 1998), 465.

22 Mémoire, 24 July 1918, *AFGG* 7/1, annex 276 (English translations in both British and US official histories).

23 David Stevenson, *With our Backs to the Wall: Victory and defeat in 1918* (London: Allen Lane, 2011), 116; Zabecki, *German 1918 Offensives*, 271.

24 See the daily intelligence reports in 15N 5.

25 *AFGG* 7/1, appendice 1, p. 365.

26 Ibid., appendice 6, p. 383.

27 Pétain to Foch, 31 July 1918, and Foch to Clemenceau 20 July 1918, ibid., annexes 403, 178.

28 Fayolle, *CS*, 294 (entry for 5 August 1918).

29 *AFGG* 7/1, 109.

30 Rawlinson diary, 6 June, 11, 19, 23 July 1918, Churchill Archives Centre, Cambridge.

31 Ibid., 26 July 1918.

32 Foch to Haig, 28 July 1918, *AFGG* 7/1, annex 354.

33 Buat diary, 25 July 1918. Buat had now replaced Anthoine as chief of staff.

34 Ibid., 28 July 1918.

35 Yves Tremblay, 'Raymond Brutinel et la guerre de mouvement', in Roche Legault and Jean Lamarre (eds), *La Première Guerre Mondiale et le Canada: Contributions Socio-militaires Québecoises* (Montréal: Editions du Meridien, 1999), 195–224.

36 *AFGG* 7/1, 155–8.

37 Fayolle, *CS*, 295 (entry for 9 August 1918); GQGA war diary, 11 August 1918, 26N 1.

38 Haig diary, 8 August 1918, typescript and manuscript versions differ; First Army war diary, 8–9 August 1918, 26N 20.

39 See Humbert, 'Lettres d'un chef à ses fils', *Revue des Deux Mondes*, 1 September 1922, 133.

40 Barescut diary, 10 August 1918.

41 *AFGG* 7/1, 196–8; Mangin's 'note', 10 August 1918, ibid., annex 609; Fayolle, *CS*, 295 (entry for 10 August 1918).

42 Haig diary, 15 August 1918.

43 GQGA JMO, 15 August 1918.

44 *AFGG* 7/1, 204.

45 Ibid., 256–7.

46 Report #43 PC, 13 August 1918, 17N 348.

47 First Army, Weekly report, 17–23 August 1918, 16N 1390. The postal control commission had read 36,047 letters on which they based their judgement.

48 André Kahn, *Journal de guerre d'un juif patriote 1914/1918* (Paris: Editions Jean-Claude Simoën, 1978), 319.

49 QGQA JMO, 4 August 1918; Buat diary, 4 August 1918.

50 For the row over this change of plan, see Elizabeth Greenhalgh, *Foch in Command*, 430–7; David F. Trask, *The AEF and Coalition Warmaking, 1917–1919* (Lawrence, KS: University Press of Kansas, 1993), 100–6.

51 Hirschauer Carnets de Guerre, 12 September 1918, Z30947 SHD/DAA.

52 *AFGG* 7/1, appendices 5 ter, 5 quater, 9. The casualty figures are for a slightly longer period, 1–25 September 1918.

53 Hirschauer Carnets de Guerre, 15 September 1918; Pershing diary, 20 September 1918, Library of Congress.

54 Robert B. Bruce, *A Fraternity of Arms: America and France in the Great War* (Lawrence, KS: University Press of Kansas, 2003), 262.

55 Note sur le moral des troupes d'après le contrôle postal, pendant la période du 14 au 24 septembre 1918, 16N 1485/4.

56 E. Petit, 'L'Aviation française en 1918', *RHA* 1968/4, 165.

57 Williamson Murray, *War in the Air 1914–1945* (London: Cassell, repr. 2000), 71; Hoeppner, *Germany's War in the Air*, 167.

58 Directive, 3 September 1918, *AFGG* 7/1, annex 938; Pétain to Foch, 8 September 1918, ibid., annex 1036.

59 Intelligence report #1548, 13 September 1918, 15N 5, gave 196 German and 2 Austrian divisions, but still 68 in reserve. See also *AFGG* 7/2, annex 11.

60 *AFGG* 7/1, 333.

61 Note pour le général commandant le G.A.C., 8 September 1918, ibid., annex 1039; 'Situation de l'Artillerie à la date du 26 septembre 1918', Gouraud mss, PA-AP 399, vol. 41, dossier 1, Archives diplomatiques, Paris.

62 Buat diary, 19 August 1918.

63 *AFGG* 7/1, 348–50.

64 *AFGG* 7/2, 122–6.

65 Fayolle, *CS*, 304 (entries for 1 and 5 October 1918).

66 Foch to Pétain, 4 October 1918, *AFGG* 7/2, annex 137; Buat diary, 17 October 1918.

67 Graziani, Résumé sommaire des événements des 15 et 16 juin 1918, 15N 45.

68 Martha Hanna, *Your Death would be Mine: Paul and Marie Pireaud in the Great War* (Cambridge, MA: Harvard University Press, 2006), 254.

69 *AFGG* 7/2, ch. 20.

70 Hanna, *Your Death would be Mine*, 263.

71 Herbillon, *Souvenirs*, 2: 330; Général Mordacq, *Le Ministère Clemenceau: Journal d'un témoin*, 4 vols (Paris: Plon, 1930), 2: 286.

72 All comments from reports in September 1918, cited in Nicot, *Les Poilus ont la parole*, 492–3.

73 Calculated from the table in Michel Goya, *La Chair et l'acier: L'invention de la guerre moderne (1914–1918)* (Paris: Tallandier, 2004), 430.

CHAPTER 9

1 Cyril Falls, *History of the Great War: Macedonia*, 2 vols (London: HMSO, 1933–35), 2: 67.

2 Conversation between Reichskanzler and Ludendorff, 9 October 1918, in Erich Matthias and Rudolf Morsey (eds), *Die Regierung des Prinzen Max von Baden* (Düsseldorf: Droste Verlag, 1962), 117.

3 Glenn E. Torrey, *Henri Mathias Berthelot: Soldier of France, Defender of Romania* (Iaşi/Oxford/Portland: Centre for Romanian Studies, 2001), 268.

4 *AFGG* 10, 591.

5 *AFGG* 8/3, 470–9.

6 Unpublished letter of 30 September 1918, reproduced in André Ducasse et al., *Vie et mort des Français 1914–1918* (Paris: Hachette, 1962), 454.

7 *AFGG* 9/1, 48, note 4.

8 Général Mordacq, *Le Ministère Clemenceau: Journal d'un témoin*, 4 vols (Paris: Plon, 1930–31), 1: 105.

9 Pisani's report cited in Yves Jouin, 'Hedjaz 1916–1918: Les compagnons de Lawrence', *RHA* 1965/2, 107–21, here p. 117.

10 *AFGG* 9/1, 91. See also Vincent Cloarec, *La France et la question de Syrie (1914–1918)* (Paris: CNRS Editions, 2010, pb edn), 356–8.

11 *AFGG* 9/1, 226–7.

12 Ibid., 208.

13 Cloarec, *Syrie*, 379.

14 *AFGG* 9/1, 152–64.

15 IC 84, 30 October 1918, CAB 28/5, TNA.

16 Elizabeth Greenhalgh, *Foch in Command: The forging of a First World War general* (Cambridge University Press, 2011), 452.

17 On this episode see ibid., 454–7; and Elizabeth Greenhalgh, *Victory through Coalition: Britain and France during the First World War* (Cambridge University Press, 2005), 254–61.

18 *AFGG* 7/2, 233.

19 First Army war diary, 30 September, 10 October 1918, 26N 20.

20 *AFGG* 7/2, 95.

21 First Army war diary, 18 October 1918, 26N 20.

22 *AFGG* 7/2, 186.

23 Ibid., annex 406.

24 Ibid., annex 444.

25 Ibid., annex 202.

26 Fayolle, *CS*, 307–8 (entries for 28, 30, 31 October 1918).

27 Fayolle's instruction *AFGG* 7/2, 116, and annex 199.

28 Ibid., 204.

29 Général Mangin, *Comment finit la guerre* (Paris: Plon, 1920), 210.

30 Fayolle, *CS*, 306 (entries for 21, 22 October 1918).

31 *AFGG* 7/2, 214.

32 Fourth Army medical officer's report, cited in Julie d'Andurain, Le Général Gouraud, un colonial dans la Grande Guerre (PhD thesis: Université de Paris IV, Sorbonne, 2009), 522.

33 Note #4935, 21 October 1918, *AFGG* 7/2, annex 329.

34 Greenhalgh, *Foch in Command*, 474.

35 *AFGG* 7/2, 239–40.

36 The various studies are in 16N 1715.

37 GQG Note, 26 August 1918, ibid. On the Lorraine proposal, see Jean-Baptiste Duroselle, *La Grande Guerre des Français 1914–1918: L'incompréhensible* (Paris: Perrin, 1994), 408–10; Frédéric Guelton, 'L'Offensive de Lorraine, une approche historiographique critique', in Rémy Porte and François Cochet (eds), *Ferdinand Foch (1851–1929): Apprenez à penser* (Saint-Cloud: SOTECA Editions 14–18, 2010), 177–87; and Guy Pedroncini, *Pétain général en chef 1917–1918* (Paris: PUF, 1974), 422–9.

38 Pétain's comment to Jacques Isorni, his lawyer and biographer, made in prison after the Second World War is cited in Guelton, 'L'Offensive de Lorraine', 185.

39 For Foch's views, see Général Weygand, *Mémoires: Idéal Vécu* (Paris: Flammarion, 1953), 626–6, 630–1; for Pétain's views see the Rapport du maréchal commandant en chef les Armées françaises du Nord et du Nord-Est sur les Opérations en 1918: La Campagne défensive, part 6: 'La Bataille de Champagne', which reproduces the Foch–Pétain correspondence.

40 Cited in Gras, *Castelnau*, 382.

41 Pétain, Rapport, part 6: 'La Bataille de Champagne', 30.

42 Fayolle, *CS*, 323 (entry for 7 January 1919).

43 Anthoine deposited the text with the Bibliothèque de l'Institut in Paris, in a sealed envelope marked 'may be opened on 1 January 1972'. It was published in *GMCC* 156 (1989), 105–7.

44 Weygand, *Idéal vécu*, 631, note.

45 For more details on the transport crisis, see Greenhalgh, *Foch in Command*, 492.

46 *AFGG* 11, 791.

47 Clark report, 17 October 1918, box 2, E18, RG200, NARA.

48 Daniel Halévy, *L'Europe brisée: Journal de guerre 1914–1918* (Paris: Editions de Fallois, 1998), 277–9.

49 Etudes et documentation diverses, 15NN 8/1.

50 Foch's remark made to the conservateur of the Bibliothèque de l'Arsenal, cited in Ducasse et al., *Vie et mort*, 459.

51 Unless stated otherwise, all the information for this section is taken from Laure and Jacottet, *Etapes*, ch. 8.

52 Telegram from French liaison officer to war ministry and GQGA, 13 November 1918, *AFGG* 7/2, annex 574.

53 The details of the Vrigne–Meuse operation are described in Alain Fauveau, 'Le dernier combat: Vrigne-Meuse, 10 et 11 novembre 1918', *RHA* 251 (2008), 18–34. The author wonders whether the operation to cross the Meuse, which cost so many lives at such a late stage in the war, was justified.

54 Cited in Bruno Cabanes, *La Victoire endeuillée: La sortie de guerre des soldats français 1918–1920* (Paris: Editions du Seuil, 2004), 45. The priest's name was Georges Guitton.

55 General Debeney, Première armée du 4 août au 11 novembre 1918: Résumé des faits journaliers, n.d., AWM 26/476/1, Australian War Memorial, Canberra.

56 Statistics vary, and may not count exactly the same categories. See Greenhalgh, 'A French Victory, 1918' in Ashley Ekins (ed.), *1918 Year of Victory: The end of the Great War and the shaping of history* (Auckland: Exisle Publishing, 2010), 89–98.

57 Colonel Larcher, 'Données statistiques sur les forces françaises de 1914–1918', *RMF* (May 1934), 198–223, and (June 1934), 351–63. See also Frédéric Guelton, *L'armée française en 1918* (Saint-Cloud: 14–18 editions, n.d.), 76–80.

58 *Historique du 227e Régiment d'Infanterie 1914–1918* (Dijon: Imprimerie R. de Thorey, 1920).

59 Note on troop morale, 29 November 1918, 16N 1485.

60 Halévy, *Europe brisée*, 381.

61 Louis Barthas, *Les Carnets de guerre de Louis Barthas, tonnelier (1914–1919)* (Paris: Francis Maspero, 1978), 550.

62 Georges Bonnefous, *Histoire politique de la Troisième République*, vol. 2, *La Grande Guerre, 1914–1918* (Paris: PUF, 1957), 429–31.

63 Jules Maurin and Jean-Charles Jauffret, 'Les Combattants face à l'épreuve de 1914 à 1918', in Guy Pedroncini (ed.), *Histoire militaire de la France*, vol. 3: *De 1871 à 1940* (Paris: PUF, 1992), 292–3. See also Antoine Prost, 'Die Demobilmachung, der Staat und die Kriegsteilnehmer in Frankreich', *Geschichte und Gesellschaft* 9: 2 (1983), 178–94.

64 Cabanes, *Victoire endeuillée*, 312–15.

65 Poincaré, *Au Service*, 11: 109.

66 Antoine Prost, *Les Anciens Combattants et la société française 1914–1939*, 3 vols (Paris: Presses de la fondation nationale des sciences politiques, 1977), 1: 49.

67 Cabanes, *Victoire endeuillée*, 327–31.

68 Jean Lacouture, *De Gaulle: The rebel, 1890–1944* (London: HarperCollins, 1993), 54. Charles de Gaulle, *Lettres, notes et carnets 1905–1918* (Paris: Plon, 1980), has photographs of the ticket and thankyou postcard between pp. 288 and 289.

69 Georges Cahen-Salvador, *Les Prisonniers de guerre (1914–1919)* (Paris: Payot, 1929), 281–2. Cahen-Salvador directed the POW service in the war ministry.

70 Pierre Hervet, 'Les nécropoles français de la captivité', *GMCC* 147 (1987), 105–10.

71 Judith M. Hughes, *To the Maginot Line: The politics of French military preparation in the 1920's* (Cambridge, MA: Harvard University Press, 1971), 22–3.

72 Letter written from Mainz by a soldier in Eighth Army, cited in Cabanes, *Victoire endeuillée*, 219.

73 Raymond Poincaré, *Au Service de la France: Neuf années de souvenirs*, 11 vols (Paris: Plon, 1928–74), 11: 359.

74 Prévisions sur la résistance que pourrait opposer l'Allemagne à une invasion des Alliés', 5 May 1919, 14N 50/1.

75 Conversation between President Wilson, M.M. Clemenceau and Lloyd George, and Baron Sonnino, 16 June 1919, in Paul Mantoux, *The Deliberations of the Council of Four (March 24–June 28, 1919)*, 2 vols (Princeton University Press, 1992), 2: 461–72.

CHAPTER 10

1 Michel Goya, '1918: L'armée motorisée française gagne la guerre', in Christian Malis (ed.), *Guerre et manoeuvre: Héritages et renouveau* (Paris: Economica/Fondation Saint-Cyr, 2009), 141–59, here p. 149.

2 Général Herr, *L'Artillerie: Ce qu'elle a été, ce qu'elle est, et ce qu'elle doit être* (Paris: Berger-Levrault, 1923), 86, note 2.

3 Guinard et al., *Introduction*, 208. See Antoine Prost, 'Compter les vivants et les morts: l'évaluation des pertes françaises de 1914–1918', *Le Mouvement Social* 222 (2008), 41–60.

4 See the summary in Frédéric Guelton, *L'Armée française en 1918* (Saint-Cloud: 14–18 editions, n.d.), 19–29.

5 Rémy Porte, *La Mobilisation industrielle: 'Premier front' de la Grande Guerre?* (Saint-Cloud: 14–18 editions, 2005), 287.

6 Guinard et al., *Introduction*, 125.

7 Clemenceau to Pétain, 21 October 1918, 6N 88; Raymond Poincaré, *Au Service de la France: Neuf années de souvenirs*, 11 vols (Paris: Plon, 1928–74), 10: 372 (entry for 3 October 1918).

8 Ibid., 139–42.

9 Goya, 'Armée motorisée', 150.

10 Guinard et al, *Introduction*, 169.

11 Ibid., 171–2.

12 For an overview see David Stevenson, *With our Backs to the Wall: Victory and defeat in 1918* (London: Allen Lane, 2012), 173–84.

13 Michel Goya, *La Chair et l'acier: L'invention de la guerre moderne (1914–1918)* (Paris: Tallandier, 2004), 290.

14 Janet Morgan, *The Secrets of the Rue St Roch: Hope and heroism behind enemy lines in the First World War* (London: Penguin, 2004), 341.

15 Henri Navarre et al., *Le Service de renseignements 1871–1944* (Paris: Plon, 1978), 22.

16 Guinard et al., *Introduction*, 196–7.

17 See Jean-Jacques Becker's introduction to Annette Wieviorka (ed.), *Justin Godart: Un homme dans son siècle (1871–1956)* (Paris: CNRS Editions, 2004).

18 Antoine Prost, 'Le désastre sanitaire du Chemin des Dames', in Nicolas Offenstadt (ed.), *Le Chemin des Dames: De l'événement à la mémoire* (Paris: Stock, 2004), 137–51; Historique du Service de Santé, 16N 2309.

19 Prost, 'Désastre sanitaire', 145.

20 Ibid., 150.

21 Denis Rolland, *Nivelle: L'inconnu du Chemin des Dames* (Paris: Imago, 2012), 238.

22 Prost, 'Désastre sanitaire', 148–9.

23 Médecin principal de 1ère classe Uzac, 'Le Service de santé dans les armées engagées du 15 au 31 juillet 1918', *RMF* (November 1922), 344–71.

24 Ibid., 365.

25 Dr Léon Barnard, *La Défense de la santé publique pendant la guerre* (Paris/New Haven: PUF/Yale University Press, 1929), ch. 12.

26 Porte, *Mobilisation industrielle*, 303.

27 Olivier Lepick, *La Grande Guerre chimique 1914–1918* (Paris: PUF, 1998), 256–75.

28 Anthony Clayton, *Paths of Glory: The French Army 1914–18* (London: Cassell, 2003), 207.

29 Guelton, *L'armée française*, 90, 89, 91.

30 Guinard et al., *Introduction*, 153; Porte, *Mobilisation industrielle*, 287.

31 Goya, *La Chair et l'acier*, 431. Figures are based on Laure and Jacottet's study, but Goya does not explain how he has evaluated the figures for firepower.

32 Guinard et al., *Introduction*, 164.

33 Gilbert Hatry, *Renault: Usine de guerre 1914–1918* (Paris: Lafourcade, 1978), 84–5.

34 Ibid., 69.

35 Charles Christienne and Simone Pesquiès-Courbier, 'L'effort de guerre français dans le domaine de l'aéronautique en 1914–1918', in Gérard Canini (ed.), *Les Fronts invisibles: Nourrir, fournir, soigner* (Nancy: PUN, 1984), 238–40.

36 Buat diary, 5 and 30 December 1916, ms 5390/3, Bibliothèque de l'Institut; Paul Guillaumat (ed.), *Correspondance de guerre du Général Guillaumat 1914–1919* (Paris: L'Harmattan, 2006), 158.

37 Goya, *La Chair et l'acier*, 292.

38 Ibid., 290; Guelton, *L'Armée française*, 43–5, lists the numbers and types of gun in March and November 1917.

39 Goya, 'Armée motorisée', 148.

40 Erik Le Maresquier, 'L'Approvisionnement des chevaux pendant la guerre de 1914–1918', in *Congrès national des sociétés savantes* (Nancy-Metz, 1978), 295–304.

41 Guinard, *Introduction*, 181–2.

42 See Stevenson, *With our Backs to the Wall*, 225–32. On the Allied organisations see Elizabeth Greenhalgh, *Victory through Coalition: Britain and France during the First World War* (Cambridge University Press, 2005), 239–46. On the 'service automobile' see André Doumenc, 'Les transports automobiles pendant la guerre de 1914–1918', in Canini (ed.), *Les Fronts invisibles*, 371–80.

43 The ideas in this paragraph are borrowed from Guelton, *L'Armée française en 1918*, 56–7.

44 Less than 1 per cent of communes lacks a monument, and in those cases there is usually a plaque bearing names in the church: Antoine Prost, 'Les monuments aux morts', in Pierre Nora (ed.), *Les Lieux de mémoire*, vol. 1 (Paris: Gallimard, 1984), 223, note 4.

45 Général R. Alexandre, *Avec Joffre d'Agadir à Verdun* (Paris: Berger-Levrault, 1932), 120, n. 4.

46 Marc Bloch, *Ecrits de guerre 1914–1918* (Paris: Armand Colin, 1997), 146.

47 Rachel Chrastil, *Organizing for War: France 1870–1914* (Baton Rouge, LA: Louisiana State University Press, 2010), ch. 4.

48 See Judith M. Hughes, *To the Maginot Line: The politics of French military preparation in the 1920's* (Cambridge, MA: Harvard University Press, 1971), 27–30.

49 Philippe Boulanger, 'Le Refus de l'impôt du sang: Géographie de l'insoumission en France de 1914 à 1922', *GMCC* 188 (1997), 3–26.

50 Philippe Boulanger, *La France devant la conscription: Géographie historique d'une institution républicaine 1914–1922* (Paris: Economica/Institut de stratégie comparée, 2001), 329–33.

51 All the information on pensions is taken from Antoine Prost, *Les Anciens combattants et la société française 1914–1939*, 3 vols (Paris: Presses de la Fondation Nationale des Sciences Politiques, 1977), 1: 55; 2: 18–19, 23–24.

52 Ibid., 55, 19.

53 The register contained 1,325,290 names in November 2003: Prost, 'Compter les vivants et les morts', 52.

54 Olivier Faron, 'Une catastrophe démographique', *L'Histoire* 225 (October 1998), 46–8.

55 Sophie Delaporte, '15 000 "gueules cassées"', ibid., 40.

56 Clémentine Vidal-Nacquet, 'Le couple pendant la Grande Guerre: un sujet d'histoire?', note 31, online at http://centenaire.org/fr/societe/le-couple-pendant-la-grande-guerre-un-sujet-dhistoire, accessed 21 January 2014.

57 Fabienne Bock, *Un Parlementarisme de guerre 1914–1919* (Paris: Belin, 2002), 59.

58 Ibid., 117.

59 Fabienne Bock and Thierry Bonzon, '"Il faut que vous sachiez ce qui se passe chez nous": 246 lettres de militaires français au Parlement en 1917', in André Loez and Nicolas Mariot (eds), *Obéir/désobéir: Les mutineries de 1917 en perspective* (Paris: Editions La Découverte, 2008), 167–80.

60 Général Mordacq, *Le Ministère Clemenceau: Journal d'un témoin*, 4 vols (Paris: Plon, 1930–31), 2: 105–7.

61 CSDN meeting, 27 October 1920, 2N 4.

62 Louis Mairet, *Carnet d'un combattant* (Paris: G. Crès, 1919), 174.

63 Louis Barthas, *Les Carnets de guerre de Louis Barthas, tonnelier (1914–1919)* (Paris: François Maspero, 1978), 376 (October 1916).

64 Général Valluy, *La Première Guerre Mondiale*, 2 vols (Paris: Larousse, 1968), 2: 321.

65 Haig diary, 12 October 1915.

66 Wilson diary, 24 October 1918, DS/Misc/80, Imperial War Museum, London.

67 Brigadier-General Sir J.E. Edmonds, *Military Operations France and Belgium 1918*, 5 vols (London/Nashville TN: Imperial War Museum/Battery Press, 1993 [1947]), 5: 584.

68 See Jennifer D. Keene, *Doughboys, the Great War, and the Remaking of America* (Baltimore/London: The Johns Hopkins University Press, 2001), 124–5.

69 Général Weygand, *Mémoires: Mirages et réalité* (Paris: Flammarion, 1957), 11.

70 Fayolle, *CS*, 320, 322, 331 (entries for 14, 26 December 1918, 16 June 1919).

71 Anthony Adamthwaite, *Grandeur and Misery: France's bid for power in Europe 1914–1940* (London: Arnold, 1995), 62–3.

72 Lecture in Wülzburg camp, exact date unknown, in Charles de Gaulle, *Lettres, notes et carnets*, 2 vols (Paris: Plon, 1980), 1: 536.

73 The correspondence is in Fonds Joffre, pièces 419–24, 14N 3.

74 Général Weygand, *Mirages et Réalité*, 63.

75 Mordacq, *Ministère Clemenceau*, 4: 25, 28, 29.

76 Elizabeth Kahn Baldewicz, Les Camoufleurs: The mobilization of art and the artist in wartime France, 1914–1918 (PhD thesis, University of California, Los Angeles, 1980), 318.

77 Fayolle, *CS*, 353 (entry for 14 July 1919).

78 Louise Weiss, *Mémoires d'une européene*, 3 vols, vol. 1: *Une Petite Fille du Siècle 1893–1919* (Paris: Albin Michel, 1978), 303.

79 Leonard V. Smith, Stéphane Audoin-Rouzeau, Annette Becker, *France and the Great War 1914–1918* (Cambridge University Press, 2003), 172–5; André Ducasse, Jacques Meyer and Gabriel Perreux, *Vie et mort des Français 1914–1918* (Paris: Hachette, 1962), 480–1.

Bibliographic essay

The purpose of this essay is to evaluate very briefly some of the most important secondary works cited in the notes, and to give some guidelines for further reading about France's Army, in light of the continuing avalanche of publications in French and in English marking the First World War's centenary. Preference is given to recent scholarship, but, where relevant, older works are cited, as well as significant websites. Not all works mentioned here appear in the notes. A collaborative bibliography, both excellent and comprehensive, is to be found on the website of the International Society for First World War Studies (www.firstworldwarstudies.org). For recent French theses, search www.theses.fr.

General works

The 103 volumes of *Les Armées Françaises dans la Grande Guerre* (*AFGG*), the French official history, constitute the vital first port of call. The text volumes are dry and dense, but the gold lies in the thousands of documents appended to each one. As the volumes are now out of copyright, the Bibliothèque nationale de France (BNF) has digitised them all, except for the map volumes, and they are downloadable as pdfs from the library's vastly stocked Gallica website (gallica.bnf.fr). The files are word-searchable, giving them an edge over the printed volumes. The BNF has also digitised the unit histories supplied by the Bibliothèque de la Guerre (part of the Service historique de la Défense in Vincennes). Newspapers of the First World War period and the professional literature, such as the *Revue militaire française*, *Revue de l'Infanterie*, *Revue militaire générale* and the *Revue des Deux Mondes* are also downloadable from Gallica.

Unit war diaries are available online on the Service historique's 'mémoire des hommes' website (www.memoiredeshommes.sga.defense.gouv.fr), but require downloading a page at a time. These are of variable quality, mostly handwritten. Unfortunately they are usually of use only for establishing the unit's whereabouts, basic operations and casualty lists. For documents such as after-action reports, it is necessary to consult the operational records in Vincennes: series 16N for army headquarters, 18N for army groups, 19N for armies, 22N for corps, 24N for divisions and 25N for regiments. The published inventories of all the N series for the First World War are accessible online (www.servicehistorique.sga.defense.gouv.fr/contenu/pages/fonds-archives.html).

Among published works on the French Army, William Serman and Jean-Paul Bertaud provide an invaluable update to Guy Pedroncini's edited papers in the

Histoire militaire de la France. In English, Robert A. Doughty is indispensable for greater detail on strategy and operations than could be provided in the present work. Anthony Clayton complements Doughty by giving more 'practical' information in useful appendices. More such information is found in Sumner and Embleton's brief guide to the French Army in Osprey's 'Men-at-Arms' series. The War Office's 1914 handbook on the French Army has been reprinted. The Franco-American volume in Cambridge's 'New Approaches to European History' series, *France and the Great War*, is more useful for the home front than for the army.

Although personal diary records must be used with care, two are invaluable because they cross the civil–military boundary: those of the parliamentary deputy and soldier Abel Ferry, and Colonel Emile Herbillon, the liaison officer between GQG and the French government. Ferry's notebooks, originally published in 1957, have now appeared in fuller form, together with some letters and a good introduction. Herbillon is useful because, unlike in Britain, no minutes were taken at cabinet meetings, and so he provides a window into governmental thinking. Poincaré must be read with a grain of salt, as there are significant differences between his original daily notes (where they are extant) and the eleven volumes of his published memoirs. The last volume on 1919, however, is a straight transcription, published posthumously. The memoirs of Joffre and Foch (both translated into English) should be taken as a rough operational guide only, despite their frequent use by many Anglophone historians. They were produced by their staffs and are very dry.

Two further general sources must be mentioned, as they are both informative and well illustrated. The publisher SOTECA 14–18 Editions produces a monthly magazine with articles written by qualified historians, such as those in the French Army's Service historique. Also it publishes important monographs and re-editions – for example, Rémy Porte's annotated edition of General Sarrail's memoir of his command in Salonika – and a collection 'hors-série' on specific topics. These include the Dardanelles, the Somme, and Frédéric Guelton's highly informative study of the French Army in 1918. The second general source is the Service historique's own in-house journal, *Revue historique des armées*, which publishes themed issues. These make interesting comparisons possible between, for example, the treatment of the anniversary of 1916 in 1966's and then 2006's issues.

Like the curate's egg, conference proceedings constitute an occasionally good source. The research presented at the annual conferences in the Historial at Péronne has rarely reached a wider audience, but the proceedings are starting to appear: see John Horne's edited volume on 1915, for example. The Crid (Collectif de recherche international et de débat sur la guerre de 1914–1918) has made its conference proceedings more accessible, and its website (www. crid1418.org) is a goldmine of reviews and articles, news and conference announcements. It publishes an online newsletter and has pages in English. (See also below for 1917's military operations.)

The contribution of France's colonies has received greater attention recently. In English, Richard Fogarty's comprehensive treatment includes a long essay on sources. In French, Jacques Frémeaux and Marc Michel have both written extensively on colonial troops. Frémeaux covers all France's colonies, not simply those in Africa, and has useful tables.

Finally, an overview of the directions which the French historiography is taking is provided by the 1998 conference proceedings edited by Jules Maurin and Jean-Charles Jauffret. It now needs updating. The BNF's database of theses, SUDOC, indicates over sixty doctoral theses on the First World War, awarded or in process, since the turn of the century, yet few of these are on strictly military topics. The BNF's catalogue shows over 170 titles published on the Great War in 2012 and 2013 alone, but again few of these deal with the French Army or other military questions. Recent trends follow the 'cultural turn' that is so evident in English-language works. The 1917 mutinies and the rehabilitation of those executed during the war have inspired much writing (see below); the attics of grandparents' homes are giving up their hidden diaries and letters, and huge volumes of these, often published locally, are appearing. The 'sociology' of the 14–18 generation, including the female half of the population and those too young or too old to fight but not to suffer occupation or deportation, attracts many young researchers. Local studies have also proved a popular topic.

Clayton, Anthony, *Paths of Glory: The French Army 1914–18* (London: Cassell, 2003)
   France, Soldiers and Africa (New York: Brassey's, 1988)
Doughty, Robert A., *Pyrrhic Victory: French strategy and operations in the Great War* (Cambridge, MA: The Belknap Press of Harvard University Press, 2005)
Ferry, Abel, *Carnets secrets 1914–1918 suivis de lettres et de notes de guerre* (Paris: Grasset, 2005, revised and expanded edn)
Fogarty, Richard S., *Race and War in France: Colonial subjects in the French Army, 1914–1918* (Baltimore, MD: Johns Hopkins University Press, 2008)
Frémeaux, Jacques, *Les Colonies dans la Grande Guerre: Combats et épreuves des peuples d'outre-mer* (Saint-Cloud: SOTECA 14–18 editions, 2006)
Guelton, Frédéric, *L'Armée française en 1918* (Saint-Cloud: SOTECA 14–18 editions, n.d. [2008])
Herbillon, Colonel Emile, *Du Général en chef au gouvernement. Souvenirs d'un officier de liaison pendant la guerre mondiale*, 2 vols (Paris: Tallandier, 1930)
Horne, John (ed.), *Vers la guerre totale: Le tournant de 1914–1915* (Paris: Tallandier, 2010)
Maurin, Jules, and Jean-Charles Jauffret (eds), *La Grande Guerre 1914–1918: 80 ans d'historiographie et de représentations* (Montpellier: UMR 5609 du CNRS–ESID, 2002)
Michel, Marc, *Les Africains et la Grande Guerre* (Paris: Karthala, 2003)
Ministère de la Guerre. Etat-Major de l'Armée, *Les Armées françaises dans la Grande Guerre*, 103 vols (Paris: Imprimerie nationale, 1922–38)
Pedroncini, Guy (ed.), *Histoire militaire de la France*, vol. 3 (Paris: PUF, 1992)
Poincaré, Raymond, *Au Service de la France: Neuf années de souvenirs*, 11 vols (Paris: Plon, 1928–74)
Serman, William, and Jean-Paul Bertaud, *Nouvelle histoire militaire de la France* (Paris: Fayard, 1998)

Smith, Leonard V., Stéphane Audoin-Rouzeau, Annette Becker, *France and the Great War, 1914–1918* (Cambridge University Press, 2003)
Sumner, Ian, and Gerry Embleton, *The French Army 1914–1918* (London: Osprey, 1995)
War Office. General Staff, *Handbook of the French Army* (London/Nashville TN: Imperial War Museum/Battery Press, repr. 1995)

The French Army as an institution

The classic text on the military in society is that by Raoul Girardet. It is supplemented by the relevant essays on the role of the military in the Third Republic, published in two edited collections: *Serviteurs de l'état* and *Militaires en République*. Leonard V. Smith's study of 5 DI, with its analysis of the renegotiation of the relationship of authority between citizen soldiers and the high command, has been extended in an interesting work by Emmanuel Saint-Fuscien on authority and obedience, using the discipline in 3 DI as its exemplar. A recent study of soldiers' reading habits by Benjamin Gilles complements Audoin-Rouzeau's earlier study of trench newspapers. The latter work has been translated into English. The large collection of trench newspapers held by the Bibliothèque de Documentation internationale et contemporaine in Nanterre has been digitised, in collaboration with the BNF's Gallica.

Other aspects of the institutional life of the army have been studied: chaplains (Boniface); shirkers (Ridel); soldiers on leave (Cronier); demobilisation (Cabanes); prisoners-of-war, both military and civilian (Annette Becker); and 'anciens combattants' or veterans (Prost). The last-mentioned has been translated in a very truncated version, and readers should consult, if possible, the original three-volume thesis. The rare survival of both sides of a marital correspondence provides an unusual insight to life at the front (Martha Hanna). A similar marital correspondence has survived between the writer and doctor, Georges Duhamel, and his wife Blanche.

Audoin-Rouzeau, Stéphane, *Men at War 1914–1918: National sentiment and trench journalism in France during the First World War* (Providence, RI: Berg, 1992)
Baruch, Marc-Olivier, Vincent Duclert (eds), *Serviteurs de l'Etat: Une histoire politique de l'administration française 1875–1945* (Paris: La Découverte, 2000)
Becker, Annette, *Les oubliés de la Grande Guerre: Humanitaire et culture de guerre, 1914–1918: populations occupées, déportés civils, prisonniers de guerre* (Paris: Noêsis, 1998)
Boniface, Xavier, *L'Aumônerie militaire française (1914–1962)* (Paris: Cerf, 2001)
Cabanes, Bruno, *La Victoire endeuillée: La sortie de guerre des soldats français 1918–1920* (Paris: Editions du Seuil, 2004)
Cronier, Emmanuelle, *Permissionaires dans la Grande Guerre* (Paris: Belin, 2013)
Duhamel, Georges et Blanche, *Correspondance de guerre 1914–1919*, 2 vols (Paris: Honoré Champion, 2007)

Forcade, Olivier, Eric Duhamel, Philippe Vial (eds), *Militaires en République 1870–1962: Les officiers, le pouvoir et la vie publique en France* (Paris: Publications de la Sorbonne, 1999)

Gilles, Benjamin, *Lectures de poilus 1914–1918: Livres et journaux dans les tranchées* (Paris: Editions Autrement, 2013)

Girardet, Raoul, *La Société militaire de 1815 à nos jours* (Paris: Perrin, 1998)

Hanna, Martha, *Your Death would be Mine: Paul and Marie Pireaud in the Great War* (Cambridge, MA: Harvard University Press, 2006)

Mariot, Nicolas, *Tous unis dans la tranchée: 1914–1918 les intellectuels rencontrent le peuple* (Paris: Seuil, 2013)

Prost, Antoine, *Les Anciens combattants et la société française: 1914–1939*, 3 vols (Paris: Presses de la Fondation nationale des sciences politiques, 1977)
In the Wake of War: 'Les Anciens Combattants' and French Society 1914–1939 (Providence, RI/Oxford: Berg, 1992)

Ridel, Charles, *Les Embusqués* (Paris: Armand Colin, 2007)

Saint-Fuscien, Emmanuel, *A Vos Ordres? La relation d'autorité dans l'armée française de la Grande Guerre* (Paris: EHESS, 2011)

Smith, Leonard V., *Between Mutiny and Obedience: The case of the French Fifth Infantry Division during World War I* (Princeton University Press, 1994)

Military operations

David Stevenson's chapter on French strategy in *Great War, Total War* is a good brief introduction to put beside Robert Doughty's *Pyrrhic Victory*. William Philpott's stable of doctoral students in King's College London is producing valuable work on the French Army at the operational level (House and Krause below).

The major battles of 1914, the Marne and First Ypres, have received recent treatment. Both Herwig and Beckett have treated all belligerents equitably, rather than recounting the battle from a single-nation perspective. Sewell Tyng's account of the Marne is well worth reading. Zuber's work on the battles of the frontiers reads like staff college papers; Simon House's recent doctoral thesis gives a more balanced picture of the fighting in the Ardennes, and Damien Baldin and Emmanuel Saint-Fuscien have written a readable account of the fighting at Charleroi. Prete's first volume of his trilogy deals solely with the Franco-British relationship, hence Joffre's overall role in 1914 still needs further study. Bourachot tends towards hagiography.

The fighting in 1915 remains a gaping hole in the historiography. There is memoir literature, but operational accounts are rare, although gaps are beginning to be filled – Jonathan Krause on Second Artois, for example. Despite Cassar's work, the French presence at the Dardanelles is little known, even in France. The Salonika expedition is better served, but only at the political and strategic levels (Dutton and Tanenbaum), although Fassy deals with command of an inter-allied force and the notes to Rémy Porte's edition of Sarrail's memoir provide a useful corrective.

The battles of 1916 are much better known. Horne's book on Verdun is still worth reading, despite its occasional errors, and should be supplemented by General Bernède's work, whose study of Verdun is very well illustrated with modern photographs and that publication rarity, fold-out maps. The Somme has been taken over as a British battle, despite the similar numbers of French troops present, who did rather better than the BEF and at lower cost in casualties. The Somme département has put a lot of effort into battlefield tourism, and its closeness to the Channel makes it accessible to British visitors. They should read Philpott's study of the Somme, which makes up for the previous neglect of the French contribution to that long battle.

For too long the events of 1917 have been dominated by the mutinies and their repression, and then by the role of Pétain in restoring the French Army to offensive health. Denis Rolland has written a long-overdue account of the Battle of the Aisne, making a very fair assessment of Nivelle's role. The collected essays in Nicolas Offenstadt's edited volume on the Chemin des Dames are all interesting. The mutinies and military justice in general (see below) have stirred polemics. The late Professor Pedroncini's classic account has been challenged by Leonard V. Smith's study of one French division and by André Loez, who has shown how Pedroncini occasionally distorted the evidence. Loez's published book is a cut-down version of his doctoral thesis. The Crid's website has a useful database of all the documented acts of indiscipline. The only extended study of the battles of the second half of 1917 is Pedroncini's analysis of General Pétain's command. Unfortunately, it was written before the archival holdings in Vincennes were catalogued, hence it is very difficult to find the documents that he cites.

The 1918 fighting is frequently treated from a national perspective, despite the fact that, on the Allied side, it saw the most international of all the First World War's battles. David Zabecki's excellent account of the German operational failures in the first half of the year is balanced by noting British and French reactions. David Stevenson devotes the first two chapters of his *With our Backs to the Wall* to the German offensives of March to July and the Allied responses between July and November, but deals with all belligerents; hence the space devoted to the French Army is small. The essays in Duppler and Groß provide an overview of the war's end but are written, once again, each with a national perspective. Michael S. Neiberg provides a notable exception with his analysis of the July battle that marked the turning-point for the Allies and Germany alike – from German successful offensives to Allied counter-attack and push to victory.

Baldin, Damien, and Emmanuel Saint-Fuscien, *Charleroi 21–23 août 1914* (Paris: Tallandier, 2012)

Beckett, Ian F.W., *Ypres: The First Battle, 1914* (Harlow: Pearson Education, 2004)

Bernède, Allain, *Verdun 1916: Le point de vue français* (Le Mans: Editions Cénomane, 2002)

Bourachot, André, *Joffre: De la préparation de la guerre à la disgrâce 1911–1916* (Paris: Bernard Giovanangeli, 2010)

Cassar, George, *The French and the Dardanelles: A study of failure in the conduct of war* (London: George Allen & Unwin Ltd, 1971)

Duppler, Jörg, and Gerhard P. Groß (eds), *Kriegsende 1918: Ereignis, Wirkung, Nachwirkung* (Munich: R. Oldenbourg, 1999)

Dutton, David, *The Politics of Diplomacy: Britain and France in the Balkans in the First World War* (London/New York: I.B. Tauris, 1998)

Fassy, Gérard, *Le Commandement français en Orient, octobre 1915–novembre 1918: Étude historique d'un commandement opérationnel français à la tête d'une force militaire alliée* (Paris: Economica, 2003)

Herwig, Holger H., *The Marne, 1914: The Opening of World War I and the battle that changed the world* (New York: Random House, 2009)

Horne, Alistair, *The Price of Glory: Verdun 1916* (London: Macmillan, 1962)

House, Simon J., *The Battle of the Ardennes, 22 August 1914* (PhD thesis, King's College London, 2012)

Krause, Jonathan, *Early Trench Tactics in the French Army: The second battle of Artois, May–June 1915* (Farnham: Ashgate, 2013)

Loez, André, 'Si cette putain de guerre pouvait finir': Histoire et sociologie des mutins de 1917 (PhD thesis, Université Paul Valéry, Montpellier III, 2009)

14–18, Les Refus de la guerre: Une histoire des mutins (Paris: Gallimard, 2010)

Neiberg, Michael S., *The Second Battle of the Marne* (Bloomington, IN: Indiana University Press, 2008)

Offenstadt, Nicolas (ed.), *Le Chemin des Dames: De l'événement à la mémoire* (Paris: Stock, 2004)

Pedroncini, Guy, *Les Mutineries de 1917* (Paris: PUF, 1967)
Pétain général en chef (1917–1918) (Paris: PUF, 1974)

Philpott, William, *Bloody Victory: The Sacrifice on the Somme and the Making of the Twentieth Century* (London: Little, Brown, 2009)

Prete, Roy A., *Strategy and Command: The Anglo–French coalition on the Western Front, 1914* (Montreal/Kingston: McGill/Queen's University Press, 2009)

Rolland, Denis, *Nivelle: L'inconnu du Chemin des Dames* (Paris: Imago, 2012)
La Grève des tranchées: Les mutineries de 1917 (Paris: Imago, 2005)

Sarrail, Général, *Mon Commandement en Orient* (ed. Rémy Porte) (Saint-Cloud: SOTECA Editions 14–18, 2012)

Smith, Leonard V., *Between Mutiny and Obedience: The case of the Fifth Infantry Division during World War I* (Princeton University Press, 1994)

Stevenson, David, 'French strategy on the Western Front', in Roger Chickering and Stig Förster (eds), *Great War, Total War* (Cambridge University Press, 2000)

With our Backs to the Wall: Victory and defeat in 1918 (London: Allen Lane, 2011)

Tanenbaum, Jan Karl, *General Maurice Sarrail 1856–1929: The French Army and left-wing politics* (Chapel Hill, CA: University of North Carolina Press, 1974)

Tyng, Sewell T., *The Campaign of the Marne 1914* (London: Oxford University Press, 1935)

Zabecki, David T., *The German 1918 Offensives: A case study in the operational level of war* (London/New York: Routledge, 2006)

Zuber, Terence, *The Battle of the Frontiers: Ardennes 1914* (Stroud: Tempus, 2007)

Tactics and doctrine: pre-war and developments

There has been an unbalanced emphasis, particularly among American historians, on the *offensive à outrance*, the pre-war doctrine that supposedly sent against German machine-guns men in their visible red trousers, armed with their bayonet and a will to win. For example, Porch is highly critical of the French Army. Queloz presents a less febrile picture, and Cosson shows what the French Army took as lessons from the South African and Russo-Japanese wars.

Essential reading here is Michel Goya's study of the French Army's vast improvements; he links developments in equipment and improved tactical doctrine to the industrial mobilisation discussed below. It awaits a translator. Changes in artillery and infantry tactics are still covered best in the inter-war volumes by General Herr and Colonel Lucas. Although tanks are often considered a British invention, the French were just as keen to seek and exploit new weapons. Tim Gale's recent doctoral thesis (King's College London again) on the creation of France's tank force and the development of tank doctrine has documented this.

Cosson, Olivier, *Préparer la guerre: L'Armée française et la guerre russo-japonaise, 1899–1914* (Paris: Les Indes savantes, 2013)
Gale, Tim, *The French Army's Tank Force and Armoured Warfare in the Great War* (Farnham: Ashgate, 2013)
Goya, Michel, *La Chair et l'acier: L'invention de la guerre moderne (1914–1918)* (Paris: Tallandier, 2004)
Herr, Général, *L'Artillerie: Ce qu'elle a été, ce qu'elle est, ce qu'elle doit être* (Paris: Berger-Levrault, 1923)
Lucas, Colonel Pascal, *L'Evolution des idées tactiques en France et en Allemagne pendant la guerre de 1914–1918* (Paris: Berger-Levrault, 4th edn, 1932)
Porch, Douglas, *The March to the Marne: The French Army 1871–1914* (Cambridge University Press, 1981)
Queloz, Dimitry, *De la Manoeuvre napoléonienne à l'offensive à outrance: La tactique générale de l'armée française 1871–1914* (Paris: Economica/EPHE IV Sorbonne, 2009)

Industrial mobilisation and new materiel: artillery, aviation and tanks

As the sub-title of Rémy Porte's study reveals, mobilising a country's economic and industrial resources is just as important, if not more so, as mobilising its manpower. The records of both Army Commissions show how vital the parliamentarians considered industrial mobilisation to be. These are in the Archives nationales (series C) for the Chamber of Deputies, and in the Palais du Luxembourg for the Senate. The latter are in poor physical condition; the former are handwritten for the most part and awkwardly bound. The volumes in the Carnegie Institute's series on the social and economic history of the war are still relevant: for example, Arthur Fontaine's volume from the French series, which has been translated into English. The voluminous papers of one of the war ministers and one of the armaments ministers may be consulted in the Archives nationales, for both Painlevé (313 AP) and Albert Thomas (94 AP) seem to have kept every scrap of paper. Among Clemenceau's papers that survived his end-of-life cull, now in Vincennes (series 6N), only a few folders remain dealing with armaments and aviation.

Michel Goya's work, described above, should be read in this context also. In English, Patrick Fridenson's collection of essays on the home front has been translated. John Godfrey's book is more concerned with political economy than with industry itself, but is good on Albert Thomas. For tanks, see Goya and Gale above. Aviation is better served in popular literature, since many of the best-known aces were French.

The contribution of women in factories to produce the munitions, as well as their nursing and other more militant activities are covered in Margaret Darrow.

Darrow, Margaret H., *French Women and the First World War* (Oxford/New York: Berg, 2000)
Fontaine, Arthur, *French Industry during the War* (New Haven, CT/London: Yale University Press/ Oxford University Press, 1926)
Fridenson, Patrick, *The French Home Front, 1914–1918* (Providence, RI: Berg, 1992)
Godfrey, John F., *Capitalism at War: Industrial Policy and the Bureaucracy in France 1914–1918* (Leamington Spa/New York: Berg, 1987)
Porte, Rémy, *La Mobilisation industrielle: 'Premier front' de la Grande Guerre?* (Saint-Cloud: SOTECA, 14–18 Editions, 2005)

Intelligence

The study of intelligence gathering and interpretation is a burgeoning sector of First World War studies. In the French case, this has been stimulated by the return from Russia of many of the documents that the German Army took from Vincennes during the course of the Second World War and transported to Berlin, whence the Russian Army removed them in turn. A first tranche of boxes arrived in the 1990s and was catalogued, but the arrival of a second tranche caused a re-think, and both sets were withdrawn to be re-catalogued, a process that is not yet complete. The inventories for those series that have been completed (9NN, for medical matters, 15NN for Allied headquarters and 16NN for GQG) are available from the SHD website.

Two recent theses by serving French Army officers have used this returned material: Olivier Lahaie and Michaël Bourlet. More generally, Forcade's early chapters are helpful; Lastours deals with cyphers.

Still worth reading are the memoirs of those involved during the war: Armengaud (aerial intelligence), Cartier and Givierge (cyphers). Givierge's long account is in the manuscripts division of the BNF. The only reliable overview in English is in Douglas Porch's two chapters in his wider study of the French secret services.

Armengaud, Général, *Le Renseignement aérien: Sauvegarde des armées* (Paris: Librairie Aéronautique, 1934)

Bourlet, Michaël, Les Officiers français des 2e et 5e bureaux de l'État-major de l'armée (août 1914–juin 1919) (PhD thesis, Université de Paris IV, Sorbonne, 2009)

Cartier, François, 'Souvenirs du général Cartier', *Revue des Transmissions* 85 (July–August 1959), 23–39, and 87 (November–December 1959), 13–51

Forcade, Olivier, *La République secrète: Histoire des services spéciaux français de 1918 à 1939* (Paris: Nouveau monde editions, 2008)

Lahaie, Olivier, Renseignement et services de renseignement en France pendant la guerre de 1914–1918 (PhD thesis, Université de Paris IV, Sorbonne, 2005)

Lastours, Sophie de, *La France gagne la guerre des codes secrets: 1914–1918* (Paris: Le Grand Livre du Mois, 1998)

Porch, Douglas, *The French Secret Services: From the Dreyfus Affair to the Gulf War* (New York: Farrar, Strauss and Giroux, 1995)

Military justice and military medicine

The work of the former head of the service historique, General André Bach, is a mine of information on courts martial between 1914 and 1916. For the critical year of 1917, see military operations above. Interest has been sparked by cries for rehabilitation of those condemned for acts that nowadays would be attributed to stress or combat fatigue or shell shock. The topic has fed into the left–right divide that separates French historians of the First World War. Antoine Prost's online report on behalf of the Mission du Centenaire provides a balanced summary of the debate.

Medical aspects of the war have also become a popular topic of research: Lastours, for example, on facial disfigurement. Two former 'Médecins-chef des services' of the French Army, Alain Larcan and J.-J. Ferrandis have produced a new and well-illustrated history of the medical services. Prost has done a sterling service in the matter of casualty statistics by synthesising the various figures used by historians and politicians.

Bach, General André, *Fusillés pour l'exemple 1914–1915* (Paris: Tallandier, 2003) *Justice militaire 1915–1916* (Paris: Vendémiaire, 2013)

Kalifa, Dominique, *Biribi: Les bagnes coloniaux de l'armée française* (Paris: Perrin, 2009)

Larcan, Alain, and Jean-Jacques Ferrandis, *Le Service de santé aux armées pendant la Première Guerre Mondiale* (Paris: Editions LBM, 2008)

Loez, André, and Nicolas Mariot (eds), *Obéir/désobéir: Les mutineries de 1917 en perspective* (Paris: Editions La Découverte, 2008)

Prost, Antoine, 'Compter les vivants et les morts: l'évaluation des pertes françaises de 1914–1918', *Le Mouvement Social* 222 (2008), 41–60
'Quelle mémoire pour les fusillés de 1914–1918? Un point de vue historien' (Ministère des anciens combattants, 2013) at www.ladocumentationfrancaise.fr/var/storage/rapports-publics/134000666/0000.pdf (accessed on 28 January 2014)

Allies and the enemy

Franco-German relations have dominated the twentieth century, despite the risk that concentration on the Western Front between 1914 and 1918 skews perceptions of what was a 'world' war. Apart from the joint work of Jean-Jacques Becker and Gerd Krumeich, the hostile relationship during the war years has received little attention, although Wencke Meteling's work comparing the experiences of the local regiments of Frankfurt an der Oder and Orléans covers both home and western fronts. By contrast, much has appeared on the 1920s and 30s, most prominently by Jacques Bariéty.

Attitudes towards France's Allies have not been studied in great detail, other than at the level of high command. My own analysis of the French views of the inexperienced British during the Battle of the Somme ought to be extended to 1918, when Allied units were mixed together to meet successive crises. There is a very brief study of 1918 by Jean Nicot, using the postal control commission reports, and a recent doctoral thesis by Chris Kempshall. Franziska Heimburger's forthcoming thesis on the role of language in this international cooperation will be illuminating. Most of the literature on the principal relationship, that with Russia until 1917, concentrates on the pre-war. The doctoral thesis by Ioannis Sinanoglou is now over forty years old, and the forthcoming volumes on Russia's Great War and Revolution will provide the fruits of more recent scholarship. Bruce's work on the Franco-American alliance shows how much the AEF owed to French training and equipment, but is too romantic about mutual relations.

For Romania see Glenn E. Torrey's work; for Italy see the papers in the 1973 conference proceedings on France and Italy during the First World War, and work by Cappellano and Le Moal, who has also written on Serbia. The Greek connection is usually treated from the Salonika expedition perspective (see military operations above), but Mitrakos ranges wider. Vincent Cloarec's thesis on the Middle East has been re-published recently.

Bariéty, Jacques, *Les Relations franco-allemandes: Après la Première Guerre Mondiale 10 novembre 1918–10 janvier 1925 de l'exécution à la négotiation* (Paris: Editions Pedone, 1977)

Becker, Jean-Jacques, and Gerd Krumeich, *La Grande Guerre: Une histoire franco-allemande* (Paris: Tallandier, 2008)

Bruce, Robert B., *A Fraternity of Arms: America and France in the Great War* (Lawrence, KS: University Press of Kansas, 2003)

Cappellano, Filippo, 'Les relations entre les armées italienne et française pendant la Grande Guerre', *RHA* 250 (2008), 53–65

Cloarec, Vincent, *La France et la question de Syrie (1914–1918)* (Paris: CNRS Editions, 2010 [1988])

Greenhalgh, Elizabeth, '"Parade-ground soldiers": French Army Assessments of the British on the Somme in 1916', *Journal of Military History* 63: 2 (1999), 283–312

Heimburger, Franziska, Une Mésentente cordiale? Les langues et la coalition alliée sur le front de l'ouest de la Première Guerre mondiale (PhD thesis in process)

Kempshall, Chris, Unwilling Allies? : Tommy–Poilu Relations on the Western Front 1914–1918 (PhD thesis, University of Sussex, 2013)

La France et l'Italie pendant la Première Guerre Mondiale [Proceedings of conference held in Grenoble, September 1973] (Grenoble: Presses universitaires de Grenoble, 1976)

Le Moal, Frédéric, *La France et l'Italie dans les Balkans, 1914–1919* (Paris: L'Harmattan, 2006)

La Serbie du martyre à la victoire 1914–1918 (Saint-Cloud: SOTECA 14–18 Editions, 2008)

Meteling, Wencke, *Ehre, Einheit, Ordnung: Preußische und französische Regimenter und ihre Städte im Krieg, 1870/71 und 1914–1919* (Baden-Baden: Nomos, 2010)

Mitrakos, Alexander S., *France in Greece during World War I: A study in the politics of power* (Boulder, CO: East European Quarterly, 1982)

Nicot, Jean, 'Perception des Alliés par les combattants en 1918 d'après les archives du contrôle postal', *RHA* (1988/3), 45–53

Sinanoglou, Ionannis, France looks Eastward: Perspectives and policies in Russia, 1914–1918 (PhD thesis, Columbia University, 1974)

Torrey, Glenn E., *Romania and World War I: A collection of studies* (Iasi/Portland, OR: Center for Romanian Studies, 1999)

Henri Matthias Berthelot: Soldier of France, defender of Romania (Iasi/Oxford: Center for Romanian Studies, 2001)

The Romanian Battlefront in World War I (Lawrence, KS: University Press of Kansas, 2011)

Index

Military ranks are given as at first mention